GOAT BROTHERS

Goat
Brothers

LARRY COLTON

D O U B L E D A Y

New York London Toronto Sydney Auckland

PUBLISHED BY DOUBLEDAY
A division of Bantam Doubleday Dell Publishing Group, Inc.
666 Fifth Avenue, New York, New York 10103

DOUBLEDAY and the portrayal of an anchor with a dolphin are
trademarks of Doubleday, a division of Bantam Doubleday Dell
Publishing Group, Inc.

Library of Congress Cataloging-in-Publication Data

Colton, Larry.
Goat brothers/Larry Colton.—1st ed.
    p.   cm.
1. Colton, Larry.   2. United States—Biography.   3. Journalists—United States—
Biography.   4. College graduates—United States—Biography.   I. Title.
CT275.C696A3   1993
973.92′092′2—dc20
[B]   92-25067
CIP

ISBN 0-385-24407-X

To Steve, as promised back in 1979

1962 GOAT BROTHERS' HELL WEEK SHOPPING LIST

1   12-inch trout
3   dozen eggs
1   box of Kotex pads
1   argyle sock
1   small bell
1   can of Aunt Jemima syrup
6   Walla Walla onions
1   dozen Trojan rubbers
1   burlap bag
1   Kotex belt
1   four-foot red ribbon
1   Tabasco sauce
1   bag of marshmallows
1   swat paddle
1   ten-pound block of ice
1   bottle of Heet analgesic balm

Report to Big Ben at bottom of pledge stairs at *precisely High Noon* on Friday!

Prologue

When in doubt, gallop.
　—French Foreign Legion axiom

It was a full midnight moon, as I remember it. Lots of stars over the High Sierras. August 1979. My best friend, Steve Radich, and I were sitting in folding chairs in front of the wood-framed tent we were sharing with our daughters. It had been seventeen years since we'd first met as fraternity brothers at the University of California at Berkeley.

He handed me the bottle of José Cuervo Gold and I took a swig. No glass, no lime, no salt. Tough guys. We were both going through "trial separations" from our wives. They both had subscriptions to _Ms._, one a nurse, the other an art therapist.

Steve defined masculinity. At least my version of it. I envied his good looks—thick dark hair, brown eyes, lean and firm body, deep resonant voice. At Cal he had been a three-year letterman on the football team. Big Man on Campus. He walked down Telegraph Avenue in 1963 and coeds' heads turned; he roared into the fraternity driveway on his motorcycle as if he was some sort of James Dean. He had it. A good student too. And at the age of thirty-five, still regarded as one of the most tenacious and agile rugby players in Northern California.

We had come to the Sierras with our daughters to attend the Lair of the Bear, a family camp for Cal alumni. I wasn't sure if it was the sweet redolence of the sugar pines, or the straight shots of tequila, or the fact that we were the only single fathers in camp, but we were, as the apologists of the men's movement would later label it, doing some heavy-duty "bonding." At the time, we just thought we were a couple of close buddies getting snockered and shooting the shit.

We talked about women. "I want them all," he claimed. Moderation wasn't his thing. We agreed that there was a major disparity between the way it was when we were chasing girls in college and the way it was a decade and a half later. Things had changed. No news flash was necessary. We knew all the new words—vulnerability, intimacy, communication, equality. But that didn't make us Renaissance men. I told him that I had just read *Loose Change* by Sara Davidson, a book about three sorority sisters from Cal and the changes they'd been through in the sixties and seventies. He had read the book too.

"You should write the male version," he said. "Tell *our* side of the fuckin' story."

And that was how I came to write this book.

I didn't go back to my home in Portland, Oregon, after the week in the Sierras and start cranking out the chapters right away. Events and heartbreaks conspired to keep me from it for another eight years, but not a day went by that I didn't think about my long-lost Pi Kappa Alpha (Pi KA) fraternity brothers, the guys who'd stood with me on the cusp of manhood. We weren't a contrived men's group who sat in beanbag chairs, sipped lemon-flavored mineral water, and talked about our feelings. What we liked to do was gather around alcohol like cavemen to fire and talk about the 49ers or the snooty blondes in the Kappa house across the street. Or sometimes we had burp contests. We were *the* jock house at Cal. Half the brothers played a varsity sport, and hardly a week went by without somebody from the fraternity getting his picture in the *Daily Californian*, typically crossing the goal line or home plate. And we taught each other how to relate to women.

We weren't a house full of blue bloods—we came from middle-class and blue-collar California backgrounds. And being among the best and brightest of our Sputnik-era high schools, we weren't dummies either. Of course, the beatniks on campus accused us of being button-down, mindless anti-intellectuals doomed to lead lives of fatuous desperation in the suburbs. So what? We didn't join the fraternity to sit around and discuss Kafka or Nietzsche or civil rights. We were there for the existential crunch. Pi KA's place in the intellectual universe was not an issue we pondered. According to our calibrations, Pi KA *was* the center of the universe, home to the greatest guys ever. We were accruing social skills (i.e., drinking, twisting) that would, no doubt, be more important than anything we memorized in Cliffs Notes.

When I graduated in 1965, I moved away from California, and over the years, lost track of these fraternity brothers, except Steve. As I began to zigzag through the eighties, I wondered if they too had been swallowed by the seismic cracks of social change. Did they have as much trouble trying to cross the great cultural schism of the last three decades as I had? Were they all divorced and wondering what to do with the kids after the nineteenth trip to the zoo? Did they still wear madras? Did they cheat on their wives? Had their table manners improved?

From a distance I could imagine them self-confident, settled, secure. They would be wearing their Ray•Bans, driving down the freeway in their hogmobiles talking to their brokers on their cellular phones. Or maybe they were the brokers. The vision was unsettling. My idea of an investment opportunity was *two* discount pizza coupons on the refrigerator door.

Or maybe they were all nifty guys at loose ends . . . or thoughtless Casanovas . . . or unfinished boys still caught in the eternal search for the Perfect Woman. Or maybe they had all been happily married twenty-two years and were deacons at the church. Who knew?

There was only one way to find out.

In 1987 I set out on a journey in search of these men. I traveled the freeways, dirt roads, and cul-de-sacs of California, tracking them down, reconnoitering with the past. I was in full gallop. Eventually, I chose to relate the stories of five men. We were not all in the same pledge class, but still, we had all been goats . . . that's what the actives called us in Hell Week. In addition to Steve and myself, I picked Jim van Hoften, Loren Hawley, and Ron Vaughn . . . not just because of the checkered lives they have led but also because of who they were back in the fraternity. Or rather, who I thought they were, which, I would soon discover, was not necessarily who they really were. Lots of secret lives back then.

In 1962, Jim (a.k.a. "Muldoon") van Hoften, an engineering major from Burlingame across the Bay, was a big, broad-shouldered scowler, hunched over his textbook for Physics 4, one of the required classes for the criminally mathematic. He and I roomed together in the fall of that year—that was the scary Cuban Missile Crisis semester—and for the life of me, I couldn't figure why we had pledged this guy, a Lumpy Rutherford in a house full of Ricky Nelsons. It took me twenty-five years to finally figure it out. He fooled us all.

Then there was Loren (a.k.a. "Hayseed") Hawley, the rawboned country bumpkin who showed up with a pound and a half of press clippings
from the Yuba-Sutter *Appeal-Democrat* pinned to his Marysville High
letterman's sweater, supposedly the greatest jock in the history of Yuba
County. And maybe Sutter County too. At the Purple Passion Party, our
annual function that would one day make the drunken loutishness of
Animal House seem like sherry hour at the faculty club, he got laid atop
the pool table. Or so the legend proclaimed. The last I'd seen of him in
1965, he was riding off into the sunset with Miss California in his red
'57 T-Bird convertible, an infectious grin headlighting his way, looking
every bit like a guy bound for terminal boyhood.

Everybody's friend in the fraternity was popular Ron (a.k.a. "Herbie")
Vaughn, a good-looking, bighearted student-athlete. He was talented on
the gridiron and obsessed with becoming an architect. He had a big-
busted, blue-eyed, blond girlfriend in the Theta house to drool for. But
the thing that I remembered most about Ron was the rumor that he was
"part nigger." That's how we talked in the fraternity back then. It seemed
unlikely—he was as white as everyone else in the house, and besides, Pi
KA was a fraternity whose national charter excluded anybody who wasn't
white. So I never asked him about it. But that's what the rumor was.
Anyway, he seemed destined for great things.

I spent days, weeks, months, and eventually years probing the intimate
details of these men's lives. We camped, golfed, drank, schmoozed,
boated, traveled back in time. I sat in their dens and living rooms, listening to their tales of manhood. And boyhood. They confessed things I
wouldn't have guessed in a million Hell Weeks back in the days of the
New Frontier.

The résumés were impressive: astronaut, professional athlete, Ph.D.,
Marine, millionaire, mental patient.

The places they'd hung out were the datelines of the times: Gulf
of Tonkin, Haight-Ashbury, outer space, inner space, Beverly Hills,
Lompoc Federal Penitentiary.

I talked to their friends, enemies, high school sweethearts, college
girlfriends, wives, ex-wives, parents, and in one case, the county coroner.

I didn't set out to write a social history, or an attack on the women's
movement, or an essay on the territory of masculinity. I just needed to
tell the stories of five fraternity brothers. I was compelled.

1962 GOAT BROTHERS' VOCABULARY

arch: throw up
beaver: female
bird: throw up
bong: blackball from fraternity
book: study
brown helmet: rejection
cat's ass: excellent
cinch: failure notice
d.c.: dumb cunt
dollies: girls
fartless: lazy
Fern: local bar
fox: grade of F
Freddy: fraternity man
greenbagger: beatnik
guyner: Negro
hawk: watch girls
hog: eat
hogules: food
honger konger: Oriental

horndog: ugly girl
joy boys: homosexuals
knobby: blow job
Mick: easy class
pimp: ridicule
pimpy: uncool
pop: cocktail
rack: sleep
ralph: throw up
rat fuck (r.f.): prank
re-zee: nap
roll: flunk out
Sally: sorority girl
scarf: eat fast
shoot: girl watch
short hitter: bad drinker
snuffy: pledge
trebs: breasts
trou: pants
walk: skip a test

PART ONE

California College Days

Know that, on the right hand of the Indies, there is an island called California, very near to the Terrestrial Paradise.
   —From *Las Sergas de Espladián*, by Garci Ordóñez de Montalvo, fifteenth-century Spanish writer

1

Larry

The American ideal is youth—handsome, empty youth.
  —Henry Miller

I checked myself one last time in the steamy mirror. It was the morning of Freshman Orientation in Dwinelle Plaza and I was ready—new penny loafers, Sta-Prest cotton pants, button-down oxford shirt. A splash of Old Spice and a dab of Brylcreem and I was on my way, down the creaky old stairs and out the front door of my Berkeley rooming house.

It was September 1960. On a campus of 23,000, I did not know a soul. Not one person. Except the baseball coach, George Wolfman, who had gotten me set up in the rooming house, a run-down, weathered Bay Area brown shingle at the corner of Bowditch and Haste (later to be razed and turned into the northeast corner of embattled People's Park). It looked like the Bates Motel. Cobwebs covered the front porch. The ceiling in my third-floor garret slanted at a 45-degree angle, and unless I stood in the middle of the floor, I had to stoop. Being six-three wasn't always an advantage. I missed Mom and Dad.

The day I left home Dad said goodbye with a handshake and an admonition to "keep my nose to the grindstone." Mom stood on the porch in her apron, waving goodbye, tears rolling. I wouldn't have admitted it at the time, but I had a little mist going too. I'd had a great childhood. In the Colton household, we never had to deal with swings in temperament

—there weren't any. Things were always good—standard middle class, Ozzie and Harriet stuff, no alcoholism, no wife beating, no gaping psychic wounds. My biggest childhood scar, I guess, was on my twelfth birthday, when I asked for a Mickey Mantle glove and instead I got a cheapo mail-order Sam Mele model. Sam Mele was a no-name banjo hitter for the Washington Senators.

I also missed Dexter. He was my best buddy back in Westchester, the suburb of sameness in L.A. where I'd grown up. We played a zillion hours of sports together. We never smoked or drank, but we did cut school once and drove to the Coliseum in his chopped, channeled, and lowered '51 Chevy to see the Dodgers' first game in L.A. in 1958. He had freckles and unruly red hair and looked like Tom Sawyer after shock therapy. He was going into the Marines. I'd never heard of Vietnam.

The blisters from my new shoes were killing me as I hurried down Telegraph Avenue, headed for campus. A light fog picketed the Bay Area, but patches of blue gave promise to picnic weather. At the corner of Telegraph and Bancroft, next to the construction site for the new Student Union, I approached a long row of card tables that lined the sidewalk. They were strategically placed a few inches off University property, each table stacked with pamphlets for off-campus issues: the NAACP advocating fair housing in Berkeley; Bay Area Young Republicans advertising Jackie Robinson's appearance for presidential candidate Richard Nixon; Slate, the left-wing student political party, seeking contributions for its defense fund for students arrested in the May protests and riots in San Francisco against the House Un-American Activities Committee (HUAC) hearings. I didn't stop to browse.

It was a new decade on campus. The May arrests had triggered a statewide salvo at the Berkeley campus. Critics were calling it the Little Red Schoolhouse or Moscow Jr. Politicians, including Nixon, were campaigning for stricter enforcement of the 1951 University rule prohibiting Communists from speaking on campus. A California Senate subcommittee report had labeled the University "subversive . . . with sympathy to Communist front organizations and a constantly growing disrespect for constitutional authority." University president Clark Kerr, who had argued that the ban on Communist speakers should be lifted, was accused of "opening the gates to Communists and anyone else to utilize the University property as a brawling ground for political controversy." Kerr publicly defended the students, assuring the critics that "there aren't going to be any riots."

I didn't care about any of that. What I knew about Cal was that its football team, led by Joe Kapp, had been to the Rose Bowl two out of the

last three years, and its basketball team, coached by Pete Newell, had
been to the NCAA finals two years in a row, and its baseball team,
coached by George Wolfman, was one of the best on the West Coast. I
hadn't come to Cal to listen to Communist speakers. I had two fixed
collegiate goals: to become a big-league shortstop and to get laid for the
first time. I declared "undecided" as my major.

I had zero intention of joining a fraternity. In fact, I was confused
whether it was sororities or fraternities that had boys.

At Freshman Orientation, an assistant dean addressed the 4,000 new
students, all of us from the top 10 percent of our high school classes.
"Half of you will *not* graduate from this university," he warned. "The
academic competition will be fierce."

I wasn't too worried. After all, I had come in third in the Westchester
American Legion essay contest on "What the Bill of Rights Means to
Me." But whoever read my freshman English entrance exam wasn't im-
pressed. I flunked. I had to take Subject A, also known as Dumbbell
English.

I went to the freshman get-acquainted dance in the Student Union.
That was a bold step. At Westchester High I was paralyzed with a Fear of
Dancing—I hadn't gone to the prom or the Winter Wonderland Ball or
any of the sock hops. It wasn't that I was a pimply misfit or couldn't get a
date. I had the credentials—senior class president, captain of the baseball and basketball teams, honor society president. What I didn't have
were the moves. Or the confidence. Mr. Cool couldn't bop. That was my
high school secret. It got so bad that when I was asked to the Spinsters'
Hop by Margaret Alexander, who had a body better than Gidget, I went,
but I sat on the sidelines the whole evening with my leg propped up on a
chair, telling her I sprained my ankle at basketball practice. I even had it
wrapped in an Ace bandage.

But there I was in the Student Union, leaning against the wall, surveying the action, the lights down low, the band playing "In the Mood." A
pretty brunette with a beehive hairdo walked my way and took a spot
next to me. I checked her out with a sidelong glance. Very tasty. But I
couldn't get up the courage. I couldn't get out the words. What was I
supposed to say? "Read any good Cliffs Notes lately?" "Want to come
back to my creepy rooming house and dust with me?"

I never knew what to say to girls. It went all the way back to Tonia
Barclay in the sixth grade. She was the Brigitte Bardot of Kentwood
Grade School—blond hair, sleepy blue eyes, upturned nose, sultry pout,
impressive young curves. We sat on opposite sides of the classroom.

During the Pledge of Allegiance, I stared at *her*, not the forty-eight stars on the flag. In "drop drills," I fell to my knees under my desk, pretending to cover my eyes from the primordial flash of the Russian hydrogen bomb that was incinerating downtown Westchester, but really I was peeking across the floor at *her*. One night she called my house. What a shocker that was. She asked me if I liked her. Mom was standing right next to me when I picked up the phone. Tonia was wanting a commitment, a verbal show of affection. What a silly concept, I thought. Absolutely I liked her. I stood next to her at recess. What more did I have to do?

"No," I lied, hanging up.

"Who was that?" asked Mom.

"Dexter," I answered. I always lied to my mother about girls. Probably something to do with the old Oedipal thing.

Tonia went on to be the femme fatale of Westchester High, the sexiest girl in school, cruising by me in front of my locker as if I was invisible. I'd blown it. I felt awkward around girls. They seemed unknowable. Nobody had ever told me about the birds and bees . . . not my parents, not Dexter, not my health teacher at Orville Wright Junior High. Until I reached high school, I thought screwing was when a boy put his hand on a girl's breast and twisted like he was opening a jar. Really. The first time I "accidentally" masturbated, I thought for sure I had done permanent damage, like curdled my urine or something.

The brunette took her beehive elsewhere, leaving me to contemplate my next move. I overheard two guys talking about her ugly calves as she walked away. That made me feel better. I'd always been swayed by the tyranny of locker-room opinion. Like with my first date in high school. Her name was Bonnie Hayes—she was cute, perky, member of the drill team, girls' vice president, lived in a big house in Playa Del Rey. Pretty bitchin', I thought. Then I heard guys talking in the locker room. "She's not that cute," they agreed. That did it. I never asked her out again.

I never even came close to getting laid in high school. Actually, I was more interested in finding a steady girlfriend. Pam West was as close as I got to going steady. She was smoky, voluptuous, elegant—all of that— Lee Remick and Kim Novak rolled into one. We went out ten times our senior year. And ten times I never even kissed her good night. Not even a little peck at the front door. We never even held hands. But I was in love. Full throttle. But I didn't know how to go about telling her. I guess I figured she should have got the message after I asked her out ten times. You know, deeds, not words.

One day after school I saw her talking in front of her locker to Don

Callicoat, the linebacker and captain of the football team. He was the Stanley Kowalski of Westchester High, shoulders wider than Sepulveda Boulevard. Pam was looking up at him all puppy-eyed and moist. My heart dropped to my desert boots. I called her that evening to go to the library.

"I have to put my hair up in rollers," she explained.

I drove by her house. Callicoat's customized candy-apple-red '50 Ford was parked in front. I knew it was his because I could see the streetlight gleaming off his "Nobles Car Club" emblem in the rear window. The Nobles were the closest thing Westchester had to a fraternity, a club of hot-rodders with souped-up engines, greased-down hair, and Elvis sneers. They were shop-class guys. I had no doubt I could whip them all in a spelling bee. The windows to Callicoat's car were so steamed he and Pam wouldn't have noticed if President Eisenhower's motorcade rolled by.

I left the get-acquainted dance at the Student Union without having met anyone. As I walked down Telegraph past the Mediterranean Cafe, where all the beatniks in berets were inside jabbering on about poetry and existentialism and weird stuff like that, I vowed to do something about this Fear of Dancing. How else was I going to make it with the girls?

Cal had not been my first choice for college. I wanted to go to Stanford, but my SAT score put me into the category of the mathematically impaired. Sorry, the rejection letter said, try again. That saved Mom and Dad about a cool twenty grand . . . if my math was correct. My baseball scholarship (grant-in-aid) at Cal would pay for my $160 yearly tuition, plus I was to get $100 a month for clipping the grass around the track stadium. When I was growing up, we had a Japanese gardener to do the mowing and edging around our modest stucco tract home.

During the summer before college, several major-league scouts had come by the house to talk. The Dodgers and the Red Sox both offered a $16,000 bonus, but Dad, who dropped out of Santa Monica Junior College during the Depression to go to work trimming blueprints at Douglas Aircraft for sixteen cents an hour to support his parents, thought I should go to college so I could have an education to fall back on in case I got beaned or something. I agreed. A couple good seasons at Cal, I figured, and they'd be talking a hundred grand. I didn't lack for athletic chutzpah.

Basically, I arrived at Cal tabula rasa. Handsome, empty youth, with a cannon for an arm. I flunked my first midterm. It was in Sociology 1A, a class of 600 students. The essay question asked us to "detail the impact of the military-industrial complex on the organization man." Huh? Dad was the quintessential company man for Douglas, having never left after the Depression, driven by a quest for security, working his way up from sixteen cents an hour to become office manager of the Missiles Engineering Department, on his way to thirty-eight loyal years with the company. But I didn't write about that in my blue book. I really didn't know much about what Dad did, except there was always enough money to buy me a new glove, even if it wasn't always the one I wanted. Sometimes he let me use his Shell credit card. Otherwise, my red-and-white '55 Ford Sunliner convertible, which he bought, was running on empty. I went to see the TA in his office.

"Obviously, you don't grasp the concepts," he said, sitting there in his corduroy coat with patches on the sleeves, rimless glasses, and Brillo-pad hair.

"I thought it was going to be a true-false test," I said.

I wasn't doing very well in Physiology 1A either, a course I was taking to satisfy part of my science requirement. One day I was sitting in my lab section in the Life Sciences Building, fidgeting uncomfortably in my itchy ROTC uniform, waiting for the TA to show up, wondering if maybe I should have signed that bonus contract with the Dodgers. The class stirred when the TA entered. He wore a white lab coat. Trailing behind him on a leash was a puppy. On a campus patrolled by a hundred dogs, this was the cutest I'd seen, a springer and black Lab mix, with white feet and a white tuft. Students got up to pet it.

"Take good notes," he advised. "This'll be on the final."

He lifted the dog onto the lab table, stroking its head with one hand, pulling out a syringe with a long needle with the other. He didn't mess around, injecting the needle quickly into the dog's chest, pushing the plunger. The students gasped.

"The dog doesn't even feel this," he claimed, his voice calm and detached.

The dog whimpered a pitiful yelp, then its eyes rolled back in its head as it went into convulsions. The TA grabbed it to keep it from shaking off the table.

"It's already dead," he observed.

He put on surgical gloves and slit open the dog's belly, starting the slice at the white tuft. As twenty lower-division, non-science students watched, he slowly pulled out the insides—liver, kidney, intestines, and finally the heart—methodically detailing the physiological functions, organ by organ. I had never heard of the word "vivisection." I got a C–.

I missed my dog Buffy, a blond cocker spaniel. Her only flaw was that she always tried to intercept the rubber ball I endlessly threw against the side of the garage.

It was time to get to work on my Fear of Dancing. I drove south on Telegraph Avenue to Oakland, parking my Sunliner on a side street—just in case anyone was following me. Then I sneaked in the side door of the Arthur Murray Dance Studio. This wasn't cool, I knew, but it was desperate times.

"What's included in the introductory package?" I asked.

For fifty bucks, I was told, I would learn the basic steps of the cha-cha, waltz, samba, fox-trot, rumba, swing, and tango.

"I just want to be able to dance slow and do a little bopping," I requested.

"That's *not* the way we teach it at Arthur Murray!" snapped the manager.

I paid the fifty dollars. At the end of my second private lesson, after spending the hour stumbling through the mambo, my instructor, who knew she was Carmen Miranda, led me off the floor. Told me I didn't get the concepts.

I quit, not even bothering to ask for a refund or a take-home diagram of the steps.

Desperation. With the surfer look waxing into vogue, I bought a bottle of Lady Clairol "Light 'n Bright," figuring that maybe I could dazzle the coeds with the sun-bleached look. Instead, my hair turned a rusty copper. I had to shell out a buck fifty for a crew cut.

More desperate times. My new best friend on the freshman baseball team, Bill Harrison, dropped out of school to return to Fresno to be near his father, who had suffered a serious heart attack. And another new friend, Kevin Brown, a catcher on the freshman team, killed himself playing Russian roulette. But I was hitting the ball well, leading the team in RBIs and stolen bases. Scouts were at every game.

It was the summer following my freshman year, which, other than freshman ball, had been pretty discouraging—one date and a 2.2 g.p.a. But I was sure things would pick up my sophomore year. Dave Dowling and I had put down a deposit on a modern two-bedroom apartment on Hearst Avenue on the north side of campus. Dave was a wacky left-handed pitcher and chemistry major from Chehalis, Washington, who had a curveball that fell off the earth. He had turned down an offer from the St. Louis Cardinals for $25,000. I had visions of pretty coeds coming over to bake our T-bones and watch "Surfside Six" with us. We had both been invited to join the Pi KA fraternity, but had declined—I'd heard grisly stories of pledges being swatted and dumped naked and blindfolded in the middle of the Golden Gate Bridge. No, thanks.

Mom was in the kitchen packaging up a box of dishes and utensils for me to take back to Berkeley. She was always taking care of business for me. During the fifties, Hazel Colton—"Haz" to her friends—was compiling the portfolio of an era: Cub Scout den mother, PTA secretary, bridge club president. She drove my older sister Barbara, the Honored Queen, to Job's Daughters meetings; she worked the concession stand for my Babe Ruth League games; she volunteered at the polls every election day. She liked Ike, kept a bowl of plastic fruit on the dining-room table, and stacked the bookshelves with *Reader's Digest* condensed versions. She shopped for our meat and potatoes at the new Ralph's Market on Sepulveda Boulevard and for my back-to-school Peggers at the new Broadway Department Store, our link to the haute couture of Westwood and Beverly Hills. She could get cynical with the best of them, but her counsel on life was usually brief and pragmatic: "Don't drink from the carton . . . no bouncing the ball in the house . . . close the door so you don't let the flies out." At no time did she instruct me on how to deal with members of the opposite sex. But the cookie jar with the clown face was always stocked with a fresh batch, usually chocolate chippers. For Christmas, I gave her pot holders, aprons, and spatulas. That's what was on her list.

The phone rang. It was Dave Dowling calling long-distance. He'd changed his mind on the apartment—or rather his parents had—and he'd gotten the last opening in the dorms. "Sorry," he said.

"So where are you going to live?" asked Mom.

"I guess I can join a fraternity," I replied.

"A fraternity?" she said, raising her eyebrows. "Do you think that's such a good idea?"

2

Loren

It's my life, I live it, criticism be damned.
  —Framed motto hanging over
  Loren's bed as a teenager

Loren kissed his mom goodbye. His dad had already left for work without saying goodbye or wishing him good luck on his big venture. Not that Loren ever expected anything from his father.

"Promise you'll call me tonight," Genevieve Hawley instructed her only child.

"I will," he lied.

He stopped at the end of Sweezy Street, ready to head out of Marysville, sitting tall behind the wheel of his new olive green '60 Plymouth Fury, a graduation gift from Pop and Eddie—that's what he called Earl and Ethel Graves, his maternal grandparents. The 383 cubic inches of V-8 "Sonoramic Commando" power couldn't get him out of town fast enough, away from the discord between his mom and dad.

Everybody in Marysville knew the Hawley family. Loren's dad, Hal, a strong, barrel-chested man, was a popular coach and p.e. teacher at Marysville High. Lots of winning teams, lots of friends at the Elks Lodge. Genevieve was a part-time receptionist for Dr. Parkinson, the family doctor who treated just about everyone in town at one time or another. And of course for the last three years it was damn near impossible to pick up a copy of the Yuba-Sutter *Appeal-Democrat* without seeing a photo of Loren. Best athlete in Yuba County. Probably forever. All-Sierra Foothill League in football, basketball, track, baseball. Scholarship offers up the whazoo. Notre Dame wanted him. So did the Air Force Academy. He was also a member of the California Scholastic Federation, the statewide honor society, and played trombone in the school band, once playing at halftime at a 49er game at Kezar Stadium. He had so many gold balls and all-league trinkets that there was enough for two charm bracelets, one for his mom, the other for Sue Morgan. She was the sheriff's daughter, head cheerleader, class valedictorian. They'd been going together, on and off, since his sophomore year when he first asked her to dance at the sock hop in the school's cracker-box gym after the Yuba City game.

But neither Sue, nor Dr. Parkinson, nor the subscribers to the *Appeal-Democrat* knew what really went on at night behind the doors at 1315 Sweezy Street. Loren wasn't sure what bothered him most, his dad's drinking or his mom's meddling.

Marysville had been his universe. The house on Sweezy Street, located in a subdivision four blocks from the high school, was the only house he'd lived in. Except for the hardwood parquet floor in the kitchen, the Hawley house was identical to the houses on either side. It was a great place to play—family room in back, wide street, sloped curbs, friendly neighbors, young elm trees, a park at the end of the block. Neighbors on Sweezy Street didn't bother to lock their doors.

Marysville, population 7,200 in 1960, is located forty miles north of Sacramento on a tongue of lowland between the Yuba and Feather rivers, protected by levees on both sides. It is named after Mary Covillaud, a survivor of the ill-fated Donner Party, which froze coming over the Sierras in 1846 and whose survivors had to eat the dead. In 1955, when a devastating flood threatened to wipe out the city, Hal helped man the sandbag crews while Genevieve and Loren fled out of town with a caravan of other mothers and children, spending two nights at a ranch in the nearby foothills. For two days, Loren, thirteen, was pursued around the ranch by twelve-year-old twin sisters. "That's when I first realized my son was going to have his way with girls," Genevieve later observed.

Leaving for college, Loren drove his Fury down Bridge Street, where he had gone cruising to Andy's Drive-In a million times in Mike Monahan's light brown customized '46 Plymouth coupe with the nickname "Baby Shit" pinstriped across the rear fender. Genevieve thought

Monahan, a tough kid who worked nights pumping gas at his dad's service station in Yuba City, was a bad influence on her son.

Loren crossed the Feather River and headed out of town, driving west through the surrounding farm country, fertile flatland rich in grains, vegetables, and fruit trees. He passed Trowbridge, population 42. That's where Genevieve grew up on her parents' ranch, and that is where Loren spent the fondest days of his childhood, away from the friction of Sweezy Street. He idolized Pop and Eddie. And in return, they doted on him. They would drive into Marysville to pick him up for the weekend, chauffeuring him to his choir practice at the Presbyterian Church or to his Little League games. On his tenth birthday, Pop gave him Sugarfoot, a chestnut gelding, and in the summers, Loren rode Sugarfoot to the swimming hole down the lane, tying him to a tree while he swam and played. The next year, Pop built him a motorized go-cart with a 35-horsepower Briggs & Stratton motor, using an old pontoon from an airplane as the body. Loren painted it fire engine red with an 86 on the side. That was the number of Vern Nagler, his favorite player on his dad's team at the high school; Nagler would go on to play for the Cleveland Browns. And then there was the Fury for graduation.

Genevieve, a large, robust woman, big-boned like her son, claimed Pop was more of a father to Loren than Hal. Loren tagged after Pop everywhere. It was Pop who played catch with him and taught him how to work with tools and build things—the things Hal was always somehow too busy to do. When Loren begged to harrow the field one hot summer day, Pop turned him loose on the tractor. But before Loren had even finished the first row, the scorching heat blowing off the engine sent him running for the shade of the porch and a tall glass of Eddie's hand-squeezed lemonade. Still, it was Pop and Eddie's dream—and Genevieve's too—for Loren to go off to college and then return home to work the land that had been in the family for three generations, to continue the family tradition.

As he approached the exit on U.S. 40 for Berkeley's University Avenue, he still had to make a choice. Stanford or Cal. Jack Curtis, the head football coach at Palo Alto, was expecting him. So was Marv Levy, the new head coach in Berkeley. Loren had told both coaches he was coming. (NCAA letters of intent for college athletes were not enforced in 1960.) Sue Morgan was expecting him too. She was already enrolled at Cal in premed. He'd told his mom and dad he was going to Cal. But he wasn't sure.

"What the hell," he said, taking the University Avenue exit.

Parking his Fury in a red zone on Telegraph Avenue, he bounded toward campus to inform freshman football coach Mike White that he had indeed arrived. He passed Vaughn's Clothing, where a semiannual 2-for-1 sale lured students inside with the promise of free cigarettes and an eight-ounce Coke. As he crossed the street, he turned and ogled a tall blonde as she entered Cal Books. In the distance was the Campanile, the 307-foot Berkeley landmark in the middle of the campus. He gawked—he'd never seen anything taller than Pop's silo back home.

He was a rawboned six-four, 185 pounds, broad-shouldered and wide-eyed, his ice-blue eyes drinking in everything in sight. He had bushy eyebrows and his brown hair was neatly trimmed; he wore Levi's, a white T-shirt, and a big-toothed grin. He never broke stride passing the card table with the political literature.

"Howdy!" he declared, bursting into Coach White's office.

Coach White, a handsome young assistant, lean and gung ho, looked up, startled. He hadn't been convinced that Loren was coming, despite what he'd been told. "Terrific!" he responded, offering a hydraulic hand-shake.

There were scholarship forms to complete. Loren was receiving a grant-in-aid . . . tuition, $50 for books, $100 a month for room and board. "Have you thought about what you'd like to major in?" asked Coach White.

"Shoot, I don't know," he replied. "What do they have to offer?"

"We'll get you set up with an academic adviser," said White. "Where are you going to be living?"

"Shoot, I don't know," he replied. "My friend Stan Parkinson from back home told me I should join his fraternity."

Few issues on the Berkeley campus in 1960 generated more debate than the one over the value of the Greek system. The controversy was fueled by the death on the USC campus of a Sigma Kappa pledge who choked to death on a piece of raw liver soaked in olive oil—the ambulance attendants found him lying on his stomach, dressed in a burlap bag. After that incident the dean of men at Cal sent letters to every fraternity reminding them that hazing had been prohibited by the University for ten years and that the legislature had passed a bill that would cut off aid to any public school that sanctioned hazing that caused bodily harm. Meanwhile, the University's student body store continued to pocket money from the brisk sale of fraternity paddles . . . the ones used for swats.

In Sacramento, a bill had been introduced that sought to prevent freshmen from pledging, maintaining that "pledges are forced to deal with exaggerated social pressures when they should be concentrating on their books." In an article titled "Old Fraternity Handshake Losing Its Grip," *Newsweek* maintained that the Greek system was on its way out and "rituals, frantic hazing and whoop-'em-up parties to promote brotherhood are slowly sinking into the horizon." When fraternities across the country refused to eliminate discrimination clauses in their national by-laws, critics opened fire. The *Daily Californian* was filled with angry letters to the editor charging the Greeks with, among other things, providing "an anti-intellectual atmosphere" and a "false brotherhood." One student wrote: "No amount of brotherhood, solidarity or closeness can justify their pitiable loss of identity. They wear their pledge pins like a cross; they form an amorphous clot of nonentities."

But the predictions of the death of the Greeks on the Berkeley campus were premature. In 1960, membership in the forty-seven fraternities on campus was 2,700, which represented 22 percent of the male student body. That was up 5 percent from the previous year. An editorial in the *Daily Californian* declared that fraternities and sororities were "valuable instruments in maintaining the cohesive values vital in the lives of our 'anonymous youth.'"

Loren parked his Fury in the yellow zone in front of the Pi KA house and hurried across the bone-dry front yard to the front door. He entered, not bothering to knock, pausing in the vestibule. Nobody was in sight. Drapes were drawn, cigarette butts floated in half-empty beer cups, the *Chronicle* sports page littered the floor, a photo of Orlando Cepeda staring upward at the paint peeling from the ceiling. Of the forty-seven fraternities at Berkeley in 1960, Pi KA was *the* ugliest. A forty-year-old three-story stucco box, it was painted a washed-out pink. The narrow front yard was devoid of landscaping, and the interior of the downstairs —living room, pool room, TV room, Ping-Pong room, and card room— was Genevieve Hawley's worst nightmare: paint peeling from the walls, beer stains covering the rugs, furniture ripping at the seams, dust collecting in the corners. The mounted deer head on the card-room wall had both eyes gouged out, Marlboros dangling from its mouth, and a jockstrap strung between the antlers like a slingshot. The dining room was in the basement, a dark, dank medieval dungeon, with a low-beamed ceiling, three long oak tables stained a dark brown, and dusky walls decorated with broken wooden goalposts from games long forgotten. Across the driveway was the fraternity annex, a two-story white clapboard, even scrungier than the main house. It was the target of repeated warnings from the Berkeley fire marshal, who threatened to shut it down unless the wiring was brought up to code.

Despite the architectural and aesthetic deficiencies of the house, it was geographical paradise. Located at the corner of Piedmont and Durant avenues, it was a short walk from campus or Telegraph Avenue, and, what would be even more important to Loren, it was at the epicenter of all the best sororities, providing an endless stream of nubile coeds parading by the front window.

He spotted Stan Parkinson coming down the stairs. "I'm here!" he announced. "When can I move in?"

Parkinson, blue-eyed, handsome, solidly built, first-string lineman, fraternity vice president, biology major, had known Loren since childhood. Genevieve worked for his father, who had doctored Loren through all his boyhood traumas, including the serious bout with encephalomyelitis when he was five and the broken knuckle he got in a fistfight on the eve of the big basketball game his senior year against the dreaded Yuba City Honkers.

"Hold on," said Parkinson. "The brothers have to vote on you first."

Loren fit the Pi KA image—athletic, outgoing, energetic, not too serious, not too academic, native Californian. But unlike almost all of the other members, who were from the suburbs of the big cities, he was small-town. Rough-hewn. He got his pledge pin that evening anyway.

He was just falling asleep on the top bunk over his new roommate and pledge brother, John Stassi, a freshman tackle from Sacramento, when he felt somebody shake the end of his bed. It was one of the actives.

"Phone call. It's your mom."

"Tell her I'll call tomorrow."

"She sounds pretty worried," the active replied. "Better do it now."

Loren slowly eased his long frame out of bed, taking his time getting to the phone. "What'ya want?" he grumbled.

Genevieve wanted to know why he hadn't called. She also wanted to report that Hal had gone out drinking and wasn't home yet.

"What am I supposed to do about it?" Loren asked.

She wondered aloud how she was going to be able to cope with Hal's excesses without Loren around to help her.

"You'll figure it out," he answered. He hung up, realizing that Berkeley might not be far enough away to escape the tug and pull.

It was Monday morning, first day of classes. Loren was walking across campus with Stassi, his inseparable new best friend. Stassi was the one who labeled him "Hayseed" as soon as he saw Loren unpack his orange tie with the painting of the rainbow trout jumping out of the turquoise stream.

Stassi, the son of a Sicilian grocer, had already appointed himself Loren's collegiate shepherd, convinced Loren was going to need help in the Big City. He talked him into signing up for exactly the same schedule of classes he was taking: Norwegian 1A, ROTC, History 4A, Physics 10, Subject A, and freshman football. They made a contrasting pair: Loren was tall, fair-haired; John, nicknamed "Swampfox," was stocky, dark-complected, with a dry wit. Loren had already told him all about the love of his life, Sue, and how she was "already spending twenty-five hours a day in the library before school even started."

Back in Marysville, Loren's buddies called Sue a "touch and smile girl." In other words—no action, lots of tease. She and Loren had spent many nights parked out on Slaughterhouse Road next to the levee, doing lots of heavy petting, but not going "all the way." According to Loren, that wasn't the reason for all their breakups. He claimed it was because she was always trying to tell him what to do. Just like his mother. He also maintained that every time they broke up, there was Genevieve, sticking her nose in his business. Like the time Genevieve was playing Tripoli with her gal friends and Mrs. Martin got to mewling as to how her daughter Marcie, known to the guys in the locker room as "Lassie" for her resemblance to the TV star, didn't have a date to the school dance, and Genevieve volunteered Loren, refusing to let him wiggle out of it. After that the guys in the locker room started calling him "Little Lorrie," accusing him of having to go home at lunchtime so his mother could serve him his warm milk. Or there was the time one of his friends on the basketball team, trying to help him lose his cherry, gave him a pack of Trojans and fixed him up with a girl reputed to be the "biggest punch-board" at Yuba City High. The proof of her loose morals was that she went out with guys in junior college. Loren didn't score, and the next morning Genevieve found the Trojans in the back pocket of his jeans. She flushed them down the toilet. "You're too young for this sort of stuff," she advised. That was before Loren finally broke into the victory column in his senior year with Deanna Beverly, the saucy redhead who was always passing him notes in geometry class. One night he waited until Hal and Genevieve were asleep and then crawled out his window and pushed the family '57 Chevy halfway down Sweezy Street before jumping in and driving to room 22 of the TraveLodge, where Deanna was babysitting for her aunt. According to Loren, he sat down on the bed and the next thing he knew "she was walking it right on in there." According to Deanna, she "created a monster that night."

Loren and Stassi settled into their seats for their first-ever collegiate class. They sat in the back row of the crowded lecture hall in California Hall and awaited the arrival of their Physics 10 professor, Nobel Prize winner Dr. Edward Teller, known as the "father of the hydrogen bomb." The word in the Pi KA house was that Physics 10, a lower-division course for non-science majors, was a big Mick. Dr. Teller, who also taught Physics 186, an upper-division course for physics majors titled "Peaceful Uses of Nuclear Explosions," was allegedly too busy with his research to worry about a freshman class.

"So are you and Sue going steady?" Stassi asked.

"She thinks so," answered Loren, eyes glued to a willowy brunette walking up the aisle in a pleated skirt and white blouse. He elbowed Stassi. "Holy shit!" he exclaimed. "Never saw anything like that back in Marysville. She's breeding stock."

She continued up the aisle, and to his wonderment, sat down in the empty seat next to him. Her name was Donna James, a freshman math major from an L.A. suburb. She was an AO Pi pledge and already had a boyfriend, a Zete with *two* Corvettes. Loren barely heard a word of Dr. Teller's lecture, spending the hour eyeing Donna out of the corner of his eye. After class, he was tight on her heels as she left California Hall and headed across campus. He eased alongside and wasted no time in boldly asking her for a date.

"I'm flattered," she replied with a smile, "but I already have a boy-friend."

After she'd gone her separate way, he turned to Stassi. "Swampfox," he avowed, "don't worry about a thing. I'm gonna wear down her resis-tance."

They walked a little farther, then he added, "Maybe I'll major in phys-ics. I liked that class."

Loren stood next to Stassi in the back of the circle of freshman football-ers, his helmet under his arm, a grin on his face. Coach White was addressing the team, reviewing the game plan for Saturday morning's contest at Memorial Stadium against the UCLA frosh.

"Did you see the way Donna smiled at me after class?" whispered Loren.

Stassi didn't answer, nodding for him to pay attention. The freshman team was 3 and 0, and Loren was first-string left end, catching a touch-down pass in the team's first game against San Jose State; he had also played halfback. Coach White, who had called Loren the "best athlete on the team," was distracted by the whispering. He took a step forward and fired the football at him, nailing him right in the chest. Loren didn't flinch.

"Damnit, Loren!" yelled Coach White. "Pay attention. Get serious!"

In his own carefree way, Loren was serious. He loved the sport—the hitting, the competition, the games, the press clippings. It was the tedium of practice where his mind wandered, usually to girls, Donna in particular, although he had yet to wear down her resistance despite a month of solid effort.

After practice he headed back to the fraternity. He was like a kid at summer camp around the house, always smiling, horsing around, avoiding his studies . . . an only child suddenly surrounded by forty playmates. But he hated being a pledge. The rules. The harassment. A Pi KA pledge, like a military recruit, was required to follow a rigid—and sometimes arcane—list of dos and don'ts: achieve a 2.0 g.p.a. (or repeat the pledge semester); memorize weekly pledge lessons—songs, fraternity history, Greek alphabet, bylaws, preamble, founding fathers, etc.; complete daily cleanup chores; wear a pledge pin, use the back (pledge) stairs, answer the phone, move cars in the driveway, and attend study table from 7 to 10 P.M. Monday through Thursday at Kroeber Anthropology Library. By the end of his first month, Loren had violated every rule, not out of rebellion, but because he was usually off on his own little cloud, having fun, relishing being away from home.

He walked in the front door, and was greeted by a hulk of an active known around the house as "Big Ben." It was not a friendly greeting. Big Ben was a business major from Sacramento and a bullnecked second-string lineman on the varsity who liked to take out his off-the-field aggressions on the pledges. He was part of the old guard in the fraternity who believed in hazing hard. Ruthless. Verbal. Physical. Any way he could. He ordered his swat paddles by the dozen.

"Be in my room in five minutes!" Big Ben snapped.

Twenty actives were lined against the walls when Loren entered the room. Big Ben stood in the middle, a swat paddle gripped tightly in his meathook right hand.

"Bend over and grab your ankles," he ordered.

"What did I do wrong?" pleaded Loren.

"Shut the fuck up!"

Loren looked around the room, his eyes imploring his old hometown buddy, Parkinson, to intercede. No chance. He assumed the position.

"This is for doing a horseshit job cleaning the toilets!" barked Big Ben, unloading. The sound crackled through the room, the force of the blow lifting Loren off his feet.

"And this is for not wearing your pledge pin to class!" Big Ben swung even harder.

"And this is for being such a dumb fuckin' hayseed!"

The third blow shattered the paddle, the top half flying across the room like a helicopter, the handle still in Big Ben's hand. Stunned, Loren turned and stomped out of the room, welts already rising on his ass. He flew out of the main house and charged across the driveway to the annex, stopping at the bottom of the stairs on the first floor.

"Motherfucker!" he screamed, slamming his fist into the wall. Plaster flew in every direction.

He marched into his room and began stuffing his clothes into his suitcase. "Who needs this shit!" he yelled, throwing his pledge manual against the wall. "I quit!"

3

Ron

This is a sad case. A girl in one of Ron's classes is very smitten with him. Her folks have discovered that he is one-eighth colored and have forbidden their meeting. She has cried to me and cannot understand her parents' views! Her folks questioned him and he admitted that it was true.
—Counselor's notes, Los Angeles High, 1958

Good-looking Ron Vaughn walked briskly by the noisy TV room filled with fraternity brothers watching the 49ers and the Rams. He was off to the library to study for his midterm in Calculus 1.

"You book too much," yelled Loren. "Come and watch the game."

"Ah, I better not," said Ron, who had dissuaded Loren, his pledge brother, from quitting.

Loren leaped out of his chair and pulled him into the room. Ron laughed—he liked Loren's considerable vigor. But as he took a seat on the arm of the couch, he couldn't relax. He was in college to become an architect, not to watch the 49ers.

He was a handsome six-two, 190 pounds, with curly black hair, soft brown eyes, and a bashful smile, uniquely graceful and at the same time awkward. There was about him this wonderful and human mixture of confidence and insecurity, an amiable, softhearted guy. At Los Angeles High School he had been Boys Senior Board president, first team in football and track, and winner of the Roman Award, the honor given to the school's scholar-athlete of the year. He was serious-minded, private, always on the go, consumed with his studies, art, and football practice. He desperately wanted to be an architect just like his father, just like his grandfather. He was also the first Negro in the ninety-two-year history of Pi KA. But nobody knew that at the time. Not for sure, anyway. There were whispers. But that's all they were.

On the television screen, 49er quarterback John Brodie dropped back in the pocket and lofted a high arching spiral toward the corner of the end zone. Leaping high above the defenders to pull it in for a touchdown was wide receiver R. C. Owens.

"Look at that fuckin' jigaboo jump!" yelled Big Ben.

Ron picked up his books and walked out the door, ignoring the racial epithet . . . as usual.

He was not "one-eighth colored" as his high school counselor wrote. He was 100 percent. According to California law, a person with any mixed blood was legally "colored." There was no percentage—you either were or you weren't. Ron was. But he looked as white as anyone else in the fraternity.

He was an only child, his entire childhood spent in L.A. in the house his father designed and built on a lot on Twenty-sixth Place that had once been part of a goat farm. It was in a neighborhood near the corner of Adams and Western boulevards, four miles from downtown at the western edge of the city's middle-class minority population. In the late 1800s, it had been *the* affluent part of town, its families having made fortunes in gold and shipping, its houses large brick mansions along Adams Boulevard. After the Depression, many of the old estates were torn down for subdivision, the rich moving west to Beverly Hills and Bel Air, the first hint of white flight setting in.

The Vaughn family tree was the amalgamation of America the melting pot. Ron's mother and father, Ralph and Betty, were both light-skinned "people of color." Ralph, born and raised in Washington, D.C., was a tall, thin man, handsome and courtly, well bred. His skin was olive, a pigment darker than his son's. Ron's paternal great-grandmother was thought to be half Sioux, an exotic woman with jet-black hair, high cheekbones, and erect posture; his paternal grandfather, Roscoe, was light-skinned, a strict disciplinarian who was the superintendent of the trade school program for minority students in the D.C. School District and a practicing architect. Ralph, a graduate of the University of Illinois in 1932, was teaching the theory of design and the history of architecture at Howard University when he met Betty Fry, Ron's mother, who was working at the university as a librarian. She was tall, urbane, sophisticated, well read, a former Queen of the May while she was a student at Howard. "She's as beautiful as any movie star," Ralph told his friends. They made a striking couple, heads turning when they walked down D.C. streets together. According to the oral history of Betty's family, her maternal great-grandfather was a runaway slave who fled to Pennsylvania and married a Quaker woman. Betty, whose skin was the color of milky cocoa, was born in Washington, D.C., where she attended segregated schools all the way through college. Her brown-skinned father was a prominent Washington, D.C., dentist; her mother was a light-skinned "person of color" active in the city's bustling minority social circles. Although Betty and Ralph could both pass as white, they grew weary of Southern racial discrimination—segregated schools, segregated drinking fountains, segregated restaurants. In California, they were convinced, it would be different. Color wouldn't matter. California was a window to the future, a certifiable paradise, a place where anybody could become middle class. It would be the ideal place to raise a family. They moved to Los Angeles in 1937.

During World War II, Ralph worked as a set designer for M-G-M, the first Negro to be hired in production design by a major Hollywood studio. When the war ended, he began moonlighting as an architect—one of his first jobs was to design a remodel for Schwab's Drugstore on Sunset Boulevard, where Lana Turner was discovered and where Ron worked as a delivery boy in high school. Ralph dreamed of going into business for himself, and in even wilder flights of fancy, he dreamed of being a painter, an inventor, a modern-day da Vinci. But with a wife and small son to provide for, he stayed the course at M-G-M. When a strike shut down the studio in 1946, however, he didn't want to be the first Negro set designer *and* the first Negro scab. An honorable man, he walked the picket line, and when he quit the strike to open his own architect's office, he contributed all his savings to the union's strike fund. From the first day he opened his own business, he was swamped with work, helped by the easy availability of FHA loans—remodels in Beverly Hills, a restaurant in Encino, an apartment building in Venice, homes in Watts. He rode the Southern California building boom, leasing an expensive new office with marble floors on Wilshire Boulevard. He went into partnership with an architect with a Harvard degree, hired a staff of fourteen, bought a new Cadillac, and gave the Pontiac to Betty.

But with success came long hours at the office. He was too busy to do the things dads were supposed to do with their boys. There were no trips to the park to play catch, no closeness. The only sporting event he took

Ron to was a wrestling match at the Olympic Auditorium between Gorgeous George and Antonio "Argentina" Rocca. When Ralph came home at night, either he was too exhausted to do anything but plop into the easy chair and have a martini or else he went out to the garage, which he had converted into a studio, and worked on his drawings. Ron liked to bring his paper and drawing pencils to the studio and sit on the floor behind him, working on his own drawings. That was their game of catch.

For succor, Ron relied more on his mother, who had a busy schedule of her own. In addition to her job as a librarian with the L.A. School District at Foshay Junior High, she belonged to the NAACP, volunteered for the ACLU, and actively campaigned for local Democratic candidates. In 1954, when Senator Joseph McCarthy's witch-hunt echoed all the way down to Foshay School and authorities began pulling "subversive" books off the shelves at her library, including *Huckleberry Finn,* she fought back, speaking out against abridgment of the First Amendment on KNXT's community affairs program. Fearing recrimination, however, she wore a black veil, hiding her face from the camera. In addition to being a social activist, she was an active socialite. Well dressed and image-conscious, she took pride in her large circle of friends. Ralph was fond of accusing her of trying to enlist them in every social club in Los Angeles, making jokes about her spending more time with a martini glass in her hand than a frying pan. Most of their friends were other middle-class minorities. Most of Ron's friends were white.

When Ron was a small boy, Ralph and Betty agreed that race was not going to be a major issue in his upbringing. They were determined to have him grow up in an integrated neighborhood, attend integrated schools, eat in integrated restaurants. They wanted him to have it easier than his grandfathers, men who knew the dogs of Jim Crow. Race was rarely a topic of discussion at the Vaughn dinner table. When it was, Ralph always advised the same thing: "Everybody in the world is colored," he'd say. "Just be Ron Vaughn. The shade of your skin isn't important."

In high school, Ron made a conscious decision not to bring up the subject of his race. If somebody asked him about it, he would *admit it was true,* but it was clear to him that life was less complicated for white people. Who'd ever heard of black pride in the fifties? Although most of his close friends had been to his house and knew of his racial background, with most of the other kids in the school he was "passing" as white. He didn't think of it that way. After all, he believed he had a sense of who he was. He was just trying to walk a middle ground. Be friends with everybody. L.A. High was the most integrated school in the city. He was asked to join one of the school's all-white fraternities, but declined, not wanting to openly align with any one race. At lunchtime, when the students segregated themselves in the cafeteria, Negroes in one corner, whites in another, Orientals in another, Ron signed up to guard the parking lot from trespassers and hubcap thieves so he wouldn't have to make a choice between Negro and white.

In 1958 he wasn't worried about deep-seated issues of racial identity or what was happening at Central High in Little Rock. His concerns were more immediate—getting good grades, scoring touchdowns, earning a scholarship. Football had become a big part of his identity, neither Negro nor white, but male. Ralph and Betty could afford to pay for his college education, but it was critical to his self-esteem and concept of masculinity that he pay his own way. But when he graduated from L.A. High, despite his scholar-athlete award, he received no scholarship offers.

Ron was studying in his room in the fraternity annex at his drafting table —an old door he had sanded smooth and rested on two sawhorses. A *kaboom* suddenly shattered the calm. Walls shook and large chunks of plaster fell from the ceiling, crashing on his table, covering his drawing with a powdery white film. His first thought was Khrushchev had dropped the big one. Or that it was an earthquake—the house was only a thousand yards from the Hayward Fault, the second largest in California. It was neither. In the room directly overhead, Loren was up to his newest prank—jumping off his dresser and landing with a thud, knocking loose the plaster, hopefully to fall on Ron's head.

"Knock it off, Hayseed!" Ron yelled. He wondered if Loren ever studied.

There was a knock at his door. He ignored it, but the pounding persisted, and when he went to open it, there was Big Ben, a snarl etched across his bulldog face. "The brothers want to see you up in the SMC [president's] room in five minutes," he ordered.

Ron took a deep breath. This was it, he figured, his big moment of truth. The SMC room was where all official fraternity business took place, and was normally off-limits to pledges. He was sure this was the night he would be asked to sign an oath of allegiance to Pi KA and all it stood for . . . including the "White Clause." In other words, this was the night he would be asked to officially declare his whiteness in writing.

Pi Kappa Alpha was a national fraternity whose strength was its Southern chapters. Founded at the University of Virginia in 1868 and headquartered in Memphis, Tennessee, the fraternity adopted a White Clause in 1911 when it began expanding across the Mason-Dixon Line, designating itself as a "society of white college males." The University of California chapter endorsed this White Clause when it was founded in 1912.

For years the fraternity's national Supreme Council argued forcefully that it was a private, self-perpetuating society, free to adopt any qualifications of membership it chose. Until the fifties, the clause was never challenged, but as segregated aspects of American life, private and public, started coming under attack, state-supported institutions, such as Cal, began arguing that restrictive clauses violated state law. Beginning in 1950, each biennial national Pi KA convention discussed eliminating the clause, but each time it was overwhelmingly voted that the White Clause be kept.

"Keep it white!" the delegates chanted. "Keep it white!"

In 1958, under mounting pressure, a committee recommended the clause be stricken. The Berkeley chapter, already considered by national officers as somewhat of a maverick for refusing to conform to the sacrosanct national fraternity traditions of owning a fire engine or holding an annual Dream Girl of Pi KA pageant, voted to have the clause removed, a vote reflecting more the personal politics of the chapter's delegate, Clay Smith, than the members' rabid egalitarianism or commitment to civil rights. Nationally, the proposal was once again overwhelmingly defeated in a vote of its 120 chapters . . . and the fraternity remained white.

In 1960, when Ron pledged, only four national fraternities still retained racial or creedal restrictions in their charters: Alpha Tau Omega, Sigma Nu, Sigma Chi, and *Pi KA*. When he accepted the pin, however, he did not know any of this. Nor did any of the members know for *sure* that he was a Negro. Just as he had in high school, he had made a conscious decision when he came to Cal not to bring up the subject of his race unless somebody asked him. And given that he looked as white as Big Ben or anyone else, that was extremely unlikely.

Ron had not come to Cal directly from high school. After graduating from L.A. High, he joined the Coast Guard Reserve, serving his six months' active duty sailing up and down the coast of California. He figured that was the easiest way to fulfill his military obligation. Following active duty, he enrolled at Los Angeles Valley Junior College, hoping to earn a football or track scholarship to a major university. It was still vital to his sense of self-respect that he pay his own way to college. But he separated his shoulder in the second football game and missed the rest of the season. So much for his hopes for a football scholarship. And at the Bakersfield Relays, the big track meet of the junior college season, he spaced out for the start of the 880 relay and missed his race, waking up just in time to see the competition cross the finish line. So much for a track scholarship.

He came to Cal in September 1959, relying on his parents' money, spending his first year living in a dorm and practicing every afternoon as a redshirt walk-on with the football team, determined to impress the coaching staff into giving him his coveted scholarship. Cal was a school proud of its recent athletic accomplishments, but Ron had chosen to come to Berkeley not because of its athletic prowess but because of its School of Architecture, reputed to be the best in the state.

One of his first friends at Cal was Bill Grey, an accounting major who was one of the four Negroes on the football team. One day after practice Ron overheard Grey talking in the locker room about his new Redd Foxx album, and when Ron expressed an interest, Grey invited him to his apartment to listen to it. The next day Grey told his girlfriend about this white guy on the team who knew all the words to "Washing the Titanic." The girlfriend's mother, it turned out, was good friends with Ron's mother in L.A.

"I got news for you, honey," the girlfriend said. "That's no white boy."

Slowly, the whispers about Ron's background spread through the football team. But those who heard them willfully chose not to ask him about it . . . and he didn't say anything. Jack Trumbo, a Pi KA who was a nephew of blacklisted writer Dalton Trumbo and, like Ron, a redshirt sophomore on the football team majoring in architecture, had not heard the rumors of his racial background. He invited Ron to lunch at the fraternity. Ron was a good guy—that's what he knew for sure.

The thought of joining a fraternity wasn't something Ron had considered. He wasn't interested in being part of an exclusive group, white or Negro. His impression was that a fraternity was a bunch of immature guys running the halls, never studying, acting silly, swilling beer. He had been drunk only once—it was his senior year at L.A. High when he went to Rosarita Beach below Tijuana for spring break with three friends and they downed a quart of tequila and spent the day chasing burros in the sand dunes and throwing up in the surf. But he had met a dozen Pi KAs through football, and they made a convincing case for living with a group of people who shared a common interest. In the Coast Guard and in junior college he had been around guys who had nothing in common. Strangers. Same with the dorms, where everyone went his own way with no sense of unity or belonging. In the Pi KA house, which was the only fraternity he visited, everybody seemed to share at least one common interest: sports. He'd heard the arguments about fraternities being anti-intellectual, but as far as he was concerned, he got all the "intellectual" stimulation he needed studying about structure and design eight hours a day. He wasn't interested in spending all day in class and then coming home to discuss Proust. Another convincing argument for joining was that it might give a boost to his anemic social life. His only dates his first year were when Jackie, his green-eyed blond girlfriend from L.A. High, and Joyce, a plump but sexually enthusiastic girl he'd met in an art class in junior college, flew up to visit him. Although he liked both girls for a variety of reasons, each of those visits ended with him feeling guilty that they thought he had enticed them into coming to the Bay Area purely for sexual reasons. He had been raised to equate sex with commitment. No matter what all the guys in the locker room said.

When he was considering Pi KA's offer to join, he worried that somewhere down the line he would be asked to sign an oath pledging allegiance to a whites-only organization. He wasn't sure what the fraternity's policy on racial discrimination was . . . or even if they knew he was Negro. He did know that the University had recently mandated that all fraternities and sororities eliminate all restrictive racial or religious clauses from their constitutions by 1964 or else have their doors closed. But that was four years down the line, and hopefully by then he would be an architect.

Without discussing the decision with his parents, assuming they would tell him what they always told him—that race shouldn't be a factor—he pledged. He figured he would deal with issues of race within the fraternity as he always had . . . he would quietly ignore them. Unless, of course, he was asked to sign a White Clause. If that happened, he would quit the fraternity.

Ron walked into the SMC room for his moment of truth. Twenty actives lined the wall. Big Ben, Pi KA Sultan of Swat, was standing in the middle, brandishing his ubiquitous paddle.

"Was that your faggot little Karmann-Ghia I saw parked in the driveway yesterday, blocking my way?" he bellowed.

"Yes," answered Ron.

"Then bend over and kiss your ass goodbye!"

Whack! Whack! Whack!

"Now get your ugly ass out of my sight!" said Big Ben.

Ron hurriedly returned to his room, breathing a sigh of relief, his ass on fire, his semi-secret identity still intact.

4

Jim

Rush is the process whereby the "inners" select from the "outers" who will join their elite group based on five minutes of amorphous conversation.
  —*Daily Cal,* 1961

Stern and solemn, Jim stood on the corner of Piedmont and Durant, listening impatiently to Ralph's chatter. All Jim wanted was to get out of his coat and tie, borrow Ralph's flathead Ford, and go see his new girlfriend, Patty, who was still a junior at Mills High back home in Burlingame across the Bay.

"One more house," insisted Ralph, pointing toward Pi KA "This is supposed to be a bitchin' house."

Jim scowled. It was rush week 1962. Fifteen fraternities in three days of formal rush had taken its toll: too many handshakes, too many beers, too many amorphous conversations. He wasn't good at the small talk. He'd almost reached the point where he didn't much care which house he pledged . . . anything just to end the ordeal. He was even willing to join one Ralph didn't—despite their pact to stick together. Ralph was bugging him with his constant yammer and ubiquitous shit-eating grin. In the three days they'd been in Berkeley, they had rushed every house together. Jim was beginning to feel as if Ralph had *never* been out of his sight—grade school, Boy Scouts, Mills High football, cruising Mel's. They'd grown up three doors apart. Now, here they were again, freshmen at the Big U together, rushing fraternities. It wasn't that Jim was looking to ditch Ralph—he was still his best friend—but there was a part of him that hoped they didn't end up in the same frat. Ralph could be such a pest, like when he used to walk in the van Hoftens' house without knocking and make himself at home.

Ralph knocked on the Pi KA door. No answer. He knocked again. Still no answer. "Let's go," said Jim, edging away, always the cautious one. "You can't just walk in."

Undaunted, Ralph entered the vestibule, Jim reluctantly following. Nobody was in sight. Where was the rush chairman? Why weren't the members lined up in starched white shirts to greet them as they were at the other houses?

"What a shithole," Jim whispered, surveying the mess. "Let's beat feet."

Ralph continued deeper into the pit, Jim still following, mad at himself for playing the marionette, always letting somebody else pull the strings. Even Jim's decision to rush didn't feel like his own. His mom, who was an Alpha Chi Omega when she went to Cal in the thirties, and his older brother Scott, who was a Lambda Chi Alpha at Stanford, had told him he'd get lost in the black hole of such a big university if he didn't rush. He wasn't convinced. So why was he rushing? It wasn't to meet girls—he was already going steady with Patty . . . they'd even talked of getting married in four years when he graduated. He was joining a fraternity because, well, he wasn't sure.

Al Nelson, a first-string halfback, walked down the stairs and breezed out the front door, ignoring Jim and Ralph.

"That was Al Nelson!" exclaimed Ralph.

"So?" replied Jim.

"He's a great runner!" bubbled Ralph, a galaxy of hero-worshipping stars twinkling in his eyes.

"I could give a shit," said Jim, moving toward the door.

Another member walked down the stairs. It was Ron. "Can I help you guys?" he asked politely.

"We're here for rush," announced Ralph.

Ron smiled. Was this rushee joking? Didn't he know that Pi KA didn't bother itself with formal rush, relying instead on informal rush, a practice of bringing rushees by for lunch during the year—it could be an old high school buddy, a classmate, or, in most cases, a teammate. Pi KA was like the Masons: you had to know somebody to get invited in. Formal rush, the brothers believed, was a tedious series of phony handshakes and empty questions. ("Where're you from?" . . . "Oh, do you know

Chip Benson?" . . . "What's your major?") That was mindless chatter for the SAEs. So were sorority hostesses and noisy rush parties. Other fraternities bragged of the best rooms, or the best parties, or the best intramural teams. Pi KA bragged of its straight-ahead, broad-shouldered guys.

"How do we get to meet the guys?" asked Ralph. Jim cringed at his friend's brazenness.

"A lot of them will probably be at the Fern tonight," suggested Ron. "Try there."

Cal wasn't Jim's first choice. He had hoped to go to Stanford on a Navy ROTC scholarship like his brother Scott. He certainly had the qualifications—3.95 g.p.a., upper-five percentile on SAT scores, three-year varsity letterman in football and swimming. But when he went before the Navy ROTC scholarship review committee, he froze, coming off as a young man with all the personality of wax paper. This, coupled with his low scores on the leadership part of his written exam, torpedoed him.

There was no way his parents, Adriaan and Beverly van Hoften, could afford Stanford. Adriaan was promising to foot the bill at Cal, but Jim had learned early on that when it came to matters of finance, his father was not like the other dads on the block. In fact, Adriaan was not like other fathers in many ways.

Jim's biological father, Roger Cameron, died when Jim was only one. Jim grew up knowing almost nothing about him—who he was, what he did, how he died. Nor did he have any curiosity to find out. When Jim was six, his mother married Adriaan, who had immigrated from Holland after World War II. As far as Jim and Scott were concerned, Adriaan was their "real" father.

But in an era that demanded sameness, it bothered Jim that his father was a bit of an eccentric, unlike other dads. To the other kids on the block, Adriaan was a pied piper—a convivial, multitalented man who painted pretty pictures, played folk songs on his guitar, fixed anything that broke, whistled Beethoven's Fifth Symphony. But to Jim, he was pedantic, unorthodox, a reason to feel different when different wasn't cool. Even their two-story, two-bedroom redwood-shingled house—the only house Jim would live in until going off to college—was unlike any of the other houses on Hoover Street. Rustic, quaint, set back from the street, shaded by tall firs, enclosed behind an eight-foot cedar fence, it looked more like a chalet in the Swiss Alps than one of Burlingame's labyrinth of one-story bungalows with their red-tile roofs.

What bothered Jim most was that Adriaan, a commercial artist and illustrator, always seemed to be either out of a job or discontented with the one he had. Jim had lost track of how many ad agencies his father had quit or been fired from. Jim suspected it probably had something to do with his dad's obstinate, know-it-all attitude. The family was always stressed about money. There were many months when his mom, an executive secretary for Sylvania and then the Crippled Children's Society, earned the only income. That wasn't the way it was supposed to be in the fifties: dads were supposed to go to work at the same time every morning, moms were supposed to stay home and take care of the kids.

It wasn't that Jim didn't recognize Adriaan's eclectic talents. Adriaan was teaching him mechanical and carpentry skills, and a can-do, do-it-yourself spirit; when Beverly's mother came to live with the family, it was Adriaan who converted the garage into a studio apartment for her, with Jim's help. During the Christmas holidays, Adriaan would spend long hours artistically wrapping presents and brightly decorating a small trailer to look like a sleigh for the ride to relatives in Sacramento . . . but in truth, the wrapping was better than the gifts. It was always something: bankruptcy; the bank coming to take back the family Pontiac; the sheriff hauling Adriaan off to the clink for unpaid parking tickets. When Jim was in the eighth grade, Adriaan promised him a dollar for every A he brought home on his report card. The next semester, when Jim brought home straight A's, Adriaan promised payment in full . . . as soon as he got his next paycheck.

Beverly, a taciturn woman, tall and solid, always retreated to that place inside herself, quoting chapter and verse from *The Power of Positive Thinking* by her spiritual guru, Norman Vincent Peale. She and Adriaan shared backgrounds of lost family affluence. Adriaan's family had lost its oil refineries during World War II, and Beverly's father was taken down by the stock-market crash of 1929. Prior to that she had spent her childhood living in luxury on a large estate in San Mateo on the Peninsula, attending exclusive private schools, wearing the finest clothes, taking ballet from the best instructors. Her mother, Hilda McCurdy ("Mun" to her two grandsons), was one of the first women to earn a Phi Beta Kappa key, graduating from Indiana University with a degree in Latin; Beverly's father was a prominent federal judge who had successfully invested in blue-chip stocks. But the Crash of '29 wiped out the McCurdy family fortune, financially and spiritually breaking Judge McCurdy. He died when Beverly was still in high school. But in 1936, despite the lean times of the Depression, she graduated with a B.A. in English from Cal. After the death of Jim's natural father, she went to work as a secretary and question-and-answer columnist for the Fresno

Bee. That's when she met Adriaan. He was working as a graphic artist after immigrating to California's San Joaquin Valley following the war. The fact that he was still alive was testimony to his firm Dutch resolve. Born and raised in Rotterdam, Holland, he was a graduate of the prestigious Rotterdam Academy of Arts and Sciences and the London Royal Academy. In May 1940 he had stood on the balcony of his parents' home in Rotterdam and watched the Luftflotte II unleash what was at the time the largest aerial bombardment in history, flattening the city. The bombs stopped two blocks from the van Hoften home. Adriaan immediately enlisted in British Army Intelligence (the Dutch had no army) and was assigned to the Dutch Resistance. One of his assignments was to supply English bombers the coordinates to his father's oil tanks to prevent the Nazis from capturing them. He sat on a hilltop and watched the bombs turn a million dollars of his family's oil into a blazing inferno. In January 1943 he was captured by German SS officers while trying to supply the Resistance with handguns. He spent eighteen months in a prison camp, his weight dropping from 150 to 90. Twice the camp was hit by Allied air strikes, killing over 12,000 POWs. He was to be transferred to Auschwitz, Poland, but when the guard came to take him away, there was a mix-up with his papers and he was released by mistake. The Nazis even gave him money for the bus. By the time the Gestapo realized its error and came looking for him, he was back in Rotterdam, hiding with a Dutch family sympathetic to the Resistance. For six months, he lived in an attic without sunlight or room to stand up. His meals were handed up to him in the middle of the night. He had paper and pencil for drawing, but eighteen months in a prison camp had not only taken its physical toll, it had also sapped his creative energy. When the Germans surrendered on May 7, 1945, he emerged from the long, dark chrysalis of hiding, his youth the hard shell he abandoned as he crawled toward the light. But his stubborn Dutch resolve was secured for life. He would pass on that fortitude to Jim.

Despite Adriaan's strong will, it was the maternal side of the family that had the most influence on Jim. When he was a boy, it was Mun, the Phi Beta Kappa, who was waiting for him when he got home from school, ready to help him learn geography, sentence structure, equations. Every night she gave Jim and his brother Scott five vocabulary words from the dictionary, challenging them to make as many anagrams as they could. She gave them a telegraph set and taught them the Morse code. Mun and Beverly were anchored, pragmatic, and for a boy who, above all else, just wanted to fit in, that was more important than being able to whistle Beethoven's Fifth Symphony.

. . . .

Returning to the fraternity from physics class, he stopped in the drive-way to watch a two-on-two basketball game in progress, admiring Loren's athletic grace. But after three weeks in the fraternity, Jim was wondering if Loren ever studied. The fraternity and academics, he had discovered, seemed to be the antithesis of each other.

He went to his room and opened his textbook for Physics 4, a require-ment for engineering majors. Jim had signed up for engineering because, well, that's what somebody suggested he take. The first midterm was still two weeks away, but he was already in early panic, a hundred pages behind in the reading. He'd been the salutatorian of Mills High; achiev-ing good grades had been one sure way of feeling good about himself. With Scott getting a 3.8 g.p.a. at Stanford, he had high standards to reach.

He slammed his book down, unable to concentrate over the din out-side his door. Radios blared, conversations droned, balls bounced off the walls, and rising above it all was a full-volume mating call from one of the brothers standing on the second-floor balcony, the shrill noise di-rected at two perky Alpha Delta Pi's walking by.

"Doesn't anybody ever study around here!" Jim yelled.

"Piss and moan, piss and moan," a voice yelled back. "That's your new name. Piss 'n' Moan." Jim didn't appreciate that nickname any more than the first one he had been given—"Officer Muldoon." That name came from the TV show "Car 54, Where Are You?" His sidekick Ralph was "Officer Toody," although everybody in the house had amended it to "Toad."

Jim was having his doubts about Pi KA. He sensed he didn't fit into any of the cliques—football player, baseball player, drinking club mem-ber, pinned to an Alpha Delta Pi. Nor could he foresee it happening. He didn't even feel tight with his own ten pledge brothers, and that was the group, according to the pledgemaster, that he was supposed to be closest to. Ralph was his only clique.

And Pi KA was having its doubts about him. Nobody could explain for sure how it was that Muldoon and Toody had been pledged. The nearest anyone could figure was that they showed up at the Fern and a shitfaced brother pledged them as an r.f. Nobody would take credit and nobody could remember voting on them in rush meeting. But they were all moved in and had paid their first month's house bill ($100). The debate now centered on who was the bigger nerd . . . the grumpy Jim or Ralph the pest?

Jim had never quite cracked the in crowd at Mills High either. Not that he didn't want to. Who didn't? Those were the fifties, when being different wasn't fashionable. He wanted a ducktail—but his mom had said no. He wanted pegged pants—and his mom had said no again. It wasn't that Jim was really all that different from the other kids. He just didn't have quite enough of what it took to travel with the top dogs. No car. Too much baby fat. No cheerleader for a girlfriend. In his junior year he came up with a plan to close the gap. He taught himself how to sew and secretly pegged a pair of flared pants, doing it an inch every other week so his mother wouldn't notice. Of course, neither did the cool kids. And it wasn't as if he locked himself in his room and played the high school hermit. He was a joiner. Boy Scouts. Math Club. Church teen group. He was on the football team, although that didn't get him a lot of notice either—he toiled anonymously at left tackle on a team that won one game in three years. He swam breaststroke on the swim team too, finishing third in the Peninsula League finals, but that didn't exactly make him Troy Donahue with the girls. His parents didn't even show up to watch his meets.

Jim was a teenager who played it strictly by the rules. Except one. That was the time he let himself get talked into going with Ralph and two other buddies to hot-wire a brand-new Bonneville "pussy wagon" that belonged to an uncle of one of the boys. They took it cruising—or "making the loop," as the kids in Burlingame called the five-mile stretch of El Camino Real between King's Drive-In in Burlingame and Mel's Drive-In in San Bruno. It was an American Graffiti good time until the Bonneville's carburetors caught fire and the engine went up like a torch. When the other boys fled on foot, Jim ran too, mad at himself for being too much the follower. But at least they got away.

He struggled with his self-esteem, and joining Pi KA hadn't done it much good. The thought of turning in his pledge pin had crossed his mind. It was more than just the noise level. He was intimidated by all the jocks. Not by the fact that they were jocks—he liked to think he was a jock too, of sorts. What intimidated him about the jocks in Pi KA was that there were so many super jocks, guys who had been all-world in high school and were now stars in college. He had toyed with the idea of going out for freshman football until he saw the likes of Loren and Ron, athletes who were more muscular, more agile, and faster than he.

He also didn't think he measured up in terms of cultural hipness. He didn't watch much television or go to many movies. Sometimes after lunch the brothers would sit around the living room quizzing each other on the Top 10 hits on KYA. Jim didn't know the Shirelles from the Ronettes. Nor could he rattle off the stats of Juan Marichal or Joe "the

Jet" Perry. Ralph, on the other hand, knew the middle names of every player on the upstart Oakland Raiders. And when it came to fashion, Jim had packed his entire wardrobe into one small suitcase. He did, however, buy a new madras shirt to start college.

He also perceived a class difference. It seemed to him as if he was the only guy in the house without a shiny new car, or a big spending allowance from home, or a scholarship. He suspected none of the other guys had gotten up at four o'clock every morning in high school to deliver newspapers, as he did, or had collected for Fuller Brush in the summer so they could buy their own ski equipment and pay for their lift tickets, as he did. When his mother had told him there was no money for a new pair of desert boots, he picked avocados off the tree in their backyard and sold them door to door until he had enough for the boots.

Despite all his reservations about Pi KA, he was resolved to stick it out. He just wished he felt better about himself, about the fraternity.

He hurried past the entrance to campus at Bancroft and Telegraph, quickening his pace, ignoring the crowd that was hissing the disheveled speaker on a soapbox, a character the *Daily Californian* had pejoratively dubbed the "Sandaled Prophet of Peyote" for his outspoken advocacy of the use of narcotics. Jim didn't have time to stop and listen. He was on a mission.

He hustled past the Terrace, one of the hangouts for the beatniks on campus, then up the steps of venerable Harmon Gym. The sign inside the front door instructed freshman crew to meet in room 130. Slowly, he entered and glanced around the room. It looked like a Tarzan convention, thirty-five chiseled young men, all of them full of muscle. He felt like the Pillsbury Doughboy.

In the front of the room, standing tall and reproachful in a Cal navy-blue windbreaker, varsity coach Jim Lemmon surveyed his new recruits. Seated behind him were three distinguished-looking men in business suits. Lemmon was one of the most successful crew coaches in the country, with a reputation for his strenuous daily practices and his demand for academic excellence. Jim didn't recognize the three men in suits, but he remembered Lemmon from the freshman registration line. In a sport with no scholarships, Coach Lemmon recruited by standing at the end of the reg line every year, stopping every male over six feet and asking him if he wanted to try out for crew. When Coach Lemmon had approached Jim at the end of the line, Jim responded with a shrug of the shoulders and an "I'll think about it." After all, what did he know about crew? His only experience was rowing a boat on a Boy Scout camping trip. But the more he thought about it, the more it piqued his interest. Rowing a boat every day, he thought, might be a good way once and for all to firm his body and get rid of his final layer of baby fat. That was the reason he had initially turned out for swimming in high school. But the job wasn't finished—at six-three, 210 pounds, he wanted to lose about 15 pounds. It might also be a good way of feeling better about himself athletically in a house full of Jim Thorpes.

Coach Lemmon addressed the gathering, talking of commitment and conditioning. "There'll be days you'll go home from practice so tired you won't be able to open a book," he warned. "But you will. Crew has traditionally had the highest g.p.a. of any sport at Cal. And I intend to keep it that way."

Cal crew also had a tradition of winning, representing America in the 1928, 1932, and 1948 Olympic Games. Coach Lemmon introduced the three men behind him, each a former Cal rower and an ex-Olympian. They all stepped forward and proudly held up their gold medals for all in the room to see.

"America will be sending an eight-man crew to the Olympics in Tokyo in 1964," announced Coach Lemmon. "Need I say more?"

Returning to the fraternity that afternoon, Jim walked with a new purpose in his stride.

Now all he had to do was survive Hell Week.

5

Steve

All acts of hazing are specifically forbidden, including any type of physical harassment, psychological embarrassment, degradation, or infringement on the individual's academic efforts. Also forbidden is the consumption of any liquid or solid matter as well as any activity that is illegal or contrary to the individual's genuine moral or religious belief.
—Pi KA Pledge Manual

It was the night before Hell Week 1962. To ensure a good night's sleep, Steve and his nine pledge brothers had rented adjoining rooms at the Shattuck Hotel in downtown Berkeley. For the four months of their pledge semester, they had been listening to apocalyptic threats from the actives about how horrible Hell Week would be: swats until they hemorrhaged, nude marches across the Bay Bridge, live goldfish for dinner, and worst of all . . . *the biting, tearing pain.* Whatever that was. Steve double-checked to make sure he had everything on his Hell Week shopping list.

"Why the Kotex?" asked Ralph.

"Relax, Toad," Steve said calmly. "We'll find out soon enough."

Steve had a sense of calm. Then again, he had a sense of commotion. It was all part of his uncharted duality . . . a guy who tunneled into his finance textbook until midnight, then inhaled beers until closing; or a Zen-like athlete who sat quietly in the locker room before the game, then charged all over the field like a man possessed. On the freshman football team he was the starting right end on both offense and defense, leading the team in tackles.

"Gotta be tough," he counseled Toad.

Pi KA's Hell Week was allegedly the toughest on Frat Row. Maybe it was because it was a jock house filled with tough guys who thought the road to manhood was paved by a swat paddle. Or maybe it was a legacy of a generation of alumni who were veterans of World War II or the Korean conflict, men who battled through school on the GI Bill, men who'd faced death at Guadalcanal or Pork Chop Hill and weren't about to let peach-fuzzed boys from the new suburbs dance for free. Or maybe it was a male rite of passage, an arcane tradition handed down from the founding fathers. Or maybe there was no explanation and it was just a brainless exercise in degradation. Whatever the reason, Hell Week was an integral ingredient of the fraternity, as much a part of becoming a brother as learning the secret handshake. It was a private ritual never to be revealed, never to be questioned. Surviving was a badge of honor.

When Steve was still in Crocker Grade School in Sacramento, his friends began to notice a recurring trait: he liked to take risks. When he played football on the playground, for example, he ran head-on into waiting defenders rather than try to evade them; when he rode his Schwinn to Pratt's Drugstore to read Bugs Bunny comics with his best friend, Don Cobleigh, he darted fearlessly in and out of traffic on busy Land Park Drive, often with his hands off the handlebars.

Everybody agreed he was bold, tough, daring. There were conflicting theories, however, on how he got to be that way. His parents, Frank and Mary Radich, wondered if it had its roots in what happened when he was seven years old in 1951. The family was returning to Sacramento on U.S. 40 one evening from a Sunday outing to San Francisco. It was a well-traveled but not a particularly dangerous stretch of road—a flat ribbon of four-lane highway cutting through the Sacramento delta and the fertile farmland separating California's capital city and the Bay Area. Frank was going 60 miles an hour in his new Chrysler Windsor as he passed the Dixon turnoff. In the back seat, Steve and his two brothers, Frankie, five, and Mike, eight, were fighting, the usual pushing, shoving, establishing lines of death. Suddenly there was a rush of cold air, and older brother Mike was hollering that Steve had fallen out the door onto the highway. Frank slammed on his brakes, and when he ran back through the darkness, screaming out for his son, shielding his eyes from the onrushing headlights, there was Steve sitting by the side of the road, bloodied and bruised, but cool and calm, undaunted by his brush with death.

His brother Mike, who openly admitted he resented Steve for getting what he thought was favored-son status from Frank and Mary, believed Steve got his toughness from always having to defend himself against a spiteful older brother. When Steve was nine, Mike shot him in the ear with a BB gun; when he was ten, Mike hit him in the kneecap full force with a shovel. "I wanted to hurt him," said Mike. Denise Radich, the youngest of the four children, believed the toughness came from Steve's endless battles with his parents. Steve agreed. He couldn't remember when he wasn't at war with his dad. No matter what he did, it never seemed to be good enough. Frank Radich was a Croatian immigrant who had come to America with nothing, and had worked hard his whole life to grab a share of the American Dream, and he expected the same effort from his children.

On the surface, the Radichs fit the 1950s American portrait. They lived in a middle-class neighborhood, took family vacations to Tahoe and Santa Cruz, sat down at the dining-room table on Sunday afternoons for a big dinner of roast beef or a leg of lamb; they all pitched in with the family business, a small salad dressing and mayonnaise company. The boys played Little League, went to Scout meetings, excelled on the teams at McClatchy High . . . Denise got straight A's and took ballet . . . Mary sang soprano in the church choir, chaired the PTA, and served as Den Mother . . . Frank captained his bowling team, sponsored his sons' Little League team, belonged to the Chamber of Commerce and the City Planning Commission, joined a country club, served as Exalted Ruler of Sacramento BPOE Lodge Number 6, and contributed to the Democratic Party. In the forties, he purchased the financially troubled Sacramento Solons, the city's minor-league baseball team, and was hailed by the Sacramento *Union* as the "savior of professional baseball in the Capital City." Another piece of the American Dream realized.

But like Loren, who was a year ahead of him, Steve couldn't wait to leave home for college.

At precisely high noon on Friday, Steve and his pledge brothers, including Don Cobleigh, his best friend since the first grade, somberly walked in the back door, single file, burlap bags slung over their right shoulders. They were greeted by a tribal war chant . . . twenty-five actives gathered in the living room around a pony keg, chugging themselves into a ceremonial frenzy. The sacrificial goats had arrived. The curtains were drawn, jailing the room in midnight darkness; the front door was barricaded. The sign on the front porch read: "Initiation in progress. No visitors."

"Up against the wall, assholes!" screamed Big Ben.

For Big Ben, Hell Week was his chance to play DI, a reason for his military crew cut. A Marine reservist, he ran his life by the clock and by the book—he got his nickname because every morning at precisely seven o'clock he stormed onto the pledge sleeping porch and boomed out reveille with his foghorn voice. He enjoyed taking the art of hazing to new highs, or lows. His partner in abuse was business major Bobby "the General" Nichols, the shortest member of the fraternity, a fourth-year ROTC spit-shined cadet looking forward to entering the Army after graduation. He never walked to class—he strutted.

"Steve, how about a cold one before we get this show on the road?" asked Big Ben, offering his beer. Steve reached for it. Big Ben threw it in his face.

Steve wiped the beer from his eyes, resisting the urge to deliver one of the forearm shivers that Coach White taught him. After ten deafening minutes of insults, and ten more minutes of running in place, with active tripping, shoving, throwing beers, Big Ben ordered the games to begin.

"Get naked!" he bellowed. "It's time to find out if you pussies are *men* enough to be Pi KAs.

Steve stripped, the General strutting around him, knocking him off balance, stomping on his clothes. "Oh, excuse me," he said, picking up Steve's shirt. "Let me wash it." He spit on it.

"On your backs!" Big Ben ordered. "I wanna see eleven dicks pointing to the sky. Or in your case, Toad, pussy."

The actives watched and snickered as the pledges spread-eagled on the hardwood floor. "Bring on Aunt Jemima!" actives chanted.

Steve felt the syrup ooze into every crevice and orifice—eyes, armpits, hair, testicles. Next came a layer of garbage: coffee grounds, rancid cottage cheese, yesterday's oatmeal, whatever had been rescued from its final journey to the Berkeley dump. Some actives used spatulas to spread it on; others scooped it with their bare hands and fired it like buckshot. Then came the eggs, delivered every way possible: cracked over heads, plopped down throats, fired from across the room. Big Ben kneeled down next to Steve and used a black crayon to draw the circles of a target on his face, obscuring his handsome, rugged features, rendering him faceless. Steve's nose was the bull's-eye. The General scored a direct hit, then cracked a half dozen jumbo eggs into his empty beer cup and handed it to Steve. "Chug it, Pretty Boy!" Steve did as instructed. Ralph was ordered to his knees, then told to suck a yoke off the hardwood floor.

He too followed his instructions. Steve took another direct hit, this one running up his nostrils.

"Okay, you cunts!" barked Big Ben. "Get dressed!"

The Kotex pad was the first item of apparel, bonded to the crotch by the syrup. Then came the red ribbon, one end tied to the penis, the other end tied to the bell hung from the neck. The General clanged Steve's bell, and the vibrations carried down the red ribbon, right to his pecker. He quickly learned that the only way to ease the pain was to stand on tiptoes, releasing the tension. Next came the trout, stuffed inside the argyle and hung from the neck, where it would rot and stink for the rest of Hell Week. The burlap bag was the quintessence, instantly adhering to the sticky skin.

"You know what you are?" asked Big Ben, his finger boring into Steve's chest.

Steve shook his head.

"Of course you don't know what you are," Big Ben snarled. "You're too stupid to know anything. So I'll tell you what you are. You're a fuckin' goat, that's what. *A goat!* You're the dumbest species on earth, lower than whale shit at the bottom of the Mindanao Strait. Do you know where the Mindanao Strait is?"

Steve shook his head.

"I know," volunteered Ralph.

"Shut the fuck up, you worthless Toad!" yelled Big Ben, ordering Steve to do fifty push-ups. When he reached forty, Big Ben planted his size-12 wing tip in the middle of his back and flattened him to the floor. "What's the matter, cunt, can't you finish? I thought you were supposed to be so fuckin' tough."

Back on his feet, Steve stood at attention as Big Ben pointed to his pledge brothers. "Do you know who these assholes are?" he asked.

"My pledge brothers," said Steve, eyeing Cobleigh next to him, soaked in garbage and syrup from head to toe, egg dripping from his earlobes, struggling to get comfortable in his burlap bag.

"Wrong!" Big Ben explained. "They are your goat brothers!"

Steve and Cobleigh, like their goat brothers Jim and Ralph, had known each other since early childhood. The baby-faced Don knew him better than anyone, including Steve's own brothers. When they were growing up, sometimes it seemed as if Steve spent as much time at Don's house as he did at home, the two of them just sitting in Don's room, quietly reading, their close friendship not requiring anything more. Don, whose father was a bartender, didn't realize it at the time, but Steve often came to visit seeking shelter from the storm at home.

Steve was attracted to Don's light, breezy personality. Hardly a day had gone by that the two of them weren't together: walking to Crocker Grade School, playing on the same Little League team, riding bikes to California Junior High, sharing a tent on Boy Scout camping trips to the High Sierras, double-dating after football games. At McClatchy High, Don was the quarterback, Steve was the end; Don was the better student, Steve was the better athlete, twice making All-City in Sacramento as a 165-pound defensive end. Don knew better than anyone of Steve's daring—he'd watched him climb trees and throw his body at onrushing fullbacks . . . but it was the quiet side of his personality he liked the most. The generosity. The concern. He knew how hard Steve worked to do well—in sports, in school, in everything. In grade school, Steve had a slight speech impediment, pronouncing his r's as w's. Kids at school teased him, calling him Steve "Wadich." He diligently worked on the problem, and by junior high he had overcome it.

Don also admired Steve's resourcefulness and ingenuity. Like the time they were driving Mr. Radich's company pickup back from the all-night initiation ceremonies for the 36 Club, a McClatchy High fraternity. Steve was the president and most popular. His steady girlfriend, Linda Leigh, often accused him of preferring to be with his buddies in the club more than with her. At the Chug-a-lugathon Dances at Governor's Hall at the State Fairground, he abandoned her for long periods of time to revel with his friends, greeting each of them with his trademark head butt. Anyway, Steve was tearing along Highway 4 about thirty miles from Sacramento, driving like he was at the Indy 500—which according to a profile of him in the McClatchy High *Prospector* was his secret ambition. (And according to that same profile, his favorite pastimes were skiing and listening to the Ray Coniff Singers, and his future goal was "to make a lot of money.") He had promised to have the pickup back by noon, and if there was one thing Steve was afraid of, it was incurring his father's considerable wrath. They were out in the middle of nowhere, fifteen miles from a gas station, when steam began billowing from under the hood, blowing the radiator cap right off. Steve calmly pulled to the side of the road, climbed into the back of the truck, and started priming the half-empty keg. He filled two pitchers with warm beer, then poured it into the radiator. A couple minutes later, he and Don were laughing and smiling, cruising down Highway 4 into Sacramento, the pickup belching toward home.

. . . .

"Hell Week won't be over until you all can sing this song," ordered Big Ben. "The lyrics hold the secret of life." He put on operatic tenor Jan Peerce's recording of "The Bluebird of Happiness," a song suggesting that when the world seems dark and full of hate, it is important to hold one's head high so as to see the ray of light and love shine through. With "The Bluebird of Happiness" on endless repeat, the goats lined against the wall. A garbage can—known as the "barf bucket"—was set in front of them. Big Ben handed a large pitcher of dark brown liquid to Cobleigh, instructing him to drink as much as he could and then pass it to the next goat. It was a "goat shake"—molasses, vinegar, Worcestershire sauce, mustard, coffee, and prune juice.

To whet their thirst, Big Ben strolled down the line and heaped a tablespoon of garlic salt on each tongue, ordering them to swallow. Then he commanded them to take five bites of a "happy apple" (red onion).

Cobleigh took two long swigs of the goat shake and passed it to Steve. "Is that all you're going to drink, you pussy?" barked the General. "I guess you don't care if you fuck over your other goat brothers."

Steve drank the rest of the contents, sparing his goat brothers. Big Ben appeared with two more pitchers, starting them at both ends of the line. By the time the pitchers reached Steve in the middle, four goats had puked into the barf bucket. He too vomited.

"Toad, do you like your goat brothers?" asked the General.

Ralph nodded.

"That's nice," said the General. "Now climb in the barf bucket and dance! I wanna see you twistin'."

Ralph stepped into the garbage can and danced in his goat brothers' vomit.

And then Steve did too. Barefoot.

A three-inch layer of vomit covered the bottom of the barf bucket. The goats neared the end of a solid hour of calisthenics. Steve felt the Kotex pad chafing his crotch, the burlap yanking at his pubic hairs, the garlic salt numbing his nostrils.

He eyed Ralph at the end of the line, a sad sight, struggling through his sit-ups. Next to him was Jim. Steve was surprised at how tough Jim was, strong, stoic in his pain. Steve asked himself why he was putting up with it. There was no logical answer. He was on automatic pilot, brain disengaged, giving in to the process and the degradation, abdicating all power and responsibility to the actives. If chugging raw eggs, dancing in the barf bucket, and churning out sit-ups by the hundreds was what it took, then that's what he'd do. He loved the fraternity, its maleness, its group-think. He was at ease from the first day he pledged, never questioning his decision. Not for a second. He could handle the abuse. Pain, he'd learned in football, was only temporary. The humiliation and dishonor of quitting, however, were lasting, and that's what he'd suffer if he ripped off his burlap bag and stormed out the door. He could survive anything Big Ben could dish out.

Two A.M. was the worst time. That's when actives staggered in from their dates, full of booze and sexual frustration, taking it out on the goats. The easiest time of Hell Week was the Goat Olympics, which opened with the Marshmallow Relay Race, an event in which goats sat their naked butts on blocks of ice and waited for a teammate with a marshmallow wedged up his ass to waddle across the room and deposit it for the next leg of the race.

"Losing team eats the marshmallows," threatened Big Ben.

Another event of the Goat Olympics was Drink-Till-You-Puke, a simple game of drinking water until whatever food was left in the stomach was flushed up. Fire Drill was the toughest event, each goat racing nonstop from the basement to the third floor ten times with a mouthful of Tabasco sauce, spitting it on a smoldering fire in a wastepaper basket. By the last trip, legs wobbled and mouths and lungs burned. The last event, Under-the-Rug, was the most dangerous. The goats stripped off their burlap bags and crawled under a thick Pylon carpet. They had five minutes to smoke a long Dutch Masters cigar to the nub and get back in their burlap bags. Thick cigar smoke choked their lungs. Actives swandived onto the rug. (This event was canceled when a goat with asthma nearly choked to death.)

Day turned to night and back again. Actives worked in shifts to keep up the dietary, verbal, and physical assault. The stench from the garbage and rotting fish was overpowering.

Steve lost track of time. When would it be over? How many more push-ups? The worst part was not knowing. But that was part of the mind game . . . to keep the goats in the dark, literally, figuratively. Maroon them, mentally, physically. Promise them a glass of cold milk, give them a warm goat shake. Tell them they could go to sleep in five minutes, then keep them running in place for thirty minutes. Tease them with images of showers and clean sheets, then douse them with more syrup.

After forty-eight straight hours, the sleep-deprived goats, their Kotexes askew and their hair crusted with egg yolk, were marched upstairs to the

"goat head," a small water closet on the third floor barely large enough
for two men, let alone ten hulking goats. The goat head was the initiates'
only sanctuary. No active dared to penetrate the stench.

"You get five hours to sleep," Big Ben yelled.

The goats twisted like pretzels, trying to get comfortable. Jim curled
around the toilet, instantly asleep. Ralph huddled in a corner, shivering.
He had been up on the roof with a broom, assigned to stand guard
against a possible Russian invasion, Toad against the Red Baron.

"Wake up in there!" yelled Big Ben. "Get downstairs!"

Groggily, the goats filed out the door. It had only been five minutes.
More mind games, more sleep deprivation.

It was the fourth night of Hell Week. Shoehorned into the goat head, the
goats were too weary to resist. There were blisters and lesions from the
chafing of the burlap. "When is it going to be over?" whined Ralph.

Steve shrugged, refusing to give in or complain.

"Are you goats ready for the *biting, tearing pain?*" asked the General,
banging on the door. "Let's go!"

The General herded the goat brothers onto the third-floor sleeping
porch. Actives brandishing swat paddles lined the room. "You're the one
I want," growled Big Ben, waving his paddle in Steve's face.

During Hell Week two years earlier, a 210-pound active returned from
his date and pushed a goat against the wall, instructing him to keep his
hands at his side. Then he slugged him in the jaw, knocking him cold.
That was the closest the goats ever came to mutiny. After that, cooler
heads among the actives prevailed and the hitting or swatting of goats
during Hell Week was outlawed. But as Steve and his goat brothers stood
surrounded by a roomful of swat paddles, they didn't know that.

"Take off your burlap!" ordered the General.

The actives blindfolded the naked goats, tying their hands behind their
backs. Then, like captured enemy pilots, each goat was led single file up
and down the stairs for twenty terrorizing minutes, each step greeted
with a shove, a push, a poke in the back, a slap in the back of the head.
Pots and pans banged, actives howled. Back on the sleeping porch, the
goats were ordered to lie down on their backs. The cold linoleum felt
good on Steve's angry skin.

"Every active in this chapter," said the General, walking down the line,
his voice controlled, "has experienced the *biting, tearing pain.* It is what
makes us brothers in the bond."

"Now we'll find out what you goats are made of," added Big Ben.

From his place at the far end of the line, Steve heard Ralph cry out in pain from the other end, and then stumble out of the room. Then another goat wailed, and another. As the tortured cries got closer, his body tensed, his mind flailed. Then it was Jim's turn next to him. None of the goats were tougher, more impervious to pain than Jim. But he too moaned. Now it was Steve's turn.

"Here it is, the *biting, tearing pain,*" whispered Big Ben, kneeling next to him, pouring analgesic Heet straight onto Steve's crotch, sending him writhing around the floor. It was as if someone had taken a blowtorch to his testicles. But he refused to cry out.

With balls afire, he was led down the stairs into a room filled with beer-fueled actives, all whispering and tittering. He stood center stage, naked, blindfolded, hands tied.

"Before passing into the bonds of brotherhood," Big Ben said, "you must face the Morals Committee. Truth is demanded."

The Morals Committee? Steve had never heard of it. Big Ben explained that the ointment that had just been applied to his balls was a sacred Mayan emollient that for centuries had served as a medicinal lie detector that would cause the blood vessels to enlarge and burn if he lied.

"Huh?" Steve thought, too punch-drunk to think about lying or telling Big Ben he was full of shit.

The questions started simple—name, hometown, major. Steve was majoring in business. Then the actives, as they did with all the goats, leaned closer, better to hear the questions of the Sexual Inquisition. It was a room of voyeurs probing the private lives of their would-be brethren, hoping to find out who were the ladies' men, the braggarts, the underachievers.

"Are you now or have you ever been a queer?" asked Big Ben.

"No."

"Do you masturbate?"

"Yes."

"How often."

"Once or twice a week, I guess."

"Have you ever been laid?"

"Yes."

"How many times?"

"I'm not sure. Do you mean how many different girls?"

"Girls. Times. All of it."

Steve thought for a moment. His testicles were still burning. "Five different girls," he answered. "And I'd say about sixty or seventy times."

"Are you fucking that high school snatch of yours back in Sacramento?" asked Big Ben. "I sure hope so, because why else would you be running home every other weekend?"

Steve knew Big Ben was referring to Linda, whom he had been dating for two years. She was his first love. True love. Tormented love. He had brought her down to Berkeley for a party, but because he was embarrassed to have the brothers see him with a high school girl, he'd whisked her back to Sacramento while the night was still young. That was one of the immutable Pi KA commandments—no high school girlfriends. Linda was enrolling at Cal next semester, and that worried him . . . her coming to Berkeley would cramp his style, keep him from becoming the campus Romeo he'd like to be.

"Yes," he replied.

"How many times?"

"Twenty, maybe."

Blindfold still in place, he was guided out of the room into the bathroom across the hall. "Down on your hands and knees!" the General instructed, steering him toward the toilet. "To prove you're *man* enough to be a Pi KA, you have to do something now that all the brothers have done. Ready?"

Steve nodded.

The General guided his hand into the toilet. "You must now . . . partake of a brother's feces!"

Steve hesitated.

"Don't think about it!" urged the General. "Just grab one and take a bite!"

Steve did as instructed, reaching into the toilet, forcing the squishy floater into his mouth. He gagged down a small bite, swallowing quickly, his taste buds annihilated by garlic salt and goat shakes.

He heard a zipper fall.

"Now open your mouth and partake of a brother's piss!" ordered the General.

He felt the warm spray bounce off the roof of his mouth and trickle down his throat. "Swallow!" ordered the General.

His brain was too fogged to protest; he did as he was told. Suddenly, a hand reached around and untied his blindfold. Big Ben was looming over him with a big smile, offering him an ice-cold Coors. His goat brothers were there too, sipping beers, smiling, examining the bananas floating in the toilet and the vinegar in the squeeze bottle.

"Congratulations!" beamed Big Ben, shaking his hand. "Hell Week's over. You are no longer a goat. Welcome to Pi KA, Brother Radich."

6

Ron

From the body of guilty deed, a thousand fears and haunting thoughts proceed.
—William Wordsworth

Ron listened to assistant coach Bill White's instructions at practice, but the words somehow weren't getting through. He was exhausted, his brain an oatmeal soup after staying up all night to complete a project for Design 1N. All he wanted to do was curl up and go to sleep. The advice of the dean of the School of Architecture echoed through his mind: "You can't major in architecture and be involved in extracurricular activities too," he'd said. "You won't have the time or energy."

"Run a fly," ordered Coach White, the young ($8,000 a year) offensive-line coach under young ($16,000 a year) head coach Marv Levy.

Ron had earned his coveted scholarship with his hustle and hard work as a redshirt, and now as a sophomore he was alternating between third and fourth string. He had yet to get in a game, but unless he screwed up something fierce at this day's practice, he would be on the traveling squad for Saturday's game in South Bend against Notre Dame . . . which for a college football player was a trip to Mount Olympus to touch the hand of Zeus.

Ron had no illusions about the pros or being an All-American or anything grandiose like that, although he hoped he might work his way up to first string before his eligibility was over. For now, however, he was happy to be on the squad and getting a free ride, although an athletic scholarship at Cal in the early sixties wasn't exactly champagne and caviar. His benefits included no standing in long registration lines, all the cafeteria food he could eat at training-table dinners during the season, and a $100 monthly grant-in-aid that required fifty hours of campus work at two dollars an hour. His job during the week was to report to the maintenance shed of Building and Grounds, grab a rake or broom, and go wherever on campus the foreman assigned him. Some days he just leaned on his rake and watched the coeds go by. On Sundays in the fall he reported to Memorial Stadium to help sweep up the mess left by the crowd that had been there the day before to watch the Golden Bears play. And he made a few extra bucks selling the four tickets he received for every home game. He didn't have to worry about his parents using them. They had only come to see him play once in high school. The thrill of football was something lost on Ron's father.

"Run the damn thing right this time!" barked White.

The fly pattern was the hardest pass for Ron to catch. Even on eight hours' sleep he had trouble running forty yards at full speed and then looking up to catch the ball coming over his shoulder. He had already dropped his first two attempts. It was ironic that he had such trouble with it, considering it was a fly pattern he ran when he was thirteen years old that was one of the major coming-of-age events in his young life. It happened at Normandie Park in L.A.

He was in the seventh grade at Mount Vernon Junior High in Los Angeles, just entering adolescence, trying to establish his place in the universe, his quest compounded by the fact he had grown five inches in a year, a gawky, thin-chested kid with long skinny arms and legs. That was one problem. Another problem was that he believed that Negro males were supposed to be tough. He didn't feel tough. Nevertheless, he had ridden his bike to Normandie Park—his Armageddon, his land above the 38th parallel—to meet Tony Aquilar and Richard Chew, his best friends. Normally, he wouldn't risk coming to Normandie Park, the farthest frontier of his world: it was small and hostile, with dirt playing fields, netless basketball rims, a tetherball pole with no ball, and teenage thugs huddled in dark corners, smoking and cursing. Tony said he saw a switchblade there once.

But Ron had something to prove, if not to Tony and Richard, then to his own teetering self-confidence. It bothered him that he still cried and got scared so easily. In fact, he worried so much about how the other boys perceived him that he dropped out of the Saturday-morning art class his mother enrolled him in, fearful that he would be labeled a sissy. *Real* boys didn't do art. The last time he'd come to Normandie Park, three older Negro boys, the meanest-looking guys Ron had ever seen, ganged up on him, the biggest one slugging him in his pipe cleaner of a chest, knocking him to the concrete, bringing tears. But he'd come back, riding his bike, carrying his football, inexplicably pulled by the magnet buried deep in the Y chromosome that draws a boy to his limits, challenges him to step beyond the ignominy of boyhood. But where were Tony and Richard? As he waited, a thick fog rolled in. Finally, he spotted silhouettes walking briskly across the field. "Oh no," he mumbled. It was the three tough guys, coming out of the fog, right at him. He squeezed his handlebars, studying his chances for escape. It was hopeless, Custer surrounded at the Little Bighorn, no time to make a run for it, no time to explain that he really wasn't as white as he looked. But this wasn't about color. This was about courage and valor and the Y chromosome factor. Slowly, he dismounted.

"Can you catch?" asked the big one. "Go out for a pass!"

Ron hesitated, analyzing his situation. If he went out for the pass, chances were good he'd never see his ball or bike again. If he stood his ground and refused, chances were good he might not see anything again. He had arrived at a passage in life where he was going to have to make a stand or else run like a chicken. He suddenly wished his father had taught him how to fight rather than how to use a T square. For Ron, speed, not strength, was his capital. He put down his kickstand, handed over his ball, then took off on a fly pattern across the field, into the fog, a ghost through a steam room. Legs churning, he charted his route home . . . around the cemetery, by the Foster's Freeze, down Arlington Boulevard. How would he explain it to his mother? She would undoubtably tell him to go back and stand up for his rights. That's how she was. But hope springs in youth, and with one last glance he looked over his shoulder . . . just in time to see a blur falling from the mist. Tilting forward, arms outstretched, he caught it in his fingertips, pulling it to his body. A miracle catch! Better than Willie Mays's at the Polo Grounds. Better than Crazy Legs Hirsch in the end zone of the Coliseum. Those were only games. This was more. There was no high-five, no end-zone spike, no Ronnie Shuffle. Those rites of manhood hadn't been invented yet. He tucked the ball to his side and trotted back, ready for more pass routes. Dusk had surrendered to evening when he finally returned home, eager to share the details of his greatest male triumph. But how could Ralph, a gentle man and an artist, possibly relate? Or how could Betty, a mother and a woman, conceivably understand? They were both, as Ron saw it, going through that difficult age all parents go through when they just don't get it, too busy making a living.

But now, seven years later, hard as he would try, he couldn't master the over-the-shoulder catch. Not even with Coach White glaring at him.

Ron liked Coach White—it was for the same reason he had liked his coach at L.A. High, Joe Edelson. They were tough, no-nonsense men; Ron always knew where he stood with them. That was important to him. He wished his father was more that way, tougher, more disciplined. Too many times he didn't know where he stood with his father. Ralph was more like Coach Levy—distant, preoccupied, concentrating on the bigger picture.

"Go!" screamed Coach White, who liked Ron, thinking he had potential to be a first-stringer. He also realized that Ron was a young man with priorities, his studies coming before football.

Ron ran down field, punchy from lack of sleep, his legs churning in slow motion. He was outside his body, looking down, watching himself suddenly veer to the right, a top losing its spin. His legs buckled and he crashed to the turf. He struggled to get up, but everything was spinning, fuzzy, caught in a vertigo. He closed his eyes, seeking balance. When he opened them, Coach White was standing over him.

"What's wrong?" White inquired.

"Nothing," blurted Ron, stumbling to his feet.

"Then get back there and do it right!"

Ron steadied himself, trotting unsteadily back to the line of scrimmage for another fly pattern. He would survive and go to South Bend to watch the game from the end of the bench. But between the demands of his studies, football, and the fraternity, he wondered if something wouldn't have to go.

The mood was perfect: Frank Sinatra on the hi-fi, the lights down low, his parents not due home for hours, Jackie snuggled close to him on the couch, rekindling their old high school flame. It was Christmas vacation 1961. The phone rang.

He ignored it.

He wasn't going to let anything disturb the moment. Jackie, blond, green-eyed, five-nine, pretty, had been his one and only true love. They met as juniors at L.A. High. Jackie had been the Amy Vanderbilt of L.A. High, never meeting a club or activity she didn't want to join: Junior Girls Board; president of her sorority; honor student; Job's Daughters; High Teens (at the Methodist church on Wilshire Boulevard). On weekends she worked in her mother and stepfather's stationery store in Santa

Monica. Her mother was an alcoholic; her real father died when she was three. On her first date with Ron to "A Night in Shangri-la," the junior prom, Ron almost called off the date when she came down the stairs wearing a gold kimono, a black obi, dark eye shadow, and her hair dyed black. He thought she looked like a Chinese hooker, and as soon as the dance was over, he asked her to go home and rinse out her hair and change her clothes before he would take her out to dinner at Ciro's on the Sunset Strip.

The phone rang again. He ignored it again.

In their senior year, they had been informed by the principal that he had received a phone call from an angry parent demanding that they not be allowed to attend the prom. Even though L.A. High was an integrated school, interracial dating was taboo, and this angry parent, whoever it was, objected to Ron and Jackie's relationship. Jackie, who knew of Ron's background before they ever went out, suspected the complaint came from the father of one of her girlfriends, a man who would hold the phone in front of her face every time she visited, telling her that if she and that "nigger boy" ever got married, their children would be as "black as this phone." Ron suspected it was Jackie's stepfather, who ignored him every time he came to pick up Jackie. The principal left it up to them whether or not they went to the prom, and they did go. Ron's decision to attend was not because he saw a chance to take a stand against racism. He had no interest in being a crusader. His reasons for going were more primal—he was in love with Jackie and wanted to go to the senior prom. Nothing more came of the parent's phone call . . . except the impression it left on Ron.

He slipped his arm around her on the couch, ready to make his move. And once more the phone rang.

"Don't you think you should answer it?" she asked.

Ron shook his head. It had been over a year since he and Jackie had done "it," and he didn't want to take any chance on letting this romantic mood get away. Sex had become part of their relationship in their senior year, although it was something that confused Ron at the time. He knew he was going off to the Coast Guard and then to college to become an architect, and there was no way he would be ready to commit to anything permanent for a long time. Jackie was a "nice" girl, not some cheapie for a quick thrill. He felt guilty after he'd left for college, worried that he'd used her. They'd never talked about it, but Ron was pretty sure she would have said yes if he asked her to marry him. It was true—she would have. But on this romantic night, Ron wasn't thinking about marriage, or guilt, or running fly patterns. He just wanted to get laid.

Once more the phone rang. Persistently. Nine, ten times. Finally, he got up to answer it, taking the call in the kitchen, surprised to hear the voice on the other end. It was Joyce, his erotic, heavyset friend whom he'd met in advanced art class at Valley JC. He hadn't seen her since spring break when he'd gone to her apartment in Hollywood for sex. She'd written him a letter two months later, informing him that she was late for her period. He'd stuffed it in the bottom drawer of his desk at the fraternity and tried not to think about it, figuring he'd hear from her again if she was pregnant. When she never contacted him, he assumed everything was okay.

"I need to see you!" she said urgently.

"How about tomorrow?" he asked.

"No," she pleaded. "I need to see you *now.*"

"About what?"

"Please! You've gotta come over." Her voice had gone from urgent to hysterical. "I'll tell you when you get here," she pleaded.

"Okay, I'll be right there," he promised.

Returning to the living room, he sat back down next to Jackie. "I have to run an errand for my mom," he said. "Wait here. I'll be back in thirty minutes."

He drove his mom's white Buick Roadmaster to Joyce's apartment near Sunset and Gower where she lived with her mother, a wardrobe lady for Paramount Studios. On the radio the news out of Birmingham was distressing—the Freedom Riders' bus had been firebombed. But that was Alabama. This was California and things were fine with Ron.

Until now.

Joyce answered the door in her robe, a box of Kleenex in her hand. She looked terrible, no makeup, hair unbrushed, red puffy eyes. She'd gained more weight and her warm smile was gone.

As soon as he entered the apartment, she led him down the hall to her bedroom, slowly pushing open the door, pointing toward the bed. In the dim light, he could see a small bundle on top of the bedspread. He inched closer.

"What's this?" he asked.

"It's your son," she whispered.

His heart crashed to his size-11 penny loafers.

She said the baby was one day old. She had delivered it herself, right there in her bathroom.

"Are you sure it's mine?" he asked.

"Positive," she answered. "Look at him. Is there any doubt?"

Indeed, the baby had Ron's black hair, the long Vaughn face. There was no doubt.

"Shouldn't you and the baby be in a hospital?" he asked.

No, she assured him, she and the baby were all right, and besides, there was no money. Tears tumbled down her swollen cheeks.

"What are we going to do?" she asked.

We? What was he supposed to do? Quit school? Forget about being an architect? Go back to his summer job as a delivery boy for Schwab's Drugstore so he could spend the rest of his life supporting a family he didn't want? He'd never been so instantly sure of anything in his whole life.

"We can't keep it," he announced.

Her tears turned to sobs.

He wanted to hold her, tell her everything would be okay. He couldn't. A voice inside him told him to be strong, invulnerable, decisive, distant. The responsibility of fatherhood was beyond him.

"I could raise it myself while you're finishing school," she suggested.

"Be realistic," he said, surprised at the force in his voice. He knew he was right. How could *she* support it? Sell her paintings on the sidewalk? Her mother barely made enough to pay rent, and her father was out of the picture. "It wouldn't be fair to the baby," he added.

"So what are you saying?" she asked.

He didn't want to discuss it—he had to act. He picked up the phone and called the operator for the number of City of Angels, the hospital where he was born.

"What are you doing?" demanded Joyce.

He didn't reply, dialing the hospital. "I just found an abandoned baby," he said. "Can you tell me what to do with it?"

The switchboard operator asked his name and phone number. He hung up.

"What did they say?" wept Joyce.

"I'm supposed to take it down there," he lied.

"But I don't want you to," she said.

He cupped her hand in his. "I know this is the right thing to do," he whispered.

He picked up the baby in its blanket and edged toward the door. He had never held a baby before. Joyce was too weak, too drained to resist. "I'll call you," he promised. Then he walked out the door, stiffly cradling their son in his long arms.

He drove west on Sunset in his mom's Roadmaster, passing Ciro's, where he and Jackie had gone after "A Night in Shangri-la." The baby slept. He didn't know where he was going. His world was spinning.

He remembered a building he'd driven by many times, one in which nurses could be seen walking patients in a courtyard. It was in the Valley, he thought, somewhere close to Bob's Big Boy. It felt safe . . . a good place to take a newborn baby.

He turned right on Laurel Canyon, the Roadmaster lugging up the hill, past the mansions and movie stars' homes, over Mulholland Drive, then down into North Hollywood. His mind was a Christmas fog. Was Bob's Big Boy on Magnolia or Burbank Boulevard? He stopped at a signal next to two girls in their daddy's T-Bird.

"Where's Bob's Big Boy?" he asked.

They smiled and signaled for him to follow.

At Bob's Big Boy, he turned and headed back over Laurel Canyon. The baby stirred—but thank goodness, he wasn't crying. Ron tried to think of a lullaby; he turned on the radio instead. The Tokens were singing about the lion sleeping in the jungle, the mighty jungle. "Awheeeemaway . . . awheeeemaway."

Maybe he should just leave the baby on a park bench, he thought. Or maybe he should take it back to Joyce and let her raise it by herself. No, absolutely not, he reassured himself.

He drove through Beverly Hills toward the La Brea tar pits. That's what he felt like—a dinosaur stuck in the goo, trying to get loose. He was close to Jackie's house. Oh shit! He'd forgotten all about her. No doubt she'd given up and gone home. How could he ever explain this?

Near Hancock Park, he spotted a sign for a nursing home. He turned into the parking lot and shut off the engine. The baby's cry pierced the night.

Perspiring, heart pounding, he approached the nurses' station, the baby in his arm. A gray-haired woman behind the desk offered a generous smile.

"I just found this baby on the steps of an apartment building of a friend of mine," he stammered. "Nobody in the apartment knows who it belongs to."

"Who could do such a thing?" the nurse wondered.

He said he didn't know what to do and he was late for an appointment. "Can you take care of it?" he asked, head down.

She said she would, promising to call the county hospital and the police.

He thanked her and handed her the baby, then turned for the door, no last hug, no final glance.

"Young man," she called. "I need to get your name and address. The police will probably want to talk to you."

He stopped at the glass door. All he had to do was keep going, out into the December night and gone. Who would know?

He returned to the counter and left his name and address.

There was a small article on a back page of the L.A. *Times* about a student finding an abandoned baby, but Ron was never contacted by the police. He worried about Joyce. He couldn't just desert her. She was anguished, suffering. But a stronger voice told him he couldn't turn back. They talked on the phone. He explained what he'd done, telling her again that it was for the best. She wanted the baby back.

He felt guilt, a thousand fears and haunting thoughts proceeding. He needed to talk to someone. He had no preacher to turn to, no fraternity brother he could share something so personal with. How could he when he couldn't even talk to them about something as basic as his racial identity? He went to his father, more for reassurance than anything else, validation that he'd done the right thing. It felt odd—he had never talked confidentially or intimately with his father—but telling him about the baby brought a new closeness and sense of trust.

Ralph listened, then calmly assured him that he'd done the correct thing, and yes, the baby would be better off, and yes, Ron was right when he said that finishing his education was what was most important.

"This should be our secret," advised Ralph. "We don't need to tell your mom. She'd only worry. Get back up there to Berkeley and put this thing out of your mind. And remember, Ron, it's not the baby's fault."

7

Larry

The only thing necessary for the triumph of evil is for good men to do nothing.
—Edmund Burke

When it was my turn during Hell Week to enter the crowded Inquisition Room and reveal the intimate details of my sex life, I was doomed to share my big secret . . . that I was a six-three, 175-pound, flat-bellied, nineteen-year-old virgin.

"What kind of worthless goat are you?" demanded Big Ben.

Embarrassed and humiliated, that's what species of goat I was. I stood there stark naked, blindfolded, hands tied, surrounded by every active in the fraternity, my balls on fire . . . and I was confessing that I didn't have what it takes to get past first base.

"Do something about it!" charged Big Ben.

I hurried in the front door of the fraternity after baseball practice and found a line of a dozen brothers serpentining its way from Jim "Jayhawk" Nixon's third-floor room down the stairs to the second floor.

"What's up?" I inquired.

"It's a gangbang," Ralph replied. "There's a nympho in Jayhawk's room!"

It figured that Jayhawk would be involved. He was the fraternity's resident voyeur, a moon-faced transfer from the University of Kansas. The windows of his third-floor room faced west, offering a spectacular panorama of the Bay, which he enjoyed, but not as much as his view of Freeborn Hall, a girls' dorm a block away. He kept a mounted telescope focused on its windows. On the wall over his stack of *Playboys* was a scale drawing of the dorm, a square representing each room. Inside each square were notations reminding him of peak viewing times. He hawked endlessly, memorizing girls' schedules, planning his day around it, missing meals, skipping classes. He knew which girls never pulled their curtains. He kept a tally sheet on the wall, awarding himself three points for every totally naked girl, two points for breasts, one point for bra and panties. His total was in the hundreds. He took pride in his diligence.

Nobody knew for sure who the "nympho" was or where she came from . . . at least nobody was admitting it. Somebody said Big Ben found her wandering across campus and talked her into coming back to the fraternity. Somebody else claimed she'd screwed half the Betas the day before and they referred her to us. According to those who had already been in the room, she was incoherent.

"She just sorta lays there," said Ralph. "But she must like it. She's not complaining. I could see come running down her leg, so I just took a blow job."

I decided I'd rather be a virgin than thirteenth in line. I went downstairs to play Ping-Pong, ignoring the barking, ignoring the reality, ignoring the responsibility. I didn't think about the possibility of rape. Nobody was holding a gun to her head, I told myself. It was just a harmless gangbang. Boys being boys. I did nothing.

After the siege, she walked downstairs. I guessed her to be eighteen, although everything about her—her face, clothes, hair—was so worn and disheveled it was hard to tell. Her eyes were sunken, vacant; her body ransacked.

A pledge drove her into downtown Berkeley, dropping her off on a street corner. Thirty minutes later she was back, walking up the stairs to Jayhawk's room. Steve rescued her, leading her back outside, pointing her down the street. Dazed and disturbed, she disappeared into the night, never to return.

The debate over compulsory ROTC was a major issue on campus in 1961—all males were required to take it for a minimum of two years. A student had been expelled for staging a one-man sit-in on the steps of Sproul Hall, the administration building. In an editorial, the politically moderate *Daily Californian* joined the criticism:

The ROTC program is intellectually inferior, interfering with personal liberty, forcing a quasi-military discipline, teaching obsolete tactics with out-of-date weapons, and the severest lapse in the record of the university as an institution of high intellectual caliber.

The saber rattling over the construction of the Berlin Wall and the shooting down of a U-2 spy plane over Leningrad was unsettling, as was the prospect of mandatory military service after graduation, but for the life of me, I couldn't figure out how my marching around Cal's Edwards Field was helping to make the world safe for democracy. My disdain for ROTC was not as much moral or political as it was visceral: I dreaded putting on the itchy wool uniform once a week; I dreaded goose-stepping around like a toy soldier; I dreaded the gung ho student officers who thought they were the second coming of General Patton; I dreaded spit-shining my military shoes; I dreaded studying the kill-or-be-killed philosophy of President Kennedy's military adviser General Maxwell Taylor. I was learning the muzzle velocity of machine guns and the chain of command. What did that have to do with my becoming the Dodgers' shortstop? Intellectual rock bottom came when the sergeant assigned a paperback titled *Hits Count* the week before we went to the shooting range. It had cartoons and anecdotes about hillbillies who kept missing the target but finally learned how to kill when they pretended the enemy's head was a pumpkin on a fence post. The book's concluding sentence was: "Knock 'em dead on the first shot."

I felt like Beetle Bailey. At the shooting range—my first (and only) time firing a gun—I missed the target completely on my initial five shots with my M-1. "I've never seen anybody miss everything," said the sergeant. When we took our M-1s apart to clean them, I couldn't get mine back together.

During inspection I got a demerit for unshined shoes and dirty brass buttons. I started to worry I might flunk out because of scuffed-up Army shoes. Then I overheard two cadets in my platoon talking about Penny Shine, a spray-on polish. It worked like magic. At the next inspection, the sergeant saw his reflection in my shoe tops. I got a platoon commendation for three weeks in a row. But then I pulled the shoes out of the closet to get dressed for drill and the leather had cracked—there were more lines across the top of my shoes than an L.A. road map.

But somehow—I guess it was because I aced the test on the tactics of the Spanish-American War—I pulled a B, beefing up my anemic g.p.a. As luck would have it, the University yielded to criticism and dropped mandatory ROTC . . . just as I finished my two years.

. . . .

I was at bat in the top of the tenth inning at USC's Bovard Field. Scoreless tie. The league opener my sophomore year. The Bears against the defending NCAA champs. The evil Trojans. Lots of big-league bird-dog scouts in the stands. Dad was there too. It was the biggest game of my young life. As I dug in at the plate, I had one thing on my mind—not gangbang, not my midterm in Poli Sci 1A on Monday, not the New Frontier. I was thinking home run. Hero time.

My season was off to a rousing start. In the team's first twenty games, I was leading the team in batting average and RBIs, hitting cleanup, alternating between shortstop and right field. The *Daily Cal* dubbed me the "prize sophomore phenom."

Baseball was my ticket to self-confidence. Academically, I was intimidated in the classroom, never joining in class discussions, still undecided on a major. With girls, I felt insecure, afraid of getting shot down, no clue what they were thinking . . . although liquor and the twist had gotten me over my Fear of Dancing. But as soon as I put on my jock I felt fixed in my place in the world. It was as if I had decided at an early age— or maybe it was decided for me—that baseball would be the one thing in my life that would best define me. It was something I could do better than others, giving me a distinct identity, a unique potential. I excelled, both in my eyes and to those around me. I had devoted an inestimable amount of hours throwing a rubber ball against the side of the garage as a boy, allowing baseball to not only define my life but to design it. It allowed me to walk on campus quietly knowing that if I flunked every class, I still had pro baseball as my hole card. In my dismal freshman year, after I flunked my sociology midterm and the TA told me that I "didn't get the concept," my first impulse was tell him to tune in the World Series in a few years and then tell me who didn't get the concept.

I settled into my stance to lead off the top of the tenth, the same stance I had been using since I was five years old. I eyed the Trojan hurler. His first pitch was a fastball, low and inside. My meat. I swung from my rear end, and in that moment of pure baseball ecstasy, I felt the 33-ounce Louisville Slugger tingle in my hands as the ball screamed on a line toward deep right center. (I batted left-handed.) Back, back, back. But not quite enough. It caromed off the top of the wall for a stand-up double.

As I took my lead off second, thinking about where would be the best place to store my All-American trophy, the pitcher whirled and fired to the shortstop sneaking in behind me. I was picked off. As I schlepped back to the dugout, Coach Wolfman, a congenial, low-keyed man, screamed at me.

"Shithouse mouse, Colton!" he roared. "Take us right out of the game." The next batter singled, a hit that would have scored me. We didn't score that inning. I prayed for redemption.

In the bottom of the tenth, the USC leadoff hitter drilled the first pitch halfway to Guam and the game was over. Head down, I retreated to the dugout, taking a seat at the end of the bench. Hard as I tried, I couldn't hold back the tears.

I had only cried twice since reaching puberty. Once was the night North Hollywood High beat us in the quarterfinals of the L.A. city basketball play-offs; the other time was the day I left home for college.

The SC players jubilantly filed by our dugout on their way to the locker room. They spotted me crying in the corner, and jeered. We played them again the next day, and every time I came to bat, their bench jockeys unloaded.

"Here comes the crybaby!" they yelled. "Pussy! Cunt!"

I struck out three times.

I hated to strike out, especially in front of Dad, who never missed a game and always found a way to take off work to come see me play. He never criticized or yelled or acted the Little League Father Fool; I wanted so badly to do well in front of him. As a boy I waited in the driveway for him to come home from work, ball and glove in hand, barely giving him a chance to get out of his car. He'd lay his coat across the fender of his '53 Pontiac, roll up the sleeves of his white shirt, and start tossing, a scuffed-up baseball going back and forth, not much talk. Or better yet, he'd take me to the diamond at nearby Loyola University and hit me grounders at shortstop, sending me deep into the hole for the backhand, or have me charge the slow chopper over the pitcher's mound. He didn't coach; he just hit grounder after grounder. He decided when it was time to quit. On the way home, I noticed the blisters on his hand.

Baseball, I suppose, was the sure way for him to let me know I was a boy, as well as *his* boy. He loved the sport. It wasn't complicated; it was a world whose rules we could grasp. Sex, religion, the Korean War, McCarthyism, death—those were beyond us, too uncomfortable to discuss. He'd played some ball at Venice High, but he never talked much about the details of it, except once when he told me about the grand slam he hit to win the game against archrival Santa Monica High. Dad was of a generation of fathers who lived by the motto: "Don't complain, don't explain." My father, Neldon Colton—"Nellie" to his friends—never thought to flail me with tales of his austere youth.

The Venice of my dad's youth was past its halcyon days as *the* resort spot of L.A., a faint trace rubbed out by Hard Times, its distinctive charm rapidly deteriorating, covered in grime from the nearby oil wells. It was home to retired couples and families who had fled downtown L.A. It was cheap. That's what attracted the Coltons, who had moved to California from Vernal, Utah, in search of terrestrial paradise after Grandpa's sheep ranch failed. What kept them there was my dad's job loading clay pigeons on the Venice Pier. Grandpa was going through one failed dream after another: a gold mine in Northern California, raising sheep in the Aleutian Islands, selling cemetery plots. During the summers, whenever Dad had a spare dime, he rode the Pacific Electric red car downtown to Vernon Park, home of the minor-league Vernon Tigers. He got a free ticket into the games by shagging foul balls in batting practice and throwing them back onto the field.

When the Depression hit, times were bleak around the Colton house. Grandfather walked the streets in search of work. Dad dropped out of junior college, where he was the sports editor of the school paper, hoping for a career in journalism. He went to work at Douglas Aircraft, a company he would stay with for thirty-nine years, eventually working his way up to be the office manager of the engineering department. It was at Douglas that he met Hazel Storm, a secretary just moved to California from Indianapolis. When they went out on New Year's Eve in his brand-new '36 Ford, it was the first date of his life. He was twenty-four. He would never date another woman. Casanova he wasn't.

In the summer of '62 I acquired my first muscle car, which I hoped to parlay into sex. My '55 Sunliner convertible, which was sporty and cute but not getting me laid, bit the dust when a gust of Santa Ana wind howled through a rip in the convertible top and tore it off the frame, sending it flying down the San Bernardino Freeway like a tumbleweed. I traded it in topless on a '60 Chevy Impala, with 309 cubic inches under the hood, column three-speed, scavenger pipes, and moon hubcaps. I didn't know 309 cubic inches from a dipstick—I'd taken geometry in high school, not auto shop. My counselor said geometry would do me more good in the long run.

I used the Impala for my summer job. I was the chauffeur for Shari Lewis, the puppeteer. She was living in Brentwood for the summer while she played the lead in *Bye Bye Birdie* at the Santa Monica Civic Auditorium. This was no fancy limousine job—I drove her around in the Impala and she sat in the front seat unlimbering her vocal cords as we cruised down Wilshire Boulevard on the way to her performances. Sometimes the battery went dead and she would have to get out and push. But she was a good sport. I always left the engine running when I went to the door to pick her up.

That was the same summer I began to experiment with a new drug: pitching. I discovered that standing on the mound with the ball in my hand was like sitting behind the wheel of my Impala—I had the power. When I blew a fastball past the batter, sending him dragging back to the dugout, it was basic caveman stuff. Conquest. I liked being in control, the center of the action. I didn't have to chatter it up as I did at short-stop, none of that "hubba hubba, fire that rock" lingo.

I was walking off the diamond at Sawtell Field in Westwood after my first nine-inning performance, a one-hitter, when a loud voice called my name. "Forget about hitting," the man said. "You've got a big-league hose."

He was a heavyset man, frenzied, Italian. I knew he was a scout because I'd seen him at other games. Scouts were never hard to spot. They were tanned and flamboyant and wore bright Ban-Lon shirts, alpaca sweaters, gold golf slacks, and shoes with tassels. They carried stop-watches and little black books; they were ex-mediocre players with fingers gnarled from too many foul tips and teeth stained from too much tobacco. They struck me as a sad lot, the lowest rung of the baseball echelon, men clinging desperately to the only thing they'd ever known. But whenever one walked in the park, my heart beat a little faster, I threw a little harder, I hustled a little more.

The man handed me his card. His name was Tommy Lasorda, a new scout for the Dodgers in Southern California. "When you're ready to sign, make sure you call me," he said. "The Dodgers will make a pitcher out of you." I thought he was a dork.

The Minnesota Twins were also interested in making a pitcher out of me. They invited me to Dodger Stadium for a tryout under the watchful eye of manager Sam Mele before their scheduled game with the Angels. I brought Debbie to the tryout with me. She was a tall, athletic blonde from west Los Angeles who was a senior in elementary education at Long Beach State. She sat in a box seat while I went into the clubhouse to put on a uniform.

With Mele watching, I aired it out on the sideline, showing him my best heat. My fastball was rising that day. Slugger Harmon Killebrew stood by the plate and flashed a thumbs-up sign. "Take a shower, then come see me in my office," said Mele.

After my shower I stuffed a Twins uniform into the bottom of my athletic bag, figuring it would make a nice souvenir for Debbie. Then I went to Mele's office, taking a seat across the table from him and Jesse Flores, a Twins scout. I didn't have an exact bonus figure fixed in my head, but I was thinking somewhere in the $50,000 range if they wanted to get me to abandon the fraternity good life. That's what top prospects were getting.

"Looks like you gotta work on that curveball," said Mele. He sounded gruff. "But we'd like to sign you."

Flores pulled a contract out of his briefcase. At that same moment the equipment manager stuck his head inside the door. "Young man," he said, "did you take one of our uniforms?"

"I thought I got to keep one," I fibbed.

Mele eyed me suspiciously. Flores set the contract on the table. "How does a six-thousand-dollar bonus sound to you?" he asked.

I looked at Flores, then at Mele. Should I tell him I was insulted? That my worst childhood scar was receiving a cheapo Sam Mele model glove when I had my heart set on a Mickey Mantle?

"I'll think it over," I said.

Debbie and I stayed to watch the game. She surprised me by knowing who Zoilo Versalles was. I didn't know girls knew stuff like that. To my bigger surprise, she volunteered to go buy the beers. I didn't know girls ever bought the drinks. She was twenty-two. I was twenty. I had already ruled her out as a future Mrs. Larry Colton because of the age gap, and because she wasn't quite as pretty as the Perfect Girl I was searching for. But she bought a second round of beers.

By the seventh inning, we were tanked. "Let's go watch the rest of the game from up there," I suggested, pointing to the deserted seats in the upper deck down the left-field line.

We sat alone in the top row, and bingo, she unzipped my pants, and right there in row 67 of Dodger Stadium, I got my first blow job.

I was positive Big Ben would have approved . . . although technically, I still hadn't gone "all the way."

8

Loren

Resist engaging in tricks and traps to keep the drinker away from drink.
You can't cure your parent's disease.
—Eric Ryerson,
  When Your Parent Drinks Too Much

They were atop the highest run at Badger Pass in Yosemite National Park, ready for the last run of the day. A light snow was falling. Waiting for them in Yosemite Village was their rented cabin, with its fireplace, champagne on ice, and the neatly wrapped gift Donna had spent hours making for Loren. This was to be their first all-nighter together, and despite all the previous laying on of hands, their first sex. Or so Loren hoped. The anticipation was outrageous.

"Race you to the bottom!" challenged Loren.

Donna laughed, charmed by his infectious enthusiasm and uproarious daring. But no way she was racing him down the hill. He was a maniac on skis.

After the last run, they drove through the gathering darkness and falling snow into Yosemite Village. Smoke billowed from the chimney of the lodge. A postcard scene. It had taken Loren a year after that first day in Dr. Teller's Physics 10 class to finally wear down Donna's resistance and convince her to dump her boyfriend with the *two* Corvettes. She was fond of telling Loren the turning point for her was when he got rid of his

Plymouth Fury in favor of a '57 red T-Bird convertible (which Pop and
Eddie bought for him after a pledge brother burned the Fury's upholstery with a dropped cigarette). For Loren, the turning point had been
the first time he laid eyes on her, immediately transfixed by her tall,
willowy body. She was the reigning Daffodil Queen and wore her light
brown hair piled on top of her head, accentuating her long neck. That
she had been the valedictorian of her Southern California high school
and had a math scholarship was not as impressive to him as the fact she
owned her own car, a four-door '54 Chevy Bel Air.

He had finally broken it off with Sue, the valedictorian of Marysville
High. They had gone together three years, and according to Loren, it
wasn't the fact that they had never gone "all the way" that ended the
relationship as much as it was Sue's meddling in his business and telling
him what to do. "She sounds more like my mother every day," he told
Swampfox.

He was going all out for Donna. He had already taken her home to
Marysville and introduced her to Hal and Genevieve. Though they didn't
talk about it, Donna sensed the Hawley family tension. With an alcoholic father of her own, she knew the signs. Loren also took her to the
ranch in Trowbridge to meet Pop and Eddie, and this was where she first
saw another side to his personality. He took her on a tour of the property, proudly showing her the rice fields and the fences he had helped
build with his grandfather. There was a light in his blue eyes she hadn't
known. She saw the way Pop and Eddie doted on him.

"I'm just like Pop when it comes to girls," he confessed. "I put them on
a pedestal."

He talked about someday returning to the ranch and raising a family
there. The ranch had been in his mom's family for three generations;
Genevieve was born in the ranch house. Her grandfather built it in
1887, having traveled West from New England, not in search of the gold
that was bringing so many to California, but in hopes of finding rich
farming land. He purchased 5,000 acres and built fences, barns, sheds,
corrals, and a two-story house with two fireplaces and a huge kitchen.
He planted wheat, oats, barley, rice, almonds. In 1920, when Genevieve
was five, her grandfather was electrocuted installing power lines to the
house. For the next ten years, her Uncle Ed ran the ranch while Pop
worked as a brakeman for Western Pacific, assigned to the Sacramento–
Red Bluff line. Uncle Ed, however, was more interested in moonshine
than in plowing the land, and the property quickly deteriorated. The
weeds took over, the bills piled up, and then the bank served the foreclo-
sure notice. But Pop, known throughout Yuba County as a man of his

word, drove to the courthouse and promised to save the land. He quit the railroad, and for the next twenty-five years worked tirelessly, seven days a week, planting, harvesting, repairing. He regained credit from the bank and the respect of his neighbors. He did all the work himself— plumbing, carpentry, electricity. Genevieve worshipped him, shadowing him across the property as he went about his chores. He was not a religious man, rarely going to church, but he often started each morning by walking out into the front yard and devoutly gazing across his land, declaring with outstretched arms: "This is my church!" (Although it was really a farm, it was called "the ranch" by the family.) Genevieve loved the land too, growing up a big, solid farm girl, feeding the horses, harvesting the wheat, milking the cows. But despite her vigor, her mother hovered over her like a watchdog, worrying, waiting in the middle of the road for her to get home from school, even when she was twenty years old and commuting to business college in Sacramento. Hal would later complain that Genevieve inherited her mother's domineering nature, and was using it to smother Loren.

After dinner at the Yosemite Lodge, Loren and Donna returned to the cabin. He built a fire and poured the champagne. Sitting cross-legged on the rug in front of the blaze, she took her hands off of him long enough to hand him the gift-wrapped package. It was matching nightshirts in Cal's blue and gold colors. She had sewn a large 46 (his football number) on the back.

When they awoke in the morning, she wasn't sure if it was the intoxication of the champagne, or the sex, or the beauty of Yosemite outside their window, but she had never felt so close to anyone. She knew they would someday marry.

Loren was standing at the front window, ogling all the sorority girls walking down Piedmont. "Oh no," he moaned. His mom, the new president of the Pi KA Mothers' Club, was coming up the sidewalk. She was bringing new curtains for the living room. The old ones had gotten annihilated during the raucous Purple Passion Party.

"We need to talk," said Genevieve.

He assumed it was something to do with his father. Sometimes he felt like his mother's therapist, the way she was always spilling her problems to him, telling him what a louse Hal was. But then again, maybe she wanted to butt into his love life . . . to probe him for details, to find out why he broke up with Sue, or to make sure he and Donna weren't going to do something foolish.

Genevieve talked him into going for a ride with her. They drove to

Herrick Hospital in Berkeley, where she marched up to the third floor and signed the papers to have Hal committed to the hospital's alcohol recovery program, reputed to be one of the most successful in California. The doctors warned that it would be tough: padded cell, men in white coats, d.t.'s,

"Dad's not going to go for this," predicted Loren. "How are you going to get him here?"

"You're going to trick him," Genevieve answered.

Hal Hawley, Loren's dad, was a strong, handsome man, broad-shouldered, with piercing blue eyes and a formidable presence. He was born in Sutter, California—population 250, twenty miles north of Marysville —a second-generation Californian of English-Irish descent. He grew up on a ranch in "The Buttes," which is what townsfolk in Sutter called the small mountain range east of town, listed by Rand McNally as the smallest mountain range in America. Most of the family's income came from its almond orchard.

As a boy, Hal worked before school and during the summers, toiling for his parsimonious parents, milking the cows and hauling sixty-pound burlap bags filled with almonds. His mother was an old-fashioned homemaker—biscuits and gravy for breakfast, apple pies for dessert, handmade clothes for the family. She even sewed her own underwear and made shirts for Hal out of chicken-feed sacks. On the rare occasions she left the house, it was to go to church or to the market. In the afternoons, she stood at the kitchen window, watching her four children running barefoot across the field, racing their father on the tractor.

In high school Hal gained notoriety as the best athlete in Sutter County. He attended San Jose State on an athletic scholarship, where he was a four-year letterman in four sports and was elected to the school's Hall of Fame. During Prohibition he earned extra money by bootlegging alcohol for his fraternity brothers. Some think that's when he fell under the influence. Others suggest that he started in 1932 after his personal disaster at the Olympic trials in Los Angeles. The experts had considered him a cinch to make the team in the high hurdles. In the final heat, he was leading the race approaching the last hurdle. But he got off stride and tripped, landing chest first on the new red cinder track of the Coliseum, ending his Olympic dream.

When he met Genevieve at a party in Sacramento in the summer of 1938, she had just graduated from business college and was working as a secretary. It was a festive gathering, women in summer frocks, men in white dress shirts—lots of barbecued ribs, potato salad . . . and alcohol. Genevieve was in the kitchen when he introduced himself, offering to fix her a drink. "I should have known right then," she later said.

According to Genevieve, the day that Loren was born, Hal showed up at the hospital so snockered that "he didn't know if he'd had a rabbit or a boy." For Loren, it was a boyhood of no games of catch with his dad, the coach . . . no fishing trips to the lake with his dad, the fisherman . . . no praise for good report cards from his dad, the teacher. Hal never held him as a baby. Whenever Loren woke up crying in the middle of the night, Hal's response to Genevieve was always the same: "Get up and take care of *your* baby!" On the nights he didn't go to the bar or the Elks Lodge, Hal sat in his chair, reading his paper, drinking his vodka. During summers, it was Loren and his mother who drove to the rented cabin at Clear Lake for the family vacation. When Loren reached high school, Hal stepped down as a coach, saying he didn't want to be accused of favoring his own child. He did go to most of Loren's games, but it infuriated Genevieve when he would stand up and boast how that was *his* son down there scoring all those touchdowns.

It was a beautiful Saturday morning in April in the upper Sacramento Valley. Hal was sitting in his easy chair, reading the sports page. He looked up, surprised to see Loren walk in the front door. "What are you doing here?" he asked. "Don't you have spring practice today?"

"Yep," enthused Loren, handing his bag of laundry to Genevieve, then pulling Hal out of his chair. "Come on! You're coming back to Berkeley with me."

"What for?"

"To watch me practice," he said.

"I've got things I need to take care of today," Hal hedged.

"You should go," encouraged Genevieve.

"We'll have dinner at Spengler's," said Loren. "It'll be fun. We'll come back tonight."

Hal continued to resist, claiming he had a function at the Elks Lodge. But Loren insisted, practically dragging him out the door as Genevieve waved goodbye.

The dew was still on the alfalfa as they drove out of Marysville and through the Sacramento delta. Loren had the top down on his T-Bird. Sailing down the highway, wind in their faces, they made a handsome father-and-son picture, the best athlete of Sutter County, circa 1930, and the best athlete of Yuba County, circa 1960. For Loren, it was a rare chance to be alone with his dad. He told him how Coach Levy had elevated him to first-string flanker, and how there was a good chance he would be starting as a sophomore in the fall. Levy was impressed with Loren's athletic talents, describing him as "all corners, nothing but elbows and knees when he goes up for a pass." He also called him "the guy you'd want if you were casting the country bumpkin."

"Take this next exit," said Hal as they approached Davis.

"Why?" asked Loren.

"I'll pick up a six-pack."

Loren didn't slow down, holding steady at 70 miles per hour.

"Why didn't you stop?" asked Hal, eyeing his son suspiciously.

Loren ignored him, eyes on the highway.

"There's a little store at the next exit," said Hal.

Again, Loren didn't slow down. "You don't need a beer," he said.

"You sound like your mom!" countered Hal. "Now stop at the next store!"

"Might as well sit back and relax, 'cause I'm not stopping until I get to Berkeley," Loren bristled.

Hal surveyed his son. There was a determination in Loren's eyes he'd never seen, an anger he'd never sensed.

"What the hell's goin' on here?" he demanded.

"I'll tell you what's going on," replied Loren. "I'm taking you to Herrick Hospital to dry out."

"Like hell you are!" snorted Hal. "Turn this car around!"

"No!"

"I'm warning you, Loren. Pull over or I'll jump out!"

Loren kept his foot on the accelerator.

Hal pulled the handle and leaned against the door, a burst of air rushing through the car.

Loren reached across the front seat, grabbing his father by the back of the neck in a vise grip, pulling him away from the door. Hal fought to get free. The more he struggled, the tighter Loren squeezed, pushing his head toward the glove compartment with his right hand, holding on to the steering wheel with his left. He was still going 70 miles an hour.

Hal continued to fight, but it was a mismatch: he was a thick five-eleven, 190 pounds, softened by alcohol; Loren was six-three, 190 pounds, hardened by collegiate football. He kept squeezing, Hal's face turning an angry crimson.

"Let go!" Hal pleaded.

"I'll let go if you promise not to try something stupid again," said Loren. "Promise?"

Bent over, head pressed to the glove box, Hal didn't respond.

Loren squeezed tighter. "Promise?"

"Okay," said Hal.

For forty-five minutes they drove in silence toward Berkeley, Loren with one eye on the road, the other on his father, who sat slumped against the door.

Nearing the University Avenue exit, Loren broke the silence. "If you try to get away, I'll just chase you down," he said.

"Why are you doing this?"

"Because you've got a problem," said Loren. "It's for your own good."

"Your mother's got you brainwashed," Hal said. "I don't have a problem."

Loren knew better. He had heard his mother's explanations of when Hal started drinking—the fall in the Olympic trials, running bootleg booze when he was in college. But that didn't explain *why* he drank.

At the hospital, Hal went meekly from the parking lot into the lobby and up the elevator to the Recovery Center on the third floor, Loren right next to him, hand on his elbow. They stopped at the admittance desk.

Hal was shaking. "Please don't do this to me," he pleaded, tears filling his eyes. An attendant in a white jacket approached. "I'm begging you, Loren."

Loren, who'd never seen his father cry, turned abruptly on his heel and disappeared down the hall.

His fraternity brothers would never know.

9

Ron

When I observe the men who surround me in Washington and when I reflect that the Secretary of State, the Secretary of Defense, the Chairman of the Atomic Energy Commission, the Director of the CIA, and the Ambassador to India are all graduates or former students of this university—I am forced to confront an uncomfortable truth, and so are you, that the New Frontier may well owe more to Berkeley than to Harvard.
—President John Kennedy,
UC Charter Day Speech,
March 23, 1962

Ron rushed out of class and across campus, zigzagging his way through the waves of students. He needed to get to the athletic department office before Coach Walsh left for practice. This was his last chance to plead his case.

Ron always seemed to be in a hurry. He liked it that way. By staying on the go, he didn't have to deal with the haunting truth. He had returned to Berkeley, and as his father had suggested, he told nobody about the abandoned baby. It was a deep, dark secret from all the fraternity brothers. He stuffed it into a back corner of his thoughts, keeping focused instead on his studies and football. Joyce, the baby's mother, had called in tears once when he was in L.A., hoping to enlist his support in getting the baby back, but by then it was too late. Ron would later learn from his father that the child had been put in a foster home in Glendale.

He had no shortage of things to keep him occupied. He was consumed with getting his degree, studying obsessively. He had earned a reputation with his professors as one of the most artistic students in his design courses; in his advanced math and calculus courses, however, he struggled, barely passing. It was not for lack of effort—he didn't waste time sitting around the fraternity drinking beer or playing pool and Ping-Pong. At nights he studied at "the Ark," which is what students called the brown shingle building housing the architecture department, and when they turned off the lights, he went across the street and studied at the laundromat because it was quieter than the fraternity.

In football, his efforts had paid off in being elevated to first-string right end at the start of his junior year, playing both offense and defense. (It was still one-platoon football and players were required to go both ways.) He was a player with speed and agility, but what the coaches liked best was his serious attitude and hustle. He'd caught a touchdown pass at Penn State and another against Missouri, but against Washington he'd dropped two passes, missed key blocks, and got bulldozed on defense. Reviewing the game films on Monday, Coach Walsh jumped all over him, demoting him to second team.

Nearing Walsh's office, he began to have second thoughts. He didn't want to appear the crybaby. But the upcoming game against UCLA on Saturday was special, the one game more than any other that he wanted to start. It would be at the L.A. Coliseum in the shadow of his boyhood home; his hometown friends would be there. So would Ralph and Betty. In high school he had dreamed of someday running out of the Coliseum tunnel onto the storied field where he had gone as a boy to watch Bob Waterfield and the L.A. Rams. But what was even more important to him was that he would be playing head to head against Joe Zeno, his best buddy and teammate from L.A. High.

Ron admired Joe, a tough, broad-shouldered, hard-nosed Italian boy from Massachusetts, whose parents had divorced when he was in the seventh grade, shipping Joe and his younger brother to California to live with an aunt. In high school, Joe paid for his own clothes, worked twenty hours a week as a tree trimmer, delivered the Sunday L.A. *Times* on foot, carried a B+ average, and played quarterback and linebacker on the football team. Ron envied Joe's tenacity and self-reliance . . . which is what he saw as his own tragic flaw, his softness, his lack of mental and physical toughness. During the summers they worked as counselors at Troy for Boys, a sports summer camp near Lake Arrowhead. At the end of one day they raced up a steep ski lift, Joe running in heavy work boots, Ron wearing his new white Converse low-tops. Ron was the faster runner, but Joe won. And although it was Ron who won the student-athlete award their senior year, it had been Joe who got the scholarship offers.

Ron knocked softly on Coach Walsh's door, then entered. "What's up?" asked Walsh.

Ron started to stammer. Walsh intimidated him even more than Coach Levy. It was Walsh who glared at him at practice when he screwed up. "Do you have a minute?" Ron asked.

Walsh nodded. He liked Ron and the way he came to practice and gave 100 percent every day. He too had heard the whispers about Ron's background, but that was not something he thought about. He and Levy had different views of Ron's role on the team. Levy, a Phi Beta Kappa in English, saw Ron as a "nice, hardworking guy but with no exemplary skills." Walsh, however, thought he was an "excellent athlete" whom the coaching staff improperly relied on more for defense than catching passes. The problem, Walsh thought, was in Levy's conservative winged T, a system that didn't take advantage of Ron's speed and movement. Of course, Walsh never discussed this with Ron. Player-coach communication was still years away.

"I'd like to talk about getting my starting spot back," Ron said tentatively. "The UCLA game is really important to me."

"What makes you think you deserve it?" asked Walsh. "You played lousy against the Huskies."

Ron looked at Walsh sitting behind his desk, and suddenly tears welled in his eyes. He started backing toward the door. How embarrassing, he thought, to cry in front of his coach. If Walsh sees the tears, Ron could kiss the first string so long. So he believed.

"Why is this game so important to you?" asked Walsh.

Embarrassed by his own emotions, Ron turned to shield his face from Walsh. "My friend Joe Zeno starts for UCLA and it would mean a lot to me to play against him," he muttered, then abruptly exited, head down, angry at himself.

By Saturday, he had battled his way back to the first string. He got his wish to start against the Bruins, and it was just as he'd dreamed . . . charging out of the tunnel to the sound of the Cal Marching Band, his parents in the stands, Zeno across the field. But the Bruins creamed the Bears that day, another loss in a one-win season. Ron did, however, stick with the first team the rest of the year and win the most improved lineman award.

.   .   .   .

Ron was excited. President John F. Kennedy was coming to Berkeley to speak at the University's Charter Day ceremonies on March 23, 1962, at Memorial Stadium, and Ron was one of a handful of athletes chosen by the coaching staff to serve in the student honor guard that would form a corridor for the presidential party to march through on its way to the speakers' platform.

In many ways, Ron mirrored the Kennedy image—young, vibrant, bright, earnest . . . and full of secrets. He was enfranchised in the New Frontier, if only in terms of image and youth and the fact his parents actively campaigned for Kennedy. But the Bay of Pigs? Vietnam? He didn't know about that stuff. He knew about the new Peace Corps and John Glenn's ride in the *Friendship* 7 and the photogenic First Family. Happy stuff.

But serious trouble loomed in Berkeley for Kennedy's appearance. One potential problem was the weather. Three straight days of rain and blustery winds had pummeled Northern California, threatening to drench the city's pirouette in the national spotlight. Small-craft warnings were up from Point Reyes to Santa Cruz. Eighty-five thousand tickets had already been distributed, and with a forecast calling for more rain, the prospect of switching the speech to 8,000-seat-capacity Harmon Gym loomed as a logistic nightmare.

But of even more concern to University and city officials was the potential for an embarrassing student protest. Student activism was gaining a major foothold on campus, and two groups were promising mass demonstrations: Students Against Nuclear Testing and the Ad Hoc Committee for March 23rd. In an open letter to the *Daily Californian,* the protesters assailed Kennedy on numerous issues, including: military spending; the Bay of Pigs; supporting dictators; failure to make "even minimal steps to full citizenship for the Negro"; and committing U.S. troops to a war in Vietnam "without consulting the American people."

Berkeley was tense. To the members of the Pi KA house, picketing the President was unthinkable, treasonous. To counter the planned demonstrations, Winged Helmet, an interfraternal service organization, circulated a petition on Frat Row and in the dorms welcoming Kennedy. In one day they gathered 7,000 signatures. The University appealed to the demonstrators not to disrupt Kennedy's visit; the conservative Berkeley City Council appealed to the University to "silence the effrontery of the protesters;" the Berkeley *Gazette* called the demonstrators' disrespect to the office of the President "beyond comprehension;" the *Daily Californian,* while defending the students' right to protest, maintained that demonstrations would "besmirch the reputation" of the school; and a group calling itself Charter Day Support Committee announced plans for a pro-Kennedy demonstration on campus to outshout the protesters. They distributed banners proclaiming: "All the way with JFK on nuclear testing."

As the day of JFK's visit neared, officials feared an ugly confrontation.

Ron awoke to sunlight jitterbugging through his windows, bathing his small single room in an airy light. Washed clean by the rains, the sky was a Chamber of Commerce blue. Daffodils bloomed. Classes were canceled. The bells of the Campanile tolled across campus, charged by the electricity of the day. At least the weather was cooperating. But as demonstrators gathered, officials held their breath.

Ron got dressed and headed for campus. On Bancroft Avenue, 600 members of the strident Ad Hoc Committee assembled, carrying pickets, passing out anti-Kennedy leaflets; and on the steps of Sproul Hall, 300 supporters of Students Against Nuclear Testing sat in silent vigil, many of them holding pictures of babies burned in Hiroshima. But Ron breezed right by them, barely registering their presence. He was on a desperate mission to the office of his TA in Calculus 1 in hopes of talking him into letting him retake the midterm he'd flunked.

Arriving at the architecture office in "the Ark," he knocked on the door. The light was on but there was no answer. He tried the doorknob. It opened and he stuck his head inside. The TA was nowhere in sight, but sitting on top of his desk was his grade book. Ron leaned his head back out the door, furtively looking up and down the hallway. He heard footsteps—but it was only a student going in the opposite direction. Then with a hasty turn, he sidestepped to the desk and picked up a pen, quickly crafting his F into a D.

Walking back across campus, he had already made himself a solemn promise that after he graduated he would take the course again and legitimately learn the material. He felt it was his moral obligation to his future clients so that one of his designs would not tumble to the ground like a house of cards. But for now, it was more important that he pass the class.

The expected showdown on campus between the demonstrators and the pro-Kennedy forces never materialized: the protesters marched up Bancroft to the stadium without incident and quietly dispersed; and only seven people showed up to march in support of more nuclear testing. University officials and the Berkeley police breathed a huge sigh of relief.

In his room, Ron donned a ceremonial cap and gown, ready to head to the stadium and take his place with the honor guard. On Piedmont Avenue in front of the fraternity, shirt-sleeved students and citizens hustled by in waves, eager to get good seats. Pledges directed cars into the parking lot at four dollars a spot, twice the fee for football games. Vendors stood on every street corner, selling hot dogs and miniature American flags. Small children rode atop parents' shoulders. The Straw Hat Band strutted down the street to the tune of "Chattanooga Choo-Choo."

Ron entered sun-splashed Memorial Stadium through the north tunnel, just as he did on Saturday afternoons in the fall. But this was different. The stadium was jammed to capacity, delirious in its anticipation, enough energy to jump-start Berkeley. A thunderous chant echoed up Strawberry Canyon: "JFK . . . JFK . . . JFK."

The President's long, black, bulletproof Cadillac arrived, surrounded by a phalanx of motorcycle police. Under the stands, Kennedy stepped from the limousine, greeted by dramatic arts professor Garff Wilson, the University's Chairman of Public Ceremonies and Protocol (and Pi KA alumni adviser). Professor Wilson helped Kennedy into his doctoral robe and handed him his mortarboard. Inside the stadium, the people were on their feet, cheering.

University president Clark Kerr was the first in the presidential party to walk out of the tunnel into the stadium, followed by Chancellor Edward Strong, Governor Brown, and Secretary of Defense Robert McNamara (a 1949 Cal grad). The Cal Marching Band was playing "Hail to the Chief." Greeted by a tumultuous roar, Kennedy stepped from the shadows into the sunshine, removing his mortarboard, his hair shining in the sunlight. Ron strained to see his President.

Slowly, Kennedy made his way through the faculty, guests, and corridor of the honor guard, the roar of the crowd growing even louder. He passed in front of Ron, an arm's length away. "He's not as tall as I thought," whispered Ron after he'd passed.

After accepting an honorary doctor of law degree from regent Edwin Pauley, Kennedy stepped to the dais, waving to the ovation. It was the largest crowd he would ever address. As he began to speak, his Back Bay accent carried to the top of Strawberry Canyon. He spoke of a week of "momentous events" around the world: the end of the long struggle in Algeria, a renewed quest at Geneva for nuclear disarmament, the foreign ministers of Russia and the United States meeting once again on the subject of Berlin. The crowd cheered mightily when he included on his list of momentous events his wife Jackie's visit to India and her "first and last ride on an elephant."

He spoke on a theme of "a new confidence alive in the country." His message was clear and prophetic—democracy, not Communism, would carry the world toward freedom: "The emerging world is incompatible with the Communist world order," he proclaimed. But the crowd saved its loudest cheer for when he talked of Berkeley's role in the New Frontier.

Standing in the middle of the honor guard, Ron applauded, caught up in the electricity, his guilt temporarily swept clean . . . no thoughts of his cheating, no thoughts of his abandoned son, no thoughts of his hidden identity. He was part of Camelot.

Ron peered through the curtains of his motel room at the Holiday Inn in Durham, North Carolina. On Chapel Street outside his window, fifty well-dressed Negroes marched in a circle, singing hymns, carrying pickets, blocking traffic. Standing on the sidewalk, angry whites yelled racial epithets, threatening violence. Ron's stomach churned. This wasn't Camelot.

It was October 1962, a month of heated racial tension in the growing civil rights battle: President Kennedy had called in 3,000 federal troops to help enroll James Meredith and quell rioting at Ole Miss; black churches in Georgia had been burned; the lunch-counter sit-in movement had fueled angry confrontations across the South; and now, the Cal Bears, in Durham for a game against the Duke Blue Devils, had found themselves at the center of the latest battle. As the headline in the *Daily Cal* put it: "Team Tangled in Integration Dispute; Negro Pickets Surround Players' Hotel."

At issue was the Durham Holiday Inn's decision to suspend its policy of segregation by allowing the Cal football team and its Negro players to stay at the motel. The protesters were saying that the motel should be open to all Negroes, not just football players. There was a rumor that leaders of the demonstration would approach the Negro players and ask them to refuse to stay in the motel and to boycott the game in a show of solidarity. Ron hoped it didn't come down to that. He had mixed emotions, certain only that he didn't want to be involved if other players weren't. He was there to play football. The Negro players had not discussed what they would do if asked.

The confrontation in Durham had been building for several weeks. Gordon Carey, program director for the Congress of Racial Equality, considered it important enough to fly down from New York to help organize the demonstration. In previous months, the Durham Holiday Inn had been the site of periodic sit-ins by CORE, but those demonstrations had stopped when the motel manager promised to integrate the motel beginning with the Cal football team's arrival. But the manager had reneged. "I can't afford to integrate," he told a reporter for the *Daily Californian*. "People just don't like niggers around here. By God, you can't force us to do something we don't want." On the eve of the arrival of the Cal team, two students from nearby North Carolina College, an all-Negro school, had tried to eat in the motel dining room. They were kicked out, and the next day when the team bus arrived, picketers surrounded the motel, asserting that the motel's decision "to accept the California Negroes is a ridicule for the North Carolina Negroes rather than a victory for integration."

Ron continued to look through the curtains at the demonstrators in the street. He admired their conviction and courage. But at the same time it made him feel uneasy about his own ambivalence over his racial identity and commitment to civil rights issues. In Berkeley he could walk by the CORE card table on Bancroft and not feel guilty—he had midterms to take, practices to attend. His contribution to the cause, he rationalized, would be his degree and his work as an architect.

But what was happening out there on Chapel Street was different, not as easy to ignore. Maybe it was because it was the Deep South and there were angry whites across the street and the bigotry was intense and palpable rather than subtle and restrained as in Berkeley. It was forcing him to think about issues and questions within himself that he'd just as soon leave buried. He wasn't ready to deal with the civil rights movement or face questions of black and white. But those were brave people down there on the street, carrying pickets, standing up for what they believed, risking their lives . . . and there he was, peeking through the curtain, unable to even talk about issues of race with his teammates or fraternity brothers, too self-absorbed, too obsessed with getting his degree. Where was his ethnic pride? he wondered.

For its part in the controversy, University officials were trying to stay clear of the dispute. Pete Newell, Cal's athletic director, termed the situation "a local problem which does not concern us as an athletic representative of the University." Coach Levy agreed: "This will not affect us at all," he said. "We are here to play a football game."

Ron left his perch at the window and joined his teammates in the motel dining room for the team dinner. He took a bite of his steak and looked up, startled to see a Negro demonstrator enter the room and approach Coach Levy. The room was suddenly silent. The man asked Coach Levy for permission to talk to a spokesman for the Negro players. Levy pointed him toward John Erby, a co-captain and lineman. Ron admired Erby, who was articulate, not afraid to take a risk. Although they were friends, he and Erby did not socialize. Erby knew—or had heard—Ron was Negro but they had never discussed it.

The demonstrator hurried to Erby's table and they talked in hushed voices, Erby nodding his head. The conversation ended quickly and the man exited the dining room. Erby had told him that he agreed with the cause but a University of California football trip was not the time or place to make a statement.

Once again, Ron would not be required to stand up and be counted. Cal lost the game 22–0, and Ron turned in his worst performance of the year, never getting into the flow. In the postgame locker room, he threw up.

10

Jim

. . . Why should you row a boat race? Why endure long months of pain in preparation for a fierce half-hour that will leave you all but dead? Does anyone ask the question? Is there anyone who would not go through all its costs, and more, for the moment when anguish breaks into triumph—or even for the glory of having nobly lost? Is life less than a boat race?
—Justice Oliver Wendell Holmes, Jr.,
   Yale commencement speech, 1886

October 22, 1962. Jim trudged up the front steps of the fraternity, weary from a long day in engineering classes—he was taking Chemistry 2, Physics 4, Calculus 3 . . . definitely no Micks. Passing the mail table in the vestibule, he noticed the pile of mail for Loren. It was getting bigger every day. The big mystery in the house that semester was: *Where was Loren?* He didn't return to school in September. Nobody knew where he had vanished to, including the football coaches, who were counting on him as a starter. All Genevieve would say when contacted was that he had left the state and he might be back in the spring, or he might not. Jim didn't much care—he and Loren were dipoles.

He walked into the TV room, surprised to find it packed, everybody staring somberly at the screen. "What's up?" he inquired.

"Pack your bags, Piss 'n' Moan," answered Big Ben. "We're going to war."

President Kennedy had just delivered a national address informing the nation that missile sites were being prepared on the "imprisoned island" of Cuba. The brothers' normal ribaldry was silenced. Smiles were forced. We had all listened to talk before about a third world war and seen photos of the destruction of Hiroshima and Pacific atolls. But we could sweep those into a corner, apart from reality. We could ignore conflicts in Laos or Vietnam or Angola. Or even Berlin. Those were remote and foreign and unreal. But Cuba, naval blockade, missiles ninety miles from Florida—that was too close, too real. It punctured our synthetic cocoon. That's what it said in the *Daily Cal.*

"Nothing I can do about it," said Jim, shrugging his shoulders.

But in the days that followed, the tension was inescapable. He continued his routine—going to class, working out with crew, studying, piss-and-moaning about the noise. He met Ralph for a Coke at the Bear's Lair in the new Student Union. The knotty-pine Lair, with its big stone fireplace and suspended racing shell was a favorite fraternity hangout in between classes at 10 A.M., noon, and 2 P.M., while the Terrace, thirty yards away, was a gathering place for the "greenbaggers" to drink coffee, write poetry, view San Francisco, plot anarchy.

On campus, impromptu debates on Kennedy's strategy drew large and vocal crowds. Jim didn't participate—he just went to class. Detailed campus emergency evacuation plans were posted at Sather Gate; professors canceled lectures to discuss the crisis; Governor Brown postponed a campus visit and flew to Washington, D.C., for an emergency governors' meeting on civilian defense called by Nelson Rockefeller; a headline in the *Daily Cal* quoted political science professor Eugene Burdick, author of *The Ugly American,* as saying World War III was "inevitable." Nobody was talking about Saturday's football game against Penn State; students walked through Dwinelle Plaza in ghostly silence, ears glued to transistors for the latest update, the same transistors that three weeks earlier had been tuned to the Giants versus the Yankees in the World Series. A straw poll by the *Daily Cal* revealed that students backed Kennedy's naval quarantine by 7–1.

On Saturday morning, five agonizing days after Kennedy ordered the blockade, the crisis reached its darkest hour: A U-2 spy plane was shot down by Cuban antiaircraft fire, killing the pilot. Khrushchev told Kennedy he would not remove the missiles unless Kennedy agreed to take NATO missiles out of Turkey, an offer Kennedy refused. The world shuddered. Jim and Ralph finished their pledge chores, then headed to Memorial Stadium for the Penn State game.

It was a crowd weary of a week of nuclear brinkmanship that arrived in

Strawberry Canyon hoping for an upset, praying for peace. The Golden Bears were 1 and 3 on the season and were heavy underdogs to the Nittany Lions. By the end of the first quarter, the gloom was even thicker as the Bears fell behind 14–0. Then into the game for the first time during the season trotted talented sophomore quarterback Craig Morton, who had been hailed as the savior of Cal's football fortunes until he suffered torn knee cartilage when Coach Levy had him returning punts on the first day of fall practice. Doctors had originally forecast he'd be lost for the season.

Morton, six-three, 205 pounds, ruggedly handsome, charismatic, was already the Big Man on Campus. Everybody wanted to be in his inner circle of friends. One of the most fiercely recruited athletes in California prep history, he had turned down a reputed $50,000 bonus out of Campbell High to turn pro in baseball. Pi KA had put the big rush on him, bringing him by the house several times for lunch, inviting him to every party. With all the football and baseball players in the house, it was a lead-pipe cinch he would pledge, and he did one night at 2 A.M. at the Fern . . . only to reconsider in the sober light of day and jilt the brothers by pledging Beta Theta Pi . . . which he promptly depledged, deciding that being awakened at 4 A.M. to mop the floor wasn't a top priority for him.

Upon entering the game, Morton rifled six straight completions, two to Ron, driving the Bears to a score, the touchdown coming on a pass to Pi KA Al Nelson. Jim, usually a stoic rooter, was on his feet, cheering. A dazzling 73-yard scoring drive had lifted the spirits of the 45,000 in Memorial Stadium. The missile crisis was temporarily forgotten.

Cal lost the game, 23–21, despite a record-shattering performance by Morton, but at the Pi KA house after the game, there was reason for smiles. Not only had Cal's football messiah arrived, but Khrushchev had blinked, ordering the missiles dismantled. Standing by the keg, Jim overheard several of the brothers planning a Cuba Libre party for later at the Fern. He wondered if he would be invited. They said nothing to him. Wasn't he cool enough for them? Wasn't a fraternity supposed to be one for all and all for one? Or some hogwash like that?

He walked away, head down, looking for Ralph so he could ask him if he could borrow the "Toadmobile" to drive home to Burlingame and see Patty. As far as Jim was concerned, she was the best thing going for him. They were in love, and he didn't care how much shit he caught about having a high school girlfriend—Patty seemed more mature than most of the so-called sophisticated sorority girls he'd met. And not only that, she was absolutely crazy about him. Maybe she wasn't ever going to be Big

Game Queen, but she was plenty pretty enough for him, with big eyes, cute face, and short hair.

He felt a tap on his shoulder. It was Steve, smiling wide. And why wouldn't he be smiling? Steve had everything going for him . . . athletic scholarship, movie-star handsome, girls goo-goo after him, guys wanting to be his friend. Jim thought Steve a bit untamed, especially when he drank, but otherwise a straight-ahead, no-bullshit kind of guy. Jim appreciated the fact that Steve called him Jim instead of Piss 'n' Moan like everybody else. "There's going to be a Cuba Libre party at the Fern tonight," said Steve. "I've got room in my car."

And so the big missile crisis was washed away in a flood of rum and Cokes, Jim feeling just a little bit better about the future.

A cold afternoon wind was blowing in off the Bay as Jim approached the Ky Eybright Boathouse on the Oakland Estuary for the start of crew practice. He wasn't worried about the cold; it was his rubbery limbs and heavy eyes that had him worried. This was the most important day of his budding rowing career, a chance to move up to first boat, and he'd had only three hours' sleep, exhausted from cramming for his Engineering 118 midterm.

Helping carry the shell from the boathouse to the water, his legs wobbled under the weight. He settled into his seat, afraid to close his eyes for fear he'd fall asleep and tumble right out of the boat into the chilly water of the estuary. As he grabbed his oar and waited for the start of the first race, it seemed inconceivable that his weary body could respond to the challenge of back-to-back races. (The competition for first boat was determined by racing two boats, then having two opposing rowers change seats and race again, the difference in times settling who was first boat.)

The race began, and like an aquatic praying mantis, his boat sliced through the water. The Oakland Estuary was a narrow shipping channel shared by oceangoing cargo vessels, Coast Guard cutters, Navy destroyers, and the Cal crew. The race course covered three miles, finishing at the Fruitvale Bridge, a great vantage point for spectators . . . if there happened to be any. On race days, the Coast Guard patrolled the course, keeping it free of large boats. By comparison, the course had less traffic, fewer turns, and calmer water than Boston's Charles River, site of many of the big East Coast races. Still, the wind coming off the Bay, coupled with the wash of the large boats, made rowing in an eight-man shell difficult . . . even on those days when Jim had logged a good night's sleep.

For Jim, the chance to move up to first boat was not so much about dreams of Olympic gold in Tokyo as it was about basic self-worth. Every practice, he had learned, was a battle with primal pain. In high school football he'd been blindsided by linebackers, but that was pain inflicted by an opponent and not in every game. In crew the pain was self-inflicted, guaranteed in every race and every practice. Even in swimming he could pace himself, and in football there were huddles every few seconds, but a crew race was a 2,000-meter oxygen-sucking sprint, the pain grabbing hold right from the start and lasting seven torturous minutes. He had also learned that crew wasn't an instant ticket into the Pi KA clique of jocks. These were guys who knew touchdowns and line drives. How could he explain the thrill of feathering to Big Ben, the agony of washout to Steve? Would Loren—wherever he was—understand the subtle heroism of the last twenty painful strokes of the day?

In a way, crew had made Jim feel even less a part of the fraternity than before. There were days he spent more time at the boathouse than at the fraternity. He went to engineering class all day, then bummed a ride with other crew members to the estuary ten miles away and rowed himself weary, not getting home until after supper, which was the main social event of each day at the house, a time when all the brothers gathered together to click and clatter. He ate cold leftovers by himself in the kitchen, then went to his room, opened his engineering books, and tried to block out the noise, feeling isolated.

The race neared the finish line, Jim pulling hard from his starboard seat in the second boat, lactic acid pouring into his muscles, draining what little anaerobic energy he had left. He held on to the finish line, barely, his boat only a length behind, the closest they had come to beating the first boat. He slumped forward in his seat, spent, gasping, wasted, silent. He knew the language of crew, which meant he didn't talk about the pain, much less succumb to it.

Crew described how Jim wanted to see himself: it was the essence of giving 110 percent, a triumph of will, the power of mind over body, sacrifice; it was a chance to excel and reach beyond his limits without having the natural athletic ability of a Loren Hawley. It was a sport with form and purpose, a gathering place for Type A personalities. It was the opportunity to feel good about himself in a house of jocks. It was the epitome of teamwork—eight strong men and a coxswain in a 25-foot shell, all working in unison, each man stroking to the count—if one man fell out of sync, the whole team suffered; it was the Puritan work ethic; it was, when everything fell in place, the ego of the individual sublimated to the ego of the group. That—not barf dancing—was what fraternity was about for Jim.

Crew was not without its rivalries and jealousies, but Jim enjoyed the special comradeship. In a strange way it was like Hell Week—only those who'd been through it could really know what happened. As straining as it was, he looked forward to facing the afternoon chill coming off the estuary, or walking into the bleakness of Ky Eybright Boathouse for an early-morning practice. He knew there would be no pro contract, no photos in the *Daily Cal*, just a lot of hard work and oxygen depletion. That's what it meant to be a jock.

Ten minutes after the first race he was churning through the water again in the first boat, his arms numb, stroking by memory, face etched in pain. At the finish line, it was a dead heat. He slumped forward again, his whole body shaking. He was still second boat. But he knew what Justice Holmes meant when he wrote of the glory of having nobly competed.

11

Steve

Never confuse "I love you" with "I want to marry you."
—Cleveland Amory

It was Peggy Pendergast's wedding reception, a lavish Sacramento affair held in the spacious backyard of Peggy's parents. Peggy was eighteen and Linda's best friend. The day was gorgeous: cloudless blue skies, beautiful guests, white-jacketed caterers, trays of champagne, green-and-white awnings. Linda, dressed in her blue taffeta bridesmaid gown, stood under an awning, watching Buddy (that's what she called Steve) stagger across the lawn toward her, a bottle of champagne tucked under each arm, mayhem in his eyes.

"Things could get wild," she whispered to her friend Margaret, another bridesmaid in taffeta.

It was 1963, the summer before Steve's sophomore year. Linda would be heading to Cal too, starting her freshman year. For several months she had sensed him pulling away. He always seemed to have a reason why he didn't have time to see her that summer: he was too tired from his job picking pears in the orchards near Courtland; he had to lift weights to bulk up for football; he had to help his dad pack mayonnaise jars; he had to go to Berkeley to talk to the coaches. She had the feeling she was just a convenience. But when she asked him if he wanted to stop seeing her, he said no, reassuring her he still loved her. He could be so convincing, so charming. And it was true—he did love her. She was his first big love. Once, after making love, he held her in his arms and cried. "You make me so happy," he said. She wanted to believe him. But it was an agonizing time for her.

It wasn't always that way. The first time Steve asked her out—to the junior prom—she was convinced she was the luckiest girl at McClatchy High. As far as she was concerned, he was *the* best-looking guy in the whole school. All her friends had a crush on him. Whenever she saw him at his locker, he was surrounded by his buddies, the center of attention. She wasn't the cheerleader type she imagined he would date. She was shy, studious, self-abasing, her only school activity the Spanish Club. She was pretty, but she didn't believe her looks—chestnut-brown hair, big China-blue eyes, a slender figure toned by ten years of ballet—were the stuff to nab such a big catch. After the prom, she wrote in her diary:

I wore a white satin dress and gold brocade. Buddy wore a white tuxedo and looked so handsome. After the dance we ate dinner at the El Miramar. I was so nervous I splattered sour cream all over the table. Our dinners cost $8.22. We had a real good time at the prom and lots of fun afterwards too. We arrived home at 3:45 A.M. I just hope Buddy had as much fun as I did.

They dated every weekend—he took her to a Kingston Trio concert and to the 36 Club's Moonshiners Ball. It wasn't just his good looks and sexy deep voice she liked. What hooked her was how thoughtful and attentive he was, even a bit old-fashioned: he liked to hold her hand when he walked her to class; he put his arm around her at the show; he phoned her almost every night; and when he found out she was in the Spanish Club, he joined too, writing her love notes in Spanish. She was also attracted to his family—the way they always ate meals together and went on summer trips—even though he claimed his dad was always picking on him. Family was something she didn't have. Her parents were divorced and she hadn't seen her father in ten years. She loved to listen to Steve talk about his camping trips with the Boy Scouts—that was another of those old-fashioned things she liked. She thought it sweet when he saw a photo of John Kennedy holding Caroline and talked of how much he too wanted to have a family of his own someday, and how he would give anything to have a daughter so angelic as Caroline, and how he looked forward to the day he and his future wife would go to Slavic folk dances and to the State Fair with their children. Linda, a Presbyterian, wanted to be part of it, dreaming of being Mrs. Bud Radich. He had been raised a Roman Catholic, and she liked the idea of

him being a good Catholic boy from a respected family. She was prepared to make whatever sacrifices or changes it took to convince him of
her conviction. He abstained from meat on Fridays, so she quit too.

Steve wasn't zealous about his religion, but he had learned his cate-
chism and developed a faith in the Church's moral code as a boy. He
admired the priest at Holy Spirit Church, who could be merciless with
him in confessional but was generally tolerant of Steve's declining piety.
Unlike the Church, Steve was beginning to see moral questions in tones
other than strictly black or white. He had been raised to treat authority
figures with respect and obedience, but he was questioning decisions,
especially his parents'. Still, he remained faithful, on the surface anyway,
to the doctrines of Catholicism, admitting to Linda that it bothered him
that her parents were divorced. She apologized.

Until they met, her life had been ballet. For eleven years she had
danced two hours a night, three times a week. But it was no longer her
driving passion. He was all that mattered. She invited him to a recital
and when he came she felt childish, immature. She quit ballet the next
day. Her life revolved around him. When he called, she dropped everything—friends, schoolwork. She felt out of control, and uneasy and insecure, especially after he told her what his older brother had advised him:
"Mike said I was stupid to settle for one girl when I could have as many
as I wanted."

They went to see *Splendor in the Grass,* and were convinced that it was
their movie—a story of first love, true love, eternal love, of painful teenage sexual frustration and confusion. In the movie, Natalie Wood and
Warren Beatty, whose name is Bud in the film, are a high school couple
who are madly in love but trying desperately to stave off their sexual lust
until after they are married. They seek guidance from their parents and a
minister, but are turned away as merely in puppy love. Unable to control
his sexual urges, Beatty takes up with the class tramp. Wood offers herself to him, but he turns her down because she is *too good* for premarital
sex. When he goes off to college, she has a nervous breakdown.

Life for Steve and Linda had imitated film as they battled their sexual
urges. Steve had sought guidance from his priest, confessing that he and
Linda were driving nightly to the sexual brink, lickerishly tempting the
hands of the devil. The priest advised him to see Linda only when other
people were around. In his senior year at McClatchy High, the question
for him was how long would Linda continue to be *too good?* He began to
back off, and Linda braced herself, sure he was about to dump her when
he suggested they not see each other for a while. Her friends had warned
her from the beginning that he was a heartbreaker. Her fears were con-

firmed when she went to his house one night and he opened the door, shirt untucked, hair disheveled, and she looked over his shoulder, spotting her worst blond nightmare, the class tramp, sitting on the living-room couch, sweater untucked, hair disheveled. Linda cried all the way home. But he charmed his way back into her heart, telling her that he was worried that they were "getting too close," and before long they were regulars at the Motel Sex. They used a condom. Once.

He moved her way at the wedding reception, taking a long swig straight from the champagne bottle. "My parents went to Tahoe for the weekend," he said. "I've got the house to myself."

She smiled but didn't reply, determined not to let him reel her in again, not this day anyway, no matter how handsome he looked in his blue blazer.

"Maybe you should slow down a little," she offered.

He took another swig.

She worried, as usual, that if she turned him down he would take off with someone else—she was sure that there were plenty of girls at the reception who would gladly depart with him. Or maybe he would never call again, leaving her to stare at the barren walls of her sanitarium like Natalie Wood, with nothing to do but forlornly read in her diary how he once told her she was *too good* to have sex with.

"We don't have to do anything," he said. "We can just talk."

"I don't think it's a good idea," she replied.

He continued to persist . . . he could be so persuasive, so sexy, so wildly enthusiastic. She felt herself caving in. "Okay, I'll go," she said. "But under one condition."

"What's that?"

It was that Margaret would go with them. That way, figured Linda, there would be a buffer. Nothing could happen.

"That's a shitty idea!" he countered.

But an hour later the three of them were speeding down Land Park Drive in Steve's white three-speed Falcon (which Frank and Mary helped him buy). He had a scowl on his face and a bottle of champagne between his legs. Approaching a line of cars waiting for a signal, he suddenly accelerated, passing the cars on the right, his wheels riding up on the sidewalk.

"Slow down!" yelled Linda.

He slammed on the brakes, stopping in the middle of the intersection. "Have it your way." He smiled, slowly creeping forward, 5 miles an hour in a 30-mile-an-hour residential zone.

"Take us home!" she implored.

"Fuck that shit!" he spewed, punctuating his obscenities with his foot, first on the brake, then on the accelerator.

"Buddy!"

He drove faster.

"Why are you doing this?" she asked.

He turned onto his street and screeched to a halt in his driveway. Inside the house, he marched to his bedroom, motioning for her to follow. Reluctantly, she did, mad at herself for once again being his puppet. Margaret waited in the living room.

He stood in front of the mirror, struggling to unloosen the knot in his tie. She reached up to help, their eyes meeting. If it was mayhem she saw in his eyes before, now it was absolute anarchy. He slapped her hands away, then uncoiled with the back of his hand, the blow ricocheting off the side of her shoulder to the back of her head. She tumbled backward into the wall, sliding to the floor like Raggedy Ann.

Was this really happening? Was this the same old-fashioned boy who talked about family and folk dancing and her being *too good?* What about all those love notes he passed in Spanish Club?

She leaped to her feet and bolted past him, through the kitchen, out the back door, across the driveway, her taffeta bridesmaid dress flowing in the breeze. He pursued, stopping abruptly when she ran to the neighbors' front door and rang the doorbell. He jumped in his car and sped away.

That night her mother offered words of advice: "The only thing worse than him hitting you," she counseled, "is if you let it happen again."

The next morning he called, his voice bright and full of summer, as if nothing happened. "Let's go to the river," he said.

"You must be kidding," she exclaimed.

He wasn't. He remembered nothing of the reception or going to his house. Total blackout. She filled him in on the ugly details.

Against her mother's advice, she went to his house. He was subdued, filled with contrition. She had never seen him so pained, so repentant, so vulnerable. He put his head in her arms and cried, begging forgiveness, promising change.

"I love you," he whispered. "I can't wait until we're at Cal together."

Pretty seventeen-year-old Linda had been a student at Cal only two weeks when she set out on foot from her Sigma Kappa sorority house in search of a doctor's office. Walking south on Telegraph Avenue, scanning both sides of the street, she felt as if she was about to throw up.

She hoped Steve was right—that it was just a case of freshman nerves that had her sick to her stomach every morning. What girl wouldn't be stressed out after what she'd just been through . . . leaving home for the first time, agonizing through rush, registering for classes, wondering when Steve would call.

The trauma of starting Cal had been building for her all summer. There were the normal concerns—which sorority to join . . . what to major in . . . how many skirts to pack. But those things would all fall into place, she figured. It was Steve who kept her up nights worrying. After the blackout incident, he'd been more affectionate than ever, holding her close after they made love, telling her how pretty she was, gushing on about how lucky he was to have her. He could make her feel so wonderful and beautiful. Still, she couldn't escape the feeling of being pulled in with one hand, pushed away with the other. She was coming to Berkeley, invading *his* territory.

This would be her first doctor's visit by herself. Too embarrassed to ask any of her new sorority sisters to recommend one, she stopped at the first office she reached, nervously approaching the receptionist window in the crowded waiting room.

"I think I might have a hernia," she whispered.

The receptionist patiently explained that this was a podiatrist's office and that she probably needed to see the family practitioner down the street.

She and Steve hadn't even discussed what they would do if, God forbid, she was pregnant. They had agreed only that she would call him with the results at exactly eight o'clock at the Durant Hotel. That's where he'd be with the varsity football team, sequestered on the eve of the 1963 season opener against Iowa State. "Keep your fingers crossed," she said.

Steve stood at the window of his fifth-floor room at the Durant Hotel, staring out at the Campanile silhouetted against the night sky. Built in 1902, the noble Durant Hotel had long been used to house visiting dignitaries to the University—Theodore Roosevelt, Woodrow Wilson, Robert Frost, Prime Minister Nehru had all stayed there. Visiting professor Aldous Huxley was calling it his temporary home. Steve felt as if he'd been there forever, waiting for eight o'clock and the big news.

It was 7:55. He turned and continued to pace, praying Linda wasn't pregnant.

"Holy shit, Rat!" said Loren, his roommate for the evening. "Sit down and relax. You'll do fine tomorrow."

Steve sat on the edge of the bed and stared at the television, unable to concentrate. Loren was watching "77 Sunset Strip." Steve picked up his playbook and leafed through the pages, unable to concentrate on that too. He stared at the phone.

He wasn't about to confide in Loren what he was really worried about. Not that he didn't like Loren . . . there weren't many guys he'd rather party with. But this was a private matter; he hadn't discussed it with anyone, not even Don, his closest friend, or with Ron, who had been his fraternal big brother as a pledge, a guy he respected as much as anyone, admiring Ron's maturity and work ethic. But talking about intimate stuff? As his father had taught him, a man was supposed to deal with his own problems, not burden other people with them. Loren, who was back in Berkeley after his mysterious disappearance, lived by the same code. He had admitted where he'd gone during his absence—Ricks Junior College in Idaho—but he had told none of the brothers the reason he'd gone. Or that he'd committed his dad to detox. Secrets. Secrets.

Steve hated to think about the options if Linda *was* pregnant. He knew his dad would blow a major gasket. Steve was the first in the family to go to college, and sometimes he had the feeling his education meant more to his father than it did to him, that a degree from Cal was the final stamp of approval on Frank Radich's immigration papers, the exclamation point on all those thousands of twelve-hour days he toiled so that his children could reap the best America had to offer.

At exactly eight o'clock, the phone rang. Steve sprang across the room to answer it. "The test was positive," said Linda, her voice trembling.

"All right!" exclaimed Steve, thrusting his arm in the air. "That's a load off my mind."

Linda paused quizzically. "I don't think you understand, Buddy," she said. "Positive means I'm pregnant."

"Oh, shit!" he blared, banging his fist on the table.

"Do you want to talk about it?" she asked.

"Not now," he answered. "Tomorrow after the game." He slammed down the receiver.

"What was all that about?" queried Loren.

Steve stared at the wall, the enormity of Linda's pronouncement echoing through his brain. He could see his future swirling down the drain—football, Pi KA, graduation, his chance to be a big Romeo on campus. He saw himself trudging home from work from his father's mayonnaise plant; he saw himself burping the baby while all his buddies were out partying.

"Oh, it was nothing," he finally replied. "You know, just typical girl bullshit."

For the first time since the Joe Kapp years, pundits were giving the Bears an outside chance of going to the Rose Bowl. The keys, they said, would be an improved defense and the passing of junior quarterback Craig (a.k.a. "Hummer") Morton. Steve was going to be starting at defensive left end as a sophomore, and possibly seeing some action on offense too. He had bulked up over the summer, but at six-one, 192 pounds, he was small for a defensive lineman. Around the fraternity, he was low-key about his rapid rise to first string, rarely talking about football, treating it as just one part of his collegiate life. But as soon as he walked through the locker-room doors, he was intensely competitive. His freshman coach, Mike White, had raved about his attitude and tenacious play. White had heard stories of Steve's wild side, but he only knew him as a serious, tough-minded student-athlete. Coach Levy considered him a recruiting plum, an athlete that other schools would be sorry they over-looked. Cal was the only school that offered him a scholarship.

Steve wasted no time asserting his presence in his first game, slicing through blockers on the first play to nail the Iowa State runner for a 2-yard loss. He was all over the field, relentless in his pursuit, helping the Bear defense to start the season impressively, holding the Cyclones to a lone touchdown through the first three and a half quarters. Unfortunately, the ballyhooed Bear passing game was being grounded. With five minutes to go, the score was knotted 8 to 8. Then with the ball in their own territory, Morton faded back and hit Loren streaking all alone down the right sideline with a 58-yard bomb. Loren waltzed into the end zone untouched. The Cyclones' last-gasp drive ended when Steve chased down the quarterback and threw him for a 12-yard loss, a perfect ending to a game he had dreamed of since boyhood.

In the winners' noisy locker room after the game, Loren and his new best buddy, Morton, were snapping towels and making plans to go see the dancers doing the swim and the hully-gully at the Condor in North Beach. They both had the hots for one of the waitresses, Carol Doda. Steve quietly showered and got dressed in his gray slacks and blue team blazer, his jubilation tempered by the task ahead.

The postgame crowd packed the front yard of the fraternity. Steve edged his way through, receiving the admiring pats on the back. His smile was strained. Proud Mary and Frank waited near the front door.

"I don't blame you for not smiling more," greeted Frank. "You guys played lousy." How typical, thought Steve . . . wondering what it would take to hear an encouraging word from his father. "Why didn't Levy put you in on offense?" asked Frank. "You should have said something to him."

"Fuck you," muttered Steve under his breath, easing away.

He spotted Linda, neat and prim in her pleated skirt and white blouse, the sorority uniform for the rooting section. "You were great, Buddy," she said, thinking how rugged he looked, the gash across the bridge of his nose only adding to his appeal. She wanted to hug him, but didn't, certain he would resist.

"We need to get going," he said softly.

"Why are you off in such a hurry?" asked Mary.

"None of your damn business," he replied, leading Linda away. Mary wondered what she'd done to deserve such rancor. This wasn't the first time; in fact, it had been going on since high school. She couldn't figure it out—she'd done all the things a mother was supposed to do—tuck her kids in at night, pack their lunches, dress their wounds. But Steve could be so resentful, so rude.

They drove in silence, winding their way up into the Berkeley hills, parking on a turnout on Grizzly Peak Boulevard. To the west the panorama was spectacular, the late-afternoon sun painting San Francisco in a coat of crimson.

They turned toward each other. "What are we going to do?" Linda asked, her voice faint and fragile, her eyes pleading.

He knew what she wanted—to get married and have the baby. But it made no sense. He was barely nineteen, she was seventeen. How was he supposed to support her . . . drop out of school and pick pears for $1.80 an hour? Go to work for his dad and argue every day? That's not what he wanted. He wanted to get his degree, go to the Rose Bowl, date pretty coeds. He loved being a part of the fraternity.

He took her hand. "I'm really sorry this has happened," he said. "I love you, but I don't want to be married."

"Why couldn't it work?" she pleaded, a tear rolling down her cheek. Then another.

"It just wouldn't," he said.

"So what am I supposed to do?" she asked.

He shook his head, confused. He had already dismissed the idea of abortion. Maybe it was because of his brush with Roman Catholicism as a boy; or maybe it was because he'd heard grim stories of coat hangers and girls bleeding to death. Whatever the reason, abortion wasn't an alternative. Not for him. Not for her.

"Maybe you should go away somewhere and have the baby," he suggested.

"And then what?" she asked.

"Give it up for adoption."

"I won't do that," she cried. "I won't give up our baby."

He leaned over and put his arms around her, holding her tight. Seconds passed, then minutes as they held each other, no words, just tears.

"Buddy, I love you so much," she whispered. He held her tighter.

Night was falling when he dropped her off at the sorority. "I'll call you tomorrow," he promised, kissing her on her tear-stained cheek. "We'll talk about it some more then. But you have to promise me one thing . . . you *absolutely* cannot tell anyone. This has to be a secret."

Then he joined Loren and Craig at the Condor.

Loren burst into Steve's room. "Come on, Rat, get up!" he bellowed, pulling him by the arm. "You're coming with me."

Steve was exhausted—physically from practice, mentally from the strain of trying to reach a decision. To go with Loren, he knew, required energy. Action always followed the exuberant, swirling Hayseed, who reminded Steve of a windup toy that bounced off of every wall in the room, never running down. Loren thought Steve a good-time guy, but maybe a bit too serious and studious unless someone was there to pour him the Coors.

"Where we going?" Steve asked, reluctantly dragging himself off his bed.

They were off to visit Donna at the AO Pi house. "I figured you should come along and check out the new tomatoes," said Loren. "Donna says they got a great new crop this rush."

They were greeted at the front door by a pert sophomore. As she went to call Donna on the intercom, Steve turned to Loren. "That's a great butt!" he extolled.

"Well, hot damn, boy," returned Loren. "Make a move."

Steve made his move that evening, calling to invite her out for a drink. They went to McNally's on College Avenue and drank Irish coffees. She was even prettier than he first thought: soft dark brown hair, hazel-green eyes, demure smile and a "great butt." Her name was Ayris (pronounced Iris) Hatton, and compared with other sorority girls he'd met at Cal, she seemed unpretentious, honest, peaceful. There was something delicate and appealing in her manner, and he was instantly smitten . . . and so was she.

On the surface, they appeared a mismatch: he was a six-footer, assured and outgoing, she was five-four, reticent and quiet; he liked football and beer, she loved painting and sunsets. But they connected. Right there in McNally's. Even before the Irish coffees kicked in. She too was the child of a tough-willed immigrant, coming to Berkeley partly to escape a parent's reproachful eye. Her father, a small, reproving man, was a Lebanese Catholic who owned Hatton's of Hollywood, a popular restaurant on Vine Street with the movie colony. Ayris had grown up in Westwood and was majoring in history, although art was her passion. She knew of Steve not by his reputation as a promising Cal football star —she had never been to a football game—but by the fact her sorority sisters ranked him high on their list of campus dreamboats.

After finishing a third Irish, he drove her pell-mell back to the sorority so she could make her 11 P.M. weekday curfew. She accepted his offer to go out Saturday night after he returned from his trip to Illinois to play the Fighting Illini. She rushed upstairs to tell Donna the news. "He's not at all what I expected," she said. "He's so shy and sweet."

Steve spent the next week problem solving by denial. He and Linda talked only once. On Saturday he was in Champaign-Urbana for the Illinois game. In the third quarter, with the Bears' offense unable to move the ball, Coach Levy inserted him in the game at receiver to replace Loren, who had pinched a nerve in his shoulder. The first play was a sweep around his end, his assignment to block the middle linebacker. He charged off the line, drawing a bead on big number 50 rumbling in his direction. As he lowered his helmet, they collided full force, Steve bouncing backward like he'd been hit by a runaway beer truck. He had just been pancaked by All-American Dick Butkus. He staggered off the field under his own power, head ringing, through for the day with a concussion. He'd already had one concussion in high school, except on that occasion he returned to the huddle so dingy and babbling that quarterback Cobleigh had to signal time-out and call the coach out on the field to come and take him away. The Bears lost 10–0.

Battered and bruised, Steve and Loren were greeted at the San Francisco Airport by Ayris and Donna. They drove back to Berkeley in Donna's '54 Chevy, stopping at JV Liquors on University Avenue to pick up a case of beer, then to the Travel Lodge, where they all checked into one room. For a sorority girl to sign out for an overnight was a daring thing, even on a fifteenth date, but Ayris reasoned that with Donna there too, it was innocent enough. They all stayed up the night, drinking beer, throwing pillows, bouncing on the bed, laughing, talking. Ayris and Steve pretended they didn't know what was going on when Loren and Donna went into the bathroom and closed the door, emerging fifteen minutes later, smiling shamelessly.

That next night Steve called Linda in Sacramento. She had checked out of school and moved back home with her mother, telling her sorority sisters she was homesick and was transferring to Sacramento State.

"Buddy, I want to be married and have the baby," she sobbed.

"I don't," he reiterated.

Steve eyed his father across the table, measuring his reaction. They were sitting in a booth in Larry Blake's Restaurant on Telegraph Avenue. Steve had just informed him that Linda was pregnant. Talking to his father had never been easy—even in good times Frank could be obdurate, recalcitrant—but making him take off a half day's work to drive to Berkeley so he could tell him he had knocked up his seventeen-year-old girlfriend was daunting.

"What should I do?" asked Steve.

"What kind of dumb question is that?" Frank replied, glaring. "You're gonna do the honorable thing."

Honor was a big thing with Frank Radich. He was a driven man, a strong man, toughened by the sparse times of his childhood. Tall and handsome—a trait he passed on to Steve—he embodied one archetype of the American Dream realized: the rugged, determined individualism of the immigrant pioneer. Born in 1910 to peasant parents in a small Croatian fishing village located on one of the hundreds of long, narrow islands that parallel the Dalmatian coast, Frank was raised in a one-room, windowless house with a dirt floor, no water, no electricity. When he was one year old, his father emigrated to America, promising to send for Frank and his mother when he found steady work. As soon as Frank was old enough, his mother, a devoutly religious Roman Catholic, taught him how to row across the channel to get to church and to market. When he was ten, he and his mother finally emigrated to America, joining his father in Sacramento, where he had found work with the Southern Pacific. At the age of eleven, when his father went out on strike, Frank got a job after school sweeping floors and stacking vegetables at Purity Market, a small neighborhood grocery. For the next fifteen years, he worked at the market every day—no vacations or time off, not even when he broke his leg. At sixteen he quit school and went to work full-time, supporting the family. He even saved enough to buy his own car.

And then in 1936 at the age of twenty-six, as America struggled to get back on its feet from the Depression, he took $400 of his own money, borrowed another $300, and bought his own business, a small grocery at the corner of Fifteenth and Q streets near the new state capitol. On a trip to pick up fruit and vegetables from one of his wholesalers, he met pretty blue-eyed Mary Vickers, a secretary who was on her first day on the job. She was painfully shy, unable to look directly at him when he asked to see his bill. Friends would later claim that she was so shy that she changed clothes in the closet the first five years they were married.

As with so many immigrants, Frank's work was his easel, his way of integrating into his new culture, his way of creating. His passion was to make a better life for his family; upward mobility drove him. And as with so many immigrants who fathered first-generation Americans, his relentless drive for perfection and his entrepreneurial success were sometimes lost on his children, particularly Steve, who experienced him as distant, demanding, disapproving. Frank's constant pushing rubbed against Steve's own tenacity, causing them to butt heads, all the heights and depths of the Slavic temperament possessing them both, generosity and cruelty, arrogance and humility.

"You're gonna marry that girl!" Frank ordered.

"But I don't want to," Steve replied.

"Should have thought of that before you unzipped your pants."

"What about school? And football? And everything else?"

"I can't believe what a stupid thing you've done," Frank said. "I'll guarantee you'll never get one red cent from me the rest of your life if you don't marry that girl."

It was agreed that Steve would come to Sacramento and a meeting would be held between the two families. Frank would break the news to Mary. There was much to iron out—finances, college, a wedding, the baby, where to live.

Linda nervously approached the Radichs' front door. She was the first to arrive—neither her mom nor Steve nor Frank were there yet. This would give Linda a few minutes alone with Mary—a chance for a little heart-to-heart with her future mother-in-law. That was good, she figured. She'd never felt comfortable with Steve's mom. It wasn't that Mary was ever rude—in fact Linda wished her own mother spent as much time with her as Mrs. Radich devoted to her family—but Mary could be so fortified, so austere.

Mary was also Slavic, born in Montana in 1917, the fourth and youngest child of Serbian immigrants. Her father, a miner, died of brown-lung disease when she was one. Two years later her mother married Steve Vickers, also a Serbian immigrant, and in 1927, believing California was the promised land, he moved the family to Jackson, a small town in the foothills of the Mother Lode country, forty-five miles southeast of Sacramento. Jackson was a bustling mining town and the county seat of Amador County, where the discovery of gold by James Marshall in 1849 triggered the great California gold rush. Jackson became a destination for miners from around the world—Chinese, English, Italian, Spanish, Serbians. The Serbians were so enamored with the town that they constructed St. Sava's Orthodox Church atop a hill overlooking the townsite, the mother church of the religion in North America. Down the hill from the church, Mary's stepfather opened a small market, stocking it with fresh vegetables and fruits from the fertile farmland nearby. He worked seven days a week, demanding the same of Mary and her two brothers and her sister. Within ten years, he was one of the richest merchants in Amador County. He bought a large plot of land near the center of town and built three houses, moving his family into one and renting out the other two. He dominated his home like a despot, allowing only Serbian to be spoken in the house. Outward demonstrations of affection were forbidden. Love was repressed. Mary's mother was subservient, assigned to the kitchen (which was built in the basement so she'd be able to withstand the scorching summer heat). In school, Mary was an excellent student, winning the Amador County spelling bee in the ninth grade, graduating from high school second in her class. But she was not allowed to date or pursue her interest in dance. Life was confined to school, work, family, and church. Religion was the cornerstone of the family. Frank was the first—and only—man she ever dated. It was a slow-moving romance, taking him three years to finally propose. When she announced to her father, a devoutly religious Serbian Orthodox, that she was marrying a Roman Catholic Croatian, he threatened to disown her. The Serbians and the Croatians had been warring since the sixteenth century and for her to consider such an act was blasphemous. The fact that Frank was a hardworking, honorable man made no difference. As the wedding date approached, she was a nervous wreck, unable to sleep or eat, losing thirty pounds. She had never disobeyed her father. But she went through with it, marrying Frank, not in St. Sava's in Jackson as she had always dreamed, but in a civil ceremony performed by a justice of the peace in Carson City, Nevada. The newlyweds agreed to a religious compromise: sons would be raised as Roman Catholics, daughters as Serbian Orthodox. That still wasn't good enough for Mary's father. He disowned her, refusing to talk to her. In time, however, Frank's work ethic and determination to succeed would win him over.

Linda knocked on the door. Mary opened it, surprised to see her son's girlfriend standing on her doorstep. "What are you doing here?" she asked. "I thought you were at Cal."

"Don't you know about the meeting?" asked Linda timidly.

"What meeting?"

"Mr. Radich didn't tell you?"

"Tell me what?"

Linda braced herself, paralyzed at the responsibility of telling this woman that she was soon to become a grandmother. "I'm pregnant," she blurted. "There's supposed to be a family meeting here to discuss what's going to happen."

Mary, who attended church twice weekly, closed her eyes, scanning the universe for a hidden reservoir of strength. "I knew this would happen, the way you two were carrying on this summer, staying out all night," she said. "How could you have let this happen? How can you do this to Buddy?"

Linda felt steamrolled . . . it seemed inconceivable that this woman could respond so coldly, so unfairly. They didn't speak, sitting across the living room from each other, waiting for the others to arrive. Mary, too, felt bowled over.

It was a meeting of tense faces and clipped voices. A decision was reached that Steve and Linda would be married by a justice of the peace on October 20, 1963, in Reno. Until the baby was born, Linda would stay in Sacramento with her mother, and Steve would continue to live in the fraternity and go to school. With his scholarship, plus money from summer jobs and assistance from Frank and Mary, he wouldn't have to drop out. There was no suggestion of Linda working.

Steve felt trapped, knowing he would be getting married out of duty, not love. Duty to Linda; duty to his father. "I'll marry you," he said tersely, looking straight into her huge blue eyes. "But it's not what I want. We're not going to live like married people. And I don't want you telling anybody we're married. I want this to be a secret."

She nodded, Pollyanna clinging to the hope that once they were actually married, he would change.

On Saturday, October 19, Linda turned the radio to the broadcast of Cal's game against San Jose State in Berkeley, listening for Steve's name to be called. He'd promised to pick her up at her mother's house three hours after the end of the game, then they would drive to Reno and, as he put it, "get it over with." She had a sinking feeling he wouldn't show.

Against San Jose State, he played like a man possessed in a 34–13 victory, helping to hold the Spartans to under one hundred yards on the ground. When he dressed quickly after the game, none of his teammates had the slightest inkling where he was off to. Nor did any of his fraternity brothers have a clue, not even Cobleigh.

In Sacramento, Linda paced her living room, stopping to check her watch and peek out the curtains every trip across the floor. He was late. "He's not coming," she told her mother. "I knew it."

A car finally pulled into the driveway. She ran to the curtains. It was Steve in his Falcon, still wearing his blue Cal blazer. Her heart, she thought, was going to fly out of her chest when he held out his hand and there in his palm, looking to her every bit as glorious as the Hope diamond, was a thin gold wedding band.

Her eyes glistened and she was filled with hope. They drove to Reno and were married by a justice of the peace, spending their honeymoon night at a small motel, Linda insisting on accompanying him to the office, smiling as she watched him register as Mr. and Mrs. Buddy Radich.

The next day they returned to Sacramento. When he pulled the Falcon into her mother's driveway, Linda invited him in. "I gotta get back to Berkeley," he said, the motor running.

"What about next weekend?" she asked. "Shall I come down there, or do you want to come to Sacramento?"

He tightened his jaw. "I have midterms coming up," he said. "I don't think I'm gonna have time."

"You can study here," she offered, touching his hand.

He pulled away. "I told you that we're not going to live like a married couple," he said curtly. "Don't you understand?" She nodded, choking back tears, then watched him drive away.

That night back at the fraternity, he called Ayris to ask her out for Saturday night, inviting her to go see Peter, Paul, and Mary at the Berkeley Community Theater. She accepted, of course. Why wouldn't she?

Steve Radich was about to embark on his secret life.

12

Larry

Sexual intercourse began! In nineteen sixty-three.
—Philip Larkin, poet

It was 1963. My junior year. My twenty-first year. I was still, technically, a virgin.

But as I squeezed my way into the bleachers of jam-packed Harmon Gym, I was not, for the moment anyway, thinking about getting laid. I was about to attend my first political speech. It wasn't because the growing activism on campus had converted me into a flaming radical . . . I had to be there because it was an assignment for History 173B, the history of the Reconstruction. The scheduled speaker was author James Baldwin.

I was not intellectually curious about black culture . . . or any other culture, for that matter. College for me was fraternity and baseball, with education a distant third. I'd finally declared a major—communication and public policy, which was a hodgepodge of courses described in the 1963 General Course Catalogue as "a field major offering the student a broad range of courses to train him to effectively communicate governmental or business policy to a wide range of audiences." Whatever that meant. I signed up for it because it had the easiest classes and because there were ten girls for every guy. All I wanted was a degree. As long as I didn't flunk out, I didn't care what my g.p.a. was. Unless I got in a bad train wreck, it was clear that pro baseball was still in my future. My hole card. My big dream. I hadn't made All-American yet, but the scouts were still hanging around, tossing out bonus offers in the low five figures. After I'd struck out 19 against UC Santa Barbara in my pitching debut start for the Bears, they all now wanted to sign me as a pitcher—I was slated to be the ace of the Bear staff my senior year. But I had made up my mind that I would get my degree before embarking on a career in pro ball. I was having too good a time in the fraternity. Ping-Pong in the morning. All the grilled cheese sandwiches I could eat. Eightball in the afternoon. Food fights for dinner. Forty great drinking buddies. And a front-row seat to some of the best-looking girls in California. I was in no big hurry to get on with my life. Or bog myself down with heavy intellectual overload. Coach Wolfman said I was "too laid-back." Somebody else said it was the "Malibu Mentality." But I wasn't completely oblivious. I did get an A in ROTC the last semester it was required.

Baldwin entered the gym and the overflow crowd of 9,000 rose in unison to give him a thunderous two-minute standing ovation, the type of reception I might have expected for Sandy Koufax. A short man with a leonine head and heavy-lidded eyes, he was dressed in a dark double-breasted blazer and spoke extemporaneously. His words electrified the audience. "I'm not going into details of police dogs, fire hoses, and paddy wagons," he said. "You already know about such things." He was referring to the arrest of 2,543 demonstrators in Birmingham, Alabama, that week. The newspaper was filled with photos of the defiant Bull Connor and George Wallace, and of Negroes flattened to the sidewalk by the fire hoses. He spoke of the "the adolescent nightmare of segregation" and how "nothing will be achieved by violence."

Philosophically, I supported the civil rights movement. But that was easy. They weren't moving into my neighborhood. There had been zero Negroes at Westchester High, zero Negroes on the Cal baseball team, zero Negroes in Pi KA. I'd heard the rumors about Ron being part Negro, but as far as I was concerned, he was as white as me. Baldwin's speech was not an epiphany, but I was curious enough to stop at the Student Nonviolent Coordinating Committee (SNCC) recruiting table on Bancroft Avenue and pick up a brochure. I was no more interested in volunteering to go to Mississippi than I was in swimming the Atlantic Ocean . . . but I got interested enough in SNCC that I decided to write a term paper on it for Speech 190. I sent away for more literature, went to the library to research magazine articles. I was into the project. My first big honest academic effort.

Cheating was not openly encouraged in Pi KA, but it wasn't discouraged. A file of old tests and essays existed, as did an index of phone numbers of professional term-paper writers. For my speech and society class, I paid a woman twenty-five dollars to write a paper on President Kennedy's speechwriter, Ted Sorensen. If the President could pay somebody to write his stuff, so could I. I (she) got a B. In another class the assignment was to write a paper to persuade. I procrastinated, then the night before it was due I plagiarized a magazine article titled "The Career Woman," a composition to be put under glass at the American Museum of Male Chauvinism. The opening sentence read: "The American male is the victim of one of the most negative advancements in the history of mankind—the working wife." The concluding sentence read: "Women are becoming defeminized, and this could precipitate the biggest disaster in America since the Depression." My instructor, a male, gave me an A.

I skipped more classes than I attended. Certain professors permitted professional notetakers to attend their lectures. These notes—called "Fybate Notes"—were printed and sold on the open market for twenty cents a lecture or four dollars for the whole semester. The notes were better organized than anything I could hope to do. It was possible, with creative scheduling, to take all "Fybated" courses in a semester, which meant attendance at class was only necessary for midterms and finals. I was the best Ping-Pong player in the fraternity.

The debate over the perceived conflict between fraternity and academic values escalated on campus in 1962, and it was an incident involving two members of Pi KA that was at the center of the storm. Late one night during a pinochle game in the card room, Al Nelson, starting halfback and captain-elect of the football team, was expressing concern about his Political Science 101 midterm. Steve Thompson, the son of a Sacramento judge, a bright poli-sci major with an eye on a career in government and politics, said not to worry—he would take the test for him and guarantee a B, thus preserving Nelson's athletic eligibility. In a class of 400 students, Nelson's absence wasn't likely to be noted. So they thought. On the morning of the exam, Nelson stayed home at the fraternity and Thompson went to Wheeler Auditorium and breezed through the test. The plan would have worked except Nelson's TA did happen to notice he wasn't in the auditorium. Nelson, a Nordic god, was not hard to find in a crowd. And when a blue book showed up with his name on it, it was only a matter of hours before the two goat brothers were suspended from school for a semester and Nelson was ruled ineligible for football and stripped of his captaincy. The incident captured weeklong headlines in the San Francisco *Chronicle* and the *Daily Cal*. A deluge of vitriolic letters to the editor decried the lack of moral and academic values in fraternities.

But for my term project on SNCC, I was going legit—no plagiarism, no hired writers. I turned in an original 66-page thesis. When I received a B, I was disappointed. The following semester, a flirty blond Delta Gamma from Santa Barbara, a girl I was hoping would help me end my technical virginity, took the same course from a different professor. When she complained to me that she didn't have time to write a thesis, I volunteered to let her use my SNCC paper. My professor had written all his comments on separate sheets of paper. The night before her paper was due, she borrowed my typewriter, changed the title page into her name and turned it in, 66 pages, word for word. My words. She got an A+. And I didn't get laid.

I walked down Bancroft Avenue, curious to find out what all the commotion was. I passed two protesters carrying pickets: "U.S. Foreign Policy Is Nhu Diem Good!" "Mme. Nhu Fiddles While Monks Burn!"

For a week the big bold headlines in the *Daily Cal* had bannered the controversial visit to the campus of Madame Nhu, the flamboyant and outspoken sister-in-law of South Vietnam's President Diem. The notorious "Dragon Lady," who had appointed herself arbiter of her country's morals, was scheduled to speak in Harmon Gym. Classes had been canceled. I had no intention of attending the speech . . . I just thought it might be interesting to saunter down to the gym and check out the demonstrators and the dollies.

It was October 29, 1963. Madame Nhu's visit had caused the biggest stir in Berkeley since President Kennedy's appearance eighteen months earlier. Her remarks about "Buddhist barbecues" had intensified American uncertainty about Diem's desirability as president. Vietnam was suddenly a major issue on campus. Berkeley would be the last stop on her fractious cross-country tour to drum up support for the Diem regime. At Harvard and Columbia she had been pelted by eggs from protesters. Headlines in the *Daily Cal* were predicting "the most massive demonstration in Bay Area history." Slate and the Ad Hoc Committee to Protest the War in Vietnam had mobilized protesters and were encouraging hecklers to disrupt her speech. University officials and the Berkeley police were gearing for the worst. It was the first time I was more than subliminally aware of the debate over Vietnam.

Most of my thoughts and energy had been going to Mary. We had met at a party in Playa Del Rey over the summer. She had just graduated from El Segundo High and was working as a receptionist for a finance company. She had no plans to go to college, which didn't make any difference to me because she was cuter than Sally Fields. She wore her hair in a beehive, smoked Montclairs, and sang along to the songs on the radio. On our first date we parked in front of her parents' house until 4 A.M., steaming the windows of my Impala. Nobody had ever kissed me so passionately or pressed her body against mine so hard. On our second date she turned to me with her big blue eyes and cooed, "I'm falling in love." No girl had ever said that to me before. "Me too," I confessed. Before long she was calling me "Poophead" and I was calling her "Tiger." At long last, for the first time in my life, I had a steady girlfriend. Oh, be still my beating heart. We would have three kids, we decided. But she was determined to wait until we were married to have sex. We went to see *Days of Wine and Roses* at the La Tijiera Drive-In and spent the whole movie in the back seat dry-humping and drinking Bali-Hi. On the way home she threw up all over my leg. When school resumed in September, she talked her parents into allowing her to move up to San Jose to live with an aunt. I assumed we would start doing "it" now that she was away from home. Every weekend I commuted to see her, driving her back to Berkeley to show her off to the brothers, putting on hundreds of miles between Friday and Sunday. She hung on my arm, nibbled on my ear, whispered sweet nothings . . . but I couldn't talk her into the Motel Sex. Close. Very close. But no penetration.

"I can wait," I lied.

We talked a lot on the phone. "I keep thinking of those girls up there in Berkeley and I'm afraid you will forget me," she said.

"No way," I replied.

"I think a lot about us getting married and I want to very much, but I'm scared," she said. "I start thinking that I should go to college or maybe travel and I get all screwed up! Larry, I love you and I don't ever want to lose you and I want to get married, but darn it, then I start wondering if I will wish I'd gone to school in a few years. I don't want you to marry a dumb broad! What do you think I should do, Larry?"

"Well . . ."

"I keep thinking about what you told me last weekend in Berkeley."

"What?"

"You know, about what it's going to be like in a few years when all I will have to talk about are the kids and gossip about the neighbors, when you would rather discuss the crisis on the moon or some darn thing. What can we possibly have in common in five years? No more parties and boozing and doing the things we enjoy so much now. Those days will be over someday, ya know. I doubt if you'll still be calling me Tiger in five years."

"Yes, I will."

The demonstrators were chanting and carrying signs as I continued down Bancroft. Berkeley police cars had barricaded Dana Street in front of the gym. In a last-ditch effort to avoid trouble, the student senate had urged students and faculty to greet Madame Nhu's speech with "the dignity of a silent protest."

I heard somebody call my name. It was Steve. He was heading into the gym and bid me to join him. "What the heck," I said, falling into stride.

In my unofficial ranking of the Guys I Most Wanted to Be Seen Walking Across Campus With, Steve ranked just a notch below Morton, the only thing holding him back from being Number One being Craig's superior press clippings. Those clippings hadn't done much good against the Trojans the previous Saturday, the Bears getting thumped 36–6. Steve was still limping from being run over by All-American tailback Mike Garrett and the "Thundering Herd." I could see that. What I couldn't see was his marriage license, his wedding ring, or anything else to indicate he had tied the knot ten days earlier. I didn't even know Linda existed. Not in my wildest dreams would I have guessed he was hitched. Mary and I had seen him at Peter, Paul, and Mary with Ayris.

"So do you think we should be giving aid to the Diem regime?" he asked.

Huh? I hadn't yet figured out whose side we were supposed to be on, north or south, let alone the names of the players.

"I think we should cut his ass off," he said. "It's an oppressive regime." I nodded.

Steve's intellectual curiosity and interest in world affairs surprised me. He didn't seem the type. But he was taking a poetry class, and I'd notice him sitting in his room sometimes reading weird books about Zen and foreign stuff like that. And it wasn't even for a class. If I hadn't seen him screaming drunk and dropping trou so many times, I would've sworn he was half bookworm. I guess that's one of the reasons I found him so interesting. That and his good looks. There were always girls buzzing around him. Mary drooled every time she was around him.

An anxious and equivocal crowd jammed together on the hard bleachers as Madame Nhu was led into the gym under heavy guard. Steve and I were sitting directly over the aisle where she entered. Our eyes were riveted on Le Thuy, her beautiful, petite eighteen-year-old daughter walking at her side.

A courteous applause greeted Madame Nhu as she stepped to the

podium, surprising her audience with her charm and wit. She was forceful in her charge that the Communists were behind the Buddhist suicide
burnings and in her claim that the Communists could be defeated only
with continued American aid. Her speech was greeted not with silence
but with a mixture of hissing, applause, and laughter. (The press would
later call the reception "polite" and a "fair hearing.")

When her speech concluded and the anticipated disturbance didn't
happen, University officials breathed easier. Her guards led her and Le
Thuy from the podium. As they passed under our aisle seats, Steve
leaned over the railing and waved his arms, trying to get her attention.
She glanced up, and for a moment their eyes met.

"Madame Nhu!" he shouted. "I want to fuck your daughter!"

Steve burst into my room. "Let's go!" he exclaimed, pulling me down the
hall. It was a Monday night.

We were in my Impala and headed toward Albany, just north of Berkeley, before he explained. Loren had just called from the three-bedroom
apartment he was now sharing with Morton and Jerry Olson, a fun-
loving, life-of-the-party teammate of Craig's from freshman football.
Jerry's father owned UC Corner, a paperback bookstore on Telegraph.
The apartment had gained a fast reputation as a major Party Place.

"Hayseed says they've got more horndogs than they can handle and
they need some reinforcements," said Steve.

It sounded pretty good to me. Mary and I had pledged our fidelity. But
. . . she was fifty miles down the road, and nothing would probably
happen anyway. Besides, I could use a few beers to help ease the pain in
my right shoulder. A few days earlier I had played wide receiver in the
second intramural football game in the fraternity's history, and on the
first play of the game I ran a crossing pattern over the middle . . . and
got into a bad train wreck. The doctor at Cowell Hospital said it was the
worst separated shoulder he'd ever seen. I couldn't sleep at night, spending long hours sitting under a hot shower. The water was eroding the
figure-eight cast around the shoulder. The doctor had also said that he
couldn't promise that I'd be able to play in my senior season or that my
arm would ever be as good as it was. The pro career—the one I'd
dreamed about forever—was in serious jeopardy. I was bummed.

Steve and I walked in the open front door of the apartment. Morton
was sitting on the couch with three girls. The lights were out. Vince
Giraldi was on the hi-fi. I didn't know the names of the girls but I
recognized them. They were Phi Mus . . . or "Fucking Moos" as they
were called in the Pi KA house. It wasn't the best-looking sorority, but

allegedly it was the horniest. Olson was working the late shift at his dad's store, and Loren, who had not confided to me why he had vanished to Idaho for a semester, was already off in his bedroom with the fourth Fucking Moo. Morton was just grinning, a beer in hand.

Craig and I were friends from the baseball team, roommates on road trips. He was the center fielder, a man among boys. Six-four, 210 pounds, rock hard, gifted. Ruggedly good-looking, with bright blue eyes, strong chin, ruddy complexion, quick wit. He was from Campbell, a small suburb at the south end of the Peninsula, and his father, a glass-blower, had kept a strict, forceful hand on him while he was growing up. He and Loren were making up for lost time at Cal, heavy into the party circuit. His weekends were reserved for Vicki, a pretty Santa Monica blonde determined to capture the star quarterback; Loren's weekends were for Donna. But on weeknights, they played the field. Relentlessly.

I went to the refrigerator to retrieve a beer. My shoulder was killing me. All I found was the cardboard from a long-gone pizza and a mustard dispenser from Mel's Drive-In. Not even any milk. I checked the cupboard. A couple of cans of tuna and a box of Cheerios. I scooped out a handful.

When I returned to the living room, Craig and one of the girls had already disappeared into his bedroom, and Steve was following another girl into the other room, his pants already down to his ankles. He tripped hurrying into the room.

I sat down on the couch next to the remaining Fucking Moo. Her name was Cindy, she said. She wore her brown hair in a flip, her glasses were thick, her legs skinny, and her breasts big.

"What happened to you?" she asked, pointing to my sling.

Obviously she hadn't seen my picture in the *Daily Cal* after the injury, so I told her.

"Would it make it feel better if I rubbed your back?" she asked. "Why don't you take off your shirt." We slid to the shag carpet.

After knowing Cindy for five minutes, she was already touching me in spots Mary had failed to explore in thirty dates. With my one good arm, I pulled her toward me, reaching behind her to unhook her bra. Who was I fooling? I didn't know how to unsnap it with two hands, let alone one. It didn't matter—she did it for me. We were naked in seconds. Well, almost naked. I didn't bother to try to get my khaki pants off over my shoes, afraid she'd change her mind. I climbed on top. No slow hand. No ear nibbling. Just full speed ahead. It was over quick. Real quick. For me, anyway. It had taken me twenty-one years, five months, sixteen days, and about eight seconds, but I was no longer technically a virgin. I was in the club. I rolled off onto the shag carpet, pulling up my pants.

"Are you leaving already?" she asked.

"Yeah, I have a midterm tomorrow," I lied, heading for the door, not waiting for Steve.

Sexual intercourse began! In nineteen sixty-three.

13

Loren

Every town in America has a "criminal" abortionist.
—*Newsweek,* August 13, 1962

Stripped to the waist in their apartment living room, best friends Loren and Craig cautiously circled each other, each of them ready to pounce, 415 pounds of natural muscle . . . no steroids, no long hours in the weight room . . . just two great bodies gifted from God. Both were smiling, laughing. And both were determined to flip the other, pin him to the gold shag carpet. Intense competitors, even in a friendly wrestling match. It was the second of three falls—Loren won the first.

Loren had caught a lot of flak from the brothers when he'd announced he was going to move out of the fraternity and into the apartment with Craig. That violated one of the cardinal tenets of Pi KA—only seniors were allowed to live out of the house, a rule intended to provide a sense of unity and togetherness instead of the feeling of a motel with guys moving in and out at their whim. It wasn't that Loren didn't like the fraternity—he thrived on being around the guys, the horseplay, the friendly atmosphere. But he wanted to live with Craig. And if the brothers didn't like it, then tough shit.

He had returned from his sojourn to Idaho with a renewed determination to follow the motto that had hung over his bed as a boy: "It's my life, I live it, criticism be damned!" Other than Donna, Craig was the only person who knew the real reason he had fled to Idaho—it was to get away from his parents, his mom's meddling, his father's drinking. Hal had started back up with the booze again after being released from Herrick Hospital. By taking a semester off from Cal to go to Ricks Junior College, Loren had figured, it would give him a thousand-mile breather from the tension on Sweezy Street. It did. Genevieve couldn't just pop in unannounced to pull him into the fire. At Ricks he got straight A's, skied every weekend, and wrestled on the team. Undefeated. That's why he was sure he was going to whip Craig's butt.

When he moved out of the fraternity after returning from Idaho, some of the brothers discussed bonging him. It didn't happen, but the move caused some hard feelings. Several brothers accused him of being Craig's remora, part of the entourage of sycophants that had become attracted to Craig's notoriety. It was one thing to have your picture in the *Daily Cal,* but Craig's name and picture were constantly in the *Chronicle* and the Oakland *Tribune.* He was national copy. Big time. Touted as a Heisman Trophy candidate. And for the people around him, he was a first brush with fame and glory. For his part, Craig remained low-key and modest about his stardom, or as much as a normal twenty-year-old jock could when finding himself the BMOC, the focus of the Bay Area media, and a darling of the coeds.

Knocking over the Danish modern coffee table, Craig jumped in for a quick step-over toehold, pinning Loren to the carpet. The force of their fall shook the whole apartment building. Craig jumped up, raising his arms in triumph.

"I let you win," claimed Loren, climbing to his feet. "Your puny little ego couldn't take it if I kicked your ass twice in a row. Let's go, motherfucker! Next one's for all the marbles."

Loren wasn't, in fact, one of Craig's remoras. Craig liked all the things about Loren that appealed to everyone—his energy, his free-spirited attack on life. They had much in common, especially sports. They were two of the best athletes in the history of Northern California. Craig had been an all-star basketball player in high school too, and they loved going one-on-one, very physical against each other. Craig also liked Loren because, unlike some of the other players on the football team, he wasn't jealous of Craig's notoriety and special treatment. Loren just wanted to have fun. And so did Craig. They also shared a common thread of having battled their fathers growing up.

As they stalked each other in the center of the floor, there was a knock at the door. It was Donna. She was dressed in four-inch high heels, black cocktail dress, pearls. She had come to pick up Loren—they were due at a pinning party in five minutes. Loren had completely spaced it out.

"You haven't even showered yet," she said, eyeing her sweaty grappler. She had, in the past, jokingly accused him and Craig of being "queers," preferring to smack each other on the butt rather than spend time with their girlfriends.

As Donna headed for the couch to wait for Loren to hurry and get ready, two Fucking Moos who had been sitting in the kitchen during the main event walked back in the living room.

"I can explain," Loren sheepishly pleaded.

"Damn you, Loren!" Donna yelled. In a fury, she bent down and removed one of her shoes, firing it at his head from ten feet. He ducked and the shoe whizzed by his ear, the heel sticking into the thin plaster like a dart. Donna whirled and hobbled back out the door.

For two weeks her shoe hung over the couch, the only artwork adorning the otherwise barren walls. And Loren won the third fall with a perfectly executed modified fireman's carry.

It was a glorious March day in the Bay Area, azure sky, blooming dogwoods, spring fever owning the campus. Loren had sweet-talked his way back into Donna's heart. In fact, they were now pinned . . . engaged to be engaged. They bounded down the steps of the AO Pi house, holding hands, off for a walk up Strawberry Canyon. The walk was his idea, a spur-of-the moment detour before going to rugby practice at Memorial Stadium.

Rugby was the newest passion in his life. The perfect sport. He loved its action and contact. There were no plays to memorize; at practice, the coach, Dr. Miles "Doc" Hudson, rarely even required the team to go through calisthenics. Loren could just go out and play uninhibited, unencumbered by the attention to detail demanded in football under Coach Levy. The loose discipline was made to order for his rollicking, happy-go-lucky style. "He's got more natural ability than anyone I've ever coached," said Hudson, a dentist originally from New Zealand who started coaching Cal rugby in 1938.

Walking past the top rim of the stadium, Loren put his arm around Donna. To her surprise he had become more attentive and affectionate since their pinning party. "Let's go up there," he said, pointing up Cheapskate Hill, the eucalyptus-covered hillside that looked down into the stadium and out over the Bay. Up and up they climbed, blazing a trail through the tall grass, lush and green from the winter rains, the silence broken only by the breeze rustling through the leaves.

Whether it was the pinning party or the night of the shoe toss, the relationship had moved to another level. At nights, Loren picked her up in his T-Bird from her job in the Reserved Book Room at the library and they drove to Mel's Drive-In on Shattuck Avenue, going inside to sit at "their" booth, holding hands across the Formica tabletop, listening to "He's So Fine" by the Chiffons on the jukebox, sipping cherry Cokes. Donna showed him pictures from *Modern Bride* of the wedding gown she wanted. They weren't actually getting married—not yet anyway—but they liked talking about it. They were agreed—it would be "the biggest wedding in the history of California." They had window-shopped for rings in downtown Berkeley, planned their honeymoon to Hawaii, compiled lists of bridesmaids and ushers. Loren would have Craig as his best man. And they would have as many kids, Loren maintained, as it took to have a boy.

Donna knew he was serious. In fact, she was convinced she knew him better than anyone else . . . including his mom or Craig. He had written her mushy letters from Idaho. She knew the real reason he'd gone there. When he came back he told her that if Hal or Genevieve wanted to say something to him, that was fine—he'd listen politely—but then he was going to do whatever he wanted, criticism be damned. He was going to be his own man from now on.

With an alcoholic father of her own, Donna could sympathize, but it was more than just their shared distress that attracted her. She enjoyed his "ah shucks, I'm just a country boy" routine, although she saw it as a ruse to hide his intelligence, the same way that his façade of jokes and platitudes was a cover for his emotions. She frequently wasn't sure whether to believe him or not, and that was part of his paradox that both frustrated and kindled her interest. He was suspicious when he walked in the door, immensely believable when he left. There were differences in their personalities: she was a pragmatic math major graduating in three and a half years, he was a flighty dreamer on a course to graduate in six years. He had, however, finally declared a major: ag-econ. She enjoyed quiet walks and Bergman films, he liked loud parties and *The Guns of Navarone;* she was always on time, he was always late. But she was hooked on his spontaneity. There was always the hint of the unexpected, the mischievous. They made love in closets and bathrooms, seizing the passion, forgetting about who was in the next room. It was all part of the vivacity, the lust. He called her "Miss Kitty," she called him "Mr. Dillon."

Atop Cheapskate Hill, sheltered by the trees and brush, they sat down and looked westward toward the Golden Gate. It was not, however, the spectacular panorama that was on their minds.

"Won't you be late for practice?" she asked.

"Maybe," he answered, proceeding with the moment. As usual, birth control was neither used nor discussed.

Donna was positive that it was that afternoon on Cheapskate Hill when she got pregnant. Loren thought it happened on a weekend trip they took to Lake Tahoe with Craig and his girlfriend Vickie. But there was no disagreement about what they should do.

"We've got the rest of our lives to have kids," said Loren. "It'd be dumb to tie ourselves down now."

As much as she loved him and wanted to someday have a family with him, she knew it was too early. His head still swiveled every time a pretty girl walked by; and he still talked of marriage in terms of his parents— arguments and unhappiness—the husband drinking himself into oblivion, the wife bitching away. He wasn't ready for marriage and children, and neither was she. She wanted her degree and teaching certificate . . . to prove to her father that she hadn't come to Berkeley just to find a husband.

In 1963 the issue of abortion was still being debated on a relatively muted level in America, even though almost every town had its "criminal" abortionist. Sherrie Finkbine, an Arizona housewife, had sparked the first serious public debate on the issue when she fought to have an abortion because she had taken thalidomide, a drug known to cause severe birth defects. At the time, the law in all fifty states forbade therapeutic abortions (dilatation and curettage) except in cases where the mother's life was threatened. The public was beginning to call for change, charging that existing abortion laws were hypocritical and causing unnecessary fatalities. The Sex Information and Education Council estimated that, of the approximately one million abortions performed annually in the United States in the early sixties, less than 1 percent were done in a hospital by a physician under circumstances that had any semblance of legality. Five thousand women annually were alleged to have died at the hands of nonprofessionals . . . in back alleys . . . on kitchen tables. Tabloids headlined gory stories of abortion victims found dead in pools of blood with knitting needles puncturing the uterus.

Donna had heard stories of girls who had gone to Tijuana and paid $500 for abortions performed in dingy back rooms. She'd sooner have Loren perform the abortion than go to Tijuana. They decided to wait until school was out in June. That would give them time to find a safe place, and hopefully to come up with the money. She would be three months along.

"I've heard it's safe up to six months," she said. They also agreed not to share their secret.

After finals, Donna drove home to Southern California and confided in her mother, asking for the money. "You'll have to ask your father," Mrs. James replied.

Donna's father had caused her emotional pain her whole life, making her feel guilty about everything she did. It seemed unfathomable that he would agree to pay for an abortion when he wouldn't even pay for her education. The only way she could approach him, she decided, was to surprise him at his insurance office and get him to go out to lunch, then ply him with martinis.

She coerced him to take her to the Pig 'n' Whistle in downtown L.A., his favorite restaurant. He was on his third martini when she told him she was pregnant.

"I need your help, Daddy," she pleaded.

"I'm not responsible for your actions," he said, signaling for the check. "Get your damn boyfriend to pay for it."

Genevieve and Eddie were waiting in the living room when Loren walked in the door, returning from his summer job driving a forklift at a peach-packing plant. He could tell by their icy glares he was in trouble.

"What are you going to do about this?" asked Genevieve, holding up the letter Donna had written to inform him that her father had turned his back. He had left it sitting on his desk.

"What are you doing reading my mail?" he yelled.

"That's not the point, young man," countered his grandmother. "How could you let this happen?"

After listening to Loren's protestations about them snooping through his private stuff, Genevieve and Eddie agreed not only that they would pay for the abortion but that Donna could come to Marysville and stay in the family room on Sweezy Street until the situation was resolved.

Donna quickly downed her scotch on the rocks. "Let's have a couple more," encouraged Loren. They were sitting at a table in a dimly lit bar in downtown Sacramento, a half hour before Donna's appointment down the alley with the abortionist. The man was not a doctor . . . he was a tailor.

Donna had been living at the Hawleys' house in Marysville for a

month, sleeping in the family room. Genevieve had done everything possible to make her feel comfortable . . . or as much as she could under
the circumstances . . . unwed girls in Marysville weren't exactly objets
d'art to be taken to Elks Club luncheons or weekly Tripoli games. It was
Genevieve who'd arranged the appointment with the abortionist, a man
reputed to be the best in the area—he performed operations one night a
week in a small upstairs room over his tailor shop in downtown Sacramento. It was Pop and Eddie's money that was paying for it. But as
thankful as Donna was to Loren's family, she also felt sad and hurt that
she was facing the biggest crisis of her life, an issue of life or death, and
it was her boyfriend's family, not her own, who was providing the financial and emotional support.

She held Loren's hand as the waitress delivered another round of
scotch on the rocks. As far as she was concerned, Loren had been an
angel during the crisis, lending more emotional support than she ever
expected, continually telling her how much he loved her, bringing her
cards and flowers. She had always considered herself a private person,
but she was telling him things about her personal life, especially about
her father's emotional abuse, that she'd never shared with anyone. Loren
was her best friend. She was more sure than ever that they would someday marry.

After thirty minutes and another round of courage, they left the bar
and walked down the dark alley, stopping at the bottom of a stairwell.
Loren watched as Donna climbed the steps and disappeared behind the
door. She was six months pregnant.

Donna paid the $600 in cash and followed the abortionist into a small
room. There were no release forms to sign, no insurance papers to fill
out.

"You shouldn't have waited so long," he said, motioning for her to take
off her skirt and underwear and to lie down on a table covered with
white hospital paper.

There were no framed diplomas or mounted pictures, just blank white
walls and a large gooseneck lamp. There was a small sink in the corner
with a medicine cabinet. The room wasn't much bigger than a large
closet, but at least it was clean. She was grateful that Loren was just
down the back stairs.

"Legs up," the abortionist/tailor ordered.

He went right to work, inserting a catheter through her vagina into her
cervix, forcing air into her uterus. The pain was excruciating. "It will take

a couple days for the fetus to abort," he explained. "Go home and stay in bed."

Two days later, while Loren was at work, she felt sharp cramps in her lower abdomen. She headed for the bathroom. "I think I'm constipated," she informed Genevieve.

She aborted the fetus in the toilet. Standing and staring down at it, she was curious, never having even seen an infant baby, let alone a fetus. It was about the size of her fist. She leaned closer, realizing it was a boy.

Her first thought was that she should save the remains, just in case she needed proof of what happened. Maybe she should show it to Loren when he got home? But why do that? Why put him through that anguish?

She called Genevieve into the room and pointed to the fetus floating in the toilet. Then she flushed it away.

14

Ron

There are only two courses open to Negroes. One is to become a puppet of the white power structure, the other is to be independent and really speak for the Negro people.
—Malcolm X,
  UC Berkeley speech,
  October 11, 1963

Ron hustled from his architectural design class in "the Ark," walking quickly to Dwinelle Plaza, taking a position at the rear of the crowd, surprised by its size (7,000) and fervor. Normally, he was too busy pursuing his degree to have time to attend political speeches or to loiter at the entrance to campus and listen to student radicals denounce Clark Kerr and the Regents. And philosophically, he was more comfortable with the moderate tenets of the NAACP (which his mother belonged to) or Martin Luther King, Jr., than with the harsher ideas of separatism and violence being espoused by the Black Muslim movement. But when it was announced that Malcolm X would speak on campus, his curiosity was piqued.

It had been a year since the incident at the Holiday Inn in Durham and much had happened in the civil rights movement: Martin Luther King, Jr.'s "I Have a Dream" speech in Washington, D.C.; the Birmingham church bombings that killed two young black girls; Medgar Evers being gunned down in front of his house in Mississippi. Malcolm X's appearance was being sponsored by Slate, the radical student political party, which had originally been denied permission to bring Malcolm X to the campus on the grounds that such an appearance was in violation of both University and state constitutions enforcing the separation of church and state. But student activists persisted, maintaining that the purpose of his talk would be the explanation of Black Muslim views on social problems, and the University finally consented.

A rally calling for the immediate withdrawal of United States troops from Vietnam was scheduled for the same time at the corner of Bancroft and Telegraph, but it had been canceled when protesters began drifting away to hear Malcolm X. Next to the podium where he would speak was a blackboard upon which were drawn American and Islamic flags. Between them were the words: "Which One Will Survive the War of Armageddon?" Under the American flag was written: "Christianity, Slavery, Suffering, Death." Under the flag of Islam was written: "Islam, Freedom, Justice, Equality." Ron thought the message a bit overstated.

Malcolm X stepped to the podium and spoke of the "hypocrisy of America's white liberals" and predicted failure for the "Catholic administration's" civil rights program. He warned that the destiny of America and "all the black people who fall for the white man's false promises" hangs in the balance. "Flee for your lives and save yourselves," he concluded.

Ron hustled back to the fraternity for lunch. He admired Malcolm X's courage and conviction, but the message was threatening, raising more questions of his own identity. He had never overtly shown pride in his Negro heritage or culture, traveling instead the easier path of "white" society. Not making waves. How could he rationalize Malcolm X's call for black separatism and rebellion when he lived every day camouflaged in an all-white fraternity where words like "spook" and "jungle bunny" were part of the institutional racist lexicon? He couldn't.

"Pass those tuna sandwiches down this way," he requested.

He had already shoved Malcolm X's fiery call to arms to that back corner of his mind where he locked away other complex and disruptive thoughts. Such as the child he'd abandoned. He was thinking instead of his blind date for Saturday night.

She walked down the staircase at the Kappa Alpha Theta house and Ron couldn't believe his good luck. Her name was Kristi Duncan and she was a ravishing, blue-eyed, blond history major, buxom and rich. She looked as if she just stepped off the beach at Malibu, but she was from Oklahoma City. Her grandfather had struck it rich in the oil run, acquiring thousands of acres of oil and gas leases; her father, a Southerner and a staunch segregationist, had taken over the family business, and despite a weakness for good bourbon, made tons of money. Kristi had attended the best private schools, and after graduation from high school headed west to spend two years at all-girls Mills College in Oakland before talking her daddy into letting her transfer to Cal and join a sorority. She had a new powder-blue VW convertible and a good sense of humor. Ron was her first date at Cal.

They walked across campus to a party at the Beta house, spending the evening sitting alone on the front porch, talking quietly. She too couldn't believe her good luck, a first date with a handsome football player, so polite, not at all like other guys at the party waving their arms and goosing each other. He wasn't trying to get her drunk or impress her with his football exploits; he wasn't what she expected of a fraternity jock. On the walk back to the sorority, she surprised herself by reaching for his hand. Sorority girls, she'd been told, weren't supposed to take the initiative, not even holding hands. Sparks were flying. She didn't tell him about her boyfriend who was studying in Rome. Ron didn't tell her he was a Negro.

To everyone in the fraternity, Ron appeared to have it made when it came to girls. He was well built, good-looking, at ease, courtly, sanguine. But that's not how he felt. He had always been awkward around girls, growing up with no sisters, no female cousins, and no girls on his block to rehearse his approach. When he was ten his mother signed him up for the Jack-and-Jills, a pre-teen social club. At his first event, a hayride down Crenshaw Boulevard, he timorously sat to the side, watching the other kids frolic in the hay. He felt detached, the oddball, wishing he was home. But he stayed, not wanting to displease his mother. In the seventh grade he went to a party, and while the other kids danced to the sounds of the Crows and Hank Ballard and the Midnighters, he sat anchored in a chair, getting up only to pour himself another glass of punch. When his mom arrived to pick him up, the twelve-year-old hostess ushered him to the door. "Don't come back," she said. That wasn't as humiliating, however, as the time he went to Washington, D.C., with his mother to visit relatives and tagged along to a park with several boys and girls from the neighborhood. As far as Ron was concerned, the boys were the coolest guys in the universe—they wore chinos, cussed, and had been out with girls. They were all sitting in a circle when the coolest one suddenly leaned over and kissed the girl next to him. The girl blushed and the boy flashed a Romeo's grin. Figuring that must be the cool thing to do, Ron grabbed the girl to his left—he didn't know her name—and pulled her toward him, catching her by surprise. Rolling on top of her, he pressed his body against hers and began to grind, glancing back to make sure the cool guy was watching, approving. The girl shrieked and pushed him off. Everyone laughed. Ron was instantly embarrassed. In his high school relationship with Jackie—whom he hadn't seen since that fateful day he left her sitting on the couch while he drove off to discover he was a father—he always felt bottled up, hiding his feelings with a smile or a joke. At the letterman's award assembly when he was named L.A. High's student-athlete of the year, he got choked with emotion and had to walk out of the auditorium to regain his cool, and when Jackie came after him, he buried his head in a drinking fountain and waved her away, embarrassed at his tears. Just before leaving for Cal, he had painted a portrait in acrylic of the two of them standing side by side, each of them with melancholy, downturned expressions. It was in somber shades of forest green and grays. When he was finished, he stuck it in a drawer and never showed it to her.

He dated only white girls.

He was in his room working on his secret project when he looked out the window and saw Loren zip into the driveway and leap out of his convertible. Loren, who still ate lunches at the house and was a regular at the Ping-Pong and pool tables, was headed toward Ron's room, which was the only one-man room in the fraternity, a converted kitchen on the first floor of the annex. It was also the only room in the house with its own private entrance. Now that Ron and Kristi were a hot item, there was plenty of verbal speculation at the lunch table as to what the two lovebirds might be doing behind closed doors. (Although there was no house rule forbidding girls in the rooms, it was a rarity, mainly because of the privacy factor and because "nice" sorority girls weren't supposed to venture into fraternity bedrooms.)

Ron shoved his secret project into his closet just as Loren entered. But he wasn't quite quick enough.

"What's that?" Loren inquired, going straight for it.

"None of your business," Ron replied, blocking the way.

No luck. Loren pushed him aside and pulled the project out of the closet. It was a papier-mâché mouse with whiskers, red coat, and sombrero, a handmade version of the one Kristi had gushed over when they saw it in a store window on Shattuck Avenue in downtown Berkeley.

"Oh, isn't that sweet," cooed Loren, exiting as quickly as he'd entered. "Boy, has she got you pussywhipped."

Ron didn't think of it in quite those terms, but he was indeed in love. The mouse was to show Kristi what he was having trouble putting into words—a special gift to let her know how much he cared. Verbal expressions of affection weren't his specialty.

He figured he was going to need all the help he could get to persuade her to choose him over Bill, her boyfriend who was spending his junior year studying in Rome. Kristi finally had told Ron about Bill. He was formidable competition—he and Kristi had been high school sweethearts in Oklahoma City, and he had also come to college in the Bay Area, attending Santa Clara down the Peninsula. It was assumed by their families back in Oklahoma that they would someday get married.

Ron, however, was still holding back his secrets. What if the truth scared her off? She seemed open-minded, progressive, but he wasn't ready to take that chance. He wanted one girl to be close with, to call his steady girl . . . and Kristi was it. He didn't want to blow it.

They sat on a love seat in the Theta date room, other couples drifting in and out of the room. Ron had been over the speech a hundred times, but always in his room, alone. Now it was for real; Kristi's piercing blue eyes disturbed his concentration. She leaned forward, puzzled; he seemed so earnest. She had never seen him so uneasy. She had no idea what this was all about.

It was time for the truth—that's what it was all about—they had confessed their love, slept together, made plans to visit each other's families, talked about the future. He'd never felt so nervous, so filled with anxiety, so vulnerable.

"I have some Negro blood in my family," he blurted.

She studied his eyes. Was this a joke? No, his face was too serious.

"It's not a big percentage," he continued. "But it's important that you know that about me."

Kristi was stunned. The thought of him being a Negro had never entered her mind.

Tears started to fill his eyes, and he was suddenly embarrassed, not at what he'd just said, but at the fact that he always turned soft when things got emotional. He'd cried in front of Jackie; he'd cried in front of Coach Walsh; and now he was all teary-eyed in front of Kristi. He was mad that it was so hard for him to express his feelings.

"Why did you wait so long to tell me?" she whispered.

He told her he was afraid that she might not want to see him anymore if she knew.

"That's silly," she replied, assuring him that she had fallen in love with him because of the person he was, not the color of his skin. "Why would you think it would make any difference?"

Because it was 1963 and her family were segregationists and she lived in a segregated sorority and he was filled with self-doubt . . . that's why. "I don't know," he answered.

The more she thought of it, the more astonishing it seemed. Not that he was a Negro. Now that she studied the features, yes, maybe she could see that. But what was so amazing was that he had just confessed his race. *Confessed his race!* The concept was mind-boggling.

He took a deep breath. "There's something else you need to know," he said. "I fathered a child last year."

He explained the circumstances, and then he cried. For two years he had told nobody of the baby he had abandoned, keeping all his guilt and haunting thoughts bottled up inside. Now it was pouring out, unchecked, tears streaming down his cheeks right there in the Theta date room with another couple sitting ten feet away. Number 88 in the football program, big and tough Ron Vaughn, crying like a baby. He apologized. She promised him that none of it mattered, that she loved him. She had never seen such emotion, so unlike her other boyfriend, a person so stoic and in control of his feelings.

Back in his room, Ron was both relieved and despondent—happy to have it off his chest but sure that his revelations had lessened her opinion of him. Not because of what he'd told her—she seemed to be understanding, open-minded—but because he had been unable to control his emotions like a man.

15

Jim

No one tests the depth of a river with both feet.
   —African proverb

A light haze from the lumber mills clouded Grants Pass, Oregon, as Jim drove out of town toward the launch site at Graves Creek Bridge on the Rogue River for the last raft trip of the summer. And what a great summer it had been. Except for one thing. The river had won.

"Not this time," vowed Jim. "I'm gonna do it right!"

He had scored, thanks to Coach Lemmon, the perfect summer job in 1963 following his freshman year—a river-rafting guide for trips sponsored by the Sierra Club. The first half of the summer had been spent running the middle fork of the Salmon River in Idaho—known as "the River of No Return." And for the last month he'd been working the Rogue—known as "the Scoundrel of the Pacific." And it had turned out to be a scoundrel too, dumping Jim at notorious Rainie Falls his two previous trips.

Back in June when Coach Lemmon called him to ask if he wanted the job, he couldn't believe his good luck. He loved adventure and the outdoors—his fondest memories of childhood were the camping trips he took to the Sierras with the Boy Scouts and the overnight camp-outs with Ralph in the hillsides near Burlingame. Guiding tourists down whitewater rivers seemed too good to be true—challenge, exploration, and responsibility. The only drawback was that he wouldn't get to see Patty for two months. They were going hot and heavy.

The Rogue is a scenic ribbon cutting through southwestern Oregon and spawned by melting snow in the High Cascades near the royal-blue waters of Crater Lake. Alternately serene and tumultuous, the Rogue winds, rushes, and crashes 128 miles downward through mixed conifers and evergreens, slicing its way between towering cliffs, rock-studded canyons, and craggy rims to eventually empty into the Pacific. The 84-mile section that Jim would be rafting chisels through one of the most magnificent wilderness corridors in America. (Zane Grey built a cabin on it; Debbie Reynolds rode down it in *How the West Was Won,* as did John Wayne and Katharine Hepburn in *Rooster Cogburn.*) Fishermen know the river for its bountiful runs of spring chinook and fall steelhead; nature lovers know it for its wild salmonberry, Indian rhubarb, azaleas, and scarlet California fuchsias; Jim knew it for its brawling, spuming chutes and rapids, and in particular Rainie Falls, a treacherous 15-foot vertical drop into a boiling cauldron below. Most rafters portage around it.

As the flotilla prepared to put into the river for the five-day journey to the Pacific, he surveyed the Forest Service map, the names of the white-water passages ringing with adventure—Devil's Stairs, Wildcat Rapids, Deadman's Bar, Thundering Whiskey Creek Falls, and Battle's Bar . . . where, according to legend, 500 U.S. Cavalry troops in the Indian War of 1850 wiped out 200 Rogue Indians, mostly women and children. It was the danger of Rainie Falls, however, that had his attention. He knew too well of its terrifying power. It was only a mile and a half into the trip, barely enough time for the spray of the river to wipe away the cobwebs of a rowdy evening in a lumberjack bar.

A morning mist curled through the tall Douglas firs as he shoved off with his three passengers, followed by five other rafts. They were immediately tested by the rapids of Graves Creek, waves washing over the bow. He sailed through without a hitch, drifting through tranquil pools, admiring the rusty red bluffs and narrow, steep-sided cliffs. The surrounding wilderness was alive with black-tailed deer moving through the sugar pines and hemlocks. Ospreys and otters cavorted in the water. Ahead, he could hear the pounding and hissing of dangerous water.

Rainie Falls was named after a prospector who had been killed by Indians. It was rated Class VI on the international scale, meaning the risk of injury, even death, was real. More than one rafter had lost his life trying to navigate it. Few even dared to try.

Nearing the falls, Jim steered his raft to the riverbank. He and his passengers got out and walked to the upper lip to stare down into the spinning fury.

"No way," his passengers agreed.

"I'm going for it," he quietly determined. He instructed his passengers to unload their personal belongings and meet him below.

He stood at the side of the river, visualizing how he would do it this time. His first time over the falls he had immediately been sucked into the swirling eddy, his raft spinning around, bouncing broadside off a truck-sized boulder and flipping over backward, launching him and the supplies into the river. The last things he saw as he went under were ears of corn spinning past his head. All he could do was hold his breath as he went over the falls. It was thirty seconds before he bobbed to the surface in the lapping waters below, unscathed except for the missing corn and his bruised ego. The corn turned up twenty miles down the river. On the second trip, he bounced off the same boulder, only instead of flipping over, he went down the falls backward and out of control, caroming helplessly off the rocks below. It was an improvement, but hardly a victory. He spent the rest of the week plotting strategy for his third and final run at it.

Alone on his raft, he rowed back into the river. The exhilaration of rowing to the edge of danger was unlike anything he'd experienced, an adrenaline high he'd never known. Religion and praying were useless, not that they were part of his attack anyway. There were no teammates or coaches to blame. Just him competing against the forces of nature. It was mind over matter, he pretended.

As he approached the dastardly boulder, he pulled hard on his oars, using all the considerable strength he'd developed in crew. Plus all the concentration, all the singleness of purpose. It worked. He navigated Rainie Falls perfectly.

His victory cry echoed down the canyon walls, his fist thrust skyward, the moment captured on film by one of his passengers onshore. It was a picture of Jim van Hoften that none of his fraternity brothers would see. They saw instead a staid and stiff Jim, grousing about the mindless chatter in the hallway that was making it hard for him to study for his midterms in Intermediate Structural Analysis and Introduction to Fluid Mechanics. They did not know of Jim's adventuresome spirit and quiet determination. They just thought he was boring.

Nearing the end of his sophomore year, he felt pressed—his classes getting more difficult, his crew workouts getting more strenuous, his involvement in the fraternity getting more distracting. He had been appointed goatherder, an assignment usually reserved for the likes of Big Ben. He was fragmented, worried he couldn't keep up. Something had to go.

Pressed for time, he hurried across campus on his way to Harmon Gym. Walking by Sproul Plaza and Ludwig's Fountain (named after a short-haired German weimaraner that had become a campus celebrity for fetching balls out of the fountain), he ignored the circle of students gathered around a bellicose speaker. Who knew what the issue was? Foreign policy? Fair housing? Jim didn't care.

The change in the campus atmosphere since he first arrived in Berkeley was startling. The State Senate Fact-finding Subcommittee on Un-American Activities had characterized the campus in its biennial report as "bearded beatniks, pressure groups, malcontents, hordes of marching pickets, and an inconsistency on conformity toward the Left." This was 1963. Despite the objections of conservatives, the Regents had lifted the University's controversial long-standing ban on Communist speakers. The fall semester then opened with a swirl of new controversy over deepening racial issues: CORE was recruiting campus volunteers to picket downtown Berkeley merchants over minority hiring practices, including Mel's Drive-In; the Berkeley Junior Chamber of Commerce had refused to allow a UC Negro to escort a queen candidate to the Football Festival, setting off a maelstrom of protest. ("We had to protect the mental and physical well-being of the girls no matter what," explained the Jaycee chairman.) The controversy over growing American involvement in Vietnam was continuing to heat up, with speakers mounting soapboxes at the corner of Bancroft and Telegraph daily to speak out against American intervention. Not even Fraternity Row was exempt from the rising tide of controversy—six of the forty-seven fraternities and sixteen of the twenty-two sororities were refusing to sign the University-mandated antidiscrimination clause. Pi KA, however, had signed it. "It's just a piece of paper," allowed Big Ben. "We'll just bong any nigger dumb enough to walk through the door."

Jim walked briskly up the steps to Harmon Gym. He didn't have time to clog his mind with campus causes. He was nineteen and apolitical. The closest he had come to being enfranchised in the New Frontier was when his applied mathematics class was canceled (as were all University classes) for Peace Corps director Sargent Shriver's appearance on campus. He didn't go to listen to Shriver or Madame Nhu or any of the many other prominent speakers who appeared on campus. He had no deep or abiding curiosity to know the details of the Bay of Pigs, or civil rights legislation, or the Diem regime. Politics were unsolvable, and he was a pragmatist, not an idealist. He wanted things he could study and master, like formulas, equations, and Rainie Falls.

He was clear about his purpose at Cal: to get a degree in engineering, even if he didn't know what he was going to do with it. He had, however, in his rare flights of fantasy, allowed himself to think about victoriously crossing the Olympic trials finish line in the number two seat of the Cal crew. His hopes soared when he rowed first boat on the freshman crew all season, a team that won the West Coast Regatta at Long Beach, avenging its only loss of the year to the University of Washington freshmen. His weight had dropped from a baby-fat 205 to a steel-hard 180. His self-image shot up. There were bigger guys in the house, quite a few of them in fact, but few were stronger. But his sophomore season had not gone as well. He never got off the junior varsity.

As he knocked on Coach Lemmon's door, his mind was made up. He was going to quit crew. It had not been an easy decision. But first boat on the junior varsity wasn't enough payback for the drain of donating four hours out of every day. As much as he liked his teammates and the pride in working toward a common goal, he knew his future was in engineering, not rowing. Competitive sports had been an integral part of his life since junior high; there had always been a practice to attend after school. He'd never had illusions about being a super athlete or someday turning pro—sports were a diversion, a way to be part of a group and feel better about himself. Crew had done that for him, even if he never got his name in the paper or the brothers didn't understand the valor of the sport. But it was time to face reality.

It would feel strange, he thought, not to belong to a team anymore, not to have to push his body to the limit. But if he was going to have any chance of getting into a good graduate school or finding a decent job, then he was going to have to do better academically. His 2.8 g.p.a. wouldn't cut it.

Still, as he took his seat in Coach Lemmon's office and glanced at the wall filled with photos of Cal's winning crew tradition, a part of him hoped Lemmon would ask him to stay, maybe even plead with him, promise him a seat on the first boat next season.

"I think I should quit to concentrate on my studies," Jim said.

"A wise decision," replied Coach Lemmon. "Education must come first." He reached across the table and shook Jim's hand. "Good luck and study hard."

16

Steve

The campus was quiet everywhere.
—*Daily Cal*, November 25, 1963

It was Friday morning, November 22, 1963, the day before the Big Game. Cal versus Stanford. With a victory in Palo Alto, the Bears could salvage something of what otherwise had been a crummy 3–6 season, the high hopes of the Iowa State opener long since deflated. For Steve personally, it had been a decent sophomore season. Third in tackles, seventh in minutes played, knocked cuckoo by Dick Butkus.

He was sitting in the rear of his classroom in Wheeler Hall, his mind drifting from his Finance 1B lecture. Normally, he was an attentive student—he knew he had to be, thinking of himself not as gifted as the competition, just as he did in football. He wanted good grades, already beginning to think of business grad school or law school. Money and success were important, a way to prove himself to his demanding father. But on this day his mind was elsewhere. It was on Ayris, whom he had been dating for two months. And it was on Linda, whom he had been married to for one month. She was coming down for the Big Game with his parents. He had seen her once since the wedding in Reno.

He pulled out his *Daily Cal*, scanning the front page. There were stories about the game, a missing coed, discrimination in local housing, and Slate trying to get the Regents to turn over power to the faculty and students. Good luck on that one, he thought. He flipped the page and read about Dr. Teller giving a speech declaring that President Kennedy's proposed nuclear test ban treaty with the Russians was dangerous and wouldn't work. And a story about the students' vote to remove fallout shelters on campus. And a story about Ashley Montagu's book *The Natural Superiority of Women*. That was a book definitely not on his top-ten list.

Finally, the class was over and he walked outside into the gray, dreary morning, heading for the Freddy Tree, a California oak in the middle of Dwinelle Plaza where fraternity men congregated between classes to eyeball the coeds and debate important issues of the day, such as whether it was going to be grilled cheese or tuna for lunch. Or whether or not the AD Pi's were all prick teasers.

Steve stopped at the Freddy Tree, surprised to find nobody there. In fact, the whole campus seemed to be deserted. A girl ran through Sather Gate. "They've shot the President!" she wailed.

No, that couldn't be possible, he thought. He hurried to the Student Union, where students were huddled around speakers that normally broadcast nothing but cheerful, lilting Muzak.

There was no laughter, no noise, only people speaking in whispers.

He ran all five blocks up Bancroft to the fraternity. Maybe when he got there he would find it was all a big joke, like "War of the Worlds." But the brothers were all congregated in the TV room and Walter Cronkite was delivering the grim news.

"Sonuvabitch," whispered Steve, his words echoing the murmur heard everywhere.

Everyone stared, disbelieving. Although Steve wasn't yet old enough to vote, he considered himself a Democrat like his father, perceiving the world the way Kennedy spoke of it . . . in homilies of hope and effort. He admired Kennedy for his charisma, youth, family, hair. Loren entered the room, and even his bulb was dimmed.

"I wonder if there'll be a Big Game tomorrow," he posed. Steve had forgotten all about the game. Somberly, he went to his room, numbed.

The game was postponed. He called Linda in Sacramento. She was crying. When she'd first heard the news, she was at her ob-gyn.

"Are you coming home?" she pleaded. "I want to be with you."

He said he couldn't, lying about a team meeting on Saturday and a midterm on Monday. Then he called Ayris, and they spent that gloomy weekend together, holding each other, seeking comfort, talking. She was convinced his public bravado, the craziness she'd seen at parties, was only a cover for his shyness. They talked about family.

Like Steve's father, Ayris's Lebanese father emigrated to America, settling in Ohio, changing his name to Hatton. He opened a Middle Eastern restaurant in downtown Cleveland, specializing in shish kebab. Business was good and he hired a waitress, a fifth-generation American of French, Irish, and English descent who was raised on a small farm near Charles City, Virginia. They married three years later, a union that friends half jokingly said was his penurious way of getting her tip money. Ayris was born in Cleveland, the youngest of five sisters and a brother. During World War II, when her father's business went bad, he loaded the family into the Packard in the middle of the night and moved to California. In Los Angeles, he opened another restaurant, Hatton's of Hollywood (years later to become the Vine Street Bar and Grill). Mrs. Hatton talked him into adding baked Virginia ham to the Middle Eastern menu and the place soon became a popular hangout for movie stars. Ayris and her sisters worked as waitresses, turning in their tips to their father at the end of each day. Business boomed and the family moved into a large Art Deco home in fashionable Westwood—six bedrooms, swimming pool, terraced garden, stainless-steel banisters. The next-door neighbor was a producer for the "Mickey Mouse Club" and arranged for Ayris and her sisters to work as extras in movies, including *Friendly Persuasion*. Ayris was the first of her sisters not to attend UCLA, choosing to come to Berkeley, mainly to get away from her father. She wanted to major in art, but her father insisted she major in history. "What good is a degree in art?" he asked. "What good is a degree in history?" she replied.

After the first good snow of the winter, Steve took Ayris skiing at Squaw Valley. They rode the ski lift to the top of the highest slope. "Shouldn't I be starting on something a little easier?" she asked. This was her first time on skis—no instructions at the lodge, no bunny hill for practice.

"Don't be a wus," he replied. "Go for it!"

She looked down the hill, positive he was wrong. But he was so charming, so persuasive—that's how he'd convinced her to drive up to Squaw for a day of power skiing and then back to Berkeley for a party at Loren's. If it was up to Ayris, she would just as soon unstrap her rented skis, pull up a rock, and simply enjoy the grandeur of the Sierra scenery. Mountains, she thought, were to be painted, not conquered.

"Meet you at the bottom!" he yelled, pushing off straight down the slope.

Against her better judgment, she followed. Five seconds into the first ski run of her life she was careening out of control. As she tumbled through the snow, her adjustable bindings didn't release, pinning her leg beneath her. She heard the bone break. Steve was already over the ridge and out of sight.

It took the ski patrol twenty minutes to carry her off the mountain. The pain was excruciating and the diagnosis was worse—a segmented fracture of the tibia, two weeks in a hospital, six months in a cast to her hip.

It was another forty-five minutes before Steve finally peeked his head into the first-aid room. "I'm sorry," he said. "I would have been here sooner. I didn't know. It's such great powder today . . ."

He drove her 90 miles an hour back to Berkeley and Cowell Hospital, carrying her to the admittance desk. As they waited for her to be checked in, he began to fidget.

"Why's it taking so long?" he wondered.

"Why are you in such a rush?" she asked.

"I don't want to be late for Loren's party," he answered. "You don't mind if I go without you, do you?"

And that is when Ayris began to think that maybe this handsome young man wasn't exactly whom she thought he was. During her two-week stay in the hospital, he came to visit, once, bringing her a box of chocolate-chip cookies.

"Did your mother bake these for you?" she asked. He nodded. Actually, Linda baked the cookies.

Waiting for Steve to arrive, Linda studied herself in the mirror. She was six months pregnant, and for the first time, she felt attractive. For their big "date," her mom had bought her a stunning new China-blue maternity dress. She'd gotten her hair done. They were going to see the movie *Tom Jones.*

It had been a glum time for Linda. For the first three months after they were married, she saw him three times, always a quick visit, twice at a Motel Sex. He rarely called. He continued to make it clear he didn't want to be married and didn't want the baby. She hated lying to her friends about why she had dropped out of Cal and moved back home, telling Steve she wouldn't lie about being married anymore. But even when she told her friends she was married, it was embarrassing trying to explain why they weren't living together. She asked him if she could move to Berkeley. "I love the fraternity," he said. "I'm not moving out." It would have been easier for her if he was callous or raised his voice, but he was usually courteous and understanding. But inflexible. She was afraid to ask him what he was doing with his spare time and he didn't volunteer. She clung to the hope that as time went by he would soften, change his mind, want to be married, let her move to Berkeley, and live with her in an apartment. But the more she pushed, the more trapped he felt. When she phoned the fraternity and left messages for him, he didn't return the calls. He thought it easiest if his actions, or his inactions, did his talking.

She heard a car approach, nervously checking herself in the mirror one last time. It wasn't him. She continued to primp.

After Christmas she had resumed her push to move to Berkeley, even suggesting that she would get an apartment and he could keep living in the fraternity but just come and visit. "I can't stop you from coming," he answered, "but I won't change my mind."

Still, she hoped. In January she informed him she was moving down to the Bay Area. Her mother agreed to pay for an apartment. When he said he would help her look for a place, she felt her first glimmer of hope. It wasn't a promise to move in together, just an offer to help. But he insisted that she had to live in Oakland, away from the campus. They found a small, unfurnished one-bedroom near Lake Merritt, ten miles from the fraternity. It was clean, modern, and spartan. The furniture was hand-me-downs from her mother. There were no pictures to hang; her only silverware was what Steve stole from the fraternity; her only cooking utensils were an electric skillet and toaster her aunt gave her as a wedding gift. (There'd been no gifts from Steve's side of the family.) She didn't know how to cook. She was eighteen and living by herself in a city where she had no friends, no car, no phone. She passed the time reading and watching TV—"My Favorite Martian," "Petticoat Junction," "The Patty Duke Show"—anything to keep her mind off how unhappy she was. She kept hoping he would surprise her and come to visit, but he rarely did. Her big venture each day was walking to the corner market, or to the phone booth to call him. Glum times indeed. The nights when she couldn't reach him, she tried to convince herself he was at the library, even if it was Saturday night. He had never promised that theirs was a death-do-us-part commitment or that he wouldn't go out with other girls . . . and she continued not to press him on it, blindly hoping that because they were married and because he had shown some feeling for his Roman Catholic moorings in the past, he would honor the vows they'd taken. On the occasions he did come to visit, he doled out just enough affection to keep her holding on. Then he'd disappear back into the fraternity woodwork, maintaining his secret, feeling guilty, seeing Ayris.

But now she was all smiles as she heard his footsteps approach the apartment door. All smiles and nerves. This would be their first time out in public since she'd moved to Oakland. The movie was in San Francisco.

She opened the door. He stepped back to look her over, and with one glance, she was transformed from a glowing young mother-to-be in a pretty blue dress into a dumpy hausfrau in a gray sack and babushka. She fought back the tears.

At the theater, as they waited in the refreshment line in the lobby, he spotted two teammates from the football squad. He quickly turned his back, hoping they wouldn't see him. But they did, approaching with their dates.

"Hold in your stomach," he whispered. He couldn't hurry into the darkened theater fast enough.

On the drive home over the Bay Bridge, she took his right hand and guided it to her stomach. "Do you feel the baby kick?" she asked.

"No," he said, quickly pulling away his hand.

At the apartment, she invited him in to spend the night. "I really should get back to the fraternity," he said. "I've got a ton of studying."

The next morning, in tears, she called her mother, asking her to come and get her. By nightfall, she was out of the apartment and living back in her room in Sacramento. But she hadn't given up.

"He'll change when the baby comes," she said. "I know it."

He called Ayris to ask her to meet him at the International House on Piedmont Avenue for a Coke. "I don't think so," she replied, cold and distant.

"What's wrong?" he asked. "You're not still mad at me for only visiting you once in the hospital, are you?"

"No."

"Then how come you sound different?"

"How can you be so dishonest?" she asked, starting to cry.

"What are you talking about?"

She had found out he was married. Linda had told a friend, who told a friend, who told a friend in the AO Pi house, and pretty soon the word had reached Ayris. At first, she refused to believe it. It was too incredible to believe . . . that this delightful and affectionate, if maybe a little wild and impetuous guy had kept such a huge secret from her.

"I can explain," he stammered. "It's not like we're really married."

Ayris didn't buy it. She hung up, devastated. How could he do this to her? Did he have no respect for her? She felt betrayed.

. . . .

Steve stood next to Linda's bedside at Sutter Hospital in Sacramento, holding her hand. She was about to be wheeled off to deliver the baby by cesarean. He leaned over and kissed her on the forehead.

"I love you," he whispered.

Her prayers had been answered. In the weeks leading up to her due date, he had changed, sending her cards and flowers, calling her every night from Berkeley to check on her condition. He came home on weekends and felt the baby move. For the first time since they were married, she felt more than just a flicker of hope. When his father called him at the fraternity to tell him Linda had started labor, he was out the door and at the hospital in record time. For fifteen hours he sat at her side, offering encouragement.

"You're the greatest," he said as they wheeled her away.

It was a seven-pound-ten-ounce boy, Dennis. Mother and baby were doing fine. When Linda came out of the anesthetic, there was a beautiful bouquet of long-stemmed roses from Steve next to her bed. But no Steve. He was already on his way back to the fraternity, a bottle of champagne between his legs, a six-pack at his side.

Nearing the Dixon exit—where he had fallen out of the car and bounced across the highway as a small boy—he felt nature call. He took the first off-ramp, relieved himself by the side of his white Falcon, then sailed back onto Interstate 80, accelerating to 85 miles an hour again. He thought it odd that all the headlights seemed to be coming straight at him. But he kept going, weaving in and out of them . . . being the race car driver he wanted to be . . . going eastbound in the westbound lanes.

He'd gone five miles by the time he realized his big mistake, moving over to the shoulder. When he reached the first exit, he crashed through a barricade, shattering his windshield. He escaped unscratched, Mr. Lucky. There was only one problem: the California Highway Patrol was right there to slap the handcuffs on him.

The next day at the fraternity, everybody laughed when he related the details of his night in the drunk tank. His new nickname was "Wrong Way Radich." The only part of the story he neglected to tell was the part about his wife and baby.

17

Ron

There is no more evil thing in the world than race prejudice. It justifies and holds together more baseness, cruelty, and abomination than any other sort of error in the world.
—H. G. Wells

It was late at night and Ron was in his room working on a set of drawings for his senior design project, a modern, form-follows-function layout of a Safeway supermarket. He had invested months on the assignment, the most important work of his academic career. Three quick raps on the floor directly over his ceiling interrupted his concentration. That was the secret signal from Kristi. It meant she was sneaking down to his room.

It was his senior year, 1964, and he had moved out of the fraternity, taking a job as the Theta houseboy. In exchange for changing light bulbs and fixing leaky faucets, he received $100 a month and free rent in the servants' quarters, a small private room, which just so happened to be conveniently located directly under Kristi's room. They'd had a few daring midnight trysts—very risky stuff, because if they got caught, Ron would be out of a job and Kristi would be out of the sorority. They had agreed to cool it for a while and take their romance-making elsewhere. That's why he was surprised to hear her knock.

Ron had enjoyed his three years in the fraternity. Despite the distractions and the racial jokes, it had provided a sense of belonging, a few close friends, and an escape from the demands of his studies. He was relieved that he had never been asked to sign a White Clause. He was also done with his football eligibility, no longer on scholarship. There had been no offers from the pros or All-American laurels, but he was proud of what he had accomplished—his climb to first string, his two varsity letters, a touchdown pass against USC, a victory over the Rose Bowl champion Washington Huskies, the praise from Coaches Walsh and White. Pleasing his coaches, like pleasing his parents, had been very important. But what he was most proud of in his athletic career were not the touchdowns or the tackles, but the fact that football had allowed him to pay his own way through college so that he didn't have to depend on his parents' money. That had done wonders for his self-esteem.

As he listened to Kristi's footsteps overhead, he hurried to get himself in order, splashing on a quick dab of Aqua Velva and Right Guard. One thing that he'd learned in the fraternity, strangely enough, was better hygiene. He'd never used deodorant until he pledged. A couple of complaints from the brothers had squared him away.

He peeked out the window, just to make sure the housemother wasn't outside snooping around. He had to admit he enjoyed these clandestine rendezvous. And it wasn't as if their love affair hadn't already survived some nervous moments. There was that day Ron tearfully *confessed* his race and his abandoned baby. Kristi didn't flinch at that one, reaffirming her devotion, although she sometimes wondered if he was attracted to her because of her blond hair and blue eyes, antithetical to his own background. They really didn't talk much about it, but she had the impression he was ashamed of his Negro heritage. It was just the gut feeling she had. For Ron, the most threatening time in the relationship had been over spring break when Kristi flew to Rome for a week to decide once and for all if there was anything left between her and her old boyfriend, Bill. She'd admitted to Ron that she was still torn between the two of them. For five days he lived on eggshells while she was in Italy, not going out, feeling suspicious and insecure. If she truly loved him, as she said she did, then why was she going to see Bill? It was hard for him to believe, despite her assurances, that his teary-eyed admissions hadn't caused her to have second thoughts. Unable to take the suspense, he had called her hotel in Rome to put in his last-minute bid. Bill was there. She couldn't talk. But when Ron picked her up at the airport, the verdict was good. What he had thought were his weaknesses—his vulnerability and sensitivity—were what had won her heart. But he didn't know that. Another nerve-wracking ordeal was when he went to Oklahoma City to meet her family and friends. Before their arrival, Kristi had admitted to her staunch segregationist father that Ron had "a trace" of Negro blood in his background. "But he's not *really* Negro," she explained. It was a tense and formal three-day visit, Ron assigned to sleep in a back bedroom. He felt awkward, out of place. But he was able to persuade Kristi's father that he was a "personable and polite young man." Mr. Duncan told Kristi that he doubted Ron actually had any pure "nigra" blood. "It's probably Egyptian or something like that," he concluded. Kristi's mother pulled Ron aside to grill him on his goals in life and his intentions with Kristi, wanting to know if he loved her daughter and planned to marry her. "Someday," he hedged. But as much as he loved her—which was a lot—he wasn't ready to make a permanent commitment. Not until he had his degree and was comfortably employed.

He heard Kristi's footsteps approach his private entrance at the rear of the sorority. She knocked lightly and he quickly ushered her inside. She was wearing a Lanz nightgown, her blond hair piled atop her head. She looked more sexy than usual, he thought. He moved to hug her. That's when he noticed her teary eyes.

"Look at this," she said, handing him a piece of notebook paper. A sorority sister had anonymously slipped it under her door. It was a crude drawing of a vagina, the words "Nigger Lover" scrawled across it.

"What should we do about it?" she asked.

Ron thought for a few moments, then suggested the same path he had followed his whole life regarding issues of race. "Ignore it," he advised.

Ron waited anxiously for Kristi to return from the opulent Claremont Hotel in the Berkeley hills. She'd gone there to meet her mother, who had flown out from Oklahoma to discuss something "very, very important."

Things were going well for him as he entered his final semester. His senior design project was selected for display in the department archives. He had put months into it, spending long hours at the Safeway in Montclair, an Oakland suburb, following shoppers all over the store to determine a more efficient and cost-effective floor plan. His final design included shelves stocked with only one product sample to reduce storage space, computer ordering, and drive-up windows where the goods would be picked up.

He had already been offered a job. It was with Paul R. Williams, a highly respected black architect in L.A. In 1937 Williams had hired Ron's father when Ralph and Betty first moved to California from Washington, D.C. Ralph thought so much of Williams that he'd named him Ron's godfather. Ron's only reservation about going to work for Mr.

Williams was that he didn't want to be hired on the basis of nepotism. But it was an excellent opportunity, a comfortable place to put in his three-year apprenticeship before gaining his license. He was considering the offer.

Things were also going well between him and Kristi. He took her to San Francisco to see *Mutiny on the Bounty;* they went for sunny Sunday drives in the Berkeley hills in his Karmann-Ghia, ignoring the wind rushing through the holes he'd drilled in his floorboard to drain the rainwater that poured in through the leaky roof; they talked of someday getting married and how Hawaii would be the best place to raise their children "because color doesn't matter over there." It helped Ron's sense of security thinking that Bill was out of the picture. The only thing he worried about was whether Kristi would be willing to wait for him while he got himself established as an architect.

But that was something to worry about down the line. As they met in the Theta courtyard after she'd returned from her meeting with her mother, he could tell from the anguish on her face that there was a more immediate problem. She was distraught. Her father, sensing that things were getting tight between the two of them, had called a friend of his in L.A., a prominent car dealer and close friend of actor Ronald Reagan. Mr. Duncan instructed his friend to hire a private investigator to check into Ron's family background. "Find out whatever you can about that boy," he said. When the report came back that both of Ron's parents were "Negro" and Mrs. Vaughn was involved with the NAACP and the ACLU and Mr. Vaughn campaigned for Negro politicians, Mr. Duncan promptly dispatched Kristi's mother to California to issue an edict: either Kristi break it off with "that nigger boy" immediately or else she was on the next plane back to Okie City, cut off dry as a bone from Daddy's oil money. Forever.

Kristi had no money of her own, and without her father's money she had no way to pay for college, or rent, or new madras skirts, or gas for her VW. Her mom said that Daddy would take away her car too.

For Ron, marriage wasn't an option. How could they afford that? He had twenty dollars to his name. And there was no way—zero—that he would ever go to his parents for money. Mr. Duncan had them trapped. Ron couldn't quit school to get a job—not when he was this close to graduating, not when his degree was his ticket to the future. And as far as Kristi quitting school to go to work to support him, well, he would just as soon stand in the breadline.

"What if we just saw each other secretly?" he asked. "How will your father ever know?"

"He'll have us followed," she promised. Ron believed her. After all, the man had already hired a private detective once. And money was obviously no hindrance to him. Ron knew now why he hadn't had good feelings about Mr. Duncan when he stayed at Kristi's house.

Sitting on a bench under a eucalyptus tree in the courtyard, they held each other, emotionally steamrolled. The relationship was over. Mr. Duncan would win.

Ron lay on his bed in his room, staring at the ceiling, listening to Kristi's footsteps overhead. On his portable hi-fi, the melancholy sound of Joan Baez tormented his soul. These were tough times. Very tough.

It had been three months since he and Kristi had been forced to stop seeing each other. He was in despair. Angry at Mr. Duncan for being a racist asshole; upset at Kristi for not having made more effort to stand up to her father—maybe she hadn't loved him as much as she claimed; and mad at himself and feeling guilty for not stepping forward to make a commitment, for always putting his precious degree above all else, above love and what he thought was moral and right.

But it was too late to do anything about it. Six weeks after Mr. Duncan's edict, the ceremonial candle was passed around the dinner table at Kristi's sorority, and it stopped when it came to Kristi. She and Bill, who was back from Rome, were engaged. They would marry in June.

The more Baez sang, the lower Ron sank, seeing himself as a guy who ran away every time he was asked to step up and accept responsibility—about his baby, about his racial heritage. What kind of a man was he? Malcolm X was preaching black pride and he was knuckling under to a Southern bigot.

He turned off Baez and walked outside his room, spotting Kristi and Bill walking arm in arm toward the courtyard, the same courtyard where he and Kristi had sat so many times, holding hands, sharing intimacies, being in love. This was too much to bear. He circled the courtyard, stopping on the other side of the eight-foot cement wall. He chinned himself to the top, peering down at them from behind. They sat on a bench, whispering words of love, just as he and Kristi had done on that same bench three fortnights ago. He retreated to his room to torture himself with more Baez.

He hung up the phone, unsure what to think. It was Kristi. She'd called to say she wanted to talk. She was on her way over.

Graduation was near. He had quit his job as Theta houseboy and moved into a room in a quaint vine-covered brown shingle on the north side of campus. He hadn't told anyone about Mr. Duncan and the stuff with the private eye. That was too intimate, too painful. He'd told friends he and Kristi split up because he couldn't give her the commitment she needed. That wasn't a total lie, he rationalized.

He had become an academic recluse, grinding toward graduation. For escape it was more Sinatra and Baez . . . more melancholy. And a little Lightning Hopkins too.

"Just to talk and find out how you're doing," Kristi had said on the phone. "I still care about you, Ron. I always will." But why, he wondered, did she *really* want to see him? He put on a little more Right Guard and Aqua Velva.

Hearing her footsteps, he was giddy with anticipation, hopeful and nervous, trying to guess her motive. Had she changed her mind about marrying Bill? Did she want to make love one last time? There had been something unmistakably tempting in her voice when she'd called, he thought.

He opened the door, admiring her in the porchlight. He was home alone. She was dressed as usual, her standard plaid skirt, white blouse, button-down-the-front sweater . . . but somehow her hair seemed blonder, her body more voluptuous and inviting. Never had he seen her look so beguiling.

They sat on the couch and exchanged pleasantries. She and Bill were moving back to Oklahoma after the wedding, she said; Ron told her that he'd decided to take the job with Mr. Williams in L.A. Their eyes met. He saw the caring he'd known so intimately. Impulsively, he leaned toward her, his body pressed against hers. She stiffened, her hands between them. He continued pushing against her until they tumbled over backward onto the couch. He tried to kiss her.

"I didn't come here for that," she gasped, pushing him away.

He pressed on, throwing his arms around her, pulling her back toward him. She struggled to get free.

"Let go!" she shrieked.

Startled, he fell back, embarrassed, humiliated.

She sprang to her feet and headed for the door. "I can't believe you did that," she said.

"I'm sorry, I'm sorry," he pleaded.

"How could you?" she asked, walking out the door.

As she drove away, he stood at the window, watching her baby-blue

VW convertible disappear down the hill. All he could think of was to get away and to have the days hurry past so he could receive his coveted diploma and escape to L.A., where he wouldn't have to drive down streets filled with memories of her. He desperately wanted out of Berkeley and to get on with his life. He'd had enough of college.

18

Larry

Westchester Moundsman Signs Substantial Bonus Contract.
—Westchester *News Advertiser*

I paced the living-room floor of our Westchester house, staring at the phone, praying it would ring. Paul Owens, the head West Coast scout for the Philadelphia Phillies, had promised to call by noon. It was 12:30.

The news in August 1964 was lousy: the bodies of three civil rights workers had been found buried in a red-clay dam in Mississippi; the Gulf of Tonkin Resolution swept through the House and Senate; President Johnson announced a major troop call-up.

But I had my own problems. In my senior season at Cal it was hard to tell what was louder—the sound of the crack of the opponents' bats against my fastball or the echo of the footsteps of the scouts jumping off my ship. My shoulder separation had kept me out of the first month of the season, and when I did finally get back into action, I was a collegiate launching pad, the USC bat rack starting to jump as soon as I walked out of the locker room. Coach Wolfman kept advising me to "throw through the pain," which was like a shrink telling a schizophrenic to snap out of it. At the end of the school year in June, the scouts who had been following me since I was a junior in high school were vamoosed. The last I saw of Tommy Lasorda, he was heading over the hill, on his way to another pile of lasagna.

During the summer after my senior season, I played on a semipro team in Culver City and showed faint signs of recovery. The New York Mets and Yankees both hinted that they were interested again, but then poof, they disappeared down the road. By August, the only team still keeping an eye on me was the Phillies. But they weren't exactly knocking down my door.

I was distressed. For seventeen years I'd focused on one objective: when I was seven I made my sister Barbara pitch to me in the driveway so I could practice my drag bunts; when I was thirteen I didn't join the Boy Scouts because it would interfere with Babe Ruth League practice; when I was twenty I had my first sexual experience at Dodger Stadium. Baseball was my life. How could they have said I didn't want it enough? What was I supposed to do . . . slide headfirst into the dugout to prove I had the fire in my belly?

If Mr. Owens didn't call, I had no clue what I was going to do with the rest of my life. It was going to be pretty hard landing a cushy public relations job with Rawlings Sporting Goods based on my 2.18 g.p.a. and my 5–7 record as a senior at Cal.

I didn't talk about my despair—men weren't supposed to discuss their fears and anxieties. My father didn't. I just went about my summertime business, working on my tan, hammering down Coors, dry-humping with Mary, who had moved back to L.A. when I did in June.

Mom watched me pace the living room. She'd been a witness to all the hours I'd banged a ball with a taped bat with the kids in the neighborhood, all the summer days that Dexter and I played over-the-line at Westchester Playground. She always packed me a lunch so I wouldn't have to waste time coming home to grub. She had an investment too— all the hours at the Babe Ruth League concession stand, all the hours spent stitching up torn uniforms and sewing elastic into the bottom of my baseball socks so I would look sharp. "It's not whether you win or lose," I'd tell her. "It's how you look in your uniform."

The phone rang. I tripped over Buffy in my rush to answer it. It was Mr. Owens.

"I really want to sign you, but . . . ," he said, stopping to clear his throat.

I braced myself for the final guillotine.

"But I'm afraid I can't get to your house with the contract until tomorrow morning," he continued.

Excuse me? Did I hear that right?

The Phillies not only wanted to sign me, they would give me a "substantial" signing bonus of eight grand and a first-year salary of $500 per month . . . plus, if and when I made the big-league team for ninety days I would get another eight-grand bonus. I was to report to minor-league spring-training camp in Leesburg, Florida, in March, and was tentatively assigned to spend my first season in Bakersfield in the Class A California League.

"What'ya think?" asked Mr. Owens.

What did I think? I think I would have paid them to sign. I also thought Tommy Lasorda and the rest of those ship-jumping, leather-skinned, Ban-Lon-wearing, bogus scouts were moles. This was better than that night in row 67 at Dodger Stadium. This was better than that night on the shag carpet at Loren's apartment. This was better than anything. I was going pro!

I called Dad at work, telling his secretary to pull him out of a meeting. He was even more excited than I was. I would have called Dexter, but he was in Marine boot camp at Camp Pendleton, getting ready for Vietnam.

Mr. Owens said he'd be at the house at noon on Saturday with the contract.

It was a quarter past noon and I was nervous, peering out the curtains, hoping to see Mr. Owens's car pull into the driveway. The phone rang.

Oh no, I thought. He was calling to tell me the Phillies brass had nixed the deal, deciding to invest in a couple of new hot-dog machines instead.

I cautiously lifted the receiver. Whew! It was just Mary, calling to ask if she should pack her cocktail dress. As soon as the contract was inked, we were going to hop in my Impala and highball it up Interstate 15 to Vegas for a quickie one-night celebration. I'd already booked a reservation at the Tally Ho Motel in the forty-dollar luxury suite. We had finally, after more than a year together, broken the sexual ice. Once. In Craig Morton's bed. Afterward, she had fallen into a funk, feeling guilty, brooding for a week, vowing that we wouldn't do it again until we were married. She hadn't promised me that we were going to do "it" in Vegas, but I was hopeful. It would, at the very least, be our first time in a motel, our first time spending the whole night together. I wasn't sure if I was more excited about signing the contract or about seeing Mary naked in the luxury suite at the Tally Ho. The one time we'd made love was under the covers with the lights out and our tops on. We'd even joked about getting married at the Chapel of the Chimes. "Who says I'm joking?" she'd said.

Owens pulled into the driveway in his Chevrolet. He wasn't flamboy-ant and leathery like the other scouts—he was a tall man, lean and angular, college-educated, soft-spoken, a cross between Gary Cooper and Henry Fonda. He wore a gray business suit and was accompanied by Carl Smith, a Phillie bird dog who had managed my semipro team and recommended me to Owens.

Mom was wearing her best summer dress and Dad had done something that I had never known him to do in all the twenty-two years that I'd been acquainted with him—he cut short his Saturday-morning golf game after nine holes so he could be there for the big event. I was spruced out in my best fraternity togs—cotton wash-and-wear pants, white socks, and a three-button, short-sleeve pale yellow and blue striped shirt. In my wallet I had two hundred bucks for Vegas that Dad was fronting me. And no condoms.

We all sat down at the mahogany dining-room table, Mom serving up cups of Instant Folgers. I didn't drink coffee. The All-American Boy. Mr. Owens told my dad he thought I had a good chance to make the big leagues in three or four years.

"I wouldn't be signing him otherwise," he said.

Dad was milking the moment. If I hadn't been the one with the fastball, I might have thought from the huge smile he was wearing that he was the one who was signing. In a way, I guess he was. I just wanted to get my John Hancock on that contract and get my Impala out on that highway to the Tally Ho.

An hour later and Dad was still rambling on about the history of the hook slide, or some darn thing. Mary called twice, wanting to know what was taking so long. I liked her eagerness. At last, Owens pulled the contract out of his briefcase. "Where do I sign?" I inquired. But first Dad had to go over it word for word like an SC law student. I called Mary.

"Don't forget to pack your bikini," I said.

"It's gonna be winter before we get there," she said. I continued to like her attitude.

And then finally—after all the years of dreaming, plus two tortuous hours at the dining-room table—I was a pro.

The floor was shaking and the walls were vibrating. Everybody on the dance floor at the Pi KA house was doing the surfer stomp. I was standing by the keg, arguing with Mary.

"Let's just forget it and go dance," I shouted, trying to be heard over the band.

"I don't want to dance," she snarled, turning to greet Steve with a big smile, the first one I'd seen from her all day.

It was the fall semester of '64, two months after I'd signed my contract. After depositing my $6,400 after-taxes bonus into Security First Savings, I'd returned to Berkeley to complete the last twelve units I needed to graduate. I moved out of the fraternity into an apartment in west Berkeley on Roosevelt Street with three other jocks, two of them baseball players, the third a basketballer. It was a standard, thin-walled, college-town apartment—beer-can pyramids, dart holes in the walls, broken Danish modern furniture, hair in the sink, empty milk cartons in the fridge, no dish-washing liquid, no vacuum. On Halloween when the trick-or-treaters came and caught us unprepared, I handed out handfuls of Cheerios, making sure my fist was all the way into their bags so they couldn't see what was coming. On her first visit, Mary had walked in the door and immediately started a cleanup crusade, demanding we mop the kitchen floor. We had no mop. Shel Buch, the basketball player roommate, ordered her to get off the rag.

As the band played on, it wasn't the dirty dishes in the sink that had Mary so upset. Our relationship was crumbling fast. Part of the problem was that other than the fact we were both from California and our mothers hung wash under the same sun, we had nothing in common. Another part of the problem was sex. It started the infamous night at the Tally Ho. After our romantic night of celebration on the town, we had come back to the suite, and while I went into the bathroom to spiff up my act, she plopped down on the bed, passing out colder than a cucumber until checkout time, cocktail dress and all. "You're not mad at me, are you, Poophead?" she asked the next day as we left town. "Not at all," I lied, the Chapel of the Chimes fading in the distance. When I returned to Berkeley in September, she stayed in L.A., but being the new big spender on campus, I flew her up to the Bay Area on weekends. We had fallen into a sad routine: lousy, boozy, guilt-ridden sex at the Flamingo Motel on Friday night, followed by sulking, surly, sexless Saturdays, then a desperate shot at patching it up on the ride to the airport on Sunday.

We were in the middle of one of those sulking, surly, sexless Saturdays when I handed her my beer at the fraternity party and excused myself to go upstairs to the bathroom. When I got back, she was out in the middle of the dance floor doing the hully gully with Steve, looking up at him all gaga-eyed and cutesy. I thought about marching out the front door right then, but I didn't. After the end of the song, I stepped between her and Steve, my back to him. He didn't know I was pissed; I didn't know he was married.

"I think we should go," I said.

"I don't want to!" she snapped.

I took a step toward her, and before my foot hit the floor, she unloaded from deep left field, the palm of her hand catching me flush on the cheek, spinning my head, the slap echoing through the room. Fifty heads turned to stare. The band froze. I stomped across the floor and out the door, cheek stinging, pride on fire. She followed, and although no more blows were struck, that was our last night together.

Two days later I met the future Mrs. Larry Colton . . . or the first one anyway.

19

Steve

Oh, they had to carry Harry to the ferry,
Oh, they had to carry Harry to the shore,
And the reason that they had to carry
Harry to the ferry was that
Harry couldn't carry anymore.
   —Cal drinking song

Linda sat on the edge of the bed, getting angry as she watched her husband get dressed. They were in a room at the Motel Sex in West Sacramento. Linda's mother was babysitting Dennis while they went out to "dinner." Linda was mad at herself for once again falling prey to Steve's charm, for once again allowing herself to believe that there was a chance their marriage would work. She was hooked on hope. But she now believed that all he really wanted was a quickie at the Motel Sex.

   The reality of the relationship was that it had been four stormy years and an endless chain of disappointments . . . like the way she had gotten her hopes up the last month of her pregnancy when he was all sweet and tender and sending her flowers. She didn't see him for a month after the baby was born. Dennis was now five months old and Linda could count on one hand the times that Steve had held his son. She'd thought that maybe his parents would help persuade him to be more of a father, but every time she brought the baby to Frank and Mary's, she sensed them backing away.

Steve continued to get dressed. He too was mad, feeling trapped, resentful. He had been forced into being a husband and a father against his will. He resented his father for stubbornly making him marry Linda; he resented Linda for not agreeing to give up the baby for adoption. He felt guilty that Linda was suffering—he cared about her—but the way he saw it, it was a giant mistake from the beginning. And as far as he was concerned, it wasn't his fault—he'd been honest through the whole thing, always making it perfectly clear that he didn't want to be married or have a child. He had told her about Ayris, and although Ayris had told him to go shit in his hat, he was content to let Linda think that Ayris was still hot for his program.

"So, tell me about her," Linda asked, as Steve stood in front of the mirror, combing his hair.

"What's there to say?" he replied. "I have her wrapped around my little finger."

That was the final straw. How could he be so cavalier? she wondered. If he talked that way about Ayris behind her back, surely he must be saying the same thing to Ayris about her. At that moment, although she'd never met Ayris and knew almost nothing about her, she felt a bond, a sister doomed to anguish.

"Take me home!" she demanded.

She did not hear from him again until their son's first birthday. That's when he sent her ten dollars and a note telling her to buy Dennis a nice present with the money.

Steve and Don looked at each other with forced smiles. Then they threw up.

It was the annual drink-till-you-drop initiation run in the eucalyptus groves of the Berkeley hills for Beta Beta, an elite interfraternity club on campus. To be initiated, the neophytes had to make ten round trips up and down a steep 200-yard incline, stopping at the bottom of the hill each time to refuel with another Dixie cup filled with gin and grapefruit juice and a tequila floater. Steve and Don, whose drinking days together went back to the 36 Club at McClatchy High, were ready to head up the hill for the sixth time. Both had already barfed twice.

According to those in the ultra in crowd—which unbeknownst to all but a dozen select fraternity men was the super-secret and exclusive Gun Club—Beta Beta was the penultimate interfraternity club on campus. At the bottom rung of the social ladder was Winged Helmet, a service organization that raised money for charities, collected petition signatures for political causes (such as welcoming Kennedy to campus), and didn't serve booze at its functions. Next up the ladder was Skull and Keys, which borrowed elements of Harvard's Pudding Club and Yale's Skull and Bones. Founded in 1889 with a motto of "Surreptitious, Clandestine, Loyal," Skull and Keys was originally a drama club, but over the years it developed into more of a social organization than a drama society, although every spring the club produced a ribald play, a production that was noted more for alcohol consumption than theatrical merit. Steve had played the lead role of Buttman in "The Adventures of Buttman and Rawbun," a play written by his pal Cobleigh. Being a member of Skull and Keys was a prerequisite for belonging to Beta Beta, a club that made no pretense of putting on plays or raising money for handicapped kids. It was a drinking club. Period.

Steve, who liked to think he had the stomach to digest scrap iron, had prepared for the initiation run by coating his stomach with half a loaf of white bread and a quart of milk. But everybody knew he couldn't handle three beers, let alone ten Dixie cups of killer booze. His drinking had become infamous on Fraternity Row. His framed caricature hanging next to the stuffed deer head in the fraternity den depicted him in his number 87 football jersey, crashing through a police barricade, a bottle of booze in one hand, a wasted look on his face, a pretty girl at his side. It was titled "Wrong Way Radich." And his reputation was not limited to the fraternity. A profile of him on the sports page of the *Daily Cal* was titled "Radich: 87 Proof."

On one level, his excessive drinking made little sense—he admitted he didn't like the taste; he seemed happy, vital, strong; he was admired, a standard for masculinity. But drinking was a way of life in the fraternity . . . it was as accessible as milk, its use not only condoned but celebrated . . . declining to drink was to be set apart from the crowd. Ron was the closest the fraternity had to a teetotaler. Alliance with the brothers was most easily gained by way of the keg, and in an uncomfortable stage of life, drinking was a common denominator, a river of communication in a land of the laconic, a way to be sociable and meet people. For Steve, alcohol helped mask the aches and pains of football and an unhappy marriage and a critical father. Or maybe it was because he had an irresistible chemical demand for alcohol. Nobody knew for sure, nobody worried about it. Pi KA was a fraternity, not a recovery unit. Drinking was a ceremonial part of the glorious passage, a way for young men to win the spurs of manhood. Three Coors made Steve a man amongst men. So he thought.

At the end of the seventh lap, he stopped to down another Dixie cup. Two gulps into it, the color drained from his face and his eyes rolled. Hands on hips, he bent at the waist and vomited again, chunks of regurgitated Wonder bread spewing from his mouth and nose. It was a manly sick. He took off up the hill again, but halfway up he staggered and fell. "Timber!" someone yelled. Down and down he rolled, through the eucalyptus leaves, not stopping until he deadened against a moss-covered log. Don moved to help him to his feet. It was no use. He was out for the count.

And they had to carry Steve to the car. And the reason that they had to carry Steve to the car was because Steve couldn't carry anymore.

.

Steve was hanging out at the Freddy Tree. He had come to campus to gape and gawk.

In the fall of 1964 the campus had become a great place for gaping and gawking, and not just at coeds. It was a three-ring sideshow, a cultural transformation taking place right before Steve's eyes. The Terrace, the popular student commons across from Sproul Hall, looked like one giant coffeehouse, awash in sandals and goatees. The music of Baez, Dylan, and the Beatles had replaced Jan and Dean. Madras was a vanishing fabric. An atmosphere of unrest prevailed. Student activists had gained a secure foothold in campus politics—Slate dominated the student senate, and according to some observers, it also controlled the *Daily Cal.* Protesters at the corner of Bancroft and Telegraph avenues daily passed out leaflets denouncing LBJ's policies in Southeast Asia.

The biggest issue on campus, however, wasn't the escalating presence of American advisers in Vietnam—it was civil rights. Despite Berkeley's 20 percent black population and its increasing reputation for liberalism, the city was bitterly divided over desegregation: black shoppers were not welcome downtown; there was discrimination in employment and segregation in the public schools; an open-housing ordinance was voted down; and less than 4 percent of the University student body was black.

Activists were fighting back. The Berkeley chapter of CORE was picketing the conservative Oakland *Tribune* and conducting shop-ins against Lucky Markets (a strategy of loading up shopping carts with food and then deserting them in front of the checkout stand). Anti-Barry Goldwater pickets were organized to protest alleged racist overtones in his presidential campaign; card tables soliciting donations and sign-ups for SNCC and other civil rights organizations were set up at the edge of campus. It was those card tables more than anything else that had University officials worried.

For two years, a conflict had been brewing between the administration and student activists over the use of the campus for off-campus political causes. University policy prohibited it. The activists had won two mini-battles, the first when President Clark Kerr and the Regents voted to have the ban on Communist speakers on campus lifted, the second when a "Hyde Park" free speech area on campus was established where speakers no longer had to give seventy-two hours' advance notice, although some critics questioned what authority the University had to compel students to step across a line before they could say what they wanted.

The administration had always allowed the card tables to exist at the corner of Telegraph and Bancroft because it was not University property. But as activists flocked to the corner like pigeons to bread crumbs, administrators and Regents worried that these "blue-jeaned and unshaven malcontents" were hassling passersby for money to support civil rights causes, creating a "bad image" for the University as a sanctuary for beatniks. Alex Sherriff, assistant dean of students, argued that it was the University's duty as "moral guardians to protect the clean-cut students from these agitators."

At the start of the school year, officials had declared that they had reexamined old maps and the University technically owned the property at the corner of Telegraph and Bancroft and the card tables had to go. The fuse was lit. Activists who had spent the summer of '64 working for SNCC in Mississippi facing the threats of the Ku Klux Klan were not about to back down to bureaucrats from academia. They accused Kerr of caving in to right-wing local politicians. Kerr, who was rumored to have turned down a cabinet post in the Kennedy administration, maintained that University policy covered all political groups—in other words, Students for Goldwater couldn't solicit on campus either. Defiantly, the activists escalated the conflict by moving their tables into the middle of Sproul Plaza, joined by the conservative Goldwaterites.

But as Steve left his perch at the Freddy Tree and walked toward Bancroft Avenue, where the debate raged, he wasn't thinking about issues of free speech. Spotting Ayris walking up ahead, he hurried to catch her. By the end of the day, she was riding through the Berkeley hills on the back of his new Honda 350—the motorcycle he'd borrowed from South City Honda in Sacramento, the new business his father had just purchased. Ayris couldn't have known it at the time, but her wild ride with Steve, which she thought was already finished, was just beginning.

20

Larry

The situation in Berkeley is anarchy.
  —Governor Pat Brown, referring
   to the Free Speech Movement,
   December 4, 1964

My roommate Shel, a member of the junior varsity basketball team, and I were hanging out at the Freddy Tree. As usual. Catching the afternoon shoot, and playing Nods, a popularity contest we'd invented in which a point was awarded every time somebody nodded or issued an unsolicited verbal greeting in our direction. (It was against the rules to go fishing for nods.) Shel, a good-looking guy from North Hollywood with curly black hair, blue eyes, a sarcastic wit, and terminal angst, was a harsh critic of my social cool—in particular, my relationship with Mary.

"Shit-can her," he advised. "She's a d.c."

From our position at the Freddy Tree we could see a crowd gathering on the other side of Sather Gate in front of Sproul Hall. "Arrest us all!" they chanted. "Arrest us all!"

As we debated whether to go investigate, I spotted a vision of loveliness walking down the steps of Wheeler Hall, a girl so beautiful she took my bonus away. She was wearing a matching yellow sweater, skirt, and headband. If Mary was Sally Fields, this girl was Sophia Loren. Tall, dark-haired, exotic. My eyes autographed her every step as she walked past us.

"Hi, Shel," she greeted with a movie-star smile

"How do you know her," I exclaimed, watching her walk away.

She was a friend of Janet Goldberg, Shel's girlfriend. Her name was Denise Lee, a sophomore art major from Beverly Hills. She lived in an apartment, and according to Shel, her mother was a movie star. He couldn't remember if it was Dorothy Lamour or Vivien Leigh. I conceded the Nods championship to him.

"Ask Janet to get me a date," I beseeched.

We left the Freddy Tree to check out the chanting and the commotion in front of Sproul Hall. Three hundred students, most of them sitting, were surrounding a University police car and blocking it from moving. Locked in the back seat was activist Jack Weinberg, a summer volunteer for SNCC in Mississippi. He had just been arrested for setting up an "unauthorized" recruitment table for CORE in front of Sproul Hall. A tall, thin, wiry-haired demonstrator took off his shoes and climbed atop the police car, a fierce moralism etched on his face. His name was Mario Savio, a senior in philosophy, who had also been to Mississippi that summer. He called Kerr and the administration "a bunch of bastards," and compared the policeman who had arrested Weinberg to Adolf Eichmann and the removal of the tables to an "act of emasculation." The demonstrators listened, transfixed.

I too was transfixed, not by Savio's call to civil disobedience, but by the ravishing daughter of the movie star standing on the other side of the crowd.

The unfolding unrest on campus in October and November 1964 was good theater—the passion, the chaos, the novelty—a living lab on civil disobedience, the essays of John Stuart Mill and Henry David Thoreau in 3-D. Things started getting seriously weird following the suspension of Weinberg and seven other students for setting up tables on campus to recruit for off-campus political causes. Their supporters, led by Savio, formed the Free Speech Movement (FSM) and lifted a self-imposed moratorium on their political activities, reopening their on-campus recruiting, setting up card tables in front of Sproul Hall in defiance of the University. Savio accused the administration of political oppression and abrogating the Bill of Rights.

Fearing a confrontation, the University postponed taking any action against FSM's disobedience. Every day, students gathered in Sproul and Dwinelle plazas to listen to impassioned speeches on both sides of the debate. On November 24, 300 students staged a two-hour sit-in on the second floor of Sproul Hall, singing Beatles songs and Christmas carols. There were rumors of a student strike. FSM leaders stepped up their criticism of the administration; Savio asserted that the University's opposition to FSM was a "master plan of the Regents to intimidate and suppress students." He accused them of treating students like IBM cards. I loved the University.

The majority of students on campus still opposed the movement. Winged Helmet, the interfraternity service organization, circulated a petition calling for "differences of opinion among free men to be settled by orderly and responsible negotiations and a belief in the support of law, order, and responsibility." Free speech, the club argued, was not an unrestricted license to question instructional authority.

It wasn't just Frat Row that challenged FSM: an editorial in the *Daily Cal* (which some accused of being controlled by Slate) vigorously maintained that the FSM leaders did not represent the majority of opinion of the student body; the student senate, while endorsing the free speech rights of students on campus, urged students to go to class and stay away from the "militant demonstrations" so that it would not appear the movement had more support than it actually did. "FSM no longer has the extension of on-campus political rights as its goal," a spokesman for the senate claimed. "Its present plans for civil disobedience are directed solely toward meaningless harassment of the University."

I was ambivalent, especially after Shel broke the news that he had gotten me a date with Denise for Friday night. There was, however, a minor caveat. "Janet said to warn you that Denise is not into jocks or fraternity guys," he said.

"No problem," I answered.

On Friday, December 4, 1964, the day of my Big Date, I got up at noon and headed for my outpost at the Freddy Tree. The campus had erupted. It started Thursday afternoon with a massive pre-sit-in rally on the steps of Sproul Hall, Joan Baez singing "The Times They Are A-Changin' " and "We Shall Overcome." After she was finished, 1,000 demonstrators marched into the building and began the largest sit-in of an American university, vowing not to leave until their demands were met. When they occupied all four floors, hundreds of black-booted officers from the combined forces of the University police, Berkeley police, Oakland police, Alameda County sheriff's deputies, and California Highway Patrol circled the building, waiting for orders to drag them out. It was late Thursday night when word spread that the demonstrators had broken into the office of president emeritus Gordon Sproul and were trashing it. It wasn't true, but Edwin Meese III, a conservative assistant Alameda County prosecutor who was stationed in campus police headquarters in the basement, panicked. He called Governor Brown in Sacramento and urged him to send in the police. Brown ordered the protesters arrested, and at 4 A.M. police moved in and began dragging demonstrators out of the building.

When I arrived on campus in the afternoon, demonstrators were still being hauled out. They came headfirst, feetfirst, anyway the police could drag them; they bounced down the steps and were tossed into waiting buses. Fraternity men cheered. I watched, a curious and silent spectator to history, worried more about my Big Date than issues of free speech. It would take 367 policemen twelve hours to carry out 773 protesters in the largest mass arrest in California history. The University was in the national spotlight on the six o'clock news.

I was having trouble believing freedom of speech didn't exist on campus. From every nook and cranny students were questioning authority; every day was a verbal brawl. I didn't understand why FSM was so intent on castigating Clark Kerr. Wasn't he the same guy who'd told Nixon and the Regents in 1962 to keep their noses out of who spoke on campus? I certainly didn't feel oppressed or part of what one protester called a "robot factory."

On the other hand, why was the University so upset about a few card tables on campus? Who cared? So what if these people jingled their little collection jars? I was a big boy . . . if I didn't want to listen to these pasty-faced bohemians, I could just walk on by. Mario Savio didn't have to go to my baseball games; I didn't have to go to his speeches. Basic First Amendment stuff. For me it came down to an issue of style over content, or as one student put it in a letter to the editor in the *Daily Cal:* "I don't deny the virtue of some of the goals of these grub-niks, but I question the repugnant, nauseating manner in which they represent their ideas. I suggest that these 'thinkers' and 'campus leaders' rearrange their schedule to include an occasional bath and haircut."

I nervously knocked on the apartment door. I was ten minutes late. On purpose. Didn't want to seem overanxious. Otherwise, I would have been there four days earlier. Denise's roommate, a friendly girl of Japanese ancestry, ushered me inside. I noticed a poignant charcoal drawing of two teary-eyed black girls embracing in front of a burned-down church.

"Denise painted that," said the roommate. "She painted everything that's in here." The walls were filled with art. My walls were filled with dart holes.

Denise appeared from out of her bedroom. I was willing to head straight to the Chapel of the Chimes, but I thought she might think that was rushing things a bit. So I introduced myself instead. She was prettier than the law allowed in 1964: five-eight, aquamarine eyes, thick dark brown hair, perfect complexion, drop-dead smile. I wasn't afraid of Janet's warning—I told her we were going to a Cal basketball game at Harmon Gym and a party at Pi KA. What else was I going to do? Take her to the art museum and stand there with my thumb up my butt?

"I've never been to a basketball game," she said.

"It'll be fun," I promised. I couldn't wait to get there. I was thinking about maybe just walking right out into the middle of the court during the game, stopping the action, so everybody could see me with her.

As we settled into our seats, I asked her what she thought of the FSM arrests. I wanted her to know I wasn't just another dummy jock, that I had my ear tuned to current affairs. She said she didn't feel the administration was suppressing our freedom of speech but she had gone to the pre-sit-in rally.

"I wanted to hear Joan Baez," she explained. "She has the voice of an angel."

"I really like Connie Francis," I said.

"You're funny," she said.

Denise's famous movie-star mother was not, I would later learn, Dorothy Lamour or Vivien Leigh. It was Hedy Lamarr, the woman billed during the late forties by M-G-M as "the century's most beautiful woman." Denise was the obvious genetic benefactor of her mother's classic European elegance. Her father was John Loder, the third of Hedy's six husbands. (Denise had taken the last name of her mom's fifth husband, Howard Lee.) Loder was a British actor whom Joan Crawford once called the "most handsome, well-built Englishman I ever met." (The critics called him "wooden.") Denise had attended Stockbridge, a private prep school in the Berkshires of western Massachusetts, studied in Paris for a year, and gone steady with a classmate by the name of Chevy Chase. She had her own car, a '59 T-Bird hardtop.

But we didn't talk about cars, family, or ex-sweethearts that first date. I pulled out my A material, including singing her a medley of Beatles songs in my Donald Duck voice. I modestly told her, ah shucks, that I'd signed with the Phillies. "Is that football?" she asked. At the Pi KA party I frugged, swam, monkeyed, and shimmied—all my best moves. On the way back to her apartment, I asked her out to dinner in two weeks—I was sure somebody as gorgeous as she was dated up well in advance. She accepted. She also kissed me good night, a hot, steamy embrace that fogged the Impala windows. I felt like asking her what she wanted to name our firstborn right then and there.

In the two weeks leading to our second date, I did not call her. I was following the prescribed Pi KA method of courtship, which theorized that to capture a woman's heart, it was best to be reserved, aloof, and indifferent. To pursue too hard, which was to send flowers and mushy cards and call on the phone, was uncool. "Girls like it when they don't know what you're thinking," the brothers advised. "They want a challenge. Otherwise, they'll walk all over you." Denise walked by the Freddy Tree and waved and smiled in my direction. I waved and smiled back, then looked the other way. I wasn't about to let her walk all over me.

In winning the battle, Clark Kerr lost the war, vastly underestimating student and faculty support for the movement, especially in the aftermath of the arrests. The activists' strategy had been to have the arrests take place in front of the student body and the media, believing that the sight of the police forcibly dragging students out of Sproul Hall would win the hearts and minds of the faculty and students. The tactic worked: there were charges of police brutality; the prosecution, which was led by Edwin Meese III, was criticized for proceeding too zealously; and a poll in the *Daily Cal*, which headlined the arrests as "A Hard Day's Night in Sproul," revealed that in the week following the arrests, 55 percent of the students now backed FSM, while 38 percent were against it and 7 percent were neutral. That was a dramatic shift from before the sit-in. And by a vote of 824–115, the faculty endorsed the demands of FSM. Savio declared total victory.

In the weeks that followed, the University gave in to the demands of FSM, opening the campus to off-campus political activity. It was impossible to ignore the upheaval, but I was doing my best. I took Denise out to dinner at Vanessi's in San Francisco, pretending I knew all along what antipasto was.

"Would you like a nice Pinot Noir with your dinner?" asked the waiter.

"Indubitably," I answered.

I was graduating in six weeks and leaving for spring training, so I stepped up my pursuit of Denise, defying fraternity advice. Over Christmas vacation we went to parties in L.A. and to see *Goldfinger* at Grauman's Chinese Theater in Hollywood. Denise got embarrassed when I butted into the line. When I picked her up at her mom's two-story Cape

Cod in a ritzy neighborhood in Westwood, she whisked me out the door
before I had a chance to meet the famous Hedy.

"Mom's being weird these days," she explained, mentioning something
about another divorce. I was still trying to figure out what antipasto was.

I brought Denise to Westchester to meet Hazel and Nellie. "You're so
lucky to have such normal parents," she said.

Back in Berkeley after vacation, I was desperately cramming for my last
finals. I kept having a nightmare that I would flunk my Geology 10 final
and they wouldn't let me go to spring training until I took the course
over again. In this dream Gene Mauch, the Phillies' manager, was standing outside the clubhouse and screaming pop-quiz questions at me about
sedimentary rocks and stalagmites. It was hard to study, my mind preoccupied with Denise. There was a sense of urgency to our relationship. All
I wanted to do was be with her. She seemed so much more sophisticated, cultured, and worldly than I. That's because she was.

I had loved Mary, but that was a pony ride at the fair compared to the
wild gallop across the frontier I was on with Denise . . . even though I
still hadn't said one word to her about how I felt. Couldn't she guess? I
was afraid to take the risk. What if she didn't feel the same way? I
thought she did, given the way she kissed me and went out with me every
time I asked, but how could I be sure? How was I supposed to know
what girls thought? Cal didn't have any courses in that. We still hadn't
talked about love or made it.

I walked into the Life Sciences Building for what hopefully would be the
last exam of my college career, my head so crammed with memorized
facts about meandering rivers and volcanic mountains and glacial flows
that I was afraid to sneeze for fear my brain would come through my
nose. I was flunking the course, having attended class only once all year,
too busy hanging out at the Freddy Tree, and unless I got a C on the
final, my nightmare would come true. This was it—four and a half years
of college down to one last test. Two outs, bottom of the ninth, full
count.

The TA handed out the test. I quickly scanned the twelve short-essay
questions. Hooray! I knew enough about every question that I was sure I
could fluff my way through it. When I turned in my blue book and
walked outside into the bright California sunlight, I knew I had aced it.
Look out, world, here I come with my degree in communications and
public policy and my final g.p.a. of 2.18. There would be no cap and
gown, no graduation ceremony, no shaking hands with Clark Kerr . . .

and no more 2S deferment. LBJ had just announced another major call-up.

To celebrate my academic achievement, Denise and I drove to Sausalito and sat on a dock at the edge of the Bay, feeding bread crumbs to sea gulls, making up stories about their families. She told me that she wished I wasn't leaving. The feeling was mutual, I confessed. That night, with Johnny Mathis playing on the hi-fi, we made love for the first time on the living-room floor of my apartment. With no guilt afterward. To graduate from college and to have that happen all in one day . . . wow! I also got a new set of Wilson golf clubs from Mom and Dad.

The next morning I packed my belongings, and Denise and I headed south on Highway 101, making it as far as Oxnard, fifty miles north of L.A., where we checked into a motel and did not get out of bed for twenty-four hours. How lucky could a twenty-two-year-old guy be? I had a college degree, a contract to play the national pastime, $5,200 left in savings, and a gorgeous girlfriend. Considering what a crummy freshman year I'd had, Berkeley had worked out pretty well for me. Maybe things were starting to get sort of weird in places like Saigon and Selma, but those towns weren't on my map.

"This may be a silly question," Denise said as we pulled to a stop in front of her mom's house. "But do you think we should have been worried about birth control?"

21

Loren

. . . a big, husky carbon copy of the original clean-cut All-American boy . . . the greatest thing for the American image since "The Star-Spangled Banner."
—Description of Loren in the Brisbane *Courier-Mail,* July 1965

When Donna found out she was pregnant for the second time, she was positive of one thing . . . she wasn't going back to the abortionist. She had a better idea. Loren, however, was skeptical of this new plan.

It was August 1964. He had stayed in Berkeley for the summer because he couldn't face going home to Marysville and listening to his parents yap at each other, and because he wanted to work out every afternoon at Edwards Field with Craig in preparation for their senior season. Craig was being tabbed to battle Roger Staubach and Joe Namath for All-American quarterback honors, and Loren wanted a piece of the action—by catching enough of Craig's passes, he figured, he could catch the eye of the pro scouts and get drafted. He and Craig were spending long hours diligently perfecting their patterns and timing. After practice, instead of chasing girls as they'd done the previous year, they went separate ways, Loren to the apartment on Warring Avenue he was now sharing with his football and rugby teammate Tom Blanchfield, Craig to the apartment on College Avenue he was now sharing with Vickie, his wife. Loren, who had been an usher in their Santa Monica wedding, missed the good old days of the front-room wrestling matches and Fucking Moos.

He was nervous about Donna's plan. Very nervous. But both of them were as positive as they had been at the time of the first pregnancy that they weren't ready to settle down and raise a child. Donna had been stood up too many times and had found too many telltale signs of his other "tomatoes." Earlier in the summer she'd walked in the open door of his apartment and found him sitting on the couch, as cozy as could be, with one of her sorority sisters. She weathered that disaster. It wasn't easy for her to abandon the passion and the pain they'd shared. They'd known each other since the first day of their freshman year and she couldn't imagine being with anyone more exciting, more adventuresome. They'd had so many good times together, like the night they won the swim dance contest at Big Al's on Broadway in San Francisco. And she felt closer to his family than to her own. After all, it was his grandparents who had paid for the abortion, and it was Genevieve whom she called to look at the fetus in the toilet. If that wasn't closeness, she didn't know what was. She was convinced Loren loved her, in his own way, but marriage wasn't on the immediate horizon. She could wait.

The decision to have another abortion was the easy part—the difficult part was figuring out where to have it done and how to pay for it. Loren couldn't ask Pop and Eddie to pay for a second abortion—that was asking too much—and Donna wasn't about to go through the humiliation of asking her parents again. Her father had barely talked to her since the first one. The $200 in cash she and Loren had between them was about $300 short of what they would need.

Loren was waiting when she arrived at his apartment. She carried a grocery bag that contained a clean sheet, a flashlight, hair curlers, and a piece of plastic tubing that she'd just purchased at Berkeley Toy and Hobby, the kind of tubing used as a fuel line for expensive model cars.

"Are you sure this is what we should be doing?" Loren asked.

"I know what I'm doing," she answered, filling a pot with water and putting it on the stove to boil, then dropping in the tubing and a large curler. She instructed Loren to clear the newspapers and dishes off his desk and spread out the sheet.

"I don't know about this," he said, his voice trailing off.

"I trust you, Loren," she said. "You're the only person in the world I'd let do this to me. Look at it this way. If we were on a camping trip and you got bit by a rattlesnake and I had to cut your leg open to save you, I would. This is the same thing. I'm only six weeks pregnant. It's not like last time."

After the water was boiling, she removed the curler and tubing and set it on top of the sheet. Then she took off her skirt and underpants and scooted up on the desk, spreading her legs, and inserted the hair curler in her vagina to prop it open. Then, using the flashlight to see, Loren slowly eased the piece of plastic tubing inside her as she instructed, carefully moving it back and forth against the walls of the uterus until they were convinced the fetus was destroyed.

It was the first play from the line of scrimmage. Loren could hardly contain himself, so pumped up he was growling. Under overcast skies, a capacity throng of 76,780 fans had jam-packed its way into Memorial Stadium in Strawberry Canyon for the 1964 Big Game. Cal versus arch-rival Stanford. The final game of his collegiate career.

It had been a disappointing final season for Loren and the Bears. It started for him on the first day of fall practice when head coach Ray Willsey, a gruff, chain-smoking advocate of hard-nosed football who had replaced the fired Phi Beta Kappa Marv Levy, switched Loren from flanker to strong safety. So much for all the summer hours working on routes and timing with Craig. But Loren adapted quickly to the change. The coaches were convinced he was a natural, better suited to the less disciplined, more aggressive demands of the defensive secondary. At six-four, 215 pounds, he was the largest and strongest defensive back on the team, able to outleap any receiver in the league. For all his casual and whimsical approach to the game, he was a tough, aggressive player, a huge hitter who loved to bury his helmet and pads into the guts of flankers coming his way. In a game against Miami at the Orange Bowl early in the season, he intercepted a pass in the end zone to thwart a last-second Miami drive and preserve a rare Bear victory. But going into the final game, the team had won only two games, despite an All-American season by Craig. A victory over Stanford, however, would salvage some of the pride. In the previous year's game—postponed a week because of Kennedy's assassination—Loren fumbled a look-in pass from Craig on the Bears' 20-yard line late in the game, setting up Stanford's winning score. He was looking for redemption.

As Stanford's offense came to the line for the first play from scrimmage, he prowled his spot on the field, eyes fixed right on the eyes of the flanker, daring him to come his way. And the flanker did, turning to catch a short flare pass just as Loren arrived like the afternoon Greyhound into Marysville. The contact was heard in Sutter County, and the Stanford trainer had to help his Looney Tunes player off the field. It was a hit that would become the signature shot on the 1964 Cal highlight film. It was also about the only good thing that happened all day. The Bears lost 20–3, the third time Loren had tasted defeat at the hands of the archrival Indians.

He could not remember the last time he had cried—maybe it was at the drive-in in Marysville when he saw *Shane*—but as he tucked his helmet under his arm and trotted off the chewed-up green turf of Memorial Stadium for the final time, he was close to tears, uncharacteristically melancholy. Football had been a big chunk of his identity, affording him pampered status, an outlet for his energy and aggression. As fans poured across the field, he dodged his way between them, trying to get to the locker room as fast as possible, not wanting to lose it in public.

"I like the way you hit," a greasy-haired stranger said, trotting alongside him.

"Thanks," Loren grumbled, not slowing down, in no mood to chitchat with some low-life used-car-dealer kind of a guy. The stranger continued to keep pace.

"Here's my card," the man said as they reached the goalposts. "Don't be surprised if we give you a call next week."

As Loren headed up the north tunnel for the final journey, he glanced down at the card. The man's name was Al Davis, general manager of the Oakland Raiders.

"Another fuckin' schooner for my boy here!" Loren yelled to the bartender, his arm draped over Steve's shoulder. "We gotta get his head screwed on straight. He's talking dumb!"

It was the spring of '65. They were in the Rathskeller, Loren's fiefdom. Located downstairs at Larry Blake's Restaurant two blocks from campus, the loud and bawdy Rathskeller was as much a part of Berkeley tradition as the Campanile or Sather Gate: beer was served in schooners the size of goldfish bowls; sawdust covered the floor; water pipes hung from low ceilings; ex-rugby players tended bar. And the louder and more raucous it got, the better Loren liked it. It was where he went to hang out with "the boys." On this day he was trying to do a sales job on Steve, hoping to convince him that it was in his best interest to come with the Cal rugby team on its scheduled summer trip to Australia. Steve, who, like Loren, was an outstanding rugby player, was maintaining that he needed to stay in Berkeley to go to summer school so he could graduate on time in four years. To Loren, the thought of missing out on the rugby trip to Australia was blasphemous. He was going to make the trip, no matter what. Not even Al Davis and the Raiders were going to stop him.

"Rat, think of all that Aussie pussy just waiting for your big hammer," he encouraged, leaning his crutch against the bar, the one he was using to hobble around on after the knee surgery he'd had following his rugby injury in a game against the University of British Columbia.

Al Davis was, in fact, trying to discourage him from going to Australia. In the 1964 pro football draft, the Raiders had made Loren their ninth-round pick, signing him to a contract in Davis's office the day before the draft to hedge a bit on the expected bidding war between the established NFL and the upstart AFL, a feeding frenzy that was being fueled by the AFL's new $36 million TV deal with NBC and the new league's eagerness to sign the top collegiate stars, such as Namath, Staubach, Morton, Butkus, Gale Sayers, and John Huarte. Other than the Raiders, however, none of the other teams had shown any interest in Loren, except for one little nibble from the Cowboys. Still, Davis had given him a slick sales pitch: that the AFL would soon be on a par with the older and more prestigious NFL; that the city of Oakland was going to build a modern new stadium so they would no longer have to play their games in cracker-box Frank Yuell Field next to the Nimitz Freeway; that Loren would be playing in his own backyard. All that sounded fine to Loren, but what really caught his attention was when Davis said the Raiders would pay him a $12,000 salary (nonguaranteed) with a $2,500 bonus in training camp. It was nowhere near the guaranteed $150,000, three-year deal (plus an XKE) the Dallas Cowboys were giving to his best buddy, Craig, but it beat driving a forklift at the peach-packing plant in Yuba City. Davis and the Raiders' management were unhappy, however, that Loren had blown out his knee playing rugby. And if he went to Australia in the summer, a trip that would overlap the start of the Raiders' training camp, well, he might as well kiss off any hopes of pro football. Steve, who still had a year of eligibility left and pro aspirations of his own, couldn't believe that Loren would even be thinking about going on the trip and jeopardizing his chance with the Raiders.

"Fuck Al Davis and the nag he rode in on!" blustered Loren. "I'm going to Australia, and if he doesn't like it, fuck him!"

He turned to watch his professor for ag-finance, who was also his adviser, walk down the stairs and take a seat in a booth in the rear. A minute later, Loren was sitting across the table from him, ordering two more schooners, trying to fast-talk his way into a passing grade. He launched into his thickest "I'm just a country boy" routine, regaling the man with stories about how he used to ride his Grandpa Earl's tractor to help him turn under acres of wheat for the government's soil-bank program. This wasn't the same professor whom he'd tried to humor with a midterm blue book filled with nothing but jokes—that little trick didn't work—but as he signaled for still another round of schooners, the professor's appreciative smile gave hope that there was still a chance he might pass ag-finance, a must if he had any hope of graduating any time before the end of LBJ's administration.

It was near closing when Loren walked his professor up to Telegraph Avenue, his arm around him as if they'd been great pals for years. They said goodbye, then Loren headed for a phone booth to call Donna and see if she wanted some late-night company. It was a familiar call.

Donna had survived the second abortion. And then, incredibly, she'd gotten pregnant again. But instead of going to the back-alley abortionist or Loren's apartment, this time she found a doctor who prescribed her ergot, a pill veterinarians use to induce labor in cows. It produced the desired miscarriage. She had already graduated from Cal and moved to Marin County, where she was teaching algebra at Novato High School and feeling alone, abandoned, despondent, sometimes even suicidal. Loren was tossing her morsels of emotional support, usually late at night, but it wasn't enough. She was spending her nights developing lesson plans in her small studio apartment in San Rafael while he was back in Berkeley, playing the college Casanova, wowing the coeds with his contract with the Raiders. But because they had been through so much together, and because of all the pain she had suffered, he was having trouble cutting her completely loose, feeling a sense of obligation. From Donna's standpoint, however, that sense of obligation only seemed to happen after midnight, but usually, feeling lonely and in need of his crumbs of support, she'd give in. He would promise to be there for dinner the next evening, then not show. It was difficult for her to admit it was over. She had become so attached. Nobody had ever known her as he had, and she was sure nobody ever would. When they were alone, he could be intimate, romantic, and ever since that passionate night in Yosemite Valley, she had believed that they would someday marry. She had been willing to sacrifice everything for him. But now he was bailing out. What bothered her most was that he wouldn't come right out and tell her to her face that it was over. He was acting it out—not calling for days, failing to show up, ignoring her. That was his solution, she believed —to hide, to keep moving, to avoid responsibility. The last time he'd called, she couldn't figure out if she was his sister or his daughter or his girlfriend or his mother. As helpful as Genevieve had been through the first abortion crisis, Donna felt she was smothering Loren. It was as if Genevieve had been unable to find satisfaction in her marriage to Hal, so she was putting all her eggs in Loren's basket, never letting him alone, making it hard for him to have room for somebody else. That's what

Donna felt anyway. She was depressed, feeling theirs was a tragic lost love.

Her phone rang, waking her. She knew it was him. She let it ring, then rolled over and went back to sleep. No more, she vowed. She'd suffered enough.

On the Qantas flight to Brisbane, he outlined his goals for the trip: "Kick some ass and get me some Aussie pussy." He accomplished the latter before jet lag even set in. The rugby part of the trip, however, was expected to be more difficult. The Bears were arriving in Brisbane riding a 24-game winning streak, but the Australian rugby press was predicting the "Yanks" would get their "comeuppance" against the vastly more experienced Australians.

Rugby had become the great passion in Loren's life. At a time when campus unrest, not sports, was bringing the national spotlight to Berkeley, the rugby team had raised $25,000 for its trip to Australia. The team was undefeated, and although no official rankings existed, Cal was arguably the best side in America, handily defeating Notre Dame, USC, UCLA, and the University of British Columbia. *Sports Illustrated* called Berkeley the "rugby capital of America." Excellence in rugby was not new to Cal, the tradition starting in 1906, at a time when football was under attack for being too savage. From 1906 to 1915, football was banned at Stanford and Cal and the Big Game was a rugby match. But when football resumed, rugby did not die. Matches regularly drew crowds of 10,000; coeds wore "I'm a rugger hugger" buttons; and Cal had gained an international name in the rugby world, not only for its winning but for the combination of verve and casualness with which its players approached the sport. Under coach Miles "Doc" Hudson, discipline was loose, made to order for Loren. Doc Hudson called him "the best natural player" he'd seen in his thirty years of coaching. Nicknamed the "King of the Line-Out," Loren excelled at leaping over opposing players to capture the ball. A full-page color photo of him soaring above a line-out against Notre Dame appeared in *Sports Illustrated*. Not even his pal Craig could claim that.

Prior to the team's first game in Brisbane, one of the local newspapers assigned a young female reporter to cover the initial practice for the women's section. She focused her story on Loren, calling him "the greatest thing for the American image since 'The Star-Spangled Banner.'" The caption under a photo of him lying shirtless on the grass read: "Isn't he scrumptious?" And when she asked him about dating habits back home, he replied: "Most of the boys on the team have a girlfriend—or maybe two or three!"

In the first game, the Bears played Queensland University to a 9–9 tie, stunning the local press, captivating the Australian fans with their wide-open, all-or-nothing style of play. One columnist wrote: "The Golden Bears brought a new conception of the game to Brisbane fans. Their spiraling gridiron passes, bone-shuddering tackles, and obsessive chase for the loose ball make them the most exciting rugby players since the Fijians of 1952."

Everywhere they played—Armidale, Sydney, Melbourne, Canberra, Auckland—record crowds applauded their speedy hard-nosed game. Games were televised and had to be moved to larger stadiums to accommodate the demand to see what one Sydney writer called "the daring and determined approach of the wonderfully built and free-spirited Californians." The players were billeted with local families and treated like royalty, given all the ale they could drink. Loren showed no signs of having undergone knee surgery four months earlier. Back home, the Bay Area sports sections gave front-page coverage to the tour, a photo of Loren leaping high above a line-out showing up in the Raiders' office.

The team finished its tour with a 5–2–2 record, the losses by a total of only six points in matches played in driving rain and mud. Loren, in no hurry to get back to the Raiders' training camp in Santa Rosa, accompanied the rugby team for an extra week in Fiji and Tahiti. He also arranged to have Diane, a tall brunette Delta Gamma he'd been dating before the trip, meet him in Hawaii for a week. He notified the Raiders that it would be another two weeks before he could make it to camp.

Davis told him to buzz off.

When Loren bounded off the plane in Oahu, he heard a familiar voice call his name. He turned, and there to greet him with a lei, resplendent in a flowered muumuu, was his mother. "Surprise!" she exclaimed. She drove him to the hotel in her rented Jeep with the pink-fringed top, his chaperon for the week.

Loren hurried across campus toward the Ag-Econ Building. It was the fall of '65. Instead of enrolling at Cal to finish up his remaining ten hours to graduate, he'd taken a job as an assistant manager for the Product Finishing Company, a cabinet-painting firm in Emeryville owned by an avid booster of Cal football. He was enticed by the $700-a-month starting salary and the loose hours that gave him the freedom to wander Berkeley and pick up girls. When he got back from Australia the

Raiders had told him that they would "consider" inviting him to training camp next year.

He walked into the office of his adviser, his old drinking buddy from the Rathskeller. He told him about the great rice harvest his Grandpa Earl had, and how the Raiders wanted him to be on the taxi squad, and how he just wasn't going to have time to go to school that semester.

"What about in the spring?" the professor inquired.

Loren shook his head. That's when the Raiders wanted him around for mini-camp and public relations, he claimed.

"Guess that means you won't be coming to school next fall either," said the professor.

"It's going to be a long season," allowed Loren.

Well, in that case, deemed the professor, the only thing to do was waive those pesky last ten hours. "I'm convinced you know the material," he said.

And with that, Loren Harold "Hayseed" Hawley was a graduate of the University of California, Berkeley.

22

Jim

U.S. to lose Vietnam, asserts Vietnamese visitor . . . 10 months, 10 years, it doesn't make any difference.
—Daily Cal,
    September 30, 1965

The bleachers behind the backstop of the San Quentin softball field were packed. Murderers. Robbers. Rapists. Thieves. Jim, the left fielder for the heavy-hitting California Department of Bridges, stepped to the plate, bases loaded, the game against the prison inmates on the line. (The San Quentin team played only home games.)

"Hey, batter!" yelled a convict, shaking the wire fence. "I got money on this game. Better strike out if you want to get out of here alive."

Jim stepped out of the box and smiled.

"I ain't joking, motherfucker!" expressed the convict.

It was July 1965 and Jim was working for the summer as a student engineer for the Department of Bridges. It was the third summer in a row he'd landed a good job. Following his adventures as a river guide, he'd worked as a surveyor for the U.S. Forest Service in King's County, south of Yosemite, part of a four-man crew that went into the forest with axes and chain saws to cut down trees for logging roads. For his job with the Department of Bridges, which he got on recommendation from one of his structural engineering professors, he worked in a big office in San

Francisco, sitting in the middle of a sea of drafting tables. His responsibility was to help on the advanced planning for a new bridge being proposed for the Bay, one that would run from Alameda on the east side to Hunters Point near Candlestick Park. He developed his own design, a long suspension bridge with tied arches, and it was one of only two selected by his supervisor for consideration. A picture of it appeared on the front page of the *Chronicle*. (The bridge idea was shelved the next year in favor of Bay Area Rapid Transit.)

He nervously dug in at the plate, eyeing the pitcher. He wasn't exactly Willie Mays with the stick, but with his strong arms, hardened by three years of high school swimming, two years of collegiate crew, and summers in the woods, when he did connect he could go seriously way deep.

"Don't forget what I said, asshole!" a voice called out.

The first pitch arched perfectly over the plate, right into his wheelhouse. His eyes widened, his muscles tensed, and he swung from his heels. And on this day, there was no joy in San Quentin. Mighty Muldoon had connected. A grand salami . . . the ball last seen headed out over the Big House toward Alcatraz.

Walking through Sproul Plaza on his way to his fluid mechanics class, he stopped to watch the daily swirl of activity. It was like being in the television department of Sears, every set turned full volume to a different channel. A student claiming to be a member of the Filthy Speech Movement, the latest incantation of FSM, stood on the steps of the Student Union and yelled, "Fuck!" Nearby, a gathering of students demonstrated for the Sexual Freedom League, a free love group protesting the administration's refusal to allow dirty movies on campus. Everybody but Jim, it seemed, was wearing a button or carrying a picket for a different cause: "Legalize Abortion," "Save the Redwoods," "Donate Blood to the Vietcong," "Smoke Marijuana," "Fuck the Draft," "Join the Peace Corps," "Batman Is Ugly."

He had moved out of the fraternity at the start of his senior year in September 1965, renting an apartment in Oakland with Darrell Connell, an architectural student who had also worked for the Department of Bridges over the summer. After three years of living in the house, Jim was glad to be out. The fraternity had never been a comfortable fit. Now he was looking forward to graduating and getting out of Berkeley. He didn't like what was happening on campus.

It was a far cry from the Berkeley he arrived at in 1962. Following the FSM sit-in and arrests, the campus had become a maelstrom of dissent and a center for the new student movement that was sending shock waves across America. Berkeley was suddenly at the radical forefront, students calling out for a new style of American life, no longer willing to accept the revered values of contemporary society and the Establishment. Angry voices denounced the bourgeois traditions of affluence and capitalism. There was a sense that the young must take control. At the Mediterranean Cafe on Telegraph, sandaled intellectuals discussed issues of personal salvation and spiritual enlightenment. To Jim, a former Boy Scout and the son of Republican parents, these people were nothing more than scrofulous bohemians. He had come to the University to get an education, not to carry pickets and change the world. He was apolitical, a part of the vast and voiceless majority of the student body who either didn't care or didn't approve of the dissenters. (In 1965, University officials estimated that only 3,000 of the 27,000 students actually marched in picket lines, while another 7,000 were in sympathy with the protests when the cause was perceived as good—i.e., Vietnam or FSM— but were too busy studying to become actively involved.)

As he continued his trek to class, he spotted a girl who'd been a classmate at Mills High in Burlingame. She carried a protest sign advising LBJ to end his "dirty little war." Jim shook his head, astonished at the girl's fervor. He approached.

"Stop wasting your time!" he advised. "You're here to get an education. Go to class!"

He wasn't interested in picketing the war, but then again, he didn't want to go fight in it either. His older brother Scott, who had gone to Stanford on a Navy ROTC scholarship, was in submarine training, getting ready to ship off for the South China Sea. As far as Jim was concerned, that was enough contribution to the war effort from the van Hoften household.

By the end of 1965, Vietnam had replaced free speech and civil rights as the big issue on campus. It was impossible for Jim to walk across campus without seeing antiwar protesters. He couldn't escape it: the *Daily Cal* carried full-page ads paid for by students and faculty asking President Johnson to stop the war; at Charter Day, when keynote speaker Arthur Goldberg, American ambassador to the United Nations and a spokesman for American policy in Vietnam, was introduced to the crowd of 15,000 at the Greek Theater, half stood up and walked out. Jim was in the library studying.

What had been a remote battle in an unknown land two years earlier was now front-page news; the fighting from the nameless hamlets and jungled mountains was a part of the changing American consciousness;

the body bags were coming home; and as Jim neared graduation day, General William Westmoreland, *Time's* Man of the Year, was calling for more troops . . . and getting them. Jim believed in the righteousness of the American cause in Vietnam, he said, but like college seniors all across the country, he was faced with the grim prospect of being called to Vietnam, with its monsoon mud, baked heat, and deadly guerrilla warfare. He needed to figure out a way to miss that road trip.

He had always been one to go along with the crowd. When Ralph suggested they go out for football in high school, he thought it sounded like a good idea; when his mother and brother suggested he join a fraternity at Cal, he signed up for rush. And at the end of his junior year, when Patty began talking earnestly about getting married, it seemed like a reasonable thing to do: they had been going steady since his senior year in high school; their families got along great; neither of them had ever dated anyone else seriously; and they were in love . . . and love couldn't wait for him to finish his military service, or grad school, or whatever he decided to do after graduation. The decision was simple. She accepted his proposal of marriage. The wedding was set for June 1966.

It was time to dodge a bullet. He set out across campus for his appointment with his senior academic adviser, Hans Albert Einstein, who, according to the rumors in the School of Engineering, was some sort of distant relative of his famous namesake. Jim didn't care if the guy was related to Moses. All he wanted was for Professor Einstein to give him a four-star recommendation to grad school so he could stay home and watch the war on TV.

His academic record at Berkeley was the tale of two halves. His freshman year was marked by cinch notices and repeated warnings from his parents to get his act together. Hampered by the demands of crew, Pi KA, and his studies, he finished his sophomore year with a g.p.a. of 2.8 . . . which was above the Pi KA average, the third worst of the forty-seven fraternities . . . but 2.8 wasn't going to get him into Caltech or somewhere brainy like that. That's when he decided to drop crew, which wasn't a good move for his Olympic chances, but a wise decision with respect to his standing in the classroom. In his junior and senior years, he received straight A's, establishing himself as one of the brightest students in the School of Engineering.

He still wasn't sure what field of engineering he wanted to specialize in out there in the real world. His major was civil engineering, considered to be the easiest of the engineering majors, but he was attracted primarily to classes or professors he found interesting, rather than a course of study leading in a specific career direction. His first adviser, T. Y. Lin, who invented a prestressed concrete that would revolutionize building, was instrumental in his developing an interest in structural engineering. Jim excelled in analyzing loads and forces and its application in building bridges and dams, lessons he put into practice in his winning design for the new bridge across the Bay. He also cultivated an interest in hydraulic engineering, considered to be the toughest field of study within civil engineering. He enjoyed studying about fluid forces and flows, as well as the challenge of the more difficult courses. But he still didn't know what he wanted to do with his life . . . or how he was going to avoid the military after he graduated. His only hope for avoiding the draft after graduation, he concluded, was grad school. That would give him another two years on his 2S deferment, and hopefully, the war would be over by then. He had new reason for hope: at the start of his last semester, Secretary of Defense McNamara was declaring that the war was going so well that draft calls would be cut in half by 1967.

Jim entered Professor Einstein's office to ask for guidance. With his excellent grades in his junior and senior years, he qualified for Cal's graduate program, but he wanted to get away, to find a school with no campus unrest.

"What are you looking for in a graduate school?" asked Einstein.

Jim had two main requirements. He wanted a school that would give him financial assistance and was close to great skiing. Einstein knew just the place. It was on his recommendation that Jim was awarded a $250-a-month position as a research assistant in the graduate school of engineering at Colorado State University in Fort Collins, just a hop, skip, and a chair lift from some of the best slopes in America, a great place for newlyweds to start a life together and to watch the war from, no protesters in sight. Jim could hardly wait.

They were married at the First Presbyterian Church in Burlingame with a hundred guests in attendance. Patty, who had completed two years at San Mateo Junior College, was twenty; Jim was twenty-two. His best man was Darrell Connell, his roommate his senior year. Ralph, the only Pi KA in attendance, served as an usher. A week earlier at Ralph's wedding, Jim had been the best man. After a brief honeymoon to Tahoe, the newlyweds moved into an apartment in Oakland; Patty worked in a bank while Jim went to summer school to complete his final twelve hours. He had frugally squirreled away money from his job the previous summer.

Jim graduated in August 1966. As he and Patty headed east out of town on Interstate 80 in his newly purchased '64 roundback Volvo with their skis on top, he was glad to be leaving Berkeley and its chaos. He would later recall his years at Cal and the fraternity as the worst of his life.

23

Steve

It was a full moon, the Thursday night before Cal's '65 league opener against the Washington Huskies. Senior Steve Radich had reason to be howling: he and Ayris were going hot and heavy; he was pulling a B average in his bus ad classes; and after being smashed 48–6 by Notre Dame in the nationally televised season opener, the Bears were on a roll. In a 24–7 win over Air Force, Steve, who had been switched from defensive end to linebacker after bulking up to 210 on weights and protein drinks, was named Pac 8 co-player of the week with USC's Heisman Trophy winner, Mike Garrett. Bay Area sportswriters were comparing him to Les Richter and Matt Hazeltine, the two greatest linebackers in school history; he appeared to be a lead-pipe cinch to be drafted by the pros. The future was bright.

But things were about to change.

He arrived at the weekly Thursday-night Gun Club meeting, parking his motorcycle in front of the Tomb, the club's secret meeting place, a concrete bunker hidden behind a wall of trees at the foot of the Berkeley hills. He entered, joining the other eleven members in the club's traditional opening chant:

"Keep the cunt out! . . . Keep the cunt out!"

He took a long swig of gin, the club's sacrament, then passed it to his chum Don next to him. They both placed their sacred, never-to-be-lost book of poems on the ceremonial table in front of them and smiled. It was meeting time. Man time. Macho time.

The Gun Club was a secret society of fraternity men, its existence known only to its members and alumni, all pledged to silence. It sat high atop the interfraternity pyramid; its members selected who was admitted into Beta Beta and Skull and Keys below it, and ultimately, the Gun Club itself, the supreme inner circle, the Who's Who of Fraternity Row. So named because it originally met at Landigunner's Bar in San Francisco when it was founded near the turn of the century, the club convened by candlelight every Thursday at 7 P.M. in the Tomb. Members talked of a bond that was ten times stronger than their other fraternal affiliations, a bond based on the club's exclusivity, secrecy, ritual, and the belief that they were truly the dozen most cat's ass guys on campus. Its alumni roster included Chief Justice Earl Warren. It was a club with a history of almost no jocks, the theory being that jocks were too involved with their sports and too dedicated to their training to be able to participate in the weekly debauchery of the Gun Club. Steve was the first football player to make the inner circle in almost a decade.

The club's initiation ritual was part of the bond, taking place on a stage in a rental hall in San Francisco in front of alumni and members. Steve's performance was legendary. Like every other inductee, he was brought individually in front of the members and ordered to drop his pants, then told he would be timed to see how long it took him to screw Betsy, reputed to be the biggest "nigger whore" in Oakland, the copulation to be witnessed by all those present and the time recorded in a sacred log. After several agonizing minutes, with the members yelling and passing the gin bottle, Betsy was finally brought out. But instead of being a "nigger whore," she was a silver-handled, sixteen-ounce flagon filled to the brim with gin and beer, to be downed within two minutes. Upon finishing off his sixteen ounces, Steve took one step forward, then barfed all over the Gun Club alumni seated in the first row.

The weekly Gun Club meetings were a ritualistic combination of straight shots of gin, personality analysis, and poetry reading, sort of a drunken T-group session to the sound of Rudyard Kipling. Presiding over each meeting was the Hebe (pronounced "heebee"), the only junior in the club. The Hebe (who in mythology was the Greek goddess of youth and the cupbearer to the gods), wore a red wig, brought the gin, maintained order, and led the opening chant that set the club's decidedly macho tone. He was also responsible for calling on each member to read a selection from the prized red book of poems, a book that included only male poets, i.e., Jack London, Mark Twain, Robert W. Service.

Steve loved the Gun Club, thriving on its essential maleness. He stood to recite Service's "Willy the Lady," the club's signature poem, raising his voice loud and strong when he reached his favorite verse:

> ". . . The world is full of women, and the women full of wile;
> Come along with me, Willy, we can make you smile!
> Come and have a Man-Talk . . ."

After the meeting, Steve, Don, and Terry Holberton, their close friend and fellow Gunner, adjourned to the Fern to continue their drinking. It was after midnight when he called Ayris, who had moved out of the AO Pi house and was living in an apartment on Channing Way. Their romance was full-throttle. Almost. She still found it difficult to completely trust him, knowing that he had kept his marriage to Linda a secret so long. But he was now promising, unequivocally, that it was over between him and Linda and that the divorce papers had been filed. It was true. He'd made it clear to Linda, however, that since it wasn't his idea to get married, he wasn't going to pay for the divorce. The papers were sitting unsigned at a lawyer's office. When Ayris, whose father was a Lebanese Catholic, asked him how Steve could rationalize a divorce with his Roman Catholic upbringing, he explained that he and Linda had been married by a justice of the peace, not a priest, so therefore the marriage was never sanctified by the Church. Ayris could buy that. What she had trouble with was his penchant for getting blotto and then calling her in the middle of the night, wanting to come over and get affectionate. Usually, she would refuse, telling him she'd see him in the morning when he was sober. These lapses into loutish behavior embarrassed and confused her. Seemingly, his sole purpose was to get hopelessly, helplessly drunk, which was so unlike him when they were alone and sober and he was being tender and gentle and talking of his dreams and holding her hand.

"Not tonight, Steve," she said on this Thursday night, rolling over to go back to sleep.

But he was a young man not easily deterred . . . and he had the impressive linebacker press clippings to prove it, like the one in the Berkeley *Gazette* that said he had been "nothing short of brilliant this season . . . smelling out plays like a beagle and scattering blockers like a lawn mower scatters grass." With Holberton riding on the back of his Honda 350, he roared up Telegraph on his way to Ayris's apartment. Despite the hour, he was wearing his usual riding attire—Levi's, white T-shirt, and aviator sunglasses. Joe Cool.

Arriving in front of Ayris's apartment building, he parked his motorcycle on the sidewalk and studied his route to her third-floor unit. The security gate was locked. He asked Holberton, an amiable, ruddy-complected intramural boxing champ from Santa Monica, to give him a boost. Up he shimmied, Tarzan, using a drainpipe to propel him upward. As he swung out to grab the railing of the third-floor balcony, his hand slipped. "Oh shit!" he yelled, falling like a rock, caroming off a railing below, landing with a thud on the sidewalk. He clutched his side.

The X rays at Cowell Hospital showed two cracked ribs. The doctor bandaged him up and released him, but recommended he avoid contact for a month. That would mean he wouldn't be ready until the Big Game, the last game on the schedule . . . and that would be the end of his shot at All-Coast, and maybe even the pros. A headline in Friday afternoon's *Gazette* declared: "Cal Grid Romeo Hurt in Fall from Balcony."

At practice on Friday, dressed in gray sweats, his cracked ribs tightly taped, he stood in the middle of Edwards Field, gasping for air, not about to surrender to the pain. And he was definitely in pain.

"Go, Rat, go!" chanted his teammates, who had formed two parallel lines for him to run through. "Go, Rat, go!"

Coach Willsey, whom Steve preferred to Coach Levy because of his tougher style, had responded to Steve's claim that he was well enough to play on Saturday against the Huskies by telling him that he'd let him play if he could run ten consecutive 60-yard wind sprints at the end of Friday's practice.

"One more to go, Rat," his teammates encouraged, clapping their hands in unison. He couldn't catch his breath. Every step was like being smashed across the back with a two-by-four. This was the *biting, tearing pain*, even more than the Heet on the testicles.

Standing at the end of the players' corridor was Willsey, a short man, his thick arms folded across his chest, a Marlboro dangling from his lips. He had been scowling and mute during each of Steve's first nine sprints, all of which had been accompanied by the robust cheering of his teammates and the *biting, tearing pain*. There were more physically gifted athletes on the squad, but nobody commanded the respect of his teammates as much as Steve.

"Let's go, Romeo," yelled Willsey, "stop stalling."

Steve took off, each step pure torture. But there was no doubt in his mind, or his teammates' minds, or Willsey's mind, that he would make it. When he crossed the finish line, Willsey just turned and walked off the field, saying nothing, lighting another Marlboro. Steve, too, just turned and headed off the field, still refusing to bow to the pain.

On Saturday, the Bears beat the Huskies 16–12, the first time in eight years that Cal had won three games in a row. Steve, taped like a mummy and shot full of cortisone, went down with a badly sprained ankle in the third quarter. He would hobble through the rest of the season, but never close to full power again. In an embarrassing 56–3 shellacking at the hands of All-American Gary Beban and the UCLA Bruins, he was knocked senseless, his third brain concussion of his career.

On pro football draft day, his name was not called. Though he would not admit it to friends at the time, he shed a tear. Playing linebacker in the NFL, he had hoped, might have been a good way to prove himself, once and for all, to his old man.

June 11, 1966, was a glorious sunny day in Strawberry Canyon's Memorial Stadium. Steve, dressed in his navy-blue cap and gown, sat up straight in his metal folding chair, listening attentively to the commencement speakers. There were some students in the Class of '66 who had chosen not to participate in the graduation ceremonies as a sign of protest against the University, and there were others who had refused to stand during the playing of the national anthem as a sign of protest against America's policy in Vietnam. But for Steve, the chance to walk across the stage and receive his diploma was the crowning achievement of his young life, better even than anything he'd accomplished on the football field. He had studied hard, and despite his frequent excursions into debauchery, pushed himself at exam time, graduating from the School of Business Administration with a 2.9 g.p.a., the first in his family to complete a college education. It gave him an important sense of self-respect, and it was, he felt, his greatest gift to his father, the hardworking immigrant who'd come to America with nothing and dedicated his life to providing for his family. For all their differences, Steve knew what his degree meant to his father. Frank and Mary were in the stands, just as they had been for every athletic contest he'd ever played in in the state of California.

Sitting a few rows in front of him was Ayris, also in her cap and gown. They were in love, but what the future held for their relationship, neither could say. After the ceremony, she was returning to L.A. with her mother; Steve was going to Sacramento for a party his parents were throwing in his honor, then in July he was leaving for Calgary, Alberta, having accepted an invitation to try out with the Stampeders of the Canadian Football League. There were no guarantees. But it was worth a shot.

He was sad to be leaving Cal. He loved his four years in Berkeley and all the activities: Football. Pi KA. The Gun Club. He had even enjoyed being a witness to FSM and the campus unrest. Cal had taught him to be open to new ideas and had unlocked his intellectual curiosity. But his future was unclear. He was twenty-two . . . he had a degree in business, an invitation to try out for the Stampeders, a wife and child, a serious girlfriend, and a new 1A listing with his draft board.

The graduation speeches and the ceremony ended, and as he rose with his fellow graduates for the singing of "Hail to California," he felt a lump in his throat and a tear in his eye.

> Hail to California, Alma Mater dear—
> Sing the joyful chorus
> Sound it far and near,
> Rallying 'round her banner—
> We shall never fail—
> California, Alma Mater. Hail! Hail! Hail!

PART TWO

Postgrad

Vietnam Vietnam Vietnam, we've all been there.
   —Michael Herr, *Dispatches*

24

Ron

West Berkeley is to the University as Gary, Indiana, is to the Louvre.
—Ron Fimrite, *Sports Illustrated*

Sitting at his drafting table, Ron stared off into space, lost, unable to concentrate. It was 1965 and he had been on the job as an apprentice architect for Paul R. Williams, his godfather, for six months.

"Ron, can I see you in my office in five minutes?" said Mr. Williams, a good-looking man of fine features, deep voice, and an assured, dignified presence. "I want to talk to you."

There was something stern and ominous in Mr. Williams's tone, Ron thought. Was he being called on the carpet? Fired? He had that same knot in his stomach he did whenever Coach Walsh had glared at him for missing a block. The week before, Mr. Williams, one of the first nationally recognized Negro architects with a large clientele, had summoned him to his office to discuss making a $1,200 mistake in one of his drawings and for submitting a design on a remodel of a Negro fraternity house in Southern California that would cost four times as much as the client had to spend.

Ron was churning inside. On the outside he looked vigorous and full of pride. He had an apartment in Manhattan Beach, a degree from Cal, and a sporty Triumph Herald he bought from a woman in Santa Monica. But inside he felt unenthused, disconnected, restless. He had thought about leaving L.A. Part of it was knowing that Daddy had helped get him the job. He didn't want to be riding his father's architectural coattails—it was the same pride that had made earning a football scholarship at Cal so important to him.

He was going through the motions at work, finding it hard to stay on task. He felt ineffective, inadequate . . . mad at himself for not forcing himself to learn. The job had great potential—Williams was well respected, there was a diversity of projects. How lucky could a guy fresh out of college be? He had already worked on the designs for a Fedco building on La Cienega Boulevard and an African Methodist Church in downtown L.A.

But the truth was, he wasn't enamored with Mr. Williams's style—it was like his father's style, too conservative. Ron was interested in new concepts of design—that's what he had excelled in at Cal—but in the real world of architecture, there were details to consider—building codes, costs, time. That seemed like such an intrusion on his art. He wanted to design modern masterpieces, not worry about wiring regulations.

Mr. Williams had been generous with his help, covering Ron's $1,200 mistake. But Ron wasn't about to go to him with what he needed help with the most—his broken heart. He hadn't talked to anyone about what had happened between him and Kristi. It still hurt. He had gone to Hawaii right after graduation to try to forget the pain before starting his job with Williams, and while he was in Honolulu he received a letter from her, sort of an "it was nice knowing you, goodbye forever" missive. After he read it, he sat under a palm tree and cried.

He'd hoped that moving back to Southern California, away from the memories and the Berkeley streets they had walked down together, would help heal the hurt. It hadn't. He felt lost in L.A., which seemed to him, as Raymond Chandler once said, a city rich and vigorous, but a city lost and beaten and full of emptiness. He got depressed every time he listened to the news: Malcolm X murdered, Vietnam buildup, marchers beaten in Selma. He was sharing his Manhattan Beach apartment with Roger Popper, a goat brother from Pacific Palisades who was working toward his Ph.D. in psychology at UCLA. Ron envied Roger's élan. He was touseled-haired, good-looking, glib, intellectual, great volleyball player, the only Pi KA with a Phi Beta Kappa key. There was a certain mystique about Roger . . . witty and charming, yet aloof and detached. Their apartment was three blocks from the beach in a neighborhood swimming with beautiful women. Roger liked to hang out at Cisco's, a local hot spot, and Ron sometimes tagged along, always feeling out of place. The routine was usually the same—they would walk in and lean against the bar, surveying the action. Two minutes later, Roger would be deep into existentialism with the blonde of the night, and Ron would be standing to the side, feeling timorous, marooned.

His transition from the relative warmth and comfort of college to the real world was off to a shaky start. He no longer had the luxury of closing off the world while he lost himself in his studies. That's what he'd done for five years, focusing all his energy on his degree. In Berkeley, whenever he'd thought about one of his serious issues . . . the baby he'd abandoned, the broken relationship with Kristi, the racial-identity stuff . . . he'd just swept it under the rug and opened his textbook, reassuring himself that a degree would cure everything, guarantee success.

But now that he had his coveted diploma, he found himself sitting at his desk at work and brooding about things gone wrong. There was no homework at night for escape. Swilling cocktails and trying to pick up "chicks" at Cisco's wasn't helping. He had wanted to get away from the central L.A. area where he grew up, but the beach scene felt awkward— the surfers, the stews, the parties, the parade of tans in beach thongs and bathing suits. It was too casual, too hang loose. He was a college graduate and felt an obligation to be responsible and wear button-down collars and wing tips.

He had no connection with anybody his own age. As much as he admired Roger, they traveled in different worlds, sometimes going days without seeing each other. And his old high school buddies were either moved away or married. His high school sweetheart, Jackie, had married too. He missed the male companionship the fraternity and the football team provided. He joined a Los Angeles rugby team, hoping to make friends that way, but he felt more like a mascot than one of the players. He traveled with the team to a tournament on Catalina, drinking the beer, singing the bawdy songs, even going so far as to commandeer a bike and ride it off a pier . . . all in an impotent attempt to be one of the guys. The harder he tried to connect, the more removed he felt. He wasn't close to anyone at work.

He was spending more and more time with his parents, joining them for social gatherings with their friends. They tried to get him involved in their campaign efforts for the Democratic Party—Ralph was the treasurer for Jack Hawkins, a minority candidate for the L.A. City Council. But there was no connection there either. Sitting around a living room with a group of people in their fifties discussing Mayor Sam Yorty wasn't his idea of a fun night. It felt as if he was regressing to adolescence, spending too much time trying to be the perfect son again. He was no longer Ron . . . he was back to being dutiful Ronnie. He appreciated his parents' passion and commitment to civic issues and civil rights causes, but he wondered if their time might be better spent getting their own house in order. Betty was drinking more than ever and Ralph's business was sailing into perilous financial waters, overextended.

He walked into Mr. Williams's office, taking a seat across the desk. Mr. Williams cleared his throat, a father about to deliver a lecture, or in this case, a godfather.

"I've been worried about you, Ron," he said, softening his tone. "You don't seem yourself. Is something bothering you?"

"No," lied Ron, smiling. "Everything's fine."

Two weeks later he moved back to Berkeley.

His lemon of a Triumph Herald sputtered and coughed as he crossed the Bay Bridge, heading home to his empty house after another day on the job in San Francisco. It was the summer of '65 and he was now working as a junior draftsman at $600 a month for Joseph Esherick, a small, avant-garde firm in San Francisco. And he was living in a small, stucco, two-bedroom, run-down bungalow in west Berkeley near Emeryville, an ethnically mixed neighborhood, many miles from the stews and Coppertone eddy of Manhattan Beach, and a far cry from the stately fraternity and sorority houses of Piedmont Avenue and the rustic brown shingle homes of the professors and professional people in the Berkeley hills. He still felt disconnected.

He took the Ashby Avenue exit off the freeway, driving through the industrial and then the low-rent part of town, his part of town. Despite its growing reputation as an educated, cultured, and radical enclave, racism was still a fact of life in Berkeley. The city was governed by conservative Republicans who controlled policies through the Berkeley *Gazette,* meetings at the Elks Club, and the City Council. Landlords and realtors openly discriminated against minorities, even though the minority population of the community had grown from 4 percent in 1940 to 12 percent in 1950 and to 23 percent by 1965. A city that had been virtually all white had become in less than a generation a racially mixed community, with the concomitant tensions. Despite the racial mix, 99 percent of the Negroes lived in the flatlands of West Berkeley, which was becoming the political and cultural backbone of the city, home to the culturally diverse population that would form its permanent character. It was a neighborhood of unemployment, low-cost housing, and crime.

Ron walked into his house, not even bothering to go to the fridge. There was nothing in it, and even if there was, he wasn't hungry. His appetite, once so ravenous that he could devour four plateloads of fraternity macaroni and cheese, was practically zilch. He sat cross-legged on the hardwood floor and turned on the TV, watching the distressing news of the Watts riots—34 dead, 898 injured, 4,000 arrested, $200 million in damages, 15,000 National Guardsmen, entire blocks torched, a death toll higher than the week's losses in Vietnam. And it was happening in the shadow of his boyhood backyard, not Saigon, not Birmingham, not Newark.

He watched the rioting and the looting and remembered all the times he'd gone to Watts as a child with his parents. He was torn. Of course Negroes had a right to be frustrated and angry, he thought, but he wasn't convinced that gave them the right to go rampaging through the city, abdicating all responsibility to society. He felt his own deepening sense of frustration—at the injustices, at his own lack of involvement. If he believed in eliminating injustice, shouldn't he be conducting himself in a more active way? It was almost as if he was still back there at that window in the Durham Holiday Inn, watching the demonstrators, feeling guilty, hiding behind the curtain. Watts was another stick of kindling on his smoldering inner turmoil, the same old self-identity stuff that he had been ignoring for years. Who was he? If he was Negro, shouldn't he be conducting himself in a more masculine way? To be a Negro man in America, he thought, was to carry a certain signature, a distinct persona —tough, macho, fearless. So where was that coolness and bravado? As far as he was concerned, he didn't measure up as a Negro man; he was inadequate, not tough enough to punch back. He was sure his ancestors wouldn't approve of his lack of participation, his failure to express his ethnic identity. His feelings went back to his middle-class minority childhood, back when the kids on the block hit him and instead of fighting back, he ran home to Mommy. In high school and college, football had helped ease those feelings of inadequacy, giving him a stack of masculine press clippings to prove his mettle. But football wasn't tied to real issues of black and white—it was just a sport, not who he was. In the summer of his junior year at Cal he had spent time in Watts, going there to visit with a friend, Jim Bates, a former star football player from Manual Arts High, an inner-city school. They listened to Marvin Gaye records and hung out. To Ron, it was almost as if Bates was trying to teach him how to be a Negro, exposing him to L.A. Negro culture, introducing him to Negro girls. But he was afraid to step across the line, choosing to stay undeclared. In his mind, to say that he belonged to one group—Negro or white—meant that he had to cut his ties with the other. He knew he was Negro, but he said nothing, ignoring the issue, preferring to trudge ahead as always, just as his parents had instructed him. But subconsciously it was the fifties California culture, vanilla in color, that he had adopted as his own, despite having grown up on a block with no white people and having attended a grammar school that was two-thirds Negro. He had learned at an early age that white was the color of privilege and acceptance in society, and the most important thing to him, by his own admission, was acceptance. He desperately wanted to be liked and to succeed, and the easiest road was the one that was white. To broadcast his blackness was to jeopardize his chances. So why risk it? Why make life tougher than it already was? When he joined the fraternity, he liked the lifestyle and shared the values of some of the brothers. He had pushed aside personal issues in order to belong. When guys started slinging around racial epithets, he removed himself, became an observer, figuring as long as he didn't deny he was Negro he was being honest. Nobody ever asked. Because he was "passing" as white he got to see real racism, unrestrained bigotry—goat brothers watching football on TV and rooting for the tackler to "knock the nigger's head off." And because he was associating primarily with white society, he was creating his own dual identity, building a complex. It was a case of confusion more than denial. He turned off the news.

"Are you sure you didn't move to San Francisco just to get away from me?" he asked.

Trude Kiestler, a tall, thin twenty-three-year-old, with high cheekbones, long, straight black hair, and a confident smile, stopped in the middle of the sidewalk and looked at him askance. They were on a walk near her apartment in Pacific Heights.

"That's ridiculous," she said. "How could you even think that?"

"I'm really, really sorry," he said.

He first met Trude shortly after moving back from L.A. She was living in Berkeley at the time, working in the ticket booth at the Shattuck Theater to help support herself and her art classes. What attracted him, even more than her good looks, was her presence and her thick Austrian accent. At first, their relationship had proceeded smoothly—dinners, movies, Sunday walks in Tilden Park. Trude was a film buff. Her roommate was French and Ron enjoyed just sitting and listening to them talk —it seemed so international, so worldly. Being around them was forcing him to examine the dating habits he'd learned in the fraternity, which suddenly seemed so juvenile and immature, where sex was the target and guys encouraged relationships that didn't last, and if you thought otherwise you were square and weird. He'd become convinced that the two biggest loves of his life—Jackie and Kristi—had failed because he'd been too focused on himself and getting his degree, driving them away because he wanted sex but wasn't able to commit. He was determined not to make the same mistakes with Trude. He even alluded to marriage as sort of a trial balloon, but she quickly dismissed it as "silly talk." When she moved to San Francisco to take a secretarial job with Fireman's Fund Insurance, he began to wonder if he was trying to move too fast, if she'd moved to get away from him. Maybe he had acted too impetuously. It was hard to know. He was confused as to what was the right speed. The last time he had talked to her she had mentioned that she was applying for a job as an overseas stewardess.

"Have you heard anything more about your stewardess application?" he asked as they continued their walk.

Yes, as a matter of fact, she had been accepted and would be starting training in Kansas City in a month.

Ron stopped. "You're doing this to get away from me, aren't you?" he said, suddenly picking her up and putting her on his shoulders.

It scared her and she made him put her down. "What's wrong with you, Ron?" she asked. "You've changed in the last two months. What happened to the easygoing guy I first met? I don't even know you anymore."

That was the last time he would see Trude. She became a stewardess and on one of her first flights, a military charter, the plane crashed on takeoff in New Jersey, killing everyone aboard.

He sat at his drafting board, lost in his head, his mind a million miles from his work. He was startled by a tap on his shoulder. It was his boss, Joseph Esherick.

"Can I see you in my office?" asked Mr. Esherick.

Ron desperately wanted to do well on this job. Esherick, a tall, dignified man whose firm would later win the prestigious American Institute of Architects award for the firm of the year, was on the front edge of design, originating his own unique Bay Area style of architecture, one that was sensitive to the natural environment. He was also a professor at Cal, and Ron had impressed him with his creativity and earnest attitude, enough so that when he applied for a job, Esherick hired him on the spot. In Ron's eyes, Esherick was light-years ahead of the design style of either his father or Mr. Williams in L.A. He had been assigned to work on the Cannery, a new shopping and restaurant center near Fisherman's Wharf. It wasn't glory work—he was checking blueprints, deciding where to put drain spouts, choosing toilet fixtures—but he felt honored to be working with such a distinguished architect as Esherick, awed by the skills of the other architects. So why then, he kept asking himself, wasn't he thrilled to get up and go to work and rub elbows every day with the best and brightest of California's T-square-and-triangle set? Why was he having so much trouble concentrating?

"I just wanted to see if everything's okay with you, Ron," said Mr. Esherick. "You seem a little off lately. Anything the matter?"

"No," answered Ron. "Everything's fine."

As he put on the brakes in front of his house, he winced, the sound of metal against metal grinding on his nerves. In a state where you are what you drive, he was an accident waiting to happen. The electrical system of his Triumph Herald was shorting out and every morning he had to flag down somebody on the street to give him a push to get it started. The car also had a broken headlight, no turn signals, and four unpaid mechanical-violation tickets sitting on the dashboard.

He hurried into the darkened house and headed for his bedroom, stumbling over a pile of dirty pants and shirts. It wouldn't do any good to flip on the light. Pacific Gas and Electric had turned off the power. The water was shut off too. For two weeks he had been living in the dark and showering at Harmon Gym on campus on his way to work, except on those days when he was running late and didn't have time. On those days he just used a lot of extra Right Guard.

He had the money to pay the bills, but he was trying to save every penny he could from his weekly paycheck. He wasn't sure why. Maybe for his getaway. His roommate, Dave Powell, had moved out without paying his share of the bills, claiming he didn't owe anything because Ron had been mooching all his dope.

It was Powell, a blond, goateed, unemployed carpenter, who gave Ron his first taste of marijuana. They had met at Edwards Field—Ron had gone there to watch the football team practice, thinking that a revisit to his old blocking grounds might lift his spirits. They struck up a conversation on the sideline, continued it over a pitcher of beer at Kip's on Durant Avenue, and a few weeks later they were roommates. The first time Powell handed him a joint was the first time Ron had ever seen marijuana. Drugs had never been part of his world. Not in the fraternity, not at parties, not at work, not on Telegraph Avenue. "Everybody's doing it," maintained Powell. Reluctantly, Ron tried it. And liked it. It loosened him up, he believed, and made him think profound thoughts.

He rummaged through his top dresser drawer, hoping to find enough seeds and stems to roll together one joint. No luck. He walked back into the living room and sat down in the dark, plotting his course for the evening. Maybe John Albert was having one of his parties. Trude had introduced him to Albert, a Negro art professor who lived on the north side of campus and was known for his eclectic parties—women in saris, men from Harlem, dope of Mexico, people talking about Langston Hughes and Timothy Leary. Guests at Albert's parties wore sandals, not wing tips or penny loafers.

Socially, Ron wasn't sure where he fit. Was he part of the growing counterculture? A nine-to-fiver? A jock? He joined another rugby team, Peacock Gap in Marin County, a squad made up mostly of ex-Cal football players, but he quit, feeling more removed than ever. And he was totally out of sync with the fraternity scene.

Sitting in his dark and empty house, no milk in the refrigerator, no water in the faucet, he pondered his place in the cosmos. Where to go? What to do? Maybe if he moved to San Francisco, he reckoned, it would be a fresh start. He could walk to work and not have to worry about getting a push every morning. That was one incentive. So was getting out of Berkeley, a place he no longer felt connected to. Again. Yes, he concluded, he would definitely move to San Francisco. That was the solution. He hoped.

25

Larry

Hedy Takes a Pitcher-in-Law
  —*Life,* July 23, 1965

Denise and I pulled to a stop in front of her mom's house in Westwood. We had been to see Ike and Tina Turner at Ciro's on Sunset. It was after midnight and all the lights were out. In the morning I was leaving for spring training in Florida . . . and who knew when we would see each other again. Soon, I hoped, a boy in love. I had given her fourteen cards on Valentine's Day.

"Good, Mom's asleep," she said. "We can go in, but we've got to be really quiet. I don't want to deal with her."

We tiptoed into the living room, keeping the lights off, wasting no time finding a cozy spot on the floor behind the couch. Denise's room was upstairs next to her mom's and she didn't want to risk it. This would be our farewell embrace.

I still hadn't met the mysterious Hedy. Denise hadn't said much about her, referring to her only as her "weird mom" and mentioning something about her "problems." I assumed she was talking about Hedy's much publicized divorce, her sixth, this one from L.A. lawyer Lew Boies, a messy affair with charges that he attacked Hedy in a drunken rage with a baseball bat. My father used a baseball bat to hit me grounders.

I had made no effort to plumb Denise for details of her family background. I thought she was half Jewish, but other than that, I didn't know much. I knew nothing about her past sex life except that she had that high school boyfriend with a weird name . . . Chevy Chase. She was gorgeous—that's all I needed to know. I didn't know if Hedy was a millionaire or broke. I hoped she was a millionaire.

I knew that Denise and I came from different worlds, although just how polar I had no idea. My parents were from Utah and Indiana, hers were from Vienna and London; Hazel was PTA secretary, Hedy didn't cook; my dad came to all my ball games, Denise hadn't seen her father, John Loder, since she was three—no birthday cards, no phone calls, no love. She did, however, have a childhood of material abundance—big houses, expensive clothes, maids, chauffeurs. When she was ten, her mom walked into her room and found her making her bed. "Don't do that," Hedy ordered. "That's why we have maids." In the exclusive River Oaks section of Houston, where Denise lived when Hedy was married to millionaire oilman and fifth husband Howard Lee, she was chauffeured to school every day in a limousine, always ducking down in the back seat and making the driver drop her off a block away so the other kids wouldn't think she was different. Every trip out into the public with her famous mother was a public spectacle . . . people pushing and shoving, flashbulbs popping. Denise didn't like it.

Her childhood had also been one of cultural abundance. Despite the divorces and the distortion of Hollywood, Hedy, who spoke six languages, insisted that music and art and the best of European culture be integral parts of Denise's and her brother Tony's lives. Family gatherings centered on the Steinway. Denise had to watch "Omnibus" every Sunday. Art became her passion; she spent endless hours in her room painting pictures, the one thing that brought her consistent praise. In the ninth grade—after Hedy moved back to California following her divorce from Lee—Denise attended Beverly Hills High. With the exception of Candice Bergen, none of her friends were the children of movie-star parents. In the tenth grade, she and her brother were sent to Stockbridge in Massachusetts, a private boarding school with an emphasis on the arts. She was happy to be away from the social pressure of Beverly Hills High and the insecurity of her mom's notoriety, mood swings, and erratic Hollywood lifestyle. Denise traveled to Europe to study in Paris her junior year. In my junior year at Westchester High, I traveled to Tijuana with a friend who was getting his '53 Ford customized with tuck-and-roll upholstery.

"Oh no!" uttered Denise. "I just heard Mom's door open."

Suddenly, a lithe silhouette appeared at the top of the staircase in a slinky silver nightgown. We dove onto the couch, frantically pulling on our clothes. There wasn't time to zip up. I placed a throw pillow over my lap.

"I heard voices," said Hedy, her thick Austrian accent descending the stairwell ahead of her.

"Larry's here," replied Denise.

"Oh good," Hedy said, "I'd like to meet him."

I didn't dare stand for my introduction to "the century's most beautiful woman." She took a seat in the chair opposite us, the room bathed in shadows, lit only by the faint light from the lamppost across the street.

Hedy talked nonstop for an hour, a meandering stream of consciousness about USO War Bond tours, Judy Garland, being on the set at 5 A.M. Whatever. It was a verbal knuckleball and I couldn't get a glove on it, the words floating by, disintegrating in the dim light. Then she made her exit, ascending the stairs, disappearing back into her room.

"Now you've met my mother," sighed Denise. "Weird, huh?" She was no Hazel Colton, that was for sure.

Denise and I kissed long and passionately, her goodbye tears staining her mascara. I cried all the way home. Love hurt. Tomorrow I was going pro.

Flying to minor-league spring training camp in Leesburg, Florida, I wondered what to expect and which farm team I would spend the season with. The Phillies' six Class A teams (Eugene, Ore.; Portsmouth, Va.; Bakersfield, Calif.; Spartanburg, S.C.; Miami, Fla.; and Huron, S.D.) all trained in Leesburg, and which team I was assigned to depended on how well I did. I imagined big ol' farm boys from Kansas able to throw through the side of a barn, and surly sons of steelworkers squeezing the sawdust right out the end of their Louisville Sluggers. I felt like I did walking to Orville Wright Junior High to start the seventh grade, jittery as hell, positive all the ninth-grade boys were going to beat me up and pull down my pants.

We were lodged in the Magnolia Hotel, which was right out of a Tennessee Williams play—weeping willows brushing against the windows, rocking chairs on a long veranda, Early American furniture, lace doilies in the lobby. But it was a *down* sort of place . . . the phone and the television were *down* the stairs, the bathroom was *down* the hall, the coffee shop was *down* the street, and the Negro ballplayers were *down* the road, segregated to another hotel. Mom had neatly folded my clothes in my suitcase, hiding the chocolate-chip cookies under my white boxers. I set Denise's picture on my nightstand.

Located in the middle of the state and billed by its Chamber of Commerce as a "pleasant surprise," Leesburg was surrounded by lakes filled with largemouth bass . . . and alligators. That's what Moose Johnson, one of the coaches, told us at rookie orientation.

"Don't be doing no fuckin' swimming in none of the fuckin' lakes around here," he instructed. "Fuckin' gators bite your leg off. Make it fuckin' hard to hook-slide."

Moose was a crew-cut blond, squat-bodied, bowlegged, gravel-voiced, tobacco-chewing ex-minor-leaguer who would be coaching the team in Spartanburg. I hoped I got assigned somewhere else, preferably to Bakersfield. That way I could be close to Denise, and Dad could come and see me pitch.

"I want you fuckin' pitchers to keep a warm-up jacket on your arm between innings," Moose advised, draping a jacket over his right arm to demonstrate. "And for you fuckin' left-handers, you guys put it on this other arm."

Moose and the other coaches promised to keep a tight rein on the 180 ballplayers in camp, many of whom were away from home for the first time, hormones blazing. Only ten of the players were Negro or Latin. At twenty-two, I was one of the oldest players in camp and one of only a handful with a college education. By the end of the second day my nickname was "the Professor." I didn't tell them I had a 2.18 g.p.a. Our only pay was five-dollars-a-week laundry money. We got box lunches at the ballpark and chits for breakfast and dinner at the Tradewinds Cafeteria, a ten-minute walk from the hotel. That's where I met my first bowl of grits. No wives or cars were allowed in camp. Curfew was 11 P.M., and nobody was allowed to leave the city limits.

"You're here to be ballplayers, not no fuckin' Casanovas," bellowed Moose.

Being a Casanova in a town where alligators outnumbered the girls was tough. I saw *Inside Daisy Clover* with Natalie Wood, the only movie in town, three times. Every night I walked down to the pay phone next to the First Florida Bank, pulled out my bag of quarters, and called Denise in Berkeley, spending $200 of my remaining bonus in the first two weeks. We burned up the lines, repeating how much we missed each other and how we couldn't wait to be together again. We had talked of marriage, but that was something for down the road, we agreed, maybe in two years when she graduated from Cal, or when I made the major leagues. We weren't engaged, nor had we taken any vows of celibacy. It was just understood, unspoken, like most of everything else between us.

At the ballpark, my locker, which was three nails and a milking stool, was located next to the toilet. A sign warned players not to flush when the shower was in use. My baggy uniform was heavy gray flannel, and in the Southern-fried heat it was like burlap in Hell Week. I was number 128. Although they issued me a size 7 1/8 hat for my 7 1/4 head, I was lucky, because the guy who had worn it the year before had already stretched it a couple sizes.

I lockered next to a skinny eighteen-year-old freckle-faced pitcher who could hum that pea. He was known to all his friends back home in South Carolina as Flyrod. He'd had a tough time deciding whether he wanted to be a ballplayer or a stock car racer—he kept a picture of his new four-barrel Plymouth Sports Fury next to his nails. One day before practice— it was the week President Johnson called in 3,000 National Guardsmen to protect demonstrators in their second attempt to march from Selma to Montgomery to register black voters—I asked him what he thought of the civil rights movement.

"Back in South Carolina I'm known as a 'nigger lover,' " he said, coating his face with zinc oxide.

"How so?"

" 'Cause I think they should give 'em a break," he said. "Just hang 'em from low trees. That way the bottoms of their feet can scrape the ground. Gives 'em hope." I had never seen segregated drinking fountains before Leesburg. But I'd heard a lot of "jokes" like that around the fraternity.

In my first intrasquad game, I pitched three innings. Nine batters up, nine batters down. Four strikeouts. "Nice fuckin' job," said Moose. I was surprised the caliber of player wasn't better, convinced that there were fifty players in camp who couldn't have made first string at Cal, and yet there they were, running around under the hot Florida sun, some of them with bonus money falling out of their wallets. Of course, nobody talked about how big their bonus was or how much they were making. Management liked it that way, so that during contract time in the winter nobody could say that so-and-so was making such-and-such. Only movie stars and the FBI had agents.

Across the street from the main field was a pockmarked sandlot that was used as an auxiliary diamond for batting practice and fundamentals. It was Baseball Hell, a gravel pit with bases, known as Diamond 2. Fly balls hit into deep left center disappeared into a swamp and nobody volunteered to retrieve them. Practice on Diamond 2 was halted the day Papa Alligator slithered out of the reeds to sun himself in left field.

"Put a fuckin' uniform on him!" yelled Moose.

After a month of being cooped up in Leesburg with Flyrod and the mosquitoes, I broke the rules and fled the city limits. It was with Doreen. I met her one Sunday morning at the Tradewinds Cafeteria. She was a doe-eyed blonde home from Georgia Southern University on vacation, and she suggested we take a drive down Route 44 to check out the spring-break action at Daytona Beach in her daddy's white Oldsmobile convertible. That sounded like an American cultural phenomenon more intriguing than shagging balls on Diamond 2. I couldn't resist her soft Southern drawl. Or her Southern great bod. Flyrod had even started to look good.

"Y'all have a girlfriend back in California?" she asked.

"No," I answered, taking another swig of beer as we cruised into Daytona. I'd never seen guys wearing loafers without socks before, or cars on the beach. Baseball was teaching me lots about culture already.

It was two hours after curfew when Doreen and I returned to Leesburg, parking around the corner from the Magnolia. My roommate, a pitcher from California, had been released the day before and I had the room to myself. I invited her up, telling her we'd have to sneak up the back stairs so the coaches wouldn't see us. She accepted, but made it clear she could only stay for a few minutes. "Now don't y'all go getting any ideas," she said. I figured I'd hide Denise's picture before she noticed.

We were walking around the rear corner of the hotel when Moose suddenly appeared. Leaving Doreen behind, I took off like a big yellow Sports Fury, around the block and down the street. When I snuck back, Moose was gone. And so was Doreen, forever. But there was a note pinned to the door of my room. It was from Paul Owens, the scout who'd signed me. He had been promoted to executive director of the Phillies' minor-league spring-training camp. The note instructed me to report to his room . . . "no matter how late it is."

"Damnit, Larry," he snapped, sitting on the side of his bed in his underwear. "You've got a bright future in this game. Don't be stupid and fuck it up!"

The next day I received a notice from the Selective Service System that my draft status had changed from my 2S deferment to 1A. It was the same day President Johnson upped the ante, launching Operation Rolling Thunder, a long campaign of air strikes by Navy jets against North Vietnam.

I loaded the bat bags into the baggage compartment, part of a rookie's rites of initiation into the baseball fraternity, then boarded the "Iron Lung," the team bus. In twenty-four hours I would be making my pro debut. Bob "the Whale" Wellman, the robust manager of the Eugene Emeralds of the Northwest League, the highest of the six Class A farm teams in the Phillies' system, had tabbed me as the starting pitcher for the league opener, a road game against the Wenatchee Chiefs, a Chicago Cub farm club. I was already pooping in my pants.

The Iron Lung was baseball's answer to the "goat head." The exterior looked like it had been used as the target for the Oregon bowling team; its original red-and-white paint job had lost its sheen in the Harding administration. Top speed was a rivet-rattling 50 miles an hour. It had no air conditioning, no toilet, and only two windows that opened. Half the seats were broken and springs pressed skyward through the ripped upholstery. In the rear, the last two rows of seats had been taken out and replaced by two makeshift beds, which were nothing more than six-foot planks of plywood, with no mattress, no pillows, no blankets. One was reserved for the starting pitcher, the other for the catcher. I opted for a seat in the second row, directly behind the Whale, seated in the manager's traditional shotgun seat. I could live with the broken seat back.

We rolled out of Eugene in a drizzling rain, ten hours to go to Wenatchee. A game of hearts dominated the middle seats. "Lock up your women, Wenatchee!" cried a voice from the rear. "Here come the Emeralds!" A thick cloud of cigarette smoke drifted overhead.

Seated across the aisle from me was Jim Perkins, the only Negro on the team, an outfielder. He was from Compton, California, and had huge shoulders that tapered down to a 31-inch waist. He was soft-spoken, friendly, and could hit the ball "a fer piece," but this was his sixth year in A ball, and maybe his last. According to the scuttlebutt, he "jaked" it when he wasn't hitting well, a term I'd already heard applied to several Negro players.

I was learning the baseball jargon, and much of it had to do with "chasing pussy," the sport within the sport: a "mullion" was an ugly girl, a "safety" was a sure thing in the next town, an "Annie" was a baseball groupie, and a "Bruce" was a homosexual. I wasn't sure why, but a couple of the players had started calling me Bruce. Maybe it was because I'd been to college. Or because I didn't chew tobacco. Or because I was from California. I could only guess.

Two hours out of Eugene the Iron Lung caught fire, smoke and flames pouring from the engine. For five hours we stood by the side of I-5, waiting for a backup bus, taking turns hitting fungoes off of an overpass and bowling baseballs through the passing cars at tin cans across the freeway.

"Welcome to the bush leagues!"

It was daybreak when we finally pulled into beautiful downtown Wenatchee and checked into the hotel, a dump that made the Magnolia seem like the Fontainebleau. I hadn't slept a wink on the bus, staring out the window at the evergreens passing in the dark. In the seat behind me, the shortstop snored and farted the night away. And this was what I had been dreaming about my whole life.

A crowd of 616 fans ventured out of the apple orchards to brave the 39-degree night air and witness the season opener. In California I'd never played in weather below 75. My mound opponent for the Chiefs was Lee Meyers, who would gain his fifteen minutes in the baseball spotlight three years later when he married actress Mamie Van Doren. But that night belonged to me. I struck out four of the first five batters and got a hit my first three times at bat, including a line-drive double off the top of the right-field wall to drive in two runs. I ended up with a seven-hitter, striking out eight. We won 6–4, and the way I figured it, I already had one foot in Cooperstown. I didn't even wait until we got back to the hotel to phone Dad, calling him collect from a pay phone right outside the ballpark.

"I didn't have my good stuff," I swore.

It was the perfect place to start a marriage . . . the grandiose All Saints Episcopal Church on Rodeo Drive in Beverly Hills . . . with arched corridors, forty-foot stained-glass windows, red-tiled roof, flowered courtyard. The weather outside was idyllic, 80 degrees, gentle ocean breeze, smogless blue skies.

Denise was a nervous wreck.

I turned to watch her walk down the aisle toward me, so beautiful in her white wedding gown, the rays of sunlight through the stained-glass window backlighting her radiant dark hair. So elegant the audience uttered a collective gasp. They couldn't have guessed the chaos.

This was not a shotgun wedding, but rather a napalm marriage, one shaped by American foreign policy in Southeast Asia. When my Uncle Sam told me he needed me front and center at the induction center on July 12, I quickly revised my long-range plans and proposed to Denise in room 7 of the Continental Motel in Eugene. She accepted and we set the wedding date for July 10, 1965. (Married men were exempt.) We had known each other four months, three of which I had lived in another town. I had, however, learned a few more things about her: she wasn't half Jewish and her mom wasn't a millionaire anymore. Darn it. We talked more about the future than the past. The bright lights and a career in Hollywood were not what she sought. She wanted normalcy and a family, like what she saw when she sat in the breakfast nook at my house, watching my mother fixing dinner in the kitchen and my father practicing his putting on the rug. I still didn't know for sure if she was a virgin when we met and she didn't ask me how many girls I had slept with. (It was four—Mary and three Fucking Moos.) But I wasn't getting married to get laid or to dodge the draft. I was in beaucoup love. I was twenty-three, she was twenty.

All the details and planning for the wedding had fallen on her shoulders—reserving the church, ordering the invitations, organizing the reception, registering for china, coping with her mom. I was in Eugene, pitching away, set to fly in the day before the wedding. Hedy was in a fog, either unable or unwilling to do much of anything. Denise suspected it was a combination of the fall from public adulation, too many divorces, and money worries. Hedy's latest romantic interest was a twenty-five-year-old, unemployed French artist. Hedy was fifty-two. Denise also suspected that the burden of Hollywood and the silver screen and being "the century's most beautiful woman" had chewed up her mother, much as it had her friend Judy Garland. And Marilyn Monroe. Hedy was no longer the glamour queen or top box office, and now her beautiful daughter was getting married and leaving home, such as it was.

Denise had sent a wedding invitation to her father in Argentina, not quite sure what she was expecting in return. For him to walk her down the aisle? A trust fund? An apology for not having contacted her in sixteen years? He responded with a Hallmark card signed: "Best Wishes from Your Father." She threw the card in the trash and cried.

At the wedding-rehearsal dinner at the Tail of the Cock restaurant on La Cienega Boulevard, I had introduced Hedy to Mom and Dad. It was Ward and June meet Delilah. They didn't say boo to each other the whole evening. I had never seen Mom so tense, her jaw clenched too tight to chew. Hedy was Hollywood, and Mom wanted nothing to do with it. And Hedy, evidently, wanted nothing to do with suburbia.

Denise continued down the aisle, escorted by Neal Marvin, a gentle, silver-haired prop director at M-G-M who had long adored Hedy and was as close to a father as Denise had ever had. My best man was Tony, Denise's younger brother. I picked him so I wouldn't have to choose between my friends. I might have picked Dexter, but he was in Danang.

"I now pronounce you *man and wife*," said the preacher.

We walked back down the aisle between the 300 guests. Hedy had not invited any of her show-biz friends, not even Bette Davis, Denise's godmother. It was a church full of aunts, uncles, friends, and fraternity brothers. I didn't invite Jim; Loren was in Australia; Steve was in the last pew with Ayris; and Ron was circling the block in his Triumph Herald, too embarrassed to come inside the church because he didn't have a date.

We walked out the door, shielding our eyes from the Beverly Hills sunlight. Waiting to greet us was a small phalanx of news photographers, bored paparazzi on a slow news day. They waited until Hedy exited, then cameras clicked and popped. The caption under our picture in *Life* would read: "It was a posh wedding in Beverly Hills and former film star Hedy Lamarr, 52, looked as radiantly happy as she had at all six of her weddings."

She wasn't happy at all.

"I can't wait to get out of here," whispered Denise.

After the reception at the Santa Ynez Inn, Denise and I changed into our getaway clothes—she in her hot-pink skirt and jacket, me in my blue-gray sharkskin suit—then headed to Hedy's house. My parents were right behind us in their car, Hedy right behind them. The plan was to quickly unwrap the wedding presents, pick out the essentials we needed to start housekeeping, then load them into a U-Haul and drive to Eugene in Denise's '58 Thunderbird. The team had given me four days off. The car and trailer were already hitched and ready to go in Hedy's driveway. So was Denise's trousseau.

"Let's get this over with fast," urged Denise.

Hedy had recently moved from Westwood into a ranch-style three-bedroom house on a secluded dead-end street in Coldwater Canyon, a mile north of the Beverly Hills Hotel. The house was in disrepair, weeds growing between the cracks in the patio, shrubs dying, no water in the swimming pool.

Dad and I carried the gifts into the house and spread them around the living room. Denise and Hazel sat on the floor, unwrapping; Hedy sat in a couch, Tondelayo on her throne, observing. It looked like sale day at Filene's Bargain Basement—wall-to-wall toasters, place mats, pillowcases, monogrammed towels, silverware, knickknacks, electric doodads. The silence between Hedy and Hazel loudened. I occupied myself packing the U-Haul.

"Which toaster should I pack?" I asked, pointing to the three we'd received.

"I don't know," replied Denise. "Mom, which one do you think we should take?"

"Why don't you ask her?" she pouted, nodding toward Hazel.

"I'm asking you," said Denise.

"What the hell do I care what toaster you take?" replied Hedy. "God knows I always had a toaster for you."

"What's that have to do with it?"

"It has everything to do with it," said Hedy. "But obviously you don't understand."

"What don't I understand?" asked Denise.

"That I've given you the best years of my life. Do you think I enjoyed getting up at five A.M. to go to the studio and work all day long? I sacrificed everything for you and your brother. For what? To get treated like this?"

"Treated like what? What have I done to you?"

"Everything. Nothing. You wouldn't understand."

I definitely didn't understand. This wasn't bases-loaded-two-out-in-the-ninth tension. That kind of tension was make-believe and manufactured, governed by rules and managers and played out on grassy fields with a case of beer waiting in the clubhouse. This tension was real—mother-versus-daughter warfare. A surreal Hollywood psychodrama. I wasn't prepared. I'd never heard Haz and Nellie raise their voices . . . now I was in the middle of a family minefield, grenades exploding, a mother groping in the twilight of lost glamour, a daughter wanting to escape. It was "the century's most beautiful woman" clinging to her little girl while Ward and June and their $8,000-bonus baby stood in the middle, mouths down to our suburban shoes. Hazel looked at me as if I was standing at ground zero and the bomb was already out the bomb-bay door. Dad continued to carry things to the U-Haul, undisturbed, just another day on the putting green.

"Who gave you that?" asked Hedy, pointing to a large, expensive crystal bowl sitting in the middle of the floor.

Denise closed her eyes, realizing she had forgotten to make a list for thank-you cards of who gave what. She started writing feverishly.

"How could you forget?" huffed Hedy.

"I just did."

"Forgot? Did I forget to take care of you? Answer me that."

Denise stiffened. "Mom, you haven't lifted a finger for this whole wedding."

"Haven't lifted a finger?" screamed Hedy. "Let me tell you what I've done. Who do you think paid for your whole life?"

Denise waved her arms. "I don't want to hear it. I just want to get out of here."

"Good . . . go ahead and leave. I don't give a damn! You can stay with the Coltons next time you're in town."

Denise handed me the last box to pack, a set of green plastic glasses with flowers and fruit painted on the side, given to us by my Aunt Florence. Denise followed me toward the U-Haul.

"You're not taking those ugly things, are you?" asked Hedy.

"Yes," replied Denise.

"I guess you don't care about good taste and culture and everything I've taught you . . ."

Denise stepped out the sliding-glass doors onto the patio, then pivoted abruptly, facing her mother, who was adrift in a sea of wrapping paper.

"Fuck you, Mom!" she screamed, giving the finger with both hands. "Fuck you!"

I'd never heard her say "poop" or "damn," and now she was yelling "fuck you" at her mother in front of God and Hazel, who stared in disbelief. Dad just kept on packing.

"Let's get out of here," pleaded Denise.

I set the box of glasses into the U-Haul, then shut the door and closed the trunk of the T-Bird. Finally, we were ready to exit, to start our life together. I reached for the car key. It was locked in the trunk. And we didn't have a spare.

To the west—beyond the empty pool and the bougainvillea and the palm trees—the sun was starting to set and the California sky was turning a beautiful crimson. But things were already dark at Hedy's. I slammed my hand against the U-Haul, then went inside to call a locksmith. He said it would take two hours before he could get there. Oh great, I thought, plenty of time for a cozy little family dinner . . . we could drink from our green plastic glasses and have all the toast we wanted—that is, if Hedy had any bread in the house . . . or if Denise didn't have a nervous conniption . . . or if Hazel or I didn't implode first.

Without saying a word, I walked out the front door and headed up the driveway.

"Where are you going?" asked Denise.

"For a walk," I answered, not looking back.

Aimlessly I ambled. And thought. Thinking and walking. Down one Coldwater Canyon street, up another. Staring into space. Staring at the expensive houses. Twenty minutes later I was standing in front of the entrance to the Beverly Hills Hotel. Dressed in my turbocharged sharkskin, surrounded by XKEs and Continentals and Fleetwoods, I was mentally overwhelmed and emotionally underequipped. I wasn't thinking about the injustice in Watts or the Marines in Danang or the race to the moon. I was thinking about me. I had a mother and a mother-in-law sneering at each other like the Hatfields and the McCoys; I had been married three hours and I was already walking away.

But I was no longer 1A.

I looked up into the gathering darkness, turned, and headed back to the house. When I walked in the door, Denise was in tears and Hedy was in a back bedroom. My parents had left. Mom literally threw up when she got home.

Mercifully, the locksmith arrived to liberate the key. At long last, we were ready to go. "Are you going to say goodbye to your mom?" I asked. Denise shook her head.

Twenty minutes later, stuck in traffic on the Ventura Freeway, I turned to her. "So how do you like being Mrs. Colton so far?" I asked. She cried all the way to the Vandenberg Inn in Santa Maria. When we arrived at our apartment in Eugene two days later, there was a telegram from Hedy that triggered more tears. I interpreted its terse message to mean that Denise had been disowned. A few days later, Hedy sent us a new color television, leading me to conclude that either I had misunderstood the telegram or Hedy had undergone a dramatic change of heart and decided not to disown her daughter after all. Or maybe she forgot that she had sent the telegram. In any case, I was happy to be married.

26

Ron

We have to smash down the walls.
—Huey Newton

Another Friday night alone in the city. Head down, eyes to the floor, he slinked into the small corner market around the block from his basement apartment on Union Street in San Francisco and headed for the junk-food shelf. With his back to the cashier, he scooped a package of Hostess Ding Dongs into his coat pocket. Then fled into the night.

Back in his dimly lit kitchen, he opened the Ding Dongs and set them on the kitchen table in front of him. It was his low-budget dinner, pretty much the same one he'd had two weeks in a row, most of them stolen. With a knife and fork, he cut them into quarters. On the busy sidewalk outside his small window, people were walking and chatting—the Great Society coming alive on a Friday night on the modish Union Street. But for him, it was another restless evening alone, out of dope, out of sorts.

The move to San Francisco hadn't cured his funk. Slowly, methodically, he ate half his dinner, pausing to lick his fingers. He walked to the window and peered out beneath the blind, watching a couple stroll by holding hands. They looked so natural, at ease, relaxed. Why couldn't he be like that with girls? he wondered.

He wasn't stealing Ding Dongs for lack of money. He couldn't explain why he was doing it, just as he couldn't explain why he was depressed.

He was making decent money—$600 a month at Joseph Esherick, socking half of it away into a savings account, probably to buy a new car. His Triumph was ready for the junk heap, the rear end now crumpled like an accordion after the emergency brake failed on an incline near Union Square and the car crashed into the side of a taxi.

He put his second Ding Dong in the refrigerator, then got himself ready to go pay a visit to Maureen, a redheaded legal assistant who lived a few blocks away. He checked himself in the mirror. He looked bad, maybe worse. The sparkle was gone from the eyes; he was no longer a robust collegiate athlete—he was wan and pale.

At Maureen's, he buzzed her apartment. No answer. Just as well, he thought, turning to leave. The real reason he was there was to mooch a joint, and if she was there, he'd have to lie about why he'd come. Not that he didn't like her. She was pretty and funny and bright, working for a prestigious law firm. She was a Cal grad and they had dated briefly before he met Kristi. But he felt as if he was using her . . . for her sex, her pot, her company on lonely nights. That didn't feel right—he'd grown up in the fifties and knew that boys weren't supposed to take advantage of girls. He was confused by the new morality that was afoot in America and the old sexual barriers coming down.

Maureen was a connection to the past. Seeing old college friends made him uneasy—he worried that they would be judging him, talking behind his back. He turned down invitations to parties with ex-teammates or Pi KAs, afraid that he wouldn't be dressed well enough, or that somebody might ask him what happened between him and Kristi, or that everybody would think he was weird because he didn't bring a date. He didn't have the tools to explain himself.

Walking to the rear of Maureen's apartment building, he glanced up, noticing that her second-floor window was open. He checked to see if anyone was watching, then quickly climbed atop a brick wall and hoisted himself through her window. He went directly to the dresser in her bedroom where she stashed her pot. Hearing footsteps approaching down the hall, he grabbed some dope and stuffed it in his pocket, then climbed out the window and walked home. Back at his kitchen table, he smoked a joint and polished off his second Ding Dong, thinking profound thoughts.

He sat at his drafting table, trying to get up the nerve to go knock on his boss's door. He was worried that Mr. Esherick would try to talk him out of quitting. Or maybe that he *wouldn't* try to talk him out of quitting. Or that Mr. Esherick would say, "You're right, Ron, you are doing a horseshit job and you should think about another career, something a lot less challenging."

Ron felt as if he'd failed on his last project. His assignment had been to render preliminary design and program development for a children's mental retardation ward at the Langley Porter Psychiatric Center of the University of California Medical Center in San Francisco. He had poured himself into the project. The state had asked for preliminary designs because it was studying the possibility of changing the method of caring for severely and moderately disturbed children—moving away from warehousing toward the establishment of residential care facilities in the community, with homelike environments, activity areas, and sleeping quarters. As part of his research, he had gone to a state hospital to observe existing facilities, his first exposure to the severely disturbed. Viewing the hydrocephalic children was distressing, bringing up old guilt over the son he'd abandoned. Was the boy healthy? Did he have good parents? Where did he live? Ron was hoping that in some way his work on the project would serve as penance, but instead it only intensified his guilt. The project had also raised new levels of anxiety about his professional competence. Most days he left the office feeling overmatched, guilty about his contribution, embarrassed that he wasn't handling his share of the work. Because the Langley Porter job was a health-care project, there were rigid code specifications to follow . . . codes he knew nothing about. By coincidence, Steve Thompson, one of his goat brothers, was working for the state in Sacramento as a researcher for the Department of Finance and had been assigned to write an evaluation of Esherick's design proposal for Langley Porter. While he was in San Francisco gathering information for his evaluation, Thompson spent a night on the couch in Ron's apartment, surprised and concerned about the plight of his old fraternity brother. It wasn't just the Ding Dong wrappers on the floor, or the hair in the tub, or the pile of dirty dishes in the sink. It was the lost and troubled look in Ron's eyes. In the morning Thompson was awakened by a naked woman walking through the apartment, a go-go dancer who had stopped by to see Ron on her way home from work. Ron apologized profusely, worried that Thompson, who was married, wouldn't understand the situation and think him unfit to be working on a project for handicapped children and Esherick would lose the bid. Thompson did, in fact, recommend that the state not fund the project, but it was because of budget cutbacks, not Ron's morality. Nevertheless, Ron thought he was partially to blame.

He knew a lot of his thoughts were irrational, but there didn't seem to be anything he could do to control it. Weird thoughts kept filling his head—he imagined himself levitating down the sidewalk, he saw dead dogs stacked in a corner, he watched clouds making love. He wondered if it had something to do with a strange evening he'd spent with a woman named Katrina, a potter he'd met at one of John Albert's eclectic parties in Berkeley. He'd gone to her apartment and they sat cross-legged on the hardwood floor, listening to sitar music, surrounded by everything saffron, drinking Red Mountain wine from earthen goblets, toasting each other with interlocked arms. When he left the apartment the next morning, he walked outside and saw vivid colors and breathing flowers and pulsating sidewalks. He wondered if she'd slipped him LSD. And maybe that's why he was thinking such strange thoughts, feeling so light-headed.

His courage finally corralled, he walked into Mr. Esherick's office and hurriedly told him he thought it was in everyone's best interest if he resigned. Much to his relief, Mr. Esherick didn't tell him to think about another line of work. Nor did he try to talk him out of it. He was saddened by Ron's condition, telling him to take some time off and sort things out.

On September 27, 1966, Governor Pat Brown broke off his reelection campaign tour in his race against Ronald Reagan to fly to San Francisco, where angry Negroes had set fires, broken windows, and looted stores in retaliation for a white cop's shooting a Negro youth fleeing in a stolen car. Brown ordered in 2,000 National Guard troops and 300 Highway Patrolmen to the Hunters Point District near Candlestick Park. The next day the unrest spread to the Fillmore District on the northwest side of town. Nine people were shot.

From his apartment, Ron followed the news reports on TV, watching helmeted police with shotguns and automatic rifles, marching ten abreast down the street. He saw Guardsmen in jeeps, carrying 105 mm recoilless rifles. This wasn't Selma—this was five miles away. It didn't make any sense. Neither did the news that two U.S. Marine planes in Vietnam had bombed a friendly village by mistake, killing twenty-eight Montagnard tribesmen and destroying a hundred homes. Nor did the panhandlers outside his front door.

He had moved again—his fourth move in a year—this time to a run-down apartment building on Hyde Street, around the corner from the downtown YMCA. Vagrants and winos sprawled in front of the entrance. Sirens filled the night. Mice roamed the halls. When he walked outside, he tossed his spare change to the panhandlers on the curb.

He felt pinned down, under siege. Who were the good guys? Who was he? The summer of 1966 had been hostile, blacks across America striking back—Chicago, Cleveland, Philadelphia, Omaha, Dayton, Atlanta. The more he watched of the riots and the more he read of James Meredith, or Martin Luther King, Jr., or Stokely Carmichael—men with the courage to stand up to the fire hoses and the dogs and the shotguns—the more he questioned his own values. The emergence of Black Power militancy was particularly unsettling. When he was growing up, overcoming prejudice was to be done quietly, slowly, within the system. Ralph and Betty spoke out through their work, or political campaigning, or the NAACP. He was raised to play by the rules, to embrace moderation and the conciliatory approach of men like Booker T. Washington. In high school, when he'd confronted the black nationalism preached by Marcus Garvey, it struck him as being too radical.

The doctrine of the Black Panthers and the espousal of violence made him uncomfortable, much the way he felt that day in Dwinelle Plaza listening to Malcolm X call for a separate black nation. But it was forcing him to make a closer examination of his own identity at a time in his life when he was already confused. To him, the new stronger and more strident voice from the Negro community was asking him to make a conscious decision: either he was a Negro for civil and economic rights at any cost or he wasn't. There could be no middle ground, no more walking the line, no more pretending he was just one shade on a big happy continuum. How could he openly embrace both cultures when men like Huey Newton were proclaiming it was hypocritical for Negroes to patronize white society? It was a call to arms.

The summer riots and the sight of armed National Guardsmen marching toward his neighborhood were evoking a greater sense of partnership with the goals of the Black Power movement, not with its violence, but with the need to smash down walls . . . his own walls . . . to start anew. He had no commitments, no self-worth. What he had was a smorgasbord of guilt, beating himself up over the racial issue, flailing himself for his failures with women, for abandoning his son, for doing poorly at work. The state's decision to veto the Langley Porter project weighed heavily on his mind—he was convinced that emotionally disturbed children needed proper facilities, not warehousing, and he had let them down. He was a failure as an architect, a father, a son, a man. So he thought.

He had to get away. Unjumble his mind. Change his lifestyle. The answer, he decided, was to go on an odyssey across America and figure out who he was.

. . . . .

The assistant supervisor of the San Francisco clinic for retarded children followed him to the door to thank him, but it was too late. Ron had just handed her $1,500 in cash from his savings, telling her to make sure it went to help the children, then turned abruptly and hurried out the door without leaving his name.

Somehow, in the fog that was now shrouding his mind, he hoped that this munificence would help absolve his sins of abandoning his son and failing on the Langley Porter project. It was his second act of philanthropy of the day. His first stop had been Lowell High near Kezar Stadium, where he drove his Triumph up to the door of the auto shop, flipped the keys to the teacher, and said, "Give it to one of the kids."

He bought a '64 VW Bug and hit the road. But before he could go out in search of himself across America, he needed to try to unload one very large piece of excess baggage that he'd been carrying around for four years. He drove to L.A. and contacted the family service agency that had handled his son's adoption. He confessed that he was the father. He knew the agency wouldn't reveal where his son was, but he hoped that by coming clean it would help relieve some of his guilt. And if the boy ever did decide he wanted to know who his real father was, then Ron's name would be on record.

Maybe he would go his whole life and never get to meet his son. But at least now there was a chance.

It was October when Ron headed east out of L.A.: the pill was six years old; "Bonanza" and "The Red Skelton Show" were one-two in the Nielsens; and according to John Lennon, the Beatles were more popular than Jesus. Sitting behind the wheel of his Bug, Ron had no specific destination, only vague ideas in his head and $200 in his pocket. He had not gone far when he came up with a plan—or maybe he'd had it in the back of his mind the whole time and just didn't want to admit it. He would go to Chicago. But first he would go to Oklahoma City and see Kristi. It had been two years since she had dropped the bomb on him, but he knew their relationship had ended with so much left unsaid and unresolved. He had so many questions for her. Did she ever think about him? Was she happy? What would she have said if he had asked her to marry him?

He drifted through the Southwest, zigzagging across New Mexico and the Texas panhandle, sleeping in the back seat at night, waking up with the light of morning. Maybe he'd take a detour to Dallas, maybe not. The more he drove, the deeper inside his head he traveled, searching for answers to questions he didn't know. He passed the turnoff to Dallas and thought about Craig, who was now with the Cowboys, a world beyond

Ron's grasp. He and Craig had not been close at Cal, and even if they had been, he'd be too embarrassed to go see him now.

On the outskirts of Oklahoma City, six days and 1,600 miles after his odyssey had begun, Ron stopped at a pay phone and looked up Kristi's number under her husband's name. But what if Bill answered when he called? Should he hang up? Ask for Kristi? And what was he supposed to say to Kristi when he did reach her? That he was sorry? That her father was a racist butt hole?

He dialed the number. It rang once, twice, then he hung up. What if Kristi didn't want to talk to him? He dialed the number again. Bill answered.

"Is Kristi there?" Ron stammered.

"She's not here right now," Bill said. "Can I take a message?"

"Just tell her Ron called," Ron answered. He got back in his car and left town, no explanation, no attempt to call back. His odyssey continued.

Standing on the sidewalk in front of a tall office building on Michigan Avenue in Chicago, he shivered against the cold gray November day, his only protection a light windbreaker. He was down to his last two dollars.

Initially, he had come to Chicago to see Mr. and Mrs. Henderson, friends of his parents. He felt he owed them an apology. Just before he'd left on his odyssey, Ralph and Betty had invited the Hendersons' beautiful twenty-one-year-old daughter to their house for dinner. She was a senior at USC. Betty had it in the back of her mind to do a little matchmaking for her son. After she and Ralph went to bed, Ron had tried to put an unexpected and inappropriate move on the beautiful daughter on the living-room couch. She protested—loud enough to wake Betty—and to send Ron into another embarrassing tailspin of guilt. Maybe by coming to Chicago and apologizing, he figured, he could relieve some of that. But once he got to town, he reasoned no apologies were necessary.

Nothing had been going right for him in the Windy City. When he'd first arrived, he picked up a young hippy hitchhiker, who told him a tale of woe. Ron felt so bad for him that he gave him $75, leaving himself with only $25. That made him feel better. For a while, anyway. Disheveled and in need of a shower, he had driven to the Roosevelt Road slum area on the South Side, not far from the Cage Park district, where two months earlier angry whites had thrown rocks and a knife at Martin Luther King, Jr., setting off a night of violent rioting. He was turned away at a flophouse hotel, one with bars on the windows and beds for ninety cents a night. He went to another one down the street. Same result. He couldn't figure it out. Was he being discriminated against because he looked like a white boy? He checked into the YMCA.

For two weeks he had been walking the cold and windy streets of Chicago, talking to himself, trying to fight off the chill. But there was something noble about it, he told himself, being down and out in the American heartland, in the City of Big Shoulders. He sat at the edge of the Chicago River, staring at the murky water, the wrapper from his Ding Dongs blowing off in the breeze. He applied at the *Tribune* for a job as a newspaper boy. Maybe he'd stay the winter. Sorry, they said, no openings.

As he continued to stand in front of the tall building on Michigan Avenue, he watched two businessmen exit the building. They both wore expensive topcoats.

"Any spare change?" he asked, needing a dime for a phone call.

The two men looked the other way.

"Assholes!" he mumbled.

He muttered to himself about the injustice—he had given $1,500 to help handicapped kids and $75 to a needy hitchhiker, and now these assholes in their fancy topcoats coming out of their fancy offices wouldn't even give him a lousy dime. Didn't they understand that he wasn't the normal panhandler, that he had an architect's degree, that he once caught touchdown passes against USC and Penn State, that he once had a beautiful sorority girlfriend?

He went to a phone booth and called Sam Stassi, an ex-goat brother and football teammate, who was attending dental school at Northwestern. Sam was from Sacramento, a 190-pound offensive guard when he was at Cal, the older brother of Swampfox, Loren's close friend. He had a dry wit, a four handicap in golf, and a new wife. Ron was not about to beg him for money—that would be too humiliating—but at least Sam would be a friendly face. They made plans to meet at a bar on Rush Street. Sam invited Jess Pittore to join them. Jess was another ex-goat brother and football teammate, a smooth-talking, handsome Italian from Napa who was working for a Chicago travel agency.

The last time either Sam or Jess had seen Ron he was hale and fit, a varsity receiver. When he walked in the bar, gaunt and drawn, 165 pounds, their mouths fell to the sawdust floor. "Looks like you walked here from California," observed Jess. Shortly after their beers arrived, a fight broke out two tables away, a wild melee—chairs flying, bottles breaking, fists flailing. Sam and Jess leaped atop their chairs for a better view. Ron didn't budge, staring into his beer, hands folded, ignoring the bedlam. Later, when order was restored, Sam invited him to his house in Des Plaines for dinner and to meet his wife.

"We gotta get some food in you," he suggested.

"I don't want to be an imposition," said Ron. "If I get in the way, just tell me and I'll go." He insisted on following in his car.

Twice on the way to Des Plaines, Sam had to pull over to make sure he hadn't lost Ron. When he turned into his driveway, signaling Ron to pull in behind him, Ron just kept going, down the block, around the corner, and into the night, no wave goodbye, no explanation. He didn't want to mooch, he didn't want to see a happy couple. His odyssey continued.

27

Loren

I have never thought of equality when I thought of women. I have always put them on a pedestal.
—John Wayne

He couldn't keep his eyes off her. She was the best-looking thing he'd ever seen. Auburn hair, five-ten, blue eyes, cover-girl smile, legs to eternity. There were a few beauty judges around the country who agreed with him. She was an ex-Miss California. And if that wasn't enough, she was also the winner of the Swimsuit Competition at the Miss America Pageant in Atlantic City, dazzling Bert Parks and millions of TV viewers in her shocking electric-pink swimsuit.

"I want her," he declared as she ran past him.

"No way she'll go out with you," predicted his roommate, Tom Blanchfield. "She's a priss."

"We'll see," he replied.

He and Blanchfield, an ex-football teammate who the brothers in the Pi KA house thought was either the dullest guy on campus or the most conceited, were standing on the sidelines at Kleeberger Field, one of the University's intramural facilities. Watching sorority girls play powder-puff football had suddenly become Loren's favorite spectator sport. Especially now that he'd discovered his fantasy woman, the ex-Miss California, who was the star flanker for the undefeated Delta Gamma juggernaut and a sophomore majoring in communications and public policy at Cal with a 3.4 g.p.a. She was well rehearsed in the company line about Miss America being a scholarship pageant, not a beauty contest.

It was fall 1965. Loren, the assistant sales manager of the Product Finishing Company in Oakland, was still in a collegiate mentality, focused on the good times, definitely in no rush to settle down. Surprisingly, the Raiders had agreed to give him another chance to come to training camp. But that was not for another seven months. Until then, he would work a little, play a lot. He no longer had to worry about the draft board—the doctors had declared him 4F. The knee injury he'd suffered in rugby, though not bad enough to keep him out of Raider camp, would keep him out of Vietnam. He maintained that he would have willingly served.

As the ex-Miss California returned to the sideline, her jersey splattered with mud, Loren's eyes hung like Slinkies, demanding a reply. She ignored him.

He turned to Blanchfield. "She's as good as mine," he said, winking.

He sat on a stool on the raised platform behind the cash register at UC Corner on the corner of Telegraph and Durant, his head on a swivel, watching all the coeds walk by. He was already ten minutes late for his first date with the former Miss California.

"Mercy!" he declared. "That little tomato's not wearing a bra. Very sweet!"

He was a regular at UC Corner, the busy paperback book and sundry items store. It wasn't a love of Balzac or Hemingway or the out-of-town newspapers that drew him there—it was a great girl-watching perch. He also had sort of a proprietary interest in the store, which had been a Berkeley landmark for twenty-five years. Craig was now part owner, having invested $10,000 of his bonus from the Cowboys into the business, which was owned by Lester Olson, the father of Craig and Loren's ex-roommate, Jerry Olson, who was now managing the store. Mr. Olson had encountered financial troubles—rumor had it that he was losing big at the racetrack—and Craig had stepped up and helped bail him out with a ten-grand infusion of cash. Loren, Craig, and Jerry had kicked around the idea of opening another UC Corner, maybe on the north side of the campus or in Davis, with Loren managing it. But that little entrepreneurial venture could wait. First, he had his sights set on becoming an all-pro defensive back . . . and getting close to the former Miss California.

He picked her up at the sorority and walked her to his car, a '64 Ford

Galaxy that his boss said would be better for his business image than the '57 T-Bird he'd been driving. Waiting for them in the back seat were three rugby teammates whom he had brought along for support, sort of designated shit-givers in case the former Miss California tried to get too snobby or prissy on him.

Loren had no ambivalence about how things were supposed to work in a relationship. It was simple: men were the master class, the recipients of privilege and power. Women stayed at home with the kids and their feelings; men worked in the world and made the big decisions. "It's a man's world," he liked to say. And manliness meant being in control, taking charge. In the World According to Hayseed, women's preordained status in life was to come in and try to influence a man's life and tell him what to do. Or change him. Or blame him. Or make him feel guilty. It was ingrained in them when they were little girls, he said. And he was determined not to let a woman tell him what to do. No girl was going to boss him around, not even the former Miss California.

Despite warnings from her sorority sisters that he was a fast-talking, compulsive seducer, the former Miss California had accepted his offer to go see *Cat Ballou* because, in her words, she wanted to find out for herself who this big wolf was. He had a thing or two to learn about her too. She was determined to have people realize she was more than just the winner of the Swimsuit Competition. Raised on a cul-de-sac in a bedroom community in the East Bay, she was the oldest of four children. Her father, a high school teacher, was a retired Army officer, a stern disciplinarian, slow to express affection or approval. In high school she'd been the classic high achiever—honor society, majorette, winner of the Science Fair, member of the swim team. It was her father who entered her in the local beauty contest, even helping to hem her dress the afternoon of the pageant. She won that contest, and finally Miss California, performing a Juliet Prowse rendition of a jazz baton dance in the talent competition. She looked like Priscilla Presley. In her onstage interview, she named her mother as the woman she most admired. At the Miss America Pageant in Atlantic City her victory in the Swimsuit Competition was not enough to wash away her disappointment at not winning the Big Title. She retreated backstage in tears, positive that she had let down not just her family and supporters but all of California. Still, for winning the Miss California and the Swimsuit Competition, she received a college scholarship and a full wardrobe, including a mink stole. She traveled the state for a year on a public appearance tour and received a new Oldsmobile that she got to trade in every 3,000 miles, each new model bearing a Miss California plaque on the door. At Cal, she was a serious student, irritated by the tactics of the demonstrators, resenting the campus disruptions. She was there to learn, hoping to parlay her good looks, poise, and education into a career in business. To earn extra money, she modeled fashion shows in San Francisco.

By the time Loren pulled his Galaxy into the theater parking lot, he had decided he would not be needing the services of the three goons in the back seat. This ex-Miss California, he'd decided, was not such a "snobby tomato" after all.

"You're dismissed, boys," he said. By the end of the movie, he and the new love of his life were holding hands.

The former Miss California drove Loren's Galaxy over the Golden Gate Bridge, hurrying to get to the Oakland Raiders' training camp in Santa Rosa. He had called her from his motel room, telling her to get there as fast as she could. There was an urgency to his voice that she had never heard before. It was August 1966.

Their relationship had taken off like gangbusters right from that first date. He'd applied his full-court press, demanding her time and attention. And she willingly obliged, convinced he was the most powerful, take-charge, dynamic guy she could ever imagine, the exact opposite of her strict father—spontaneous, passionate, outrageous in his emotions. And because he was four years older than she, he seemed so much more worldly, mature. The fact he was soon to be an Oakland Raider didn't hurt either. The only drawback to the relationship from her standpoint was that he had made it hard for her to keep up with her studies. He was ready to party seven nights a week, tracking her down at the library and enticing her to come have beers with him at the Rathskeller, smothering her with his relentless energy. It was Balzac who said that beauty could "never be won by a languid lover," and Loren, even though he wasn't up on his Balzac, had taken her on tour with him—a double-date ski weekend at Tahoe with Craig (whose marriage to the Santa Monica blonde had been annulled); a homey weekend at the ranch house with Pop and Eddie. She sensed he was making a concerted effort to bring her into his family circle. He wanted a one-on-one relationship, he said, and so did she. When she asked him about the other women in his life, he assured her they were a thing of the past. "Ask my friends," he said. "They'll tell you how much I've changed for you. All the other women I've been with are down here on one level, and you're way up here on a pedestal."

She took the Santa Rosa exit off Highway 101 and drove to the team's motel. She'd been there to visit him a few days earlier, their picture appearing in the Oakland *Tribune* with a caption about the former Miss

California visiting her boyfriend, the former Golden Bear, soon to be a Raider. Loren was optimistic about his chances for making the starting unit. He had the size and the leaping ability, and figured that it didn't hurt that his ex-coach at Cal, Bill Walsh, was now a Raider assistant under head coach John Rauch. In his first preseason game, he'd knocked down two passes and recovered a fumble in the Astrodome against the Houston Oilers. He and his training-camp roommate, Fred Belitnikoff of Florida, were the rookies getting most of the media attention.

She pulled into the motel parking lot, surprised to see him standing in front of the office. In the year that they had been dating, she was hard pressed to remember him ever being on time. On the pavement next to him were his suitcase and athletic bags. He wore a long face.

"The assholes cut me," he said, throwing his bags in the back. "They had their team picked before camp ever opened. Didn't make a damn bit of difference how I did."

They rode in silence back to Berkeley. She had never seen him so downcast. In fact, she'd *never* seen him down at all. In the back of her mind she wondered if he had taken it seriously enough in advance. He hadn't worn himself out in preparation—no long hours rehabilitating the knee in the weight room, no long wind sprints or stair climbing, no midnight oil pouring over the playbook. His knee felt fine, he'd said, and his natural athletic talent had always carried him through . . . so why change anything? She didn't question him on it. He said the coaches had asked him to stick around and be on the taxi squad, but he had better things to do with his life than go to practice every day and hope somebody got injured.

"Who gives a shit anyway," he said.

Unaccustomed to seeing him down, she didn't know what to say or how to comfort him. She knew him well enough to understand that beneath the anger and the "I couldn't give a shit" attitude, his pride was wounded, but that he was too proud to admit it.

"So what's next for Loren Hawley?" she asked.

A good question. In many ways, he mirrored the political face of California. Despite the state's accent on the new and the young and the liberal, and for all its casual lifestyle, the Golden State was riding a new tide of political conservatism, Loren tight astride it. He wanted to move away from Berkeley, unhappy with what he saw happening to his alma mater. He was part of what political analysts were calling the "Berkeley backlash" that Ronald Reagan hoped to ride into the governor's mansion. Reagan was making Berkeley an issue in the campaign, playing to the growing fear of California taxpayers that the campus was nothing more than state-supported anarchy, a place of "drugs, sex, and treason." In a speech he'd suggested that Cal's football team might have more success if it was allowed to "put cleats on sandals."

For the first time in his life, Loren was faced with life without the security of football. Now the real world loomed. His degree in ag-econ had been a path of least resistance, not an expressway to a career. What he had going for him more than anything else was an abiding belief that he could accomplish whatever he chose to do. All he had to do was figure out what that was. He wasted little time in deciding his new goal —to make money. Lots of it.

He rolled over in his bed, opening one bloodshot eye, trying to remember where he was. Someone was shaking him.

"Y'all gotta get up!" pleaded a voice, shaking him again. "I'm never gonna make my flight."

He rolled back over, pulling the sheet over his naked body. Through the Johnnie Walker fog, he vaguely remembered—he was at Craig's apartment in Texas. He and Craig, who had been nominated for Bachelor of the Year in Dallas, had been out nightclubbing into the wee hours, just as they'd done every night since Loren had been in town; they had charmed two Braniff stewardesses back to the apartment. The soft Texas accent rattling around his brain belonged to Cindy. Or was her name Mindy? In the throes of midnight passion, he'd promised to drive her to the airport to catch her morning flight to Denver. Now in the cold reality of morning he was suggesting she take a cab.

"There's no time," she implored. "Y'all promised. Come on!"

Slowly, groggily, he swung one long leg to the carpet, then the other, fumbling to pull up his boxers. He was a sorry sight: his hair pointed south toward the Alamo and north to Amarillo. His breath smelled like a cattle drive. He had come to Dallas not just to party with Craig, as he had on previous trips, but also to attend a two-week sales training course for College Life, an insurance company that he'd told the former Miss California was his new ticket to fame and fortune. He'd told her this shortly after he'd returned from British Columbia, where he'd gone to try out for the Lions of the Canadian Football League, a venture that had lasted only four days because, according to him, he didn't like their style of football. With College Life he was being trained to sell deferred policies to college seniors, and according to the sales executives, he was a natural for the insurance business with his gregarious, outgoing, assumptive style. He could be in the Millionaires Club in no time, they assured him. Still, it was hard for him not to be a tad envious of Craig's lifestyle—the easy money, the cars, the adoration of playing for the Dallas Cowboys. It wasn't that Loren begrudged his old roomie the success and notoriety—in fact, he'd heatedly argued Craig's case to anyone in Dallas who'd listen that the Cowboys would be better off with Craig starting at quarterback instead of Don Meredith. Loren knew how physically tough Craig was—they had been in two pier-six brawls together, once in North Beach in San Francisco when they took on what seemed like the whole bar, escaping just as the paddy wagons came, the other time when they went toe to toe with two skiers in a snowy parking lot in Squaw Valley, Craig winning on a TKO, Loren knocking his guy into lullaby-land. But Loren also knew how frustrated and discouraged Craig was over Coach Tom Landry's insistence that it would take a minimum of five years before he was the starting quarterback. Loren had even offered to serve as Craig's agent to plead his case to general manager Tex Schramm. Craig agreed to let him do it when and if the need occurred. There was nobody he trusted more than Loren.

"Hurry up!" urged Cindy.

Loren stumbled into Craig's room, sitting on the edge of his bed, waking him with a wet-willy. "Coach Landry's here," he said as Craig opened one eye. "He wants to go over the game plan against the Redskins with you." Craig lifted his head off the pillow, only to have Loren shove it back down. Loren walked to the dresser to get the keys to "the Golden Ram," Craig's new gold Buick Riviera, then headed for the front door.

"What about your clothes?" asked Cindy.

"No time," he said.

Wearing only his boxers, he drove to Love Field, arriving at the Braniff terminal with minutes to spare. He told Cindy to give him a call whenever she was in the Bay Area, blowing her a kiss goodbye. And then, on the way back to Craig's apartment complex, he ran out of gas on the busy Northwest Highway, a mile from the nearest gas station. No money, no clothes.

It was a gray November morning, an arctic wind blowing down from the north, the temperature near freezing, much colder than he thought it ever got in Texas. His only hope, he concluded, was to make a run for a gas station . . . because surely nobody would pick up a guy in his underpants. Teeth chattering, he started jogging barefoot along the highway. Horns honked, drivers waved, but nobody stopped to pick him up. His boxers flapped in the breeze.

At the gas station, he stood behind the ethyl pump, eyeing a peroxided blonde in an El Dorado waiting for service. This was his big chance, he thought, an opportunity to utilize all that he had been taught in training class and to go for the assumptive close and get her to buy him a gallon of gas and then give him a ride back to the Golden Ram in her nice big warm Cadillac. He knocked on her window. She drove away.

Eventually, he begged the attendant into advancing him the gallon of gas, then ran back to the Golden Ram, the arctic wind chilling him to the bone. And he would eventually make it back to the Bay Area, where the beautiful former Miss California was waiting to pick him up at the airport.

"How did it go?" she inquired.

"Two years," he answered. "I figure that's about what it'll take me to make my first million."

28

Larry

If I could get back in baseball, I'd climb onto that minor league bus and I'd ride and ride and ride through the night, and I'd thank God for every mile.
—Garland Shifflett, former minor-league pitcher

I trudged up the steps to our Berkeley apartment on College Avenue in the worst mood of my life. I had been stuck in traffic for three hours in our new Chevy Super Sport, first on the Bay Bridge on my way home from my off-season job as an inside sales rep in the Abrasive Division of 3M in South San Francisco, and then trying to get through the clogged streets of Berkeley, where demonstrators were marching down Telegraph Avenue in a massive protest organized by the Vietnam Day Committee (VDC) as part of the International Day of Protest, the largest demonstration against the war to that point.

"Bunch of ugly assholes!" I grumbled as I walked in the door.

"They're not either," countered Denise.

"Whatever," I retorted, yanking off my tie and heading for the liquor cabinet. "I don't want to argue about it."

She followed me into the kitchen. "Aren't you going to say anything?" she asked, twirling like a model.

"About what?" I asked.

She whirled again. "Notice anything different?" she asked.

My shoulders sagged. Her beautiful shoulder-length dark hair—so thick and lush and sexy—was gone, sayonara, chopped short and swept into a pile somewhere on a beauty-parlor floor.

"What'ya think?" she asked.

On another day and in another mood, I might have been able to politely lie. "I hate it," I answered.

She turned and sprinted to the bathroom, slamming the door behind her. A voice instructed me to apologize, to go to her and comfort and hug her and tell her she was still the most beautiful woman I'd ever laid eyes or hands on. Instead, I went to the kitchen and grabbed a carton of eggs from the refrigerator.

"I'm going down to Telegraph Avenue," I snorted, heading for the door.

"Why?" she sobbed.

"To nail a few of those assholes!" I announced.

It was October 15, 1965. We'd been married three months. For the most part, it had been pure bliss. For me, anyway. Denise and Hedy were doing fine too, their relation going along as serene as a walk in a convent garden. For now, anyway. I decided that figuring out the dynamics of their tug-of-war was beyond me; I was content instead to watch "F Troop" and "The Joey Bishop Show." Marriage had been good for my career—I won my first six games after the wedding, the write-up in the local papers following each game always mentioning my famous mother-in-law. But nothing about Hazel. I finished the season 13–9, with a 2.89 earned run average and a .328 batting average. John Quinn, general manager of the Phillies, mailed me a registered letter, notifying me that the Phillies had picked up my contract. I would be going to 1966 spring training with the MAJOR-LEAGUE TEAM! That was the bliss part. The ugly part was that I also got a registered letter from the Selective Service board informing me that it too was picking up my contract. They'd changed the rules on me. Due to the massive buildup of troops in Vietnam, married men were no longer exempt. I was 1A again. The letter ordered me to report to the U.S. Army induction center in L.A. on December 1, 1965. "I guess we got married for nothing," I remarked. Denise didn't laugh.

We had moved to Berkeley after the season ended in Eugene. Denise took art history classes at Cal while I commuted to my $500-a-month job with 3M, in which I sat at a desk and phoned customers to inform them about the latest in sandpaper. I lived for the lunch wagon, and my doughnut breaks, and the start of spring training, and the brace of V.O. on the rocks I would slug down while watching "Leave It to Beaver" reruns on the new color TV. The Phillies were trying to get me into a

National Guard unit, and like all major-league teams in 1965, they had hired a front-office military specialist whose job it was to help protect their prospects by getting these players into the National Guard or the Army Reserves, which were considered safe havens, unlikely to be activated. (No profession had a higher occupational immunity to the military draft than baseball.) But so far, the Phillies' military specialist had not had any luck in getting me into a Guard unit.

My pockets loaded with eggs, I stormed down Channing Way toward Telegraph, armed for battle. In addition to the torchlight march from the campus to the Oakland Army Depot, an afternoon teach-in had been held on campus, featuring poetry readings by Allen Ginsberg, Lawrence Ferlinghetti, and Paul Goodman. The *Daily Cal* had urged students to "read VDC literature, attend the teach-in, listen to their points, and follow your conscience." The City Councils of Berkeley and Oakland had refused the VDC a march permit, but protest leader Jerry Rubin and the marchers were proceeding anyway, vowing to keep it peaceful. According to the rumors, the Hell's Angels were waiting at the Oakland city line to turn them back. The National Guard was on alert. And I was pissed.

I still knew nothing of the history, economics, or religion of Southeast Asia, other than I thought Madame Nhu's daughter was pretty sharp. I had no moral, philosophical, or political objection to American involvement in Vietnam. I had been raised a faithful believer in the purity of America's purpose. I assumed there was a valid reason we were sending troops there. I just didn't want to be one of them.

The last of the 7,000 marchers were parading by UC Corner, cast in a jaundiced light from the pale yellow glow of the sodium streetlights. Berkeley policemen in their khaki-colored uniforms lined the sidewalk. Signs everywhere urged Johnson to "bring the boys home."

My issue wasn't one of foreign policy. On this night I was upset about the politics of style and appearance and Jerry Rubin and his grubby friends blocking my route home, making me late for my rump roast. And Denise getting her damn hair hacked off. It mattered not that I had gotten married when I did to avoid the draft. Or that I was begging the Phillies to get me into a Reserve unit. What mattered was that these Bob Dylan lovin' beatniks were pissing me off. The difference between me and them was tonsorial. And about 45 miles an hour on our fastballs.

"It's Friday night!" I yelled as they passed by my spot in front of the Rathskeller. "Get a date!"

I was aching to unlimber a couple sidearm hummers at these bohemians on parade. But alas, I didn't. Some quick math and I realized I was seriously outnumbered. I wandered downstairs to the Rathskeller and inhaled a couple schooners and talked to Loren about the Bears' chances against the Washington Huskies in tomorrow's game. This was the same day that Steve, who was still in his senior year, ran the ten wind sprints with cracked ribs. Meanwhile, at the Oakland city line, the marchers were being turned back by 300 Oakland policemen. They resumed their march the next day, only this time they were stopped by the Hell's Angels, who were waiting for them. The confrontation turned rough, and before it was over, several marchers were hospitalized and five bikers were jailed, their bail of $26,400 paid for by the Conservative Action Committee, a group sponsored by the Young Republicans.

After returning to the apartment, I promised Denise that I would not get so hostile when I was upset, and she promised me her hair would grow out.

It was the day after Thanksgiving 1965. Denise and I had come to L.A. for the holiday and were driving down Avalon Boulevard in Watts, on our way home from visiting our friends Lola and Jim Perkins, a teammate from my first year in pro ball. They lived on the edge of Watts, and our route back to Westchester took us close to the battle scars from the riot zone. I had ventured into Watts and Compton numerous times as a teenager for baseball games, never feeling threatened. But that was then. I locked the doors.

Actually, I was more nervous about getting shot in the Mekong Delta than in Watts. I was scheduled to report for my induction physical in a week, the Phillies still unsuccessful in getting me into the National Guard.

"Pull into that gas station," Denise instructed.

"Are you gonna throw up?" I asked. She had not been feeling well. I thought maybe she'd had too much leftover cranberry sauce and pumpkin pie.

"I need to make a quick call," she replied.

"A phone call?" I asked, glancing around. "Can't it wait?"

It couldn't. A couple minutes later she hung up and returned to the car. She had called the doctor.

"Guess what?" She was beaming. "You're going to be a father."

I had always been one to keep my emotions in control. But not this time. I shouted for joy, my voice echoing through the riot zone. This was even better news than the day I found out I was on the big-league roster. Baseball wouldn't last forever . . . a child would. And so would, I believed, a trip to the Mekong Delta . . . which I no longer had to worry about. Married men with children—or expectant wives—were exempt. They would have to fight that "Dirty Little War" without me.

February 20, 1966. Denise was four months pregnant as I carried my equipment bag into Jack Russell Stadium in Clearwater, Florida, the site of the Phillies' training camp. It was my dream come true, my father's dream come true. I had reached the highest level, one of the elite few to make it to the doorstep of the major-league fraternity.

"Who are you?" asked an eager young boy poised with pad and pen.

"Larry Colton," I replied, setting down my bag, ready to sign my first big-league autograph. The boy turned and ran with his pad and pen to all-star outfielder Johnny Callison walking in behind me.

Realistically, my chances of making the Phillies' twenty-five-man roster and going north with the big club were slim. On the average it takes four years in the minors to make the major leagues, and for every minor-leaguer who makes it, a hundred fall by the wayside. And that doesn't count the millions who never make it off the sandlots. I was the only player off the Eugene club to make the Phillies' forty-man spring-training roster.

Despite the odds, I had hopes. Stranger things in the history of the game had happened . . . a couple shutout innings here, a strikeout there—and who knows? All of a sudden manager Gene Mauch might decide I had the stuff. That's the way I dreamed it, anyway.

As I walked into the clubhouse, nobody rushed up to shake my hand or welcome me to the fold. I passed Mauch's office and he didn't even look up. In the center of the clubhouse, the ace of the staff and the team's player representative, Jim Bunning, was holding court, waxing senatorial. I wasn't about to interrupt him to introduce myself. Sitting on a stool in front of his locker, Richie Allen, the allegedly temperamental star slugger, was perusing the daily racing form. No way I dared to approach him.

I scanned the lockers, looking for my name. A hand fell upon my shoulder. It was Unk Russell, the crusty old equipment man. He was pointing me toward a small, dank cubbyhole adjacent to the main locker room. It was known as "Scrubbini Row" and it was home to the fifteen players in camp whom Unk deemed least likely to go north. My locker was crammed all the way in the far corner. But at least it wasn't three nails and a milking stool. Other differences from Leesburg struck me right away, such as the fact that big-leaguers got all the fresh-squeezed orange juice they could drink after practice, and big-leaguers didn't have to worry about showering and flushing at the same time.

Watching the other players' file into the clubhouse, I felt out of place. These were men I'd read about in the paper and watched with my dad on "The Game of the Week" or at Dodger Stadium: classy first baseman Bill White; slick-fielding shortstop Bobby Wine; stylish left-hander Chris Short. It seemed weird that I was putting on my uniform right there in the same locker room with these heroes. Well, almost the same locker room. Bo Belinsky entered. He was the fallen glamour boy of the game, author of a no-hitter with the Angels, lover boy to the starlets. Hedy had met him at a party in Beverly Hills over the winter and he had scribbled a warning to me on a cocktail napkin that Hedy had delivered to me: "Good luck with Mauch!" he'd written.

A reporter for the Philadelphia *Daily News* approached, making his way past the other players in Scrubbini Row. He introduced himself, asking me if he could interview me after practice. I felt honored yet self-conscious that he would single me out over players with more experience.

"I want to ask you a few questions about your mother-in-law," he added.

"Sure," I said. What could I tell him? That she'd worked on my curveball with me over the winter? That Denise hung up on her the night before? Or was it Hedy who hung up on Denise? I could never keep it straight. The peaceful walk in the convent garden was a blitzkrieg this week.

Denise had accompanied me to Clearwater, a cranky cross-country drive in which we stopped every two miles so she could relieve herself, the baby pressing against her bladder. We were renting a spacious four-bedroom oceanfront house on Clearwater Beach, sharing it with Gary "Suds" Sutherland and his wife, Karen, also pregnant. Gary was a quiet, unassuming rookie second baseman from USC who had hit a homer off me in my senior year at Cal. We had decided to live together to save money. Our salaries didn't begin until the regular season started, so until then we would be living off of the $16.50 per diem we got in the big-league camp, which would drop off to $4.00 when we got sent to the minor-league camp. Dad had agreed to cover my car payment until my first paycheck.

On my way out of the clubhouse, proudly wearing my Phillie uniform, I passed the photographer for Topps bubble-gum cards. The word on Scrubbini Row was that Topps took pictures of only those rookies whom Mauch anointed most likely to make the club. The photographer motioned toward me. Could it be? No, he was signaling to pitcher Ferguson Jenkins behind me. I wandered onto the lush outfield carpet where players were beginning to gather for calisthenics. Some played pepper, others softly tossed the ball back and forth, laughing and sharing tales of their winters. I stood off to the side, feeling like a Jones at a Smith family reunion. Where was Dexter when I needed him? Vietnam, that's where.

Standing erect on the bullpen mound, I gripped the ball, my fingers across the seams. "No, no," patiently instructed pitching coach Calvin Coolidge Julius Caesar Tuskahoma "Cal" McLish, a dark handsome man, half Indian. "Hold your curveball with the seams. Put the pressure on your middle finger. Don't choke your grip, keep it out on the fingertips. Then when you throw it, snap your wrist at the last second, like you're pulling down a window shade. Make sure you concentrate on the target. Don't release the ball too soon and don't throw across your chest. And then bend your back and follow through. Be ready to field your position. Got it?"

Huh?

I stepped back off the rubber, trying to digest his curveball tutorial. For me, baseball had always been a simple, uncomplicated game, a game of reactions—swing level, throw hard, catch the ball when it comes in my direction. I approached the game the same as I did a serving of mashed potatoes . . . I didn't think about it—I just did it. I never read how-to books, or studied techniques of other players, or contemplated the Zen of the sport. My pitching philosophy in college was to rock and fire and go for the punch-out. Nothing fancy. The hardest part of the game for me growing up had been learning how to get my stockings to stay up straight.

"With your heat," said McLish, "if you can come up with a good, sharp-breaking hammer, you're gonna be a big winner."

The bullpen catcher, Bob Uecker, squatted low and gave me a knee-high target. He was a lousy hitter in the twilight of a doomed-for-obscurity career, and I judged from the scowl on his face that he would have preferred to be just about anywhere else in America than there in that blistering Florida bullpen warming me up. There was no simpatico between us.

I went into my windup, my brain overloaded as if I'd been up all night cramming for a midterm in Curveball 1A: I gripped the ball with the seams; I kept my eye on Uecker's target; I bent my back. Just as McLish had told me. But I held on to the horsehide too long, snapping off a wicked 58-foot overhand yellow hammer that bounced in the dirt and then caromed off Uecker's unprotected kneecap into the outfield grass, sending him yelping to the trainer's room for emergency help, the wus.

"Gotta concentrate," said McLish as I headed across the white line to throw batting practice.

My first hitter was Richie Allen, a player of immense reputation who stepped into the batter's box menacingly waving his 42-ounce nightstick. Richie was a friendly guy, well liked by most of his teammates, respected by all for his unparalleled talent, able to hit a baseball ungodly distances. But it was no secret that he was his own man, traveling to his own set of rules, with no love lost between him and Mauch, who was a fiercely competitive and intense man, arguably the keenest baseball mind in the game, a manager whom the players referred to behind his back as "Napoleon," or "the Little General," or in some cases "Asshole." I was thoroughly intimidated by Mauch, feeling his steely blue eyes boring a hole right through me as I stood on the mound ready to pitch to Richie.

For a rookie, pitching batting practice presented a dilemma. On the one hand, it was a chance to crank up the express and impress the Little General; on the other hand, it was a chance to piss off the veteran hitters who were in the batting cage to work on their stroke and not to face Man Mountain Dean on a mission to make the Hall of Fame the second day of spring training. As Richie dug in, I opted to be a polite rookie and serve it up nice and juicy for him.

It was also no secret that Richie hated spring training and would just as soon be at the racetrack. Or in the cocktail lounge. He was not one to waste energy in the batting cage, content to just swing easy and try to gulp, hit the ball right back at the pitcher. I was determined to pitch him inside so that he would pull the ball and spare Denise the pain of being a single parent. Anything from the middle of the plate out he tended to rip back through the box. About pecker high.

My first pitch was a room service fastball on the inside half of the plate. He lazily flicked his wrists and the ball absolutely, positively rocketed off his bat. It was out of the yard at the 370 mark in left center before I could even adjust my cup. More determined than ever to pitch him inside, I fired the next pitch. Whoops. The ball had barely left my fingers when I started ducking. There was no pitching screen, just empty air between me and his lethal 42-ouncer.

All I saw was a blur, defenseless to stop it. At a speed I later estimated at 5,000 miles an hour, the ball hit me on the inside of my right thigh, scant inches from the external part of my reproductive system, then ricocheted off the other thigh all the way to the foul line. I crumpled to the ground, writhing, sure I was sterilized, or dead. Players rushed toward me, but not Mauch. I could see him out of the corner of my tears, standing next to the cage, arms folded, pissed off about the delay, wondering when this Berkeley pussy out on the mound was going to get up and start hurling again.

I did not think of myself as a particularly courageous man. My previous coaches, I thought, questioned my intestinal fortitude. But with Mauch, who had yet to utter a word to me, leering in my direction, I picked myself up and continued to throw. To be a man was to play in pain, so they said. By the time I reached the trainer's room after my stint on the mound, *both* legs were already a solid black and blue all the way from the kneecap to the crotch.

But there was nowhere else on earth I wanted to be.

Spring training is an inspiration for poets: the morning dew sparkling on the verdant outfield grass, the aging vet and the rawboned rookie battling for a spot, the crack of the bat echoing through the grandstands, the brilliant spring blue sky and the harbinger of a new season. But as I stood doubled at the waist, gasping for air along the left-field foul line, the poetry of the experience was lost on me. I felt as if I was going to puke.

"One more wind sprint," ordered McLish.

I had reported to camp and the ultimate challenge of my baseball existence in the worst shape of my life. All the way through college, physical conditioning was something I'd never thought about—I'd been naturally lean all my life, no matter how much I'd eaten. And I ate a lot. I was fleet afoot and never tired. I'd finished my first season in Eugene weighing 175. But married life and a steady diet of V.O. and six dough-nuts from the 3M lunch truck every day had ballooned me to a flabby 215. It was as if I went to bed in September a six-three, hard-bodied bean pole and woke up in February a tub of guts. I hadn't worked out at all over the winter. But nobody, not Mauch, not McLish, said anything about it to me. Maybe they thought I'd always been gooey in the middle. The only reference I heard was by the writer from the *Daily News*, who referred to my "beefy midsection" in his article.

"I'm not planning on running the ball to the plate," I rationalized.

Evidently, the Phillies weren't too interested in having me throw the ball to the plate either. When the team started playing exhibition games in the Grapefruit League, I sat anchored in the bullpen, fighting off the gnats and the ultraviolet rays of the Gulf Coast sun. Nothing was said to me. McLish abandoned work on my curveball. Uecker eyeballed me as if I was a root-canal surgeon, worried that I was going to ask him to warm me up. The low point was the evening Suds and I went to the greyhound races in Tampa and I lost the last twenty dollars I had to my name. I had to call Dad to wire me fifty dollars to get me to the next infusion of meal money. I was pretty sure that back in those years when I was hounding Dad to play catch with me in the driveway so that I could be a big-leaguer when I grew up, he didn't think he would have to pay my rent in spring training too.

I was almost looking forward to the inevitable "Visit from the Turk," which is what the players called it when Mauch prowled the field, calling players aside to tell them they were being shipped to the minors for another season. At least that way I would be able to find out if he knew my name. (These were the days before players wore their names on the back of their double-knits.) On the bright side, Denise was getting a good tan sitting next to the Gulf of Mexico every day, feeling the baby kick. There was nowhere else on earth she wanted to be. I thought.

I finally did get the call from the Turk, only instead of Mr. Little General himself breaking the news to me, he sent Sergeant McLish to deliver the word. I packed my bag and said goodbye to the limitless fresh-squeezed orange juice and Scrubbini Row, heading for a hot, sultry season in Macon, Georgia, in the AA Southern League.

"Work on that curveball, Dave," directed McLish.

"The Coffin," the Macon Peaches team bus, chugged through the piney woods of Alabama, shimmers of July heat rising off the scorching two-lane asphalt of U.S. 80. We were on our way to a three-game set with the Montgomery Rebels, a Detroit farm club. I climbed up into the overhead luggage rack, hoping to catch a nap before my assignment on the mound that night. I was gunning for my fifth straight win. The bus, which was used in the off-season to haul the Bibb County chain gang down to the Ocmulgee River to bust rocks, was a sauna on wheels. But personally, I was happy to be on board and participating in a slice of Americana—the minor leagues—where normal rules of society governing spitting, scratching, farting, and cussing were waived. We were twenty-two athletic egos postponing adulthood, a fraternity, a family, a team, a mobile bachelor party. We slept until noon, played penny-ante poker until dawn. We had our own unique set of mystics, our own secret signs, our own in-house language. We sat naked in locker rooms together, drank ourselves silly in bars together, hung out in hotel lobbies together. If Pi KA was anti-intellectual, the Macon Peaches were anti-brain wave.

On the outskirts of Tuskegee, we rolled past a campaign billboard plastered with a large picture of expiring two-term Alabama governor George Wallace and his wife, Lurleen. It read: "Vote for Lurleen and Let George Do It."

"I'd be happy to let Lurleen do a tongue stand on my fuck stick," someone crowed. "She's not bad for an old broad."

It was too hot and sticky to sleep. And noisy. A debate was raging in the rear of the bus, not about Lurleen's commitment to civil rights, but over which ballpark in the league offered the best beaver shots. Outfielder Rich Barry, a blond golden boy from California and the team's leading "pusshound" and home-run hitter, adamantly argued that it was Montgomery because somebody had drilled holes in the rear wall of the dugout, making it possible to peek right up into the grandstands and see up dresses.

"Check it out tonight if you don't believe me," he maintained.

As the Coffin continued to lurch through Alabama, passing ten miles from where fraternity brother Don Cobleigh was living in a sharecropper's shack in preparation for his Peace Corps trip to Kenya, I was worried about Denise. She had seemed distant the last few days, although I hadn't probed for an explanation. Part of it, I guessed, had to do with the fact that she'd spent much of the summer worrying about her mother. It had not been a good year for Hedy: critics had panned her performance when she hosted "Shindig," a pop music show; she was fired from *Picture Mommy Dead,* her first starring role in over a decade; she had briefly entered a hospital for treatment of nervous exhaustion; she was having editorial problems with her biographer; and she was arrested for shoplifting $86 worth of merchandise from the May Company on Wilshire Boulevard (including a $40 two-piece knit suit, a $3 pen, a $2 necklace, eight greeting cards, and a 40-cent makeup compact). The story had splashed across front pages all over the country. According to Hedy, who was reportedly carrying $14,000 in personal checks and valuables in her purse at the time of her arrest, it was all a misunderstanding and she had just "forgotten" to pay. A jury later acquitted her, but Denise was agonizing.

Another reason she had been on edge, I assumed, was because she was overdue and was afraid the baby would come when I was on the road. It had been a rough pregnancy, complicated by a bad case of toxemia, a broken air conditioner in our sweltering Macon apartment, and what she presumed was my lack of enthusiasm about the impending arrival of our child. "You never want to touch my stomach and feel the baby kick," she asserted. "You act as if you're embarrassed to be seen with me because I'm big and pregnant. Sometimes I think the only reason you want this baby is because it's keeping you out of Vietnam." I told her that wasn't altogether true, that I wanted the baby for tax reasons too. "Can't you ever be serious?" she asked. "Do you have to make a joke about everything?"

It bothered me that she thought I didn't care. True, I wasn't a huggy-feely, touchy-mushy kind of a guy, but I didn't know any man who was. I was raised to focus on the external world, not the internal stuff. Plus, I was traveling in a world where shouting at Lurleen Wallace billboards was considered a display of affection.

I had entered into marriage with a clear notion of roles. My job was to be concerned about paying the light bill and keeping my curveball down; her job was to worry about having the baby and when to take the roast out of the oven. I'd help with the dishes . . . if I had time. Denise had gotten mad at me when I didn't want to go shopping for a bassinet with her. "I'm pitching tonight," I explained. "I need to rest. It has nothing to do with not being excited about the baby. Sometimes I think you forget that baseball is my career and our livelihood, not just some kids' game I go play for fun."

She cried. And as usual, I couldn't deal with the tears, unable to comfort her. I reacted to her tears as if they were barbed wire. I didn't know why.

In my heart I was looking forward to being a father, preferably to a son. But I was looking forward to parenthood in the same way I anticipated a ninth-inning rally—I didn't jump up and down and scream and holler. I just watched quietly and hoped it went well for our side. We were married . . . what more could I say?

I was committed to the marriage, being faithful, resisting the temptations of the road, staying out of pickup bars. Wasn't that what commitment was? After road games, I'd go back to my hotel room to watch Johnny Carson or read. My only deviant behavior was in Mobile when I stood in a line of ballplayers outside a prostitute's room in the hotel, a scene reminiscent of the fraternity gangbang. But instead of going inside the room, each player crouched in front of the door and peered through the keyhole. Finally it was my turn. The bleached-blond prostitute sat naked on the edge of her bed using tweezers to methodically pluck crabs from the pubic hair of her john. There was a lot of time to kill on the road.

Another possible explanation for Denise's down mood was that the life of a baseball wife wasn't as romantic as she'd first thought—she was tired of my being gone half the time, tired of having no money in the bank (my bonus was already spent), tired of not being near her friends, tired of the petty jealousies and cliques among the other wives. "They're more competitive than their husbands," she observed. She was trying to fit in and be part of the group. But in truth, she felt on the outside looking in: she was into art and film and the Beatles, other wives were into soap operas, cosmetics, and Loretta Lynn; our apartment walls were filled with her paintings, other players' walls were blank. She attended most of the games, even when I wasn't pitching, and was learning the game, but baseball was still foreign turf to her—she'd gone to a high school where the headmaster didn't allow the school band to play at soccer games because it was too militaristic.

She was also having difficulties adapting to Southern society. For instance, there was the night we were taken out to dinner by a wealthy Macon businessman, a gray-haired man in his fifties. Denise suspected he had hopes of getting to meet Hedy through her; I was willing to give him the benefit of the doubt because he was taking us to the fanciest restaurant in town, a place that wasn't in our minor-league budget—I was raking in a cool $600 a month. Over salad the conversation turned to Julian Bond, the recently elected twenty-five-year-old pacifist whom the Georgia state legislature was refusing to seat because he had spoken out against U.S. policy in Vietnam and had expressed sympathy with draft resisters. Denise voiced her admiration for Bond's politics. I was suspicious she liked him more for his good looks.

"I don't care what you say, dumpling," replied the businessman. "A nigger's a nigger. They're only one step ahead of the apes."

Denise, who roomed with a Negro girl at Stockbridge, turned and whispered that she thought we should leave. I glanced up at the waiter bringing my thick-cut New York steak smothered in mushrooms, and urged a more moderate response. Later, over dessert, the businessman boasted of his friendship with gubernatorial candidate Lester Maddox, the hard-line segregationist who'd first gained notoriety for standing in front of his restaurant with a baseball bat to keep out Negroes. (The polls showed Maddox running comfortably ahead of his main opponent in the Democratic primary, a moderate state senator from Plains named Jimmy Carter.) Denise wanted to nail the guy between the eyes with her strawberry cheesecake. I wouldn't have let her waste good food like that.

I was definitely learning about the politics of Jim Crow firsthand as I traveled to the other cities of the Southern League (Charlotte, N.C.; Asheville, N.C.; Columbus, Ga.; Montgomery, Ala.; Mobile, Ala.; Knoxville, Tenn.; Evansville, Ind.). Nowhere was it more evident than in Macon: Negro fans were segregated in a roped-off section of the left-field bleachers known as "the Coal Bin"; our team picnic had to be called off because the Ku Klux Klan showed up for a rally and bonfire; the batboy's father made him quit because he didn't want him being in the same clubhouse with our three "nigger" players. On the ball club, racism was held beneath the surface in the name of team harmony and there was no overt racial tension, but there was very little socializing off the field or off the bus between the whites and Negroes. In most of the towns we traveled to, despite the passage of the Civil Rights Act of 1964, the Negro players stayed in segregated hotels and ate in segregated restaurants. On our first road trip of the year to Montgomery, I had naïvely asked Leroy "Cat" Reams, a Negro outfielder from Oakland, if he wanted to go out to dinner with me after the game. He just stared at me as if I had some sort of death wish.

I wasn't about to go bragging to the neighbors in our Macon apartment complex about my 66-page term paper on SNCC. The racial climate throughout the South that summer was incendiary—after James Meredith was peppered with bird shot on his march from Memphis to Jackson in June, Stokely Carmichael called for Black Power to bring the whites "to their knees." My mission in the South that summer was not to fight for civil rights—not at all. I was there to work on my curve and move on up to Philadelphia.

On the road to Montgomery, the Coffin pulled into the parking lot of a small greasy spoon cafe nestled in a clump of tall pines. I was the first one inside, taking a seat at the counter. The lone waitress, a big fat woman wearing her hair in a net, served me a glass of water and watched the rest of the team straggle in. She spotted the Negroes entering.

"We don't serve no niggers here," she blared.

Our manager, Andy Seminick, a tough, bald-headed, barrel-chested, gruff-talking, fast-spitting man who as a player caught the entire 1951 World Series with a broken wrist, glared at her. He was the Phillies' catcher in 1947 when Jackie Robinson first broke into the league.

"Then you don't serve none of us," he growled.

I was surprised at his swift and decisive response. I had thought of him as a fair and decent man, but not as a champion of civil rights. Yet upon closer thought, it was consistent with his constant preachings of the importance of being a team. We all knew that if there was a brawl on the field, Andy would be right there in the center of it, sticking up for his players, regardless of color.

There was no hesitation by any of the players to vacate the premises. I assumed the Negro players appreciated the support, but I could only guess. We were a baseball team, not a traveling encounter group. As I rose off my stool, I poured the water out of my plastic glass onto the counter, then fired a riser over the cash register, scoring a bull's-eye into the middle of a pyramid of plastic glasses, sending them flying in all directions. The waitress ducked. I figured it was better than trying to get her to read my term paper on SNCC, the one which deserved an A.

Despite the humidity and two gopher balls on hanging curves, I was still on the mound against the Montgomery Rebels going into the bottom of the eighth, the score tied 4–4. The only really good pitch I'd thrown all day was back at the greasy spoon.

I had started the season poorly, losing six of my first nine decisions before winning four in a row. My curve wasn't exactly the talk of the league, nor was the occasional slider or change-up I used. But I was around the plate with all my pitches, walking fewer than two per nine innings, striking out seven. My biggest problem, according to Seminick, was my lapses in concentration. He was right. I could sail along like Dizzy Dean for five or six innings, then go la-la-land and start thinking about the nutcake with the rifle in the University of Texas Tower, or about Denise and I going to see *Who's Afraid of Virginia Woolf?* on our day off, or some darn thing. Next thing I'd know, my hanging curve was sailing off toward downtown Little Rock.

I walked the Rebel leadoff hitter on four straight pitches to start the bottom of the eighth. I could see Seminick move up to the top step of the dugout; I could also see a righty and a lefty warming up in our bullpen. My guess was that if I didn't get the next hitter, I was soaping up in the shower.

I asked the ump for a new ball, then stepped off the mound to rub it up, my back to home plate. As I gazed up into the Alabama night and the Confederate flag hanging limp from the center-field flagpole, my mind started doing one of its wandering acts . . . I wondered if Denise had started labor . . . or if that fat waitress would vote for Lurleen. Stepping back on the mound, I glanced toward the dugout, not at Seminick, but at the other end, where two players had their backs to the field, their eyes glued to the holes in the back wall, peering up the dresses of women in the grandstands. I could have been pitching naked to Babe Ruth and they wouldn't have known.

My next pitch was a pitiful hanging swerve that the Montgomery newspaper reported this way the next morning: "As the son-in-law of actress Hedy Lamarr, 24-year-old Larry Colton knows all about curves. He knows they can be good—and dangerous too. The Macon right-hander saw three of his curves hit out of the park last night."

·   ·   ·   ·

When Denise announced it was time to leave for the hospital, we were sitting on the couch watching "The Dating Game."

"Can't you wait until after the show?" I asked.

She wasn't amused.

After she checked in at the front desk, she disappeared through the doors to the labor room and I went to the fathers' waiting room. There had been no Lamaze. But I'd come prepared, bringing two books to get me through the long wait—*The FBI's Most Famous Cases* and *How to Invest in the Stock Market*. I read, I paced, I talked with the other expectant fathers, and then finally after eighteen long hours, a nurse walked into the room holding my new child, a healthy baby girl. We had already decided her name would be Wendy Denise Colton.

"Isn't she gorgeous?" cooed the nurse, handing me Wendy.

I took her in my arms (Wendy, not the nurse). I didn't tremble, I didn't weep, I just *felt* love. A whole different kind of love. I didn't care if Wendy thought Julian Bond was better-looking than me. But I didn't think she was gorgeous yet. She looked like a prune with eyes.

"She's beautiful," I testified.

It was several hours before I got to visit Denise. "You don't seem excited," she said.

What did I have to do? I'd brought her flowers and a card. I'd sat in the waiting room for eighteen hours. I'd missed work. I'd called my parents and Hedy from the hospital. I'd bought cigars to pass out in the club-house. I'd decorated the apartment for their homecoming.

"Okay, I'll admit I'm a little upset," I said.

"Why?"

"Because I missed 'The Dating Game'."

She cried. I wasn't sure why and I didn't ask.

29

Steve

Our success in Vietnam in the first quarter of 1966 has exceeded our expectations, but 18,000 more troops are needed.
—Robert McNamara, Secretary of Defense

It was cut-down day for the 1966 Calgary Stampeders, and as Steve walked off the practice field under the boiling August sun, he had a sense of doom, a gut feeling that his football-playing days were about to be axed to a halt. Still, he hoped. Sweat dripped from every pore.

He had been invited to training camp on the recommendation of Cal coach Ray Willsey, who had sold Stampeders' coach Jerry Williams on Steve's toughness and determination. Steve had come to Calgary bulked up, reporting to camp at 218 pounds, his neck so thick he couldn't button the top button of his dress shirts.

He had plenty of incentive to make the team, including a $20,000 salary and the chance to keep alive his hopes of making the NFL and proving all those scouts wrong. But even more than money or vindication, it was the self-esteem that motivated him. Football had always been a big part of his life, maybe the biggest, the one area more than anything else that gained his father's approval, proved his toughness, verified his work ethic. When he was in his uniform and opponents were flying at him from all directions, he didn't have to think about family or love or living up to responsibility and expectation. All he had to do was hit anything coming his way. There was no gray area in the sport—his job was to knock the other guy on his butt. Period. If he did, he got approval, reveling in it. If he didn't, well, there was the next play, the next game. He had a linebacker's mentality. What he lacked in size or natural ability, he made up for with his absolute focus and concentration. He wasn't one to stand in the middle of the field and gaze up into the sky and think about world events or his date to see *Who's Afraid of Virginia Woolf?* with Ayris. His attitude was his strength—he took it seriously on the field, but kept it in perspective, never too high in victory, never too brooding in defeat.

He had been all business in camp, arriving at the team's training facilities at Mount Royal College with Greg Palomountain, a six-foot, 180-pound safety from Cal who had also been recommended by Willsey. They had driven straight through, twenty-four hours nonstop from Berkeley to Calgary, barreling across Nevada and Idaho at 120 miles an hour like Tod and Buzz from "Route 66," Steve in his new '66 Fastback Mustang 2+2, Greg in his Corvette Sting Ray. Camp had been a boot-camp atmosphere . . . in bed every night by eleven o'clock in their dorm rooms on the Mount Royal campus, up at 7 A.M. for breakfast in the cafeteria before daily doubles in the 95-degree heat. There were no sightseeing junkets to nearby Banff National Park or girl-chasing forays into the nightlife of Calgary. Steve abstained from beer. His only social life outside of his teammates were his letters and phone calls to Ayris, who was living at home with her parents in Westwood following graduation, working for a computer company on Wilshire Boulevard in downtown L.A., managing a keypunch department that handled magazine subscriptions. And hating every minute of it. Her diploma in history was stuffed in a desk drawer and so were her acrylics and sketch pads. She rode to work down Wilshire Boulevard every morning on a Honda CM91, a scooter Steve had gotten for her off his father's lot at South City Honda.

Steve hadn't spent much time thinking about what he would do if he didn't make the Stampeders. That was negative energy and he liked to stay focused on the positive, although he knew his odds weren't good. Each Canadian team was allowed only fourteen American players, and the Stampeders, it seemed, had invited every linebacker in North America to try out, plus every starter was returning, each of them with necks wider than Manitoba. His only appearance in an exhibition game had been one quarter against the British Columbia Lions, in which he neither distinguished nor embarrassed himself. He did not complain to the coaches about his lack of playing time—that too was against his nature.

Nearing the locker room, he felt a hand on his shoulder pads. It was Coach Williams, motioning him to the side. Here it comes, thought Steve, hoping for a miracle.

"We really like your hustle and attitude," said Williams. "But . . ."

Steve braced himself.

"But we just have too many other linebackers with more size and experience," continued Williams. "We're gonna have to let you go."

And with that, the football-playing days of "Radich: 87 Proof" were over.

He was behind the wheel of his Mustang, out in the middle of nowhere —northeastern Nevada, southbound between Jackpot and Metropolis on U.S. 93. To the east, beyond Pequop and the Grouse Creek Mountains, the first crack of daylight was breaking gently over the desert floor, disturbed only by the headlights of his car. He was obsessed with making it back to Sacramento from Calgary in twenty-four hours, nonstop, 1,350 miles.

He felt lousy about being cut, especially considering that Palomountain had made the team. But he hadn't whined to Coach Williams about not getting a fair shot; instead, he chose to simply shake his hand, thank him for the opportunity, and then head to his dorm room to pack his bags. He worried about his father's reaction. Would Frank admonish him for not trying harder or not badgering the coach for a better shot? It amazed Steve that for all his success as a football player at Cal and for all his various Pac 8 Player of the Week laurels and his most improved lineman awards, Frank still had criticized him for not going to Coach Willsey and demanding that he play more at offensive end, the position Frank thought was Steve's ticket to the pros. How long would it take, Steve wondered, for his father to realize he wasn't Red Grange?

Feeling drowsy, he rolled down the window and turned up the radio, blasting himself awake with the fresh air and the sounds of "Oh, Pretty Woman" by Roy Orbison, his favorite singer. The speedometer was holding steady at 100.

Decisions loomed. For the first time in his life, he didn't have school or football. What he had was a degree in business administration and a handsome face. Joining a big corporation was an option, but that didn't appeal to him; attending law school was a thought, but he was tired of school; working for his father at South City Honda was a real possibility, but that seemed torturous—his mom was the bookkeeper at the shop and spending fifty hours a week working side by side with his parents could be worse than Hell Week. About the only thing he could think of

that he really wanted to do was board a steamer for Europe with Ayris
and spend a year traveling abroad. They had romanticized about such a
venture, talking about going to Yugoslavia so that he might get in touch
with his family heritage. But there was no chance of that happening—he
had no money, and Ayris's father, a strict Lebanese Catholic, would
approve of arms for Israel before he would let his unmarried daughter go
to Europe with a man who was still legally married.

There was an even bigger obstacle. Steve was now reclassified 1A and
it was only a matter of time until he received his notice to report for his
induction physical. Despite what Secretary of Defense McNamara was
saying about U.S. successes in Vietnam, the troop buildup was rapidly
escalating and was expected to reach 400,000 by the end of the year.

Heavy thoughts. Heavy eyelids. Steve didn't remember shutting his
eyes, only opening them to find himself spinning out of control in the
gravel of the highway shoulder. It was the first year of federally mandated seat belts as standard safety equipment, but he wasn't wearing his.
The Mustang started to roll . . . once, twice, three times . . . then
landed upright on all four Goodyears with a kerplunk. He was thrown
across to the passenger seat, but somehow, just as the gods were looking
down on him when he bounced across U.S. 40 as a boy and when he
drove drunk the wrong way down I-80 as a collegian, he climbed out of
the car, unscratched. He checked the dent in the roof, then slid back
behind the wheel, spewing a rooster tail of desert dirt into the dawn as
he accelerated back onto the highway, undaunted, still determined to
make it in twenty-four hours. Mr. Lucky rides again.

Ayris sat at a table with three of her girlfriends at the Oar House in
Santa Monica, a popular night spot with the beach crowd. Lots of great
bodies, loud rock-and-roll, and cheap beer. There was something about
the lead singer in the band that reminded Ayris of Steve. They looked a
little bit alike, and they both had a brush of the poet behind their male
intensity.

"I'm going to call Steve," she announced, finishing her second beer,
twice her normal allotment. She headed for a pay phone.

"If he asks you to marry him, say yes," advised one of her friends.

It was late August. Steve had made it back to Sacramento in one piece
and was living with his parents, visiting Ayris in L.A. the first weekend he
was home. She had missed him when he was in Canada—his touch, his
energy, his affection. She'd only been out of college three months but
already she felt a pressure building—half the girls in her pledge class
were already married. That's what sorority girls had been programmed to

do. She didn't want to be living at home, working at a boring job, hanging out at pickup bars. She wanted to paint pictures and be with the man she loved. But shacking up was out of the question. She'd been raised by a pragmatic Catholic, taught that if two people were madly in love and wanted to have sex on a regular basis, there should be a wedding ring and a steady paycheck.

Steve was twenty-two years old and he too was feeling a pressure building, that if he didn't propose before too long, she wouldn't wait around for him. There were so many things about her he loved. On the exterior she was soft and delicate, yet he knew that underneath was a strength, a durability that had allowed her to hang in there with him, even after he'd lied to her about his marriage to Linda. He loved her spunk—she wasn't afraid to stand up to him, to tell him he'd acted the horse's ass when he was drunk. And he loved the fact she shared his passion for going to Europe.

From the pay phone in the rear of the Oar House, she cupped her hand over one ear, straining to hear him over the din. "Say that again," she said.

"Let's get married," he proposed.

"When?" she asked.

"As soon as possible," he replied.

She accepted and the wedding was set for September 24, 1966, at Holy Spirit Church in Sacramento.

Ayris waited in the Mustang while Steve knocked on the door . . . Linda's door. He was bringing the divorce papers for her signature. It was three days before the wedding.

Ayris held her breath, nervous that something would go wrong. Who could blame her? Two days earlier Steve had borrowed his dad's pickup to drive to L.A. to help her move her belongings up to Sacramento. They had just passed Solvang, two hundred miles north of L.A. on Highway 101, when Ayris glanced in the back of the pickup and discovered that the new suitcase—the one that contained her wedding dress, new outfit for the honeymoon to Tahoe, diary, jewelry, peignoirs, and photo albums —had fallen off the back of the pickup. They retraced their route for a hundred miles looking for the suitcase, to no avail. She worried it was an omen of how their marriage would go.

"Would you like to see your son as long as you're here?" Linda asked. "He's taking a nap."

"I don't have time," Steve replied. "I've got a shitload of things to take care of today."

Linda's first reaction was not to sign the divorce papers, not because she was trying to cling to the marriage, but because she thought he was being a jerk. Six months earlier she had called to tell him she was filing for divorce, asking him to split the $175 cost. He refused, maintaining he had no money. She filed anyway, borrowing the money from her mother, but the papers had never been signed. Now he wouldn't even take two minutes to go look at his son.

Reluctantly, she signed, then followed him to the door. She could see Ayris waiting in the car. They'd never met. Linda remembered the time in the Motel Sex when Steve told her how he had Ayris wrapped around his finger. She wondered if Ayris knew that side of him—the one that could be so cold and self-centered. Or had he only shown her his good side, the one that was caring and affectionate?

As she watched the Mustang disappear down the street, she cried, tears of anger, tears of sadness. She wondered if her son would ever see his father again.

Ayris glanced at the clock. It was 8 P.M. and Steve still wasn't home from work. He had mentioned that he might meet a couple buddies for a quick beer on his way home, but she was starting to worry. Dinner was already cold.

She paced the living-room floor of their apartment, a small one-bedroom in a prosaic new apartment complex in West Sacramento, a place Steve claimed was a spawning ground for Montgomery Ward clerks. Ayris had done what she could to liven up its drab interior, painting the wicker furniture white, hanging several of her frameless paintings, making the most of their sparse collection of wedding gifts. But home furnishings weren't their priority. Their plan was to work and save for six months—Steve as a motorcycle mechanic for his father, Ayris as an insurance underwriter trainee—then take off for Europe. According to this plan, they would motorcycle across America to the East Coast, then catch a steamer across the Atlantic. The only thing that could possibly stop them would be a registered letter from the Selective Service board.

Soon it was nine o'clock. Then ten. And still no Steve. He had made it clear before the wedding that being married didn't mean that he had to stop going out with the guys. Ayris said she wouldn't object as long as he did it in moderation and didn't come staggering in at four in the morning. He promised he wouldn't.

At midnight, she fell asleep. When he finally tiptoed in the door at

5 A.M. in his stocking feet, he took two steps toward the bedroom, then stepped on something sharp. It was a shard of shattered glass from a broken picture frame fired against the wall in anger—the photo of them cutting their wedding cake together. They had been married one week.

30

Ron

Turn on to the scene; tune in to what's happening. Drop out—of high school, college, grad school . . . and follow me, the hard way.
—Dr. Timothy Leary

Skinnier than he was in the ninth grade, Ron paced the living room, shades drawn, deep in thought. It was 1967, a bewildering time—black rioters laying waste to Detroit, napalm scorching the flesh of Vietnam, Cassius Clay refusing to be inducted into the service. Inside Ron's head, it seemed as if the entire intellectual, moral, and cultural climate of the times—the zeitgeist—was caving in on him. He had to get out, make something happen.

He was experiencing a reality he'd never known before, living in an apartment in San Francisco on Sacramento Street, a block with no trees, lots of traffic noise, and concrete buildings pressed tightly together. He had returned to California following his cross-country odyssey, the final leg of that journey from Chicago to L.A. financed on money his father had wired him. He paid Ralph back with money he made selling Christmas candy door to door in Compton and Watts. He'd come back to San Francisco partially because he had been rehired by Joseph Esherick, and partially because he couldn't stand watching his parents' marriage going down the tubes. Betty was drinking heavily and Ralph's business was in trouble. Ron was convinced his dad's style of architecture was stuck in the Dark Ages, and that Ralph was too resistant to change, too stubborn to admit that the only hope was to fold the business and go to work for somebody else. The fact that Betty was bringing home more money than Ralph compounded the problem. Ron had heard rumors that his father was having an affair with his mom's cousin, and that escalated the resentment, adding fuel to the argument that it was Ralph who was the reason behind Betty's excessive drinking and hostility. If Ralph wasn't so weak, Ron thought, he'd put a stop to the affair and get the marriage back on track. Ron felt alienated, thinking back to his childhood and how Ralph never taught him how to fight or be tough. Maybe if he had, he wouldn't feel so sad and helpless now against all the confusion.

If America was on the verge of a mass emotional nervous breakdown, as Allen Ginsberg was claiming, then Ron was already at the admittance desk. At work he was barely able to complete the simplest of drafting tasks, his mind too jumbled most days to concentrate. He'd apologized to Mr. Esherick, who was offering to give him more time off or whatever help he needed. Ron was convinced the only reason he hadn't been fired was because of Mr. Esherick's benevolence.

His main hope for help, he believed, was Anna, his roommate. It was her apartment he was living and pacing the floor in; it was her food he was eating; it was her VW that transported him around the city. Prior to moving up from L.A., he had driven his perfectly good VW Bug to a used-car lot in Santa Monica, handed a salesman the keys and the registration, then turned and walked away as the salesman stared in disbelief. Material possessions, he had concluded, were not important.

He had met Anna, who was five years older, at a party in Palo Alto prior to leaving on his odyssey. At that first meeting, she was wearing a black miniskirt, and as soon as they were introduced, he felt her energy. It wasn't just her blue eyes or her strawberry-blond hair or her long legs, or even her thick French accent. She had a presence, a spiritual calm. Her shoulders were broad, her posture erect. She was wiser, more secure, more resolved, more worldly, and as he would soon discover, more erotic. She was born in Paris, and her family hid Jewish refugees in their attic during the Nazi occupation; she knew about survival. At the age of eighteen she emigrated by herself to California, and by the age of twenty-one she owned her own gift shop in Santa Rosa. When Ron met her she was managing a Robert Powers Modeling Agency in San Francisco, but now she was a masseuse on call for a San Francisco chiropractor. Ron asked her no questions about her work—he didn't want to have to answer questions about his own life.

Anna knew he was going through tough times, but she was sure he would soon snap out of it. He had so much to offer; he was athletic, artistic, caring. She could see herself living the American Dream with him—the house in the suburbs, children, summer vacations to Yosemite. She had attached herself, eager to nurture him back to full speed. He was willing to let her try, having come to depend on her for succor. And rides.

On this day, however, she had taken her car to an appointment. So, with the walls of the apartment closing in on him, he set out on foot, headed for Haight-Ashbury.

It was the "Summer of Love" in San Francisco. Flower power. Psychedelia. As Ron wandered down Haight Street, he was surrounded by bare feet and sandals . . . long hair and beards . . . ponchos and granny glasses . . . Indian prints and dirty jeans . . . tie-dyed T-shirts and Buffalo Bill jackets. For his part, he looked the role of the fraternity man who'd been sleeping in his car, a man long overdue at the laundry, with short hair, stained cotton pants, wrinkled dress shirt, and wing tips with holes in the sole. Dressing the anti-uniform wasn't his message. He didn't have a message. His bond with his fellow wanderers was that he looked unhealthy, pale, sallow, a refugee from the Land of the Tibetan Dead. Eyes that were supposed to reflect the joy and giving of the community were sorrowful and distant. His vacant look was not the product of chemistry. He was on a natural bummer. But he was hoping to score a joint.

He eyed a couple walking down the street ahead of him, figuring them to be potheads who would, if asked nicely, be happy to share a joint in the spirit of the day. Or maybe he wouldn't ask them. He decided to follow them. The man was stocky, the woman a heavyset redhead. They stopped to stare back at the tourists ogling them from the Gray Line excursion bus, known to the residents as the "Hippie Hop Tour."

The déclassé Haight-Ashbury district (or "Hashbury," as Hunter Thompson called it) had gained renown as the largest hippie colony in the world. It had long been a neighborhood of libertine attitudes, home to people of the arts and academia, with three-story Tudors and Victorians, small shops, integrated schools, and a reputation of cordiality and cultural range. In 1967 it had become the heart and fountainhead of the hippie subculture, an estimated 50,000 young people from around the globe converging on the area, prospective hippies lured by drugs, cheap rent, community spirit, and sexual possibilities. Ron was there to wander, not for the sex.

The theme on the street was political and social change. And love. Hip versus straight. It was supposed to be an experiment in openness and harmony that would shock the Establishment and slap the national consciousness—show moms and dads around the country that they lived in a world of violence and prejudice and hypocrisy and that there was a better way, a possibility of a community of nonviolence and no guns. And love. The focus was on grooviness and self-expression. Organic food, moral purpose, crash pads, and easy sex abounded. It was a stampede away from normalcy, with society and culture on fast forward, everything moving faster than ever before in American history in one location . . . the disenchanted, the disinterested and the defiant all thrown into one blender. Ron watched as an Aquarian Age philosopher stood on the corner shouting antiwar slogans. Behind him, bongos and kalimbas and "Sgt. Pepper" blared from open windows.

It was a social phenomenon, although to Ron it was just a place to wander aimlessly, a place where he didn't feel so weird, so out of touch. He felt more comfortable at the corner of Haight and Ashbury than he did in the Fillmore district, a black enclave nearby. He hadn't come to the Haight to make friends. He was too mistrustful and turned inward for that. Nor was he there to observe the phenomenon. He was, in fact, part of the phenomenon.

"Excuse me," he said, approaching the couple. They didn't hear him, continuing on down the street. He followed.

To its critics, the Haight was discordant, a colony of dirty, lazy deadbeats, a sanctuary for spoiled brats who wanted nothing more than to get stoned and laid and parade up and down the street in costume. The critics had a point. What was supposed to be so ennobling was an unsanitary community rampant with VD, hepatitis, garbage, and acidheads, a troubling glimpse into permissiveness run amok. These were not angry blacks that Ron was wandering with—it was a bunch of middle-class white kids who had dropped out of the suburbs to play poverty and be irresponsible, self-absorbed youth who thought they were the Adam and Eve of all revolution and that anybody who was into property and profit was a warmonger. Or at least that's what the critics of Haight-Ashbury charged.

The couple wandered into a head shop and Ron stayed outside, trying to be inconspicuous, staring into the display window with its obligatory counterculture necessities—incense, strobe lights, kazoos, beads, metal jewelry, posters of Janis Joplin at the Fillmore. The bookstore next door was stocked with all the hippest books—*Siddhartha, The Psychedelic Experience, I Ching, The Prophet.*

The couple exited the head shop, and again he followed, this time down the street and up a flight of stairs, where they disappeared into a room at the end of a long hallway. He paused outside the door, listening to their laughter coming from the other side. Without knocking, he entered. There were four people now, and a joint was being passed . . . just as he suspected. Silently, he waited his turn, smiling awkwardly, his hand extended.

The stocky man suddenly turned on him, brandishing a long hunting knife under his chin.

"What the fuck you doing here, man?"

"I'm not a narc!" Ron pleaded. "I just want to get high."

The man grabbed him by the shirt and pushed him out the door. At the bottom of the stairs, Ron paused, wondering what was wrong with him that these people did not want him there to laugh and share the spirit of peace and love with them.

It was another unproductive day at the office. He was feeling angry at himself for having spent the better part of the day fretting and stewing at his desk, frustrated that he wasn't contributing, not just at work but to society. He also felt like a burden to Anna. She was his one salvation, standing by him, reassuring him of her love, offering him his only real source of emotional support. But he felt weak, powerless, too consumed with his own thoughts to give her anything in return.

On his way back to the apartment, he stopped to wait for a bus. A slender black teenager was also waiting. Ron had never seen him before, but there was something about the boy that reminded Ron of himself at that age. The boy seemed cautious, not at all the tough macho image of the young black male. Ron studied him out of the corner of his eye, then slowly approached. The boy looked away. Ron continued to move closer, stopping a foot away, arms folded, feet spread, demanding to be noticed.

Ron leered, then stepped back and unloaded, slapping the boy across the side of his face, the same way the big kids hit him in junior high.

The boy stood dumbfounded, doing nothing. The bus arrived and he hurried aboard, Ron following close behind him, taking a seat across the aisle. They rode several blocks in silence, the boy's eyes riveted on Ron, who turned and looked away.

At Van Ness Avenue, Ron stood up and left the bus. He knew something was seriously wrong with him and he needed help.

In the days ahead, his thoughts grew even more jumbled. Then Anna returned from an appointment and told him that she had something she needed to discuss. He assumed that she wanted to tell him it was over, that she was tired of being the only one contributing emotionally.

"I'm pregnant," she declared, smiling.

She was emphatic—there would be no abortion, no giving up the baby. Ron's first thought was despair. It was all he could do to change his underwear and to find his way out the front door. No way he was ready for the responsibility of parenthood.

His attitude quickly changed. He was effusive, jubilant, a man being led to daylight after months in the darkness of a cave. A new baby would give him a second chance, an opportunity to atone for his abandoning his first child. It would be a gift, a way to absolve his guilt and to stop hating himself.

He hitched to Los Angeles to break the news to his parents. The growing distance he felt, especially from Ralph, wasn't the standard sixties alienation between parent and child. It wasn't about politics and values and money. It was about love and affection, which is what he'd always craved from them, but now he needed it more than ever; it was about conviction and a failure to understand why Ralph had thought finishing college was the right thing to do and why Betty was never told about the first child.

"I wonder if you're ready for this baby," said Ralph.

"What'ya mean?"

Ralph meant emotionally, physically, financially. He wondered if his son's troubled state of mind was because he was at loose ends professionally, not challenged in his job at Esherick. But he couldn't talk to Ron about it. In the past year, every time Ralph even talked about architecture, Ron would tune him out. Before Ron had moved back to the Bay Area, Ralph had arranged a job interview for him with the head of the Los Angeles city planning department at City Hall and Ron turned it down.

Ron ended up in Venice, wandering the streets, depressed and alone. He stopped in a liquor store and bought a fifth of cheap bourbon. It was noon when the police found him passed out on the sidewalk in front of the Planned Parenthood Clinic. They arrested him and threw him in the drunk tank for the night. The next morning he had no option but to call Ralph to bail him out.

He walked into Mr. Esherick's office and turned in his resignation, again. "I'm going to work for the post office," he announced. Mr. Esherick gave him a fatherly pat on the back and wished him well.

Ron didn't care if he delivered the mail, sorted packages, or washed the mail trucks . . . he just wanted a job where he didn't feel pressured.

His application was rejected. It was stamped: "Educationally overqualified."

So, with no money, no job, and a child on the way, he took a bus to the Langley Porter Psychiatric Center and checked himself in as an inpatient.

"I'm screwed up," he explained.

31

Larry

. . . My daughter, the wife of Philadelphia Phillies baseball player Larry Colton, is happily married and I don't think she concerns herself much with what happened to her father. She has her own life to lead.
—Hedy Lamarr, *Ecstasy and Me*

I was wearing my sharkskin honeymoon suit and my new white shoes. Denise brushed back a tear. It was February 1967 and we were at the L.A. Airport, saying goodbye for two months as I waited to board my flight to Florida and spring training with the Phillies. I had been promoted to the big-league roster again, although I figured to spend the season in San Diego, the Phillies' AAA farm club. We were broke, so while I was off to Scrubbini Row, Denise was staying in L.A. with the baby, half the time at her mom's, half with my parents. And dreading it.

The off-season had been a disaster. We lived in a quaint house with a wood-paneled den on a tree-lined street in Orinda, a country-club community on the eastern side of the Berkeley hills. With our new Buick station wagon, we looked the part of the happy young suburban couple, with the car seat and the golf clubs in the back. But we were broke. I had two jobs and bombed in both. The first was selling corporate season tickets for the California Seals hockey team in Oakland. In one month on the job I sold two tickets. The fact that I had never been to a hockey game may or may not have had something to do with my lack of success.

The Seals canned me. Then a buddy told me I could make some quick and easy money selling new Fords at a dealership in suburban Concord. I was financially desperate, so I gave it a try. In my one month on the job, I did not lure a single customer to the back room. It reminded me of my dating days in college.

Denise wasn't exactly partying down every day either, stuck at home with Wendy all day, feeling postpartum unattractive and unappreciated. Our sex life had all the passion of an international walk. During the days, when I took off in the car in a futile effort to make the big sales commission, she was stranded, alone with a colicky baby . . . no car, no money, no friends nearby. There were no parks or stores within walking distance, and Wendy wouldn't nap long enough for Denise to paint. The highlight of her day was watching Paul Revere and the Raiders on "Where the Action Is." There was no money for her to continue college, but even if there had been, her job was staying home to take care of our child. She passed the days talking on the phone to friends in Berkeley— these were friends who were attending classes, marching in demonstrations, going to parties, browsing museums.

It was time to board my flight. As we kissed goodbye, I brushed another tear from her cheek and told her how much I'd miss her. She promised to write every day . . . and she did:

February 24 . . . I cried all the way home from the airport. I can't even write about it—it hurts too much. I can't stand the thought of us being separated like this. It's so clear that we belong together and need each other. I never knew how much . . . This afternoon Hazel and I went to the Blue Chip Stamp place and I finally got the playpen and a walker . . . Tomorrow I have to move everything to Mom's. I'm not looking forward to it. I'm looking forward to seeing Mom, but I wish I could just stay here. I feel so at home with your parents and Wendy is happy here. But I could never feel right without you, Larry. I feel like we are one person.

February 25 . . . I'm at Mom's. God, I get depressed here. I was furious because I just wanted to stay at your parents'. Mom was very nice and so happy to see Wendy, but I can't help it. I can't live here. I'm just not comfortable. I don't know what to do. I'm so mixed up. I guess I'll try to live here for two or three weeks and then move back to your house . . . Everything is so screwed up around here. The phone in the kitchen is the only one that works. The phone man came at 10:30 but I had to tell him to come back later. I hope Mom's up by the time he comes back . . . Oh, Larry, you've only been gone two days and I'm miserable. I have nothing to do all day. If it wasn't for Wendy I'd go crazy. I won't ever let us be apart like this again. I feel like saying how could you do this to me—but I know it couldn't be helped . . . What should I do about our loan payment? Please tell me what to do . . . I'm crying now. I can't help it. I don't know how I'm going to go on without you. I can't wait until your letters start coming. Please write me every day.

February 26 . . . Living at Mom's is horrible one minute and wonderful the next . . . I got your first letter today and enjoyed it very much. It made me feel pretty stupid, though, because the letters I wrote you were so "mushy" because that's the way I felt. And yours wasn't. From now on, I'm going to write more like you do. I usually write such romantic letters because that's what's in my heart. Maybe you don't express yourself like I do, but you didn't sound very sad to be apart in your letter. I bet it's kind of fun to get away and go out with the boys and talk ball talk, etc.

February 27 . . . Mom and I went to Westwood and had the baby in the stroller all dressed up . . . I feel so sorry for Mom. This morning at 8 A.M. a cop was pounding on the door with a court order for her. I think it's about her book. He told me to wake her up. I got him to leave but he's coming back tonight. More problems! That's why I don't like living here! I'm going to try staying here another week. Sometimes I feel like packing up and leaving now. Like Mom is always telling me how to dress Wendy. I just wish spring training was over . . . I heard on the news last night that Jim Bunning held out for $85,000, the most a Phillie has ever gotten. Shucks! You'll double that someday!! . . . When we are together again, I am never ever going to let us do this again. It's not right. We belong together. I miss you so so much . . . Last night Mom said to me that you have never written to her— only once before we were married. She loves you, Larry, and I think it would be nice to write to her once in a while, like I wrote to your parents.

March 4 . . . I don't know how I'm going to last another six weeks. I can't live at my mother's and yet when I left her and came to your parents, it hurt her so much. It kills me because I know that she tries so hard to please me. And the baby is the only thing that brings any joy into her miserable life. Maybe in a week or two I'll go back to Mom's for a week. I'm just so mixed up and I have so many conflicting feelings about what I should do . . . I'm sorry my letters

aren't always cheerful and there are only crummy things to write
about. I know you don't like that. Sorry about that, Chief. It's just
that you don't know what a mess things are here and I'm the cause of
it all. Ick!

<u>March 8</u> . . . I just wanted to write and let you know how much I
love you. Life is so BLAAA without you. It kills me that you can't be
with Wendy during these two months and see all the changes. She's
becoming a real mischievous rascal . . . I too have been watching
"The Tonight Show" every night. It's so much better when it's in
California, but I don't like Johnny Carson as much as I used to . . .
Hey: "Do you know why they have taken all the Tampax machines out
of the rest rooms?" "No, why?" "Because the strings are too long for
the miniskirts!" Your mom told me that one. That's the most risqué
thing I've ever heard her say.

<u>March 10</u> . . . I took the car in yesterday. They replaced several
parts, fixed the steering, and gave it a complete lube job. It came to
$10. Your dad paid it and they will add it on to what we already owe
them . . . After I got the car, Wendy and I went over to Mom's (even
though she had hung up on me the night before) . . . I got your
letter yesterday and it was the sweetest, most sincere letter I've ever
received from you since we've been married. It made me feel like you
are still <u>in love</u> with me, as well as <u>love</u> me. Sometimes last winter in
Orinda I'd get the feeling that you just loved me and were no longer
in love with me. And I suppose that feeling was caused by our sexual
relationship. I'm so glad you brought it up in your letter because it
has been on my mind a great deal. I worry about our sex life and how
we can improve it. As you said, this separation will help, but it
shouldn't be that way. We shouldn't need to be apart—after all, we
can't leave each other every other year for two months just to increase
our desire. It should be there to begin with . . . My darling, I hope
you can understand what I mean. I love you so much, if I didn't this
wouldn't bother me so much. I really hope you get a book on Marital
Sex Life—or whatever they call them. Maybe you can find out what
our problem has been . . . Larry, I'm so glad you feel so optimistic
about it and I hope what you said in your letter comes true. Your
letter made me realize how wonderful you are because in your letter
you told me things about how you feel that you could probably never
say to me—and those are the things that a woman needs to hear now
and then . . . And I, too, have feelings about you that would be hard
to come right out and say. (Although I do express myself a little better

than you do in person.) . . . You are the perfect man. I mean it. You are a wonderful husband. I feel so safe being married to you. I know that you will always take care of me and Wendy and look after us. You know how to handle everything. You are so manly and I am so proud of you. You are so unwishy-washy. I couldn't stand that kind of a husband. I love the relationship our marriage is based on. You don't completely dominate me, and I certainly don't tell you what to do. You are definitely the man of the house and that is the way I want it to be. And yet I feel, at the same time, like we are partners in everything we do—each experience every day. We are friends, partners, lovers and lovers and lovers. Oh, everything is so wonderful. We are so happy together. Even though we're apart now, I am happy because we are so lucky to have found each other and our happiness together. Oh, Larry, I couldn't live without you in my life. I am yours until the day I die— and even after that . . . P.S.: We got a $27 Shell bill. What should I do about it?

March 11 . . . Mom called me tonight and gave me hell, sort of. Every time she calls she hangs up on me. I can see through it all, and I know she's just hurt. Oh—why can't this month be over with! I absolutely hate the predicament I'm in here . . . You'll be calling tomorrow and maybe you can give me some advice. I need you! The day we're back together will be the happiest day of my life—next to the day we were married, and the day I gave birth to your precious daughter . . . No, I didn't go see Blow-Up. I wanted to but I don't exactly love the idea of going to a movie with another girl. Someone might try to pick us up—or something disgusting like that. That's why I love to take Wendy with me wherever I go.

March 17 . . . I called you tonight but you were out. I can't help but be a little mad. I haven't gone out once since you've left. I haven't left the baby for one minute. I feel so cooped up I could scream. I have done nothing with anyone my own age. I feel like a vegetable! Or an old maid. Of course I'm not blaming you, but I have to let my feelings out to someone. I want you to be able to go out or do whatever you want—at least one of us should try to have fun. I know you don't like me to write about things that aren't pleasant—but these weeks have been pretty hard to take. I'm so sick of dragging the baby and all her stuff everywhere.

March 19 . . . I'm sorry, my darling—forgive me. I know our phone conversation wasn't very good but I am sad. Women can't contain their emotions as well as men can. It's stupid of me. Also, I'm about to get my period and that usually gives me the "blues," as they call it. Even if it was a crummy conversation, I still loved hearing your voice. You are always so cheerful—no matter what . . . I get furious when you tell me that they aren't giving you a chance. You're wonderful and those Phillie creeps won't even wise up to it! They don't deserve you. I bet if you were with another team you'd be at the top by now. But I guess we shouldn't expect too much—after all, you've only been in for two years. We're a lot better off than the majority of players. Just remember, when you're frustrated about baseball, that I think you're great . . . I truly am longing for you—in <u>every</u> way . . .

March 24 . . . I hate baseball for taking you away from me. But I love you enough to make up for it. This is no life for our family. We belong together, not just because we're "husband and wife," but because we just belong together—from the day we met we have . . . Anyway, I have all the faith in you in the world and in your ability. But if the Phillies don't recognize your talent soon, I don't want to keep going like this. I know you share my feelings.

March 30 . . . Honey, would you do me a favor? I've asked you before and you've never done it. <u>Please</u> write a short note to my mother. I know she causes us worries sometimes, but think of everything else she's given us—TV, crib, stroller, all my clothes, and most important of all, her love. She does love you and often says things like "Larry has never written me." It would mean a lot to her, sweetheart, so DO IT! (P.S.: Mom gave me $50 tonight for Easter. She knows that there are some things I need and she wanted me to get them.) Now she <u>can't</u> afford it, but she insisted. It'll really help us a lot, but I feel guilty too. So let's try to be as kind to her as possible. I'll try to keep most of the $ to pay bills—but I just <u>have</u> to buy some new bras—my nursing bras are a mess. I refuse to wear NURSING bras any longer!

April 7 . . . As I told you on the phone, Mom was sick all last week and it made me realize how much I love her and how hurt I'd be if I lost her. I was really worried. Your letter to her came at a perfect time! . . . Also, as I told you, my trip to San Diego to look for an apartment was a nightmare but I found a small place. I don't think $135 is too much for a two-bedroom, do you? I'm afraid it's not as nice as our Eugene, Berkeley, Macon, or Orinda places—but I will fix it up. It's in a great location—two blocks from the beach. The area is called Pacific Beach. I'm just happy we'll finally be back together. I can't believe this ordeal is almost over. Wait until you see how adorable your daughter is. She has the cutest, funniest personality . . . I'm counting the hours . . . What should we use for birth control?

32

Jim

I am not going to help murder and kill and burn other people simply to help continue the domination of the white slavemasters over the dark people the world over.
—Muhammad Ali, 1967

Jim walked purposefully across the Colorado State campus toward the Engineering Building. He had been summoned by Dr. Simons, his adviser in the department of civil engineering, and he didn't know why. It wasn't every day that the top dog called. Jim was nervous, afraid that Dr. Simons was calling him in to inform him that because of recent budget cutbacks in the department, his research assistant position was being cut. And if that was the case, it was so long grad school, hello Vietnam. His fingers were crossed as he hurried toward his appointment.

Things had been going great since he and Patty had moved to Fort Collins. Grad school had given a major boost to his self-esteem. He was away from the intimidation of his athletically more successful fraternity brothers . . . away from the shadow of his older brother Scott . . . away from his father's eccentric ways . . . away from the demand of being California cool . . . away from the anonymity of being just another student at Berkeley . . . away from the campus upheaval . . . away from Ralph. For the first time since the second grade, he and Ralph would not be living side by side. It was a relief—he had grown weary of

Ralph's relentless chatter and political campaigning for Ronald Reagan during the 1966 governor's race, although Reagan had gotten Jim's vote too.

Hurrying past the quiet Student Center on campus was a far cry from the noisy unrest of Sproul Plaza at Berkeley. He was happy not to be bombarded by pickets and love beads and the sound of the Jefferson Airplane coming from every apartment. In Berkeley there was no escaping the cultural upheaval—it was on every street corner—but at Colorado State the engineering department was a remote sanctuary, a sheltered world of academia and mathematical formulas. That was just fine with him. He was a top student, his scholarship paying for his tuition and books.

He and Patty were happy newlyweds, living in a modest one-bedroom furnished apartment near campus. They paid their bills with the money Patty made as a bank secretary and from the $250 a month Jim made working twenty hours a week as a research assistant. Life in Colorado was going great, with a paid-for Volvo, hamburger at thirty-five cents a pound, and best of all, lots of skiing. The only possible glitch on the horizon—and it was a definite possibility—was Uncle Sam. As much as Jim wanted to ignore politics, the escalating war in Vietnam and the continued call for more troops threatened his future. He had entered grad school hoping to retain his 2S deferment until he had his master's degree. But the Selective Service board was starting to go after previously exempt grad students. And now, if the news from Dr. Simons was bad and he had to drop out of school, he might as well just kiss the wife and Volvo goodbye and head on down to boot camp.

Jim had grown up in the fifties when war and the A-bomb were abstract, but now that the napalm and the grenades and the body counts were real, and with the troop count galloping toward a half million, he shivered at the enormity of what was happening in Vietnam. And what could happen to him? The student antiwar movement and a massive antidraft resistance had young men all over America burning their draft cards and fleeing to Canada, openly risking jail sentences, but Jim was not about to take such drastic measures. He considered himself patriotic and didn't question the sagacity of America's role in Vietnam. At one point, right after it was announced that grad school exemptions were being reduced, he had gone down to the Navy and Air Force recruiting offices and listened to their spiels. Just in case. A skiing buddy, who had been to Vietnam as a point man on patrols in the bush during the early days of the war and was the only member of his platoon who wasn't wounded or killed, had painted a convincing case for Jim to do everything possible not to go Vietnam as a foot soldier. This same buddy had learned to fly on the GI Bill and had taken Jim flying over Fort Collins several times in his private plane. "The only way to see Vietnam is from the air," the buddy instructed.

As Jim continued across campus, he checked his watch, hoping that whatever it was that Dr. Simons wanted to see him about didn't take too long. He and Patty were scheduled to leave for the slopes in an hour. He lived for the weekends and skiing. He had started skiing when he was thirteen, learning on a pair of cheap wooden skis at Dodge Ridge in the Sierras, spending his paper-route money on lift tickets and inexpensive ski clothes. In high school, whenever his mom would loan him the Pontiac Chieftain for the day, he was on his way to the slopes, sometimes taking Patty, who shared his love for the sport. His decision to come to Colorado State had been based largely on the fact that Fort Collins was located at the base of the foothills to the Rocky Mountains, close to great skiing and river recreation. The best times of his life had been his camping trips with the Boy Scouts, his ski weekends in high school, his river rafting down the Rogue River. One of the first things he had done after arriving in Colorado was to apply for the Ski Patrol, taking a first-aid course and putting himself through a rigid conditioning program in preparation for the entrance test. But on the day before the test, he slipped climbing a steep hill and landed butt-first on a sharp rock. The next morning he could barely strap on his skis. Still, this was a guy who'd survived Hell Week, rowed against the current of the Oakland Estuary, challenged the Class VI rapids of Rainie Falls. No way he was going to let a little bump on his rump hold him back. But halfway through the test he had to withdraw, too sore to continue. He came back two weeks later, however, and passed easily, joining the elite fraternity of the Ski Patrol. Every weekend he and Patty left Fort Collins on Friday afternoon and headed for Loveland Basin, paying fifteen dollars a month to share a miner's cabin with two other couples, huddling around the wood stove at night, drinking hot toddies to stay warm. The work was strenuous— rescuing skiers with broken legs, searching for lost skiers—but the payoff was that he got to ski every weekend, with free ski passes and no waiting in lift lines. For Jim, the Ski Patrol was an outlet for his adventuresome spirit, an escape from academia.

He was a star student. On the suggestion of his adviser, he had settled into a course of study in fluid mechanics and hydraulic engineering with a thesis topic of "Alternate Bars in Alluvial Channels." It was a thesis on the forces of river movement, analyzing the dynamics that cause a river to move sediment back and forth. He worked with a long flume, spending his days scraping and hoeing deposits of clay, silt, sand, and gravel, running varying levels of water over it, measuring movement, and creating equations that took up to five pages. It was raw scientific study in river mechanics, something that the Engineering Corps might someday use to prevent a river from flowing over its banks. He put in long hours, driven by the stimulation of scientific discovery. The thrill of silt movement and the agony of alluvial channels, however, was not the stuff of cocktail-party chatter, not that he and Patty were big on the party circuit. They were stay-at-homes, content to be together in the evenings and ski on weekends.

He reached the Engineering Building and entered Dr. Simons's office, still wondering why he'd been summoned. Dr. Simons wasted no time in breaking the good news. Jim had been selected for a prestigious National Science Foundation traineeship, which meant he would be paid $300 a month to devote all of his energy to studying and working toward his master's, a two-year program leading to a Ph.D. He would no longer have to work the twenty hours a week as a research assistant. But that was only part of the good news. Dr. Simons thought so much of his star student that he'd written a letter to Jim's draft board, advising them that Jim would be working directly under him on a river mechanics project vital to University research. The draft board had extended Jim's 2S deferment.

The war would have to proceed without him.

33

Steve

Be daring, adventurous, bold.
Have guts, nerve, backbone.
Knock down anything that gets in your way.
Charge massively!
  —From "Outline for Rhino Success,"
  Marine Corps handout

Dawn was breaking over the Sacramento Valley as he drove his Mustang into a secluded pear orchard in Courtland south of the city. He was alone. Nobody knew where he was nor what he was about to do. Not even his wife, Ayris. His induction physical at the Sacramento Army depot was in three hours.

Parked under a tree, he retrieved a brown paper bag from under the front seat and spread the contents on the bucket seat next to him. It was an ounce of marijuana. He studied it, slowly running his fingers through the pile, offering it a good-luck kiss. He had never smoked dope before, but according to what he'd read, it was supposed to constrict blood vessels and cause a temporary rise in blood pressure. That was exactly the result he was looking for, because he'd also read that the Army didn't accept anyone with high blood pressure.

He pulled a pack of Zig Zag papers from his shirt pocket, then painstakingly rolled five joints, each of them looking like a white worm with a marble in its belly. With the windows rolled up, he lit the first one and inhaled, coughing and gagging and spewing smoke. He had never smoked a cigarette. His face turned ashen as his lungs and the interior of his Mustang filled with smoke. He had been warned that first-time smokers sometimes don't get high, and that he shouldn't get discouraged . . . to just keep puffing. He finished the first joint, then lit another. And another. He checked his watch every five minutes, afraid he'd be late. It must be working, he figured, feeling his heart pounding. He turned on the car radio, and when the disc jockey on KROY announced the school lunch menu for the Sacramento Unified School District, he laughed and laughed and laughed.

The headlights of a car appeared in the distance. He ducked down, stashing the dope under the seat. He could envision himself trying to explain it to his dad if he got busted: "Honest, Dad," he'd say, "I'm really not a pothead. I was just trying to get out of military service." The car disappeared.

After finishing all five joints, he drove to the Army depot and parked a mile away, running wind sprints to the entrance in further hopes of raising his blood pressure. During his examination he told the doctor about the three brain concussions, the two cracked ribs, the broken wrist, and the sprained ankle. And during his blood pressure test, he tried to hyperventilate.

None of it worked. He passed with flying colors. His notice to report for active duty, he was told, should come within the next two months. He stuffed the rest of the dope into a shoe box at the bottom of the closet and forgot all about it.

Steve finished spreading out the tarp and the sleeping bags for the evening, then snuck up behind Ayris as she prepared a dinner of baked beans and trail mix. He threw his arms around her and held her close, gently swaying under the light rain that was falling. Lifting up the back of her hair, he kissed her softly on the neck.

"I love you," he whispered.

"What's all this about?" she asked with a smile.

"Just wanted to let you know I'm glad we're married," he said, melting her with his tenderness.

They were stopped for the evening at a roadside rest on U.S. 98 in the De Soto National Forest east of Hattiesburg, Mississippi, twelve days into their ride across the southern United States on their two lightweight Honda 90s. It was February 1967, and the rainy aftermath of a severe storm had driven them north of their planned route through Biloxi. Their destination was Pensacola, Florida, to visit friends, then up the eastern seaboard to New York, where they hoped to catch a ride on a steamer to Europe. They'd left Sacramento with $700 in traveler's checks, two passports, and a copy of *Europe on $5 a Day*.

Steve admired his wife's gritty spirit and her willingness to join him in throwing caution to the wind on this trip. At nights, they slept in roadside rests or off the side of the road, shivering in their sleeping bags—it may have been the southern route but it was still winter and freezing at night. On the highway, Steve would look back at Ayris and laugh, amused at the sight of his ethereal wife chugging along, her helmet visor splattered with bugs, her legs singed with exhaust burns, her elbows scraped raw from two bad spills, one near Big Sur, the other on the road into the Grand Canyon. He laughingly accused her of wanting to stop and ogle every flower or work of nature along the highway. She accused him of not even wanting to stop to go to the bathroom.

Before leaving Sacramento they had discussed fleeing to Canada to avoid the draft. Seriously discussed. But they decided that a life in exile wouldn't be worth it. Steve concluded that the best thing to do was to go ahead and leave for Europe as they had planned, then stay incommunicado on the road. That way, he said, when they returned to America in a year or two, he could claim he never got the notice to report. "And besides," he maintained, "the war will be over by then." Ayris was skeptical of this head-in-the-sand plan, but agreed to go along, convinced it was a better alternative than Vietnam. They were both opposed to the war, Ayris more on political and moral grounds, Steve more for personal reasons—he had things to do and places to go in his life, and spending two years in the Army seemed an eternity to a guy who considered a sixty-second Polaroid too long a wait.

"But we have to call home when we get to Pensacola to let them know we're okay," she argued. Reluctantly, he agreed.

They had come to Pensacola to visit Terry and Val Holberton, friends from Cal who'd been married the previous summer in Beverly Hills. Val, a Pi Phi at Cal, was three months pregnant; Terry, a member of the elite Gun Club and a witness to Steve's fall from the balcony, was in Marine flight school, training to be a backseater, soon to ship out to Vietnam. Steve thought Terry to be a straightforward, steadfast guy, quick-witted and bright.

Against his better judgment, Steve phoned his parents, and the news was bad: his official orders from the U.S. Army had arrived. He was to report to active duty in ten days.

"Might as well get shitfaced," he reasoned.

They went to the Oyster Bar and ordered a pitcher of whiskey sours. They were on their second pitcher when Steve passed out under the table. Terry carried him outside and poured him into the back seat of his new Oldsmobile station wagon for the ride back to the apartment. Twenty-four hours later, they were back for more. "Fuck it," said Steve, "I'm still going to Europe."

"You're going to have to come back sooner or later," said Terry, ordering another pitcher. "Then what?"

Steve shrugged. Terry, the archetypal gung ho Marine, launched into a recruitment speech. There was no doubt in his mind that the Corps was *the* elite fighting force in the world. He'd joined to learn how to fly, and advised Steve that he should do the same.

"You can be a grunt in the Army, or you can sign up for Officer Candidate School in Quantico and be with the best," Terry said. "But you can't run."

The next morning, after barfing his scrambled eggs through his nose, Steve walked into the recruiting office, squinting to read the sign over the door: "The Marines have landed and the situation is well in hand."

He sat across the desk from the sergeant major, who stood erect, hair cropped, stomach firm, face tight. The red stripe down his perfectly pressed blue pants was as straight as the look in his eyes. He explained that a Marine was somebody who didn't know the meaning of the word "can't," that the Corps was "brotherhood" . . . "esprit de corps" . . . "a way of life."

Steve nodded, his head throbbing.

The sergeant major rattled on about Marines ignoring the limits and accomplishing whatever they set out to do. He gave Steve two pamphlets, one a Marine guidepost on loyalty, attitude, and selfless service to country, the other a discourse on the secret of something called "Rhino Success" and the art of charging massively. Steve couldn't focus on either one.

But on March 14, 1967, Steven James Radich, former member of Little League, Boy Scouts, 36 Club, Pi Kappa Alpha, Skull and Keys, Beta Beta, Gun Club, and University of California varsity football and rugby teams, was sworn into the United States Marine Corps, reporting for basic training at Officer Candidate School at Quantico, Virginia. Ayris, his wife of five months, returned to Sacramento.

According to the word in the barracks when Steve arrived for the start of boot camp, the officer candidates in his class would be on their way to Vietnam in early 1968, right around Tet, the Vietnamese New Year.

34

Loren

They stood under the chandelier in the ornate mezzanine of a Paris hotel, all of them talking heatedly, all of them trying to get their points across at the same time—Loren, his mother, and the former Miss California. Passersby turned to stare, struck by the volume and intensity. And the physical presence of the three tall Americans.

What Loren had hoped would be the best time of his life, a monthlong rugby tour of England and France with the Olympic Club of San Francisco, was turning into a nightmare, a hopeless job of trying to placate the travel demands of his mother and his girlfriend. The immediate issue was where the former Miss California was going to spend the night. She'd signed up for the trip too late to get a reservation at the hotel that Genevieve was staying at across the street, and the hotel where the team was staying had strict rules forbidding women above the mezzanine. Loren had made it abundantly clear he was staying with the team; he was determined that nothing was going to cramp his fun with the boys.

"Loren, at least you could go with her and help her find a room," said Genevieve.

"I told you to stay out of my business," he responded. "Go back to your hotel!"

For Genevieve the trip was a respite from her miserable marriage. Hal's struggle with alcohol was improving—he'd been through the detox program at Herrick Hospital a second time and was faithfully attending Alcoholics Anonymous meetings while Genevieve attended Al-Anon meetings. But the marriage was still tormented, another year of separate vacations . . . and another year of Genevieve relying on her son for joy and sustenance . . . just as she'd done in following him to Miami and Hawaii. Loren was tired of the responsibility, angry at his father.

Genevieve did as instructed and returned to her hotel, leaving Loren and the former Miss California alone on the mezzanine to continue their debate. Actually, it was more of a lecture. Loren was intractable. He hadn't come to Europe to hold hands and visit castles and museums. This was a rugby trip. There was no use in her arguing. On this trip, she was the fifth wheel, maybe the sixth. Rugby was his mistress. He had been instrumental in convincing the venerable and staid Olympic Club in San Francisco to sponsor the team, a club made up mostly of ex-Cal players who'd toured Australia two years earlier. Nobody on the squad was a more enthusiastic spokesman or better salesman for the sport than Loren. Or more boisterous in the pubs. He was a touring ambassador, obsessed with winning. The team was holding its own in Europe, playing a slashing, knock-'em-down style as compared to the finesse of the more experienced European sides. Loren's long, cross-field passes and his leaping ability made him the favorite of the large crowds. He flourished in the camaraderie; that's why he liked rugby better than football—the togetherness, the comity. The Oakland Raiders couldn't match it, he thought. "Won't find any homos or suicides in rugby," he bragged.

"Why did you invite me on this trip?" asked the former Miss California, who was in her senior year at Cal and, despite her parents' objections, had dropped out of school for a quarter to come to Europe with him.

"I wanted to be with you," he answered.

She wondered if she was just there for window dressing, the pretty girl brought along to hang obediently on the arm of the big star. If that was the case, she wanted no part of it. His teammates, some of whom still thought she was too prissy, had made bets that she wouldn't last the whole trip. In London, when she'd complained about his lack of attention and threatened to leave, midfielder Tom Blanchfield, his roommate, asked her if he could help her pack, even calling the bell captain to come to the room and help her carry her bags down to the lobby. But she'd

Larry and Denise on their wedding day in 1965. (*Photo courtesy of author*)

Larry in the big leagues, 1968.
(*Photo courtesy of author*)

Larry with daughters Sarah and Wendy, 1983. (*Terri Farris*)

Larry, 1986. (*Photo courtesy of author*)

Jim triumphs over Rainie Falls, 1963.
(*Photo courtesy of Jim van Hoften*)

Jim on a mission over North Vietnam, 1973. (*Jim van Hoften*)

Jim and Vallarie, 1974. (*Photo courtesy of Jim van Hoften*)

Jim in space, 1984. (*Photo courtesy of NASA*)

Loren, starting defensive back for the Cal Bears, 1964. (*Photo courtesy of UC Athletic Department*)

Loren was arguably the best rugby player in America in 1965.
(*Photo Courtesy of Loren Hawley*)

Loren, Rita and Garrett, 1987. (*Photo courtesy of Loren Hawley*)

Hayseed doing business in 1991. (*Photo courtesy of Loren Hawley*)

Ron, Ralph and Betty Vaughn at home, 1955. (*Photo courtesy of Ralph Vaughn*)

Ron, starting end for Cal Bears, 1962. (*Photo courtesy of UC Athletic Department*)

Ron on college graduation day, 1964. (*Photo courtesy of Ron Vaughn*)

Ron and son Royce, 1977. (*Photo courtesy of Ron Vaughn*)

Steve, starting linebacker for Cal Bears, 1965. (*Photo courtesy of UC Athletic Department*)

Steve graduates from Marine Officer Candidate School, 1968.
(*Photo courtesy of Mary Radich*)

Steve and Ayris bike across country, 1967. (*Photo courtesy of Ayris Hatton*)

Steve and his daughter Filaree, 1976. (*Photo courtesy of Ayris Hatton*)

stiffened her resolve, determined to prove her pertinacity. It bothered her that Loren could be so sweet and affectionate when they were alone, yet as soon as he was around his teammates, he had to play the "big man." It was as if he had to prove he wasn't "pussywhipped." Nevertheless, she continued to be hooked on his wild, spontaneous side, so different from her own prim and proper grace. She loved to watch him play, captivated by his strength and agility. And for all the boisterous, rowdy behavior, she enjoyed the spirited gatherings after the matches.

Loren felt hemmed in, everyone demanding his time—his mom wanting to make dinner plans, the former Miss California wanting him to take her to the Palace of Versailles, his teammates wanting him to hit the pubs.

"Is a few hours of your time too much to ask?" inquired the former Miss California.

"I'm not your tour guide," he replied. "I didn't come here to sightsee."

"But this is Paris . . ."

"I don't give a splash of duck shit about Napoleon or Louis the Fourteenth or any of that. I'm here to play rugby."

"But . . ."

"But nothing. You've got two choices. Like it or take the next plane home."

"You could at least help me find a room," she pleaded.

"You're a big girl," he said. "You can take care of yourself. You studied French."

He had adopted the Satchel Paige attitude that pretty women were like buses—never run after one because there'll always be another one coming along in a few minutes. For all his private sweet talk and assurances to the former Miss California that she was his one and only, he had no intention of settling down anytime in the near future. He knew he wasn't ready for the responsibility. All his friends who'd already gotten married seemed miserable.

The former Miss California threw her arms up in frustration, then headed out the hotel door, asking directions to the nearest hotel. She headed down a side street, determined that if it was strength and independence he wanted, that's what she'd give him. But what were those footsteps following her? Afraid to look, she quickened her pace. So did the footsteps. Glancing back, she spotted a man in the shadows, a Hugoesque character—hunchbacked, dressed in tattered clothes. He was running toward her. She tightened her grip on her suitcase and started to run, not slowing down until she reached the safety of the Champs-Élysées.

"Damn you, Loren," she muttered.

This was the last straw, she told herself. Either he would change when they returned to California or the relationship was doomed.

She survived the trip, proving his teammates wrong, but on the flight home she gave him the ultimatum. "I don't understand what you want," he replied.

"You have to give more of yourself," she said. "Be willing to take a risk."

"You don't understand," he said. "You've already changed me more than any of my friends thought possible. My mother thinks so too."

It was 1967 and Loren was back in Berkeley. He rang up a sale on the UC Corner cash register, then scowled as he watched a long-haired hippie tape a Jerry Rubin campaign poster to the front window. As far as he was concerned, the mass influx of hippies on Telegraph Avenue was an invasion of the scourge of the earth, a direct threat to his new entrepreneurial spirit.

"Take that shit somewhere else," he yelled.

Loren now had more than just a semi-proprietary interest in the store. Using his considerable persuasive energy, he had convinced his grandparents, Pop and Eddie, to take out a $35,000 loan on their rice fields to help him finance his part of a co-venture with Jerry Olson and Craig—they were going to open a UC Corner next to the campus in Davis. It was his brainchild and his enthusiasm that had launched the project. He would be the manager. But until the architects and the bankers were finished drawing up the final plans for Davis, he was working at the store in Berkeley, learning the business—sales, merchandising, inventory, hassling the hippies. His job wasn't to read the poetry of Ginsberg, or the novels of Kerouac, or the Zen of Watts and Snyder—he was trying to figure out what paperbacks the hippies were reading . . . and stealing.

Telegraph Avenue had become a freakish marketplace, daily challenging his view of the world with its cultural diversity and liberal politics. He disapproved of the antiwar movement, maintaining that the world had been fighting wars for centuries, and as long as America was in Vietnam, it might as well go all out to win it. He also disapproved of the civil rights movement. "I don't mind somebody trying to better their position," he stated. "But I think lots of niggers are taking advantage of the system. There's good ones and bad ones, just like whites. But they don't deserve shit. Nobody deserves anything handed to them. I suppose they've had a bad deal, but if I was in charge, I'd shoot Eldridge Cleaver and all those Black Panthers. Martin Luther King too. Maybe there's a difference in their style, but they all have the same objective. My solution would be to call in the tanks and the Rat Patrol jeeps and mow 'em down."

To many, Telegraph Avenue was Berkeley's crown jewel. By the fall of 1967, following the Summer of Love, it had replaced Haight Street as the center of hippie life in the Bay Area. But as its notoriety increased, so did the problems—shoplifting, panhandling, vandalism. Concomitantly, there was escalating antagonism between merchants and the growing population of runaway youths and hippies. Reacting to complaints of Berkeley conservatives, the city initially adopted a policy of strict law enforcement along Telegraph to drive away the "undesirables." Uniformed policemen patrolled the street, enforcing a nonexistent curfew, checking draft cards, busting dope smokers. Loren cheered them on. The hippies were trying his patience with their stealing and littering, forcing him to spend as much time keeping an eye out for shoplifters as he did for pretty coeds. As reports of police misconduct increased, resentment and hostility in the community grew, and in an effort to help ease tensions, the Better Berkeley Committee (BBC), a coalition of students, activists, and concerned Telegraph merchants, was organized to replace the police foot patrols with an unarmed citizens' patrol. These monitors greeted people with smiles, hoping to discourage overt drug deals and the rising tide of shoplifting and panhandling. But the BBC experiment flopped and the police returned. Street people went on periodic rampages, breaking merchants' windows, including UC Corner's. The insurance company canceled the store's vandalism coverage. The Berkeley *Gazette* described the situation on Telegraph as "anarchy." To Loren, the UC Corner solution was simple: "Kick their fuckin' ass when they get out of line."

After watching the hippie put up the "Rubin for Mayor" poster, he walked outside the store and ripped it down.

"Why did you do that?" demanded the hippie.

"Because I felt like it!" he answered, grabbing the hippie by the shirt and lifting him straight up off the sidewalk, then stuffing him into a city of Berkeley garbage can. "Fuck Jerry Rubin!"

35

Ron

In the real dark night of the soul it is always three o'clock in the morning.
—F. Scott Fitzgerald

The dayroom at the Langley Porter Psychiatric Center in San Francisco was his hangout. He came there every morning after medication and took his seat in the big leather chair against the wall and observed, telling himself that he wasn't really a patient. He was just an interested spectator. He didn't do the jigsaw puzzles, or play cards, or watch TV. He just passively observed. And sometimes he paced.

The ward door opened and a black orderly entered, dressed in starched milk-white pants and shirt and polished white shoes with rubber soles that squeaked when he walked down the hall. The squeaking bugged Ron. It also annoyed him that the orderly knew what went on inside those padded rooms on the other side of the ward door and he didn't. Ron thought a lot about the padded rooms and the patients in straitjackets. And the patients with the smoked-out eyes who looked like they'd had one too many trips to the Shock Room. And what about the young residents who came into the dayroom and stood by the stainless-steel water fountain, scanning the patients? Ron eyed them suspiciously, wondering what gave these young hotshots the right to look at him as if he was some sort of monkey in a cage. In his therapy sessions he wanted to call time-out and start asking them a thing or two. Why did he always have to do all the talking?

And why did he always have to listen to the same sappy "Feelin' Groovy" song playing on the hi-fi every time he came into the dayroom? The guy across the room with the flat face and big forehead just kept playing it over and over, sitting in his chair, swaying back and forth. It frayed Ron's nerves, a Top 40 anthem to his guilt, reminding him that he'd thoughtlessly fathered one child and now had another one on the way . . . a child that he wasn't going to be able to support. All because he had been obsessed with "lookin' for fun and feelin' groovy." So he thought. He wanted to smash the record. But he knew if he did he wouldn't get to go Outside, which is what the inpatients called being released.

Ron, who had checked himself into Langley, wasn't as far gone as the Acutes or the Chronics in the other ward, but he had certainly presented the doctors with a psychiatric shopping list of symptoms and psychotic behavior: he had retreated from almost all of his friendships; he was finding it harder to focus and concentrate on external things; he laughed for no apparent reason; he burst into a rage without provocation; he misplaced hostility by striking out at innocent people; he withdrew from his parents and distrusted their love.

The doctors hadn't made it clear, at least not to him, what the diagnosis was. Maybe a form of schizophrenia. Or a psychotic break. But labels weren't his concern. He just wanted to feel normal again. But sometimes he wondered if he'd ever been normal. Even as a child he'd thought of himself as different. It didn't help that his friends sometimes weren't sure if he was white or black or invisible ink.

The door opened again and Anna walked into the room. Ron grinned, happy to see her smiling, freckled face and strawberry-blond hair. She was his Florence Nightingale come to rescue him and take him Outside. The doctors were releasing him after only two weeks as an inpatient. They had prescribed him a month's supply of Thorazine and instructed him to attend a weekly outpatient therapy session at the clinic. And if that wasn't enough, Anna was convinced she could nurture him back to health with love and affection . . . and soon they would be a beautiful family, with a husband who went to work every day as an architect and came home every evening to a wife, child, and two-car garage in the suburbs.

Dressed in his normal uniform—dirty slacks, wrinkled dress shirt, wing tips—he walked west on Wilshire Boulevard toward Santa Monica.

Alone. Aimless. Trying to get a grip. He'd lied to Anna about why he'd come to L.A., telling her it was for a job interview. He knew that's what she wanted to hear—she hadn't stopped prodding him since he'd been released from Langley. Get a job. Get a job. Get a job. That's all he ever heard from her, it seemed. "Stop nagging," he'd reply. He'd applied for a junior draftsman's position with a San Francisco firm but had been turned down. Much to his relief. He knew he wasn't ready for the responsibility. It was all he could do to get himself out of their apartment on Sacramento Street in the city, preferring to sit alone in the living room, curtains drawn, introspecting. He'd stopped taking his medication as soon as he was released, uncomfortable with its effects—the cotton mouth, the lethargy. "I'm trying the best I can," he repeatedly said. Anna persisted. He knew she'd be pissed if she found out that the real reason he'd borrowed money and took off for L.A. was to look for the son he'd abandoned six years earlier. That was money that should have gone to his new family.

As he continued his trek down Wilshire Boulevard, his search was pretty much at a dead end. He had learned that after he had given up the baby, it was placed in a foster home in Glendale until a permanent adoption could be arranged. The foster family named the infant Patrick Parker. That's where the trail ended.

Waiting for a signal to change, he was asked for spare change by a disheveled man he guessed to be a refugee from the nearby Sawtelle Veterans Center. He fumbled through his empty pockets, remembering his own unsuccessful attempts at panhandling on Michigan Avenue in cold and windy Chicago. Noticing the man's shoeless feet, he removed his shoes and handed them to him, then continued barefoot down the street.

One act of charity, he figured, deserved another. As he walked through the parking lot of the Fox and Hounds Restaurant, a valet parking attendant asked him if the brand-new Mustang idling in the lot was his. Ron said yes, the attendant handed him the keys, and the next thing he knew, he was crusing west on Wilshire, radio blaring, then north on the Pacific Coast Highway to Topanga Canyon, where he followed a Cadillac up a long winding driveway, paranoid that he was being tailed by the Highway Patrol. When the driver of the Cadillac jumped out of his car and walked to the Mustang, Ron threw it in reverse and headed back to the Fox and Hounds. He was already tired of the life of a car thief.

Instead of abandoning the car on the street, he returned it to valet parking, then walked inside and turned himself in to the manager, confessing his crime. He waited patiently in the lobby while the manager called the police, who arrived to handcuff him and haul him off to jail. He declined his phone call.

Sitting in the holding tank, he felt the glare of a large black from across the cell, a man who looked to Ron to be a jailhouse regular.

Ron decided that as long as he was going to be in jail, he might as well go for the full punishment. He walked past the black man and sat down on the edge of a bunk, peeling back the blanket off a sleeping inmate. Slowly, he slid his hands up the man's leg, fondling his thigh.

"What the fuck you doing, faggot?" demanded the black man.

"Mind your own business," Ron replied.

The black man moved toward him, then doused him with water. Ron jumped to his feet, ready to fight. Hearing the disturbance, a guard rushed to the cell and separated them. Transferred to another cell, Ron spent the night serving his self-imposed penitence for his self-diagnosed selfishness, waiting to be released on his own recognizance and return to San Francisco.

Anna finally caved in to the emotional and financial burden of trying to support him. Following one of his daily odysseys to Haight-Ashbury, he returned to the apartment and found his meager belongings heaped in a pile outside the door. Spread across the top was his Cal letterman's jacket.

"Cut loose the past and get on with your life," she directed. "Or else you're going to lose this child too."

It was 3 A.M. when Ron tapped on the bedroom window of Jack Trumbo, his former fraternity brother, football teammate, and architectural study partner. Trumbo, just back from a spiritual odyssey of his own in his VW van to Taos, New Mexico, was living in Berkeley and working for a small firm. He hadn't seen Ron in two years and was flabbergasted at the change, saddened at how gaunt and troubled his friend had become. He had heard rumors from other fraternity brothers that Ron had fallen into the clutches of LSD, but Ron assured him those rumors weren't true. "I'm fucked up on my own," he explained.

In a world he viewed as hostile, Ron trusted Trumbo. He seemed centered, compassionate, possessing inner calm and a sense of security that reassured Ron. For the next two weeks, Trumbo housed and fed him, counseled and encouraged him. He arranged a job interview with a small San Francisco firm that resulted in Ron's being hired as a junior draftsman; and he met with Anna, facilitating a reconciliation.

Despite Ron's problems, Anna had not given up hope for the great and spiritual family life with him. She also prayed for a return to the passion they had when first they met. Since her pregnancy, he had withdrawn physically. She invited him to join her for her first Lamaze class. "I'll give it a try," he pledged.

For all his good intentions, and for all the efforts of Trumbo and Anna, his fog refused to lift. He lasted only briefly on his new job, unable to complete the simplest of assignments. Each passing day seemed to elicit more strange behavior. On one of his walks he passed an auditorium where a lecture was just ending. He watched as a small circle of people from the audience gathered around the speaker, who seemed to him to be pontificating. Ron edged his way into the circle, listened for a moment, then slapped the speaker across the cheek. Before anyone could respond, he walked out the door and into the night, giggling.

Ron stared straight ahead, smiling obsequiously as Anna and the doctor explained why they had decided it was best if he didn't assist with the delivery. Without listening to them, he knew the reason why—Anna didn't think he could handle it.

Anna was beginning to worry that there wasn't much of anything he could handle. She had hounded him for days about going down to the State Welfare Office to apply for financial assistance and food stamps—there was no food in the cupboards, no money in the bank, and the baby was due in a month. When he begged off, claiming he didn't know how to do it and that it was too emasculating, she flew into a rage. "Be a man!" she ordered. And when he continued to resist, she took him by the hand and drove him there herself. He brought a letter from his outpatient psychiatrist stating that he was medically unable to work due to "severe emotional stress." The case worker at the Welfare Office awarded him full benefits for the totally disabled.

"It would probably be better if you didn't come in the delivery room," said the doctor. "It's a pretty stressful environment."

Ron nodded and smiled. On the one hand, he'd thought all along that the whole Lamaze training was silly, a bunch of self-righteous, pseudo-hip phonies sitting around on Indian print cushions and panting like a bunch of dogs, telling themselves how enlightened they were and how much more mellow their kids would be. Such bullshit, he thought. On the other hand, he was sad that this had come to pass on such a special occasion, that he couldn't be there for Anna.

On May 15, 1968, while on full welfare, he and Anna were married by a judge in a civil ceremony in San Francisco City Hall. Five days later, Anna gave birth to a son. They named him Royce, following a fourth-generation tradition of Vaughn males—Roscoe, Ralph, Ron, and now Royce.

In the ebb and flow that was his mind, Ron was euphoric.

In September they moved to Los Angeles, lured by the promise of a job for Ron and a rent-free house. Ralph and Betty, their own marriage hanging by a thread, had moved to an apartment in Marina Del Rey so that Betty could be closer to her new job as librarian at Marina Del Rey Junior High. Their house, the one Ron had grown up in, was unoccupied. The promised job was as a junior draftsman for a firm on Pico Boulevard, a position arranged by Ralph.

Anna was hopeful that all the changes—marriage, fatherhood, relocation, new job—would give Ron the psychological booster shot he needed. It didn't. According to Anna, he refused to go out socially, criticized her constantly, shunned the baby, eschewed sexual contact. He saw it the other way, that it was she who was cold and unsupportive. Mostly, he sat in the darkened living room and remembered scenes from his boyhood. The house was a small cathedral to Ralph's architectural style back in the forties before he "got conservative," as Ron put it. In the living room was a large fireplace with Mexican lava stone, a twenty-foot purple sofa, high beamed ceilings, gray bookshelves, and *no* windows. "There's nothing worth looking at," Ralph once explained to the building inspector. An indoor patio and garden in the middle of the living room were covered by a plastic corrugated roof, and on rainy nights when he was a boy, the raindrops sounded to Ronnie like BBs bouncing on a tin plate. The floor of the patio was dirt, with a marble fountain, small shrubs, and a cactus Ralph had added to give it a Mojave look. He had also added birds— canaries, finches, pigeons—and when Ron didn't deliver on his chore of cleaning up the bird droppings, Ralph covered the ground with crushed white rock, camouflaging the bird shit, making life easier for Ronnie. The exterior of the house was trimmed with natural redwood and landscaped with ivy, geraniums, pampas grass, and African ferns, and here again Ralph had made things easier on his young son by hiring a gardener after Ronnie didn't deliver on his chore of keeping the landscape trimmed. In the backyard was an incinerator with a conical top, and when he was eight, Ronnie would lie in his bed, peeking at it under his curtains, imagining it a wicked gargoyle, making himself so scared he would have to get up and go into the living room. He always wanted to be in the living room, near his mother, away from the demons that lurked outside his window.

One evening Anna and Ron went to visit Ralph and Betty in Marina Del Rey. On their way home in Anna's VW, they got into an argument.

"Pull the car over right now!" he demanded.

She refused. When she slowed down for the next intersection, he jumped out of the moving car, stumbling to the concrete. She circled the block and picked him up.

When they walked in the house, the argument continued. She slammed a door, knocking a hand-carved family tree off the wall, a piece of art that Ralph had spent hours sanding and varnishing. It crashed to the floor, breaking in half.

"You bitch!" Ron screamed.

"It wouldn't have happened if . . ."

"If what?"

"If you were a man instead of a basket case!"

He whirled around and backhanded her, the blow sending her reeling, splitting her lip.

She ran to the kitchen and phoned the police. He didn't try to stop her. He was too weary, too confused, too ashamed. "I'm sorry," he pleaded.

She pressed charges. The next day she and Royce were on their way back to San Francisco. And for the second time in a year, Ron checked himself in for inpatient treatment, this time to the psychiatric ward of Los Angeles County General Hospital. It was back to the dayroom, back to the medication, back to the shrinks, back to wondering what went wrong.

36

Larry

1968—a year that shaped a generation.
—*Time* magazine

I peered in to get the sign from Phillie catcher Clay Dalrymple. He held down one finger. Fastball. My specialty. Digging in at the plate, his fierce panther eyes glaring right through me, was Pittsburgh Pirate right fielder Roberto Clemente, the four-time National League batting champion and future Hall of Famer. In the stands, sitting with all the other Phillie wives, was Denise with eighteen-month-old Wendy in her lap.

It was the last week of 1968 spring training. The Phillies were breaking camp in two days, heading to Los Angeles and opening day against the Dodgers. All the roster cuts had been made by manager Gene Mauch. Except one. The mathematics of the situation were easy to figure—there were eleven pitchers still in camp and only ten would make the club.

My chances seemed good. Nineteen sixty-seven had been my best year in the minor leagues. Pitching for the San Diego Padres in the AAA Pacific Coast League, I won 14 games with an e.r.a. of 2.98. My curve and slider were still iffy, but Ned Garver, a Cincinnati scout, was quoted in the Indianapolis *Star* as saying, "Larry Colton is the best pitching prospect I've seen this year. I've never seen a young pitcher change speeds so effectively." During the winter, I'd pitched in the Florida Instructional League (4–0) and for Ponce in the Puerto Rico Winter League (6–2), arriving in Clearwater with a pound of clippings to staple to my chest, including one from *Sports Illustrated*: "Philadelphia's seemingly old Phils have a fine young pitcher named Larry Colton, who is married to Hedy Lamarr's daughter and did not do too badly at San Diego last year for the pennant-winning Padres. Colton is expected to help fill in for Jim Bunning, who was traded."

Roberto Clemente didn't give a rip about my clippings. This wasn't the first time I had pitched against him. I was hoping he'd forgotten our last encounter—it had been a scary one. For me, anyway. It happened in winter ball in a game in San Juan. I had been instructed that the way to pitch him was inside. Way inside . . . jam him with pitches a foot inside, right at his chest. His stance was deep in the box, so deep that it looked from the mound that he couldn't cover the outside part of the plate with his bat, but as every National League pitcher knew, he stepped into the plate and creamed outside pitches to right field and beyond. So when I faced him in front of 18,000 of his wildly devoted countrymen, I hummed my first pitch just as I'd been instructed, a whisker melody that sent him sprawling to the dirt. Slowly, he dusted himself off, leering at me with an animal intensity that took my breath away. He was the greatest hitter on the planet, the God of Puerto Rico, and if I was reading his eyes correctly, he was not pleased about being dusted by a no-name rookie. And judging from the savage booing of his rabid fans, they weren't too happy with me either. But on the next pitch, Ponce catcher Pat Corrales, a street-tough Mexican-American from Fresno, called for more of the same. I was as scared of Corrales as I was of Clemente. He sometimes walked out to the mound after I'd made a bad pitch, and with the ball in his fist, jam it into my chest with a simple directive: "Throw the ball hard, puss!" My second pitch to Clemente, another fastball, rode the Caribbean wind right up under his chin again . . . and once more he hit the dirt. Again he got up slowly, only this time, instead of dusting himself off, he dropped his bat, and with the most menacing snarl in recorded history, started toward me. He wasn't running—he was just walking confidently, an executioner on his way to another day at the office. I was already backpedaling toward St. Croix. "*¡Muerte el yanqui!*" the crowd screamed, which if I remembered correctly from my Spanish at Westchester High, could be roughly translated to mean: "Kill that no good motherfuckin' gringo and then use him for shark bait!" Or something like that. But before he got too far out of the batter's box, Corrales leaped in front of him and said something to him in Spanish. I was nearing the center-field wall at the time and couldn't tell quite what was said, but whatever it was, Clemente turned and headed back to the batter's box and the umpire signaled me to return to the country. On my next pitch, a fastball a foot outside, Clemente ripped a screaming double to right center. Corrales told me later that he simply appealed to Clemente's humanitarian spirit, explaining to him that I had a wife and child and was all for statehood for his native island.

But that was winter. This was spring, and Mauch, the God of my career, was in the dugout, his steel-blue eyes watching my every move, trying to decide if I had what it took to be a big-leaguer. In my previous outings that spring under his watchful eye, I had thrown well (four earned runs in fourteen innings). I'd even gotten a couple base hits to help my case. Still, I knew that if I screwed up in this final test against Clemente and the Pirates, I was on my way back to the minors.

Dalrymple was giving me an inside target—way inside. As I started my windup, my brain and all my baseball instincts were telling me to zip one right up under Clemente's chin again. The feisty Mauch would surely think me a manly man if I put the best hitter on the planet on his butt. But as my long right arm windmilled past my body, my heart was telling me to sneak one across the outside corner. And that's exactly where the ball went. Clemente's eyes lit up, his muscles rippled, his bat uncoiled. It was a thing of baseball grace and power, a poetic moment when an eight-ounce Rawlings baseball and a 35-ounce Louisville Slugger meet in violent harmony, a collision echoing across racial and generational barriers.

But the baseball gods were smiling on me that warm spring day. The ball rocketed off Clemente's bat, and at the precise instant when it started its ascent into the Florida ionosphere, Phillie second baseman Cookie Rojas climbed the ladder and speared it in the pocket of his Wilson A-2000, the smoke of the impact blanketing the diamond.

I pitched three shutout innings, and when I strode off the mound after the final out, I glanced up and smiled at Denise in the stands. After the game, she was waiting in our Buick station wagon with the fake wood paneling, the only car in the players' parking lot with a peace emblem and a Eugene McCarthy bumper sticker. (Two days earlier LBJ had announced that he would neither run for reelection nor accept his party's nomination.)

"Pack the bags," I declared. "We're going to the Show."

I was floating when I arrived at the ballpark the next morning. I'd called Dad to tell him I'd see him opening night at Dodger Stadium. I couldn't have scripted it any better—to start my big-league career in my hometown in front of family and friends. My only worry was whether or not the equipment man could find a hat big enough to fit my swelled head.

I passed Mauch's office. He was sitting behind his desk, talking to general manager John Quinn, an austere man who always looked to have just returned from an appointment with his embalmer.

"Colton, come in here," commanded Mauch.

In my three years in camp, those were the first words the Little General had spoken to me. I froze, as nervous as if I'd just been summoned for an audience with God and Jesus, only Mauch and Quinn were more important. I stepped into the office, thinking maybe I should genuflect. Were they going to tell me I was the fifth starting pitcher in the rotation? Or were they going to use me in long relief until I got my feet wet? I didn't much care—I was just thrilled to be there.

"We're sending you down," said Mauch gruffly.

Excuse me, Mr. Mauch, could you step aside while I throw up my pancakes and then slit my wrists all over your desk? Surely I had heard him wrong. How could they be sending me down? I'd already proved myself in AAA. And I thought I'd pitched as well as anyone in camp. What was I supposed to do? Beg? Throw a tantrum? Take it like a man?

"I think you can help us," Mauch continued, "but we want you to pitch two or three games in Triple A and then we'll call you right back up."

Sure, sure, Geno. The baseball graveyards were filled with thousands of tombstones inscribed with those infamous last words: "We're going to call you right back up." If that's the truth then, sirs, what should I do with my family? Should I trust you and send them on ahead to Philadelphia? Or do I move them to San Diego with me?

"Send them to Philadelphia," said Quinn.

I still didn't believe their promise. As I cleared out my locker and headed for the new minor-league complex across town, it was all I could do to keep from crying. I was crushed. I dreaded calling Dad and telling him I'd been cut. I stopped at a liquor store on my way home and bought a fifth of V.O.

"Did you hear the good news?" asked the clerk. "They shot that nigger Martin Luther King."

The phone rang in my room at the Mission Valley Stardust Hotel in San Diego, jarring me awake. It was 7 A.M. I figured it must be Denise calling from New York. I'd been trying unsuccessfully to reach her for two days. She and Wendy were staying with her brother Tony in Greenwich Village until I was called up . . . a promise I was doubting more than ever because I still hadn't gotten the call after giving up only two runs in eighteen innings in my first two games in San Diego.

"Hello," I said, trying to clear the cobwebs of a half dozen mai tais from the night before.

It wasn't Denise. It was John Quinn calling from Philadelphia. "We're calling you up," he said. "Meet us in Atlanta in two days."

I danced naked around the room, celebrating the dream come true. On that day, U.S. Marines were fighting to hold the ancient capital of Hue, students at Columbia University were occupying the administration building, Ron Vaughn was pacing the dayroom, and I was deliriously happy. I was going to the Show! A big-leaguer! I flopped down on the bed, waking Janet. Or was her name Janice? I wasn't sure. Either way, I had met her the night before. She was the Kon Tiki cocktail waitress in the skimpy Polynesian outfit who'd served me the mai tais. She was not, however, my first affair.

The infidelities had first started during the 1967 season. The initial tryst was with a phone operator in spring training when Denise was back in L.A. writing me all those letters. After that it was on almost every road trip of the season. These weren't groupies—minor-leaguers didn't have hordes of nubile young women waiting outside the locker room or beating down our hotel doors. These were women I met in bars, restaurants, airports, hotel gift shops. Denver, Hawaii, Spokane, Tulsa, Indianapolis. Wherever. Tall ones, blond ones, pretty ones, ugly ones . . . it didn't make much difference. As soon as the plane took off on another road trip, off came the wedding ring. Stewardesses were coveted objects with many of the players, but I preferred bypassing the competition and going for the car-rental clerks, making a move while the team waited for the luggage at the carousel. I wouldn't lie to these women . . . sometimes I'd tell the truth, sometimes I'd selectively withhold information. If they asked for my phone number, I gave them the ballpark's number. I kept my little black book stuffed in an extra pair of baseball shoes. I never used protection.

Screwing around on the road was as much a part of baseball as the suicide squeeze. In fact, it was more. It dominated conversations. "Does she have a friend?" "Cover for me if my wife calls." Most of the married players did it. Obsessively. Openly. Proudly. Our secrets were good with each other. We were a fraternity. Pitchers who worked fast on the mound and got the games over with quickly were popular—it meant more time for the neon league. A city was judged not by its scenic beauty or architecture, but by its pickup bars and by what time the ball games started . . . the earlier the better, leaving more time to prowl.

I was making up for being a late bloomer in college, I told myself, taking advantage of the new morality. I was a ballplayer in relentless pursuit of the zipless fuck, feeding that part of my ego that striking out the side and having a beautiful wife and child couldn't. Because we were in a town only three or four days at a time, I saw these transgressions as flings of the flesh, not affairs of the heart. Here tonight, gone in the morning. I had no doubt whatsoever that I was still madly in love with Denise and we would be married forever. The proof, as I saw it, was that I never had any inclination to screw around at home or during the winter. It was just a road-trip thing. The rest of the time I was content to be the family man. Denise seemed to be happier than she had been the previous year—it had been an endless summer for her and Wendy on the beaches of San Diego, Clearwater, and Ponce. And I thought my adventures on the road actually increased my desire and made me more attentive at home. I was having my cake and banana cream pie too. And now that I was going to the big leagues, it figured to get even better. As the players always said . . . the only differences between AAA and the major leagues were "better lights, better room service, and better pussy."

Janet, the Kon Tiki waitress, was too sleepy to share in my exhilaration about being called up. How could I explain the joy of having just discovered that I was going to the *Major Leagues* . . . that I was now a member of the same elite fraternity as Babe Ruth, Mickey Mantle, Ty Cobb, and Willie Mays . . . that my name would forever be logged in *The Baseball Encyclopedia?* How could a Kon Tiki cocktail waitress whom I'd known for five hours possibly understand the million throws I made against the side of the garage or the thousand summer days of playing over-the-line with Dexter? My God, I was going to Atlanta. That meant Hank Aaron. Should I pitch him inside? Outside? As soon as she left, I called Dad to share the good news.

"Congratulations," he said, "and keep that nose to the grindstone." What else was a grindstone for?

I called Denise at her brother's fourth-floor walk-up in New York. She wasn't in. "I don't know where she is," said Tony.

As it turned out, she was with her new lover, an artist from Greenwich Village.

Arriving in Atlanta twelve hours ahead of the team, I didn't even unpack before setting out in search of entertainment. It didn't take long to find it at a bar on Peachtree Street. She was a miniskirted secretary for Coca-Cola with a Miss Georgia smile. I didn't know if it was because she was impressed when I told her I was a *big-leaguer* or if it was the five Southern Comforts on the rocks that I bought her, but at closing time she came with me back to my room at the Marriott. We were still awake when the dawn came up over downtown Atlanta.

As far as I was concerned, I had things pretty much going my way . . . a big-league fastball, a big-league wife, and now big-league bimbos and better room service. With the $18-a-day meal money, I could drink up a storm and still have money left over at the end of a road trip to buy Denise a little gift. My new salary was for $8,000 a year, plus a $6,500 bonus after ninety days in the big leagues. I was twenty-five years old.

Miss Coca-Cola was gone when the team arrived at the hotel and I greeted my new roommate, Dick Hall, a tall, balding veteran reliever who looked like Ichabod Crane when he went into his herky-jerky submarine delivery. A graduate of Swarthmore who worked in the off-season as an accountant, he was one of only three Phillies with a college degree. He was friendly and quiet, didn't smoke, drink, or chase women, and the first thing he did after neatly hanging up his clothes was open up his briefcase, pull out a slide rule, and start writing down columns of numbers. I didn't know if he was figuring out his e.r.a., his taxes, or the circumference of the dugout. I didn't ask. I felt like I was back in college, rooming with Jim van Hoften and his math books. I was not about to tell him that I'd been up all night with Miss Coca-Cola.

The team dress code on the road mandated coat and tie, so after combing my short hair, also required, I got dressed and went to the lobby to girl-watch and wait impatiently for the five o'clock bus to the ballpark and my first appearance in a big-league uniform. I bought Visine to get the red out of my eyes, which had seen only an hour's sleep. I didn't want to show up on the team bus my first day wearing sunglasses, afraid that Mauch would think I was too Hollywood.

I wasn't sure what to expect in the way of a greeting from my new teammates and coaches. Was there some sort of rookie initiation I'd have to go through? Carry the bats? Sit in the back of the bus? Sing "Take Me Out to the Ball Game" in the nude? Partake of the brothers' feces? I was assured that there were no such rituals by my two closest friends on the team, Jeff James, a fun-loving, hard-throwing right-hander from Indiana, who had been my roommate the previous year in San Diego, and Gary "Suds" Sutherland, a versatile infielder from Southern California, who was my golfing partner and ex-housemate my first year in spring training.

When it was finally time to get on the bus in front of the hotel and head for Fulton County Stadium, I climbed aboard, passing in front of Mauch in the front seat. He offered no hello, no handshake, no "Welcome to the Phillies." Sitting behind him was Al Widmar, the pitching coach, who'd told me all spring how "great" I was throwing. He struck me as Mr. Insincere.

"Great to have you here," he offered. "You're in long relief tonight." In my three years in the minor leagues, I had never relieved. But with an experienced starting rotation of Woody Fryman, Chris Short, Larry Jackson, and Rick Wise, I wasn't counting on jumping right in as the ace of the staff.

"I'll be ready," I enthused.

I sat down next to pitcher John Boozer, the other college graduate, an alumnus of the University of South Carolina. He was good-natured, spoke fluent Spanish, threw a nasty spitball, and chewed tobacco around the clock—except when he was with his wife. Nobody in the league could spit tobacco more accurately than Boozer. His favorite trick was to spit a big slimy brown gob on the ceiling, then position himself under it and catch it in his mouth as it drooled down. Then do it again. He also liked to wait in hiding for guys to exit the shower and then hock a gooey on their privates. Somehow, he was likable enough not to get uppercutted for his tobacco high jinks. As the bus pulled out into traffic, he opened his window and dumped out his Styrofoam cup filled with an ugly brown juice that reminded me of a goat shake. It splattered on the front windshield of a car below.

At the ballpark, as other players hustled by the knot of kids waiting by the clubhouse door for autographs, I signed everything in sight, gladly. At my locker I proudly put on my clean gray uniform, number 21, my eyes drinking in the moment. There was no Scrubbini Row. I noticed immediately another important difference between the majors and the minors—the quality of the clubhouse spread. In the minors we were lucky to get candy bars and pop. In the Show there was ham, turkey, chicken, ribs, salads, fruits, beer . . . enough so that a guy could hog out and never have to spend a penny of his meal money.

As I walked alone up the tunnel to the dugout, my spikes echoed up the concrete runway, offering a surreal drumroll to my big-league arrival. Click clack, click clack. I felt conspicuous, intrusive, humbled, ignored, a third-grader at a sixth-graders' party. It wasn't that I didn't believe in my talents as much as it was a feeling of being uninitiated, the pledge, the new kid in the class. I was on the team but not yet a part of it. There was no big brother as there was in the fraternity to usher me into the fold. These were guys who'd made it to the majors on the strength of their arms and their bat speed, not their social skills.

As I reached the light of the dugout, the stands were still empty and the Braves were on the field taking batting practice. Oh my God, it was

Hammerin' Hank in the cage. Craaaack! A line shot over the wall. I acted nonchalant. Ho-hum, just another day at the office. When it was the Phillies' turn for batting practice, I trotted out onto the field, staring up in awe at the cavernous stadium, appreciating how much smoother the infield dirt was, how much plusher the outfield turf. I wished my dad could see me.

After batting practice I ran my wind sprints, then returned to the clubhouse to change my sweatshirt and grab some fresh bubble gum for the start of the game and the national anthem. I didn't want to miss anything. I put on my clean jersey and clickity-clacked my way back to the dugout. I checked to make sure my pants were zipped.

"Are you nervous?" asked Boozer as we stood at the top step, poised to head for the bullpen down the left-field line.

I nodded. Then he spit, scoring another bull's-eye, this time right in the middle of my nice clean jersey, dotting the first i in "Phillies" with a big brown stain.

"Welcome to the Show!" he said, laughing.

When I reached the left-field foul line, Miss Coca-Cola, for whom I'd left a pass, was sitting in the first row right behind the bullpen, waving me a greeting. Sober, I observed that she looked more like Miss Tab. I waved back. Ace reliever Dick Farrell, acknowledged to be one of the premier neon-leaguers in the majors, eyed our exchange.

"Not bad for a rook who hasn't even been in a fuckin' game yet," he said, fatherly throwing his arm around my shoulder.

The Braves threatened to break the game wide open against starter Larry Jackson in the bottom of the fifth. At the end of the inning, the bullpen phone rang. It was Widmar calling from the dugout with orders from Mauch. "Colton, warm up," he said. "Jackson's due up fourth this inning. If he gets up, we're pinch-hitting for him and you're in."

I sprang off the bench, enough adrenaline racing through my veins to win the Kentucky Derby. Normally, it took me at least five minutes to get loose. On this special night I was ready when I got off the bus. "Save something for the game, rook," shouted Farrell. I stepped off the bullpen mound, realizing that if I went into the game the first hitter I would face in my major-league career would be none other than number 44, Hank Aaron, the man on his way to breaking Babe Ruth's all-time home-run record. I suddenly needed to go potty.

As fate would have it that April night, the Phillies went down one-two-three in the top of the sixth and I did not get in the game. I was, however, credited with a "scare," which is what the men in the bullpen called it when a reliever warmed up in earnest but didn't get called into the game. I celebrated right through curfew with Miss Tab, who was looking like Miss Coca-Cola again by the time we reached her apartment. The sun was just coming up on my second day as a big-leaguer when she dropped me off back at the Marriott.

It was May 6, 1968, a chilly evening at Crosley Field in Cincinnati, top of the fifth, Reds leading 6–0, a meager crowd of 3,961 watching the action. I was sitting in the bullpen, wondering if I'd ever get in a game. All I had to show for ten days in the major leagues were two scares, the one in Atlanta and another at Shea Stadium when we were getting blown away by a Mets rookie named Nolan Ryan. I was frustrated, the novelty already starting to wear thin. Mauch still hadn't said boo to me. He was worried about bigger things, such as his job—the team was losing and he was feuding with star slugger Richie Allen.

"Colton, warm up, you're going in next inning."

The words took the chill right out of the evening. It was too late to learn a new curve; I would have to go with what I had. Every muscle and every fiber in my body was in fourth gear before I'd even lifted my butt off the bench. It didn't matter that I'd pitched in front of more fans on Bibb County Employees Night in Macon, or that the NBC camera crew wasn't there to record it for the archives, or that this was mopping up a lost cause. This was it, my major-league debut, the precise moment that I had been working toward my whole life, my father's whole life. I was about to dance the essential moment, to play with the powerful icons of my American dream. For me to be emotionally in control at a time of such dramatic personal intensity would have been to will away a tornado.

"Better think of something quick, rook," hollered Larry Jackson as I crossed the right-field foul line and walked briskly toward the mound, handing my jacket to the batboy.

I rushed through my eight warm-up pitches, a robot on hyperspeed. As the first batter made his way to the plate, I turned toward the outfield and rubbed up the baseball, the view before me locked forever in my senses—the grassy terrace in left field, the Wiedemann's billboard, the Longine's clock atop the scoreboard, the house lights twinkling on a nearby hillside. A voice from the press box high above home plate announced my name, then the batter:

"Now batting for Cincinnati, number 14, right fielder Pete Rose."

Pete Rose! Ex-rookie of the year. Charlie Hustle. I watched him dig in, taking his familiar crouched stance in his sleeveless uniform, bent at the waist, waving his bat. He was hitless in the game, trying to keep a 20-game hitting streak alive. All I knew about him was that he was an all-star and played like a maniac, the kind of hitter I hated to face, a pesky left-handed slasher.

My catcher, handsome Mike Ryan from New Hampshire, squatted behind the plate and signaled for a fastball. As I nodded in agreement, every mechanic of pitching that I'd ever been taught was forgotten. My mind was blank, Ryan's target a distant beacon, the plate a postage stamp. I rocked into my windup and let it fire, the ball heading toward the plate as if on a leisurely stroll. Rose leaned into the plate, then watched contemptuously as the ball sailed low and away.

Umpire Harry Wendelstedt signaled ball one.

Ryan put down two fingers. Curve. Gulp. Gripping the ball behind my back, I had more confidence in my ability at that instant to recite the complete works of Camus than I did of snaking a breaking ball by Petey Boy. If my infielders were chattering it up behind me, I didn't hear them. The pitch bounced two feet in front of the plate.

Rose snarled. He wanted to swing the bat, keep his hitting streak going.

Ryan walked the ball halfway back to the mound, offering words of encouragement in his thick New England accent. "Eye on the target," he said, settling back in behind the plate, signaling another fastball.

The last thing I wanted to do was walk the first big-league hitter I faced, so with that in mind, I went into my delivery and hummed an overhand express down Broadway. The salivating Mr. Rose unleashed a mighty swing, the crack of bat against ball echoing viciously through the nearly deserted old ballpark. The ball screamed into left center, rattling the boards at the foot of the scoreboard, and as I'd rehearsed a million times in spring training, I ran to back up third. No need. Rose stopped at second with a stand-up double. No need for him to slide on his belly. His hitting streak was alive.

And I was in *The Baseball Encyclopedia.*

Somehow, and I wasn't quite sure how, I got the next two hitters, Alex Johnson, a future batting crown winner, and Tony Perez, a future RBI leader, to ground out. And then, with Rose jitterbugging off third, trying to distract me, I got six-time all-star Vada Pinson to swing and miss at a slider at the knees for strike three. I floated off the mound. I had just debuted against four excellent major-league hitters and held them scoreless, pitching my way out of a tight jam. My e.r.a. was a heady 0.00. I was averaging a strikeout per inning. I was intoxicated, passing in front of Mauch in the dugout, expecting a word of praise. Nothing.

In my second inning, Lee May, a man with arms thicker than Rhode

Island, jumped out of his shoes and drilled a dreaded hanging curve for a resounding double to left to lead off the inning. The next hitter, rookie sensation Johnny Bench, grounded out to second, advancing May to third. So there I was again, a runner on third, one out, trying to pitch out of a jam. Ryan called for a fastball inside on the next hitter Tommy Helm, a smooth-swinging second baseman. And that's right where I put it, the ball rising up and in, sawing him off at the hands. His bat splintered in two, the ball blooping toward first baseman and future president of the league Bill White, who was playing in to cut off May at the plate. Sadly, from my perspective, the ball quailed just over White's outstretched glove for a cheapo single, sending May home, ending my scoreless major-league skein. Undaunted, I humped up to retire light-hitting shortstop Leo Cardenas on a grounder and then blew three fastballs by feeble-hitting pitcher George Culver to end the inning.

Mauch, still mum, pinch-hit for me, thus ending my baptism. Sitting in the dugout, my heart still pounding as if Buddy Rich was cooped up inside my chest, I wanted to keep pitching and have another shot at Petey Boy. I was ambivalent about how I'd done, upset that I'd given up a run and that I'd made bad pitches to Rose and May, but happy that I hadn't walked anybody or embarrassed myself by tripping over my spikes or something. I was still averaging a strikeout per inning. I'd earned another shot. No matter what happened in the future, I could now say that I was a big-leaguer. I was in the fraternity.

Little did I know.

Back at the Rhinelander Hotel after the game, I rode up the elevator with Mauch, just the two of us. I might as well have been one of the dentists in town for the convention. Dead silence for seven floors.

I called Dad to replay every pitch, then phoned Denise. We were living in Delran, New Jersey, across the Delaware River from Philadelphia in a large apartment complex with several other players. Denise was just starting to get acquainted with some of the other wives, but with Wendy approaching the terrible twos, she had plenty to keep her busy. Or so I thought.

On the phone, she seemed distracted, distant. "Is Wendy still up?" I inquired.

"No," she answered.

"Is something wrong? You don't sound right."

"No, everything's fine," she said.

Never in a thousand road trips would I have guessed that while I was

out making my big-league debut on the road, her paramour from Greenwich Village had driven down from New York, arriving after Wendy was
asleep, to spend the night, in our bed, leaving in the morning before
Wendy awoke.

But at least Rose didn't score.

37

Steve

Winning the "hearts and minds" of the Vietnamese people is just another cliché for war—man killing man.
   —William Corson, *Betrayal*

Loaded down with a fifty-pound pack on his muscular back, he dripped sweat from every pore as he marched single file up the hill, on maneuvers at the Quantico Marine Corps training center. In step right behind him was Glen Richards, his good buddy since the first day of Officer Candidate School (OCS) boot camp.

"Where's my limousine?" asked Steve. "My driver is late today." He scanned the dirt road behind him.

He and Glen had forged a tight friendship since their arrival at Quantico. Steve was surprised at the quality of the men in OCS, almost all of them college-educated. Glen, a fair-haired and wiry five-eleven, 160 pounds, was from Lake Charles, Louisiana, the son of Cajun French parents. He had been studying to be a teacher and "raising hell" at McNeese State when he dropped out to join the Marines, and as far as he was concerned, Steve was the best man in the class, a Marine's Marine, tough as they came, yet at the same time not a Marine, a compassionate guy who didn't have to say "Yes, sir" all the time . . . who didn't say "fuck" every other word . . . who didn't walk around with his chest puffed out to prove his mettle.

Steve had signed up for the Marines hoping to go to flight school, but an astigmatism in his left eye eliminated that option. He was going into artillery instead. With the war escalating and Westmoreland cheerleading for 250,000 more troops in a hurry, OCS had been cut from twenty-five to twenty-two weeks. It was day and night, seventy hours a week, a sprint through the training manuals . . . how to build a latrine, how to defend a trooper in military justice court, how to treat prisoners, how to lead, how to charge like a rhino, how to kill. For Steve, the physical training in OCS—the push-ups, the running, the climbing over walls— was easier than double days during football practice, and the mental harassment from the DI in boot camp had been a stroll on Virginia Beach compared to Big Ben in Hell Week. In boot camp he got eight hours' sleep a night . . . in Hell Week he got none; in boot camp he ate three square meals a day . . . in Hell Week he ate garlic salt and raw eggs.

After boot camp he became a "brown-bagger," which meant instead of sleeping on the base he went home every night to his apartment and Ayris, who was teaching art classes to Marine wives and driving to Washington, D.C., on weekends to march in antiwar protests against the Pentagon . . . with Steve's blessing. He compared the war to Hell Week in the Pi KA house—it was a bad idea over which he had no control, and if he was going to survive, his only choice would be to make the best of it, treat it as an adventure. He knew that he would be sent to Vietnam at the conclusion of OCS and there was nothing he could do to stop it. But if Ayris wanted to try, more power to her.

"Here comes your limo," said Glen, pointing to an empty troop convoy truck kicking up dirt as it rumbled up the hill.

Steve fell out of line, hoisted his pack into the back of the truck and climbed aboard, waving goodbye to his platoon.

"See ya tomorrow," he said.

He was off to football practice in his private Marine limo. His astigmatism was bad enough to keep him out of flight school but not off the Quantico football team. Every afternoon a convoy truck picked him up in the field and took him to practice. The Marine brass had decided that he was temporarily more valuable as a linebacker against VMI or William and Mary than as an artillery officer in the war against the Vietcong.

As it turned out, his tour of duty in Vietnam was delayed four months so he could finish the football season. Glen and the other members of his OCS class shipped out just prior to the Tet Offensive in January 1968. Steve arrived in Vietnam during the spring-summer lull, shortly after Martin Luther King's assassination.

It took him only one gagging breath of lifeless air after he stepped off the transport plane at Tonsonhut Air Base to stop treating it as an adventure and realize he was in the middle of the most profound event of his generation.

Heat had never bothered him, not at double days at Calgary, not when he was picking pears in those inferno Sacramento summers, not even when he was charging through the obstacle course at Quantico. But this was different. July in hell. Ardent, sapping, disgusting Vietnam heat. Even at China Beach, where he'd come with several Marine buddies from I Corps for R&R, it was hard for him to get comfortable. Tiny grits of white sand, blown by the hot, dry wind, stung his body. So did the news that Glen had been wounded when his platoon was caught in a VC ambush ten miles south of Danang in an area known as Dodge City. Glen was leading a platoon of thirty-two men, patrolling to keep 122 mm rockets from blasting the base when they were caught in a cross fire. Only five of his men survived. He received a Bronze Star and a Purple Heart and still had fragments from a grenade in his side, but after a month in a hospital in Yokohama, Japan, Glen was back in Vietnam.

It seemed odd to Steve that Marines were splashing in the waves, laughing, surfing, chugging beer, acting as if it was just another day at Malibu, while a few kilometers away, villages were being incinerated and Marines in body bags were being loaded onto the big Chinooks for the start of the journey home. He felt guilty about lying on a white, sandy beach, a beer in one hand, a book in the other. It didn't make sense—he was getting five days of in-country R&R (referred to as I&I by the troops, for intoxication and intercourse) and he hadn't even seen any action. But a lot about this war wasn't making any sense to him.

He was assigned to the 1st Marine Division in I Corps. (For military purposes, South Vietnam was divided into four parts, and I Corps, the northern sector from Danang to the DMZ, was the Marines' war.) His job was to assist in the coordination of all major artillery fire around Danang, an assignment he hated. He wanted to be closer to the action. He had requested a transfer. His first choice was to be reassigned as a forward observer (FO). An FO was out in the bush in the thick of combat, trained to call in artillery support for the troops, which made the position a prized target for enemy fire. His second choice was to lead a combined-action platoon (CAP), which was a unit sent out to win the "hearts and minds" of Vietnamese villagers.

He shifted to get comfortable on his beach towel, continuing to read *Betrayal,* a nonfiction book by Marine Lieutenant Colonel William Corson that detailed the corruption and sabotage of the American effort in Vietnam. According to Corson, America could not win a military victory in Southeast Asia—its only chance for success was to promote economic and political self-sufficiency, hamlet by hamlet, not by handing out a few packets of seed or a fistful of dollars—which was the current strategy to win the "hearts and minds"—but by CAPs destroying the Vietcong infrastructure within a hamlet, as well as establishing and maintaining security, law and order, intelligence, propaganda, and civic action. It meant constructing schools, building irrigation, repairing roads, introducing new crops, establishing credit unions, supplying materials, winning the trust and confidence of the people. Steve was convinced that such a strategy of "pacification" was the key to winning the war.

Corson's book was validating Steve's observations about the inefficiency of the American effort in Vietnam. Everywhere he turned in Danang he witnessed waste and mismanagement—too many bureaucrats and noncombatants and masters of misinformation sitting behind desks in air-conditioned offices, sucking up taxpayers' dollars, cranking out endless requisition slips and worthless information handouts . . . too much black-market corruption . . . too many American civilians working in the relative security of Danang, living in comfortable bungalows, earning "hazardous pay" bonuses that allowed them to double their salaries. The war was no more real to these paper-pushers, thought Steve, than if they were back in America watching it on Walter Cronkite, yet there they were, 30,000 of them, vicariously getting their combat thrills off the Marine private who hunted the Vietcong. Steve was frustrated, annoyed he had to deal with these people.

He hadn't come to Vietnam to spend his thirteen months behind a desk or to sip Singapore slings in the Officers' Club with Marine lawyers who thought B-52s should bomb Vietnam into an ashtray. He was a Marine and making the traveling squad wasn't enough . . . he wanted in the game, not out of any messianic anti-Communism patriotism, or because he thirsted to "kill a gook," or because he had an Audie Murphy wet dream about calling in artillery fire on his own head to win the Medal of Honor posthumously. He had a sense of duty and obligation . . . to the Corps, to his men. He'd been trained to lead.

Bored, he gathered his towel and book and headed for 11th Marine headquarters in Danang, hoping to find out about his request for transfer. He just wanted to do what he was trained to do—be a forward observer—and then get back home to Ayris and get on with his life in the real world. According to a rumor, the action was starting to heat up again in I Corps, and if everything went well, LBJ might start bringing the troops home by Christmas.

But three months in Vietnam had taught him not to trust anything he heard or read—this was a war of false facts and fictional kill ratios. If he wanted battle facts, he knew better than to look for them in the charts and graphs that were handed out in the offices in Danang. The only way for him to find out what was really going on was to talk to those who'd been out there, the ones who'd smelled and touched the death. You didn't find out how the game against Mike Garrett and the Trojans was going by asking the cheerleaders . . . you talked to the guys with the dirtiest uniforms.

He was starting to seriously question America's purpose in Vietnam. He'd talked to too many soldiers and too many officers to believe what LBJ had said about 1967 having been the "Year of Progress." Even when he was in OCS being pumped full of Marine doctrine, or even when he was finishing up his training at artillery school at Fort Sill, learning how to bring in 105 mm howitzer shells on a tumbleweed four miles away, he didn't believe in falling dominoes, or the gospel according to Westmoreland, or the company verbiage about the light at the end of the tunnel. His skepticism was based on the faces of the troops who'd been through the firefights. That's where the real truth was, in their hollow eyes.

Despite his cynicism about the conduct of the war, he embodied Marine leadership—loyal, self-disciplined, courageous, physically conditioned. He believed in the tenets he'd learned in Quantico about "Rhino Success"—that to succeed, whether it be in combat or in life, the secret was to charge massively through the jungle, always with a purpose. But the longer he was in Vietnam, the harder it was for him to reconcile his love for the Corps and his deepening disdain for the war. He was proud to be a Marine, bathed by the brotherhood, swayed by its eliteness and rectitude. But when he looked into the eyes of the troops who'd been in combat, his fellow Marines, he saw that grinding sense of loss, that unwanted intimacy with death.

He kept his doubts to himself. He had been raised by a strict father to challenge himself, not authority: when Frank told him to marry his pregnant girlfriend, he married her; when Coach Willsey told him to run ten wind sprints with cracked ribs, he ran ten sprints; when Big Ben told him to dance in his brothers' barf, he danced.

And when he walked into 11th Marine headquarters and received his new orders, he wasted no time in packing his bags. He had gotten his first request and had been reassigned as an FO on the "frontier" near the DMZ. He was going to where the action was.

38

Larry

1968 was a year when America lost its national sense of virtue.
—*Time* magazine

June 1, 1968. Wearing only a jockstrap, I sat at the table in the middle of the Phillies' clubhouse at Connie Mack Stadium, autographing baseballs, dozens of them. Signing balls was always the first order of business upon arriving at the ballpark each day, although some days I neglected to do it—not because I was too busy to be bothered, but because I felt silly doing it, as if my name didn't belong. I had been in the big leagues five weeks and all I had to show for it were the two innings against Cincinnati and a new hi-fi that was payment for being on a Topps baseball card. (When I went to the record store and brought home our first three albums—Glen Campbell, the Association, and Johnny Mathis' Greatest Hits—Denise appointed herself the new music commissioner.) In the twenty-five days since my one game, I'd pitched batting practice, charted pitches from the dugout, ate peanuts in the bullpen . . . but I hadn't even gotten a "scare." Neither Mauch nor pitching coach Al Widmar had told me where I stood. At least not verbally.

I perused the itinerary for our next road trip. We were leaving the next day for San Francisco to play the Giants and then to L.A. It would be my first trip back home to California as a major-leaguer, and even if I was gathering mildew on the bench, I was excited—the big-leaguer returns home and all that. I had lined up tickets for family and friends. And I was still dreaming of Mauch calling on me as a secret weapon against Willie Mays or to duel Don Drysdale at Dodger Stadium.

As I finished signing the balls, Sandy Padwe, a columnist for the Philadelphia *Inquirer,* sat down to interview me. Again, I felt silly, sitting in the middle of my teammates, answering questions in my jockstrap about my mother-in-law. Padwe's column was titled "Glamorous Life? Not for Colton."

> . . . Colton has learned the meaning of the word "frustration." It is written on his face and is reflected in the tone of his voice. He is not bitter, just discouraged.
>
> "It's funny," he mused in the Phillies' locker room. "The big leagues have been my goal since I was five. Then you get here and the novelty wears off in two days." Colton spoke softly. At times his voice was almost inaudible. The other players were dressing too, and Colton may have felt self-conscious talking to a reporter.
>
> Some day Colton will be a big success in baseball and the reporters will be swarming around his locker inundating him with questions about his mother-in-law, who happens to be Hedy Lamarr.
>
> Oddly, he has never seen one of her movies. "Every time one of them is on something comes up and I miss it," he said. "But then again she's never seen me pitch . . ."

June 4, 1968. The television above the bar at the Jolly Friar, a nightclub on California Street in San Francisco, was flashing the election returns from the California presidential primary. Senator Bobby Kennedy held a healthy lead over Eugene McCarthy, the candidate for whom I had cast my absentee ballot. But presidential politics weren't on my mind. Dressed in my new gold sports coat and forest-green slacks, I was zeroed in on Ingrid, a tall, blond Scandinavian stewardess for Pan Am whom I'd met earlier in the evening and was hoping to smooth-talk into spending the night. She didn't know a Phillie from a Raider, but still, the night was filled with promise. She smiled appreciatively when I told her she looked like Elke Sommer.

We were sitting at a table with my friend and baseball teammate from high school, William West Goldsborough III, a man of Kennedyesque hair and wealthy parents. He was working on a graduate degree at San Jose State. I signaled the waitress for yet another round, ignoring the fact that the team curfew of 1 A.M. was rapidly approaching. Mauch hadn't checked rooms all year, and besides, Ingrid was worth the risk.

And then the news bulletin flashed on the TV screen. The unthinkable had happened. Again.

Everything in the bar stopped—the chatter of the patrons, the ring of the cash register, the tinkling of cocktail ice. Laughter turned to silence. We stared at the images on the television screen, numbed, the news out of L.A. casting an anguished shadow over the evening, the year, the decade. The world was going nuts. But I still hoped to spend the night with Ingrid.

I excused myself to go to the bathroom, suggesting to Ingrid that we might leave as soon as I returned. She didn't respond, her sad eyes glued to the TV. I suddenly didn't like my chances.

When I got back, three guys were surrounding our table. They were all in their early twenties, white, well built, clean-cut, casually dressed, alcohol-fueled. One of them was pointing a finger at Goldsborough, telling him to meet him outside. Seems that one of the guys had said something to Ingrid, and when Goldsborough told him to buzz off, it was a "fuck you," and then another "fuck you." And that's when I walked up. I suggested we leave, handing Ingrid her coat.

"You're an asshole!" said one, stepping in front of me.

I eased around him, taking Ingrid by the arm and leading her toward the exit. Goldsborough followed, leaving the three standing at the table. Outside on the sidewalk, while Goldsborough walked down the street to retrieve his MG, I stood on the corner with Ingrid, putting in my last-ditch bid to keep the night alive. Before she could reply, she pointed over my shoulder. "Don't look now but those three guys just walked outside," she said, "and they're coming this way. They look like they want to fight."

I was twenty-five years old and had never been in a fistfight. Not once. And I was in no mood to start. I started to walk away, Ingrid walking next to me.

"Come back here, asshole," a voice instructed.

"Ignore them," Ingrid advised.

Instead, I stopped and turned to them. "What's the problem?" I asked. "I don't get it. Is the whole world going nuts? Why do you want to fight?"

" 'Cause you're an asshole,"

"I don't even know you. What did I do?"

At that moment, Goldsborough pulled up to the curb in his MG and jumped out to see what was going on. As he approached, one of the three charged him. The next thing I knew I was lying on the sidewalk, my face mashed, my shoulder throbbing, my Ingrid gone. But at least Goldsborough got the best of his guy.

I was now 0–1 in my pugilistic career, still looking to throw my first punch. I'd been blindsided before I could even unload my secret Kid Gavilan bolo punch. A second haymaker had sent me straight over backward. I'd put my hand back to brace the fall. That's when I felt the shoulder pop.

At St. Francis Hospital, where X rays revealed a serious shoulder separation, I told the doctor that my shoulder had popped out of its socket when I reached for a phone. As I walked into Mauch's office at Candlestick Park the next day, I wasn't sure what I was going to say. I wasn't too eager to confess that I'd had the shit beat out of me after curfew outside of a bar where I had just inhaled ten drinks. Mauch looked at me standing before him, my arm in a sling, both eyes black and blue.

"Just one question," he said. "Were you in a beef?"

"No, sir," I lied, explaining that a friend had accidentally hit me between the eyes with his class ring and that my shoulder popped out reaching for the phone.

He dismissed me with a roll of the eyes, telling me I would be put on the disabled list. He had bigger problems (Richie Allen) to worry about than me. In fact, Mauch was fired five days later. Since the injury was to my left (nonpitching) shoulder, I viewed this as only a temporary setback. The doctor had said I should be able to resume my big-league career in two months.

Little did he know.

It was one of those warm L.A. evenings, sun going down, the sky a hazy blanket of brownish blue-gray. I stood poised on the top step of the Phillies' dugout at Dodger Stadium, ready to take the field with my teammates. The game was sold out, 50,060 fans on hand to watch Dodger ace Don Drysdale try to add to his record string of 54 consecutive shutout innings. Sitting in the second deck behind first base were Mom and Dad.

During the construction of Dodger Stadium in the late 1950s, Dad had driven our family Buick to Chavez Ravine every month, parked on what he knew would someday be the pitcher's mound, and looked up at the army of workers forming its great shell, imagining the day when the Dodgers—and on an even brighter day, his son—would be playing there. It was a dream I inherited in spades, and was about to realize. Sort of.

It was June 8, 1968, my twenty-sixth birthday. Bobby Kennedy had died from the assassin's bullets and the Dodgers and Phillies were about to trot out onto the field to line up along the foul lines in a pregame moment of silence for the slain senator. I was wearing my sling and a

Phillies jacket draped over my shoulders. I wanted to be part of the tribute; I wanted to be a player in Dodger Stadium.

The crowd rose in unison as we filed out of the dugouts. Standing on the first-base line, I looked up into the capacity throng, my mood matching the smoky twilight haze shrouding the top rows of the stadium. It was surreal, eerily silent. Not the way I had imagined my hometown big-league debut.

I was sure there would be a brighter return.

Five weeks after the injury, Denise, Wendy, and I were back in San Diego, where the Phillies had sent me for minor-league rehabilitation, which I hoped would be temporary. Although I didn't know it at the time, the move was putting 3,000 miles between Denise and her Greenwich Village paramour.

"Get that arm back in shape and we'll call you right back up here," new manager Bob Skinner assured me.

The injury had damaged nerves in my left arm. I had no strength in my thumb and forefinger and couldn't lift my left arm above the chest. But since I was a right-hander, it was okay for me to throw . . . I just couldn't swing the bat or catch balls above my belt. But I could live with that. I knew I wasn't 100 percent yet, or anywhere close, but I was in a hurry to get back to the Show and get that big-league meal money and see Miss Coca-Cola again. I lost my first three games. At the plate, I stood with the bat on my shoulder, striking out every time. On the mound, the catcher had to lob the ball back to me so I could catch it at the waist. After each pitch, I ducked, following through so that my butt ended up facing home plate—that way if the batter drilled one back through the box, I wouldn't have to catch it with my face. The comeback was a disaster. Throwing and ducking was not working. My right arm started to hurt too. I was a grump around the apartment. And then on a road trip, I received a special delivery letter from Denise:

July 28, 1968

Dear Larry:

The first few days of this road trip were lonely and long. I was getting depressed at first because you left without seeing to anything for me. I mean you didn't put up the shade, fix the toothbrush holder, or leave a schedule and the list of hotels where you'd be staying. Then I don't hear from you for six days! All of the other wives were talking about how their husbands had called the first night, or two times already, etc., and I hadn't heard from you. Then I called you at 1 A.M.

(your time) and there was no answer. I really felt left out. For five days I didn't see any of the other wives. They're all set in their little cliques already. Finally I went over to Kay's house. There were about seven wives there. They all spend the night together and everything. I'd just as soon stay alone than go through that hassle.

We all went out to dinner and to see The Odd Couple. I felt <u>dumb</u> walking into the show with 15 other "ladies"—all of us dressed up and chatting away. How housewifey and bridge-clubby! Then we went to a Tupperware party. It was such a bore. This lady demonstrated for two hours how to use these plastic kitchen things. And to top it off, I ordered some of the stuff. Actually, I ordered good things: a lettuce crisper, a Jell-O mold, and a cold-cut keeper.

Honey, the main reason I'm writing is because there's a lot on my mind that I have to tell you. This may come as a surprise to you but I doubt it. You must share my feelings, but maybe you haven't admitted them to yourself. It's about our marriage.

The reason I'm writing instead of talking to you is because I don't think we could ever talk like this. That's just part of it. I have so many important feelings that I don't talk over with you—because I feel I can't. I honestly don't think you even could really understand them. Sometimes I wonder if you understand me at all. I don't mean to be critical at all—please don't think I'm nagging. This is so important to me.

I don't think our marriage has been open lately. Our conversations consist of "dinner's ready"—"turn to Joey Bishop"—"good night." I really feel screwed up about life and I can't even talk to my own husband about it. It's like we hold all of our <u>deep</u> feelings and emotions back. I feel so choked up from not being free with you and you never being open with me. I know that by now you think what I've written is ridiculous, but I've got to tell you.

I know we're "happy" and we don't fight—but at least on my part it's not a real happiness anymore. I was happy when we were dating and first married. I remember times like sitting on a pier in Sausalito with our arms around each other, watching the ducks and making up cute stories about them. That was the you I loved. We went dancing and had a ball. Everything was young, alive, and passionate. Now, I'm not too dumb—I know we can't be that way because of Wendy and your baseball career and all that. And I'm not saying any of this is your fault; it's us together. It's the <u>feeling</u> I miss. Now I have a feeling of crossword puzzles, watching TV, some pleasant times, but mostly just existing together out of habit. The whole time we were in

Philadelphia we never went anywhere or did anything together. We didn't go see the Liberty Bell or Independence Hall or any of the sights. You probably think I'm being unfair and outrageous and wrong. But, honey, I can't help my feelings. I've held them in long enough, and as my husband, I think you should know that I'm feeling like this. I've tried to suppress this so many times and I guess I should. I should be perfectly content and happy because I do have a wonderful family. But there's something lacking and it's just eating at me. I feel so guilty for even feeling this way.

You've always been the perfect husband—so it must be me. Honey, I'm not condemning you—or myself for my feelings. But I really think that either I've changed or you have. I just love music and dancing and the beach and everything. You seem to dislike everything I do. And all I think about is our first date when we went to your fraternity party and did the "monkey." God—I had so much fun with you.

Maybe it's because you're 26 now and your interests have changed. Or maybe it's because I'm 23. But I feel so young still and I'm not about to give up that feeling. I just wish we could do something wild once in a while, like when we flew to St. Thomas for the weekend. I sound crazy, don't I? How would you feel if you couldn't play golf anymore? Well, that's how much I want to do a stupid little thing like go dancing. I'm not a teenybopper and I don't want to be. Oh, I don't even know how to tell you. I just wish you understood me. Actually, it's me that's changed. I love mod clothes—I love long hair—I love mustaches—I love rock music. It seems like I like all the things you dislike. Maybe it's my fault for "going mod" all of a sudden. Or maybe it's your fault for getting old and boring and only wanting to stay home and watch TV or go to a movie or play golf. But I don't think it's either. It's us together.

Please don't think I'm telling you I want us to split up—because I don't. I love you more than anything. And I love Wendy so much I don't know what to do. I never want a divorce; I never want to break up our family. It's so wonderful. I don't want to end up like my mother.

I know you must have bad feelings too. I can tell by the way you act and you must know from the way I act. Our sex life is only one aspect of this emptiness in our marriage now. Honey, I don't want to hurt your feelings—this is hurting me so much—but I am so bored with our sex life. You've got to know this. It's so unpassionate that I can't stand it. Even our kiss lacks in whatever I'm searching for. It's just so dull. It's been dull off and on for years, but it's never bothered me so much until now. Maybe I should go see a shrink. I know these things settle down after several years of marriage, but it doesn't have to be this bad.

You might feel this way even more than I do. I really have no idea as to how you feel about us sexually. You <u>can't</u> be happy with it. You must have secret longings for the feeling—physical—that we don't have anymore. I do. You must be bored with me too, because I'm bored with myself. When I'm making love to you I put nothing into it. Maybe it's because I'm <u>embarrassed to be free with you.</u> I have so much passion inside me that's dying to come out. Didn't you feel anything when we saw that kissing scene in <u>The Thomas Crown Affair</u> after their chess game? I died inside when I thought of how we kiss. Maybe this is just part of becoming "oldly-wed" that I'm going to have to adjust to. I know I can't expect the passion of a first kiss to last forever. But all I want is just a little feeling put into it—put into our whole existence together.

I feel I have so much to give to a man—and I only want to give it to you, Larry. I feel like I'm beautiful and sexy when other men look at me—but when you do I feel like I should be wearing "dumpy dresses" and I'm fat. You must feel that I don't appreciate you either. I know there must have been plenty of girls that have looked at you that certain way or even offered themselves to you. I wouldn't be at all surprised. You are handsome, funny, a wonderful person, well mannered, and a <u>real man.</u> And you shouldn't be surprised to know that there have been several men interested in me. They would have loved to have had an affair with me. Of course nothing happened, but I can't honestly say that I didn't have any hidden desires. I think it's only human—people are people—and just because one gets married doesn't mean that men and women become neuter. There have been plenty of men attracted to me—but I am too devoted to you to ever let anything start. But it felt wonderful to be appreciated and <u>really wanted</u> and told I was beautiful. I don't want to give you the wrong impression. <u>Nothing</u> ever got anywhere. I just don't want you to forget that I'm a woman. Sometimes I really think you do forget. I've just become Wendy's mother, your wife and housekeeper—and not a woman. Well, I <u>love</u> being a mother and I <u>love</u> being a wife—but I want to be all of them.

God, honey, everything sounds so bad. I guess it's because I said everything at once and got carried away. Of course we have some good things going for us, but I just can't stand for our marriage to become an existence or a habit. I don't want to lose what we had when we were dating. I want to really live my life to the fullest. This might shock you or it might not because you might have felt the same way—but I have even thought of ending our marriage at times—but I realized that I couldn't because you have become so much a part of me and I would be lost without you. You and our darling Wendy are the most important things to me. I love you both beyond words.

Please think about all of this, Larry, and <u>try to understand</u> it and not condemn it. For the sake of both of us.

Yours,
Denise

P.S.: Wendy's up from her nap now feeding me on her new tea set. I miss you more on this road trip than on any other one in the three years we've been married. I love you so much. Please <u>try</u> to understand me.

I was trying to understand, but there were days when everything seemed to be destined for the toilet. My career, my marriage, America. The blind faith I'd always had in the virtue of my country and its government was gone. Too many assassinations. Too many riots. Too many dead in Vietnam. Too much turbulence. I was on fast spin. I'd sit in the dugout, and instead of thinking about pitching, I'd be bummed out about Mayor Daley, or the body bags, or some other garbage I'd seen on the news. Or worrying about Denise. But I didn't talk to any of my teammates about that sort of stuff. With them, I drank and chased women. I wrote Denise a reply to her letter:

Dear Denise,

I don't have a lot of "newsy" things to report except that my hair is longer than it's ever been. It's not as long as Tiny Tim's, but I look like a shaggy dog. I get quite a few comments on it from the other players, but I'm not going to cut it until the brass tells me to.

I am very much aware of your feelings toward our marriage. As I'm sure you understand, the horrible year I've had in baseball has something to do with my "bad attitude." I've always tried to leave my baseball worries at the ballpark and not burden you with them. Unfortunately, I have carried my unhappiness with baseball over into my relationship with you.

Honey, I think perhaps one of our basic problems stems from the fact that you are a very emotional person whereas I am not. Let me explain. I feel you are a person with a great desire to be loved and needed. An outward display of this love and need makes you feel warm inside. Loving words, shows of affection, kisses, token presents are all part of this. And I don't mean unnecessary type of affection. I believe I realize the kind of affection and warmth you want. And I know I haven't been giving you this lately. But believe me, it is not because I don't feel it in my heart. I love you more than ever. As I said, I am not a very emotional person. But I actually do consider myself an emotional person. I just hide it inside. I don't give you the affection and love you want, expecting you to take it for granted. This is very wrong on my part.

I can't tell you why I don't show my affection and love outwardly because I don't know. Maybe its because it seems unmasculine when indeed it isn't. I will put forth an effort to show my deep love and affection because it certainly can't be that much of an effort to display something that I truly feel. I could not exist without you. I need you and want you with everything I have. You are my life!

I also realize our life hasn't been too awfully exciting. I still believe we do more than the average couple. I am not too old at 26, as you implied, to enjoy going dancing or having an evening of fun. The fact that I am content to stay home is a tribute to you. I don't feel a need to escape. Anyway, get your rockin' shoes ready.

Don't think that I don't desire you physically, because I very much do. There are very few nights I don't mentally want to make love to you. Seventy-five percent of the time we go to bed, I am just too tired to make love. We stay up too late. We'll never have a great sex life as long as we watch TV so late.

One thing you mentioned in your letter did upset me. And that was that you had "desires" at certain times. I realize people are sexual animals and have desires, but your implication hurt me. This could only come from a failure on my part. I was also hurt when you said you had even thought of splitting up. I just can't imagine you would consider that. Do you really think it is that bad between us? I want to be together forever.

With all my love, Larry

39

Loren

Beat your gong and sell your candies.
—Chinese proverb

A January dusk spread over the Sacramento Valley, and at Loren's newly purchased three-bedroom California ranch house in the middle of a well-kept suburban block in Davis, an impromptu party was underway. As usual. The front door was open, the stereo blaring, the cocktails flowing.

Dressed in jeans and a white T-shirt, he walked out the sliding-glass doors onto the patio to check the steaks on the barbecue. As he walked past Craig, visiting from Dallas, he grabbed a handful of quarterback butt, then wiggled away. It was part of their "silly savage" routine. Craig blew him a kiss.

Loren turned to the former Miss California, visiting from Berkeley. He pulled a thick wad of bills from his pocket and peeled off a couple fifties. "Run down to the Safeway and pick up some more steaks," he instructed. "And get more champagne too. The good stuff." He flipped her the keys to the Golden Ram, the Buick Riviera Craig had turned over to him for the business.

Loren was the new bigger-than-life impresario of Davis, the nabob of the neighborhood, his house a nightly gathering place for his friends, his business the talk of the downtown merchants. UC Corner of Davis was up and running, financed on the collateral of Pop and Eddie's rice fields, Craig's contract with the Cowboys, and UC Corner in Berkeley. Loren was the managing partner. What he lacked in business experience and acumen, he was making up for in enthusiasm. It was his zeal and effort that had sold the bankers and launched the business.

Davis seemed a perfect location for him, a slightly inflated version of Marysville. Located in Yolo County fourteen miles west of Sacramento, it was one of the fastest-growing communities in Northern California, a town of 25,000 surrounded by farmland rich in barley, sugar beets, tomatoes, and wheat. It was also home to a branch campus of the University of California, projected to be the fastest-growing of all seven UC campuses, with a reputation for its College of Agriculture and School of Veterinary Medicine. The store's location four blocks from campus was ideal, with good foot traffic and little competition.

Loren had thrown his heart and soul into the project, involving himself with everything from the design to the construction to the grand opening. It was modeled after the successful formula of the Berkeley store—paperbacks, magazines, cigarettes, candy. But the realtors had talked him into taking it to a grander scale. He had tripled the square footage, adding an upscale billiard hall with eighteen of the most expensive slate pool tables. He also installed a short-order lunch counter that served hamburgers, fries, and soft drinks. It was all sparkle and glitz— opulent light fixtures, royal-blue carpeting, state-of-the-art kitchen equipment. "Nothing but the best," he'd said. But wait! There was more. Jumping on the latest trends, he stocked rolling papers, beanbag chairs, comic books, tie-dyed T-shirts. He carried albums on consignment from Tower Records. And when Varsity Sports, a sporting-goods store down the street, went up for sale, he persuaded Craig into taking out a loan to purchase it. They also started Craig Morton Sports, a wholesale sporting-goods distributorship selling to retailers and schools from Sacramento to the Oregon border. It was Loren's large-sized gusto and his beating the gong that put it all together, convincing the banks that consumer demand, his managerial skills, and Craig's name would create a cash cow.

For his part, Craig was happy to entrust his investments to Loren, his best friend, party partner, and business guru. Craig had not taken any business classes at Cal and was admittedly naïve about the world of finance, having neither the time nor the inclination to be involved in the day-to-day operation of a business. He was a fun-loving football player. Period. In Dallas, he had spent his first three years riding the pine behind Don Meredith, waiting his turn for the spotlight, frustrated at his lack of playing time and Coach Tom Landry's tight control. His playboy reputation and his selection as the Most Eligible Bachelor in Texas hadn't helped his standing with Landry, a devout born-again Christian. But with Meredith hinting retirement after the 1968 season, his role was soon to change.

Craig had not come to Davis on business. He was there to party with his pal. During the frustration of his first three years in Dallas, nobody had been more supportive, more encouraging than Loren, who would call him regularly, advising him to hang in there, reassuring him of his skills. Loren knew that Craig, for all his All-American press clippings and outward confidence, was congested with self-doubt and insecurities. Their relationship had become symbiotic, running deeper in private than the fast lane they traveled in public. They were both sons of hard-shelled fathers, relying on each other for unconditional moral support. They fed each other's egos. Craig would come to Loren's rugby games, offering lofty praise, not just for his athletic skills but also for his way with the women after the game It was a toss-up who was the cashing in more on the sexual revolution.

They both hoped to cash in on their new business ventures. Loren had hired friends and family to work for them: John "Swampfox" Stassi, his pledge brother, was co-managing the bookstore; Tom Blanchfield, his ex-roommate and rugby teammate, was co-managing the sporting-goods business; Genevieve was keeping the books; and the lovely former Miss California was establishing a marketing plan for the wholesale sporting-goods business. She had taken business classes at Cal and had worked in marketing and sales for a cable television company in her senior year.

For the former Miss California, who was a frequent weekend visitor to Davis, it was an unpaid position. She had been swept up in Loren's indefatigable vigor for his new entrepreneurial adventure, volunteering to organize sales strategy. With an eye on a career in business, she liked the challenge. It was also a way for her to squeeze herself a little extra time in Loren's busy schedule. Following the fiasco of the rugby trip to Europe, he had made an initial effort to be more attentive, to give more of himself to the relationship. But launching the project in Davis had consumed him. She marveled at his intensity, but lamented the invasion of their time together. He was always distracted, preoccupied, off to another meeting, surrounded by sycophants. Avoiding intimacy. Even at social events, he assigned friends to keep her entertained while he ran around being the wheeler-dealer. There were times she wished he would afford her the undivided attention he gave Craig. But she trusted Loren when he vowed he was faithful.

When she returned from the Safeway with the steaks and champagne, the plans had changed. It didn't surprise her—she'd learned early on that with Loren the plans were always changing. Mr. Spontaneous. Go with the moment. And at that moment, he and Craig were rounding up a caravan for a quick gambling-and-skiing junket to Tahoe. The casinos were calling.

"But I've got business in San Francisco tomorrow," she said.

"No, you don't," replied Loren, leading her toward the door. "You're coming with us."

How could she resist such an indomitable spirit? They stopped at Varsity Sports, opening the store to let the girlfriends in the caravan pick out complimentary ski equipment for the slopes. The former Miss California pulled Loren aside, advising him against such a generous giveaway.

"It's good promotion," he maintained.

"You can't run a business this way," she warned.

"We'll see." He winked.

40

Steve

Use bullets, not bodies.
  —American strategy in Vietnam

On a soggy hillside near the DMZ, Second Lieutenant Steve Radich huddled under his poncho, waiting for the rain to stop. The monsoons had slowed the action near the DMZ to a crawl. It was too wet even to inspect the howitzers. The sweatbox of summer had been replaced by the dankness of the endless rain. Everything stank—his fatigues, his body, the bunker, his enthusiasm for the Corps.

He'd come to the DMZ as a forward observer, and that had been fine by him—that's what he'd trained to do at Fort Sill. It was a job suited to his linebacker's mentality. An FO patrolled with the infantry and was the artillery's link with the front line, the technical expert to call in the big guns, making the position not only one of the most valuable but also the most dangerous. In an enemy ambush, the FO was a prime target for snipers—they would try to take him out before he could summon artillery help from the firebase.

But the patrols in the DMZ had been scaled back and Steve had been assigned to the relative security of what one platoon leader called the "creature comforts" of a fire-support base. The new strategy of the high command was to win firefights by sheer weight of explosives. Instead of continuing to pour infantry into the hostile countryside, a network of fire-support bases had been established. A fire-support base was equipped with heavy artillery (105 mm howitzers and 81 mm mortars) capable of offensive fire in a 360-degree circle. It was surrounded by sandbags, bunkers, foxholes, and trenches, linked together by concertina wire, the perimeter protected by claymore mines and trip flares. Further out, where the VC troops might assemble, the landscape was dotted with more mines and bangalore torpedoes, capable of wiping out an entire enemy platoon . . . or a careless patrol.

More and more resources had been assigned to supply and defend these firebases, including Steve. He had plenty of time to write in his journal:

3 Oct. 68. More of the same, nothing much doing. For a couple days last week had some shooting during early morning, but since then very little, if any. Days don't seem to be passing too slowly though. We have an easy position here and the food is outstanding. I eat very small portions (usually) to keep from getting fat. Last weekend I even ran around the compound (1 mile). I've lost most of my spare tire, only a little extra now.

He had requested transfer to the DMZ not only to be closer to the action but also to get away from the graft and the bureaucrats in Danang. He quickly learned, however, that the field had its share of inefficiency. "What's the difference between the Boy Scouts and the American troops in Vietnam?" the joke went. "The Boy Scouts are better prepared." Everything was in short supply—ammo, trucks, drinking water, patience. Concerned with his equipment, especially his "four-deucers" (81 mm mortars), he had requested new guns. Even under the best of circumstances, they were inaccurate, but the monsoons had made maintenance difficult.

9 Oct. 68. A little excitement since we've been down south. We took some sniper rounds into our area about 2145. Everyone was running around bumping into each other, scrambling to get their weapons. As it turned out, it was the ARVN living in the tree line about 100 meters from the wire, firing randomly.

As much as he loved the Corps, he doubted its game plan . . . or even if there was one. It wasn't like his experience in football, when his coaches always sent the team out onto the field with a preconceived plan of attack. What was the plan in Vietnam? he wondered. The Marines' seventy-seven-day battle at Khe Sanh struck him as a perfect example of the aimlessness of the mission. One week Khe Sanh was the fulcrum of the war against Communism, worth however many lives it took to defend it; a week later it was a worthless patch of dirt. ("The situation has changed," explained the high command.) It shook the Corps's confidence; it embarrassed Steve.

<u>19 Oct. 68.</u> Slow, slow, slow. Nothing doing except rain. 29 in. in last five days. Our position here is melting like sugar. Real soft ground, just sloughing off toward any low ground. Got Ayris in chess game via mail.

Amusing incident with one of my men. He got this girl back home knocked up, married her, had a kid, and now she's shacking up with someone else. She's trying to get all his money—even wrote to congressman to complain that he also had fiancée. He's always telling me his problems. Wants to go up north and get zapped to solve his problems. Now says there's a possibility kid isn't his. He's always smiling and grinning at me. Expects me to have solutions to all his problems. It's kind of a good feeling that he comes to me with his problems.

Steve only had to consider his own position to see the waste of resources. He was sitting on his butt, equipped with semi-obsolete weapons, supporting troops who were rusting in the rain. Even if those troops were sent into battle, they were under orders not to return fire when they went through a village. What was the sense of it? There were days he felt like firing howitzers and mortars into the empty hillsides. Why shouldn't he contribute to the massive waste of resources? Maybe it would abet ending the war early—his small way of helping to drain the American taxpayers of what was left of their commitment to a politically, economically, and militarily losing cause. And then there were days he felt he'd been sent to Vietnam for no other reason than to fill sandbags and load them onto the revetment walls. He tried to keep his mind occupied, thinking about R&R with Ayris in Hawaii. (She had moved there when he was sent to Vietnam, living in an apartment, taking art classes at the University, intensifying her opposition to the war.) He also thought about what he was going to do when he went back to the real world. Work for his dad? Go to law school? He and Ayris talked of buying property in the mountains and living off the land, escaping the madness.

<u>31 Oct. 68.</u> Happy Halloween, Rat! Last couple of weeks have been better. C Battery moved two guns to our position. Their XO came down and has been living with me. He's a good shit, and he's been great company. Before I was pretty much a loner.

On way to regt. passed a gook funeral wake. Was really colorful.

Pallbearers had a colorfully decorated casket on shoulders. Preceding the procession were the village elders and four tall poles with long yellow streamers. Also had big bass drum and cymbals beating a death dirge. Following was whole village, wailing and moaning. Funny with so much death that they still maintain their customs.

Finished rereading Corson's Betrayal. Really swayed by it again. Shows the waste.

Three days since I've heard from Ayris. Really miss her and her letters.

Returned my ballot and threw it to Hump. Looks like he's a loser. I'm beaucoup serious for war to end.

Despite his strategically remote position and the slow pace, he wasn't careless. He knew that safety in even the most protected places in Vietnam was conditional. He approached his assignment with professional, precise perfection; he paid attention to even the smallest of details. Unlike some of his men, he wasn't relying on voodoo or a rabbit's foot to bring him safely home. He had no St. Christopher medal, no picture of Ayris in his shirt pocket, no rock-and-roll "I'm a man, yes I am" lyrics on his helmet. And no ganja. He hadn't smoked dope since his failed attempt to pump up his blood pressure just before his induction physical.

14 Nov. 68. A Marine 2½-ton truck ran over a 6-year-old boy at our south gate and killed him. The next day Civil Affairs paid his parents 1,000 p's (about $10). The going price for a water buffalo is about 30,000 p's. The value of life is 1/30 that of an animal. The villagers scooped him up and took him out into the rice paddy and dropped him in. Not very sentimental and reverent, but practical and realistic, I guess.

He applied for another transfer. He was still interested in leading a combined-action platoon—those were the troops who went into the villages and rooted out the VC and worked with the Vietnamese on becoming self-sustaining. But he was even more interested in becoming an aerial observer. An AO rode in a two-seater plane, marking the countryside and calling in the artillery from the big ships anchored offshore. His astigmatism had kept him out of Marine flight school, but he'd learned that it wouldn't prevent him from being an AO.

16 Nov. 68. Went down to check out Alpha. They had a firefight west of their wire. On way out, saw dead VC lying in middle of the road, stretched out as if on cross. Completely white.

We got our 155s (howitzers) in day before yesterday. Have a lot of work to do on them. Thought I was getting feel for being officer, but with this new weapon and new people, still feel unsure of myself because I'm new at it. Within a week I should get squared away <u>again.</u> Probably will get transferred to AO as soon as I do.

From 2,000 feet, the tropical sunrise was beautiful. Or was that another napalm sunrise? Twelve months in Vietnam had warped his sense of color and light. Below, the canals and waterways of the Plain of Reeds stretched across the landscape like murky veins. To the east, anchored offshore, were the Navy destroyers of the Seventh Fleet, their huge sixteen-inch guns waiting his word to unload. He'd gotten his transfer to AO.

Seated in the rear seat behind pilot Ed "Fox" Sharney, he scanned the familiar ground below—rice paddies, riverbanks, tree lines—looking for any sign of enemy movement. He and Fox, a slow-talking, easygoing, handsome farm boy from southern Ohio and a graduate of Bowling Green, knew the terrain and the patterns of life in the hamlets below. That was their job—general reconnaissance and intelligence gathering to detect any unusual activity which might give a clue to enemy troop movements . . . then mark the target area with smoke rockets and call in the coordinates for the F-4s, or the howitzers, or the "sweet sixteens," as Steve called the Navy guns. On this flight, they were looking for signs of snipers who had been harassing the Navy boats with the Riverine forces.

"Over there," said Steve, pointing to a dozen Vietnamese squatting near the edge of a rice paddy.

Fox banked the plane for a closer look. This was the part that Steve liked the most—the banks, the rolls, the dives. He was in love with flying. That's why he'd applied to be an AO in the first place, and after four months of "birddoggin'," he was sure that the Vietnam War, if nothing else, would be his ticket to a GI Bill-sponsored pilot's license. And who knows? Maybe he'd even become a commercial pilot. Or a helicopter pilot. He dreamed of someday owning his own plane. He had lots of dreams.

They were flying a piston-driven Cessna 0-2A, an odd-looking duck with two push-pull engines, one mounted on the nose, the other at the rear of the fuselage. It was equipped with machine-gun pods, but, as always, they were flying unarmed except for the marking rockets. Their only protection was a loudspeaker, a leaflet dispenser, and Fox's ability to evade. (On previous missions, Fox, like a halfback on a naked reverse, had zigged and zagged to avoid machine-gun fire from the ground.) Top speed was 200 miles per hour, which was 85 miles an hour faster than the Cessna 0-1 Bird Dog they had been assigned to earlier.

Fox, who, like most forward air controllers, had previously flown jets, brought it in low, close to the ground, contour flying, shaving the tree-tops and the hooch roofs, trying to give Steve a better look. Sometimes it looked as if they were going right through the branches—Fox was that good. Steve had no fear.

"I can't tell if they're VC," Steve said. "Maybe they're just farmers."

He knew damn well they weren't farmers, but he was fed up with the death and destruction. He'd seen the carnage that a 3,000-pound shell from a Navy destroyer left behind, how it could wipe out a small village without bothering to discriminate between children, women, and VC guerrillas. Unless the lives of American troops were directly threatened, he was no longer going to be party to the slaughter. Fox felt the same way.

With only a month to go on his tour, Steve's fear wasn't that he would be shot down. Death was all around him and yet he felt immune to it. He was too professional, too proficient at what he did. Death, he reasoned, came to those who feared it or who didn't know what they were doing. What he feared was not death but getting caught in what he was about to do.

He radioed the coordinates to the USS *New Jersey*, then signaled Fox to clear the area. As they gained altitude, he looked back and watched as a $10,000 shell exploded, ripping a crater the size of Sproul Hall smack-dab in the middle of an empty field. He smiled and flashed the peace sign. By his calculations, at $10,000 per misdirected shot, he was making his contribution to the military waste, helping to end the war.

41

Ron

There's a place up in the hills above Mendocino called Lost. It's for any-
body who is. You find it, or it finds you.
  —Holiday, September 1968

The room was small, the walls an institutional green. Outside the window, the putrid sky was choked with smog and the hillsides baked a
parched brown. But Ron, who was approaching his thirtieth birthday,
hadn't checked himself into the psychiatric clinic at L.A. County General Hospital for the view or the decor. He was there to get a grip. Anna
had moved back to San Francisco with the baby and was thinking about
moving up the coast to Mendocino in search of tranquillity.

Sitting in a chair facing a therapist and four interns, he felt like a term
project . . . the schizophrenic on display. Or whatever his diagnosis
was. He was tired of doing all the talking. How could he make any
progress if he just blabbed away with no feedback? They seemed so
smug.

The treatment was more of the same that he'd had at Langley earlier—
taking medication, sitting around the dayroom, spilling his guts to the
therapists. With no progress. Maybe it was time to take over the session,
make something happen.

He stood up and folded his arms across his chest, glaring down at the therapists. He said nothing. This was his bold act of rebellion, his power play.

"How does that make you feel?" he was asked.

What kind of dumb question was that? Why didn't these smarty-pants in the white coats have the answers? He sat down. No use aggravating them. He might as well go back to trying to act normal. That's what he'd always done . . . the black in a white fraternity, the artist in the locker room. Tried to fit in. Don't cause waves. And that, he deduced, was what he needed to do to get out of the L.A. Club Wacko. Play the game. Just be good little Ronnie boy. Prove he wasn't different.

He sat back down. But down deep inside, he felt different, and he always had.

After two weeks in L.A. County General Hospital, he was released to a halfway house on Adams Boulevard, a converted motel a mile from his boyhood home. He had another two-week supply of Thorazine and was as confused as ever.

Ralph came to visit. They sat on opposite sides of the room, their words forced, tense. Ralph and Betty, once the model of the middle-class minority couple, were now separated. "What can I do to help you?" asked Ralph. "I think you need to get busy on a job and get your mind off all these things that are bothering you."

Ron stared out the window, not replying. As far as he was concerned, Ralph was the master of not facing facts, a man too stubborn and too proud to close the doors to his business and go to work for someone else, too irresolute to be able to give Ron the tools to deal with his problems. The rumors of Ralph's extramarital affair with Betty's cousin only added more fuel to Ron's hostility.

"Talk to me, Ronnie," pleaded Ralph, who suspected that the pressure Anna had put on Ron to get married and have a baby had played a big role in his lost state of mind, maybe even more than Ron's confusion over race or his abandoned baby.

Ron stood up and crossed his arms across his chest, glaring down at his father. He said nothing. Then he turned and walked out of the room.

Sadly, Ralph shook his head, wondering if he would ever get back the son he once knew.

Anna agreed to give their marriage another chance. Ron suspected it was a decision based on hope that he would soon recover and they would live in family harmony in Mendocino, surrounded by forested hills, cool mountain air, bright skies, and the sea sparkling through the cypress trees. For Ron, it was a second chance—with Anna, with fatherhood.

He rode a Greyhound to San Francisco, then they rented a U-Haul and headed north on Highway 1, the two-lane coastal road that winds along the rugged shoreline past logging camps, undulating moors, and miles of picket fences bordering the road. They hoped to find steady work, she as a waitress, he perhaps in a sawmill.

They weren't the only ones coming to Mendocino in search of a new lifestyle. A quaint, transported Maine fishing village with white steepled churches and gingerbread cottages, Mendocino had become a town full of runaways, the hills and woods surrounding it filled with communal societies heading back to nature. Fishing and logging no longer sustained the town's economy as it once had; the artsy and crafty and light-hearted had moved in, attracting the tourist dollar to the galleries and the head shops on Main Street.

Anna talked of living a simpler life, away from the evils of the city. Not only would it be best for Royce, it would be therapy for Ron. Relaxed. Stress-free. Away from his parents' discord. He could work, and if someday he wanted to go back to being an architect, well, they would think about that when the time came. What was important now was getting his head back on straight and taking care of his family.

They hadn't come to Mendocino to grow dope and get high—which was what brought many to Mendocino County. Pot wasn't Anna's thing, and the only thing Ron was smoking was Camels, about a pack a day. They moved into a small cottage in the woods south of town. Anna found a job waitressing in a coffee shop; Ron, however, couldn't find work. The arguments and the tension started immediately.

"I'm not going to support you," she asserted.

For the time being, Ron's job was to watch Royce, but most days that was a task too daunting. He spent long hours walking in the woods or working on architectural sketches of imaginary projects. He checked out a library book on wood sculpturing and carved a redwood bust of himself using Anna's woodworking tools, tools she'd asked him not to use. She blew a gasket. That was the end of his woodworking career. She told him to get a real career. Or else move out.

Who could blame her for feeling frustrated? She was constantly picking up after him: he left dirty ashtrays around the house; he took baths and didn't clean the ring in the tub; he rarely changed Royce's diapers; he didn't look for work. The longer he was unemployed, the more they argued. And the harder she pushed, the more he pulled away. "Stay off my back," he warned. She told him to be a man, to provide for his family, to take care of himself. His option was to leave.

She had tried her hardest to nurse him through his problems; she was a resourceful woman and had been his one shelter from his brain's storm. In return, she had gotten nothing. That's how she saw it. He saw it differently. Her intensity and strong personality, which he once found seductive, now weighed him down. He accused her of nagging. He felt isolated, alone.

He walked to a clearing in the hills called Lost, silently communing with other bewildered souls in the Haight-Ashbury of the pines. He was close to the streets of Mendocino, the same streets that James Dean wandered in search of his mother in *East of Eden*. When he picked up a newspaper, the world around him got even more jumbled: newly elected Richard Nixon was claiming he was working for peace but the bodies continued to come home in coffins; Huey Newton was in jail; the inner cities were burning. The trees were closing in on him.

Anna was at work, due home in a half hour. Royce was asleep in his crib. It was time for Ron to split. No goodbyes, no sticking around to hear one more time what a lousy husband and father he was. He hastily packed, throwing a change of clothes into a small satchel and his senior design project from Cal into his portfolio. Of his meager belongings, that's what seemed most essential to getting a fresh new start, to finding a job in L.A.

He took off on foot, heading for Highway 1 to hitchhike south. No problem getting a ride, he figured. It was 1969—picking up hitchhikers was part of the counterculture code and Highway 1 was a long ribbon of winsome youth hitting the road without any resources other than the goodwill of the drivers in the psychedelic vans. He was dressed in cotton pants and a wrinkled white dress shirt. Compared to the other hitchhikers, he looked like the *GQ* Man of the Year.

Nearing the highway, he remembered he had forgotten to leave a bottle for Royce in case he woke up before Anna got home. He hesitated at the side of the road, afraid that if he went back, Anna would return, spoiling his clean getaway. He didn't have the fortitude to tell her to her face that he was leaving. He'd left a note.

Panicked, he ran back to the house, stopping at a tavern to buy a carton of milk. Royce was crying when he walked in the door. He quickly fixed a bottle, leaving the carton out on the counter—his final goodbye to Anna. He leaned over and kissed Royce on the forehead, then headed out the door again.

At the highway, he stuck out his thumb and the first car stopped, a VW with a peace emblem on the rear bumper. The driver was a young woman, plain and unadorned, with long, straight brown hair. She was going to Mexico. Or maybe Arizona. She hadn't made up her mind yet. The *I Ching* would let her know.

As he loaded his portfolio into the back seat, a VW screeched to a halt next to them. It was Anna.

"What'ya doing?" she yelled, jumping out of her car.

"Leaving," he said. "That's what you want."

"Where's Royce?" she asked, a half-smile suddenly turning to concern.

"At home."

"You left him alone?"

"He's got a bottle. He's fine."

"Damn you," she shouted, grabbing at his portfolio.

Inside the car, the young woman calmly observed the tug-of-war as if she was watching a test pattern. Ron wrestled the portfolio from Anna's grip and tossed it back into the back seat, signaling for the young woman to pull away as he slumped into the passenger seat. Anna could only stand and watch as they disappeared around the bend.

42

Jim

Never had he been so nervous: not when he faced the *biting, tearing pain* . . . not when he approached Rainie Falls on the Rogue River . . . not when he said "I do" with Patty. He braced himself for the next assault.

"What is the fundamental weakness of Johnson's thesis on applications of stochastic processes to sediment transport rates?" asked Professor Simons.

Jim breathed a quick sigh of relief, then confidently launched into his answer. He had spent months preparing for his orals for his Ph.D. in hydraulic engineering. It wasn't just his thesis—"The Interaction of Gravity Waves and Turbulent Channel Flow"—that he had to defend. He'd been warned that he could be questioned on anything he'd ever studied in civil engineering. The Ph.D. orals were the last chance for the department to weed out the weak . . . and for him to fail now, after spending twenty years climbing toward this academic peak, would be unthinkable.

It was all part of the educational game, he realized, reminiscent of the inquisition during Hell Week, only instead of standing naked in front of a roomful of voyeuristic Pi KA actives and answering questions about his sex life to prove his fraternity mettle, he was standing in front of five tenured professors in a classroom at Colorado State University, answering questions about river mechanics to prove his academic merit. But Jim, as usual, was good at playing the game and accomplishing the assigned task, even though he doubted he would ever have any practical application for the material in his thesis. It was just an exercise in problem solving.

"How do you measure the resistance of a device in a vacuum if you can't touch it?" asked Professor Sandborn.

Suddenly Jim's heart sank. He had no clue what the answer was. He shrugged his shoulders, admitting he didn't know.

"Neither do we," said Professor Sandborn. "We were just hoping you might be able to help us come up with an answer."

Jim passed the exam.

Despite completing his dissertation and passing his orals, he still had two more years to complete before being awarded his Ph.D. He had reached a false summit, and after seven years of pounding the engineering books, four at Berkeley, three at Colorado State, he was burnt out. He was also 1A again, the draft board refusing to extend his 2S deferment.

The three years in Fort Collins had been the best of his life. It was almost as if his world didn't really begin until after he'd left Berkeley. Part of it had to do with skiing—sometimes he felt as if grad school was a three-year ski holiday. He'd spent 1967 on the Ski Patrol at Breckenridge and 1968 as an instructor at Loveland. But it was a lot more than just the slopes. He loved being married and coming home to Patty after spending all day in the lab. His self-esteem and confidence had blossomed. And academically, he was a big success . . . straight A's, recognition for his thesis, a prestigious National Science Foundation traineeship, the dean of engineering taking him personally under his wing. But his draft board didn't care about any of that anymore. They wanted him front and center, fighting the spread of Communism in Vietnam.

He had a decision—two years in the Army as a grunt or enlisting for four years as an officer. It wasn't a tough choice; he'd heard too many gruesome stories about combat from his Vietnam vet buddy on the Ski Patrol. So in the spring of 1969, with Nixon's promises of troop reductions echoing across the land, Jim applied for and was accepted into both the Air Force and the Navy flight training programs. If he had to go into the military, he decided, he might as well do it as a pilot. His brother Scott, a Navy officer, advised him that if he wanted to learn to fly, the

Navy was the way to go. Why? Because Navy pilots were the ones with the balls to land on carriers.

Despite the concerns of Patty and his parents, who thought a five-year commitment was taking too big a chunk out of his life and would be hard on the marriage and hurt his chances of completing his Ph.D., he enlisted in the Navy Officer Candidate School. Patty would return to Burlingame and live with her family while he went through his sixteen weeks of indoctrination at Pensacola. After that, she could join him and they could be together the rest of his tour. And Vietnam? It would take three years of training to become a combat pilot. And that was only if he was lucky enough to be one of the "chosen few" to survive the rigorous training. "The war will be over by then," he said.

It was May 20, 1969. In Berkeley, National Guard troops stood guard over People's Park; in Washington, Nixon endorsed the secret bombing of Cambodia; in Montreal, John and Yoko started a "bed-in" for peace; and in Pensacola, Florida, Jim reported for duty at the School of Pre-Flight in Pensacola, the cradle of Navy aviation.

He stepped off the bus at the front gate with the thirty-four other raw recruits in his class to begin Indoc, the Navy's answer to Hell Week— one week of verbal abuse, calisthenics, endless spit shines, unrelenting attention to detail. He marched in formation to the barbershop . . . much like walking with his goat brothers into the darkened living room of the Pi KA house. He was greeted by Sergeant Bodine, a Marine drill instructor. Jim was sure that if he went to the dictionary and looked up "drill instructor," he'd find a picture of Sergeant Bodine in his Smokey the Bear hat, screaming at a recruit from an inch away.

"If any of you pussies want a DOR," barked Sergeant Bodine, "I'll be happy to oblige."

DOR, Jim quickly learned, was "Drop on Request," which meant that a cadet could opt out of the Navy aviation training at any time and be reassigned to two years of enlisted duty on a ship, which, of course, was one extremely long step down the pyramid of manliness in this fraternity. At the top of that pyramid were the jet pilots.

The image of the Navy pilot was that of the macho fly-boy, carefree, heroic, decked out in his silk scarf, aviator sunglasses, and leather flight jacket. A fighter jock belonged to a select group of men, well educated, survivors of the toughest weeding-out process in all the military. According to Navy literature, its pilots were self-reliant, disciplined, responsible, patriotic instruments of national policy. According to some of their ex-wives, however, Navy pilots were intolerably narcissistic and vain-glorious.

Like many of the young men entering Navy flight training, Jim thought of it more as entering a technical school where he would acquire a specific set of skills. This wasn't a career . . . it was an adventure, much like signing up to be a river guide or to be on the Ski Patrol. He fully intended to return to his academic pursuits and civilian life after his five years. What he quickly discovered, however, was that he had stepped into the middle of a tight-knit fraternity, and he was instantly obsessed with climbing up the pyramid of flying.

And levels was what Navy aviation was all about, not levels of rank, like ensign and admiral, but indescribable levels of skill and bravery, daring and coolness, reflexes and experience that would one day be called "the right stuff" and would compel a man to hurtle through the sky like a bullet, risking death. Although it was not in any recruiting brochure that Jim had read, Navy aviation was also about death: lots of Navy career pilots died in flying accidents, and that did not include war, which the Navy did not consider an accident. And for those pilots lucky enough not to die, many more would someday have to push the ejection button and bail out of a crashing plane.

Jim and his class were ushered into an auditorium. The rumor was that the Navy had recruited more pilots than it needed and only those cadets with the best grades in Pensacola would get promoted into the jet pipeline, which was where the true fighter jocks were funneled. An officer stepped to the lectern. "Half of you won't make it!" he announced. "You'll never get your wings. And only one in thirty will become a jet pilot."

Jim returned to the barracks to find two of his classmates in tears. It could have been the breath-sucking Florida humidity . . . or the last 150 gut-busting "kahoopies" (combination push-up, mountain climb) . . . or Sergeant Bodine's verbal cannonade. The two men were gone in the morning. DOR. Gone from the fraternity, never to fly. It didn't have to be said—some men had it, some didn't. To help him endure, Jim remembered his mother's axiom: "This too shall pass."

He felt a sense of purpose and an esprit de corps with his Indoc classmates, much more than he'd ever felt in Pi KA with his goat brothers. These were men dedicated to becoming Navy aviators, the best, and therein was the fraternity, a sense of belonging. Pi KA was a social club, one he never connected to, always feeling himself the outsider. Not so at Pensacola. He fit, instantly one of the guys. With three years of graduate school, he was the senior member of the class, a little more mature, a little calmer. He was chosen class captain. The only office he ever held in Pi KA was goatherder.

Flight training, as with all levels of Navy aviation, was a series of tests to move to the next level. Each station was divided into the *haves* and the *have-nots*. Either you moved up or you were *left behind. Washed out. Shit on a stick.* To some it happened in introductory instruction. Pre-Flight, known as ground school, was Jim's first step to his wings and commission, a rigorous combination of academics, physical fitness, and military discipline, four years of Annapolis crammed into four months—long hours of classes in naval orientation, aerodynamics, leadership, engineering, aviation science, and navigation. He excelled, scoring at the top of his class academically. Grades were everything—those who lagged academically were *washed out.* He scored second in his class in physical training, breezing through the obstacle courses, easily swimming a mile with his flight clothes on, thanks to his high school swim team experience. He also did well in the officer candidate classes—he had the quality of quiet forcefulness—although he wasn't there to become an admiral. He was there to fly.

Students were quickly separated into the pilots and the "backseaters," the Naval Flight Officers (nonpilots) who became the navigators, bombardiers, radarmen, and weather observers, which were all polite terms in the brotherhood of fighter jocks for *washouts.* Nobody ever said it, but it was always implied that if you didn't get that gold bar signifying you had successfully flown solo, you had failed in a test of nothing less than your manhood. Only those promoted to a fighter squadron were still in the real fraternity.

After two weeks of ground school covering cockpit procedure, engineering, and flight characteristics of the single-engine, prop-driven T-34, Jim reported to Saufley Field ten miles west of Pensacola for the beginning of primary flight training. It was at Saufley Field that he was given his first communion with plane and sky. He did well, receiving his gold bar, elevating him one small step up the many-tiered pyramid.

After his solo came more intensified levels of training—loops, wingovers, barrel rolls, spins—and at each level more trainees fell back into the world of *washouts.* Jim steadily advanced. When he was in the cockpit, he was comfortable, in control, feeling a sense of daring and machismo that he saw as missing from his pedestrian personality. He called Patty back in Burlingame to share his enthusiasm and tell her he'd been promoted to jet school. She said all the appropriate words . . . but how could she really appreciate what he was saying? How could she share the confidence he'd gained? She couldn't. It wasn't because she was a woman or because she wasn't smart enough. Unless you were in the fraternity, it was unknowable. The Navy was keeping them apart, that's what she knew.

There were certain identifiable characteristics of the fighter jock—righteous aplomb at the O Club, big wristwatch, aviator shades, fast car. Most young pilots, full of cockiness from their new aeronautical success, fancied themselves highway daredevils as well, ready for the Daytona 500. For a graduation gift to himself after flight school, Jim bought a new '69 GTO hardtop coupe, with a 400-cubic-inch V-8 and four on the floor. Patty had rolled their VW Bug, an accident she neglected to tell him about, not wanting to worry him while he was in training.

With his new dress whites hanging in his GTO, he arrived at Meridian, Mississippi, home of the Navy's jet training school, the next level up the pyramid. He hadn't entered his new fraternity just to be a pilot—it was to be a *jet* pilot. Left behind in Pensacola were the unchosen—the prop pilots.

Patty joined him in Meridian. Most Navy couples lived in a large apartment complex, but the van Hoftens rented a small two-bedroom house, living comfortably on his $600-a-month ensign's pay. Because they would be there only six months, Patty didn't work. She stayed home, bored, waiting for him to come home, doing her best to be the dutiful officer's wife, attending the wives' luncheons and teas. But she missed California. Meridian seemed like such a small town with nothing to do. The only places to eat out were a Burger Chef and a German restaurant; the town closed down on Sundays. And she prayed there wouldn't be that dreaded knock at the door, the one every young Navy pilot's wife feared—the Navy chaplain come to inform her that her husband, her true love since the tenth grade, had piled his jet trainer nose-first into a bog and was charred to a crisp.

Jim rode to the base many mornings on his new motorcycle, another accessory of the fighter pilot. The base was carved out of rolling timber-laden and marshland terrain. To build runways, workmen had gouged hills, diverted streams, and filled in swamps. Jim was surprised at the beauty of Mississippi's piney woods. He was also surprised at the segregated life in Mississippi. Integration on the base, however, was not an issue. There were no black aviators in his class in the jet pipeline.

At Meridian, after intensive classroom study, he received 120 hours' flying time in a T-2A Buckeye, a straight-wing, easy-to-fly subsonic jet, with time devoted to formation and instrument flying. He liked the morning flights, to take off with the dawn and look down at the houses and the roads cut through the piney woods; he felt sorry for the working stiffs down below, those who had to punch the time clock every morning and didn't know the joy of riding ten tons of major military hardware into the sky. There was something primordial, almost sexual about it, the power, the thrust. In high school and college, he'd spent considerable time feeling one notch below, left behind. But flying a jet was a feeling of superiority. An attitude. It was one thing to conquer the equations of fluid mechanics, quite another to feel the afterburners kick in. He tried not to flaunt it with braggadocio. What kept his ego from running wild like a star halfback stumbling over his own clippings was the knowledge that he was still at the bottom of the pyramid. He could not yet imagine himself up where the combat pilots resided, or beyond that at the apex of the pyramid, the spot reserved for test pilots, and ultimately the astronauts. He was preoccupied with what every Navy aviator at Meridian thought about—carrier qualifications—the onerous task required to reach the next level.

Taking off from the air base in a T-2 jet, he joined a pack of six trainees and followed an instructor out over the Gulf. It was a clear blue day, little wind, calm seas—the Navy wouldn't be so fiendish as to send up neophytes in bad weather for their first carrier landing. The target was the *Lexington,* a World War II carrier stationed off the coast in the Gulf of Mexico. His heart was pounding. Never had he been so nervous. *Never.*

Every Navy pilot knew that he couldn't truly call himself a fighter pilot until he had passed the Big Test—landing on an aircraft carrier. That was not the final test, not even close, but it was the victory that allowed a Navy fighter jock to peacock into a room of Air Force pilots and know there was a line of bravery and skill that he had crossed and they hadn't.

Carrier qualifications were held back in Pensacola. Jim had signed up for an accelerated class of six weeks. Most of the unmarried pilots opted for the ten-week course, not necessarily because they wanted more training but because it was well known that the O Club in Pensacola, which looked out over the waters of the Gulf, was thick with the prettiest girls of the Florida panhandle, girls in search of macho fly-boys. But Jim was very much married. He reasoned the faster he moved through training, the quicker he and Patty could get back to California. Miramar Air Base near San Diego was the penthouse of the pipeline.

Carrier qualifications had begun with practice landings, always solo, on a carrier deck painted on the ground in the boondocks. A Landing

Signal Officer (LSO) signaled the pilot in for touch-and-go landings, grading his performance, debriefing him at the end of the day. There were lectures and movies, horror scenes of planes skidding sideways across the deck, smashing into other planes or towers, or just sliding right off the edge into the drink, or, worst of all, coming in too low and wiping out against the end of the deck. The films never showed anyone walking away from those crashes.

But no film could prepare him for the actual day. The squadron stacked up in a pattern, starting at 5,000 feet, everyone descending on the same path. Jim looked down and saw the carrier. The deck seemed like the griddle on his mom's O'Keefe & Merritt, greased with jet fuel and hydraulic fluid. It had no railing. He knew that even in the slightest of breezes the deck heaved and rolled and bounced, compounding the task of landing a jet going 135 knots on a ship going 20 knots. Tests in Vietnam had showed that the monitored heart rates of pilots coming in for a carrier landing were higher than during antiaircraft fire.

His knees trembled. The stick shook in his sweaty palms. Gliding in, he felt as if he was in a falling Burlington Northern caboose, not in an airplane. He locked in on the LSO, afraid to look over the edge. He entered the groove, ten seconds to touchdown. There was no red light, the signal for a wave-off. This was it. If he screwed up and the tail hook missed, he would have three seconds to get his jet engines back up to power to take off again. Otherwise he was in the drink.

There was no way to anticipate the violence of going from 150 miles an hour to zero in two seconds. The hook caught and the airplane jerked to a stop, the seat restraint harness locking into place. He was thrown forward like a rag doll, hanging in the straps, safely landed, his heart dancing a mighty mambo inside his flight jacket.

He was now a member of the elite club, not just because he had made it but because he would have the balls to go back up and do it again and again and again, his heart pounding and his palms clammy every time.

As good as he felt about landing a jet airplane on an aircraft carrier, he knew he couldn't truly call himself a Navy fighter pilot until he did it in combat. And that seemed highly unlikely. He still had a year and a half of training to go, and there were already more pilots in the pipeline than were needed for Vietnam. So they said.

43

Loren

We will make certain that no normal business goes on in the city while there are still troops on our streets.
—Student spokesperson, People's Park demonstration

Standing just inside the locked front door of UC Corner on Telegraph Avenue, his feet spread and his arms folded across his brick wall of a chest, Loren sneered as waves of demonstrators ran wild in the street. Berkeley was under siege. Police barricades were on every corner; National Guardsmen with fixed bayonets and gas masks lined the street; troops in jeeps scanned the rooftops, shotguns ready.

It was May 20, 1969—the same day Jim showed up at the front gate in Pensacola to start flight training. Telegraph Avenue had been a bloody war zone for five days, with dozens injured and one student dead from double-O shotgun wounds. At issue was not free speech, or civil rights, or Vietnam—it was the battle over People's Park, a disputed piece of vacant land four blocks south of campus. It was a confrontation over property, capitalism, and a way of life. Governor Reagan, who was refusing to negotiate, had called in the National Guard and three battalions of the 49th Infantry Brigade.

Loren applauded as three blue-helmeted policemen billy-clubbed a demonstrator in front of the Bank of America building across the street. Tear-gas canisters exploded on the sidewalk, sending students running helter-skelter for cover. The rumor was that chemical agents were about to be dropped on campus to disperse a crowd of 4,000 gathered in a vigil for the slain student.

The decade in Berkeley, like Loren, was flaming out, original goals abandoned, no clear-cut direction for the future. He had come back to Berkeley, not to watch the revolution, but to babysit UC Corner, which was all that was left of his once promising entrepreneurial ventures with Craig. After only one year in business, the bank had already foreclosed on UC Corner in Davis, as well as Varsity Sports and Craig Morton Sports. The former Miss California had been right when she warned of his loosey-goosey style. It was a textbook failure—no business plan, irregular store hours, money missing from the till, merchandise sitting unopened in the back room.

It had been a quick but painful collapse, with lots of bitter finger pointing, primarily between Loren and his ex-roommate Jerry Olson, who was Craig's partner in the Berkeley UC Corner store. Jerry, who had invested $10,000 in the Davis store, accused Loren of mismanagement, claiming he had taken on too much overhead, overextended their credit, and neglected the business while he lived the good life. By Loren's own admission, he had made mistakes. "I'm not a manager," he confessed. But he countered with accusations that Jerry and his family had also mismanaged the Berkeley store, misappropriating Craig's initial investment. Lawyers were called in, depositions were taken, and when it was all over, Loren and the lawyers convinced Craig to sue Jerry for a million bucks. It was settled out of court, Craig gaining control of UC Corner in Berkeley, or what was left of it. And that's what Loren was doing there— trying to manage it through its last, dying days, while Craig stayed in Dallas, wondering what happened to his investments, contemplating bankruptcy. His wasn't the only investment lost. Loren's grandparents lost the $35,000 collateral from their rice fields. Eddie was heartbroken.

If all the financial upheaval wasn't enough for Loren to deal with, Bernie Copeland, his CPA, who had helped him launch the Davis ventures and was his main business adviser, was returning from a trip to Squaw Valley with his two young sons when his car plunged off the side of the road and down a steep canyon, killing him and the two boys. Police were unable to determine the cause of the crash. Not long after that, Greg Lee, who ran the record sales for Loren in the Davis store, was hit from the rear on his motorcycle on his way home from work. Loren arrived at the emergency room just in time to see him die. And then there was another friend, John Barreveto, who died when his helicopter was shot down in Vietnam.

As he watched the demonstrators continue to run past the Berkeley store, he had no sympathy for their claims to People's Park. The property, purchased by the University in 1957 and cleared of its existing houses in 1968, was originally earmarked for development, but because of a lack of funds, the University had let it become a dirt parking lot that had become an eyesore filled with trash and abandoned cars. Several hundred students and local residents, spurred by a collective spirit and a frustration with the University's bureaucratic inaction, decided to clean up the site, clearing and leveling the ground, erecting playground equipment, planting trees, grass, and flowers. For a brief moment, the movement in Berkeley was in harmony, people working toward a common humanitarian goal, hippies and activists united, a project embodying the values they were espousing. Instead of opposing or protesting or tearing down, they were creating. It was a refreshing breakthrough. But after two weeks of work on the site, Chancellor Roger Heyns's office had issued a release stating that the University would have to put up a fence to reestablish the "conveniently forgotten fact" that the field belonged to the University. At 4:45 A.M. on May 15, hundreds of Highway Patrol and Berkeley policemen, dressed in bulletproof flak jackets and armed with rifles and tear gas, had cordoned off an eight-block area around the site. An eight-foot steel-mesh fence was erected. The next afternoon an estimated crowd of 6,000 marched down Telegraph past Loren. When they reached the park, the confrontation exploded into a major battle, demonstrators throwing rocks at the officers, the police retaliating by flooding the south campus area with tear gas. Sheriff's deputies, armed with shotguns, fired at the crowds, sending demonstrators running for protection. When the marchers couldn't penetrate the barricades at People's Park, they took to the streets, striking out against the "capitalist pig" merchants on Telegraph. That included Loren.

He was fed up with the rioting and the anarchy. Three times in the last five days bricks had crashed through the store's plate-glass windows, spraying broken glass in all directions, letting in tear-gas fumes. He had boarded up the windows with thick plywood, furious and disbelieving at what was happening to his college town, a far cry from the Berkeley he had come to at the dawn of the decade. Gone were the crew cuts, chaste coeds, and convertibles cruising down Telegraph Avenue, replaced by long-haired freaks, Army troops, and combat jeeps. He was proud to be a jock and a hawk; his only concessions to the movement were his long sideburns, bell-bottom pants, and his approval of the braless look. But as far as he was concerned, People's Park was just an excuse for a bunch of losers to riot.

In the distance he heard the thump-thump-thump of a helicopter as it swept low over Sproul Plaza, spraying clouds of nauseous CS tear gas (a type developed by the Army for use in Vietnam and outlawed for wartime use by the Geneva Convention). Students fled, reeling from the gas, vomiting. Loren applauded, again. Panic-stricken students banged on the locked front door of the store, trying to get inside to escape the rolling clouds of gas. He stood firm, smiling, flashing the peace sign.

He was able to hold his ground against the demonstrators, but it was a lost cause in the battle to hold off the creditors. By the end of 1969, UC Corner, a fixture on Telegraph Avenue since the fifties, closed its door for good. Loren was out of work.

He was also on the verge of losing the former Miss California. She'd been offered a job in public relations with TWA. If she accepted, it meant she'd have to move to L.A., which for all practical purposes would spell the end of the relationship.

After five years together, she was tired of his unwillingness to give more of himself, tired of his lack of commitment. But it wasn't easy to let go—he had been her only boyfriend all the way through college, and although they had never been officially engaged, she'd dated nobody else. He'd swept her off her feet from the beginning, moving fast, negotiating her time. It wasn't so much that he had to have her at his hip—it was more out of a need to control the show. Or at least that's what she'd come to believe. He was in charge of their social life—rugby parties, hanging out with Craig, trips to the ranch. It was always what *he* wanted to do. She had, however, willingly accepted his terms.

"Nobody's holding a gun to your head," he'd say.

She thought the carefree attitude he'd had in managing his business ventures paralleled her own problems with him—how his abundant energy and charm and charisma had gotten things off to a flying start, but then there was a lack of follow-through, no attention to details. She was convinced he could sell anyone on anything, but taking care of business was another thing. It had been frustrating to her to watch the effect the business had on his relationship with other people, especially Craig, who hadn't been able to figure out why he was losing money and didn't know how to confront Loren. In all the times that she'd been around them, she had never heard them talk about business. It was always jokes and good times. She felt sorry for Craig, thinking he'd been taken advantage of.

But she knew how hard it was to confront Loren. He was so opinionated, so dogmatic. It bugged her that he always had to get in the last word. It also bothered her that he usually had an entourage around him. He kept the door to his house unlocked and a steady stream of friends drifted in and out at all hours. From her standpoint, it was diluting the relationship. He was avoiding private time. And if it wasn't his friends, then it was the business . . . a phone call he had to make, a deal he needed to work out.

She sensed he was running away, skimming life, diving into the superficial so he wouldn't have to be too serious. He put conditions on how much he could give. He always had an excuse: "Wait until after rugby season." "As soon as I get this business mess cleared up." She needed more. His spontaneity, one of his charms that originally attracted her—the no time schedule, the never knowing what was coming next—had grown thin. She needed form and structure in her life: he returned things in worse condition than he got them; he always showed up late; he always thrust his opinion on her. And there was always the nagging suspicion, despite his denials, that he was seeing other women. She was tired of hearing how much he'd changed since he'd met her, and how none of those other women ever meant anything to him.

She accepted the job with TWA and moved to L.A. When he made no effort to dissuade her, she knew it was over.

Loren sat on the couch and watched Craig grimace as he slung another sidearm pass from five feet away into a pillow. They were in the living room of Craig's large rented house in North Dallas. It was November 1969.

"How's it feel?" asked Loren.

"Bad," replied Craig, continuing to throw into the pillow.

"Be tough," encouraged Loren.

Craig nodded, appreciative of the support. At the beginning of the season, he had finally inherited the starting quarterback position following Don Meredith's retirement—he'd paid his dues and now it was his turn. He got off to a good start, leading the Cowboys to first place in the conference. But in the sixth game, he was buried under an avalanche of tacklers and felt something tear in his right shoulder. With rookie Roger Staubach, who was back from his four years in the Navy, waiting on the sidelines, however, he couldn't afford to come out. At practice the next week, he couldn't throw and was barely able to lift his arm. But on Sunday he loaded up with cortisone and continued to play, then went back to throwing into a pillow during the week.

Loren hadn't come to Dallas to retrieve Craig's passes off the couch, however. He had come to talk business with the Cowboys.

·   ·   ·   ·

Dressed in his double-breasted suit and cowboy boots, he stared across the desk at Tex Schramm, the shrewd general manager of the Dallas Cowboys, a man noted for his tough, cold negotiating. They were sitting in the Cowboys' plush new corporate headquarters in downtown Dallas. With Loren was attorney Bob Brown, a Cal grad. They were there to try to renegotiate Craig's contract. Despite the failure of the businesses, Craig had entrusted his financial matters to Loren, a move one friend called "the blind leading the comatose."

In addition to the pain in his shoulder, Craig was in serious financial trouble; he not only had lost his investment money but had blown through his salary as well, highballing across the fast lanes of Texas, Nevada, and California on his way to his reputation as one of the NFL's leading playboys. The IRS was breathing down his neck.

Loren presented Craig's case to Schramm, claiming that if the Cowboys didn't help out Craig he would have no option but to file bankruptcy. "I don't think you appreciate how tough Craig is," said Loren. "But if he has to go through bankruptcy, I'm not so sure he can mentally handle it."

Schramm shook his head. The Cowboys had already advanced Craig money on his contract and were not willing to do it again. Loren accused the Cowboys of purposely letting Craig's financial problems get out of hand so that they would have him over a barrel, desperate to sign a new contract at any price.

Schramm shrugged.

"You're a sonuvabitch!" charged Loren.

Schramm wouldn't budge. Craig had no alternative but to file for bankruptcy. The Cowboys finished the season with an 11–2–1 record but lost in the playoffs to Cleveland, 38–14. Loren skated away without having to file bankruptcy.

The decade for Loren was winding to a chaotic close . . . and none too soon. His parents were on the verge of divorce, three friends had died, his alma mater was under siege, his business ventures were belly-up, his friendship with Craig was strained, his friendship with Jerry Olson was over, the former Miss California had split, his grandparents' investment was down the drain, he was unemployed.

So what would he do differently if he could go back and start the decade over? "Not a damn thing," he said. "I've never had a bad day."

And he believed it too.

PART THREE

Ex-Husbands
(The Seventies)

Whenever you want to marry someone, go have lunch with his ex-wife.
—Shelley Winters

44

Larry

The disturbing fact is that the vast majority of people, including educated and otherwise sophisticated people, find the idea of change so threatening that they attempt to deny its existence.
—Alvin Toffler, *Future Shock*

I was fuming, pacing the living-room floor, glancing out the window every ten seconds. Denise was an hour late with the car, which I needed to get to work. Wendy, three, was taking a nap.

It was January 1970. A new decade. Despite some disorientation, the sixties had been good to me—college degree, marriage, child, my picture on a bubble-gum card. And I had even higher hopes for the seventies—big house in Malibu, World Series ring, a son. We were living in a $200-a-month upstairs duplex in Playa Del Rey with a view overlooking west L.A. and Santa Monica Bay. I was working as a fitness instructor for Jack La Lanne Health Spa on Wilshire Boulevard, a job I hated, although not as much as the other off-season jobs I'd had selling sandpaper, used cars, hockey tickets, disability insurance, and sporting goods. And for the first time in our marriage, Denise was also working. She was a model for Nina Blanchard, the top agency in L.A., and that's where she was on this day, off doing a photo shoot, no doubt in some flimsy negligee, surrounded by gorgeous male models and artsy, sensitive photographers, no doubt taking her dear sweet time about getting home. Couldn't she at least call?

But no, I wasn't threatened.

I was also waiting for a call from the Phillies. It seemed strange that it was six weeks before the start of spring training and they hadn't even sent me my contract yet. Usually I got it in November. My phone calls to the front office had gone unreturned. "Maybe they're trying to tell me something," I'd told Denise. I'd spent the 1969 season at Eugene (which had replaced San Diego as the Phillies' farm team in the Pacific Coast League), trying to get back to where I was before my separated shoulder. I had a tolerable 11–9 record, but by the end of the season the manager, Frank Luchessi, a short, inconstant man who twice during his managing career got in clubhouse fistfights with black players on his team, had stopped talking to me, glaring at me as if I was the second coming of Abbie Hoffman. Maybe it was the love beads I wore. Or the peace sign I put in my locker. I threw a shutout and his only comment to the newspaper was: "He needs a haircut." My hair barely reached the top of my ears. (Facial hair, including sideburns, was forbidden.) I suspected he had advised the Phillies not to invite me to spring training with the major-league team, but still, it was distressing not to have received even a minor-league contract. Maybe I wasn't Bob Gibson, but I thought I at least deserved the courtesy of a Christmas card. Or something.

Denise finally called. The photo shoot was taking longer than anticipated. "It's probably going to be another hour," she said.

"Shit!" I replied. "I'm supposed to be at work."

She reminded me that she was getting paid $50 an hour, whereas I was getting $2.85. I didn't want to hear that, nor did I want to know what skimpy, sheer, see-through thing she was modeling, or for whom. When she'd first announced that she was going to try modeling, I thought it would be great to brag about my wife the glamorous model, but the truth was, which I didn't dare say to her, I wanted her to quit. I hung up, then unloaded a solid left hook to the wall, knocking to the floor her painting of the two tearful black girls outside a bombed church, shattering the glass, waking Wendy.

So far, the seventies were not going well.

On the way to my ten-year high school reunion in January 1970, Denise lamented how baseball was preventing me from having long hair. After cocktails and dinner the reunion committee handed out awards—most kids, longest married, etc. I won the prize—a pair of scissors—for the male with the longest hair.

"It's as if the sixties passed these people by," she whispered.

Dexter, my best Westchester High buddy, was there, just back from his second tour of duty to the DMZ with the Marines. I felt guilty for the abundance and security of my life. I didn't ask him about Vietnam and he didn't ask me about my baseball career. If he would have, I could have bragged that I'd just learned that I was traded to the Chicago Cubs as the player-to-be-named-later in a deal sending all-star right fielder Johnny Callison and me to the Cubs for outfielder Oscar Gamble and pitcher Dick Selma, a deal giving me a bright new outlook on my career. But Dexter and I were stuck in some kind of uncomfortable time warp, only able to talk about the games we'd played against Venice and Hollywood High back in the fifties. Denise yawned. When the band showed up and started unpacking their accordions, she requested we leave.

Pulling up in front of our duplex after dropping off the babysitter, I eyed a hippie couple strolling down the sidewalk. They were dressed in serious fringe; I was wearing a double-breasted houndstooth sports coat, black slacks, white turtleneck, and black loafers with tassels. So it must have been the peace symbol on the back of our Buick station wagon that caught their eye.

"Say, man," said the guy, "do you know where we could score a joint?"

I gave them a quick once-over, decided they weren't escapees from the Manson Family, then told them to follow me upstairs. I had just purchased a nice plump ten-dollar lid earlier that day.

It originally had been Denise's idea that we try smoking pot. I had resisted at first, but she persisted and I finally agreed to try it in the winter of '68, unaware that she'd started smoking it six months earlier. I was zonked after two puffs that first time, freaking out at the colored soap balls in the bathroom, thinking they were the greatest technological invention of modern times. We bought a lid, then another. During the '69 season, I smoked once or twice a week, although only at home with Denise and never with any of the other players. As far as I knew, none of them were dopers. The recreational-drug culture had not yet invaded pro baseball. The use of amphetamines, however, was widespread. "Greenies," as the cross-top uppers were called, were passed around the locker room like candy. I had tried a greenie once, but when my heart tried to jump over the center-field scoreboard, I swore off.

I liked smoking dope. It made me high without having to drink half of Kentucky. I could eat Dots and listen to the Strawberry Alarm Clock forever when I was loaded. Sex felt more erotic, Nixon seemed uglier. It made me, I believed, part of the movement, one with the counterculture, free from the hypocrisy of the straight world. And best of all, it brought me closer to Denise, making her think that maybe there was hope for me after all, that I wasn't doomed to wear tasseled shoes forever. That's what I thought, anyway.

But there was much about the whole movement thing that had me confused. There were days I couldn't figure out if I was married to Sophia Loren, Germaine Greer, or Harriet Nelson. Denise talked about how she would have given anything to have been at Woodstock, then went off to model for a Bank of America commercial. She told me I dressed too straight, then bought me a golf sweater for Christmas.

I wanted to be married . . . to have a wife, children, traditional roles, a family station wagon. I liked the concept. Wendy was so cute that strangers stopped us in the supermarket to admire her. I thought I was being a good daddy, giving her piggyback rides, reading her Dr. Seuss bedtime stories, quacking like Donald Duck, staying up until 5 A.M. on Christmas Eve desperately trying to assemble "Clyde," her super-deluxe rocking horse. But I also wanted to jump bones on every woman who walked by, be one with the sexual revolution.

I was sure our marriage had improved in the year and a half since Denise had written to tell me how unhappy she was. But there was always that fear that I would wake up one morning and find a Dear Larry note saying, "Sorry, you're a nice enough guy, but you're just not hip enough." What exactly hip was, I wasn't sure, but I thought of it in cultural terms—music, clothes, etc.—not in emotional terms—intimacy, vulnerability, etc. I hadn't done my case any good when I argued that Ram quarterback Roman Gabriel was more popular than Mick Jagger. But I was trying. For Christmas I gave her Janis Joplin, Iron Butterfly, and Steppenwolf albums. We went to concerts—Crosby, Stills, Nash and Young; the Rolling Stones; the Youngbloods; Three Dog Night; the Doors. In 1966 I had voted for Ronald Reagan for governor—in 1968 I voted for Eugene McCarthy; I no longer stood on the sidewalk on Telegraph with my pockets loaded with eggs. The times they were a-changing . . . and so was I. I just wasn't sure if it was fast enough to suit Denise.

Even though I thought of myself as politically in agreement with the movement, I was at the same time threatened by it . . . the anarchy of the Chicago Seven, the hostility of the Black Panthers, the sexual experimentation of the hippies. It was so much to assimilate so quickly, while at the same time trying to come up with a better curveball. It was as if I went to sleep one night wanting to be Sandy Koufax, then woke up in the morning trying to be John Lennon.

I was caught in a world in between. When I walked in the clubhouse, my teammates eyed me as if I was Che Guevara; but when I walked down Telegraph, hippies surveyed me as if I was Lawrence Welk. We went to see *Hair*, and I loved the music but squirmed at the nudity. The issue of hair seemed to capture the nether world that I was caught in— my hair was too long for baseball, too short to be hip.

It wasn't as if I had to put on an act for Denise. I truly had become antiwar; I really did love the Beatles; I sincerely did hate Spiro Agnew. But I couldn't very well show up in the clubhouse wearing raggedy jeans and a "Fuck the Draft" T-shirt if I wanted to get back to the Show. Wearing love beads under my baseball sweatshirt would have to be my contribution to the revolution.

When I walked in our duplex with the hippie couple, Denise wasn't as happy with my love-peace-and-happiness gesture as I thought she'd be. Still, she joined us as we fired away on a couple of "righteous" doobies. The guy was from Chicago, and when I told him I'd just been traded to the Cubbies, he fell to the floor, bowing toward Wrigley Field. It wasn't until the next morning that I discovered he'd stolen my nice plump lid.

It was a perfect June night for baseball in Honolulu, the temperature a balmy 83, a refreshing trade wind blowing out toward right. I had no doubt that it would be my last game in the minor leagues. My bags were packed for the Show.

I had reported to 1970 spring training in Scottsdale, Arizona, with the Cubs in the best shape of my career, trimmed down from 210 to 185 pounds, thanks to running on the beach every day, a grapefruit diet, and Jack La Lanne's Health Spa. I was sure that there would be no way that Cub manager Leo Durocher could keep me off the big-league team. The Cubs, coming off a disappointing collapse at the end of the '69 season, were loaded with all-star talent—Ernie Banks, Billy Williams, Fergie Jenkins, Ron Santo, Ken Holtzman. In Scottsdale I had a new attitude, arriving early to practice every day, staying late, running extra wind sprints, hustling after balls in batting practice, sprinting to first base in drills, drinking nothing stronger than grapefruit juice. I kept my hair short, my mouth shut, and my safeties out of sight of the Scottsdale Ramada, the team's headquarters. Denise stayed in L.A. with Wendy and modeled.

For all my hustle and clean living, I might as well have camped in a cocktail lounge. Durocher didn't even know I existed. He called me "Hey, You." I didn't pitch batting practice or intrasquad games. My only shot was two innings in a "B" squad game against the Cleveland Indians. I gave up one run. Durocher wasn't even there that day. I thought him an arrogant, pompous ass. But if he'd told me to kiss his ass, I would have puckered up and smooched away.

I was sent down to the Cubs' AAA farm team in Tacoma, Washington, an Army town hidden under rain clouds and the stench from wood-pulp mills. It felt like Fort Armpit. My spirits sank even lower when I was assigned to long relief, which was a polite way of telling a guy who had always been a starting pitcher that he was now pitcher non grata. But in my first two games in relief I pitched five innings of hitless ball, convincing manager Whitey Lockman, an easygoing, unpretentious man, to give me a starting assignment. In my first start, I threw a three-hit shutout. By June I was leading our last-place team in every pitching category, with a record of 6–1 and a 2.06 e.r.a. I was throwing as well as I had before the shoulder injury. In a feature story in Sporting News titled "A Svelte Colton Chills Coast League Bats," Lockman attributed my success to my "desire and dedication." Following another shutout, the headline in the Tacoma Tribune read: "Colton Fires 2-Hit Gem; On Way to Chicago?" Word had it that I would be called up after the game in Hawaii on June 13. My new address would be the brick and ivy of patriarchal Wrigley Field, the baseball acropolis where Babe Ruth called his shot.

But a funny thing happened on my way to meet Mr. Durocher. In the bottom of the eighth in Honolulu Stadium, with the trade wind blowing out and the score tied 2–2 and a runner on first, the opposing pitcher, veteran Juan Pizarro, came to bat. He was a big left-hander from Puerto Rico with a dozen years in the Show, hoping for one more go-round. In his previous at-bat, he had jumped all over one of my hanging curvatures for a two-run homer. I wasn't about to make the same mistake. He would get a steady diet of low heat.

The first pitch sailed in knee high and inside, exactly where I aimed. He unleashed a mighty golf swing, and the violent sound of ball and bat colliding was audible, no doubt, in Bora Bora. I didn't even bother to turn and watch. I was told later that the ball cleared a sixty-foot wall beyond the right-field fence, the first time in the history of the ballpark that such a feat had been accomplished.

The next day the Cubs bought Pizarro's contract and he was on his way to beautiful Wrigley Field. I, on the other hand, was on my way to six straight losses back in the fetor of Tacoma.

I came home from the ballpark, rolled a joint, then turned on Johnny Carson. Denise got up and turned it off. "I'm not happy in our marriage," she announced, voice trembling.

"Not happy?" I replied. "What'ya mean? How can you not be happy?"

There was something missing, she explained. I wasn't satisfying her emotionally, physically, or spiritually.

"That's a relief," I said. "I thought it might be serious."

"Don't make a joke of this, Larry," she warned.

We talked way past Johnny Carson. How could she be unhappy, I wondered, when we never argued? The more we talked, the more frustrated I got. It didn't make sense. Was I supposed to help more with the dishes? Do the grocery shopping? Let her run the finances? No, it wasn't stuff like that, she said. It was a feeling in her heart. I was confused—earlier in the year she'd told me how much she thought our relationship had improved, that I was more open and our communication and sex were better. Now she was saying our lovemaking was inhibited and lacked passion. I wished I could have told her about the compliments I'd received on the road about how passionate and attentive the other women thought I was.

"I'm not sure I love you anymore," she confessed. "And I'm not sure I can get it back. We've grown in different directions. I don't want to make love with you anymore, at least not until I change the way I feel."

I wanted to slug the wall. She had such a sense of doom. I tried seeing it from her perspective, figuring that maybe she was tired of the nomadic life—we'd been married five years and had moved twenty-one times (not counting all the moves back and forth between Hedy's and my parents'), always because of *my* career, living in strange towns for three or four months, with no family, no permanent friends, no sense of home. The only furniture we had was baby cribs and playpens. Denise had rarely complained, adjusting at each new stop—Clearwater, Macon, Eugene, Ponce, San Diego, Philadelphia—but with a couple exceptions, she had not connected with the other baseball wives. She chatted and laughed with them during the games, but they were from different worlds. The gossip, the Tupperware parties, the beehive hairdos . . . "They're all so straight," she said.

I thought that maybe Tacoma was the problem. "Hang in there to the end of the season," I offered. "I love you, Denise. I don't want to lose you." For the first time in our marriage, she saw me cry.

It was a team flight from Phoenix back to Tacoma. Sitting next to me was the squatty reserve catcher, a brusque redneck from Nebraska. He glanced down at my book, *Points of Rebellion* by Supreme Court Justice William Douglas, a call for social reform to change the violent cycle of poverty, pollution, and segregation in the country.

"That one of them Commie books?" he asked.

"Here's something you might be able to read," I replied, flipping him the finger.

For the first time in my career, I was thinking of quitting. I'd been in pro ball almost six years and had only two dinky innings in the big leagues to show for it. I was twenty-eight, an old man by minor-league calendars; I didn't want to end up one of those sad baseball characters who hung around the bush leagues forever, waiting for a good hop. If the Cubs didn't call me up after the start I'd had, I questioned if they ever would. I was discouraged and disillusioned.

My attitude had soured. Instead of ordering grapefruit juice at the bars, I ordered bourbon. I hadn't gotten a haircut in weeks. I'd quit running wind sprints between starts. And instead of talking about base-ball in the clubhouse, I rambled on about Kent State, the invasion of Cambodia, the no-facial-hair rule. I dared the other players to give the peace sign in the team photo. None did.

Baseball wasn't fun anymore. I didn't care if we won or lost . . . and we usually lost, firmly entrenched in last place. I had retreated into a shell, feeling estranged. None of my teammates had any inkling of my marital problem—we *never* talked of such things, not in the dugout, not in the clubhouse, not on road trips. In fact, I had talked to *nobody* about the problem. It was too embarrassing, an admission of masculine failure. What kind of man was I if I couldn't keep my wife happy? I wasn't about to seek marital counseling. How could a stranger know what was best for *my* marriage?

It was scary to think about quitting. Baseball had been my life. It was what defined me. I was a baseball player, then a husband, then a father. My adult life had been designed by my fastball, not my college diploma. Baseball affected every decision I made. I also believed baseball had influenced Denise's decision to marry me—if I was a shoe salesman, no matter how good, she wouldn't have married me. Baseball was glamor-ous, masculine, respected. It offered the promise of money, travel, adu-lation. I didn't know anything else; I had no other career frame of refer-ence. I had loved the game, the competition, the fraternity with the players. I loved standing on the mound being the center of attention. It was power, control. Its loss would be a loss of self, I worried. But I was ready to quit.

I continued reading *Points of Rebellion.* Justice Douglas was urging young people to rise up in protest, to be instruments of change. The book was raising questions for me about my own contribution to society. Baseball seemed indulgent, part of the Establishment. In the Age of

Aquarius, it wasn't what was hip. The country was heavy with the cruci-
ble of Vietnam and the riots at home and I was hung up about giving up
a two-run homer to Juan Pizarro. I wanted to do something "relevant."

At 37,000 feet somewhere over eastern Oregon, with an "America
Love It or Leave It" reserve catcher sitting to my left, I decided I would
quit baseball at the end of the 1970 season and become a teacher. I
didn't know what I would teach or how I would get a credential. But for
the moment, that didn't matter. I had a goal. I was reeling in the nobility
of it, excited to break the news to Denise at the Sea-Tac Airport, figuring
she would be thrilled. Teaching would provide us stability, an ingredient
she had never known.

I bounded off the plane, scanning the waiting area for her and
Wendy's beautiful faces, always a welcome sight after two weeks on the
road, no matter how many safeties I'd been with. They weren't there.
Strange. For all the road trips I'd ever been on, Denise had always been
there when I stepped off the bus or plane.

I got a ride home with another player. There was a note on the kitchen
counter informing me that Wendy was at a neighbor's and Denise was on
a modeling assignment. (She was working for a Seattle agency.) It was
after midnight when she finally got home, rather late, I thought, but
when I'd questioned her once before about another late assignment, she
glared at me as if I was Joe Friday. I told her about my big decision.

"That's great," she lied.

The score was tied 1–1, bottom of the sixth inning, one out, none on.
The batter was Steve Garvey, the promising young third baseman for the
Spokane Indians, the L.A. Dodgers' farm club. I looked in for the sign,
ignoring his Popeye forearms. I knew nothing about him personally other
than that he was a good curveball hitter and that a couple of his teammates had told me privately that he was a real Goody Two-Shoes. The
squatty redneck catcher signaled fastball. I shook him off. He signaled
slider, the pitch I'd struck out Garvey with his first two trips to the plate.
I shook him off again, motioning for him to meet me in front of the
mound.

"I want to throw a knuckleball," I said.

He stared at me incredulously from behind his mask. I'd never thrown
a knuckleball in my career. "Whatever you say," he said, rolling his eyes.

What did I have to lose? It was the last game of the season and we
were a pitiful 46 games behind powerful league-leading Spokane, a team
managed by colorful Tommy Lasorda, with a roster of future major-
league stars that included Garvey, Davey Lopes, Bill Buckner, Tom Pa-

ciorek, Bobby Valentine, Billy Russell, Tom Hutton, Charlie Hough, Doyle Alexander. It was also, I had decided, the last game of my career, my secret swan song.

I had expected to be melancholy when I arrived at the park, knowing that I had reached the end of the dream that had consumed me since childhood, but I wasn't. Maybe it was because I was occupied with thoughts of getting on with a new career—the plan was for us to move to the Bay Area, where Denise would model and I would work part-time and go back to school at San Francisco State to get a teaching certificate. Or maybe it was because I was absorbed with saving our marriage —Denise was pulling further away. Or maybe it was because I smoked three joints just before leaving the hotel, the only time I'd come to the ballpark high. By the sixth inning, however, the buzz was long gone.

Or maybe I wasn't more melancholy because I was keeping it a secret that this was my last game. I hadn't told anybody but Denise about my plan to quit, figuring I'd write a letter to the Cubs after the season. I doubted they would try to talk me out of it, although, all things considered, I'd had a decent year, with twice as many wins (13) and innings pitched (215) as anyone else on a team that had only won 45 games. In my penultimate game, also against Spokane, I'd pitched a two-hit shutout and slugged a 425-foot home run—the next day the Tacoma *Tribune* had reported that "Colton did most of the job with a sizzling fastball, prompting one of the major-league scouts on hand to remark, 'He showed me the best hummer I've seen in this league all season.'" So I felt good about bowing out of the game still with the "best hummer" in the Coast League.

My debut knuckleball against Garvey, a pitch I had been working on for years while playing catch in the outfield, did a modest little dance on the way to the plate, but missed the strike zone by a couple of counties, rolling to the backstop. I waved the redneck catcher to the mound again.

"Let's try it again," I said.

The redneck catcher shrugged and glanced toward manager Whitey Lockman in the dugout, who signaled for the bullpen to start heating up in a hurry. For the first time all season, the normally placid Whitey looked upset. I didn't know if it was my knuckleball or if it was just his frustration at the whole lousy season. Despite the fact that we had the worst record in pro ball, he had maintained supernatural patience, never losing his temper, never throwing chairs in the clubhouse, never checking on us for curfew. Not once during the season had he bugged me about cutting my hair. He treated us like adults even though we behaved like adolescents and played like shit. The low point in the season had come a few nights earlier at our team party in the Stadium Club in Tacoma beneath the grandstands, a players-and-coaches-only affair that had erased any second thoughts I had about quitting. Prior to the party I had spent several days secretly writing "An Ode to Whitey," a tribute that I planned to read to him in front of the team at the conclusion of the party. I'd hand-printed the poem on poster board and pasted pictures of each player around the border. Before I could present it to him, the players started ribbing and roasting each other good-naturedly at the podium. But the frustration of a losing season and massive quantities of alcohol quickly escalated the roast into a fusillade of meanspirited and barbed insults, and then a full-scale food fight, with cups of beer and vodka flying . . . and then, finally, fists and blood, a real barroom brawl, teammates slugging it out toe to toe. I stood off to the side, screaming, "You guys are fucked!" The redneck catcher screamed back, "Fuck you, pothead!" It was a miracle nobody was seriously hurt. When order was finally restored, I ushered Whitey to the podium. A poetry reading suddenly seemed about as appropriate as china in a bull shop, but I started reading anyway. The room fell silent, mouths dropped open. When I was finished, the players stood in unison and applauded, not for my sophomoric poetry, but for Whitey. I handed him the framed poem. His face was blank. I couldn't tell if he thought I was Carl Sandburg or Karl Marx. Without saying a word or changing his expression, he returned to his seat and continued eating his potato salad. I didn't know what he thought.

My second knuckleball to Garvey also missed the mark, as did my third and fourth attempts. As he trotted to first, I glanced toward Whitey in the dugout. He had gone from looking upset to apoplectic, obviously unappreciative of my knuckleball experiment, 46 games out of first place or not.

The next hitter was Tom Paciorek, a strapping young outfielder, stepping to the plate with 99 RBIs. I'd had his number all season, striking him out three straight times in the previous game. But I had talked to him before the game and he had expressed how important it was to him in his bid to make the major leagues to reach 100 ribbies. As I rubbed up the baseball, with Whitey now up to the top step of the dugout, it occurred to me that perhaps, in the spirit of Woodstock, I might be able to do something altruistic in my swan song.

"Fastball down the pipe," I whispered to him after wild-pitching Garvey to second.

My next pitch was exactly as advertised, cheese-whiz right down the chute. As soon as Paciorek swung and connected, launching the ball deep into the eastern Washington night, the only question was whether it would travel farther than the shot Pizarro hit. The ball had not even started to reenter the earth's atmosphere when Whitey stormed out of the dugout and headed for the mound, signaling to the bullpen.

He said nothing, just angrily motioning me off the mound. There was no goodbye, no wishes for a long and happy life, no gold watch. My baseball career, such as it was, was over.

But I was in *The Baseball Encyclopedia.*

Denise said it was urgent that we go somewhere private and talk, so we drove to a remote corner in Berkeley's Tilden Park and sat on a grassy knoll surrounded by eucalyptus. It was three days after my career-ending gopher ball. Everything we owned was stuffed into a U-Haul trailer hitched to the back of our station wagon. Friends were watching Wendy.

"Well?" I said anxiously.

She turned toward me, struggling to compose herself.

"Go ahead, say what's on your mind," I urged.

"I've fallen in love with another man and I want to be with him," she stammered. "I want a separation."

I stared up into the trees, then down at the ground, the words penetrating my brain, my heart, my every pore. *I've fallen in love with another man.* That's right, Larry, that's what she said. It felt as if the blood was draining right out of my body into a big pool on the grass. It was my worst nightmare—my wife telling me she wanted to leave me for another man. I wanted to scream; I wanted to cry; I wanted to choke her. But I sat frozen, too stunned to blink, a zillion questions stampeding my head. How long had she been screwing him? Was his pecker bigger than mine? Had Wendy met him? What would I tell my friends? What about my parents? They were expecting us in L.A. the next day.

"Who is this guy?" I finally asked.

He was a model in Seattle and they'd met on one of those "late" assignments, a photo shoot for United Airlines where they posed as a couple flying off to Hawaii on vacation.

"I knew it!" I blurted, the light suddenly clicking on.

She explained that he was really an artist and he was just modeling to make money until he sold some of his paintings. He was sensitive, open, caring, and gentle, she said, and even though he was four years younger than she, they had so much in common. They'd talked of collaborating on children's books. I thought I was going to gag. She wanted to fly back to Seattle that night to be with him. And take Wendy with her. I did gag.

She claimed they hadn't slept together yet. Right, and I was Babe Ruth. "You can admit it," I said. "I admit I've been screwing around too."

"What!"

I blurted it out. Striking back. "Hundreds of times," I said. "Every road trip." As soon as the words were out, I wanted to reel them back in.

"You asshole!" she raged. "How could you?"

Good question. I didn't have the answer . . . it was hidden too deep in my chromosomes. The Y one.

"You're the one who wants to leave and break up the family," I said.

Mine were just one-night stands. No harm intended.

And then the tears started. Hers. Mine. Not just trickles. Major torrents. Tears of rage, tears of despair.

Somehow, through the hysteria and my pleading for her not to leave, she agreed to drive to L.A. with me so my parents could see Wendy before she flew back to Seattle the next day. It would give me 400 miles to talk some sense into her, convince her what a huge mistake she was making.

We pulled into the driveway of my parents' new condominium in Marina Del Rey. It had been 400 teary-eyed miles through the blistering heat of the San Joaquin Valley with a broken air conditioner. Every time I tried to convince Denise that a separation wasn't the way to solve our problems, I burst into tears. Wendy would look at me from the back seat with her big green eyes and say, "Daddy, please don't cry." And that would make me cry even more. Pum-Pum, the fluffy eight-week-old cockapoo puppy that I had gotten her for her fourth birthday was also in the back seat, yipping and pooping and adding to my misery. When we reached a smog-choked L.A., a cop pulled me over for driving in the fast lane with a trailer; he must have thought I was crying because he was writing me a ticket. The KRLA Freeway Watch said it was the biggest traffic jam in the history of the San Diego Freeway. "Daddy, please don't swear," said Wendy. By the time we pulled into the driveway in Marina Del Rey, I was ready to explode. I was wearing sunglasses to hide my reddened eyes.

"What are you going to say to your parents?" asked Denise. "We can't just go in there and pretend nothing's wrong."

I didn't know what I was going to say. I had never let on that our marriage was anything but rosy. Nor had I told them of my decision to quit baseball. They opened the door and rushed to greet us—a big happy family reunion, so they thought—arms outstretched for Wendy. I broke into sobs.

"What's wrong?" asked Mom.

"Ask her!" I yelled, pointing at Denise.

"I'm not the only one to blame!" Denise screamed. "Tell them about all the horrible things you did!"

Mom and Dad stood dumbfounded, bowled over by this sudden emotional napalming, their son crying, Wendy crying, their daughter-in-law screaming. From family joy to total chaos in ten seconds. I grabbed Wendy and ran upstairs to the guest bedroom, followed by Denise, then Dad.

"I don't know what the problem is," he said, calmly, apologetically, "but it's upsetting your mother. I want you to leave."

His response wasn't surprising—we had always been a family that lived in domestic harmony, preferring to sweep any problems under a stiff upper lip rather than do battle. Denise, Wendy, Pum-Pum, and I got back in the car, drove to Santa Monica, and checked into a motel on Wilshire Boulevard for an all-night cryathon. I couldn't change Denise's mind. She made plane reservations to Seattle for her and Wendy (and Pum-Pum too), and in the morning the cab arrived to take them to the airport. I stood on the sidewalk and cried, watching Wendy clutch her doll, Mrs. Beasley, and wave goodbye out the back window.

Mom had been skeptical of the marriage from the beginning, not because she didn't like Denise, but because she thought our backgrounds were too dissimilar. "But I couldn't have told you that back then," she said. It had always bothered her that every time my name was in the paper it always said "Larry Colton, son-in-law of Hedy Lamarr." Never once did she read "Larry Colton, son of Hazel Colton."

"I thought your marriage was going fine," said Dad, in the only statement he would make about our separation.

Mom and Dad took me back when I returned to their condo, and for three agonizing days I sorted through everything Denise and I had collected in the five years of our marriage, dividing it into stacks—hers, mine, and the Goodwill. Every time I picked up another memory—wedding pictures, Wendy's tea set, Denise's art supplies—I wallowed in more pathetic tears. I couldn't eat. A friend called to invite Denise and me out for dinner; I couldn't admit that she had left me, telling the friend we couldn't make it because we were moving to the Bay Area in the morning. I heard on the radio that Jimi Hendrix died of a drug overdose. I was too bummed to smoke or drink, afraid it would send me over the edge.

I called Hedy, who had moved to New York. It seemed funny—that I would be calling to ask for marital advice from a woman who had been divorced six times. During our marriage, when Hedy and Denise were bobbing and weaving, hating and loving, Hedy and I remained constant. She was always friendly and cordial to me. Denise had commented numerous times how much better I got along with her mother than she did. I was hoping to get Hedy to go to bat for me, to convince Denise she was making a mistake. Hedy counseled me not to give up, to do everything I could to make sure that Denise knew how much I loved her. Her words made me feel better, although I suspected her opinion would carry little weight with Denise.

I drove back to Seattle. My only hope, I decided, was to employ civility and kindness, to quit being such a crybaby, to be strong, to shower Wendy with love and affection, to cooperate with Denise any way I could. I promised to sell the station wagon, our only real asset, and split the profit. I would give her most of the $3,000 we had in savings, keeping just enough to get me going.

I dropped off her belongings at the small cabin she had already rented on a small lake just south of Seattle. I could see evidence that *he* had been there, such as his wardrobe hanging in the closet. But they weren't sleeping together yet, she maintained. I hugged Wendy goodbye and drove away, choking back the tears, again.

As I pulled back onto the highway, I was a lost soul at the crossroads. I didn't know where I was going or what I would do when I got there. All I knew was that my pride wouldn't let me stay in Seattle. Nor did I want to go back to California. Too far away from Wendy, too many old friends to face.

I drove south on I-5, stopping in Portland, 170 miles south of Seattle. I had been there several times on road trips while playing in the Pacific Coast League; I liked the idea of being in a town where nobody knew me and I could just disappear into the pine trees, not having to explain what went wrong. Alone to sort through my gloom. I was into introspection and solitude. I checked into the Heathman Hotel, where I'd stayed on road trips. The bellhop remembered me. From my eighth-floor room, I stared down at the teenagers cruising Broadway below and recalled how only a month earlier I had joined my teammates in a water-balloon drop on those cruisers. Seemed like fun at the time.

I was shell-shocked. Within a week's time my baseball career had ended and my wife had left me. I was camped out in a hotel in a strange town where I had no friends, no family, no job, no clue for the future. I had $800 in traveler's checks, a Buick station wagon I had to sell, an ounce of dope, and two suitcases of clothes, half mod, half country club. Aimlessly I walked the streets until dawn, ignoring the steady drizzle. It was September 15, 1970, ten years to the day from when I'd started Cal. Not exactly what I had in mind back then.

45

Ron

So I used to try not to get in too deep, for fear I'd get lost and turn up at the Shock Shop door. I looked hard at anything that came into sight and hung on like a man in a blizzard hangs on a fence rail. But they kept making the fog thicker and thicker . . .

—Ken Kesey, *One Flew Over the Cuckoo's Nest*

For Ron, the second half of the sixties had been a hellish vortex, his mind buried beneath layers of guilt and confusion about racial issues, abandoned children, failed relationships, career, manhood, self-worth. Everywhere his odyssey had taken him—Mendocino, Haight-Ashbury, Chicago, L.A. County General Hospital—had only muddied the picture. Everyone who'd offered a hand—his parents, Anna, his therapists, Joseph Esherick—had been unable to get through. He entered the seventies fragile and bent, just trying to hold on.

To passing strangers, he appeared normal enough. No uncontrollable fits, no talking to voices in the dark. But to his friends and family, the change was shocking, his athletic body a shell of what it once was, his complaisant personality vanished. He had retreated inside his head, his mind filled with weird thoughts. He wasn't in therapy, he wasn't on medication. He was just trying to hold on, the fog getting thicker each day.

. . . .

As he walked in and out of the surf at Venice Beach, a thick fog hovered just off the shoreline, waiting for the sun to relinquish its hold on the afternoon. Ron, however, didn't care if it was sunny or gray—he hadn't come to the beach to work on his tan. He was there for his daily constitutional. Walking and worrying. Worrying and walking. With his denims rolled to the knees and his wing tips in hand, he assiduously sidestepped the tide pools. It was all part of the routine. He glanced at his watch, making sure he was leaving himself enough time to make it home for his vital daily elixir.

He was living rent-free in his mother's apartment in Marina Del Rey . . . with no car, no job, and no money to send to Anna and Royce in Mendocino. His parents, who had always had their place in L.A.'s middle-class minority society, had finally separated after thirty-five years of marriage and were going through a messy divorce. The battle lines were drawn. Ralph was living in Westlake Village in the Valley, trying to hold his business together, putting the finishing touches on a bid for a federal housing project that could save his firm. Betty was having the worst of it, her hard times compounded by a radical mastectomy and a mandated retirement after thirty years as a librarian with the L.A. School District. The fact that Ralph had left her for her cousin, a woman thirty years younger, didn't help. There had been a barrage of acrimonious insults. Ron had taken to his mother's side, blaming Ralph not only for the divorce but also for his own dark journey, reasoning that Ralph should have been tougher and more directive as a father instead of being a coaxer and a guider. According to Ron, Ralph was not built of tough enough moral or constitutional fiber, so therefore neither was he.

He walked across the sand, passing a blonde in a bikini, alone on her towel. "Excuse me," she said.

He never broke stride. Meeting women was out of the equation. Too many questions. Too much ambivalence. He was sexually disoriented. He had ventured into a homosexual bar on Santa Monica Boulevard, unsure of his motives. Curiosity? Boredom? He had even allowed himself almost to be seduced, but walked away, concluding that his motives were as self-centered as they had been in his heterosexual relationships, the only difference being that with girls he had done it for his own gratification, but this would have been for his own punishment, to see how low he could go. Or at least that's what he told himself.

He walked south on Lincoln Boulevard, mindful of the time. He didn't want to be late. Across the street, a crazy man shouted obscenities skyward. Ron quickened his pace, ignoring the disturbance, avoiding eye contact with everyone he passed. That too was part of his routine—

staying detached, keeping a low profile. Once, on a trip to the unemploy-ment office to check on job openings, a fistfight broke out in the line behind him and he never turned around. He just wanted to blend in with the scenery. Harm came, he believed, to those who meddled.

He wondered if there'd be a letter or a message from Anna waiting for him when he got home. Or from her lawyer. She had been to court in Mendocino County and had been awarded, based on his earning poten-tial as an architect, $325 a month in alimony and child support, a figure exceeding his monthly income by exactly $325, not counting the loose change Betty gave him. His arrearage was accruing by the day. Anna had hoped that Betty and Ralph would send money since Ron seemed to be incapable of the responsibility of supporting his son. But since Betty believed that Anna had simply used Ron to father a child, she wasn't of a mind to contribute. Anna denied she'd used Ron, and Ron believed her.

Ron walked into the apartment. Betty was sitting on the couch, a cocktail in her hand. The shades were drawn, the room awash in gloom. He tiptoed past her, apologizing, his tone obsequious, servile, like one might expect of a six-year-old raising his hand to ask the teacher if he could go potty. He wanted to stop her drinking but he didn't know how.

"I'm not bothering you, am I?" he asked, caustically.

"Oh, Ronnie, you're such a nice and nasty boy," she uttered with a smile, repeating her favorite phrase. "Of course you're not bothering me."

"Let me know if I do," he insisted. "I'll move out if you want."

There were days when he wished she would throw him out, make him fend for himself. He was thirty years old and he knew the only way he was ever going to regain his self-esteem was to get out on his own and stop mooching off Mommy. But not yet. Not until he found some kind of a job, any job.

"May I please watch TV?" he asked.

She signaled her okay. He giggled, then turned it on and settled back, ready for another daily fix from his magical pacifier.

"Ladies and gentlemen," announced TV host Chuck Barris, "welcome to 'The Gong Show'!"

Ron watched and laughed, hanging on to the edge of the couch like a man in a blizzard hangs on a fence rail.

It was 3 A.M. He dragged the vacuum behind him, opening the door into the ladies' room of the Brown Derby Restaurant in Beverly Hills. He stopped to yawn. Twenty-four hours without sleep was taking its toll.

Maybe a quick catnap would help. He stretched out on the rug in the vestibule and closed his eyes.

He was working the midnight-to-eight shift for a janitorial service, recently promoted to the Brown Derby after proving his stuff sweeping up popcorn at a seedy downtown theater. Things were looking up. Sort of, barely. This was his fourth job in two months. He had started as a stock clerk for Bullock's Department Store in Westwood. That only lasted through the Christmas holidays. Then he went to work as a dishwasher for Kelly's Prime Steak House in Marina Del Rey. Things were going along pretty well on that job until he asked the cook if he could take a cigarette break and the cook said no, so he went anyway, only to have the cook threaten him with a carving knife, a gesture Ron responded to by turning in his rubber apron. After that he worked as a switchboard operator for the Jamaica Bay Inn in Marina Del Rey, a job he quit after the first night. Too boring.

He was excited about his job with the janitorial service. At $2.60 an hour, he was making enough to have moved out of his mother's apartment into an $18-a-week room in a downtown flophouse on Hope Street . . . a positive step in rebuilding his dignity. Out of his first paycheck he was able to send $20 to Anna, which, by his calculations, only left him $11,980 behind in his support payments. He was also able to pay the enrollment fee for a class in technical drawing at L.A. Trade Tech—he was thinking that maybe he was better suited to be a commercial illustrator than an architect. Less pressure.

He still had no car, no friends, and no social life, a recluse cut off from his past, preoccupied with his inner thoughts. He traveled by foot and by bus, living on a diet of doughnuts, coffee, and Camel straights. He passed the days painting in his room or staring out the window at the winos in the alley. The zeitgeist continued to weigh heavily—the lunacy of the Chicago Seven trial, the whitewash of Chappaquiddick, reports of the My Lai massacre. He had attended a peace demonstration in MacArthur Park, not sure if he was there out of opposition to the war or because he was trying to somehow redeem himself and ease his guilt. In his twisted state, he thought the fact that he had joined the Coast Guard Reserves out of high school was yet another example of his spineless fortitude—American boys were dying in Vietnam and all he'd done for his country was sail up and down the California coast and swab a few decks. He marched in the demonstration, but when somebody gave him a protest sign to carry, he refused, afraid that it would draw attention to him. He wasn't there to make a name for himself in the antiwar movement.

It was 8 A.M. when he opened his eyes from his catnap in the vestibule of the ladies' room at the Brown Derby. He had slept through his shift, the restaurant still a mess. His boss was standing over him, telling him not to bother showing up for work again.

So he moved back in with his mother and resumed his old routines—walking and worrying and watching "The Gong Show."

Walking down the street, he noticed the slow-moving police car and the two officers suspiciously watching his every step. It didn't surprise him. He was sure the FBI had a dossier on him too.

"What are you doing in this neighborhood?" they asked.

He ignored the question, continuing to amble down the sidewalk. But when the cops moved toward him, he froze, then spread-eagled against a car as instructed.

It turned out to be a case of mistaken identity—he matched the description of a suspect in a robbery—but the incident fed his paranoia. Not just about police spying but also about the marching tides of social injustice. A few days later he walked into Marina Yacht and Sail convinced that they wouldn't sell him that nifty little 26-footer on the showroom floor because, well, he just knew they wouldn't. When the salesman told him to vacate the premises, he refused, mentioning the excesses of capitalism, demanding to see the manager. He got his wish, getting to see not only the manager but his .38 revolver too. That's when he decided he wasn't as interested in yachting as he claimed to be. His consolation was that he knew he was walking a higher moral ground . . . he wasn't contributing to the war machine or helping line the pockets of corporate greed.

Ron had spent the greater part of the sixties racked with guilt for having abandoned the child he had fathered. As far as he was concerned, that was what triggered his downslide. Then when Royce was born, he saw his chance for redemption. But now he'd failed there too, a two-time loser as a father.

He awoke from his nap and looked out the window of his seat on the Greyhound bus. The driver announced that the next stop was Willits.

"Oh shit!" he exclaimed, realizing he had slept through Ukiah, his destination. He was due at the Mendocino County Courthouse for a hearing on his request to have his child support and alimony reduced. He was expecting an angry confrontation with Anna.

When Anna originally requested $325 a month, he hadn't contested it. What difference did it make whether it was $325 or $50? He couldn't pay. Fighting it would only have made her madder. And she was indeed angry, feeling betrayed, rejected, emotionally abused. Who could blame her? She had nursed him through dark times, giving him second and third chances. And in the two years since he'd run out on her in Mendocino, she had received less than $200 for her and Royce. But now that Ron was working again—this time as a repairman for a postal-scale company—it was time to set up a realistic payment schedule. He was out of his mom's apartment, living in a small upstairs apartment in a four-plex on Longwood Street near the corner of La Brea and Venice Boulevard, his rent reduced in exchange for light maintenance. In the teeter-totter that was his life, things were on the upswing again, although just barely. His self-image still hovered below the fulcrum.

His separation with Anna had not been amicable. He'd accused her of being impatient, of not giving him enough time to get back on his feet, of constantly reminding him how miserable their life together had been for her. Thinking back on their marriage, he too was angry. It was always: "Do this!" "Clean up that!" "Get a job!" "Be a man!" There was no relief. She had turned cold and unbending, as he saw it, more like a Nurse Ratched than a Florence Nightingale. Yes, he had treated her badly, and yes, he hadn't held up his end of the marriage . . . no income, no touching, no emotional support. But she was relentless, always nagging him. Whenever he had called to inquire about Royce, whom he still wasn't emotionally ready to be a father to, she immediately took the offensive, demanding money, apologies, restitution. "How is it you have enough to pay for your rent but not your son?" she demanded.

He hitchhiked the thirty miles back to Ukiah. To his surprise, Anna was not contesting his request that his arrearage be drastically cut and his monthly payment reduced to $100. "What choice do I have?" she'd asked. The court, upon reading the testimony of his former therapists, granted his request.

His upswing was short-lived. He was laid off at work and evicted from his apartment. He felt as if he was ready for the Shock Shop.

He carried the last load of his belongings downstairs and packed it into his makeshift moving van, which in this case was two garbage cans set atop a dolly he had commandeered from the four-plex. It was a sad sight—a gaunt and troubled thirty-one-year-old man stuffing all his worldly possessions into two garbage cans. Resting on top of one can was a football autographed by all his teammates his senior year at Cal, a ball he had envisioned would someday sit in the den of the award-winning house he would design. The ball was flat, the names faded and blurred.

On top of the other can were the unassembled pieces to a homemade wooden rocking horse he planned to send to Royce. He had designed the horse himself, taking the blueprint to a patent attorney, believing he could mass-produce it and donate the profits to needy children, an act of munificence that he hoped would ease his guilt for being a failure as a father. "My fee is five hundred dollars," the lawyer had said, practicing his putting stroke behind his desk, not even bothering to look at the blueprint. It was yet another example of the dense greed and injustice Ron saw as undermining American values. His was again the higher moral cause. That's why he ignored the requests of the tenant below to stop his hammering and sawing on the project. When the tenant complained to the landlord, who had been after Ron for repeatedly falling behind on his rent and his maintenance duties, it was the last straw; eviction followed.

"Fuck you!" he muttered, as he walked down the driveway, pulling the garbage cans behind him.

He turned right on Venice Boulevard toward downtown, no idea of his destination. He was homeless, penniless, malnourished. But as low and as aimless as he was, his dignity wouldn't allow him to go back to his mother. The casters clattered irritatingly over the cracks in the sidewalk. The driver of a passing car turned to stare.

"Fuck you!" Ron muttered.

He eased the dolly off the curb, unable to stop one of his cans from sliding off. Clothes and art supplies tumbled to the pavement. He knelt to retrieve them as the passengers on a passing bus turned to stare.

"Fuck you!" he muttered.

He turned up one street, then down another, and found himself standing in front of the home of his godfather and former employer, Paul R. Williams. He pulled the cans into the garage and explained to Mrs. Williams he would be back to reclaim his belongings sometime soon. Then he set out on foot again.

As night fell on downtown L.A., he joined in prayer over his supper with the other men at the Union Gospel Mission.

46

Larry

Life is short; live it up.
—Nikita Khrushchev

I looked like a musty Buffalo Bill after a hard winter—fringe coat, shaggy hair, droopy mustache. It wasn't bad enough that I was suffering through a marital and a career crisis. Now I was convinced I was dying. It started as a painful knot in back of my right shoulder and then just kept spreading . . . from my neck to my armpit and then all the way down my right side. It felt as if I had every elephant and his brother standing on my shoulder. I was up to fifteen aspirins a day. I couldn't lift my right arm; the muscles were in atrophy; my appetite was gone.

But I wouldn't go to the doctor.

It was November 1970, two months after my last pitch and Denise's pronouncement that she was ditching me for another man. I had rented a one-bedroom clapboard house on a half acre in Garden Home, a wooded suburb of Portland. It had apple and plum trees and a pumpkin patch in the backyard. Not that I cared. I was in a deep funk, living alone in a strange city, positive I was headed to that great Coast League in the sky. Dead at twenty-nine.

Every day was the same: I woke up at noon, drove downtown in my '59 Chevy pickup camper and went for a walk along the Willamette River, then up to picturesque Washington Park overlooking the city. Walking and worrying. Worrying and walking . . . trying to figure out what went wrong, the melancholy lyrics of "It Don't Matter to Me," a sappy song by Bread echoing through my mind, its words trying to convince me that it was okay if Denise needed some time to be free to go out looking for herself, and that it didn't matter to me if she took up with someone who was better than me, because her happiness was all I wanted. I would have been more productive trying to convince myself I was Babe Ruth.

I was obsessed with putting the pieces back together. Denise was giving me just enough rope to keep me hanging on, telling me there was still a chance for us but she just needed more time to figure things out.

"Your happiness is all I want," I lied.

At night, with the rain falling outside my window, I sat at the Formica table in my kitchen, hunched over my five-dollar garage-sale Smith Corona, typing away left-handed until dawn, pouring my guts into an epic love letter. I was convinced it would make her realize that she had made a mistake and that I was changing and we could indeed have the great love she longed for.

On Friday afternoons I'd drive to Seattle and bring Wendy back to Portland and spoil her with Perfect Weekends with Dad—trips to the zoo, Big Macs, park swings, two scoops of jamocha almond fudge at Baskin-Robbins. If she made a mess, I cleaned it up. Then I'd drive her back to Seattle on Sunday night. I met Tom, Denise's new paramour. He was my worst nightmare—better-looking, better built, better hair. An early-model Patrick Swayze. Big blue Paul Newman eyes.

"Nice to meet you," I lied.

Even if I didn't have a malignant tumor, which I was sure I did, I didn't want to go back to baseball. I had bittersweet memories of my six years in pro ball, appreciating it for the friends made and the games played, disparaging it for its politics and partnership with the Establishment. I couldn't bear the thought of explaining to my teammates what had gone wrong—so much of my identity as a player had been tied to my marriage. Or so I thought. I just wanted to ruminate . . . and finish the letter.

I pondered new careers, new lifestyles: I went to a Jethro Tull concert and thought about becoming a rock musician; I read *Trout Fishing in America* by Richard Brautigan and pondered the life of a poet; I went hiking in Mount Hood National Forest and dreamed of being a forest ranger; I read *Summerhill* and romanticized about teaching in an alternative school. But mainly I just wanted to get my family back. That was my job.

I didn't date. It was weird—when I was married I couldn't wait to go on the road and sport-fuck, now all I wanted to do was be married. In two months in Portland the only person I'd met was Sandy, a slender brunette. We were just platonic friends. She was an artist, calm and centered. Some nights she sketched in the living room while I typed in the kitchen. She was my spiritual therapist, listening sympathetically as I rambled on about my busted marriage. Her only advice was that I should go to the doctor.

I finally mailed my tome to Denise, 68 typed pages, two pages longer than my thesis on SNCC. Then I sat back, and like a guy with an F going into the final, anxiously awaited her reply. And waited and waited. After a week, I called.

"I haven't had time to read it yet," she said.

"No hurry," I lied. "I know you're busy. I was just calling to talk to Wendy."

No longer able to lift my arm, I finally went to the doctor, an orthopedist. He referred me to a neurologist, although judging from his concern, he might as well have been sending me straight to the mortician. The neurologist, a pompous twit whom I decided I hated halfway through my hour wait in his outer office, probed my withered right side and looked even more concerned. I weighed 165, ten pounds less than my bean-pole days in college, fifty-five less than my chubbo spring training of 1966.

"I want to keep an eye on how this thing progresses over the next month," he said. "If it doesn't improve, I'll want to put you in the hospital for some tests."

"What do you think it might be?" I asked.

"I'm worried about two things," he replied. "That it could be a tumor on the spine or ALS."

"ALS?"

"Lou Gehrig's disease."

And I'd thought I'd heard bad news when I'd been demoted to the bullpen in Tacoma. "What should I do for the next month?" I pleaded.

"Go home and put your left hand on one side of the mirror, your right hand on the other, then look yourself square in the eyes and tell yourself there's a fifty-fifty chance you're dying."

And that's what I did. I was too numb to cry, too afraid to tell anybody, including Denise. I just went about my daily walking and worrying, alone, scared shitless. Sandy moved to Eugene, leaving me in total solitude. The nights were hardest, an unheroic, depressing confrontation with thoughts of death. It was hard to believe that just a few months earlier my picture was in *Sporting News* and I was counting the hours until I was pitching in Wrigley Field. The pain in my shoulder was getting worse. I had a hollow dent above my shoulder blade where I could reach in and grab bone. Dad, unaware of the problem, called to find out how things were going.

"Fine," I lied. "Hey, how about those Lakers!"

Denise called to say she'd finally read the letter. "I still need more time to sort things out," she concluded.

"No big rush," I lied.

I was in the hospital five agonizing days for tests, including a myogram, electroneuroanalysis, and a biopsy. (The bill, every penny of it, was covered by my baseball insurance—fortunately I hadn't gotten around to telling the Cubs I was quitting and was still under contract.) I lay flat in bed, no word from Dr. Pompous as to the results. He never even peeked his head in the door. On the sixth day, he finally showed up. He was wearing his power-of-life-and-death face. I bolted upright, which is a definite no-no so soon after a myogram. The throbbing in my head from sitting up was so intense I barfed my Jell-O all over the doctor's leg. I was aiming for his crotch.

"The good news is that it's not a tumor or ALS," he said. "The bad news is I don't know what it is. Your tests were all negative. We'll just have to keep monitoring it. You can go on about your life."

My head ached too badly to celebrate.

Sitting in my pickup in the parking lot outside of Tacoma's Cheney Stadium, I found it rather disconcerting that in five minutes I would be in the clubhouse putting on my uniform again, resurrecting my dead career. But it was for a noble cause. My mysterious malady miraculously cured itself in the spring of 1971. I was convinced that the whole episode had been psychosomatic—that I had become so tense and uptight about my failed marriage and career that I made myself sick to my shoulder. While I was recovering, I had decided, again, that I wanted to be a high school teacher. But it would take two years to go back to school and get a credential . . . and that would cost money I didn't have. So after considerable agonizing, I reluctantly signed a contract for $2,200 a month to play another season in Tacoma, figuring that by living cheaply I could bank enough to get me through two lean years of schooling. By the time I had completely healed from my mystery illness, spring training was already over and the season was underway. So I put all my belongings into the back of my Chevy camper and drove up I-5 to Tacoma. I hadn't worked out a lick and now I looked like Buffalo Bill after a bad winter *and* spring. My hair was down to my shoulders. Far out and right on. My plan was to walk into the office of the new manager, Jim Marshall, a drill sergeant sort of guy who had replaced Whitey Lockman, watch him throw a fit over my hirsute condition, then dash down to the barbershop and clean up my act to play the game.

But as I sat in my pickup in the parking lot, I had one last hope to keep me from having to play another season. I had interviewed the day before in Portland with the director of an innovative teacher intern program—it was a Harvard-developed program designed to train people with college degrees to work with minority students. In this program, the interns taught full-time, were paid first-year-teacher wages, and received a teaching credential at the end of the year. Too good to be true. The hitch was that the program wasn't accepting applications for another two months. I had begged and pleaded with the director, rattling off platitudes about children being our future and my "quest" to help society. He was a baseball fan and marveled at my willingness to quit the national pastime to become a teacher. He said he'd discuss my case with the review committee, but doubted they would make an exception. "But call me late tomorrow afternoon," he'd said. "Just in case."

I went to a pay phone under the grandstands in Tacoma and called him long-distance in Portland. "We've decided to bend the rules," he said. "You're in the program."

I bounded into the clubhouse. Only a couple of players had arrived. I said a brief hello, then walked into Marshall's office. He looked up at me from behind his desk and grimaced, his eyes racing from my hair to my fringe jacket to my faded bell-bottom jeans. He was looking at Dennis Hopper in *Easy Rider*, not the ace of his staff.

"I just got some great news!" I enthused. When I explained to him that I was quitting to become a teacher, he had the look of a man who had just been told by his doctor that the tumor was benign. He wanted nothing to do with me, I concluded, even if I did have the "best hummer" on the staff.

He studied me across his desk, contemplating his response. "Well," he said, "I guess a man has to do what a man has to do."

47

Steve

Do I contradict myself? . . . I contain multitudes.
—Walt Whitman

Ayris sat in the living room of their Sacramento apartment, watching Steve skim through the pages of the newspaper, a man too impatient to read one article all the way through. How typical of his mercurial, Gemini personality, she thought. He had been home from work for thirty minutes and already he had tinkered with his motorcycle, put on a Roy Orbison album, done 200 sit-ups, read twenty pages of Vonnegut, and skimmed the paper, back to front. She suspected that he was more restless than usual this evening, that there was somewhere he wanted to go or something he wanted to get off his chest.

"Anything the matter?" she inquired.

"No," he mumbled, his mind far away. It was such a contrast to how attentive he'd been that morning, his smile so persuasive, his charm over the legal limit.

She didn't press the matter. It wasn't because she was mousy . . . Ayris Radich was delicate but no doormat . . . it was just that she'd learned not to quiz him on his inner thoughts. He was a person who thrived on challenge, physical and mental, and would go out of his way to engage in a battle of wits, but he had an inner core that he sometimes kept reserved for himself. When she tried to penetrate it, he retreated.

He stood up and headed for the door. "I'm going back to the shop for a while," he announced. Ayris surveyed him skeptically.

The "shop" was South City Honda, where he had been working since his discharge from the Marines. His dad had him doing a little bit of everything—sales, parts, repairs—grooming him maybe to someday take over the business. Steve wasn't so sure about such a lifetime commitment, but for the time being he was content, figuring that the hassle of working under his parents' watchful eyes was less of a strain than getting lost in the shuffle of a big company. He enjoyed the challenge of troubleshooting motorcycle engine problems, and now that the shop had been selected as one of only five outlets in Northern California to carry the Civic CC, Honda's first venture into the car business, he was busy getting the auto dealership launched.

"When will you be back?" asked Ayris, who was taking classes toward a master's in painting at Sacramento State and working as a part-time bookkeeper at the shop.

"I don't know," he answered, flying out the door.

Ayris had worked hard schooling herself to accept his restless, unpredictable spirit. She doubted she would ever have the comfort of knowing for sure what he was *really* thinking or where he was *really* going when he walked out the door. It was always a possibility that she could send him out for milk on Monday and he wouldn't come home until Wednesday.

As he weaved in and out of traffic on his motorcycle, the wind felt good in his thick dark hair, which he was growing fashionably long since the Marines. He was happy to be living back in California, happy to have his military obligation behind him. He had survived Vietnam with no post-combat stress, no thousand-yard stare, no screaming nightmares. He was proud to have been a Marine, yet still convinced the war was aimless. He talked little of his experiences, not because he was ashamed to have served in Vietnam, but because he was not one to dwell in the past or the negative. Life for him was today and tomorrow, not yesterday. He preferred to think of Vietnam in terms of the friends he'd made and the GI Bill that he was using to pay for his private flying lessons. The one thing about his Vietnam experience that he did brag about to friends was how he had misdirected Navy artillery into empty fields to prevent what he saw as pointless killing. He was also pleased with his new slimmed-down look. When he joined the Marines he weighed 220, still ballooned from his days as a linebacker; four years later the bull neck was gone and he was a lean and fit 180.

His marriage to Ayris was entering new territory. For the first time the

military and the specter of war and death weren't hanging over their
heads. Their marriage had been shaped by the Vietnam War—every decision, every move, every plan. Ayris had been able to rationalize her own
antiwar sentiments and being married to a Marine by knowing that underneath Steve's Semper Fi rah-rah, he didn't accept the tenets of war
and violence. The first thing he did after his discharge was give away his
guns, a shotgun and a .30-30 rifle he'd received for his birthday as a
teenager. "I've fired my last shot," he proclaimed. Ayris was thankful that
he had come back from the death and destruction with his body and his
spirit still whole, although maybe a little more restless.

But then again, he had also come home a little more mellow, a little
more laid-back, a little more receptive to new ideas. He was as eager as
she was to escape the urban rat race and move to the country to live a
back-to-nature lifestyle. They stopped eating red meat and subscribed to
The Whole Earth Catalogue and *Organic Gardening*. Ayris learned to
bake her own bread and grind her own wheat. Steve voraciously read
books on natural farming, ecology, and do-it-yourself home building.
They made a down payment on twenty acres of land forty miles east of
Sacramento in the Mother Lode country, and spent weekends on the
property clearing a site for what they hoped would be their environmentally one-with-the-earth house. Steve talked in homilies of idealism and
reformation.

The duality of his personality—who he was when he woke up in the
morning wasn't necessarily who he was going to be come nightfall—was
a paradox Ayris wrestled with each day. She loved his versatility, but it
also kept her on the edge of doubt, never certain what was coming next.
They had traveled to Europe after the Marines, and although it was the
best time of their lives, it had been a daily reminder to her of his quick-
silver personality. For example, in England they bought an old English
Ford and he spent five days working on the engine to save money, then
when it broke down in France he just pushed it to the side of the road
and abandoned it. Her idea of touring Europe was to go slow and stroll
through the museums and cathedrals, soaking in the culture and history;
he wanted to power to the next country and soak up the culture by
sitting in a sidewalk cafe, drinking beer, and meeting people. Ayris
couldn't deny that he was a champion when it came to meeting people—
he had an eagerness about him, an immediate, sympathetic friendliness
that worked as well in Belgrade as it did in Berkeley. In Paris, while Ayris
visited the art galleries, he hung out at the American Express office,
flirting with the American girls there to cash their checks. He genuinely

liked to be around people, women and men, the more the merrier. It was his duty to keep the party going.

When he still had not returned from the shop at midnight, Ayris stared at the ceiling, suspecting the worst. Trust was not the cornerstone of their relationship. It went back to when he lied about his marriage in college. Linda was now remarried, her second husband having adopted Dennis, all parties agreeing that it was best for the time being if Steve stayed out of the picture. There was no child support, no weekend visits. Steve hadn't seen his son in five years.

Ayris stared at the phone, wondering if she should call the shop. In the past when she had checked up on him, he accused her of snooping. But knowing how poorly he held his alcohol, she always had the fear when he stayed out late like this that he was going to wrap himself around a telephone pole or a blonde. She dialed the shop.

"South City Honda," he answered.

She wasn't the type to hang up. "I was just wondering when you were coming home," she said, breathing a sigh of relief.

"I'm sorry," he charmed. "I lost track of time. I'll be home as soon as I finish working on this engine."

He hung up . . . and then went back to working on the pretty cashier he'd met at the organic food co-op.

It was 1972. Sweat glistened off his muscular shoulders as he swung his pickax, trying to clear the rocky ground for his homesite in the Mother Lode. The temperature was 103. Watching from the shade under a nearby oak tree was his friend and rugby teammate on the Capital City Recaps, Ed Forrest, a barrel-chested, rough-cut, burly Irishman.

"Take a fuckin' break, Hercules!" Ed foghorned, holding out a beer. "You're making me tired."

Steve paused, but only long enough to take a quick swig of his organic carrot juice. He was a man possessed, newly dedicated to abstaining from alcohol and women other than his wife. He and Ayris had started piecemeal construction on their house. It was to be 100 percent environmentally pure, with rock walls, solar heating, and pump water. The site, in the Sierra foothills near Shingle Springs just down the wash from where James Marshall's discovery triggered the California gold rush, was raw undeveloped land, hilly and parched and remote, dotted with California oaks, rocks, and rattlesnakes. As far as Steve and Ayris were concerned, it was Xanadu, their insurance policy against Armageddon. As far as Ed, a graduate of Santa Clara University, was concerned, it was desolate and ugly, nothing but weeds, rocks, scrawny oaks, and a nearby dump. He laughed as Steve's pickax struck mine tailings buried beneath the compact dirt, sparks flying in every direction.

"Frank Lloyd Wright couldn't fuckin' build a house here!" Ed belched, opening another beer. "But who knows? Maybe you'll get lucky and some Okie will build a plywood shack down the gulch and give you something to look at."

Steve just kept swinging, the sparks flying. He and Ed, whose father was a lineman for the 49ers in the fifties and whose wife was a good friend of Ayris, had met in college. Initially, Ed thought Steve was carrying some kind of burden, always weighted down, too serious. He soon came to realize Steve was a man of a million faces, but still, Ed had made it a career project to keep him loose, making sure he always had a beer under his nose. Ed was there for the welcome-home-from-Vietnam party Steve's parents hosted, and when Mr. Liquor took over and the party moved to a downtown bar, it was Ed who roared the loudest when Steve grabbed a fat girl by her rolls and carried her around like a suitcase. And it was Ed who always encouraged him not to go home after their rugby games, but to go out and "get fucked up with the boys." Not that Steve needed much encouragement. Ed thought that Steve was not only the best player on the team, tenacious and fearless, but also the most likely to go "Cuckoo the Clown" and keep the party going at the postgame pub.

"Give it up, Hercules!" Ed yelled as Steve paused for another swig of carrot juice. "You'll never break up this shit with that ax. Let's go rent a jackhammer and a backhoe."

"No!" replied Steve, determined to keep the project one-with-the-earth: no power tools to disturb the tranquillity; no wood except what he could recycle from old barns; no pesticides for Ayris's organic garden. Even the rattlesnakes were allowed to slither free. "Gotta keep the balance of nature," he maintained.

Steve's pride and joy on the property was an outdoor privy that turned waste into compost. It was Ayris who had first learned about the privy, reading about it in *The Whole Earth Catalogue*. It was invented by a man in Sweden, and on their trip to Europe, they had made a special side trip to Stockholm to learn more about it. The man made them his American distributor. Steve had become an expert, giving demonstrations and lectures on it around the state, receiving phone calls at South City Honda from people all over the country interested in it. Channel 13 in Sacramento had sent a reporter out to the property to interview him. His rugby teammates had taken to calling him Dr. Shit.

As he continued to dig and Ed continued to down his beers, a car approached on the dirt road, stopping at the edge of the property. A man in a coat and tie got out and walked up the hill.

"Mr. Radich," he said in a businesslike tone, "I saw you on TV last week talking about your privy. Pretty interesting."

"Would you like to take a look at it?" asked Steve.

"Well, not really," the man replied tersely. "I'm an inspector with El Dorado County and I'm here to check the house and see your building permit."

"Guess you'll have to bust me," said Steve. "I don't have one."

Not only did he not have a permit, he didn't have an approved plan, a builder's license, or any of the other legal requirements to build a house. The building inspector frowned, then slapped a red tag on the project, warning Steve to cease and desist immediately. Then he got back in his car and disappeared down the road in a cloud of dust.

"What are you gonna do?" asked Ed.

Steve popped open a beer. "Guess I'll knock off for the day and get shitfaced," he said.

"Then what?"

"Then I'll come back up here tomorrow and keep on bustin' rocks. Fuck 'em!"

48

Jim

It's better to die than to look bad.
   —Navy fighter pilot slogan

It was the summer of 1972 and Jim stood on the deck of the aircraft carrier USS *Ranger* as it sailed west beneath the Golden Gate Bridge, destined for the South China Sea. President Nixon had ordered the mining of Haiphong Harbor and the bombing of Hanoi and other key North Vietnamese targets, escalating the war. The operation, known as Linebacker I, was the first time since 1968 that American planes were striking targets in North Vietnam. The decision had stirred the antiwar movement, triggering a new round of bitter protests across America. It also had Jim on his way to combat. He would be part of Linebacker I.

He had mixed emotions about his assignment. On the one hand, he was surprised to be going. When he had entered Navy flight school in 1969, peace was allegedly "at hand" and he assumed the war would be over by the time he finished his three years of training. At each stop along the fighter pilot pipeline—Pensacola, Florida; Meridian, Mississippi; Beeville, Texas; Miramar, California—the message was always the same: the Navy already had more combat pilots than it needed. Good pilots had been washed out at every level. He had spent the last six months of his training as a recruiter, much of it on the Brigham Young University campus. (The Navy didn't recruit on the Berkeley campus.)

Vietnam seemed an unlikely possibility. But then Nixon cranked up Linebacker I and Jim was one of a handful of new pilots assigned to a RAG (replacement air group). From a family standpoint, it couldn't have come at a worse time. He was a new father, Patty having given birth to their first child, a daughter named Jenny; and he had just bought his first house, a small tract home near the base at Miramar. During his tour of duty, Patty would be working part-time as a secretary for a real estate developer.

Jim was ambivalent about the war, but he knew that in the world of pilots only those with combat experience moved up the pyramid to where they could truly call themselves fighter pilots. Not to have flown in combat was like a ballplayer having had three good years in the minors but not getting called up to the Show. But how could he explain that to Patty? From her perspective, the Navy had come between them, kept them apart for too many nights. She had done her best, attending the tedious teas with the officers' wives, suffering in silence. But she resented it. And now the Navy was going to take him away for thirteen months and send him into the middle of enemy fire.

Jim had tried to convince her, convince himself, that it wouldn't be that dangerous. That's one way he could stay sane, believing in his own aerial immortality, when of course in reality he was taking the ultimate macho gamble every time he climbed into the cockpit. That had been true even in training. It could happen barreling down the runway at 200 miles an hour, or flaming out at 20,000 feet. Inside his F-4 he had more ways of buying the farm than he could ever explain to her. But whether it was in training or in combat, death would always be the result of bad luck . . . for no *real* fighter pilot screwed up himself.

It had become hard for him to talk to Patty about what he did. Only those who shared the danger and the bravery and the fear could really understand jetspeak. At Miramar, Jim liked going to the O Club with other fighter jocks and knocking back a few cocktails and talking about the art of flying. If it wasn't the O Club, then it was a bottle of PX booze and then back to somebody's house, the wives in the kitchen, the brethren in the living room sharing the word and reveling in the unspoken air of superiority. It went with the territory, and like every young pilot, Jim had known the feeling of kicking back the cobwebs of a long night and driving to the base at dawn, fortified with coffee, braced to fly. There was nothing, however, according to those who had already done it, that could brace a pilot for flying over enemy territory engulfed in antiaircraft fire.

On September 10, 1972, as the USS *Ranger* sailed into the Gulf of Tonkin and Jim's first combat mission, Henry Kissinger announced that

North Vietnam was ready to reach an agreement by the end of October. Linebacker I was being called off in preparation for peace. Only the "piece of cake" bombing raids over South Vietnam would continue.

He walked toward his F-4, helmet under arm, flight suit snug, sunglasses shading the glare, the sun rising peacefully over the blue waters of the South China Sea. He liked the morning launches best and the tranquillity of the dawn patrol. There was an almost intoxicating smell—the taint of jet fuel riding the ocean spray—the pulsating energy of the USS *Ranger*'s deck coming alive, an orchestrated chaos, 2,500 men working in earnest, squadrons gearing for takeoff, the noise a wild crescendo . . . buzzing, hissing, the deafening roar of the jet engines. His adrenaline was pumping.

It was November 1972, fifteen miles off the coast of South Vietnam. Nixon had just been reelected, and although a peace agreement had still not been reached, the bombing of North Vietnam had not been resumed. Jim climbed into the cockpit and strapped himself in, turning to full power, saluting the catapult officer. With his hand on the stick and the afterburners kicking in, he was off like a bullet, outracing his own sound, the acceleration sucking his stomach against his spine, zero to 150 knots in the blink of an eye. Hardly the plodding shadow he cast back in Pi KA.

This was what he was trained to do, the responsibility of 50,000 pounds of lethal, fire-breathing aircraft, entrusted to him by American taxpayers; and this is what all those pilots who got *left behind* in the jet wash of the brotherhood would never experience. He was the sharp sword of President Nixon's foreign policy, armed with six 500-pound bombs, four Sidewinders, and two Sparrow missiles. On this mission he was heading deep into South Vietnam, his target a small bridge suspected of being used to transport enemy supplies. He prided himself at being as accurate with his bombs as anybody in his squad of fifteen.

He was flying wing with his section leader and close friend, a friendship that was inexorably, vitally, and fundamentally forged through their primitive quest for survival. The section leader, a sanguine, smooth-talking graduate of Annapolis, was on his second tour of duty. In between tours he had been an instructor in the Navy's new Fighter Weapons School (Top Gun) and he had hopes of someday becoming an admiral. Jim had no such lofty ambitions. If he decided to make a career of the Navy—and Patty certainly wasn't all that hot about that—he could see himself maybe being a test pilot. But right now, as he soared along at Mach I, his primary goal was to survive this mission. America controlled the sky over South Vietnam, and there was almost no chance of encountering any Migs, and only minimal chance of facing any heavy antiaircraft fire, but still, there were plenty of missing-in-action American pilots to prove these weren't purely the friendly skies. Every pilot knew that each new mission was a flirt with death . . . or another chance to look bad.

The irony of what he was doing wasn't lost on him—he had gone to college to learn how to build bridges, now he was blowing them up. Most of the time, the bombs he was dropping cost more to build than the bridges he was trying to destroy. Some days he felt as if he was doing nothing more than scattering dirt and blowing up rubber trees, although it was hard to know for sure. Rarely did he see what his bombs hit or the damage he did.

There were some days he suspected he was bombing Cambodia. One clue was that he'd been briefed by Intelligence on how to escape and evade if shot down over Cambodia. He was told he'd be on his own, however, if he strayed over Laos. There were lots of nasty stories of Laotians capturing downed American pilots, tying them to trees, cutting off their balls, and stuffing them in their mouths.

His job was to fly to coordinates, not to question what his mission was or where the coordinates were—he was being paid $12,000 a year tax-free in the combat zone to drop bombs, not to plot military strategy. Dissenting wasn't in his Navy dictionary; he didn't question the cause. Navy training offered no classes in the politics or history of Vietnam. Politically, even though he had voted for Nixon over McGovern, he considered himself neutral. But when he read about demonstrators back in Berkeley marching against the war, he fumed. How could those hippies know the horror of standing on the flight deck and watching a Russian-built SAM send a B-52 tumbling from the sky? Or having a good friend shot down on Thanksgiving eve? Or trying to weave through enemy anti-aircraft fire? Or going into a dive to avoid a heat-seeking missile, with 6 g's slamming lungs and spine to the back of the seat? For Jim, this war wasn't about political ideology—it was about making it back to the ship alive. Those people down there in those bunkers firing AA into the sky were trying to kill him.

It seemed unreal, but then war wasn't realistic to begin with and this war was even more unrealistic, especially from 20,000 feet above a country he had never set foot in. He hadn't come to Vietnam looking for hero medals. But the point was, he was out there. Putting in twelve-hour shifts. A fighter pilot in combat. Doing his duty.

He droned down on the small bridge, guided by a forward air controller's (FAC) phosphorescent smoke to mark the target. He dropped two bombs, then banked away.

"It's still standing," the voice of the FAC crackled over the radio, "but at least you covered it with dirt."

Another call came on the radio. It was for a TIC (troops in contact)—a large encampment of enemy troops had been spotted crossing a wide field. He was assigned the middle of the field, with two other planes taking the flanks. They zoomed in low, unloading their bombs. He banked away, unable to see the damage.

"I think we just blew up about three hundred gooks!" declared another pilot.

Back on the *Ranger,* he returned to his compartment, where he had a safe stocked with booze and walls adorned with centerfolds. A sign below Miss August read: "Share a screw with a friend." He poured himself a stiff shot of scotch and took out some stationery. This was insane, he thought. There was a good chance he'd just killed three hundred people, and there he was, sipping a cocktail, feet up on his desk, writing his wife back in sunny California to ask her why she wasn't writing him more often. He wondered if he should tell her what just happened. Who outside of his brotherhood could understand the insanity? He felt a million miles from the real world, from Patty, from his daughter he barely knew. "Something's really screwy here," he mumbled.

The midnight-to-noon shift was the worst. He had put in two flights before dawn, getting up at 11 P.M., his internal clock gone loony. Flying over enemy territory was spooky enough, but to do it at night while running purely on combat-zone adrenaline rather than eight hours' sleep was crazy. But the scariest thing was the night landing, trying to land a six-million-dollar fighter on the lighted deck of a two-billion-dollar aircraft carrier. His brain said one thing, the seat of his pants yet another. The deck didn't sit still because it was dark—it bounced . . . five feet, ten feet, worse in heavy seas. And if he lost his cool and had to scurry off to land at Tonsonhut Air Base, well, that wasn't how to look good. But even if he was lucky enough to make it safely down through the black and land on the pitching deck, he was graded on his landing. There was no relaxing.

He was returning to ship from a night mission, flying way up there in the dark, everything coming at him in deep shades of black—the ocean, the sky, the deck, the universe. It was a moonless night. Low ceiling. He started his descent, palms sweating, heart pounding. Gliding down to the deck out of the black, he followed the landing signal officer's instruction to adjust slightly to the left, then he set the wheels down, the plane jerking to an abrupt halt. Not perfect, maybe slightly off center to the left and maybe a damaged catch wire, but safely down. He crawled from the cockpit and was greeted by an enlisted man.

"The captain requests your presence on the bridge."

Jim smiled, patting himself on the back. It wasn't every day the big cheese dished out congratulations on a job well done. He climbed to the deck.

"Goddamnit!" yelled the captain. "They had to wave off the pilot behind you and now he's up there running out of fuel, delaying recovery, endangering the ship. This isn't the first time you've landed off center and damaged a wire! Those things cost six hundred dollars!"

"Yes, sir," Jim replied stoically.

Back in his compartment, surrounded by centerfolds again, staring into his glass of scotch, he thought it insane. He had just cheated death . . . and got his ass chewed out for it. How could that prick have the balls to be upset over a six-hundred-dollar wire—which turned out not even to be damaged—when millions of dollars in bombs had been wasted that night blowing up jungle rot? "Something's screwy here," he mumbled.

On December 18, 1972, Jim awoke, surprised to discover that the *Ranger* was now floating in Yankee Station off the coast of North Vietnam. President Thieu of South Vietnam had said no to the terms of the peace agreement, causing the talks to break down and Nixon to call for the resumption of the nonstop bombing of North Vietnam. It was being called Linebacker II. Jim's "piece of cake" missions were over. His targets over North Vietnam would be mostly bridges, railroad yards, and petroleum tanks. If the weather was cloudy he would fly with Air Force F-4s, which, unlike the Navy's F-4s, were equipped with electronic devices to help determine where the target was. When the Air Force dropped their bombs, he was supposed to drop his.

There are two primary types of air wars. One is designed to destroy the enemy's ability to make war—bombing supply lines, airfields, ammo depots, etc. The other is designed to break the enemy's will to fight, which means deliberately bombing civilian areas as part of a terror campaign. According to the Pentagon, Linebacker II was not unrestricted aerial warfare. Nevertheless, there was unparalleled devastation. The designated targets were always said to be military—rail yards, industrial facilities, airfields, SAM sites, radar installations, oil storage—with B-52s and fighter-bombers pounding away relentlessly. In the process, however, many civilians died and nonmilitary targets, such as Bach Mai Hospital, were destroyed. The administration defended the carnage by saying that if the objective was to lay Hanoi flat, the B-52s could do it.

On the first day of Linebacker II, Jim and his section leader were assigned to fly a Mig CAP (combat air patrol) for an alpha strike on Vinh, a coastal town south of Haiphong. (An alpha strike threw as many planes at the target as possible.) Their job was to fly offshore and protect against an unlikely counterattack by Migs.

As the alpha strike neared completion, and with no Migs in the area, the section leader called on the radio. "Arm up!" he ordered. "We're going feet dry [over land]."

Scared shitless, Jim followed him down for a pass over a heavily defended area. Antiaircraft fire poured at them from a bunkered installation, engulfing their planes in black smoke.

"Time to cut fuck," ordered the section leader.

"What the hell was all that about?" asked Jim as they turned and headed back to the *Ranger*.

"In case the war ends tomorrow," replied the section leader, "I wanted you to be able to say you were shot at over North Vietnam."

Jim had learned that war took sane men and made them do insane things. A few days later he and his section leader were patrolling offshore when he got the hand signal to follow. That meant that what they were about to do was unauthorized and there should be no radio contact. He followed as his section leader swooped down on a North Vietnamese junk sailing in coastal waters. The F-4s were not equipped with machine guns for strafing—but that would have been unfair anyway; this was just a scare mission. His section leader roared in fifteen feet over the junk, his afterburners searing the sail, the jet wash sending a wall of water crashing down on the defenseless junk.

Junk sport, Jim discovered, was all part of war, where it was okay to do macho things not normally in the code of ethics or safety. In war, tomorrow might not come. A pilot had to do whatever it took to stay sharp, and if he thought buzzing junks kept him at the competitive edge, then that's what had to be done.

Keeping a competitive edge was a matter of life and death for Jim. Every mission over Hanoi was a tap dance through antiaircraft fire. But on December 30, only twelve days after Linebacker II began, North Vietnam agreed to renewed peace talks and Nixon stopped the bombing. Lieutenant JG James van Hoften's final mission over North Vietnam would be one of the very last of America's long nightmare.

·   ·   ·   ·

Welcome home, Conquering Hero. Arriving back home in San Diego, he hadn't even unpacked his bags when Patty dropped a big bomb of her own—she wanted a divorce. She was in love with another man, her boss.

For four years, Jim had been soaring above the clouds, wrapped in the steel-blue armor of one of the most macho brotherhoods alive. Now he was crying like a baby. Patty was his high school sweetheart, the love of his life. Aside from a couple blind dates at Cal, she was the only girl he dated in college. His parents thought she was terrific; her parents thought he was terrific.

He started putting two and two together. No wonder he didn't get a letter from her the last month of his tour. No wonder he couldn't reach her on the phone. No wonder she was so distant during R&R in Hong Kong. He should have seen it coming. But he didn't.

"Why?" he asked.

"You've changed," she explained. "You're not the same guy I married."

Changed? Of course he'd changed. And for the better, he thought. The Navy had given him a self-confidence he never had before. But maybe that was the problem. She didn't have a degree, she didn't have a career . . . and now that Jim was a hotshot fighter pilot and almost a Ph.D., well, maybe it was too threatening. She never did like the Navy life and all that time apart. She wanted a husband who was more passionate about her than about flying. It was as if he'd put his family life on automatic pilot for four years while he concentrated on flying with the brotherhood. Now the family had crashed. Too late, Lieutenant.

He felt betrayed. He had gone off to fight in an unpopular war, flown sixty missions, dodged antiaircraft fire, sweated night landings . . . and then walked back in the door at home and got dumped. His tearful efforts to dissuade her made no inroads.

He moved into the barracks at Miramar, where he was able to commiserate with six other men in his squadron who had also been discharged by their wives upon their return from Vietnam.

"Hell, yes, I'm bitter," he said.

49

Loren

When a fellow says, "It ain't the money but the principle of the thing," it's the money.
—Frank McKinney Hubbard

On Sunday morning, December 17, 1972, as the bombs of Linebacker II fell on Hanoi, Loren was flat on his back in his room in St. Luke's Hospital in San Francisco. Sitting at his bedside was Genevieve, just as she'd done every day since his operation. She was finally, after years of bitter acrimony, divorced from Hal. Her world now revolved even more around her only child.

"You gotta leave now," said Loren, who was anxious to get her out of the room before either Sally, a perky blonde, or Lisa, a voluptuous stewardess, showed up.

"But I just got here," protested Genevieve, leaning over to fluff his pillows.

"Go!" he ordered. "I need to take a nap."

Reluctantly, she headed toward the door, asking if there was anything she could get him. "No," he said. She reminded him that he should plan on spending a week with her in Marysville after he was released. "Maybe," he said, motioning her out the door.

He was at St. Luke's recuperating from major reconstructive surgery on his shoulder, a five-hour operation in which doctors took a nine-inch strip of muscle from his leg to retie the damaged ligaments of the shoulder. He had injured it in a rugby match in Paris when two French defenders nearly tore his arm out of its socket trying to keep him from crossing the goal during the last game of the Bay Area Touring Side's (BATS) second tour of Europe. It was a painful ending to a trip that had been a big success for him—not only did he not have to cope with the distractions of touring with his mother and the former Miss California, the team won seven of its nine games and he accomplished his stated goal for the trip, which was "to fuck a Commie." In Timisoara, Romania, he scored one for international diplomacy, persuading a comely Romanian waitress from a resort on the Black Sea to lie with him in the moonlight under a spreading oak tree.

He had invited both Sally and Lisa, who were rivals for his attention, to come and visit him at St. Luke's. Both agreed, both promising to be there "sometime before noon." And what if they showed up at the same time? That was fine by him. It wouldn't be the first time he'd asked two women to meet him at the same time. His theory was that it was always good to have a backup.

The door to his room opened. It was neither Sally nor Lisa. It was somebody he was even more eager to see. The man was Lee Roberts, Loren's new mentor in the real estate business, a big-money guy in the California land rush who dealt primarily in large ranches in the San Joaquin Valley and new housing developments around Sacramento. Roberts was toothpick skinny and wound tighter than a golf ball, with slick black hair, hollow cheeks, jittery hands, and shifty dark eyes that never stopped scanning the room. He had a habit of talking out of the side of his mouth—it was as if he had a secret parcel of land to unload quick before anyone else found out about it. Rumor had it that there was Mafia money behind some of his deals. Loren first met him at a celebrity golf tournament at Lake Tahoe; Loren, who shot an 87 the first time he ever played the game, had gone to the tournament to tag along with Craig. Roberts was bowled over by his gregarious personality and told him to give him a call at his office in Yuba City if he was interested in a job. At the time, Loren was working for Boise Cascade, where he'd gone to work after the belly-up failure of his Davis business ventures with Craig; he was a divisional sales manager in recreational properties, working out of a posh office on the forty-eighth floor of the Bank of America Building in San Francisco, selling lots near Grass Valley, pulling down two grand a month, wearing tailored suits, commuting to a lavish bachelor pad in Belmont Keys in Marin County, picking up women left and right at all the Bay Area hot spots—Zack's, Pierce Street Annex, Tiger

A-Go-Go, Buena Vista. But the nine-to-five corporate life wasn't for him —there was no motivation, no niche. He didn't like working for the Man. When Boise Cascade wouldn't give him six weeks off to go on the rugby tour of Europe, he quit. When he returned to California, he called Roberts.

They were still in the feeling-out process, slightly wary of each other's motives. Roberts had volunteered to teach Loren the business. He could envision Loren, with his fast-talking, high-energy personality, as a magnet, an ideal front man to go out and pump hands and bring in the deals, a counterbalance to his own cryptic personality. His concern was that maybe someday down the road—it would take several years to learn the art of deal making—Loren might get a little too big for his business britches. Loren saw Roberts as a ticket to big money . . . he was enamored of Roberts's financial success, the business acumen, the knowledge of the deal, the cunning, the preference for doing business in Wrangler jeans and cowboy boots. Roberts's office was in Yuba City, just down the road from Andy's Drive-In, where Loren cruised as a teenager.

"So what's the doctor say about your shoulder?" asked Roberts. "When you gonna be able to get out of here so I can start showing you how to make some money?"

"He thinks I shouldn't play any more rugby," Loren replied. "But I got news for him."

At the age of thirty, he claimed that rugby was still the passion of his life. If it came down to choosing between it and women, he said, "the tomatoes would have to go." He thrived on being part of its macho worldwide fraternity. On the field was the one place where he still felt truly at home, a world with its own lingo, its own spirit. He got goose bumps standing on the pitch before the international matches when they played "The Star-Spangled Banner."

The door opened again and in bounced Sally, the pert and pretty honey blonde. She was from Texas and had the drawl to prove it. She had dropped out of SMU in her sophomore year when her mother was killed in a hit-and-run accident. Loren first met her in a Dallas nightclub on one of his trips to see Craig, after which she flew to California several times to spend weekends with him. Hers was a soft, fresh, innocent charm. In 1970 she moved to San Francisco permanently, a move Loren did nothing to discourage. She was in training to be an operations manager with Wells Fargo Bank. She was his acknowledged "main squeeze," although he repeatedly reminded her that he was not ready to be tied down and that she would be better off with somebody like a nice young stockbroker with a Chevy Caprice. Loren was driving a Continental Mark IV, another one of Craig's hand-me-down cars.

She had barely settled into her chair next to his bed when her main competition walked in. Standing off to the side, Roberts smiled, realizing he was about to witness a showdown at St. Luke's. Lisa was not the type to turn and run. She was a stunning five-eleven, curvaceous, auburn-haired stewardess for World Airways, dripping with a cosmopolitan style that belied her small-town roots. She had grown up tall and skinny in Pullman, Washington, basic middle-class, secure, conservative stuff. Her father owned a dry-cleaning business and the family spent vacations at their cabin on Coeur d'Alene Lake in Idaho. After a year as a Delta Gamma at Washington State, she and a girlfriend headed off for summer jobs at Saks in San Francisco. Lisa fell in love with the city and stayed. She was flying charters all over the globe, as well as moonlighting as a model, primarily doing print work for Macy's and local car dealers. The first time Loren spotted her she was walking across a parking lot in front of the Tiger A-Go-Go at the San Francisco Airport. Positive that he was seeing the world's most gorgeous creature, maybe even prettier than the former winner of the Miss America Swimsuit Competition, he seized the moment, hopping out of his car and coaxing her phone number. Then he didn't call. A few weeks later he spotted her again, this time across the crowded dance floor of a San Francisco disco. He was able to convince her he'd lost the number. She gave it to him again, and this time he did call. On their first date, he made a point of letting her know where he stood: "I don't want a relationship," he maintained. "I've got too many things going on in my life." She took the challenge. In the months that followed, Loren spent considerable time juggling her and Sally, convincing each they were number one.

He introduced them, then turned to wink at Roberts. The doctor entered, noticing the beautiful women on opposite sides of the bed. "Looks like the patient is recovering," he said.

"Can't complain," said Loren. "So when can I get out of here?"

"Couple more days," answered the doctor.

As soon as the doctor exited the room, Loren swung his feet over the side of the bed and turned to Roberts again. "I don't care what that quack thinks," he said. "I can't hack this place another day. I'm outta here right now. Gotta get home to watch my boy." He was talking about the Cowboys' televised playoff game against the 49ers. Craig was starting at quarterback.

Roberts handed him his clothes—red bell-bottom pants (no underpants), polyester print shirt, and patent-leather shoes with a gold buckle (no socks). "I can see I'm gonna have to teach you how to dress too," said Roberts.

The only thing that still needed to be settled before fleeing down the back stairwell was who would get to be the lucky gal to help him on with his clothes and escort him home . . . Sally, the blonde with the sweet disposition, or Lisa, the tall stewardess oozing self-confidence?

It was no contest. Lisa went for the assumptive close, helping him on with his shirt, telling him she'd have her Corvette waiting by the exit, dismissing Sally with a friendly smile.

There was little doubt Lisa had the strong personality that Loren claimed he was looking for in a woman.

They didn't have enough time to make it all the way back to Loren's apartment in Yuba City before the kickoff, so they checked into the Voyager Inn in Davis. Even though Loren wasn't saying anything, Lisa could tell he was suffering, not just from the pain in his shoulder, which he was much too macho to admit was killing him, but also from what was happening to Craig on the field. Going into the fourth quarter, the Cowboys were trailing 28–13 and Craig was having a miserable game. Despite the tension in their friendship after the Davis disaster, Loren still considered himself Craig's biggest fan.

Craig's career had been on a roller coaster since he took over as the starting quarterback in 1969. In 1970, despite his well-publicized problems with his nightlife, business failures, and the IRS, he led the Cowboys to the Super Bowl against the Baltimore Colts, but when he threw two interceptions and the Colts won, fans blamed him for the loss, especially after it was revealed he had relied on hypnosis during the season. Craig had turned on his own to hypnosis, confidentially, to help him relax, to boost his confidence, and to free him of the pain in his elbow, shoulder, and knees. In the 1971 season, booing Craig became routine at Texas Stadium, and his response only made matters worse—he would raise his arms like an orchestra leader and direct the booing, a gesture that didn't help his standing with Coach Landry, who began alternating him and then replaced him with Roger Staubach, a move Loren was convinced had more to do with the fact that Staubach, like Landry, was a "born again" Christian. But at the start of the 1972 season, just when Craig had resigned himself to sitting on the bench, Staubach was hurt. Craig responded with his best year, and although he remained the target of boos, he had led the Cowboys into the playoffs against the 49ers.

Craig and Loren's friendship had cooled. Ever since the failure of the business, there had been a gradual drifting apart—fewer phone calls, longer periods between visits, an uneasy tension. The closest it came to open rancor was when Loren talked about the losses they had suffered and Craig responded, "Yeah, well, if *we* suffered losses, then how come *I'm* the only one who had to declare bankruptcy?" Craig felt betrayed: he had trusted his two good college buddies, Jerry Olson and Loren, and ended up bankrupt. He and Loren hadn't spoken in several months. For Loren, it was a matter of principle—they had both made mistakes—but the way he saw it, they shouldn't let money come between them. And besides, he was sure Craig's bankruptcy had as much to do with his playboy lifestyle as the failed businesses. If Craig wanted to make him the scapegoat, well, that was his problem.

In the fourth quarter, Landry replaced Craig with Staubach, who came off the bench to throw two touchdown passes in the final two minutes to rally the Cowboys to victory while Craig watched from the bench.

After the game, Loren turned off the television. Lisa hinted that maybe, just maybe, he should call Craig to cheer him up. Loren declined. After all, he didn't remember Craig calling him in the hospital to cheer him up.

50

Larry

Love means never having to say you're sorry.
—Erich Segal, *Love Story*

Awash in a virtuous pride in my new teaching career, I had no second thoughts about quitting baseball. I was, however, mad at myself for not taking better advantage of the opportunity while I was in the game. For instance, why did I smoke dope, drink bourbon, and eat like a pig during my career? Why did I always dog it when it came to running wind sprints? Why was my concentration on the mound so feeble? Why didn't I spend more time working on a breaking ball and less time chasing women? Why didn't I keep my political views to myself? Why did I sit in my hotel rooms during the days instead of going out and exploring the cities I was visiting? Why didn't I walk away from those thugs in San Francisco?

Why? Why? Why?

But I was moving ahead, immersed in teaching. I had bought the whole sixties thing and was committed to carrying out Kennedy's inauguration challenge to do something for my country. I wasn't going to be content teaching Shakespeare to rich white kids—I wanted to teach basic writing skills to disadvantaged minority students. Such a noble cause. I began my intern teaching with wide-eyed optimism, staying up half the night correcting papers and preparing lesson plans.

"Today we're going to learn about the semicolon," I instructed.

"Who gives a shit!" a voice in the back responded.

Okay, so I had a lot to learn about the reality of public education. I was interning at John Adams High, a modern facility located in an integrated, blue-collar neighborhood of northeast Portland with a 40 percent black enrollment. The school was the brainchild of seven Harvard doctoral students, and the most energetic and comprehensive attempt to establish an alternative high school in an urban setting in the United States. With the pendulum of education in America swinging left, Adams High was on the cutting edge of reform, attracting extensive national attention. A cover story on the school in *Newsweek* was titled "Best High School in America?" The handpicked staff was liberal, idealistic, iconoclastic, dedicated to teaching what was "relevant." Students called teachers by their first name and were encouraged to take responsibility for their own education. In theory, it was an educational cornucopia, tossing all the latest teaching techniques into a cocked hat—interdisciplinary studies, modular scheduling, optional grading, team teaching, decentralized administration, community as classroom. In reality, however, it was a zoo—racial tension, fights, drugs, kids wandering the hall, no unified vision by the staff. Every week was a new controversy: the DAR presented the student body with an American flag and the student government refused to accept it; rest rooms were turned into extortion centers; a boy was elected the school's candidate for the city's revered Rose Festival court; School Board officials and conservative community leaders initiated an acrimonious campaign to end the experiment and convert it to a traditional school.

I sat in on a planning session for a team-taught interdisciplinary unit on the women's movement. When I proposed that we do a segment called women's rights and internal punctuation, the women on the team, all of them feminists, didn't appreciate my suggestion. For a guy who had just spent the last ten years absorbing culture through the fraternity and locker-room walls, to be suddenly team-teaching with hard-core feminists was a little like John Wayne going to work at *Ms.* My male moorings were seriously challenged. For the first time in my life I was forced to sit down and participate in lengthy exchanges of ideas with women I did not want to hop bones with. What a revelation.

I wasn't doing much bone hopping. Except for a couple of boozy one-night stands, I was still concentrating on re-wooing Denise, trying to prove how much I was changing and how I would be better for her in the long run than her artist/model boyfriend Tom. On Friday afternoons I drove to Seattle to bring Wendy back to Portland with me for the weekend, returning her on Sunday night. Denise was still throwing me just enough emotional lasso to keep me roped to the hope that our marriage could still be salvaged from the ashes. And then I met Kathi.

Her name was Katherine Elisabeth Jeffcott. She was twenty-five, born and raised in Portland, a slender five-five, crisp blue eyes, straight brown hair, high cheekbones, wholesome, well bred. She wore no makeup and dressed in peasant blouses, jeans, and sandals. Her parents lived in a spacious two-story colonial in Portland's exclusive west hills, her mother a graduate of Reed College and a perimeter player in Portland social circles, her father a prominent dentist and a frustrated, irascible artist. Kathi had a degree in sociology from the University of Oregon, where she was kicked out of the Alpha Phi sorority in 1967 for smoking dope. She was working as a bank teller and living alone in a downtown flat, going through a pound of salad and a half case of Pepsi a day.

Despite all I'd learned from my new feminist colleagues, when a mutual friend introduced me to Kathi, my first thought was that I very much wanted to hop her bones. I hadn't changed *that* much. On our first date we sat cross-legged in an alpine meadow next to the Santiam River in the Oregon Cascades, staring meaningfully into each other's eyes, surrounded by purple wildflowers and a picket of conifers that rustled musically in the breeze. We were sitting on my wool blanket that I had been awarded for lettering on the varsity three years at Cal. Our juices flowed, aided by Red Mountain burgundy and ten buttons of peyote.

"Far out," I said, pointing to a cloud shaped like a moose head.

Three days later we moved in together. Three days! We'd known each other a grand total of ninety-three hours. I had been separated from Denise for only nine months.

"Do you think we're moving too fast?" Kathi asked.

What a silly question, I assured her. How could we deny such passion? We pledged to be honest and faithful and open, all the things I'd failed at with Denise. I was determined not to repeat my mistakes. No more infidelities.

"Are you sure you're telling me the truth about it being all over between you and your ex-wife?" she inquired.

"Absolutely," I answered.

We sat on the living-room floor, passing a joint, just the four of us—me and Kathi, Denise and Tom. Weren't we being civil? Weren't we being couples of the seventies? It was important for Wendy's sake, Denise and I had concluded, that we be friends. One big happy family. But it felt weird . . . to be holding hands with my new girlfriend while I watched my wife (our divorce wasn't final) stroking the arm of her boyfriend. I was sure my mother would have thrown up on the spot.

The next day Kathi got the test back from the doctor—she was pregnant. Her diaphragm had failed. I thought she'd be upset, but she greeted the news with joy. For all her child-of-the-sixties front, she still had old-fashioned values. She had talked of maybe going to nursing school, but what she really wanted was to be a mommy, with a husband and a couple of kids and the white picket fence in the burbs.

"I don't know if I'm ready," I said. We had known each other four months. "I'm sorry."

I was in love, or at least it sure felt like it, but a voice inside me was saying that it was too soon to take on the responsibility of another child, that I needed more time to recover from the heartache of the first marriage, that I needed to finish my internship and get a full-time position.

"So *when* will you be ready to start a family?" she asked, her joy turning to tears.

"I don't know," I replied. "Could be six months. Could be a year . . . three years. Or . . . maybe I'm ready now."

The phone rang. What timing! It was Denise, and she too was in tears. I took the phone into another room. "We need to talk," she said, an urgency in her voice. She didn't want to talk on the phone about whatever it was that was bothering her. "Can you come up tomorrow?" she asked. I said I would.

Kathi and I went to sleep that night agreeing that we would think it over for a couple of days. Or rather *I* would think it over. The next morning, without telling her, I drove to Seattle to meet Denise, whom I suspected wanted to see me regarding the divorce . . . or else it was because she wanted to tell me she needed more support money for Wendy.

"When I watched the way you and Kathi were looking into each other's eyes," she said, "I was so jealous. It made me realize that I still have strong feelings for you and maybe we should go slow and really think about what we're doing."

"What are you saying?" I asked.

"I don't know," she answered. "I guess it's that I'm not sure I'm ready to lose you."

I could feel myself being reeled in. I didn't tell her Kathi was pregnant. We picked up Wendy from school and took her to a park. As we pushed her on a swing, a grandmotherly-looking woman approached. "What a joy it is to watch such a beautiful and happy family," she said.

That's what I'd been trying to convince Denise we were for a year. And now that I'd found somebody else and wasn't down on my knees begging her to come back, she was suddenly flashing serious signs of reconciliation. She admitted she was still in love with Tom and wasn't ready to flick that in yet, but now there was a chance she really did love me after all. "Oh, Larry, I'm so confused," she said. I tried to play it cool, telling her I didn't know for sure what would happen if she decided she wanted to get back together, but I knew in my heart that I would take her back in a snap. She still had that power over me.

Back in Portland, I didn't tell Kathi about the Seattle trip, but I did tell her I'd made up my mind about the baby. "I love you, Kathi," I said. "But I'm not ready. I'm sorry."

Tearfully, she agreed to have an abortion. We kept it a secret. I felt depressed, not about the moral or ethical questions, but because I knew how upset she was and because I wasn't being truthful with her. My pledge of honesty and openness had already been discarded. Denise and I continued to have secret phone conversations (but no sex).

The inquisition was about to begin. I squirmed uncomfortably, head down, studying the patterns in the Persian rug in the living room of Kathi's parents. They had summoned me to ask me my long-range intentions. Did I plan to marry their daughter? Kathi and I had been living together for almost six months, and despite their efforts to accept it, "shacking up" was frowned upon in the upper crust of Portland society.

Yes, I answered, I loved their daughter. And yes, I wanted to marry her someday. So then what's the holdup? they politely inquired. When I explained that I wasn't ready, they pushed for a reason. In their day, when two people loved each other and wanted to be together, they got married.

"I need more distance from my first marriage," I admitted.

"Are you still in love with your first wife?" they wanted to know.

"No," I lied.

Denise was continuing to ride the fence, telling me how torn she was and how it was tearing at her heart knowing how much Wendy missed me and how for her sake we maybe should get back together. I assured her that was the wrong reason.

Kathi's parents weren't the only ones putting pressure on me. When Kathi found the phone bills detailing my calls to Denise, she threatened to leave. "I'm not going to sit around forever waiting for you to make up your mind," she said. "You can't do this. Either we set a date to get married or it's over."

I was in over my head, having jumped into a relationship with Kathi before sorting through the baggage of the last one. I felt guilty—for coercing Kathi into an abortion, for sneaking around behind her back, for keeping her dangling. She loved me and was making it clear that she wanted to be together. With Denise, I still didn't know which way the wind was blowing. What I did know was that if I didn't propose soon to Kathi, she would walk out the door and never come back. I didn't want to take that risk.

We were married in a small church ceremony in Portland on February 18, 1972. My parents didn't attend. At the reception, I got drunk and passed out two minutes after we checked into our honeymoon suite at the Heathman Hotel in downtown Portland. But the bellhop remembered me.

Standing on the Pi KA front porch, I scanned the postgame crowd walking down Piedmont Avenue, looking for familiar faces, long-lost goat brothers. It was a football Saturday afternoon in Berkeley, October 1972.

Kathi and I had been married eight months and were doing rather well, I thought. There had been a few times I had pined for Denise and wondered if I had been pushed into this marriage, but those misgivings were fading. We had moved to Berkeley when I couldn't get a teaching job in Portland due to budget cuts and a freeze on new hiring. Kathi was working as a teller in a bank and I was working for Jerry Olson as a $3.50-an-hour cashier at Northside Books, a bookstore rising from the ashes of the failed UC Corner enterprises. Jerry was one of the few college friends I'd maintained contact with—I'd always been drawn to his energetic, life-of-the-party personality: he had been an usher in my wedding to Denise; I'd been out on the town with him the night before I got beat up in San Francisco in 1968; I had stayed at his house every time I visited Berkeley. In college he had looked the part of the quintessential frat boy, with the crew cut and the boy-next-door smile; a decade later he looked the part of the archetypal Berkeley hippie, with hair down to his butt and a beard to the middle of his chest. He seemed more like Rasputin than a member of the Berkeley Business Alliance. He had always been a born entertainer—the best dancer and biggest jokester on Frat Row when he was twenty, and now a decade later he was dead serious about becoming the best drummer in rock and roll. He carried his drumsticks everywhere, pounding away . . . in the car, at work, on the toilet. He was taking lessons and playing in garage bands—what made him different from other struggling Bay Area musicians was that he had his bookstore to support him and his young family. I wondered if his obsession with drumming was his way of blowing off all the pain and hostility he still carried from the UC Corner fiasco. Craig had been his best friend, and now they didn't speak. Jerry hated Loren, blaming him for turning Craig against him and for the loss of UC Corner. The very mention of Loren's name sent Jerry into a drumming frenzy. Not that Jerry was my nominee for merchant of the year—when I started to work at Northside Books, a clone of the UC Corner stores, the books were stocked not by author or title but by publisher because that was how they were shipped and it was easier to arrange them that way. Frustrated customers were walking out in droves, unable to figure out if Hemingway was published by Doubleday or Dell. I was beginning to think about opening my own bookstore, if not in Berkeley, then in Portland or Eugene.

Although Berkeley was hardly the same as it had been during my letterman days, I loved the energy, the weirdness, the intellectual current . . . such a contrast to my days on the team bus. At the bookstore, we broadcast the Watergate Senate hearings over the loudspeakers, and customers would congregate in small clusters like fans listening to the World Series, cheering each new incriminating revelation.

I had lost contact with most of the goat brothers, unaware that Jim was flying missions over Hanoi and only vaguely aware that Steve had served in the Marines. All I knew about Loren was what I heard from Jerry Olson, which wasn't very nice. I'd bumped into Ron once in 1969 at Bullock's in Westwood, where he was working as a stock boy, and he had looked so gaunt and acted so skittish that I had no reason to doubt the rumors about him being brain-fried on LSD.

Standing in front of the Pi KA house after the football game, scanning the crowd, I somehow expected that if I did spot any of my ex-fraternity brothers, they would be conservative, button-down Republicans working for Price Waterhouse and I would be the only one hip enough to have voted for McGovern and been to a Three Dog Night concert. Then I heard a familiar voice, deep and resonant, booming through the crowd. It was Steve. The last time I'd seen him was at my wedding to Denise. As fraternity brothers, I had always liked him, admiring his tenacity on the football field, his discipline in his studies, his wild streak at parties. But back then we never got to be close friends—I knew nothing about his secret wife and child in Sacramento. (Of course, nobody else did either.)

We edged our way to the keg, catching up on old times. I wasn't sure if it was cosmic vibrations, or astrological coincidence (we were both Geminis), or the free beer, or because he was so good-looking and he unlocked some deep hidden sexual confusion in me . . . whatever, we connected. He was passionate about life. His eyes lit up as he told me about the speech he was giving the next day to a group of Cal professors about his privy that turned waste into compost. It was instructive to hear him confess his own wobblings and insecurities during the past decade, admissions that would have gone unspoken in our invulnerable Joe College days. It wasn't as if we were two Alan Aldas talking about what we could do to end sexism, but it was at least a confirmation that I wasn't the only goat brother to have bounced off a few walls. I felt I'd found a soul mate. He and Ayris spent the night on the floor of our apartment. Kathi was impressed. "Talk about sexy!" she gushed.

Kathi and I spent the next weekend in Sacramento with Steve and Ayris. They took us to the Mother Lode to show us their property, and put us to work carrying rocks and hauling the wood from an old barn he had razed. I doubted I was yet ready to move to the boonies and seek such an alternate lifestyle, but I marveled at his energy and strength. He offered me a swig of his carrot juice.

"No, thanks," I said. "But I'll take a beer if you have one."

He didn't.

"If I had a body like yours," I said, eyeing his lean, firm torso, "I'd never get any sleep."

"Why's that?"

"Because I'd be up all night admiring myself in the mirror."

It seemed to me that he and Ayris were so tranquil and secure together, affectionate and nurturing. They had been married six years. I hoped Kathi and I would be that comfortable together after we'd been married that long. She was pregnant again, and this time there would be no abortion.

51

Ron

Inside the armor beats a glass heart.
—Peter Filene, *Man in the Middle*

He would teach, yes, that's what he'd do. A helping, sharing profession
. . . a career to ease his guilt for his failures as a father. He could make
a contribution to society. Help the children. None of this Age of Narcis-
sism for him. No, sir. He signed up for two classes at Loyola University
—philosophy of education and psychology of education. He also answered an ad on the campus bulletin board for a roommate in a residence hall, and moved in with another male student, nineteen years old
and full of youth. He was thirty-two. Maybe by surrounding himself with
college-age boys, he reasoned, he could go back to his halcyon days and
get it right this time.

He sat in the living room listening to his roommate and his friends
plot their strategy for a Friday evening. Maybe they would go to Carolina
Pines and check out the nude bowlers . . . or maybe they would crash
a frat party in Westwood. He retreated to his room. How could he relate?
How could he possibly explain to them where he was coming from? Did
they understand that he was once Almost-All-Coast and performed in
front of stadiums filled with fans? Or that he was twice a father? Or that
he was twice a mental patient? Or that he shoved all his earthly belongings into two garbage cans and pushed them aimlessly down Venice

Boulevard? Of course they couldn't understand. He moved out and rented a room from an elderly couple in Inglewood, commuting to school on a collapsible bike he carried to class in a canvas bag he slung over his shoulder.

He answered another ad, this one for part-time work washing and waxing cars for a leasing company in Inglewood. The perfect job, he thought—outdoors, low stress, within biking distance. He didn't have a car. He got the job and quickly established himself as the best hose-and-buff man on the lot. His boss was so impressed that he offered him a chance to transfer to the Fullerton lot in Orange County and go full-time. That meant Ron had to make a decision between washing cars and his classes at Loyola. He took the job. So much for his teaching career.

Washing cars in Orange County was fun while it lasted, but he decided there was more to life. After nine months, he stored his meager possessions with his mother and hitchhiked to Montreal. His goal was to use his credentials as a member of the United States Coast Guard Reserve to hitch a ride to Europe with the Canadian Merchant Marine. That was one of the perks of his six years in the Reserves—Merchant Marine privileges.

He had several reasons for wanting to get to Europe. First, he still harbored thoughts of one day becoming an architect, and how could he truly understand design if he never saw the masterpieces of the great architects of Europe? Second, he wanted to research the English and German roots of the Vaughn family tree. How could he ever truly understand who he was if he didn't know his own family history? Third, he needed to get away from the political climate in America. He had signed up to campaign door to door for George McGovern in Orange County, which was a little like going salmon fishing on the Ventura Freeway . . . but after being turned away at almost every house, he quit. And lastly, he wanted to get away from Anna's phone calls requesting more support money for Royce. He had been sending her a small trickle from his paycheck at the car-leasing place, but it wasn't enough to keep her off his back. Maybe he could find a job in Europe and send money back for Royce.

In Montreal, he went to the Canadian Merchant Marine office and inquired when the next ship was leaving for Europe. He was told that the Canadian Merchant Marine only sailed the Great Lakes. So much for his trip to Europe. He took a bus back to L.A.

·   ·   ·   ·

He was living with his mom again. She had moved into a courtside apartment in Franklin Villa near the Hollywood Bowl, living off her savings and pension from thirty years as a school librarian. She was still bitter about her divorce from Ralph, and spent most of her days talking to old Mr. Smirnoff. Worried about Ron's mental health, she volunteered to pay for his charter flight to Germany and a Eurorail pass. The trip was back on. He planned to stay two months, and if he could find work . . . who knows how long?

He landed in Munich, went directly to London, and checked into a hostel. He traveled the city and the English countryside (including Stonehenge) on his collapsible bike. Riding through London one afternoon he saw an advertisement for a purebred wirehaired terrier, a dead ringer for the dog he had as a boy. He had to have it. Right now. Whatever the cost. Such a dog, he hoped, would reconnect with the purity and innocence of his youth. Be a best friend.

But there was a problem. With shots and papers, the dog cost more than he had in his travel budget. So he cashed in his return airline ticket and bought the dog, naming it Llandwit after a small town in Wales. He carried Llandwit with him in a cardboard box everywhere he went in London. Llandwit was now more important to him than seeing the grand architecture of Europe or unearthing the roots of the Vaughn family tree. When he learned he couldn't keep Llandwit at the hostel or take him on the train, he called Betty, asking if she could wire him the money to get home. For three days he and Llandwit sat in Heathrow Airport, waiting for the money to arrive. It finally did. So much for the extended European holiday.

It was 1974. Ron and his father were watching a Smokey Robinson special on television in the living room of Ron's Hollywood apartment. Llandwit was at the door, scratching to get out. It was not a fenced yard, but Ron had trained his best friend not to cross the street.

Ralph looked at his son. For the first time in a decade, he was seeing a flicker of hope in Ron's eyes. Gone was the dark, brooding glare; gone were the days when Ron would walk out of the room as soon as Ralph entered. In fact, it had been Ron's idea to have Ralph move in with him. It had been a tough year for Ralph; he'd been forced to close the doors to his office after twenty-seven years. The Nixon administration had cut back on funding for federal housing projects, eliminating the project Ralph was counting on to rescue his business. To add to his problems, he and his new wife, Betty's cousin, were now separated. (Ralph's one-year-old daughter, Ron's half sister, was five years younger than Ron's son Royce.)

Ralph believed Ron's improvement was related to his new job. Ron had answered an ad in the *Times* for a job as a boy Friday for Merle Roussellot, a small architectural firm on Santa Monica Boulevard in West Hollywood. It was gofer work—delivering blueprints, filing applications, checking building codes. But it was a start. Betty bought him a new Honda CC to drive to work, his first car in six years. He was being punctual and working hard. Roussellot liked him, teasing him about the hard times of the Cal football program. Ron was given more responsibility, including drafting assignments and preliminary design sketches. He even began to think that somewhere down the line he might gain the courage to take the licensing exam. But that was a long way down the line. He was still just inching along, one fragile step at a time. Ralph crossed his fingers, hopeful he was getting back the son he once knew.

Ron got up to let Llandwit out. Just as he'd hoped, Llandwit had turned out to be a best friend, always there to greet him when he got home from work, no questions asked, tail wagging. Ron took him for nightly walks, kept him supplied in treats, let him sleep on his bed. Llandwit was the first unconditional love he'd felt in many hopeless moons. He wasn't ready yet to start dating again. Not even remotely. But he had begun to visit old friends—Joe Zeno, his best friend from high school; Jack Trumbo, his ex-fraternity brother. Both men understood that Ron was still a long way from being the Ron of old, but they too could see a new light in his eyes. Ron even got so bold as to sign up to referee rugby matches, but he quit after the first one, concluding he wasn't up to the task.

Ron opened the front door for Llandwit, then sat back down on the couch. He wasn't yet settled in when he heard the screeching brakes and the sickening thud, then the pitiful, desperate squeals of his best friend. By the time he reached the street, Llandwit was dead.

Ron stood on the sidewalk and wept.

52

Steve

. . . encouraged by the freedom granted by birth control pills and by an atmosphere of growing permissiveness concerning all sexuality, sexual roaming has become considerably more prevalent . . . what concerns us are the effects of infidelity on intimate partnerships.
—Dr. George Bach and Peter Wyden, *The Intimate Enemy*

He was obsessed. When he drove down the street, his head turned at every woman he passed. He would speed up to get a better look at the brunette in the VW ahead of him. In bars he eyeballed every woman who walked through the door. At work he flirted with women right under his father's nose. During his rugby games he was aware of every woman on the sidelines. In the Safeway he pushed his shopping cart four aisles out of the way just to get a better look at the blonde in frozen foods.

He wasn't looking for perfection. Not a "breast man," or a "butt man," or a "leg man." He focused on whatever was good—if she had nice eyes or a good sense of humor, that was enough. He didn't care if she was tall or short, married or single.

"I want them *all*," he said.

He didn't tell Ayris he wanted them *all*, but he did confess he wanted to sleep with other women, proposing that they have an open marriage. It was unrealistic and hypocritical, he said, to pretend that they could go the rest of their lives without having sex with someone else. It wasn't that he didn't love her, or that he wanted a divorce, or that he didn't appreciate her qualities—she was gentle, spiritual, smart. They shared a similar worldview. And he still liked her body. But he felt trapped, knowing that he was missing out. Monogamy was too restrictive.

Ayris did not want an open marriage. She tried to analyze why he had this compulsion. Was something wrong with her? Their marriage? Did Steve, despite his lust for women, subconsciously disrespect them? Or was it just a sign of the times? These were the seventies, a time to experiment, to try new lifestyles. She questioned herself . . . if she was so liberal and open-minded, how could she put restrictions on him? On herself? And if he truly loved her, as he said he did, what difference would it make? As long as they continued to grow together, why should she care? He wasn't saying she couldn't have affairs too. If there was any chance of the marriage surviving, she concluded, she would have to accept changes in the rules.

But she resisted in her heart, hoping that working on the property would distract him from the temptations, get him focused on building a future together. Most weekends they commuted to the land and slept in the "Pink Palace," a used trailer they bought to serve as temporary quarters. The construction of the rock house was progressing slowly, hindered by running battles with the county building inspector and the unforgiving land. The mounting marital tension didn't help. There were days they worked the land together in chilled silence, the disaffection and estrangement hanging thick in the air. She wrote in her journal:

April 24, 1973 . . . I felt so depressed this morning I could hardly stand it. I couldn't talk to Steve and I knew he needed it. We both desperately needed to touch and love but invisible resentments halted any efforts. We went to sleep last night without love and the morning was heavy and void. I couldn't eat and I couldn't talk.

It was potentially explosive and I almost wanted a cruel encounter. But slowly kind words eked out from him and finally we laughed at the animals. When I cried, he took me to the couch and we worked at it together until we felt like holding and loving each other. He put me on the bed which is on the living room floor, and he put pillows around me and wrapped me in covers and hugged me very hard. He likes taking care of me and making me feel better and slowly he succeeded enough to allow me to live this day.

Her name was Amanda, although Steve liked to call her Samantha because she reminded him of Elizabeth Montgomery on "Bewitched." She was twenty-five, single, tall and willowy, with braided blond hair. Her father was a prominent local politician; she was a graduate student in design at Sacramento State. The fact that Steve was married seemed not to deter her.

She was holding on tight, her arms around his thirty-three-inch waist as he drove his motorcycle into the lot at South City Honda. It was after closing time and everyone had gone home. He told her to wait outside while he made a quick dash into his office . . . just to double-check that his dad hadn't decided to work late. Getting caught by Frank, as far as Steve was concerned, would be worse than Ayris walking in on him.

"I've got a better idea," he said, grabbing the keys to one of the new Civics. "I'll take you to see my property. It's really peaceful there at night."

"Sounds great," she said.

Frank had appointed him general manager, which for Steve meant longer hours expanding the car dealership. Working at South City Honda was no longer just a temporary and convenient job in Daddy's shop to make money to finance the next adventure. He wasn't a motorcycle mechanic anymore; he was a businessman, his salary tied to profit. With the motorcycle business going better than ever, and a waiting list of customers lined up to buy the new cars, it was, as Frank liked to call it, a "gold mine." They were selling out their factory allotment of thirty new cars per month before they even hit the tiny showroom floor.

Because business was booming, Steve had found himself with less time to work on the property—the foundation and one wall were all that was finished. He and Ayris had put a down payment on a three-bedroom house in Sacramento on tree-lined Thirty-fifth Avenue in a middle-class neighborhood four miles from downtown. They hoped to be moved in before the baby was born. Ayris, who was still taking classes toward her master's in art, was due in May. They agreed that it would be too difficult to raise a child in the isolation of their property, especially if all they had for housing was the Pink Palace.

When Ayris first broke the news she was pregnant, he was skeptical. He knew he had the wandering eye and wouldn't be faithful. It wouldn't be fair. Not to Ayris. Not to the child. Not to himself. He didn't want to have it end up like his first marriage. But Ayris was adamant about keeping the baby, hoping that by the time May rolled around, he would be excited about being a father. He saw no choice but to go along with it. He even promised to attend Lamaze classes.

Holding a six-pack in one hand and Amanda's hand in the other, he walked across his property, a full moon lighting their way to the Pink Palace. Meanwhile, back in Sacramento, Ayris wrote in her journal:

January 26, 1974. Steve's out again and I can't get to sleep. I lie here obsessed and hating it. These nights are the worst of our relationship. Yesterday and today I could tell it was coming. I knew he was restless, tired of me, longing to break loose. It hurts me.

I feel so bound now, so lacking in freedom. I'm fat with pregnancy. Usually, I feel good with it. I feel the baby move and it pleases me. I've been happy more than sad. I'm learning so much, changing and really growing. But, physically, how odd I look. If everything was straight, if we were clear and in tune, I'd be beautiful. Instead, I'm laughable, embarrassing, fat, grotesque and funny.

And so Steve goes out. I'm certain, if he can, he'll lie with someone else, some nonpregnant, drunken chick. He's not going to stop this, ever. On nights like this, I'm so sure, so painfully aware that we can't last.

He's changed in so many ways—really become whole and seeking new levels of understanding himself. But he doesn't want to change this part of himself.

I so often think I'm too demanding, too possessive to request a change. But I can't help reacting like I do each time. I either love him and can't have this happen, or I accept it and feel very resentful and cold.

I'm afraid he's going to keep hurting me more and more. It will be worse with the baby. I'll feel more need for his love and company. I'll be less free and he'll do the same things he's doing tonight.

He told me he'd be home early, that he wouldn't get drunk. Why all this bullshit? I hate it. I hate it. I feel empty and very sad.

He was in the right-hand lane on U.S. 50 on his way back from the property, Amanda at his side, empty beer cans in the back seat. The car began to drift onto the shoulder. He swerved abruptly to get it back on the highway, but it was too late. It rolled down an embankment and flipped into a ditch, landing on its side.

The ambulance arrived to take Amanda to the hospital, where she was put in traction for severely bruised vertebrae. Mr. Lucky wasn't scratched, but he was booked for drunk driving, his second DWI. He had no choice but to tell Ayris the truth. And his dad too. The car was totaled and Amanda's father was threatening to sue the dealership for complicity.

March 18, 1974. It has been almost two months since the last time
Steve stayed out and I remember it so well. It was a night full of fears
that became truths. Everything I was dreading happened that night.
He was at the land with a "chick," drinking and got in a bad accident,
rolling a new car. It was the worst it could've been without being a
complete disaster. She was injured and stayed in the hospital two
weeks. He would go to visit her after dinner. Hopefully it's not a
permanent back problem because then he can expect a big lawsuit.

The emotional happenings were something else. All very intense but
also, for the first time, very clear. I knew I didn't have to and didn't
want to take that kind of indirect abuse. In spite of my noble efforts
to be open and accept outside relationships, I felt very hurt and
injured. But I had all night to cry and be upset. When he finally came
home at 8 A.M., I knew what I really felt I would do. For the first time,
I told him that I would leave if it happened again. I meant it and he
knew it. He cried. I was crying all the time, but still feeling strong and
definite.

Since then, he's stopped drinking—it makes a big difference. We
moved to our new house and have been very involved in fixing it up.
It's been a really positive, constructive and consuming effort. I am
also very pregnant now and with the baby moving and our childbirth
classes, the whole thing has become undeniably real. Steve is
accepting and at times really enjoying it.

There have been very few times since that night that I felt those
same hate-filled resentments. Mostly, I am content and loving, and
while he's "good," how can I not accept him as he is? No hassles
about changing.

Today, after finishing our new parquet wood kitchen floor, we came
to the land. On the way up, my soul was filled with the spirit of
spring. The earth is awake this month. It is full of new shoots and
promises of sweet fruit. Even in our own small garden patch, life is
abounding in our strawberries, peas and radishes. I love the green
hills and all the life in them. Our baby will come the same time as so
many wildflowers and blooming buds. It's beautiful and peaceful here
today, in spite of all the threats and hassles of a troubled world. As I
look down our quilt canyon and feel the movement inside of me, I
sense the mystery and the outrageous wonder of being alive.

53

Jim

On March 3, 1969, the U.S. Navy established an elite school for the top one percent of its pilots. Its purpose was to teach the lost art of aerial combat and to insure that the handful of men who graduated were the best fighter pilots in the world. They succeeded. Today the Navy calls it its Fighter Weapons School. The pilots call it Top Gun.
—U.S. Navy recruiting brochure

It was another tequila sunrise over La Jolla. He punched the snooze alarm, trying to grab another five minutes of sack time before heading out to Miramar and another day of Top Gun training and aerial dogfighting out over the desert.

It had been a rough couple of months for Lieutenant JG Jim van Hoften, dumped by Patty as soon as he got back from Vietnam, discharged in favor of another man, sent crawling to the Navy barracks to live out of a duffel bag while the new guy moved into *his* house with *his* wife and *his* daughter. Jim kept a picture of Jenny on his nightstand, saddened by not getting the chance to be with her day to day, although in reality he really never had been. When she was born, he was up to his stick-and-rudder training in F-4s, and then before she could walk, he shipped off to Vietnam. He was paying Patty $150 a month in child support.

He'd asked himself a hundred times what he could have done differently? Been more affectionate? More attentive? Of course. What guy couldn't be better at that? But the real problem, he figured, had been the Navy—the travel, the moving, the separation, the way of life. What did Patty care about taking it to zero gravity or folding back the envelope? She resented him flying with the brethren all day, then talking about it all night. He'd changed. When they met in high school, he was quiet, reserved, tentative. Now he was a fighter pilot. But he wasn't going to feel guilty for having served his country. And if Patty thought she would be better off with her new man, well, que sera. Her parents, who had always thought Jim was a great catch for their daughter, had offered to pay for marital counseling. Jim lasted one session, concluding the counselor was a "wimp" and didn't know the first thing about *his* marriage.

It was a bittersweet time. For the first time since he was sixteen, he was without Patty. That hurt. But he had moved out of the barracks into a house in ritzy La Jolla with two rock-'n'-rollin' fighter pilots. They called their new bachelor digs "the Palace." It was a rented three-bed-room ranch-style, with cactus in the front lawn, inlaid blue tile in the swimming pool, a well-stocked liquor cabinet, and a steady stream of party guests, many of them tanned and eager Southern California divorcées. The house was owned by Mike "Doo Doo" Doyle, a pilot missing in action; his parents were renting it out. (Doyle's remains were later shipped home.) Jim had the master bedroom, its centerpiece his stereo, his one big keeper from the property settlement. He had become proficient at barbecuing steaks and fixing QB Specials, a drop-dead con-coction that used a case of rum and was served out of a thirty-gallon barrel. And he was a regular at Bully's, a La Jolla hot spot that special-ized in tequila shooters, ferns, and loud shirts. That's where he hung out with "the Fools," a loose-knit collection of young lawyers, doctors, and fighter pilots who lined the bar and wore signs that said "Pick Me."

He was uncertain about his future. He still had nine more months of active duty in the Navy, including another tour of duty on the USS *Ranger* off the coast of South Vietnam. (A cease-fire was in effect, but American ships were still being sent to the South China Sea, just in case.) Until he shipped out, he was one of only eight pilots selected for training in the Navy's flashy new Fighter Weapons School, a selection he hoped might be a stepping-stone to becoming a test pilot. Every fighter jock knew that Test Pilot School was a major training ground for astro-nauts. Not that Jim had any pilot-in-the-sky dream about someday being an astronaut. He couldn't qualify even if he wanted to—at six-three he

was three inches over NASA's maximum height limit. His Top Gun classmates had nicknamed him "Ox."

After rolling out of bed and fortifying himself with a cup of Instant
Folgers, he headed for Miramar. Speeding down La Jolla Boulevard in
his Porsche 911, the sun glinting off his aviator shades, Karen and Richard Carpenter on the radio, he looked every bit the part of the cool and
collected jet jockey. Who needed Patty?

Fighter Weapons School was the Navy's newest training program, another elite fraternity, not yet well known to the outside world, but already well respected among the pilots. Jim had greeted his selection with
his usual unassuming constraint. It was an excellent training opportunity, a chance to improve his proficiency and competitive edge . . . and
if it helped him get accepted into Test Pilot School, so much the better.

Never had he had as much fun flying—Top Gun students were relieved of all other officer responsibilities. All they had to do was fly.
Three or four times a day they flew their F-4s out over Chocolate Mountain in the desert near the Salton Sea and got it on. Wicked dogfights.
Aerial artistry. Cream-of-the-crop instructors. Turning and burning and
taking it to the edge until the Top Gun won.

To Jim, Fighter Weapons School wasn't just about the glory or being
number one in the class: it was the satisfaction of being part of a select
few; it was the challenge of testing man and machine and knowing what
the limit was; it was the thrill of climbing straight up until gravity sucked
his airspeed to zero and then falling to earth like a ten-ton locomotive; it
was the sensation of his hair being on fire when he reached Mach II.

After another day of dogfighting, he climbed down from the cockpit of
his steel-blue F-4, changed out of his flight suit, and headed for the O
Club on the base at Miramar, taking his usual place at the end of the
bar. The daily happy-hour ritual was underway, the eyes of the fighter-
pilot groupies petitioning the jet jockeys, the men responding with their
best "pick me" smiles. Jim looked handsome in his blue flight suit.

He first spotted her standing behind a potted palm. She was cute and
blonde and looked like the end product of a San Diego eugenics program. She also looked to be more of an observer than a participant. He
hesitated to approach. He was not a guy with an arsenal of witty opening
lines.

"What do you do?" he asked.

She was a nursing student at San Diego State, working for the summer as a secretary for the manager of the Chief's Club. Her name was
Vallarie Davis, and she was five-five and had shoulder-length hair, brown
eyes, a confident smile. She was no stranger to the fighter-pilot come-on;

she had already dated several, none of them more than once. Tales of Mach II didn't impress her. After talking to her for several minutes, Jim excused himself to go to the bathroom. Two of his Top Gun brethren swooped in on her, anxious to put in a good word for their friend and classmate.

"Ox is really smart," said one. "He has a Ph.D."

"Am I supposed to drop my panties right now?" she asked.

She accepted Jim's invitation to go out, not because of his IQ or his Porsche or the ribbons on his shirt, but because he seemed polite, gentlemanly, unlike the other fighter pilots and college boys she had dated. In turn, he liked her sense of humor. She was brassy, feisty, irreverent . . . exactly the opposite of Patty.

On their first date they talked a blue streak over dinner; Jim admitted at the end of the evening that he'd told her more about himself in four hours than he had revealed in thirteen years with his ex-wife. Vallarie appreciated the fact that he was the first pilot she'd dated who didn't try to unhook her bra on the first night. She thought it was nice he talked about his daughter. A family man and all that.

As hot as he was for her, he was cautious about rebounding full steam into a heavy-duty committed relationship: he was enjoying life at the Palace and partying with the Fools; he hadn't totally recovered from Patty; he was leaving on another tour of duty. But it was hard to discount the attraction. Vallarie was stable and had a goal in life—to be a nurse. The overeager divorcées he'd been meeting at Bully's seemed only to be husband hunting.

Their relationship sputtered along for three months, Jim intent on proceeding cautiously. But then things began to heat up in a hurry. Vallarie kept notes in her diary:

January 5. Ox called. Came over and played Scrabble. I won. Triple points on "zip." Fun time. Got to bed at three.

January 11. Saw <u>Sting</u> with Ox. Mexican dinner in Mission Beach. Bed at 4. I like him.

January 20. Ox called. Saw his daughter. He was down. Always is after he sees her. I like him.

February 9. Went to party at Palace. Slugged down four QB Specials and passed out on his bed before party started. Woke after party ended. Asked Ox if it was a good party. We drove to Aspen Mine Company to sober up. I think I love him.

February 20. Saw <u>Exorcist.</u> I love him.

She confessed her love in her diary before saying it to him. He hadn't declared his love yet either, although when he left on a two-week mini-cruise along the California coast after completing his Top Gun training, he made a major commitment—he left her his Porsche. He wrote her almost every day, flirting with saying the magic words. "I miss the good times." . . . "Pick me when I come home." . . . "You are a beautiful person and stay that way always." . . . "I do think a great deal of you." . . . "I hope you didn't get your hair cut off. I'll never speak to you if you did." His letters were variously addressed to Vallarie Sweetheart Loverdoll Davis; Ox's Vallarie; Vallarie in Waiting. His last letter cracked the ice, sort of: "I think I'm in love with you," he wrote.

He mailed an application to Test Pilot School, sold his Porsche, and then shipped off on the *Ranger* for his second trip to the Gulf of Tonkin, bidding Vallarie a sad farewell. He had made up his mind that he would put in for his discharge from the Navy if his application to become a test pilot was rejected.

With American military involvement in Vietnam ended, his second tour was nothing more than a training exercise, or "maintaining proficiency," as the jet jocks called it—mock missions, carrier landings, staged dogfights. Tedious, repetitive stuff. It wasn't a cruise about taking it to the edge . . . it was about spit shines and haircuts. He hated to admit it, but he missed the adrenaline and madness of his first tour. He also missed Vallarie.

The response to his application for Test Pilot School was finally mailed to him on board. Nervously he opened it, his future in the Navy hanging in the balance. "We are sorry to inform you," the rejection letter began. It had nothing to do with proficiency, they assured him. It was a matter of him being 300 hours short of the 1,500 minimum hours of flying time required. For the first time since he stepped off the bus in Pensacola in 1969, he had been *left behind*. He'd gone as far up the pyramid as he was going to get. It was time, he concluded, to leave the Navy. He had no desire to go to Beeville, Texas, as a flight instructor and watch neophytes slam into the back of a carrier. Instead, he would go back to Colorado State and finish up his Ph.D. in engineering, and after that . . . he wasn't sure. He put in for his discharge and wrote Vallarie, telling her he was on his way home, eager to be picked.

After four and a half years of military service, Lieutenant JG James "Ox" van Hoften was discharged from the Navy on August 9, 1974, the day Richard Nixon boarded the helicopter on the White House lawn and waved goodbye for the last time. The Fools threw a party for Jim at

Bully's, and the next day, sitting by the pool at the Palace in La Jolla, he proposed to Vallarie. She accepted.

The wedding in San Diego on May 31, 1975, was attended by a lot of Fools and tequila. It was a marriage faintly blessed by Jim's parents, who had always considered the reserved Patty the perfect catch for their son and were slow to warm to their new sharp-tongued whirlwind of a daughter-in-law. Vallarie and Jim's mom were dipoles, with little in common except Jim. The very things that attracted him to Vallarie—her openness, spunk, and flair for the socially outrageous, traits that he wished he had more of himself—were what scared his mother.

They moved to Fort Collins. Vallarie got her first nursing job at Pouder Valley Memorial Hospital; Jim used his GI Bill and a research assistantship to work on a project in turbulence and gravity waves. Academically, his return to engineering was an easy adjustment—he had spent much of his time in the Navy involved in intense study. The discipline came easy. The hardest part was finding time in his rigorous research and study schedule for Vallarie. At nights, he burned the midnight oil at the desk in the living room of their small apartment.

"I promise I won't try to distract you," pledged Vallarie, standing over his shoulder, wearing nothing but her tan lines.

One day as he neared the completion of his Ph.D., he wandered down a corridor in the Engineering Building and spotted an ad on a bulletin board for an opening at the University of Houston for an assistant professor in hydraulic engineering with a background in wave mechanics— right up his academic alley. It would require teaching one graduate course and one undergraduate course; the rest of the time would be for research. He submitted his resume, got an interview, and was hired. Simple as that. He didn't even apply anywhere else.

"But what if I don't want to move to Texas?" mused Vallarie.

"It's a great opportunity for me," he replied.

"These are the seventies," she said. "You know, equal rights."

"Two years," he proposed. "If we hate it, we'll leave."

Vallarie could only hope for the best.

They moved to Houston in 1976. Teaching, he quickly learned, was not his passion. He was frustrated at the mediocrity of the students, many of them Iranian. He did, however, find purpose in his research, working on a paper on bioengineering for artificial heart valves. The project was at the cutting edge of research on artificial hearts being conducted by world-renowned experts Dr. James Cooley and Dr. Michael De Bakey of

Houston. He worked on high-tech experimentation with laser ananome-
try, a new way of measuring fluid flow. Utilizing his expertise in fluid
mechanics, he quickly gained recognition as an authority in turbulence
and blood flow. The earlier-model artificial valves tended to be too mechanical, flapping back and forth like toilet seats when the heart
pumped, making unnatural noises, breaking down the red blood cells;
Jim's research was vital in designing a more efficient valve to help his
team in the race against the competition, Dr. Jarvik in Utah.

Despite his immersion in his research, he missed the Navy, the camaraderie, the feeling of belonging, the adrenaline. What bothered
him about teaching was that there was no closeness on the staff—
everybody was off doing their own thing, locked away in their own
little offices, backbiting, worried about tenure or funding or know-it-all
freshmen.

He applied for the Navy Air Reserve in Dallas, which along with Miramar was one of only two Reserve bases in the country. This was no rinky-
dink flying circus he was trying to crack—Navy Reserve pilots were better than active pilots, more experienced, all of them combat veterans.
There were only four squadrons of fifteen and competition for entry was
fierce. He made it.

Monday through Friday he taught and researched at the University,
then Friday afternoon he hopped in his Datsun and drove from their
newly purchased house in northwest Houston to Dallas to spend the
weekend flying. It was demanding, 125 days away from home and hearth
a year—bombing practice over Nevada, carrier landings in the Gulf, aerial combat above the California desert. It was learning the latest in
computer technology and avionics. He was paid $8,000 a year, which
helped to supplement his $23,000-a-year professor's salary.

Vallarie, who was now a nurse in a Houston hospital, was not happy
with his being gone every weekend. "I might have to have an affair with
the milkman," she warned. "But don't worry. If I do, I promise I'll be
thinking of you."

On a Reserve training mission, his plane developed engine trouble and
he was forced to land in Denver for repairs. While he was waiting for the
parts, he saw two men step out of a T-38 and smile as they put their skis
in the back of a limousine waiting for them on the runway. He inquired
who they were. They were astronauts.

"Nice perks," he observed. "Where do I sign up?"

By coincidence, a teaching colleague entered his office a few weeks
later and dropped a flyer on his desk. It was from NASA. Applications
were being accepted for astronaut training for the new space shuttle

program. Jim shrugged. At thirty-three, he figured he was too old, and at six-three, he knew he was too tall. And besides, if he couldn't get into Test Pilot School, how could he be picked as an astronaut, the apex of the pyramid?

That night he showed the flyer to Vallarie, who was six months pregnant. She encouraged him to apply. "But before you go walk on the moon," she instructed, "go finish the dishes."

54

Larry

So few grown women like their lives.
—Katharine Graham, *Ms.,* 1974

"What will your wife say is your tragic flaw?" asked the moderator.

The audience giggled, watching the three contestants on "The Newly-wed Game" squirm. I was contestant number three, so I would be the last to answer.

No, I wasn't on television. I was participating in a takeoff of the syndicated game show for one of the basic writing skills classes I was teaching at John Adams High in Portland. It was part of a unit I had created called Marriage and the Run-on Sentence. (Other units included: Football and the Comma; Death and the Apostrophe; Paragraphs and Your Parents.) My co-contestants were two other male teachers. Our wives were waiting in the hall, ready to come in and try to match our answers. The students had made up the questions. Spelling counted.

It was 1974 and Kathi and I had been married two and a half years. We'd moved back to Portland from Berkeley in 1973 two weeks after the birth of our blue-eyed, blond daughter, Sarah Elisabeth. I had abandoned my short-lived career in the book business to accept a full-time teaching position. Kathi was staying home to take care of Sarah and was working two days a week as a nurse's aide. She was not particularly happy with her life. She talked of going to nursing school.

The kids I was teaching weren't Harvard bound. They threw punctuation at the page like a drunk at a dartboard; they couldn't spell marijuana or amphetamine, but they knew where to get it. I was using every trick I could to motivate them, even if it meant revealing semi-secrets of my private life.

My tragic flaw? That was the question. I thought Kathi might say it was that I was a dreamer. When I was pursuing the idea of opening my own bookstore, she told me to get real. "How do you propose to start a business when we can't even afford new underwear?" she wondered. Picky, picky, picky. When I told her my new fantasy was to be a writer and I was thinking about free-lancing magazine articles, she shook her head and told me to think about painting houses in the summer instead.

She thought that one of my worst flaws was my impracticality about money. It wasn't that I didn't make enough—as a teacher, that was a given—but that I wasn't sensible with what I had. My theory had always been that somehow the money would be there. "We won't starve," I'd say. I suppose it was a carryover from my baseball days when I always believed I was on the verge of winning the Cy Young Award and so it wasn't worth my time to sweat the small stuff, like the electricity bill. Kathi put it this way: "You're irresponsible!"

Or maybe she would say my biggest flaw was something a little more intangible . . . something to do with trust. Because our relationship had started off with me sneaking up to Seattle to see Denise, Kathi still didn't trust me. It didn't help that I'd told her that I had been unfaithful many times in my first marriage. She said I was a flirt. She said a few other things too: that I wasn't emotionally supportive enough, that I kept a spot reserved for myself that she couldn't penetrate, that I wasn't honest with my feelings, that I wasn't who she thought I was when we first met. She said I had been all romantic and lovey-dovey at first, but then I changed. "You talked about how much you wanted a family and I could see how much you loved Wendy," she said. "I thought you had all these old-fashioned values. But now, you're not the least bit romantic. There's always a distance."

It would have been easier if the question had been: "What was Kathi's tragic flaw?" That was easy, I thought—her lack of confidence and self-esteem. It bugged me. She was intelligent and good-looking, yet she doubted herself at every step, even when it came to things as simple as calling and ordering a pizza. "I'll get it wrong," she'd say. The shrinks would probably say it was because her curmudgeon of a father never gave her any strokes. When she talked about going to nursing school, she might as well have been considering climbing Mount Kilimanjaro barefoot. Whenever I asked her to go for a jog, or to play tennis, or to hit a bucket of balls at the driving range, the answer was always no, that I was a jock and she'd never be able to keep up. I wondered what we would do together when we were old and gray. There were days it seemed that all we had in common were sex, pot, and Sarah.

I tried to think positive. I desperately wanted the marriage to work, I tried my best to convince her I loved her, tried to be all those things I thought I'd heard the women's movement say a man was supposed to be —vulnerable, supportive, intimate. I didn't go out drinking with the boys; I changed Sarah's diapers; I was faithful. Still, Kathi wasn't happy with her life. Marriage and motherhood weren't turning out to be all she'd hoped they would.

Was it me? Was it her? Us? The institution of marriage? The seventies? The women's movement? My essential maleness? I was trying to be the good father . . . getting up in the middle of the night, helping with potty training. But I never seemed to be able to do quite enough. When we went through Lamaze, she was convinced I wasn't *really* into it, especially when I complained that the classes were at the same time as "Monday Night Football."

"What is your answer, contestant number three?" asked the moderator. I decided to go with being a dreamer as my major flaw.

Kathi and the other wives returned to the room and wrote down their answers. The game was on the line. Suspense hung heavy over room 27. The students moved to the edge of their seats. I was confident of victory. Kathi was the last to answer.

"He's not handy around the house," she responded.

She had a point. I didn't even own a toolbox. We had just bought a modest three-bedroom house for $13,000 in a blue-collar neighborhood. The upstairs windows had been painted shut: I broke the first two I attempted to fix. I bought new windows but couldn't get the glaze to work. Now the cardboard covering was starting to come off.

But I knew that down deep in her heart, Kathi didn't think that was my *tragic* flaw. She just wanted to spare me in front of my students. I never let them play "The Newlywed Game" again. Nor did I ask her for the real answer.

It was a typical rainy Saturday morning at the Colton household in mid-decade. Sarah was watching "Bullwinkle" in the living room; Kathi, who had started nursing school, was at the library studying for a midterm she was "positive" she was going to flunk, even though she had a 4.0 g.p.a.; and I was at the table in the kitchen, buried under a huge stack of hopeless essays that I had let pile up while I had been working on another free-lance article.

I had started writing for profit in 1974, and sold my first story to the *Oregonian,* a piece about minor-league baseball. I was paid $175. It took me three weeks to write it. I was euphoric. Being published tasted better than any shutout I'd ever twirled, I proclaimed. Kathi told me I was being premature when I suggested I quit teaching and write for a living. "Do you think the car insurance is going to pay itself?" she asked. I hated it when she thwarted my creativity like that. After publication of my first article, I was hungry for more. I came home from school every day and cranked at the old Smith Corona, the same one I'd used to write Denise the 68-page letter. I was having pretty good luck selling feature stories to local Portland publications, which as far as making any big bucks was concerned was a hopeless cause. But at least I was doing it. Nurturing the dream. Personality profiles, sports commentary, political issues, whatever. Usually I got three cents a word. I tried to write long. The concepts of agents, advances, kill fees, copyright, were way over my head. I was just thrilled to see my words in print. Obsessed. It was like being in *The Baseball Encyclopedia.* Immortality. As a ballplayer, I had usually walked off the field after a game and didn't think about it until I climbed back into my jock the next day. With writing, I took it with me everywhere. I was lost in composition, rewriting paragraphs in my head, plotting chapter and verse, dreaming of the great American novel. We were a month behind on our mortgage. The essays to correct were stacking up higher than Mount Hood.

Sarah burst into the kitchen—but then, Sarah, three, burst in everywhere she went. She was a buzz saw with an industrial-strength mind of her own. For a child with such an angelic face, she knew how to throw a sulk that could cross state lines, so different from the strawberry sweetness of Wendy, but just as lovable to a father.

"Daddy," she exclaimed. "There's a man at the front door. He's all wet."

I peeked through the curtains, and sure enough, there was a man shivering on the porch, drenched to the bone, hair hanging like a wet mop. It took me several seconds before I realized it was Steve. He was bleary-eyed, no suitcase, a motorcycle parked in front. I ushered him inside, surprised and elated to see him. He was on his way to Boeing Field in Seattle to pick up a plane he had bought, sight unseen, and the new Honda 350 parked in front was part of his down payment. He explained that when he left Sacramento it was 95 degrees, so naturally, all he wore was a T-shirt and jeans.

"Froze my fuckin' ass off coming over the mountains in the middle of the night," he said.

"Ummmm, you said a bad word," observed Sarah.

He wanted to shower, take a nap, and borrow some warm clothes. And then he wanted me to ride up to Seattle with him on the back of his motorcycle. "I'll fly you home in my new plane," he said.

I glanced at my stack of essays to correct. "Let's do it," I said.

Kathi and I had been to visit Steve and Ayris several times since our first reunion in Berkeley, and he had been to Portland on rugby trips. With each visit, we became closer friends. He was the only Pi KA I remained in contact with, although there was much that I still didn't know about him, such as his marriage to Linda or his push for an open marriage with Ayris.

Steve took a nap, I got a babysitter, and we were on the road, me riding on the back of his motorcycle. It was late afternoon when we reached Boeing Field. He drove the motorcycle right into the hangar where his plane was parked. I took one look at it, and my decision was irrevocable.

"I'll take the bus back to Portland," I declared.

The plane looked to be a relic from an old Sky King movie—pontoons, pregnant fuselage, propellers front and back. He said it was like the plane he flew in over Vietnam. No wonder we lost the war. I doubted it had been airborne in decades. Greasy engine parts were scattered all over the concrete floor, a ponytailed mechanic standing to the side, scratching his head, totally confused. Or stoned. I couldn't be sure. Steve surveyed his new aircraft with the admiring smile of a man who had just purchased the Concorde. The mechanic advised him that it would be ready to fly by noon tomorrow. I would have guessed the *Spruce Goose* had more chance of getting off the ground.

At noon the next day we returned to Boeing Field, and unbelievably, the plane had been reassembled and rolled out of the hangar.

"Come on," Steve enthused, "I'll take you back to Portland."

"No!" I insisted.

"At least let me give you a quick ride over Puget Sound," he persisted.

"No!" I upheld.

He was cogent in his appeal, a hard guy to say no to, charming and persuasive. But I was steadfast in my fear, determined not to go up in that bucket of bolts, especially not into a sky filled with clouds darker than a cast-iron skillet. He climbed into the cockpit like Flyin' Jack and taxied out to the runway to take it for a test spin. Defying the laws of gravity and aerodynamics, the plane lifted off the ground, the vibrating noise of its engine still audible long after it had disappeared into the black sky.

I envied, and at the same time shuddered at, the way Steve challenged physical risk. He savored it, courted it, lost himself in its cold chill. It had always been part of his charisma—the way he roared up Durant Avenue in college like some kind of James Dean . . . the fearless way he played linebacker . . . the daring way he requested to go to where the action was in Vietnam. Standing timidly by the side of the hangar wasn't his style.

I rode the Greyhound back to Portland. I would later learn that he encountered serious engine trouble on his flight back to Sacramento and was forced to make an emergency landing in a cow pasture near Mount Shasta. Mr. Lucky rides again.

55

Steve

Nothing in life is so exhilarating as to be shot at without result.
—Winston Churchill

The plane was bouncing all over the sky, Steve at the stick, trying to hold it steady, Loren next to him, holding on for dear life. They were at 11,000 feet, somewhere over the rugged Oregon Cascades, flying south, fighting the elements. Fierce head winds. Zero visibility. Ice forming on the wings. No radio contact. Fuel running low.

"This ain't good," observed Loren.

When they took off from Goldendale, Washington, near the Columbia River, Steve had calculated there was enough fuel to make it all the way back to Sacramento. But he hadn't reckoned on the fifty-mile-an-hour head winds. Or the radio going out. Or the winter storm swooping down from Alaska. He faced a dilemma: if he climbed to a higher altitude, he ran the risk of the plane icing up; if he dropped to a lower altitude, he ran the risk of slamming into a mountain, or another plane . . . although it was hard to imagine anyone else nuts enough to be flying in such miserable weather.

"We're in big trouble," said Loren, pointing to the ice on the windshield.

"We'll be all right," assured Steve.

It had been a spur-of-the-moment trip. Over cocktails in Sacramento the night before, Steve had volunteered to fly to Goldendale so that Loren could get the signature of a member of a syndicate that was purchasing an eighty-acre walnut ranch near Modesto from him for $3.4 million, a piece of property that, according to Loren, he had purchased the day before from a bank in San Diego for $2.3 million. It was his first million-dollar deal. The signed papers were in his briefcase under his seat.

"What was that?" asked Loren. It sounded as if somebody had just taken a crowbar to the rear of the fuselage.

"Just a chunk of ice breaking off from the wing," answered Steve. They were flying in Steve's leased Piper Cub . . . the Sky King Special he had landed in a cow pasture on the way home from Seattle was already aviation history.

He had pressed Loren for more details about his million-dollar deal, but had gotten only quick talk about tax shelters, double escrow, and the art of deal making. Steve had heard rumors that organized crime was dumping money into San Joaquin real estate, but Loren was jabbing and ducking, as usual, a slippery guy to pin down on details.

They had reconnected after Steve's return from Vietnam, competing against each other at the 1972 Monterey Rugby Tournament, where they were the superstars. Since then, they had kept in touch, usually at pubs after rugby games. They had more than just fraternal and athletic ties; they shared a common thread of pushing it to the edge in both their personal and business lives—alcohol, women, rugby, parents, business. But they were opposites too: Steve was reflective, a liberal Democrat concerned about the environment and social reform, a spiritual seeker toying with meditation and Tai Chi; Loren was a rock-ribbed Republican, committed to turning a deal, making the big bucks, and "getting those lazy shits in Oakland off welfare." But their friendship wasn't about politics—it was about having a good time together. Loren was involved up to his sideburns with Lisa, the World Airways stewardess, but he was careful to make sure friends like Steve knew he was a leading Don Juan of the Sacramento Valley. No one woman could tame Loren Hawley. No, sir.

"Where are we?" he asked.

"Not to worry," replied Steve.

Loren, who had 100 hours of flying time himself but no pilot's license, surveyed him dubiously. "Just get me home in one piece so I can enjoy my first million," he encouraged. He had plans to buy a small apartment unit in Sacramento.

"Gotcha covered, Big Guy," Steve replied.

He was flying blind with his characteristic sense of indestructibility. He had escaped bullets many times, physically and domestically. Such as the one he'd dodged the week after Ayris gave birth to their daughter, Filaree. During the final months of the pregnancy, he had been thoughtful and supportive, attending birthing classes, abstaining from drinking, raising Ayris's hopes that he might be settling down. He cried tears of joy in the delivery room. But on Ayris's second day home from the hospital, he stayed out all night. What made it even more embarrassing for her was that her sister was up from L.A. to help out with the baby at the time. But Ayris backed down from her vow that she would never tolerate it again, softened by his tears and his promise, once more, that it wouldn't happen again.

The plane continued to bounce through the sky, vibrating, shaking. "Look at the fuel gauge!" said Loren. It was next to empty.

"I can fix that," said Steve, adjusting the fuel-mixture control to thin the mixture and conserve fuel.

The engine coughed once, twice, then died, the propeller whirling to a halt. "Oh, shit!" yelled Loren. They were floating dead in the sky at 11,000 feet, eerily silent, the plane hanging suspended, powerless, held up only by the clouds. Then they began to fall like a brick, the whole enchilada going down, million-dollar deal and all.

Steve calmly reached toward the control panel again and readjusted the fuel-mixture. Just as abruptly as the engine had stopped, it started again, the propeller spinning back to life, the color returning to Loren's face.

"Don't be doing that to me, boy!" he shouted.

Steve nosed the plane into a gradual descent, and piloted his way down through the clouds to land safely in Klamath Falls in southern Oregon. As he rolled to a stop on the runway, he smiled, filled with the exhilaration of once again dodging a bullet.

Steve and his younger sister Denise sat next to each other on the couch in the living room of their parents' house, the only home they'd known as children. Her eyes were red and tired. He put a comforting arm around her.

It had been Steve's idea to call a family meeting and confront her about her drug addiction, convinced that intervention was the only thing that could save his sister. Her life was out of control—alcohol, heroin, attempted suicide, abusive relationships, health problems. Frank and Mary were taking a hard line, still finding it difficult to believe that their daughter was hooked on heroin.

"Denise, you blame everyone but yourself for your problems," said Frank. "You need to look in the mirror."

"Dad," said Steve in a calm voice, "she needs help."

Denise, seven years younger than Steve, was the youngest and the most intellectual of Frank and Mary's four children. She was tall, shapely, thick black hair, dark eyes, soft features, easy on the eyes. When she graduated from McClatchy High and headed off to UC Davis to major in premed, she seemed to be the girl with everything—cheerleader, honor student, Latin Club president, ballet. But in her sophomore year at UC Davis, when Steve was in Vietnam, she took a wrong turn, getting hooked on heavy drugs, dropping out of school, becoming the black sheep, estranged from the family. Her good looks turned hard.

She had become well versed in the trendy psycho-jargon of the day. By her analysis, her problems stemmed from growing up in a family that the neighbors thought was wholesome All-American but one that she believed to be a big façade, a family where love was locked away, everything kept at arm's distance, with a cold and austere mother and a distant father, a man driven by his upward mobility, setting unattainable expectations for his children, withholding approval. No matter how well she did, it wasn't enough. Or so she thought. Such thinking bewildered Frank and Mary, whose lives revolved around their four children.

To Denise, Steve was the rescuer in the family, the brother with whom she felt closest. He was the only one who had ever taken the time to sit down and listen to her, the only one who had tried to understand her pain, the only one who hadn't turned his back when she became an addict. She empathized with him in his battles with Frank and Mary. But it was ironic, she thought, that of all the children in the family, it was Steve, the star jock and the sibling who received the most attention and praise from Frank and Mary, who battled them the most.

Despite her affection for Steve, Denise knew his dark side too, his excesses with women and alcohol. She thought his problems, like her own, were rooted in his childhood . . . that he never felt loved by his mother and that his male role model for how to treat women was a father who came from a generation and a country where women weren't equals and any woman other than a man's wife or mother was put here for man's pleasure. Denise didn't think Steve's womanizing was the result of a disrespect or a hatred of women as much as it was a need for love and acceptance that he never felt at home. His philandering bothered her, because, like everyone else in the family, she thought Ayris to be saintly in her patience, a woman of indomitable strength and character.

Steve rose from the couch, anxious to formulate a plan. He suggested a drug treatment program.

"Why should we keep paying out more money?" wondered Frank. "She used the money I gave for rent to buy drugs."

"Dad," pleaded Steve, "she needs our help."

In time, with Steve's insistence, she checked into a treatment center. She would relapse again, but years later she would look back on Steve's firm stance and intervention as the first step in a long and difficult road to recovery.

His Bell bubble helicopter was his latest flying toy. He had first become enamored of helicopter flight in Vietnam and had used his GI Bill to take the lessons to get his commercial helicopter pilot's license. He had convinced Ayris that it was a good investment, and he was already making enough to cover his payments, hiring it out for five-dollar rides at the State Fair, taking water samples from the Bay for the state, drying crops for local farmers, salvaging heavy equipment. When he wasn't flying it, he kept it parked in his driveway. It was small enough to fit on a flatbed trailer that he kept hitched to the back of a pickup truck. Whenever he wanted to fly, he backed it out of the driveway, towed it to a job site or a deserted field, unscrewed the four large bolts that secured it to the trailer, then lifted straight up, using the flatbed trailer as a launch pad.

It wasn't that he and Ayris needed the extra revenue. South City Honda was a gold mine. Every time the auto transport truck arrived with another load, it was just a matter of getting the new cars cleaned up and out the door. Steve had argued and finally convinced his father that it was time to expand to a new and modern facility. This was going to be his baby. He threw himself into the project at every level . . . working with the bank on financing, meeting with the architect, negotiating with Honda for bigger allotments, shopping for a site.

He was putting in long hours. Ayris suspected his drive to push the business to new heights was to prove himself, once again, to his father, and to keep himself from getting bored. Boredom was his anathema. He needed to be doing something, even on his days off. Playing rugby, building a deck, flying. His idea of torture was sitting around watching television, even football games. Whenever he relaxed enough to read a book, it wasn't escapist novels, but rather how-to books, or philosophy, or biographies of achievers. He knew South City Honda couldn't hold his interest forever. He was exploring the world of investment capital, reading books, attending seminars. Stocks. Real estate. It wasn't the money itself, he said, or even the power that came with it. He wasn't a guy who cared about owning fancy suits, gold watches, or the latest stereo equipment. In fact, he had built his own speakers and stereo cabinets. It was the challenge of a new endeavor and the battle of wits that went with it.

On this day he had towed his helicopter up into the foothills of the Sierras to attempt the dangerous salvage of a rusty car frame somebody had shoved off a canyon wall into the American River. It was going to require flying straight down between two 2,000-foot sheer vertical cliffs. It was a job he had not been contracted to do, but was taking on himself as a project in his personal crusade to clean up the environment.

He drove to a clearing near the top of the canyon wall and went through his preflight checklist. He was wearing his usual pilot uniform: jeans, work boots, white T-shirt, and aviator shades. With all switches on, he pulled back on the handle and the helicopter slowly began to lift off the trailer. Suddenly, the aircraft vibrated violently. Straining to get airborne, it pitched forward, and as it did, the pickup truck jackknifed toward him. In a thundering, deafening crash of metal and steel, the rotor blades slammed into the top of the truck. Everything was spinning. Scraps of metal, like shrapnel, shot off in every direction. The helicopter slammed into the back of the truck, throwing Steve into the windshield.

When the dust and the flying debris and the jumbled metal finally settled, Steve rolled out of what was left of his helicopter. The pickup and the helicopter were totaled, a twisted mass of junk. He did not have to examine the wreckage to know what went wrong—he had forgotten to unscrew the rear bolts securing the helicopter to the trailer. He checked himself for cuts and broken bones, then walked away, Mr. Lucky shot at and missed again, his only injury his broken aviator shades.

He finished reading Filaree, now three years old, her bedtime story. She had fallen asleep on the couch, snuggled against his side. He gently scooped her and her "blankie" into his arms and carried her to bed, bending down to kiss her on the forehead, whispering his love.

It was a Saturday night and he was home alone with his daughter. Ayris had gone to San Francisco to visit friends for the weekend, leaving him in charge of Filaree until Sunday. Filaree was his pride and joy. He was determined to give her the fatherly affection he felt he never got . . . or that he never gave to his son, Dennis, now twelve. It had been over ten years since he had seen Dennis, even though they lived less than five miles apart. Steve continued to cling to the belief that it was best he didn't interfere in Dennis's life, and that in time they would reconnect.

Filaree was a beautiful child, with Steve's dark hair and eyes and her mother's soft disposition. Ayris struggled with Steve's behavior as a husband, but not as a father—he and Filaree had been close from the day of her birth. When she was a baby, he loved lying in the beanbag chair on the floor and putting her on his chest, holding her, rocking her. He changed her diapers; he read to her every night—Dr. Seuss, "Goodnight, Moon," "The Little Train That Could"; he played tea party, sitting in the tiny chair; he took her flying; he taught her the ABCs; he hung her a handmade swing from the giant elm in the front yard; he installed an aboveground pool in the backyard and equipped it with plastic floating turtles; he bought her a new dress every Christmas and Easter.

He kissed her good night and turned off the light, then returned to the living room . . . and called Shelley. "Ayris won't be back until tomorrow night," he assured. "Come on, live dangerously." A tall honey blonde, Shelley was a sales rep for a pharmaceutical supply company. The night they had first met he asked her what she thought was her best feature, and she looked him straight in the eye and replied, "My tits."

Meanwhile in San Francisco, Ayris had changed her mind about staying with her friends the whole weekend, deciding to return to Sacramento. It was after midnight when she pulled into the driveway. She didn't recognize the white Trans Am parked in front. Maybe it belonged to one of Steve's rugby buddies.

Walking in the front door, she saw a white purse sitting on the dining-room table. She didn't own a white purse. All the lights were off. She called Steve's name. No response. She checked their bedroom. No Steve. She peeked in Filaree's room and pulled up the covers.

Her instincts told her what her heart didn't want to believe. Then she heard muffled voices filtering down from the darkened upstairs guest room. There was a woman's voice. And the rapid shuffling of feet, like one might hear when people were trying to get dressed fast in the dark.

"Damn you, Steve!" she screamed.

She ran into their bedroom and slammed the door. She didn't want to see this bimbo. For Steve to go out and have affairs around town was one thing, but to bring another woman right into their house was the ultimate violation, the final humiliation. She knew what she had to do.

Steve quickly ushered Shelley down the stairs and out the front door, then took a deep breath and entered the bedroom. "How could you stoop so low?" yelled Ayris. "In our house. With Filaree right here!"

"I'm sorry, I'm sorry," he begged.

Ayris had heard it before. Many times. And always she had caved in to his tears and apologies, believing his promises to change. But no more. This time his tears wouldn't work.

This time she wasn't backing down.

56

Loren

If you start to take Vienna—take Vienna.
—Napoleon Bonaparte

Commitment. Why was Loren so afraid of it? That's what was on Lisa's mind as she parked her prized red Corvette next to his Mercedes in the driveway of his house in Yuba City. She had three days off before her next flight. A neighbor stopped to stare—it was hard not to notice the dazzling five-eleven auburn-haired beauty with the poured-on jeans and neon smile.

Lisa wasn't sure what to expect if she pressed Loren on the commitment issue. In the four years they had been "going together," she'd learned that the Loren she first met wasn't necessarily the Loren she now knew. In the beginning he had come on strong, telling her how "special" she was and how much he needed her. She could do no wrong. He assured her that his rocky history with women was over and that it would be different with her. Beneath his big macho exterior she saw a tenderness, an endearing little-boy quality. She was the big love of his life, he said, the only one who really counted. She believed it. He believed it. He went out of his way to impress her, flashing his money, taking her to his rugby games, bringing her home to meet Genevieve, showing off his boat and his water-skiing acrobatics. The good times flowed. He was the "Champagne King." Nothing but Dom Pérignon and the best suites at Harrah's. They were unbeatable in doubles tennis, six-four and five-eleven of grace and power covering the court like giant California condors. When they walked onto the dance floor, people stepped aside. Disco fever. He confessed his love and promised her he wanted a meaningful, monogamous relationship. "Trust me," he said. He would drop everything and charge across burning sand to be with her. She was totally hooked, so emotionally committed that she might as well have been his wife. They talked of the future.

But now the relationship was stuck. It was as if he fired off all his best moves, got her reeled in, then panicked. The phobia of being trapped. He was still in love, but now instead of its being the rockets' red glare, the fireworks were fizzling. Instead of being intimate, he was being invulnerable. He was sending double messages, contradictory behavior. He had encouraged her to move in with him, but urged her to keep her apartment in Sausalito. He bought her a beautiful watch one day, then wouldn't give her the time of day the next. He talked about togetherness, yet walked down the street two steps ahead.

She approached his front door. Or was it *their* front door? With a closet full of clothes in Sausalito and another one in Yuba City, she wasn't sure. The door was open, as usual. A low, guttural sound was coming from the living-room floor. Lisa wasn't sure what to expect, as usual.

Loren was lying shirtless on the living-room rug, grimacing, clutching his side. "There's a baseball bat in my closet," he said. "Go get it and come back in here and put me out of my misery."

She spotted the swelling in his side. It was the size of a grapefruit. "What's that?" she asked, kneeling down to examine.

He pulled away. "It'll go away," he said.

"Loren, go to the emergency room," she demanded. "Now!"

"Bullshit," he replied, slowly rising to his feet. "I'm going for a jog. I'll run it out."

Before she could stop him, he was out the door and down the street. When he returned twenty minutes later, ashen and gasping for air, the grapefruit lump was still there of course. She threatened to call an ambulance if he didn't go with her to the hospital.

The X rays revealed it was an infected gallbladder. Reluctantly, he agreed to surgery, but not before making Lisa promise not to tell anyone he was in the hospital.

"Tell them I had to go out of town," he said.

"Why can't I tell them the truth?"

"Because I don't want anyone to know I'm sick," he answered.

. . . .

In August 1977, the month Elvis died, Craig did two things that caught Loren by surprise—he became a born-again Christian, and he announced he was going to get married. To Loren, it rang like the death knell to their wild and womanizing times.

For Craig, the first six years of the seventies had been a struggle—bankruptcy, broken friendships, bench-warming in Dallas behind Roger Staubach. His name had been repeatedly dragged through the media dirt: an arrest for drunk driving; an IRS tax lien; an unsuccessful venture with a Dallas nightclub. His reputation was tarnished. In 1974 the Cowboys traded him to the New York Giants for what he hoped would be a new lease on his career. But it was only a continuation of the nightmare. The Giants were hapless, a team with no home field and not enough clean socks to go around at practice. As the team's most prominent player, Craig was the target of relentless booing by the angry New York fans. At the end of the 1976 season he was given a reprieve and traded to Denver. It was in training camp in Fort Collins with the Broncos that he found Jesus. He was listening to a radio call-in show in his room—fans were being polled on who they thought should be the Broncos' starting quarterback for the upcoming year. Craig finished a distant third. When he called his girlfriend, Susie Sirmen, a Dallas model, former "friend" of Elvis, and "a great Christian girl," she suggested he take out the Bible in the top drawer and start reading. It wasn't long after that—November 7, 1977, to be exact—when Loren and Lisa were in Dallas for Susie and Craig's wedding.

Lisa hoped Craig's apparent settling down would have an influence on Loren. But the closer she tried to get, the more he backed away. A cat-and-mouse game of commitment. She was confident he loved her, but there were days he acted as if he was some sort of hunted animal and everything she did was designed to trap him.

"You'd make a great wife," he said, "but I just don't know if I want a wife."

He continued to send mixed messages, telling her how much he wanted her in his life, then turning around and telling her she shouldn't expect anything. When they were home alone, he was often passionate and tender; around other people, he backed off, almost to the point of denying there was anything going on between them. He brought up reasons why it wouldn't work between them, rather than reasons why it could. He was excluding her from parts of his life—work, friends, trips. He could be so vague about his business deals, as if it was some big mystery that was too complex for her to comprehend. She had the impression that he was clearly trying to limit her involvement in parts of his life, setting up boundaries. Then just as suddenly he would drive her to Napa to show her a vineyard he was negotiating for, dropping names and numbers on her from out of the deep blue of California real estate.

He worked to keep the relationship at a safe distance, accomplishing it in a variety of ways—burying himself in his work, having relationships with men that excluded women. She envied how he had always dropped everything whenever Craig called, and how it was okay for him to go out drinking with the boys, but not for her to go out drinking with the girls. He complained about her being gone so much with her job, yet it suited his needs, helped to maintain the distance. A relationship with a stewardess, as far as he was concerned, was having his cake and freedom too.

She was constantly finding women's names and phone numbers on cocktail napkins, matchbooks, scraps of paper. When she confronted him, he denied there was anything to it. She wanted to believe him. Even though she had traveled to all four corners of the globe and had a sophisticated, cosmopolitan flair, she maintained her small-town, Pullman, Washington, naïveté and purity of heart; so when he reassured her that she was the most important thing in his life, she disregarded the facts and evidence, believing his stories, living on hope. She was in love and wanted to be part of his life. He was in love too, and did in fact want her to be part of his life. But he feared she would try to consume him. The way his mother consumed his father, and his grandmother his grandfather.

There were always a million and one things he had to do. They were beginning to sound to her like just more excuses to keep his distance. He was getting harder and harder to pin down on his time. "Don't count on me tonight," he'd say. Everything had to be on his time. He made plans with her, then broke them. When she talked about change, he claimed he already had; when she tried to push the relationship to the next step, he balked. She threatened to leave. But he couldn't let her walk away. He jacked up the charm, reeling her back in. She backed down from her threat.

Craig's wedding was a major Dallas social event—horse and carriage, hundreds of guests, champagne fountains. It was a marriage that surprised many of Craig's old friends who thought he was a confirmed bachelor. But perhaps the bigger surprise happened the day after the wedding when Loren took Lisa to a Dallas jeweler and bought her a large diamond engagement ring.

"But you have to promise me one thing," he said.

"What's that, honey?" she asked.

"You can't tell anyone we're engaged."

It was painful to look at. Craig's leg was one giant hematoma, black and blue from his hip to his ankle. He was in traction and the doctors were telling him he couldn't play on Sunday.

"Don't be a wus," countered Loren, standing at his bedside.

It was late December 1977, two days before the American Football Conference championship game between Denver and the Oakland Raiders, the first time in the Broncos' history that they had advanced that far. The city of Denver was going bonkers, decked out in orange-and-blue Christmas trees. And at the center of Broncomania was Craig, the born-again football messiah of the Mile High City, the team captain, and a new deacon at the First Calvary Church. Fans loved him. In his first year with the team, he had led them to a 12–2 record, the best in the league, silencing his critics. There was an ethereal quality to his resurrection. The AP and *Sporting News* named him Player of the Year. In the first round of the playoffs against Pittsburgh, he was spectacular, throwing for two touchdowns in a 34–21 victory. But he paid the price and went straight from the locker room to the hospital, where he was put in traction, his right leg so battered and bruised that he couldn't walk. His whole body ached. Fans didn't realize the pain he carried onto the field every Sunday: six shoulder operations that shot ice picks through his whole body every time he was buried under a pile; four knee surgeries that rendered him close to immobile, making him a sitting duck every time he dropped back to pass. His teammate Lyle Alzado called him "the toughest player in the NFL." Another teammate, Haven Moses, said he was "unbelievable, a born leader." A sportswriter dubbed him the "quarterback nobody wanted."

Loren had come to the hospital to check on his progress. Ironically, since Craig had moved to Denver, Loren had been spending a lot of time there too, involved in a condominium development project near Vail and an oil well leasing business called Oil Tech. He had been working on bringing in Craig as an investor in the projects. Craig's financial picture was still cloudy, but he was slowly working his way out from the past disasters of his fast living and bad investments, paying off a large bank loan and a federal income-tax lien.

"Damnit, Craig!" snapped Loren at his bedside. "You can't afford not to play Sunday. This is the biggest game of your career. You have to be out there!"

"I can't do it, Loren," Craig said, voice cracking. He had been playing organized football for twenty years, and now he was on the threshold of his greatest moment, the apex for any pro footballer, but the pain was so intense that the pills were useless.

"You'll play," directed Loren.

Nobody knew better than Loren how physically tough Craig was and all the pain he'd been through, on and off the field. He also knew that if the Broncos beat the Raiders, they would most likely face the Cowboys in Super Bowl XII, a game that would give Craig a chance to prove something to Tom Landry, Tex Schramm, and the rest of the Cowboy organization.

"If you don't play against the Raiders on Sunday," said Loren, turning to leave, "then you're not as fuckin' tough as I thought."

On Sunday, shot up with painkiller, Craig took the field against Kenny Stabler and the Raiders. He had zero forward mobility, but he was able to hobble straight back from center, which he did, passing for 224 yards in leading the Broncos to a 20–17 win. After the game, he retreated to the privacy of a locker-room hallway and cried, then was besieged by the media. He gave credit to the Lord . . . and to Loren.

"Nobody in my life has ever said anything that meant more to me than what Loren Hawley told me in the hospital," he said.

It was clear to Lisa that the big diamond engagement ring on her finger had done nothing to change Loren. If anything, he seemed to be pulling further away, firming up his escape route, programming the final demise.

He was leaving a thick trail of clues. He made no attempt to hide the names and phone numbers on his desk. It got so bad that for Christmas she gave him a fancy box to keep them in. And after a two-week trip to Arizona on business, he received a perfumed letter with a Phoenix postmark every day for a week.

"I don't know why that tomato is writing me," he maintained.

"You've obviously been giving out signals," Lisa said.

"It's her fantasy," he said. "I can't control it if she wants to write me."

Lisa backed down.

Loren was convinced Phoenix was the place to be for real estate development in the late seventies. There were some investors back in California who were none too sad at his prospective move; they claimed his only goal had been to pick their pockets. Several lawsuits had already been filed on deals that had gone awry. So far, he had managed to stay undefeated in court. "Every deal I do is clean," he maintained. The IRS, however, was beginning to wonder how he could be as clean as he was claiming. He had not filed a federal tax return in six years. That didn't seem to jibe with his nice house, swimming pool, boat, Mercedes, airplane, and various properties in California, Colorado, and Arizona.

It was clear to Lisa that his plans to move to Phoenix didn't include her. But it was hard to pin him down for concrete answers or to discuss the relationship. He justified his long absences by saying he had business to take care of, deals to close, property to view.

"The way I do business," he explained, "is to have twenty-five deals going at once. Maybe only one will work out. But I have to be on top of all twenty-five of them. I call it positioning."

Loren was in fact positioning to end it. But he felt guilty. He still loved her. In his own way. He also felt torn. It was as hard for him to commit to leave as it was for him to stay. If he had his way he could just sneak off and never have to discuss it with her. He had hoped that by leaving for long periods of time it would help accustom her to his being out of her life. And ease his guilt about having wasted her time. But how could he explain to her that her only tragic flaw was that she wanted to be with him in a permanent relationship? He couldn't.

Infidelity had always been an easy way for him to convince himself he wasn't trapped in a committed relationship. And now it was a convenient way to set it up where he didn't have to be the one to end the relationship. Except he didn't plan on it ending the way it did.

He left for Phoenix for two weeks again, driving there in Lisa's red Corvette, leaving her with his Mercedes. The Corvette was her Rosebud, but she reasoned that letting him take it with him to Phoenix was keeping the respirator plugged in.

She was sitting home one night when she heard a knock at the door. It was her insurance man. He had come to gather information about the accident involving her car in Phoenix.

"What accident?" she asked.

Loren had loaned her Corvette to the "perfume-letter lady," who smelled more like a six-pack of Bud when the police pried her from behind the wheel of the Corvette. She had crashed it going the wrong way on a one-way street. The "perfume-letter lady" wasn't seriously hurt, but the car was totaled.

Loren tried to explain. But Lisa had caved in to his stories too many times. But no more. This was the last straw. His charm and promises wouldn't work.

This time she wasn't backing down.

57

Jim

Man must rise above the earth—to the top of the atmosphere and beyond—
for only thus will he understand the world in which he lives.
—Socrates

He groaned, opening one eye, checking the alarm clock: 4 A.M. The baby
was squalling in the next room.

"Your turn," instructed Vallarie.

"But . . ."

"But nothing. Your daughter's calling."

It was November 1977. In four hours, Jim was scheduled to be on the
treadmill at the Johnson Space Center to start Day Three of his weeklong astronaut interview. He was one of NASA's 208 finalists out of
8,079 applications for the space shuttle program. Thirty-five would be
deemed to have the right stuff. He rolled out of bed, groping through the
dark to Jamie's room. She was three months old, oblivious of her daddy's
candidacy for American Hero. She needed clean diapers, now.

All the way back to that humid day in 1969 when he first soloed over
Saufley Field in Pensacola, he'd been ascending, level by level, the pyramid of aviator nobility: number two in flight school, star of the jet pipeline, sixty combat missions, Top Gun, Naval Air Reserve. Now he had a
shot at being elevated to the godly rank of astronaut. He wasn't worried
about the treadmill test—it was the interviews with the shrinks and the

panel of NASA honchos that had him antsy. Like any self-respecting fighter pilot, he didn't cotton to the world of psychiatrists and psychologists. He believed in exploring the universe, not analyzing it. He wasn't as interested in talking about his place in the cosmos as he was in establishing it.

Not that he wasn't ready to jump through hoops to get picked. Who wouldn't? Think of it. Blasting off to outer space. Talking to the President on a TV hookup. Big bucks. Huge house. Porsches. Ski condos. Freebies. Princely consulting fees. Of course he wanted it. But jumping up and down and getting all excited about it wasn't his style. Mr. Easygoing. When Vallarie had called him at his office on campus to inform him she'd rammed their Datsun into a Mercedes in a parking lot, he was so calm that she swore he was on Valium. Life would go on, he figured, with or without a smooth fender, with or without him as a Big Space Hero.

He kissed Jamie and returned to bed, falling right back asleep, almost. The squalling started again. He heaved a sigh and rolled back out of bed. What the hell . . . he didn't need eight hours' sleep to pass a treadmill test. And besides, Vallarie had her foot in his back, shoving him back into duty.

In years gone by, so the story went, the Air Force had been so hot to get their pilots chosen as astronauts that they spent days coaching them on how to dazzle the NASA bigwigs—how to talk, how to cocktail at the social gatherings, how to dress for the interviews. But there wasn't much Jim could do about his meager college professor's wardrobe. He was risking that fashion and cotillion styling weren't his tickets to outer space. He didn't shave his mustache or trim his sideburns. The only prepping he did was to learn how to count backward from 100 by sevens —somebody had warned him he'd be asked to do that.

He sat in a chair, facing the panel of ten NASA officials, including two astronauts. One might have been one of the guys who went to the moon, he thought, but he wasn't positive. Celebrity recognition was never his thing. He folded his hands on the desk in front of him. He felt less intimidated than when he had sat in front of the panel of professors for his Ph.D. orals. If he washed out back then, all those years of academic pursuit were down the toilet. Here, what did he have to lose? If he bombed, they weren't going to take away his pilot's license. Life would go on. Jamie wouldn't care.

"Starting with high school," said the NASA official, "tell us about yourself. You have an hour."

Whoa! What did they want to hear? Probably about his sports. And about teams he'd been involved with. And about his accomplishments. The right stuff. They wouldn't want to know about the wacky things—not that there was that much. NASA was into image, squeaky-clean stuff. No stories about hot-wiring the Bonneville in high school, or dancing in goat barf, or jet-washing junks, or tequila nights with the Fools and QB Specials at the Palace. They'd want to know about family. And exploring.

He launched into his answer—Boy Scouts, Mills High football, swim meets, Cal crew, Rogue River rafting, civil engineering classes, Ski Patrol, National Science Foundation fellowships, class captain at Pensacola, Vietnam combat missions, Top Gun, Ph.D. thesis, artificial-heart valve research, Mom, Dad, Vallarie, apple pie. He did not venture into emotional waters. He didn't tell them about his first wife leaving him when he got back from Vietnam. The FBI, in their investigation of the candidates, would surely verify he was no wife beater.

He maintained a clear moral tone, not too animated, not too droll. Level. Confident. Not sanctimonious or full of self. He was just trying to be himself. He left the interview room ambivalent about his performance. It was all so subjective. That's why he liked engineering. A plus B equaled C. There was a right and a wrong answer. Black and white. No gray for the shrinks to dwell in. Too bad all of life's problems couldn't be solved by an equation. Or an aerial dogfight out over the desert. Showdown at Mach I, not some leather couch with pad and pencil.

The physical exam was time-consuming, but easy. The first astronauts had showed that no great feats of physical strength or endurance were required for space flight. Ox was jogging fifteen miles a week, so a little treadmill action, even on two hours' sleep, was no sweat. His long hours with the mind probers was where it got tough. The touchy-feely stuff. He went in determined to give appropriate, astronaut-like responses. The shrinks went right for the family stuff.

"On a scale of one to ten, rate your parents' marriage."

"Ten," he answered, deciding to overlook the fact that they never came to his high school swim meets, smoked too much, and liked his first wife better than Vallarie.

"What do you like best about your wife?"

"Her sense of humor."

"What do you like least about her?"

"I can't think of anything."

"There's got to be something."

"There really isn't."

"Surely . . ."

"Well, I guess she's kinda sloppy. The house is usually a mess."

"Does that bother you?"

"Not really."

"Do you argue?"

"I'm not much of a fighter. She's always saying how she can never get me into a good argument."

He was asked whether he believed in a God. He answered that he thought something was "causing all this to be ordered," but that he didn't believe in a dogmatic God that people wrote about in the Bible. "Something is going on out there I don't understand," he said. "I guess I believe there's a person-like thing that's overseeing everything, so for nothing better, I'll call it a God."

They asked about his hobbies and he told them about the TV he was assembling and his little side business constructing hot tubs.

"Do you think you're an overachiever?"

"Well, I set goals and do it. I like to finish what I start."

"Are you a dreamer?"

"I'm more of a realist."

"Do you maintain a healthy diet?"

"Yes," he lied, assuming they wouldn't consider chips and beer at the top of the food chain.

"How much do you drink?"

He had heard tales of voluminous drinking and womanizing by former astronauts, so he reckoned that NASA would not be so pious as to think applicants were monks. "Casual drinker, I'd say," he answered. "I'll have a beer or two when I come home from work."

On the last night of his interview week, NASA hosted a social get-together in the banquet room of the NASA Bay Inn. To Jim it seemed much like a fraternity rush party—bring in the recruits, feed them drinks, make cocktail chatter, see how they mingle. Who's the mover, the recluse, the boozer? He certainly felt more comfortable schmoozing at the NASA Bay Inn than he did back in his days in Pi KA.

"At this rate," he mused, ordering his second cocktail, "I'll be through my liquor quota for the year before the end of the night."

Monday, January 16, 1978, dawned gray and wet over Houston, two inches of hail and pelting rain clogging the streets and filling the bayous, a bone-chilling wind sweeping down from Canada, temperatures dropping into the 20s, the kind of day that made Jim and Vallarie forget what a scorching humid sump they lived in most of the year. The phone rang. It was 6:30 A.M.

"Who the hell's calling at this hour?" mumbled Vallarie.

Maybe it was the chairman of the engineering department at the University of Houston, calling to tell Jim it was too cold to hold classes. That'd be just fine with him. Or maybe it was the hospital wanting to know if Vallarie was ready to come back to work . . . which she wasn't.

Jim groggily picked up the receiver. "Well, do you think you want it?" asked the voice on the other end.

Jim bolted upright, realizing it was George Abbey, director of flight crew operations for NASA. The words slammed into his brain . . . he had been chosen as one of the select thirty-five, he was going to outer space, he was at the apex of the pyramid. King of the pilots. Abbey was waiting for his response.

"Far out!" Jim blurted, his first words as an astronaut.

"Does this mean we have to live in Houston the rest of our lives?" asked Vallarie, her first words as an astronaut's wife.

Vallarie called her parents in San Diego to spread the good news.

"How much will he make?" asked her dad.

Jim's pay was certainly nothing to dance around the laundry room about. It would be $21,000. A cut in salary from his job at the University. Okay, so there wouldn't be a new mansion, or ski chalet at Aspen, or Porsches backed up all the way down the driveway, or closets full of designer clothes, or freedom for Vallarie from bedpans forever. But Jim was going to be slipping earth's surly bonds and heading for the cosmos. Far out!

"We want to throw a big celebration party for him," exclaimed Vallarie's mother.

"Oh, now I get the picture," huffed Vallarie. "I just gave birth to a baby, which was only the biggest event of my life, and I get a Hallmark card. But Mr. Space Commander gets a new job and the catering trucks start circling the block. That's okay. I'll be there like a good wife to set out the cocktail napkins and swoon over my hero."

Vallarie's protestations, of course, rode a distant back seat to the pride and delight she shared in her husband's success. She could visualize a whole new world—new friends and social standing, elegant luncheons for the spouses, majestic lift-offs at Cape Kennedy, NASA parties in swank hotels, trips to the White House Rose Garden. Maybe even a new vacuum cleaner.

"I can't wait to tell everyone I've slept with an astronaut," she said.

Technically, he was an astronaut *candidate,* a label NASA was giving the newly anointed thirty-five until they completed their first year of training. Then they would be designated as real astronauts, *true* members of the club. Jim wondered what the snobs in the in crowd back at Mills High would say about him now, now that he had been selected as one of the *Chosen Few*. The Tallest Astronaut Ever.

Of the thirty-five selected to begin training in June 1978, six were women, including Sally Ride and Judy Resnik, three were black, the first minorities ever chosen by NASA, twenty-one were from the military, fourteen were civilians. Fifteen of the candidates were selected as pilots, and twenty were designated as mission specialists to conduct scientific and engineering experiments aboard the shuttle. Because of his shortage of flying hours, Jim was designated as a mission specialist, which in essence meant that he had reached the top of the pyramid not because of his stick-and-rudder work, but because of his academic merit. His work in heart valve research had not gone unnoticed. And of all the applicants, he counted backward from a hundred by sevens faster than anyone.

He drove to his office on campus. The phone was ringing off the hook, reporters from every newspaper and TV station in Houston calling for an interview, the L.A. *Times* trying to get through. It struck him as funny. He had never been interviewed by the media. Not when he blocked a punt in high school. Not when his design for a new bridge across the Bay was selected in college. Not when he bombed Hanoi. Never. Now suddenly he was pegged by NASA as having the cool stuff of a space explorer and he needed a press agent.

"Why did you want to be an astronaut?" asked the first reporter.

Oh, where to begin? His natural quest to explore? His ascension up the pyramid? His curiosity about the universe? His search for a new brotherhood? His boredom with teaching? His patriotic calling?

"Who wouldn't?" he replied.

The reporter for the L.A. *Times* finally got through. "Do you think it will be a problem working with women in the space program?" he asked.

"It won't bother me," Jim replied. "But it might bother my wife. She's the jealous type."

That was a rookie astronaut's mistake. Vallarie's sister in Los Angeles called the next morning to read her the quote over the phone. The article was titled "Size no problem for first ox in space."

"I thought the reporter would know I was joking," said Jim.

"You know I'm not the jealous type," Vallarie bristled. "But if I do catch you messing around with one of those little space honeys, you'll be walking funny the rest of your life."

58

Larry

Writing is the hardest way of earning a living, with the possible exception of wrestling alligators.
—Olin Miller

It was Kathi's idea to go to Rooster Rock, a nude beach on the Columbia River fifteen miles east of Portland. I was a bit averse to such an adventure, but I agreed, not wanting to seem unhip, unliberated. These were the seventies.

We had been married four and a half years, and if there was such a thing as a driver's seat in a relationship, Kathi was now steering the bus. Or at least that's the way I felt. In the early days of the marriage, when I was still sneaking phone calls to Denise, it was Kathi who was insecure. But somewhere along the way, the tide turned and I was the one feeling threatened. And suspicious. I sensed that as soon as she finished nursing school and could support herself, she was going to blow me a kiss and then head on down the road, taking Sarah with her.

We spread out our towels and stripped naked. Sarah, who was three and a half, headed straight for the water. There were about fifty other nude sunbathers spread out along a quarter mile of beach. A small fleet of speedboats was anchored just off shore, the boaters all drinking beer and ogling the sunbathers, as were the people with the binoculars on the cliff behind us. It seemed I was center stage in *Oh! Calcutta!*

"You sure you want to be here?" I asked.

"Those people with the binoculars are the ones with the problem, not us," she replied.

I suspected that Kathi, who had always been relatively modest about her body, was trying to make a statement about her new liberated state of being. She was reading feminist literature and attending a women's consciousness-raising group once a week. When I asked her what they talked about at those meetings, her answer was vague, which made me leery. She talked of needing her "space." I felt barely able to claim the spot my own body occupied—she was welcome to whatever of the remaining universe she needed. When she stopped shaving her legs, I commented that I preferred smooth legs on women, making it clear that I was simply expressing my personal preference, not issuing an order. I was doing my best to be politically correct, not to cross the line of chauvinism. But I was walking on marital eggshells.

After spreading Coppertone all over my body, I pulled out a notebook and began to work on my latest free-lance article, a feature story chronicling a day in the seamy life of the Portland Greyhound Depot. I had come up with the idea after spending so much time at the depot waiting for Wendy, ten, to arrive from Seattle on her bimonthly visits. I was going to be paid only $150 for the story. Still, it was crucial money. Child-support money. With Kathi in nursing school, our finances were strained. I still had the dream of quitting teaching to go full-time at writing. After three years at Adams High, with all its chaos and all the stacks of nearly illiterate essays to correct, I was burned out. I was also embroiled in a certification dispute. Because I refused to take classes that had zero relevance to my actual teaching assignment, the hidebound school district was threatening to suspend me. The more I fought them, the more nervous Kathi got. "You've got a family to think about," she said. "You can't afford to lose your job."

Another family with a little girl Sarah's age arrived on the beach and set out their towels about fifty feet from us. In time, the little girl wandered over to us and began playing in the sand with Sarah. Soon, her naked father strolled over to make sure she wasn't bothering us. He stood next to our towel and struck up a conversation. Kathi was sitting up, eye to eye, so to speak, with this guy's penis. I was feeling uncomfortable. Here was my wife talking directly to another man's penis. I had not yet evolved to this stage of liberation. Especially considering that this guy was hung like Mandingo.

It was the last time we went to Rooster Rock.

.   .   .   .

The view from Neahkahnie Mountain was spectacular: clear blue Oregon sky, rugged coastline, steep basalt cliffs, lush conifers, the Coast Range in the distance. A nice place to start a two-day bike trip down Highway 101 and the Oregon coast.

Bill Walton, star basketball player, stared at the layer of summer fog hovering offshore and then turned to survey my yellow Schwinn Varsity with its baby seat, kickstand, generator light, and balding tires.

"You're going on *that?*" he asked, raising his red eyebrows.

I nodded, shrugging my shoulders. It wasn't the bike that worried me. It was the fact that I was barely in shape to ride three blocks to the 7-Eleven for a six-pack, let alone try to keep up with one of the world's best-conditioned athletes over steep mountain terrain. Walton was riding a custom-built, super-lightweight Falcon touring bike that cost more than my 1970 Nova.

It was August 1977, two months after Walton had outplayed Kareem Abdul-Jabbar and Julius "Dr. J" Erving to lead the Portland Trail Blazers to the NBA championship. And it was seven months after the Portland School District had canned me for failing to take the classes required to maintain my certification. My dream of being a full-time writer, much to Kathi's consternation, was underway—that's what I was doing on Neahkahnie Mountain with Big Bill . . . doing Gonzo research for a locally published book I had been contracted to write on Walton and the Blazers, a project I had yet to be paid for (which after taxes and expenses would work out to be $350 a month). But it was a gig. I was two months behind on our $200-a-month mortgage, the car insurance was about to expire, the food stamps were running out, and Denise was threatening to call a lawyer if I didn't send her the support check. My ex-wife and my wife did not share my dream of being a free-lancer, convinced I was being irresponsible. They weren't interested in hearing me talk about working in a garret in the name of Art. They wanted Cash.

"You ready to hit it?" asked Bill, pedaling away, not waiting for my response.

Bill was the counterculture's favorite jock, and I was hoping to plumb the depths of his soul as we pedaled along, to probe the enigma that shrouded him. For the most part, he had been protected from the media by his college coach, John Wooden, at UCLA and by Blazer management. There were stories of him being arrested as an antiwar demonstrator, helping harbor Patty Hearst, listening only to the Grateful Dead. But what was he really like? That's what I was there to try to find out. When he agreed to let me and a documentary film crew ride along with him for two days, it was journalistic access he had rarely granted. I had written several free-lance articles for the *Oregonian* about the Blazers in their drive to the championship and had earned a measure of trust from him.

We started to roll, followed by the film crew in their van and Bill's wife, Susan, and son Adam in their Mercedes. "Wait up, Bill!" I yelled. "I want to ask you about the time you . . ." It was too late, he was already over the crest and around the next curve, his long legs pumping like the pistons of a well-oiled machine. I was already gasping for breath, not even over the first hill. A logging truck rumbled by, nearly blowing me off the highway. Only 150 miles to go.

I had invited Kathi to come on the trip, but she declined. We had reached the point where we rarely did anything together. I suspected she was having an affair—not with Johnny Wad from Rooster Rock—but maybe the handsome professor she was jogging with at school every day —this after I had been asking her without success to go jogging with me for three years. "Damn right it bugs me," I'd admitted. Our arguments were endless. She accused me of being so absorbed with my dreams that nothing else mattered to me, including the bills or the family. She said she felt neglected. I said I felt neglected. She was as obsessed with getting a 4 point, I said, as I was with dreams of literary grandeur. Whenever I approached her, I felt her resentment and hostility. I wasn't sure where it was coming from. Yes, we had financial problems; and yes, I was a dreamer. "So what am I supposed to do?" I asked. "Go get a miserable job and work forty miserable hours a week so we can buy a new Volvo and I can be miserable the rest of my life like your frustrated father?" I was writing fifty hours a week, paying my dues, betting on the come, determined to be a writer. Damnit. I loved the creative challenge and not having to report in to a "coach" or a "principal" every day. I kept thinking Kathi's anger was coming from somewhere deeper than our financial plight. It was primal man-woman, self-esteem stuff. Issues of emotional support and respect. I did love the family, but obviously I wasn't doing a good enough job of convincing her. I didn't know what more I could do: I was still faithful, but I don't think she believed me; I complimented her on how she looked and she doubted my sincerity; I cooked dinner and she complained that the kitchen was a mess; I worked eighteen straight hours to make a deadline and she complained that I didn't make the bed. I couldn't seem to make her understand that just because I was home all day I wasn't sitting around eating bonbons and watching soap operas.

I pedaled feverishly, trying to catch up with Bill, but it was hopeless. Susan cruised by in the Mercedes and flashed her bountiful California earth-mother smile, then sped off down the road. The film crew stopped to ask if I was all right. They were hopeful I could catch up with Bill so they could record some dialogue to go with the footage of the Mountain Man and the breathtaking scenery. Both of us were wired for sound. But it was just me and the white lines of Highway 101.

I pumped over Cascade Head—or was it Mount Everest?—alone with my thoughts of my rapidly disintegrating marriage. Bill was waiting up ahead, resting, leisurely picking wild blackberries at the side of the road. A family in a station wagon screeched off onto the shoulder, jumping out of the car to snap a photo of the State Hero for the family album. The father looked up at him and asked him how the weather was up there. Bill resisted the temptation to spit on him and tell him it was raining. I chugged to a halt, collapsing, sprawling into a bed of tall grass.

"Come on!" he said, climbing back on his bike. "Gotta keep pushing."

It went on like that all day, Bill powering ahead, then waiting for me to catch up, then taking off again. When we finally stopped that night in Oceanside, I could barely lift my glass of beer. Bill wolfed down two complete salmon dinners.

I awoke the next morning stiffer than a Douglas fir. Every cell in my body hurt. "I can't do it today," I whined.

"Bullshit!" said Bill. "I knew baseball players were pussies!"

I climbed back on my Schwinn, giving in for the umpteenth time in my life to the tyranny of the locker room. I rode out of Oceanside with Bill that morning, met up with him for lunch in Lincoln City, and then watched him zoom off again into the landscape. My butt hurt so bad I had to pedal standing up. Going over Cape Foulweather, the wind blew me backward. I tried getting metaphysical, visualizing myself on the other side of the mountain, coasting down the hill. It didn't work. I had cramps everywhere—thighs, arms, eyebrows. Not metaphysical ones. Real ones. Mean ones.

But somehow I made it, rolling into our destination of Newport, Oregon, just as the sun set into the Pacific—160 torturous miles in two days. Up one hill, then up another. Hills seemingly with no down side. Into the wind. The hottest days of the year. Bill always way ahead. We'd eaten several meals together and picked wild berries by the side of the highway. So what journalistic insight had I learned about him? Not much, I concluded, other than the fact that he ate like a horse, pedaled like a machine, and hated for people to ask him how the weather was up there. It was the day Elvis died.

I sat next to him at dinner that night. A member of the film crew gave me a beanbag pillow to sit on, elevating me a foot above Big Bill. I took a long swig of beer, then glanced down at him. "How's the weather down there?" I asked.

A friend was paying me five dollars an hour to shovel dog shit and garbage out of a basement in a condemned house he had bought to turn into a rental. It was in a run-down section of northeast Portland. The people who had owned the house before had kept two Dobermans locked in the basement. The stench was overwhelming. There was standing water in the low parts of the concrete floor from where the sewer had backed up. Two rats scurried across the floor and disappeared under a pile of mildewed old clothes and newspapers. I was taking a slight economic detour to earn some cash. On this day I would be setting down my shovel early—I had to be at a suburban B. Dalton's to autograph copies of *Idol Time*, my newly released book on Walton and the Blazers. Shoveling shit in the morning, autographing books in the afternoon, writing prose at night. Chasing the dream. When I showed up at the bookstore, the line of autograph seekers stretched out the door and halfway across the mall. I strutted inside. That's when I learned they were all there to meet Jack Ramsay, coach of the Blazers, who was also there to autograph his book on coaching technique.

It was May 1978. Kathi and I had been separated a month. I was living out of a suitcase in the unfinished attic of a friend who had offered me temporary rent-free quarters until I "got back on my feet." At the rate I was raking in the free-lance coins, that figured to be sometime around mid-twenty-first century. In the separation, Kathi got the house and Sarah, I got the Nova. The transmission was threatening to go out, and I had no money to fix it. What I now had were two ex-wives wanting their child support.

It seemed like it would be easier to make a living wrestling alligators.

A month before the split, Kathi and I had been to see a marriage counselor. After seeing each of us separately, he brought us in together, looked me straight in the eye, and said, "I don't think there's any hope for this relationship."

The good news was that he only charged ten dollars. I promised to mail a check.

At that point, despite the counselor's black cloud, I was still clinging to the hope the marriage could be saved. Kathi suggested a "trial separation." "I just need some space to sort things out," she said. "I want to find out who I am." I didn't want to split up. Not again. When Denise and I had a "trial separation," I ended up feeling like a yo-yo. I could see it happening again. I was confused. And angry. My theory was that a couple was supposed to work out their problems together. I was willing to give her the rest of her life to find out who she was.

She talked of how she felt betrayed, of how I didn't turn out to be the attentive, caring family person she thought I was in the beginning. I too felt betrayed. She had come into the marriage with a Cinderella fantasy of what marriage was supposed to be, I thought, and then when she realized I was not Prince Charming, she wanted to bail out. I maintained that I was changing. I'd grown up in the fifties thinking it was supposed to be one way, but then when I got to the seventies the rules had changed. Drastically. I was doing my best to turn my boat around and go with the flow, but her response was that my change was glacieresque and she didn't have time to wait. She said I proved to her that I didn't care about the family when I let the car insurance lapse. "How could you let me drive Sarah around with no insurance?" she wondered. I saw such a complaint as a hypocrisy of the women's movement—where in the Constitution did it say that it was the husband's duty and responsibility to pay the car insurance? In the new feminist order, it seemed to me, the man was supposed to be sensitive and emotionally supportive and do 50 percent of the housework and child rearing. Fair enough. That was hard to argue. I agreed with equal pay and the ERA and *Ms.* magazine. But why didn't I get to go to journalism school and let her be responsible for paying the bills? And why was there zero chance of me getting custody of either of my daughters? Because I was a male. That's why. Where was the equality in that? I'd asked for custody and had been rejected.

A week before the separation we'd made plans to have a big talk to see if we couldn't reach some kind of eleventh-hour compromise. Ten minutes into the discussion, I glanced at her and she was sound asleep in her chair. I wasn't sure if she was narcoleptic, bored, or what. In any case, I was pissed. She had given up. I figured I might as well too, storming out of the house on my way to a half-night stand. I got home at 4 A.M. Kathi was still asleep in her chair, all the lights still on.

When she asked me to move out a few days later, I cried, a salty mixture of sorrow and anger. "If I walk out that door," I said, "I'm not coming back. I won't put any energy into getting back together." I'd been down that road before.

"That's a great attitude," she said.

And it was only a few weeks after I walked out that door that I was shoveling Doberman shit and dreaming of better days.

59

Ron

Paternity is a career imposed on you without any inquiry into your fitness.
—Adlai Stevenson

Ron parked his Honda Civic in front of Anna's house in San Francisco and checked his watch. He was ten minutes late. He had come to pick up Royce and take him to Golden Gate Park, or wherever it was a ten-year-old boy wanted to spend a Sunday afternoon with a father he barely knew. Ron was nervous, not just because he was unsure of himself around Royce, but also because he never knew what fireworks to expect from his ex-wife.

Anna was unmarried, working as a substitute teacher, living in Visitation Valley, a semi-blighted area two miles from Candlestick Park, with houses stacked side by side, no lawns and rising crime. Her small, funky wooden house sat on three-quarters of an acre; her living-room walls were covered with paintings, her bookshelves crammed with books on cooking and art. From her small earth-toned kitchen she could look to the west and south and watch the planes taking off from the airport or the fog rolling in over the hills. Her terraced backyard was shaded by a California cypress. The buckwheat sprouts and artichokes in her large vegetable garden were doing just fine. She did her own mulch.

It was 1978. For Ron it had been a long, slow climb back out of the deep dark hole that had swallowed him, but he was back functioning in society again after a lost decade, still not the same guy he was when he was number 88 for the Golden Bears (not that he wanted to be) but certainly light-years ahead of where he was back in the days when he was wandering Haight-Ashbury. It had not been a dramatic, overnight recovery, but rather a slow crawl, two steps forward, one step back . . . like when his dog Llandwit was run over. His job as an architectural associate for Merle Roussellot in Los Angeles had been crucial in helping him regain confidence, self-esteem, and a belief that he was capable of handling responsibility. In 1977, after three years with Roussellot, he had piled everything he owned into his Honda and moved to Sacramento. It was a big step. One of the reasons he moved north was career-related. Jerry Brown had replaced Ronald Reagan as governor and was releasing funds for new state building projects. Associate (unlicensed) architects were being hired. Working for the state, Ron assumed, would be secure, long-term employment. Job security was important to him. He wanted a job where he felt comfortable, relaxed, able to work within his capabilities; he wasn't interested in working on his own, or designing state-of-the-art skyscrapers, or entering cutthroat bidding competitions for jobs financed by millionaires. A job with the state would be working for *all* the people of California, contributing to the public welfare, not just the greedy special interests of a few private citizens. He had been hired on a six-month contract as an associate architect for the State Department of Parks and Recreation.

Another reason he moved to Sacramento was for social contact. Even though L.A. was his hometown, he felt isolated there, no close friendships. It was painful for him to listen to his divorced parents hurl bitter insults across town, his mother dispirited, his once proud father struggling to retain his dignity after losing his business. Ron was eager to start rebuilding friendships, and in the Sacramento area there was a network of old fraternity brothers, including Loren and Steve. One of the first things he did after arriving in town was to go visit Steve, who had heard about the problems that had befallen his fraternal big brother. Ron did not go into details of the hard times, preferring to focus on the positive. When Steve saw Ron twist his six-three frame into his tiny Honda CC, he arranged a deal for a new Civic at dealer cost.

Ron was living in a downtown Sacramento boardinghouse, his small room spartanly furnished with a bed, dresser, and hot plate. He was making monthly payments on a new J. C. Penney television, although it had been stolen three months earlier. He was hopeful of moving out of the boardinghouse into a bigger place so that he would be able to bring Royce for weekend visits. It was actually Royce, more than the job or the network of old friends, who had brought him north. Ron felt he had reached the point where he was ready to establish visitation rights and try to become a father for the first time in his life. It was not, however, going as smoothly as he hoped. He felt awkward as a parent, unprepared. Suddenly popping into Royce's life was requiring an adjustment on everybody's part, a slow earning of trust. Royce was a bright, extremely good-looking boy, with dark eyes, long eyelashes, his father's long limbs and curly black hair, and his mother's resolute personality. He was slow to warm to his father's attempt at a relationship. Ron couldn't help but wonder if part of it had to do with Anna's influence. She was still bitter. From his standpoint, she seemed determined to hold a grudge, even after ten years. Every time they spoke, she insisted on dragging up the same old dirt, reminding him of how he had deserted her, how he had failed as a husband and a father. She was making it her cross to bear, unable to let it go and get on with her life. It was almost as if she resented that he was recovering, he thought. She was making it difficult, sometimes impossible, for him to see Royce, at one point sending Royce to live with a family in Europe, forcing Ron to go to court to find out where he was. She went to court too, attempting to have Ron's wages attached. His monthly support had been readjusted to $250 and he was now making regular payments, but she still called to harass him at work. "I supported you the whole time we were together!" she railed. "If it wasn't for me you would have never gotten that job. You owe me." The way she saw it, $250 a month was not enough to compensate for the emotional and financial neglect of the past decade. She accused Ron of only wanting to see Royce at his convenience, and said that he had moved to Sacramento more to ease his own guilt than to do any meaningful parenting.

Ron got out of the Honda in front of Anna's house and stretched, working out the kinks of the two-hour drive from Sacramento. He approached the house. A note was pinned to the front door. It was from Anna, informing him that she and Royce had made other plans for the day. Sorry. Ron was left with no choice but to get back in his car and drive back to Sacramento, furious, convinced that Anna was dedicated to doing whatever was necessary to keep him from ever building anything resembling a relationship with his son.

Ron set down his beer and watched the woman walk toward his table, her eyes zeroed in on him. She had a short bob cut, painted red fingernails, and a vodka tonic in her hand. There could be no doubt—she was coming to talk to him. Steve was out on the dance floor with her girlfriend, and Loren was huddled in the corner talking business secrets with some skinny sleazeball who looked to Ron as if he belonged in porno flicks. It was Loren's mentor, Lee Roberts.

It had been Loren's idea that they come to Eddie's, a foot-stomping country-western nightclub in Marysville. For Ron this night was sort of a coming-out party, his first major socializing in many years. Earlier in the evening, he had gone with Steve to the El Mecero Country Club in Davis for the annual dinner for the Sacramento area Bear Backers, a fund raiser for the Cal football program. It was the first time Ron had dared venture to a function where he might have to answer questions from a gathering of old friends about where he'd been the past fifteen years. But Steve had insisted that he go. Steve was making a devoted effort to help usher him back into the world, regularly calling him up just to talk and check his progress, or to invite him to a Recap rugby game, or to take him out to lunch. Steve the rescuer. Ron felt a sense of comfort in Steve's presence, that he had a friend to turn to. Ron also liked being around Loren, although for different reasons. As far as Ron was concerned, Loren was the same old Loren of Pi KA days, his free-spirited energy absorbing everyone in its path. Loren made him laugh. And it was Loren who made him get in his new Cadillac after the Bear Backer dinner to ride up to Eddie's in Marysville.

"My friend told me you're weird," said the woman with the short bob cut, brazenly pulling up a chair. "You don't look it to me. But even if you are, I kinda like the weird ones."

Her name was Bertena Rogers. She was thirty-five, a peppery and seasoned fifth-generation Californian from Yuba City. She worked as a supervisor for the phone company and had two ex-husbands and a ten-year-old son. She liked her scotch straight, cussed like a cowboy, and had never been to L.A.

Bertena had already sized up Loren and Steve, figuring Loren to be too much a wheeler-dealer, sort of a sad character, Steve to be too Hollywood conceited and drunk. Ron, she thought, was very nice-looking, but definitely no Beau Brummell in his polyester brown slacks and gray corduroy sports coat with the frayed lining. She was taken aback at how polite he was. At closing time she invited him and Steve to follow her and her roommate, a tall shapely woman with an English accent whom Steve was zeroed in on, to her house for coffee. Loren, who had hooked up with a "hot tomato" of his own, gave Ron a wink and flipped him the keys to his Cadillac.

At Bertena's house in Yuba City, Steve and the woman with the English accent headed straight for the back bedroom, where Steve passed out as soon as he hit the bed. Ron and Bertena sat at the kitchen table and talked nonstop until dawn, Ron revealing very little of his crazy past. Why dredge up all that crap? The sun was just starting to come up when he finally woke up Steve to go home. Bertena walked them to the Cadillac, surprised that Steve, even in his intoxicated state, insisted on driving, and that Ron didn't even try to kiss her good night.

How was she to know that he hadn't kissed any woman in ten years?

Ron was driving down Melrose Avenue in Hollywood, returning to his father's apartment after a long day in the hot sun at Disneyland with Royce and his father. This was after a long day in the hot sun at Knott's Berry Farm the day before. Doing the Weekend Dad thing to the hilt. Stretched out in the back seat, tired and cranky, Royce, eleven, kicked a steady beat on the back of Ron's seat.

"Stop it!" Ron ordered.

Royce continued to kick away.

It was 1979. Less than three months after meeting the peppery Bertena, Ron had moved in with her and her son, commuting thirty-five miles every day from Yuba City to his job with the Parks and Recreation Department in Sacramento. At first glance, Ron and Bertena were a mismatch. She was touchy-feely, he was reluctant to hold hands; she spent money as fast as she made it, he kept to a tight budget; she was a clotheshorse, he owned two pair of slacks, brown and brown; she loved her cocktails, he rarely drank. But they were a comfortable union based on respect and need and companionship. Good friends, and lovers too. It was Bertena who pushed him to start studying for the licensing exam, refusing to accept his doubts and fears that he couldn't pass. Although the test was still months away, he was already hitting the study guide with much the same intensity that he did as a student at Cal.

He had gained a calm he hadn't known in years, branching out, reconnecting with other Pi KAs in the area. He accepted an offer from Steve to join the Recaps. He was back in shape again, weighing a trim 190, and while he didn't play the game with the reckless fervor that Steve and Loren did, he felt great about being physical again, banging into bodies, joining the guys for beers when the game was done. Everybody on the team liked him. He was also doing well at work, hired on a full-time basis, his job secure. He was assisting in the design of the restoration of historic State Park facilities. Life was decent.

"I told you to stop it!" he snapped as Royce continued to kick away. They were nearing Ralph's apartment, their lodging for the weekend, a modest one-bedroom in a clean, older neighborhood near the Hollywood Cemetery. Ralph was now retired, living off social security, with a little financial help from Ron. He spent his days painting, no school of art omitted—impressionism, modern, abstract, cubism, Ralphism. He signed some of his paintings with the name Pablo Picasso. His apartment looked more the pad of a SoHo artist than a seventy-year-old man.

"This is the last warning," said Ron.

Ron was still worried about his performance as a father. There was nothing he could do about the son he'd abandoned in 1962, but with Royce, no matter how hard he tried, he couldn't seem to break through. There was a distance, an uncertainty. It was hard for him to feel he had any control, seeing him only once or twice a month for a few hours. As much as he didn't want to, he found himself responding to Royce much as Ralph had responded to him—suggesting rather than demanding, nudging rather than shoving. It was from that weakness, Ron thought, that he had never developed the backbone to face his problems. Anna wasn't helping the situation either, still pressing him for more money, threatening to take him to court again. When she asked for money for school clothes for Royce, Ron went out and bought the clothes himself. She sent them back.

Nearing Ralph's apartment, Ron warned Royce again to stop the kicking. "You can't tell me what to do!" hollered Royce. "I don't have to obey you!"

"Yes, you do!" shouted Ron. "I'm your father!"

"No, you're not!" retaliated Royce.

Ron jerked the car to a stop at the curb and got out, pulling Royce from the back seat. The battle was on. The more Ron pulled, the harder Royce fought and the louder he screamed. A window across the street flew open, and a head popped out to watch the commotion. Ron continued to pull Royce up the street toward Ralph's apartment. There was kicking, flailing, yelling. Finally, Ron put him into a headlock and dragged him up the front steps. The neighbor from across the street called the police.

By the time the officer arrived, the screaming and the kicking had subsided and Ron was able to convince the cop that it was not a case of kidnapping or child abuse. But when Royce returned home the next day and reported the incident to his mother, Anna obtained a temporary restraining order preventing Ron from seeing his son. She promised he would never see his son again.

His career as a father, it seemed, was destined to forever haunt him.

60

Steve

. . . you do not realize that you, yourself, exist independently of your physical body.
—Jane Roberts, *Seth Speaks*

Steve was drinking cranberry juice instead of beer. In two days he was running in the Avenue of the Giants Marathon in the Redwoods and he wanted to give his body a chance. Nevertheless, he and Glen Richards, his buddy from the Marines, were at Lord Beaverbrook's, a popular Sacramento singles bar.

"Check her out," said Glen, pointing to a Suzanne Somers blonde walking through the door.

Steve's brown eyes signaled his approval.

It had been twelve years since Glen and Steve met at Officer Candidate School at Quantico. Glen, who was from Louisiana and was awarded a Purple Heart in Vietnam, suspected that one reason Steve sometimes seemed bent on careening recklessly through life was that he hadn't lived up to his own expectations for himself as a Marine, that he was disappointed that he hadn't been in a position to be ultra-daring in Vietnam and he was still trying to fulfill that macho Marine element of his personality.

"She looks eager," observed Glen.

"She looks shitfaced," said Steve, watching half the men in the place swoop in on her.

Glen and Steve had maintained their friendship after being discharged. On Steve and Ayris's trip to Europe, they spent several days in London with him—he was living there with his English-born wife. When Glen called a few years later, bummed out and broke after his wife left him, Steve invited him to come and stay with him. Glen ended up settling in the Sacramento area, enrolling in classes in elementary education, paying for rent and groceries with the $300 a month he made as the women's soccer coach at UOP and the $400 Steve paid him to work part-time at South City Honda. Steve had offered him a salesman job, but Glen was the quiet type and preferred a position detailing cars. He was also taking ballet lessons.

Steve's generosity to Glen went beyond giving him a part-time job: he let him borrow cars; he got him a spot on the Recaps; he paid his first and last month's rent; and when he saw that Glen was sleeping on the floor, he bought him a bed, couch, and dresser as a present. Whenever they went to Lord Beaverbrook's, Steve always paid, refusing to let Glen spend a dime. He also made a point of steering women in Glen's direction. Glen enjoyed being around the swirl of action that always seemed to follow Steve, but what he enjoyed most was their quiet times together . . . reading, jogging, meditating. He was also close friends with Ayris— it had been her idea to name him Filaree's godfather.

Steve and Ayris were now separated. She hadn't backed down after the night she found him with another woman in the house. She had moved to San Rafael in Marin County, where she was working as an art therapist with mental patients and dating a writer/photographer/scuba diver who was a fundraiser for Greenpeace and the Sierra Club. She and Steve had yet to file for divorce. "Who knows," Steve had said. "Maybe someday we'll circle the wagons and watch the sun go down together." He was paying her $400 a month in child support and seeing Filaree every other weekend, sometimes flying down to pick her up in his newest plane, a Bradley-Jensen single-engine, amphibian aircraft that he bought from a retired barber who had built it in his backyard. Ayris cringed every time he took off with Filaree in it.

"Looks like the blonde is leaving already," said Glen. "Better hurry if you're gonna make a move."

Steve didn't respond, preoccupied with his thoughts. Glen suspected Steve's heart wasn't in it this night and he was there only to provide him company. Or who knows why he was there. Nothing Steve did surprised Glen, like the way he suddenly announced he was going to run the

Avenue of the Giants Marathon even though he had never even run a 10K and had done no serious training other than quitting drinking for a week. The real reason he was running a marathon, he confessed, was because a woman he'd had his eye on, a reporter for the Sacramento *Bee,* said she was entering, so he signed up too, volunteering to drive up to the Redwoods with her. His hope was that on the way home they would stop at a motel.

Glen marveled at the lengths Steve would go in his pursuit of women and the depth of his obsession, and how he had plunged headfirst into the dating scene. Literally. At one point Steve's eyes had gotten red and puffy, and when he went to the doctor thinking it might be a corneal abrasion from rugby, he learned that he had a small colony of crabs living in his eyebrows. That took him out of the market for a couple weeks, but he was soon back at it, relentlessly.

Glen also marveled at Steve's physical conditioning. There had been many times when they had partied late into the night and the next morning when Glen arrived at work Steve would already be in his office, jumping rope, chugging carrot juice, popping vitamins. Steve rarely sat down on the job, always doing six things at once. Usually, one of the things he was doing was arguing with his father. The tension was constant. Steve had recently told Frank to "get fucked," and Frank fired him right on the spot. Frank, of course, hired him back the next day. Their main source of friction had become Steve's lifestyle—the drinking, the woman chasing. A steady stream of women came into the office to visit him, and it angered Frank, who complained they were "jiggling all over the place." He thought Steve had made a huge mistake splitting with Ayris. They also argued about business. Sometimes Steve's schemes backfired, such as when he ordered twenty cases of flat-tire fix-it cans and didn't sell a single one. Or his decision to advertise on television when they were already selling every car on the lot. Frank Jr., the younger brother, who was the parts manager, figured it was just another one of his brother's ego trips, a chance for him to get in front of the cameras and make himself a mini-celebrity. But there were other times Steve's ideas were visionary, such as when he insisted the company switch to computers, or when he quarterbacked the move into the new and larger showroom.

The blonde passed Steve on her way out the door. "You're cute," she slurred. He smiled, but said nothing, choosing instead to drink his cranberry juice and let her stagger out into the night. A few minutes later he and Glen left too. In the parking lot, they encountered her again. She was clinging to a light pole, surrounded by three men trying to pull her to their car, hands all over her. Steve brushed his way between them. "She's with me," he announced, hoisting her over his shoulder like a sack of potatoes.

"Bullshit!" said one of the men, reaching out to stop him.

Steve stopped. "I suggest you back off," he said politely. "Or I will have to set her down and then squish you like a little bug." The man backed off.

Depositing her in his back seat, he was unable to coax an intelligible response concerning her name or address. She was already passed out. So he drove her to his house and put her to sleep on his couch. When he left for work in the morning, she was still deep in slumber, never to meet the gallant knight who'd come to her rescue. She was gone without a trace when he returned.

Every month seemed to bring a trendy new experimentation in his seventies search for "spiritual awareness." Tai Chi. Carrot juice. Dirt biking. Megavitamins. Younger women. Meditation. José Cuervo. Avenue of the Giants. He talked of the incredible high he felt running through "the wall" amidst the grandeur of the Redwoods, but Glen knew his real high had been afterward at the motel room with the cute reporter from the *Bee*.

His latest spiritual pilot was the book *Seth Speaks*. He first came across it in the Sacramento County Jail, finding a copy on the bench in his cell. He had been sentenced to serve two weekends behind bars after pleading guilty to his third arrest for DWI. His option would have been eight weekends on the freeway litter patrol. With nothing else to do, he opened the book; the jacket flap encouraged readers to join Seth, a medium, on "a voyage inward and through the past . . . toward amazing new spiritual awareness." As he began to read, the words rang true, saying the things he'd been thinking. He underlined Seth's words in a chapter titled "The 'Death' Experience": "There is no separate, indivisible point of death, even in the case of a sudden accident. Life is a state of becoming, and death is a part of this process of becoming . . ."

Steve had always had a benign disregard for death, laughing at death scenes in movies, trusting in his own immortality. Seth was validating what he wanted to believe . . . that there was no such thing as death, that a person's spirit existed independent of his or her physical body. Not that Steve didn't care about his physical body. He was vanity incarnate, posing with other members of his rugby team for a nude calendar. He religiously followed a low-fat, natural-foods, no-chemical diet. When the judge ordered him as part of his sentence to go on Antabuse, a chemical that when mixed with alcohol in the bloodstream acts as a negative reinforcement by causing nausea and vomiting, he sought out a doctor friend, persuading him to write a letter stating that the Antabuse was having an adverse side effect on his liver and kidneys, impairing his ability to fly, drive, or do anything strenuous, including sex. It worked—the judge agreed to let him off the Antabuse.

Despite his three DWI convictions, he did not believe he needed Antabuse or any other kind of treatment. He admitted he couldn't hold his booze, but he didn't think he had a serious drinking "problem." He offered as proof the fact he could go weeks without touching a drop, and often did. He saw no reason he should abstain altogether. He was satisfied that his vow not to drink and drive again would be enough to cure his "problem."

New Year's Eve 1979 started like every day for Steve. He rolled out of bed, put on his gravity boots, and hung upside down and naked from a bar in the bathroom for fifteen minutes. It was to keep his spine aligned, which he was now convinced was vital to "body awareness."

"This is a hell of a way for a great pilot to start off the day," he bellowed, the same as he did every morning.

"Morning, Grandpa!" roared hurly-burly Ed Forrest, one of his new roommates. Ed had taken to calling him Grandpa—it had to do with the streaks of gray showing up in Steve's hair and the way he shuffled around the house every morning like an old man, dressed in his robe and slippers.

After his tofu and carrot juice breakfast, Steve returned to the bathroom to begin installing the tile in the new shower. He was determined to have the remodel of his bathroom finished for the big New Year's Eve party that night. Ed, a building contractor, was supposed to be helping him with the floor, but he was slow on the uptake, still trying to clear the cobwebs from the night before. Their other roommate, Charles Pierce Boyer III, a Dartmouth grad, rugby teammate, and wallpaper hanger, wasn't home. He was the Felix Unger to Steve and Ed's Oscar Madison.

"Get your ass in here and start helping with the floor, Ed!" yelled Steve. "If it's not finished, I'm calling off the party."

"Fuck you, Grandpa!" countered Ed, who had already called a subcontractor, too hung over to do the work himself. He also knew Steve wouldn't call off the party because it was a night filled with too much promise. Steve had invited three women, all of whom had accepted, all of whom assumed they were coming as his date. Ed could hardly wait until the fireworks began.

When Ayris and Steve first separated, it had been Steve who moved out, taking up temporary residence with Jim Baxter, a small-time coke dealer better known to his rugby teammates as "Scuzzy" in honor of his disheveled appearance and seedy friends, and then with Dale Greenbaum, an investment banker better known to Steve's friends as "Joy Boy" for his suspected homosexuality. After Ayris moved to Marin County, Steve moved back into the house, taking in Pierce and Ed, who was also going through a marital split. Steve and Ed had become handshake partners on a fix-'er-up rental house; Steve put up the down payment, Ed agreed to do the fixing up. Steve had also bought another rental, a three-bedroom brick house right next to his two-story white clapboard. He had offered it to Ayris, but she had turned him down, deciding that living next door to each other was carrying the concept of a "chummy" separation too far.

Ed's subcontractor arrived that New Year's Eve morning to start putting in the floor. He brought along his twenty-two-year-old wife, and as soon as she walked in the door, the sexual energy between her and Steve was enough to light the Christmas tree. It didn't take long before they were upstairs, tearing off each other's clothes while her husband was downstairs installing flooring.

"You're gonna get yourself shot one of these days," warned Ed after the floor and the wife had been laid. He knew he was talking to thin air, and that once Grandpa "got on the sniff," he was hopeless.

Steve had staggered the arrival times of his three "dates." The first to arrive was Maureen, a psychiatric nurse. She was a buxom and broad-shouldered six-footer, and as Ed liked to point out to Steve, she had a mustache. Steve wasted no time in steering her upstairs, convincing her there was plenty of time before the party got rolling. When they came back down, the party was starting to crank into full swing, fifty guests tooting up their noisemakers and their nose candy, including the raven-haired Helene, his second date. She owned a boutique and a great body. He soon steered her upstairs too, convincing her they needed to do it before auld lang syne, luring her with white lines that Scuzzy had given him. In the past six months he had acquired a taste for weekend cocaine, thinking it helped him stay up and drink longer. By the time he and Helene came back downstairs, Donna, a stewardess who wore her auburn hair in a Katharine Hepburn topknot, had arrived in her red cocktail dress. She was his "main" date for the evening, the one he was planning to spend the night with.

It was nearing midnight when Maureen, the psychiatric nurse, realized that she wasn't going to be the one for the midnight kiss. She pinned him against the refrigerator, demanding to know what was going on. Ed was standing a couple feet away, smiling, watching his Grandpa squirm.

"Nice mustache," he howled.

Steve wiggled free, and when the clock struck twelve, he and Donna, the stewardess, ushered in the new year with a long and steamy kiss in the middle of the dining room. Watching nearby was Helene, the boutique owner. She waited until they were done, then pulled him aside and looked hard into his eyes. "How can someone so good-looking be such a complete asshole?" she asked.

Then she turned and stomped out the door. When the brick crashed through the bay window in the living room a few minutes later, sending glass flying all over the couples dancing, Steve couldn't be sure if the culprit was Maureen or Helene. And he really didn't care. He was on his way upstairs with his fourth woman of the day, tugging at the zipper on the back of Donna's red cocktail dress.

"Come in here," ordered Steve's father, motioning him into his office at South City Honda.

Steve readied himself for another confrontation. What would it be this time? Did it really make any difference? No matter what he did, it would never be good enough.

Frank waved a piece of paper over the desk. It was the $100,000 double-indemnity insurance policy that Steve had recently canceled on his homemade plane. Because the policy was in the company name, it had come to Frank's attention.

"Look at you!" boiled Frank. "You have the body of a twenty-year-old. You eat and exercise like you want to live to be a hundred and ten. And then you turn around and do something stupid like this. You buy these planes only a lunatic would fly, then you go cancel your insurance! What happens to Filaree if, God forbid, something happens to you? Have you ever thought about that? For once in your damn life, be responsible!"

Steve turned and walked away.

61

Larry

Man was born to live, to suffer, and to die, and what befalls him is a tragic lot. There is no denying this in the final end. But we must, dear Fox, deny it all along the way.
—Thomas Wolfe, *You Can't Go Home Again*

It was a cold, drizzly morning in January 1979. I was thirty-seven, supposedly prime time for a man to hit financial and emotional maturity. Instead, I had two ex-wives, two ex-careers, and an oxidized old Nova with a broken transmission. Its only gear was reverse. On the bright side, I'd just sold a story to *Northwest* magazine for $200, a first-person account of my Christmas gig as a department-store Santa, a job I rated just ahead of shoveling Doberman shit. Six Santas sharing the same beard— it was like breathing goat barf. But the check was in the mail.

I was rushing to get Sarah ready for school. She was in the first grade, and as she did every Tuesday, she had spent the night with me. I was still living in the unfinished attic of friends who had offered me a place to crash after Kathi and I split. I had two guest mattresses, one for Sarah and another for Wendy, thirteen, when she came down from Seattle.

I was getting around town by bus and on my bike. Usually, the friends with whom I was staying let me borrow one of their cars to take Sarah to school, but on this day they were gone . . . and we'd already missed the bus.

"I can't be late," Sarah instructed. Sternly.

I tossed her peanut butter and jelly sandwich into her Princess Leia lunchbox and we walked outside to the Nova in the driveway. That's where it had been parked for two months, inert, hopeless, gathering mildew.

"Maybe it fixed itself," I hoped.

I turned the ignition. It coughed and wheezed, belching carbon. But miraculously, it started. I brushed the dust off of Sarah's seat, then backed down the driveway and out onto the street. There was no use shifting. I just kept going in reverse . . . down the block, left at the corner, then seven miles backward through the morning traffic of Portland, Oregon. I stayed on side streets, sneaking across busy intersections, waiting for cars to clear the way. My neck began to get stiff. Drivers stared in disbelief. The drizzle had turned to a downpour, raindrops sticking to the rear windshield. I stuck my head out the window, squinting through the deluge. On the radio, KGW's Skywatch announced that the morning commute was going smoothly. Easy for them to say.

A block from Sarah's school, a police siren startled me. A cop signaled me to the curb. He said he'd been following me for three blocks. I could only take his word for it—I'd been focused on what was behind me. (Or was it what was in front of me?) I pleaded my case.

"I'm dropping off my daughter, then driving straight backward to Aamco," I promised.

He must have felt sorry for me—he let me go and bid me good luck. In front of Sarah's school, I handed her the lunchbox and kissed her goodbye. She hadn't said a word the whole drive, sitting quietly, accepting backward driving as just another of her father's quirks. After watching her walk up the steps and into the school, I backed away and steered the car to a deserted parking lot, where it sat for the next month collecting more mildew while I scraped together the money to tow it.

Several months passed. I sold a few more articles, got the transmission fixed, signed the final divorce papers, and moved into an upstairs flat in an English Tudor. I read *Loose Change,* the book chronicling the lives of three sorority sisters from Berkeley in the early sixties, and it got me to wondering about some of my long-lost fraternity brothers. Had they had as much trouble navigating through the turbulent waters of the last two decades as I had? Were they waiting for their checks in the mail? Were they driving backward through the deluge? I called Steve. He invited me to come down with my daughters in August for a week with him and Filaree at the Lair of the Bear, a family camp in the Sierras for Cal alumni. The previous year he had gone with Ayris—just before their separation—joining three other Sacramento Pi KAs and their families. I told him it sounded like great fun but I didn't have the $500 it would cost.

"I'll pay for it," he enthused. "Come on. Your daughters will have the time of their lives. So will you."

Steve and I were waiting in the checkout line of the Safeway near his house. It was the eve of our trip to the Lair of the Bear.

"That's her," he whispered, nodding toward the young woman at the register, the new love of his life.

Her name was Vicki and she would have surely won the prize as the prettiest grocery clerk in California. Steve hadn't come to buy groceries —he was there to drop off two tickets to a Boz Scaggs concert that he'd bought for her. She had all-world reddish-brown hair that hung to her waist in ringlets. Her angelic face was without makeup and not even her Safeway uniform could hide her shapely body. She was twenty-two, a single mom, and according to Steve, the most affectionate woman he had taken out in the last year, as well as the only one he couldn't get into bed. Not that he hadn't tried, including a trip in his plane to a Linda Ronstadt concert and the frog-jumping contest at the Calaveras County Fair.

"I'm going to miss you while you're gone," she said with a shy smile and a buttery-soft voice. Her big doe eyes were all over him. I was invisible.

Steve and I walked outside into the hot Sacramento night. As we neared his car, the sound of squealing tires turned our heads. A gray Oldsmobile Toronado was barreling straight at us, the eyes of the driver wild and full of hate. I dove for cover behind a light pole; Steve didn't budge, holding his ground, staring right into the face of the driver. At the last second, the Toronado swerved, missing him by inches, then fishtailed to a screeching halt.

"Stay away from my wife!" screamed the driver, Vicki's estranged husband.

Steve calmly walked toward the car, his hands in the pockets of his rugby shorts. "I don't see any wedding ring on her finger," he said, his voice as unruffled as a day at the park.

"Fuck you, asshole!"

"The way I see it," said Steve politely, "you have two choices. You can either drive away like a good boy. Or you can step out of the car and let me squish you like a little bug."

The guy floored it, squealing out of the parking lot and into the night. I was still cowering behind the light pole.

"He could've had a gun," I said. "Are you nuts?"

"If he wants to kill me, he can," Steve replied. "He can crawl through my window in the middle of the night. If you're gonna die, you're gonna die."

"But . . ."

He launched into an explanation of Seth's theory of death. "Human consciousness is not dependent on tissue," he said, rambling on about consciousness of atoms and molecules and cosmic metamorphosis. "We choose our own deaths," he continued. "You can sit at a desk and be uptight and die of a heart attack. Or you can crash into a tree at a hundred twenty miles an hour. It's your choice."

I was lost, dog-paddling in the wake of his intellectual and spiritual curiosity. "Let's go get a cocktail," I urged.

We went to Lord Beaverbrook's, and when it came time to leave, he tossed me the keys to his car. He was too drunk to drive. "I've learned my limits," he said.

The sound of the chow bell echoed through the sugar pines, calling the campers to breakfast. The ringing rattled every dendrite in my system—it had something to do with six straight nights of José Cuervo Gold at the 6,300-foot elevation.

I rolled over in my sleeping bag, squinting into the Sierra sunlight filtering through the canvas top of our wood-framed tent. Sarah, Wendy, and Filaree were also starting to stir in their bunks. Steve was already up and gone, which, considering what he had been through the night before, was a feat of herculean dimensions.

This was our next-to-last day at the Lair of the Bear. It had been, as Steve advertised, great family fun in the Sierras. It wasn't, however, a wilderness-survival camp, not with its flush toilets, laundry facilities, and the hum of the blow-dryers wafting through the pines. What it had been was endless activities for every age level—swimming, horseback riding, nature hikes, tennis, crafts, bingo, hootenannies, volleyball, cocktailing. It was three prepared meals a day, and pristine scenery; it was Cal spirit around the clock, and a staff of twenty-five wholesome students off the Berkeley campus to serve as camp counselors to supervise and recreate with the kids from breakfast until bedtime. Parents were free to wander the ponderosas. Out of 250 campers, Steve and I were the only single fathers. There was one single mom. Our tent was next to the tents of three other Pi KAs and their families, all three of them classmates of

Steve's at McClatchy High: Don Cobleigh, now a contractor in Pasadena; Russ Godt, a fellow Gun Club member at Cal and now a Sacramento stockbroker; Pete Donoghue, known as "Mumbles" in the fraternity, now a lawyer.

I stumbled out of the tent, surprised to see Steve in his rugby shorts hanging upside down in his gravity boots, suspended from a wire strung between two pine trees. "This is a hell of a way for a great pilot to start the day," he bellowed. He had already run six miles . . . in his work boots. I questioned whether I had enough stamina to walk to the mess hall.

The previous night we had stampeded through another bottle of Cuervo Gold, stumbling back to our tent after midnight. Soon after we crawled into our sleeping bags, a soft voice outside the tent whispered Steve's name. It was the single mom. He grabbed what was left of the tequila and did not return until just before dawn. He had just fallen asleep, again, when another voice called his name. "Papa, I don't feel good," Filaree cried. "I think I'm going to throw up." He nursed her through what was left of the night, rubbing her back, bringing her water, applying warm washcloths to her forehead. She finally fell back asleep as the sun crawled over the Sierras' granite cliffs. That's when he laced up his work boots and took off on his high-altitude run, capping it off with a twenty-minute hang in his gravity boots. Well, actually, it was only a fifteen-minute hang because the wire snapped, sending him plummeting headfirst into the dirt and pinecones.

The marquee event of that final day at the Lair of the Bear was the Blue versus Gold men's softball game. I was billed as Camp Gold's secret weapon. "I might not play," I lied. When game time rolled around, and the sound of batting practice echoed through the thin air, and the crowd filled the rickety bleacher seats next to the field, the testosterone rallied to the call. The field, carved out of a meadow strewn with ankle-buster potholes, tree stumps, and dirt clods the size of Iowa, was not to be confused with Yankee Stadium . . . or even Diamond 2 in Leesburg. But the ponderosas in right field, my power alley, were an inviting target 200 feet from home plate. In my first two at-bats, I jacked a couple of Reggie Jackson hit-'em-and-admire-'em shots. And as the script would have it, I came to the plate in the bottom of the seventh inning, bases loaded, two outs, our team trailing by two runs. The stuff Lair dreams are made of . . . a chance to bring glory to Camp Gold. But in the most daring and unheard-of strategy in the history of Lair softball, if not all of California sports, the opposing coach ordered me walked intentionally. With the bases loaded, no less! At a family camp!! I was furious. I was honored. I yelled for Steve, who was hitting behind me, to make them pay. He swung at the first pitch and connected solidly. He was a man of robust strength, not finesse, and as the ball left his bat, it had a landing site somewhere in Nevada written all over it. But alas, there was no joy in Camp Gold that day, for when the ball finally returned from its historic flight through the thin air, there was the Camp Blue roaming fielder waiting in a distant heather to gather it in.

It was a defeat quickly washed away with more Cuervo Gold. At the closing campfire that night under the stars, surrounded by our other fraternity brothers and our children, Steve and I stood shoulder to shoulder and joined hands with the other campers to sing "Hail to California." I got goose bumps, and only the night hid my teary eyes, saddened to see such a great week draw to a close.

Labor Day 1979, a day forever locked in my memory. I sat at my typewriter transcribing the thoughts and notes I'd gathered from my week with Steve at the Lair. I'd been back in Portland two days. I didn't know if it had been the salubrious mountain air, or the Cuervo Gold, or the close confines of two dads and three daughters in a dusty tent, but for whatever reason, Steve and I were connected, so much in common. Some might have called us "soul mates." I preferred to think of us as best friends.

Much of our time together at the Lair had been spent in quiet conversation. I told him of my idea to write a book about the goat brothers. He liked the idea. "You can live with me while you're working on it," he offered. "You won't have to worry about money."

He told me things I wouldn't have guessed—that he'd been married and a father when he lived in the fraternity . . . that he'd never been in a fistfight . . . that his parents drove him nuts . . . that he'd been busted three times for drunk driving. He was a walking contradiction: he had a deep and abiding intellectual curiosity, yet he so often searched for the brainless state; he had a hunter-gatherer-survivor mentality, yet he took chances as if he had a death wish; he had a strong belief in equal rights for women, yet he sometimes treated them as if they were nothing more than receptacles for his cum.

I got up from my desk and went into the kitchen to put a pot of homemade fish chowder on the stove to simmer. The phone rang. It was Sue Goodwin Chase, Steve's next-door neighbor; she had been a Tri Delt at Cal while we were Pi KAs. They had even gone to the Purple Passion Party together his freshman year. She and her husband were in the midst of a "trial separation" and Steve had rented her the house next to his.

"I've got the most horrible news in the whole world," she sobbed. "Steve crashed his plane. He's dead."

One minute I was at my desk writing about him, the next minute he was dead. I lay paralyzed on my bed, head buried in the pillow, moving only to pound the mattress with my fist. When I finally got up and walked into the kitchen three hours later, the pot of chowder was scorched. I poured myself a shot of Cuervo Gold from a bottle Steve and I had started at the Lair. No salt. No lime. Just tears.

I drove to Sacramento for the funeral, listening to the plaintive refrain of Jackson Browne's "For a Dancer," my requiem to Steve, a song about trying to figure out what happens when someone dies, a someone you'd thought would always be around. Arriving at his house, I was greeted by a scene previewing *The Big Chill*. The Temptations on the stereo. People dancing. Lines of cocaine. Shots of tequila. Clouds of marijuana smoke. These were not the people he knew from Auto Row. Or his family. Or his goat brothers. It was the wild side of his life . . . rugby players, drinking mates, Marine buddies, hippies in ponytails, beautiful women. The house was packed. I'd never met any of them. People hugging, dancing, singing, crying. Ed Forrest stood in the middle of the dining room and threw back his head. "I want my Grandpa!" he howled.

The front door opened and in came five men who had been in the Gun Club at Cal with Steve. They were dressed in suits and ties and starched shirts. It was Wall Street walking into the New Age. The first to enter was Terry Holberton, who had been the one to talk Steve into joining the Marines in Pensacola and was now a stockbroker; he was followed by Don Cobleigh, who had spent two years in the Peace Corps in Kenya after Cal, earned a master's at Stanford Business School, and then went to work for his father-in-law's successful construction company in Pasadena. When Don had received the phone call informing him of the plane crash, he was painting the trim on the deck by his swimming pool. (It would be six years before he resumed painting.)

Don and I shook hands. Our words were forced, stiff, uncomfortable. His eyes nervously darted around the room as if he expected the vice squad to bust down the door at any second. He was clearly troubled by the disparity between the Steve he thought he knew and the apparent nature of his life in the last year. Don had been in Steve's house many times—but only when Ayris was still there. It had been well furnished and immaculately kept, the standard, adult, family home with a slight *Whole Earth Catalogue* flavor. Except for what Don saw as Steve's occasional bouts with alcohol and a little trendy mysticism, he thought him to be on solid footing, a person who had worked hard at his business, a loving father, and when sober, thoughtful and unfailingly courteous. Don had even thought him a devoted, sensitive husband. But the house he had entered this night seemed to him to belong to someone else, reminding him of the rooms at the Pi KA house—dirty, messy, no furniture, bad lighting. Worse, the people in the house were strangers who seemed to be sleazy lowlifes, loud, stoned, and obnoxious. He was disturbed by the pot and the cocaine.

Unable to reconcile the house and the people in it with the Steve he knew, Don, along with the other Gun Clubbers, left. After they had gone, I walked out on the front porch for air. Sitting on the swing Steve had hung for Filaree was a young woman, swaying slowly back and forth. She was beautiful, celestial in the moonlight. She leaned back in the swing, her waist-length auburn hair flowing to the ground. It was Vicki, the twenty-two-year-old Safeway checker. The tears in her eyes matched mine. I stood before her, silent and afraid. She put her arms around me. We stood under Steve's tree, holding each other, not saying a word. She didn't know my name. At dawn we fell into his bed. "Steve," she whispered. "Yes," I said.

The funeral was at Holy Spirit Church, where Steve had gone for confession as a teenager, and to be baptized, and to ask for advice when he and Linda were trying to fight off their teenage urges. It was the same church he and Ayris had been married in. The pallbearers carried the casket into the church, five fraternity brothers and Gun Clubbers, somber in their dark suits, eyes straight ahead; the sixth pallbearer was Ed Forrest, unshaven, bags under his eyes, glancing down the pews, winking to his rugby teammates. He was wearing Steve's slippers, no socks, sunglasses, and a dark purple suit with bright orange pinstripes, two sizes too small. Steve had bought it for him, paying five dollars at a thrift shop, so that Ed would have a suit to wear on their rugby tour to Ireland that was scheduled to leave that day.

I delivered the eulogy. I wore a beige corduroy sports coat and a blue striped shirt that I had taken from Steve's closet that morning. As I spoke, my hand rested on his closed casket. The unrehearsed words came automatically, coming from outside of me, an aural visitation, an unexpected gift of eloquence, unmediated emotions, too strong to control. I watched myself, above the room, taking it all in. I could see his parents sitting rigid in the front pew, stoic, brave, austere in their grief. Next to them sat Ayris, delicate and beautiful, tears rimming her eyes. She had last seen Steve when he dropped off Filaree after the Lair of the Bear.

When Ayris had received the phone call from Steve's parents that he was dead, she was home with Filaree, making whole-wheat pancakes, using a wheat grinder that Steve had made for her. She fell down crying, and Filaree, four, ran to the neighbors and declared, "This is the worst thing that ever happened." Ayris would never use the wheat grinder again. She and Steve had not yet filed for divorce, and there would remain a lingering sense of doubt, a relationship unresolved. Her healing would be long and painful.

Steve's first wife, Linda, and their son Dennis, fifteen, did not attend the funeral. Although they lived only five miles away in a large two-story house in the exclusive Arden Oaks neighborhood of Sacramento, they had not seen him in thirteen years. Linda had done well, owning three successful party-supply shops in the area with her third husband. Her first reaction when she heard the news of the crash was that Steve had had the last word once again. "I always knew he'd never die of old age," she said, struggling to cope with her resentment and the final loss of her first love. In Steve's obituary, Filaree was listed as his only child; there was no mention of Dennis, who had inherited his father's "bend it till it breaks" approach to life. When he was informed of his father's death, Dennis's reaction was: "Why the hell should I care? He was an asshole."

The day following Steve's funeral his father appeared in the driveway of his house. Frank walked to the garage and spotted a lawn mower Steve had borrowed and failed to return.

"Damn you, Steve," he uttered, eyes vacant, words barely audible. "I told you to bring this back when you were done."

I remained in Sacramento, staying in Steve's house, sleeping in his bed, consumed by his energy. I wore his clothes, dated his women, toasted his memory with shots of Cuervo Gold, wallowing in grief. I couldn't, as Jackson Browne's lyrics had urged, dance the sorrow away. I began to piece together facts about the crash. Dennis Velucci, his new car sales manager, who also had a pilot's license, was also killed in the crash. They had gone down in a pear orchard near the Sacramento River at Courtland where Steve had picked pears as a teenager and smoked dope until he was blue in the face trying to flunk his draft physical in 1966. Because the aircraft had dual controls, it was still not clear who was flying the plane. According to the initial investigation, the plane was practicing touch-and-go landings on a nearby slough, swooping low like a crop duster, skimming the water, then taking off again. On its third pass, it climbed back up over the pear orchard, lost power, and fell vertically to earth like a rock, nose-first. The engine, which was mounted on top directly over the cockpit, came straight down on top of them, killing both men instantly. The accident was still under investigation, a lot of questions unanswered. I had heard two rumors that were unsettling. One was that Steve allegedly had flown drunk two nights earlier, and there was a possibility that he had been drinking before the fatal flight. The second rumor, and equally troubling, was that the police had found several grams of cocaine in the plane. This rumor had it that he was involved in a big cocaine deal, agreeing to fly the goods up from Southern California, and this had been a training run. I didn't want to believe it. I had never seen him do cocaine.

The family came and took away most of his possessions. I continued to camp in his bedroom, a spartan existence, no electricity, only a mattress on the hardwood floor. I lived by candlelight and tuna. One morning I walked into the living room, startled to see Steve's mother standing there, walled inside her grief. She said she had come to look for a box of his personal papers—his estate was in total disarray—but as I watched her looking slowly around the room, I suspected she had really come in hopes of finding her son sitting in a chair, reading a book, alive and well. That's what I was hoping too.

I kept thinking about what Steve had said about how we choose our own deaths. It was so prophetic. He had lived his whole life flying dangerously close to the canyon walls and that's how he died; his Mr. Lucky routine had finally run out. I tried to read *Seth Speaks*, but I didn't grasp the message. During the days, I attempted to write, but the words wouldn't come. It was too painful. I returned to Portland.

In December, a month after the U.S. Embassy in Teheran had been overrun, I was drinking with a friend in the Veritable Quandary in downtown Portland, closing time funneling in. I signaled the waitress for a last shot of tequila.

"You gotta stop mourning this guy and get on with your life," my friend advised.

I left the bar angry—at Steve for foolishly dying . . . at the Iranians . . . at myself . . . at my ex-wives . . . at everything. Why couldn't things be happy and bright like they were at the start of the decade when I was still a baseball player, still hitched to my big-league dream, still married to Denise and thinking it would be forever? What a lousy ten years—my best friend plowing into a pear orchard, two divorces, two monthly child-support checks, two abandoned careers. I had fifty dollars in my checking account and a junk heap for a car. I had moved out of my flat and temporarily in with Julie, whom I had been dating for several months. She was thirty, recently graduated from law school, upwardly mobile, a Northwest version of Cybill Shepherd, so pure of heart and spirit that I felt like a big crumbum for sponging off of her. Given my state of mind, I had no business even inferring that I was ready for a committed relationship. I knew it and she knew it. But she let me stay with her anyway.

As I headed home from the bar, the streets of downtown were deserted. I stopped for a red light, looked both ways, then ran it, repeating the process for the next three blocks. Then I saw the flashing red and blue lights.

The cop asked me if I'd been drinking. I lied by eight drinks. He asked me to heel-and-toe. I almost fell off the planet. He asked me to recite the alphabet. I did pretty well until I got to D.

In the back seat of the squad car on the way to the precinct, with the handcuffs cutting into my wrists, I leaned forward, talking through the cage. "Hey, Copper, why don't you go catch some real crooks?" I asked. He wasn't amused. He was even less amused when I stiffened, refusing to let him put the handcuffs back on me after I'd blown a 1.6 on the Breathalyzer. Reaching behind me, he grabbed a handful of hair and jerked me to the floor, his big black boot pressing on the back of my head. My nose smashed into the concrete. He yanked my arms behind me, slapping on the handcuffs. The pain shot from my fingers to my shoulder, the same shoulder that had been separated in another drunken disaster, the night my big-league career ended in San Francisco.

In the drunk tank, I curled in the corner, head down, shoulder throbbing. Now Steve and I had something else in common . . . arrested for drunk driving. Julie bailed me out.

The good news was that a new decade was coming.

PART FOUR

Middle Age
(The Eighties)

The trick is to make sure you don't die waiting for prosperity to come.
—Lee Iacocca

62

Jim

The day will come when everyone will be famous for fifteen minutes.
—Andy Warhol

Dressed in his sky-blue flight suit, he stood at the podium on a platform waiting for the next question from the crowd gathered at the mall. He was in Cincinnati . . . or was it Cleveland? After six whirlwind days on a NASA public-speaking tour it was hard to keep track. The malls and the Rotary Clubs were all starting to look alike. Smile. Look heroic. Stand up straight. Uphold the image. Be the right stuff. He was this week's Astronaut at the Mall.

"Did you go to the moon?" a small boy asked.

"No, that wasn't me," Jim replied. Some in the crowd began to drift away, off to resume their shopping. It didn't bother Jim. The limelight for shuttle astronauts, he knew, was transitory, a Warholian blink of the public eye. He was fulfilling one of the 3,000 speaking requests annually received by NASA (most of which were now specifically asking for Sally Ride, scheduled to be the first American woman in space, or one of the program's black astronauts).

He checked his watch, anxious to get the questions wrapped up so he could get back to Houston and Vallarie, pregnant with their second child. This American Hero thing wasn't part of his laid-back, unassuming, family-man personality. He pointed to a wide-eyed boy in the front row.

"What's it like in outer space?" the boy asked. Jim patiently explained that he hadn't actually been in space yet, and that he was still in astronaut training (or "Ass-Can," as the veteran astronauts called the astronaut candidates). More people in the crowd eased away.

There had been little glamour in his first two years of training. It was basic astronaut school, learning all about the shuttle, step by step. He had discovered early on that the shuttle program, unlike the Navy, wasn't about macho take-it-to-the-envelope flying. It was learning to do it by the book. Endless memorizing. There was a manual for everything; the classroom training was intense, five hours of lectures a day—NASA spared no expense in bringing in the best instructors in astronomy, physics, orbital mechanics, flight systems, geology. Every former astronaut was brought in to talk about his mission. There were no written tests, a legacy of the original seven astronauts, who demanded that there be no competition for grades, no washouts in astronaut school. There was also no required physical fitness program. Everybody was on his or her own, expected to keep in shape. Jim jogged three miles at lunch every day, which, compared to the exertions of most of the other thirty-four astronaut candidates, was a warm-up trot.

He had come into the program expecting to be confronted with a collection of ten-gallon egos, given the star-studded résumés of the candidates. But to his surprise, what he met was a refreshing "gee whiz, I can't believe they picked me" humility. The big egos had been weeded out in the exhaustive selection process. He had never felt more simpatico with a group in his life—they called themselves "TFNG" (thirty-five new guys). In Vietnam, there had been a blood bond with the men in his squadron, a union forged by the insanity of war and the primordial instinct of survival. TFNG wasn't operating under such a deadly shadow, but it was an instantly close-knit fraternity. To Jim, this was what fraternity was *really* all about. What mattered was not how many madras shirts he had or whom he was dating, but rather the shared goal of riding a firebreathing rocket into the cosmos and sharing that brief, exhilarating moment in history at the top of the pyramid. With the TFNG the exclusivity of race and gender had been eliminated. There was an esprit de corps, congeniality, belief in the cause, singleness of purpose, and passion. Everyone was equal in pay and rank. And with but one or two exceptions, they all loved to party, Ox included. In Houston they gathered regularly at Jason's, a bar near the Space Center. And when the group went on the road to tour NASA facilities around the country (such as Huntsville, Alabama, or Cocoa Beach, Florida) or NASA contractors (such as Morton Thiokol in Colorado or Rockwell Aviation in California), the parties were uproarious. Mission specialist Judy Resnik, whose résumé included a Ph.D. in electrical engineering, classical piano, gourmet cooking, and perfect scores on her SATs, renamed Jim the "Disco Ox."

Jim asked the crowd at the mall for one last question. A man in back raised his hand. "Why spend all this money on outer space when we have so many problems here on earth?"

Jim smiled politely. He was prepared for the question—it usually came up at every press conference or public appearance. In truth, one of his main purposes on these NASA public relations tours was to sell the shuttle program to the Rotarians and the shoppers in the malls, to justify the huge sums of money being spent. All the astronauts had received instructions on the right things to say . . . quotes from Carl Sagan and Socrates about societies that lose their vision and their look to the future dying on the vine . . . or about man's need to grow and to explore . . . or about keeping up with the Russians.

Jim didn't need to be instructed in the virtue of the cause. He realized that yes, there were homeless and hungry people right there in Ohio, and yes, $800 million was a lot to spend to get a coffee-table book of pictures of the lines on Venus. "But without exploration," he concluded, "man will worm into the ground and perish. Who's to say what we will find out there?"

It was 1981. Vallarie was in the hospital after giving birth to Tori, their second daughter. Jim was about to give her a present.

"It better not be something stupid like a Dustbuster," she said. "If it plugs in, it's not a present."

Vallarie could testify to the unglamorous life of the astronaut's wife. And she usually did. For her it had been a lot of nights alone. It seemed as if Jim was on the road half the time, either off playing astronaut somewhere or else up in Dallas on weekends flying with the Navy Reserve to make extra money. They had recently purchased a new house in Friendswood, a suburb close to the Johnson Space Center, and money was tight, what with two kids in diapers and Vallarie no longer working as a nurse. It also seemed to Vallarie that on the days when Jim was home, he was always up to his elbows in one of his many home projects. His latest was a homemade plane that he and fellow astronaut and close friend Dick Scobee had invested in. It was a two-seat, open-cockpit

Starduster II, made of wood and fabric. The two men planned to fly it cross-country, even though it would have no radio.

"Hope it's not a box of chocolates," said Vallarie, eyeing her present. "My butt's too big already."

Not that Vallarie didn't appreciate how hard her husband worked or how tedious much of it was. He had just spent six months commuting to Southern California, where he spent five days a week sitting in a shuttle simulator monitoring the flight software for the reentry system being produced by Rockwell Aviation in Downey. Boring stuff. Maybe even make-work. But it was for the good of the team, a necessary part of astronaut limbo each candidate went through waiting to be assigned a flight.

The first of the nineteen scheduled shuttle launches was still two years away, but the assignments were starting to be made. To the astronauts, NASA's method of assigning flights was totally arcane, unpredictable. They had no input. Achievement was now being measured in who had been selected for a flight—the haves and the have-nots. Those who had were the anointed, going off in their little groups to begin training for the specifics of their flight; those who weren't selected were told nothing, left to sit and wait on the sidelines, like kids on the playground not picked for the kickball game. Jim was still among the unassigned. The wait was torturous. But he hadn't given up on being chosen for Mission 11 aboard the *Challenger,* which, as far as he was concerned, was the best flight, an attempt to rescue Solar Max, a satellite that had failed ten months after being launched.

He handed the package to Vallarie. "It's not very big," she lamented. "Oh, I bet it's a diamond necklace. How sweet, Ox, you shouldn't have."

She tore off the wrapping, skeptically surveying the contents. It was a hardbound copy of *Growing Up Free: Raising Your Child in the '80s.*

"You're such a romantic," she scoffed.

"Open it," he calmly suggested.

On the inside cover she discovered the handwritten poem he had composed. As she began to read, she cried:

> What will we do with the rest of our lives now that having babies is
>   through?
> Why don't we sit back and contemplate what's the best course to
>   pursue?
> It may seem that a chapter has ended,
> Especially with what you've been through,
> But the story's just getting started,

A family now, not just "me and you."
Let's first raise them with peace and tranquillity
And most of all love and stability.
We'll help them to see and to listen and learn
And to strive to develop your great family concern.
They'll laugh and have fun and love everyone.
And as the years ramble by
We'll enjoy every one
And one of these days, who knows?
Maybe a grandson.
But let's not forget what's foremost and yet so hard to keep
  properly in view.
What started all this and will simply remain
Is the love I developed for you.

                                             Love, Jim

63

Loren

Crime, like virtue, has its degrees.
—Racine, *Phèdre*

Lompoc Prison Camp, located next to Lompoc Federal Penitentiary on the site of the old Vandenberg Air Force Base, sixty miles north of Santa Barbara, is known as the country club of the federal prison system, with tennis courts, a six-hole par-3 golf course, a fully equipped gym, and no fences to stop any of the 400 inmates from taking a stroll through the eucalyptus trees and off into the pastoral countryside. Its prestigious alumni roster includes Watergate bad boys H. R. Haldeman and John Ehrlichman.

In 1982 U.S. District Court Judge Lawrence Karlton sentenced Harold Loren Hawley to one year in Lompoc and three years' probation for failure to file income-tax returns. Loren, thirty-nine, pleaded guilty to charges of not filing returns on $623,000 in income over a three-year period. As part of a plea bargain, additional charges of failing to report $483,785 in income in 1976 and 1978 were dismissed. According to the U.S. Attorney, the unreported income stemmed primarily from real estate commissions and finders' fees received from several large ranch and apartment building sales. Loren was quick to point out that he was being sentenced for *failure to file* rather than the more serious charge of tax *evasion*.

"It's a matter of degrees," he said.

After being sentenced, he flew to Lompoc by private plane, then took a cab to the prison camp, arriving at the gate wearing a powder-blue jogging suit. He had his golf clubs slung over one shoulder, his tennis racket over the other.

"Hold all my calls," he told the officials at the desk.

Lompoc was a work camp, primarily a cattle slaughterhouse and dairy. Loren's job was to hook up the milking machines to the cows every morning at five o'clock. Then he was free to open up the camp kitchen and fix himself a steak-and-eggs breakfast, maybe with some hash browns on the side. After that his day was pretty much his own.

He had come to prison camp with his usual "I've never had a bad day in my life" attitude. In fact, he claimed he was happy to be there, looking forward to the break from business and phone calls. "This is a vacation," he said. He wouldn't have to worry about his mother hounding him every day; he wouldn't have to worry about Rita, his new semi-regular girlfriend in Phoenix, bugging him about a commitment. There were those who speculated that prison was a way for him to escape the heat from deals that had raised eyebrows in Arizona. Loren just laughed at those accusations, reiterating his declaration that he'd never done a deal that wasn't clean.

He liked to spend his Lompoc mornings reading and relaxing in his bunk. In the first month he polished off James Clavell's *Shōgun* and *Tai-Pan*. In the bunk next to him was Ed, a felon who had decided that Loren was just about the smartest guy in the history of Western civilization. Ed had a potbelly, bad teeth, scabs on his arms, a Texas accent, a propensity to use the word "nigger," and a two-year sentence for mail fraud. He was hoping Loren would be his mentor and teach him the art of the deal after their release. He also wanted Loren to come with him out to the Winnebago.

The Winnebago was a weekly recreation arranged by a San Francisco pimp. It rolled into the parking lot every Tuesday afternoon and a steady stream of inmates headed off to greet it and the hookers inside. Loren declined to join the fun. "This is a vacation in all ways," he said. And besides, Tuesday afternoon was his time to go to the hobby shop to work on his leather belt.

When he first arrived in camp, the inmates suspected he was a narc. But after deciding he was a legitimate tax evader, they besieged him with can't-miss business schemes for the outside—gold, oil, real estate. To handle the requests for advice, he set up office hours in the evening for consultation. He also appointed himself the one-man entertainment and athletic director, determined to create one big happy fraternity: he turned Thursday nights into Guacamole and Domino Night; he won the camp racquetball and tennis doubles championships (although his tennis partner was shot and killed in a robbery five days after his release); he coached the camp softball team to victory in the big game of the year against the inmates in the maximum-security prison next to the camp, bringing the crowd in the big yard to its feet when he got into a heated argument after a close play at the plate and pushed the ump, a convict by the name of "Dump Truck" who was serving ten years for taking a crowbar to the side of another inmate's head.

"I don't give a shit about any crowbar," he told Ed. "He blew the goddamn call."

The prison camp was buzzing. It wasn't every day that a big-name NFL quarterback was coming to visit one of their own. As much as Loren was looking forward to seeing Craig and ironing out some kinks in their business deals, he was even more jacked up about the big basketball game that evening. The basketball games in the prison gym had become the hottest entertainment ticket in camp, standing room only, 300 inmates screaming for blood.

Craig pulled into camp in his big, shiny car. He had recently retired after eighteen seasons in pro football, quitting the game as the league's oldest player, having endured sixteen operations on his knees, shoulders, and elbow. But he hadn't come to talk football or compare scars—he was concerned with the money he had invested in Oil Tech, the oil rig leasing company owned by Loren. It was a venture that had started off hot, its penny stock skyrocketing, written up in *Time*. On Loren's advice, Craig had pumped money into it in hope of righting his financial ship. But now the bottom was starting to fall out, and new venture capital was needed, and Craig was worried he was going to lose a bundle. Again. Shades of the UC Corner fiasco.

Craig's visit was a short one. He felt uncomfortable with the fanfare his arrival had caused and with seeing his old college buddy in prison. Assured by Loren that Oil Tech would be okay, he headed on down the highway; Loren headed on down to the cracker-box gym, where his aggressive style of play had already elevated him to the status of camp legend . . . at least in Ed's mind. The games were full court, with team jerseys, heavy betting, elbows flying, bodies bouncing off the concrete walls at the ends of the court. It was Loren's kind of basketball . . . rough-and-tumble rugby-style. And this game was a grudge rematch—

the first one nearly had ended in a riot, 300 inmates refusing to return to the "dorms" after the game, the guards finally having to move in to restore order.

It did not take Loren long in the rematch to incite the crowd, turning the gym into bedlam. A six-eight slab of black steel known as "Big John," who allegedly once had a tryout with the Seattle SuperSonics, was sailing in for a lay-up on a fast break. Loren, the lone defender back to stop him, reached out and clotheslined him with a forearm, knocking Big John's feet out from under him. Everybody in the gym gasped when they heard the air rush out of his lungs when he hit the floor. Out cold. The guards had to be summoned again to quiet the frenzied crowd.

Loren's team won the game and the legend was secure. The day he was paroled, 100 inmates turned out to say goodbye. Because of good behavior, he served less than half his sentence.

Rita was pregnant . . . and wanted to keep the baby. Loren was emphatically opposed, even though he had openly encouraged her to get pregnant.

"I think you should have it taken care of," he said.

It was spring 1983. Rita was thirty-three; Loren was forty. They had met four years earlier at Houlihan's, a Phoenix nightclub. Loren had spotted her across the dance floor and moved right in. "Hey, darlin', what's your name?" he asked. She was hard to miss: five-nine, blond, blue-eyed, Scandinavian. By the end of the evening he had invited her to his house in the hills above the city. "I want you to come and see my world," he said. When they pulled up into the driveway in his Cadillac and she saw the small fleet of cars and the sprawling four-bedroom ranch house and the big swimming pool and the pinball machine in the den, she was astonished. "Is this your parents' house?" she asked in all seriousness. She was from the poor side of town—her father had deserted the family when she was a small girl. In high school she had been a pom-pom girl and a queen's attendant for homecoming, but she didn't go to college. She was working as a salesperson in major appliances for Sears and was on the rebound from an abusive relationship. As Loren poured her a glass of Dom Pérignon that first night, she was impressed. She thought he was a good dancer, good talker, "smart as hell," funny, good-looking . . . or as she told her friends the next day, "the whole package." She was also positive the competition for him had to be "unbelievable." When he had moved in for a kiss, she took a step back. "I think you're out of my league," she said. Nevertheless, they began dating on a semi-regular basis. At first, Rita made no demands or asked no questions when he dropped out of sight for weeks at a time. When she began to press him, not for a commitment, but at least for a brief accounting of where he went and what he did, he made it clear that if she wanted to keep seeing him, she better back off. "I'm doing my business," he said. He told her how much he'd already changed his lifestyle for her. "But do you love me?" she asked. He threw his arms up like a Shakespearean actor. "Love?" he intoned. "What's love got to do with it?"

For Rita, it had everything to do with it. As the relationship started to drag on, Loren satisfied with the status quo, always off chasing the next deal, she pushed for some sort of promise. She'd asked if he'd like to have kids and he said, "Sure, but not now." He told her of his dream to someday move back to his grandparents' ranch, the scene of his fondest childhood memories; it would be the perfect place to raise children—hopefully boys—away from the hustle of the city. But he wasn't ready for that yet, he said. There were too many things he still needed to accomplish. And besides, there was no mention of her being the "lucky gal" to get to share this dream with him.

Rita was positive she knew when and where she got pregnant. It was at the Sheraton Hotel in Denver when they were there for Craig's fortieth-birthday party. What made that weekend stand out for her was the fact that Loren had invited her to come to Denver with him. She was usually excluded whenever Craig and Loren got together, including two Super Bowl parties. In fact, one of her most hurtful times was when he told her that she didn't fit in with that crowd. She cried a lot over that one. She thought Craig was a negative influence on Loren and that the two of them acted like little kids around each other.

But the tears she shed over not getting invited to the Super Bowl parties couldn't match the ones when he asked her to get an abortion. "I won't do it," she asserted. "I'm a Christian." She was going to have the baby, with or without his involvement.

Loren was sure that he and Rita didn't belong together, and he had no trouble explaining why: she wasn't college-educated or well traveled; she was jealous; she was insecure; she demanded too much of his time and energy; she thought small time. "I don't give a shit about your crummy little job or what so-and-so in the shoe department said or where your manager is going on his two-week vacation," he told her. "I'm not a Sears kind of guy."

Nevertheless, he promised he would accept financial responsibility for their child. Other than that, there were no guarantees. He called his mother and asked her to come to Phoenix to "monitor the situation."

Genevieve agreed, but as far as she was concerned, Rita was not smart enough and was too possessive, definitely not the woman for her son. "I don't know what you see in her," she told Loren. And she told Rita she was wasting her time. "You might as well forget him, Rita," she said. "You're never going to know how to handle him. You don't understand him. You want more than he'll give you."

Genevieve was struggling with the direction her son's life had taken. She couldn't understand how he could be so cavalier about having gone to prison. Or why he was so attracted to money and always had to be the big spender. "It goes against the old-fashioned country values he was raised with," she said. And his way with women troubled her as well. Girls were ruining him, she believed. "He doesn't respect them," she said. "It's because they've always run after him, fawning all over him, making it too easy. He's never had a challenge with a woman in his life— it's a game to him. He works hard to capture one, then dumps her. The only one he ever really loved was Lisa. Now . . . she was special. I was proud to be seen with her. What a beauty. She would have made such a good homemaker. She was the kind who would make cookies and massage his shoulders when he came home. She appreciated fine china and nice linens. Rita's a paper-plate kind of girl." Loren reminded his mother that she hadn't been all that hot on Lisa either when he was going with her.

In November 1983, Rita gave birth to a son named Garrett Loren Hawley. Genevieve was at the hospital. Loren wasn't. He hadn't seen or talked to Rita in five months.

64

Ron

Simplify, simplify.
—Thoreau, *Walden*

Ron's life entering the eighties was a violin concerto compared to the cacophony of the bongo drums that had played daily in his head a decade earlier. He was a man who had spent the sixties and seventies in the clutches of introspection, trying to take stock and make some sense of it all. Whereas during that same time Loren or Steve would have looked at a wall in the road ahead and simply revved up to charge right through it, and whereas Jim would have looked at that same wall and figured out a way to catapult himself over it . . . Ron would have stopped in his tracks, looked intently at the wall, analyzed why it was there, what it was made of, whether or not a tunnel was possible, then he would have covered his eyes and walked away, pretending it wasn't there, getting lost on his way to his new destination.

His new destination going into the eighties was inner tranquillity . . . and to get Anna off his back . . . and to be a better father . . . and to pass his architect's licensing exam . . . and maybe even to settle down with Bertena. He was tired of everything being so jumbled. He wanted to simplify, simplify.

. . . .

He was living with Bertena and her thirteen-year-old son in her house in Yuba City, commuting to his job as an architectural associate with the State Department of Parks and Recreation in Sacramento. One of the things that had first impressed Bertena about him, in addition to his nice looks and gentle manner, was the fact that when they first started dating he would drive thirty-five miles from Sacramento to Yuba City every night to see her. He even moved in temporarily with her brother so he could be closer. She was a little gun-shy at the time, coming off her second divorce, but when he persisted, she figured that if this guy was willing to go to all that trouble, he must really like her. She pretty much had to go on his actions, though, because when it came to expressing his affection, there were no mushy soliloquies. Moments of intimacy were rare, especially after he began burning the midnight oil studying for his upcoming licensing exam.

Passing the test would not only be a big boost to his career and salary, it was crucial to his self-esteem. He was a man obsessed. "Stop saying you're not going to pass," said Bertena. "You'll do great." He had converted a shed in the backyard into a study room. Bertena was amazed at how he could be so handy and at the same time so messy; his room was cluttered with papers and blueprints, his drafting table barely visible. He was also forgetful. "Have you seen my glasses?" he'd ask. "They're on top of your head," she'd reply. His lack of attention to manners and style drove her crazy—grooming and wardrobe appeared to be afterthoughts. "You gotta get rid of those ugly polyester pants," she advised. But her advice usually went unheeded as he sailed along in his little cloud. Most of the time she couldn't even get him to argue. She'd call from work on a Friday night and say she was going to have a couple drinks with "the gals" and would be home around eight, then not come rolling in until four in the morning. The next morning he'd be all chipper and happy, asking her if she had a good time, no complaints about watching her son all evening. That she would sometimes go out with male friends didn't bother him. But she wouldn't have minded a good spat now and then to clear the air.

Bertena was the only woman he had been with since splitting up with Anna in 1969. His idea when he moved in was to keep it simple, no heavy demands, no wild spats. Moving in with Bertena, however, hadn't made it any easier with Anna. As far as Bertena was concerned, Anna was a "pain in the ass, always bitching about money." Anna accused Bertena of breaking up her family. Whenever Royce came to visit, he and Phil, Bertena's son, fought like pit bulls, neither of them appreciating Ron's attempt at mediation.

Things were not turning out to be quite as simple as Ron had hoped. He did, however, pass his exam to become a licensed architect . . . sixteen years after graduating from Cal . . . and was promoted to senior architect. He owed his success, he said, to Bertena.

It was a birthday party for a friend of Bertena's at the Ride Hotel, an old speakeasy on the Sacramento River. Normally, Ron was reluctant to attend parties, preferring to spend his free time going to movies or working on projects around the house. But for this occasion, Bertena talked him into coming . . . a decision she would regret.

They had moved from her house in Yuba City to a three-bedroom tract home that Ron had bought in North Sacramento for $500 down on an FHA loan arranged by John "Swampfox" Stassi, an ex-pledge brother of his and Loren's. It was a fix-'er-upper, Ron tackling a major remodel. Bertena had no doubt it was going to look great when he finished, but in the meantime, they were living in chaos—she would vacuum and polish, only to return a short while later to find him sanding the walls, sawdust flying everywhere.

Ron followed Bertena out onto a deck at the restaurant, where they were introduced to Connie Lesley, a tall blonde, radiant, high-cheek-boned, self-possessed, golden. As Bertena scooted off to mingle, Ron and Connie sat and talked. Connie, thirty-five, had a Ph.D. in education from Cal and was a reading specialist for the Modesto School District. Her fiancé was a lawyer. When Bertena returned to the deck forty-five minutes later and they were still deep in conversation, she didn't think much of it. After all, she wasn't supposed to be the jealous type, and if ever she'd met a one-woman man, Ron was it.

But a week later when she asked Ron to go with her up to Yuba City to visit her father, suffering from cancer, and he begged out, telling her he was driving down to Stockton, where Connie lived, to confer with her about a remodel she was considering in her kitchen, she began to suspect. In the weeks ahead, Ron and Connie continued to meet, and it wasn't always to discuss new cabinets. She was urbane, sophisticated, and talked about art and movies and things that didn't interest Bertena.

But each visit with Connie was a trip to Guilt Central. Bertena had helped nurture him in his recovery; she was the salt of the earth; and more than anyone else, she believed in him. But he felt something with Connie that wasn't there with Bertena. Part of it was physical—Connie had that blue-eyed blonde look he'd always been attracted to.

Bertena was distraught, although it was hard for her to get too self-righteous, having had a couple quick affairs in the earlier days of the relationship. But Ron had become her best friend, her lover, her buddy.

"If you'd rather be with her just tell me," she cried.

"We're just friends," he insisted.

Bertena couldn't eat; she lost thirty pounds in two months. She began drinking heavily, missing work, confronting Ron every time he walked in the door. Finally, she packed her bags and moved out, eventually ending up in the Bay Area.

Ron's affair with Connie was short-lived—she decided to marry the lawyer. Ron and Bertena reconciled, and six months after she'd moved out, they were married in a small ceremony in Reno in August 1981. The honeymoon was in Europe, taken in conjunction with a rugby trip with the Old Boys, a team Steve had played for. At the age of forty-one, Ron was one of the oldest and least rowdy players on the team, but he still enjoyed the competition, even if it took him days to recuperate after each game.

After the honeymoon, Bertena continued to live in the Bay Area, where she had been transferred with the phone company. As a manager she was making good money and couldn't afford to move back to Sacramento; and Ron had been promoted and didn't want to move either. They lived apart during the week, getting together on weekends, taking a "quality time" approach to marriage. He took her on her first-ever trip to L.A. to meet his parents. Betty's health was slipping, but Ralph was spry and active, spending his days painting and working on his inventions, his latest device a perpetual-motion machine that could "eliminate the need for fuel." Bertena thought Ralph was just about the sweetest man she'd ever met, and laughed at the way he and Ron traded jabs at each other's art and architecture. She sensed that underneath the sparring they were both quite proud of each other. Ralph was indeed proud of the way his son had rebounded, convinced Ron was over any complex he had about race, believing that whatever problems he had about it were a case of confusion rather than denial.

Ron didn't talk much about his rough times to Bertena. She knew he'd had his "crazy" period, but she didn't know many of the details. He seemed healthy enough now—that's all she needed to know. Nor did he talk much about his race. She'd known from the day they met that he was black—Loren had told her girlfriend—and she'd heard him talk about his grandfathers from Washington, D.C., one being one of the first black dentists, the other being one of the first black architects. But race wasn't an issue they discussed. They didn't discuss having children either. At thirty-nine Bertena didn't want to start another family, and she assumed Ron felt the same way. That too was a mistake.

She was going through a stack of bills on the sink when she came across a pink message slip from Ron's work. It was a phone message from Connie. "What's this about?" she asked, suspecting the worst.

They had been married a year and a half. Bertena was still working in San Francisco, only now she was living back in Sacramento, commuting four hours a day. Every weekday morning she'd get up at 3:45 to begin her journey; by the time she got home at night, she was too pooped to party. The tables had been reversed—Ron the one ready to go out, Bertena the stay-at-home.

He explained that Connie had just called to say hello. But there was something in his voice and in his eyes that told her there was more to it than that. She was right. Connie and her husband had split. Ron was seeing her again.

He denied it at first. Bertena was his friend, his wife, the person responsible for him regaining his self-confidence and self-respect. She had trusted him; she had encouraged him to keep it together with Royce. But the truth was, he had fallen in love with Connie. He just couldn't admit it to Bertena.

For several painful months, Bertena clung to the hope the marriage would last. But they had become no more than roommates, Ron spending his weekends with Connie. For Bertena, it was a tortured time. Finally, she moved back to the Bay Area. The marriage was over.

Connie and Ron had discovered that they had a strong mutual desire . . . they both wanted to start a family.

So much for simplifying.

65

Larry

So, life was good. Larry Colton had what this country is supposed to be all about—athletic ability, brains, personality and drive. No odd habits. No crazy temper. While he probably wouldn't have put Rhett Butler out of a job, he was a ladies' man, too, and had all the girlfriends any rational human being could want. Still, there was a problem. No money. Here he was 40 years old, twice divorced, the father of two daughters, living alone in one of those flaky-paint neighborhoods where America hadn't quite kept its promise. Making money writing freelance, Colton had discovered, was about as easy as truck farming the moon, and he faced Christmas of 1982 with just enough cash to buy presents for his daughters.
—Mark Christensen, *Sweeps: Behind the Scenes in Network TV*

It was a Friday night in 1981. Julie, my girlfriend and live-in companion, called home to tell me she was going to meet a couple of her lawyer colleagues for a drink after work and would be home by 7:30. I told her I'd have dinner ready. Cooking was one way for me to compensate when my cash wasn't flowing. (By all rights I should have been a gourmet chef.)

Julie and I had been together, off and on, for two years. She had stuck by me through the lowest days of my despair over Steve's death, bailing me out after my DWI, giving me a shoulder to cry on, buying the groceries, encouraging me artistically, loaning me her Honda. (My Nova was dead. Not even a reverse gear.) We had moved in together, co-signing a lease, although most months I was lucky to pay my share. "I'll pay you back when I make it big," I promised. I paid $150 a month to each wife for child support, but with an average income of $600 a month, I was often late or a few bucks short with my checks.

At 7:30 I peeked out the window, thinking I heard Julie pull in the driveway. It was a false alarm. I turned the oven down, keeping my chicken-rice-veggie casserole on warm. Then I went to my desk to work on my weekly newspaper column, "Pillars of Portland," a soap-opera parody of trendy life in Portland that a couple of independent local filmmakers were trying to convince me could be made into a television series . . . an offer I had filed with my other "I'll believe it when the check is in the bank" schemes.

Most of my friends were trying to convince me I was an idiot if I didn't marry Julie. She was bright, beautiful, and bounteous. It was hard to argue. But I had met her on the rebound from my second failed marriage, and was dubious about the marital institution. Some days I was even bitter about it: both ex-wives had been the one to pull the plug; both had blamed me for the demise; both had gotten custody; both had moved on to the greener pastures of disastrous relationships. In retrospect, both of my marriages had been mismatches . . . in temperament, priorities, and interests. Julie was the first woman I'd been involved with who actually liked to sit down with me and watch football and basketball on TV. "So what's the problem?" friends asked. "She's perfect." One of the problems was that I didn't trust myself to be faithful. Or her, for that matter. Another was that I didn't want to get married when I was still a financial *Hindenburg*. Another was a fear of failure . . . three strikes and you're out. And perhaps the biggest reason was that Julie was thirty-three and was hinting that she wanted children. I already had my quota and wasn't in the market for any more. "So what are you doing living with her?" I was asked. "That's not fair to her." The answer was that I loved her and needed her emotional support. What worried me was that I was hanging in there because of her financial support. But it wasn't as if I was dealing from the bottom of the deck— she knew what she was getting.

Eight o'clock rolled around, then 8:30. And still no Julie. I checked the casserole. It was getting crispy around the edges. I took it out of the oven, and fixed myself another gin and tonic. I began to pace, jaw set, brow furrowed. Why hadn't she at least called? Another thirty minutes crawled by. I wasn't worried that she'd been in an accident—no, I was worried that she was still at work, naked, smooching it up with one of the senior partners. Or one of the interns. Forget that this was a woman with the moral integrity of Mother Teresa. It didn't matter. Trust wasn't my main virtue. Not in women. Not in myself. By 9:30 I was fuming, ready to head downtown to one of the Friday-night meat markets. I'd show her. Only I had no car, no money for bus fare, no cash for cocktails.

It was 10:30, three hours late, when Julie finally walked sheepishly through the door, reeking of guilt and piña coladas. I was waiting in the dining room with the casserole.

"Here's your dinner!" I raged, reaching out to dump it over her head.

She threw up an arm in self-defense, sending chicken, rice, and peas flying in every direction. I picked up a handful off the rug, and even though the arm wasn't what it once was, started firing. She ran for the door, casserole peppering the room like bird shot. I reached out and grabbed her by the arm and pulled her back, then stationed myself in front of the door, arms folded, Bull Connor blocking the way. When she tried to pass, I herded her back toward the dining room, using my size as a weapon.

Then I whirled and stomped out the door and into the night. By the time I reached the end of the driveway I realized I had no place to go, no way to get there. It was the same feeling I had when I was seven and Mom and Dad were standing on the porch, waving goodbye as I ran away from home. I circled the block, rounding the corner just in time to see Julie drive away. I went back upstairs and sat down on the edge of the bed, dispirited, ashamed.

A few minutes later, Julie returned. She didn't know I was upstairs. She marched into the closet of my workroom and pulled out the box where I kept my old love letters and photos of the ex-wives and ex-girlfriends. By the time I came downstairs and peeked in the room, a blizzard had struck, my old love letters blanketing the room. I didn't bother to go in. Months after Julie had moved out, the casserole was still caked on the fern leaves, a burnt reminder of a shameful evening.

After Julie split, I barged through the singles scene, committing to nothing, wondering if I ever could. I dated three or four different women every week, spending as much time and energy on my love life as my career. In 1983 I got a call from Howard, a friend from my teaching days. He wanted to know if I'd be interested in going with him to a men's group. *A men's group?* What the hell was that? I wanted to know. Poker? Elk hunting? I didn't do either of those.

"We'll be discussing men's issues," he explained. "It's a consciousness-raising group." I told Howard I'd try one meeting. What the heck, I thought, maybe there'd be some good snacks.

Men's issues? I'd been raised in the fifties, or as my dad liked to say, "when men were men and women were glad of it." Of course I had issues. But a men's group? I'd never been gestalted or Lifesprung or any of that touchy-feely, New Age, metaphysical stuff, unless I counted the times I'd read my horoscope. Hundred-dollar-an-hour therapy wasn't in my budget.

I rode to the meeting wearing my new Oregon spring wardrobe, which was my old Oregon winter wardrobe—jeans and a flannel shirt—with the sleeves rolled up. I had to take the bus to get there, and for a guy raised in the primal L.A. freeway's shadow, that was serious cultural descent, a trip not to the minor leagues but to another game.

There were six other men at the meeting—two teachers, a social worker, a legal-aid lawyer, a graphic artist, and a part-time actor. None of us had voted for Ronald Reagan and everybody but me was either married or living with somebody. My guess was I could strike them all out. The meeting opened with a suggestion that we have a potluck for our next meeting. Next meeting? I wasn't sure I was going to last through this one and these guys were already deciding who was going to bring the pasta salad next week. At least it would be an improvement over the wimpy plate of radishes and celery I'd just polished off. I volunteered to bring ice cream.

The next topic on the agenda was compiling a reading list. I was ready to suggest *Sporting News* or Hemingway. They were tossing out titles like *The Intimate Enemy, The Women's Room, Toward a Psychology of Being.* I started to squirm. I needed some Fritos and beer. Somebody suggested we find a topic to focus the conversation. Gene, a teacher, proposed we each discuss our relationship with our fathers. One by one we went around the circle. I was shocked as each man revealed how he felt somehow abandoned by his father. The remote father. The alcoholic father. The workaholic father. Or the just plain old everyday "benign neglect" father. And these were Portland's Renaissance guys. When it was my turn to confess, I had nothing to complain about. I loved my dad, he loved me. He was a great dad. So what if he didn't hug me or tell me he loved me? Was that why I cheated on my wife? He showed me his love in other ways: he never missed a game I played in growing up; he never used physical force against me. As hard as I thought, I couldn't come up with any emotional scars . . . unless I counted the time he gave me the Sam Mele model glove rather than the Mickey Mantle I wanted.

I left my first men's group bummed out, I guess because I thought there was something desperate about a group of men all trying too hard to be Mr. Sensitive, and partly because there were no chips to dip, no Bud to bust. It wasn't that I felt uncomfortable talking about serious, meaningful issues, although for some reason I preferred to have such talks with women, or else sitting on a barstool, not in a beanbag chair nursing a Perrier. They'd have to get their own ice cream for Meeting Two.

A mid-life crisis? A male identity crisis? In truth, I had to wonder. I wasn't sure which way the wind was blowing with women. If I'd had a car, I wouldn't have known whether to open the door for a lady or not. Or if it was even okay to call her a lady. The rules kept changing. I asked a woman after making love if she was satisfied and she accused me of being hung up on performance; I didn't ask another one and she accused me of not caring about her needs. How was I supposed to know?

I was trying to understand. Vulnerable, supportive, intimacy—I knew the words—but why couldn't things be as uncluttered as they were back in the Pi KA house? Whatever happened to the Fucking Moos and the days of the male mystique?

The last question on the Portland School District's job application form asked: Why are you applying for the position of substitute teacher. Hmmmm. Because it has been my lifelong ambition. Because I love school lunches. That's what I wrote. I didn't think I could give them the real reason—I needed the $57 a day.

Substitute teaching seemed like the perfect day gig to relieve the financial pressure. It was basically being a pricy babysitter, and with no papers to correct I could be home by 3:30, ready to hit the typewriter. Maybe even start writing about my long-lost fraternity brothers. Or get going on that TV script.

Welcome back to teaching. I was officially certified by the state of Oregon to teach grades 5 through 12, *all* subjects. Spanish, shorthand, trigonometry, everything. All I had to do was wait for the phone to ring and hope I'd have enough time to get there by bus or bike. Through the rain.

The first call came on a Monday morning at six o'clock. Could I teach an eighth-grade class for the whole week? It was supposedly the toughest middle school in the district. Let's see. Five times 57. That's $285, enough to pay my rent and most of my utilities. I was out the door and on the bus in ten minutes. I wore my corduroy sports coat, the one I'd stolen from Steve's closet to deliver his eulogy.

Thirty-five students were waiting at the door. As soon as they spotted me down the hall, they smelled a sub, vultures ready to descend. I opened the door. Two boys raced to the record player in the back of the room and put on a Ted Nugent album, cranking it to full volume.

"Our regular teacher lets us do it," they said.

"Only if I can play my Barry Manilow," I countered.

There were no lesson plans and no instructions from the office. Judging from the way the kids were bouncing off the wall, my guess was that the regular teacher had slit her wrists. I was to have these same thirty-five hormonally overactive kids all day long. Math, science, p.e., spelling . . . the works. A boy in the back row was choking himself to get high; the boy next to him pulled out a tin of Copenhagen and put a pinch between his cheek and gum, then spit on the back of the AC/DC sweatshirt of the girl in front of him. She didn't notice—she was too busy ratting the hair of the girl next to her.

By the time I finished taking the roll, I was sure I was deep in the middle of *Blackboard Jungle*. Or it might have been *Lord of the Flies*. Was it three o'clock yet? I told them to take out their math books. Zero for thirty-five. Nary a one budged. Okay, I never liked math much myself. How about writing a descriptive paragraph about your family. One paper was turned in:

> My mom has brown hair and likes to sit. My stepdad has black hair, green eyes and likes to drink. I might sneak into his room at night and shoot him with his .357. Don't ask me how old my real dad is because I only see him once a year. He has trouble with his back and doesn't pay child support.

I opened the top desk drawer. There was an envelope marked "Jimmy's Ritalin." Jimmy was already at Club Speedo, sitting at his desk, mainlining Milk Duds. During the writing assignment the boy next to him started pounding on his desk and kicking his chair. I asked him firmly to stop. He picked up all his papers and books and flung them in the air. "Fuck you!" he said. I moved toward him, ordering him to the principal's office. "Don't touch me, motherfucker, or I'll sue your ass!" he yelled. "I know my rights." The boy couldn't read but he was a legal expert. When he threw his chair across the room, narrowly missing my head, I put him in a hammerlock and marched him to the office. Not exactly district policy. But it temporarily plugged the dam. Then there was the boy who called himself Captain Fantastic. He was a cross between Fonzie and General Haig. He wore full Army dress, including combat boots. He was the best artist in the class, except everything he drew looked like a shogun warrior. His favorite sport was smashing inanimate objects with his head.

Somehow, in one of the great miracles of public education, I survived the week. The rent was paid. But I didn't write a word. When I got home each day, wiped out, it was all I could do to make it to the fridge and pop a cold one. I lay down and read the sports page to find out who was the latest unhappy and unappreciated pitcher to renegotiate his million-dollar contract. During the entire week neither the principal nor anyone else on the staff inquired as to what I was doing. I could have had the students manufacturing neutron bombs and nobody would have known. Captain Fantastic would have loved it.

I left word with the substitute office that I would not accept any more assignments at that school. I managed to last six months in the substitute-teaching business before deciding that $57 a day and all the cafeteria wiener wraps I could eat wasn't worth the grief. I returned full-time to chasing the Literary Dream.

It was 1984. In a city of beautiful homes, verdant gardens, and scenic vistas of Mount Hood, I was living in a dingy upstairs flat near downtown. Actually, the apartment belonged to Sherry, whom I had moved in with on Christmas Eve after I ran out of heating oil in my rented two-bedroom, flaky-paint clapboard house. I'd showed up at her front door with my typewriter and my four-foot Christmas tree, its lights and ornaments already strung. Sherry, twenty-nine, was from New Orleans and had a degree in journalism from the University of Missouri, long legs, big dimples, a Southern drawl, curly dark hair, electric-blue eyes, and a golden retriever named Wally. She was making $700 a month as a reporter for a suburban weekly. Sometimes she let me borrow the "Prince," her slant-six Valiant. Its body looked pickled.

I had just spent six months working for $500 a month on a locally produced two-hour TV movie that was made from my "Pillars of Portland" newspaper column. The dream was to prove to Hollywood that there was talent out in the backwoods of America to revolutionize primetime television through the creation of a nationwide interlocking network of "franchised regional soap operas," all shows funded and produced by local affiliates. The project was written up on the front page of USA Today and The Wall Street Journal. It was also included in Sweeps, a book on network TV. There was one huge problem, however. The show that aired on the Portland CBS affiliate was an Atrocious Bomb. Hollywood laughed at us. So did Portland. My two partners in the project, the director and the producer, split from Oregon in the middle of the night, leaving me to deal with the unpaid bills. I had talked Rick Wise, an ex-teammate with the Phillies and a Portland resident who once pitched a no-hitter *and* hit two home runs in the same major-league game, into loaning $5,000 to the partnership, and when there was no money left in the till to pay him off, he wasn't interested in waiting in line with my ex-wives for his $150 a month. He stopped talking to me and had his lawyer sue, tacking on another ten grand in punitive damages.

"You're welcome to my Nova," I said. So much for my Dream of Revolutionizing Network Television.

So there I was again, in financial Death Valley, living with another attractive woman who was hinting about someday wanting babies. I was back to free-lancing. When I borrowed a car to drive to Rajneeshpuram in central Oregon to do a story on the Bhagwan Shree Rajneesh and his tribe of spiritual pilgrims, my friends were placing bets that I'd sign up and never come back. There were rumors that it was a sex cult. My investigation, however, was unable to uncover anything.

Then Sherry was laid off due to budget cuts. The financial picture took a turn from grim to gruesome . . . lawyers, landlords, and ex-wives all circling overhead, all wanting their checks. I'd no sooner hang up from Denise than Kathi would call.

"Why don't you get a *regular* job?" they asked.

"I have a *regular* job," I replied. "I'm a writer." They weren't buying it.

Sherry tried to be optimistic, but her confidence was drooping. She took a job cocktailing at a downtown meat market, dragging home at 3 A.M. I waited in bed, wide awake, staring at the ceiling, my male insecurity gone mojo. She walked into the room and emptied her tip money into a bowl on the dresser. It was dark and she missed, the dimes and quarters playing a sad tango on the floor. I suggested she quit.

"Why don't *you* go wait tables?" she replied.

That was one possibility, but first I had to put the finishing touches on an article I'd been working on for two weeks for *Willamette Week* on a convicted murderer. They were paying me $250. And then I read that the eighties were the decade of greed. So I demanded $275. I still didn't have an agent.

As much as I was worried about money, I was even more concerned about my daughter Wendy, who was already a senior in high school in Seattle. It had been fourteen years since Denise and I divorced and in all those years Wendy and I had stayed close—she had become a veteran of Greyhound and Amtrak. But the teen years had been a tough time for her—bitter fights with her mom, an out-of-town and broke father, no contact with her Grandma Hedy, skipping school, gaining weight, drop-out friends, and a traumatic car crash in which another teenager was killed. She rarely dated and had a low self-esteem. Her big love was heavy metal music. When she got suspended from school for cutting classes, I felt powerless. I was failing as a parent. I also felt anger at Denise for having taken Wendy away from me, relegating me to a twice-a-month parent. But even with all those weekend visits and vacations in the summer and regular phone calls, I felt guilty—that I had abandoned her, that I was a better father for Sarah, who lived only a mile away. Sarah spent two nights a week with me and got tenfold more of my attention.

I was concerned about Wendy's weight. She had a head of hair to die for and a face as pretty as her famous grandmother, but from early childhood her weight had been on a steady climb upward, and now she was a "fat" teenager. I was embarrassed, outraged, saddened. A father's Dream of Grandeur—the beautiful daughter—was lost. Instead, I had a chubby kid who listened to Iron Maiden and smoked cigarettes. Back when she was twelve she lost ten pounds once and I saw hope, praising her dietary efforts. But when she returned on the next visit and I forced her to get on the scale—a stupid move on my part—she had regained the weight. I flew into a rage, pounding my fist into the wall, sending Wendy crying into the bedroom. I was instantly ashamed of my actions, but the damage had been done. I promised never to discuss her weight again, but my disappointment was hard to conceal. I wanted to assign blame: to Wendy, for not having the willpower; to myself, for not having been the father I should have been; to Denise, for not being there every day when Wendy got home from school like a Good Mother was "supposed" to be. Denise had divorced Tom, the guy she left me for, after only two years of an alcohol-abusive marriage. (He eventually died from an overdose of rubbing alcohol while he was in a hospital in Alaska.)

In the spring of 1984 Wendy called with a surprise request. "Dad, I want to come live with you in September," she said.

I was overjoyed. For fourteen years I had dreamed about having custody, and now at long last I would, even if she was eighteen. My hope was that Wendy would move in with me, and somehow, magically, the weight would fall off. I would "cure" her problem. She would be away from her deadbeat heavy metal friends and the tensions with her mom. With me, she would maintain a proper diet and I'd be supportive, loving, all the things a father was supposed to be.

I broke the news to Sherry. She forced a smile, but clearly did not share in my joy. "Where's she going to sleep?" she asked. We were already cramped in our one-bedroom flat. "And just how do you plan to support her when you can't even support yourself?"

Minor details. I was getting, at long last, the chance to be the Good Father. "I'll figure out a way," I promised.

66

Jim

Van Hoften is nicknamed "Ox" because of his exceptional strength.
—*Time* magazine

April 6, 1984, dawned clear and bright over Cape Kennedy. Shielding his eyes from the morning glare of the Florida sun, Adriaan van Hoften was about to pop his buttons he was so proud, telling anyone within earshot that his son was up there on board that spacecraft on the launch pad. Back in the nightmare that was his in the Nazi prison camp, how could he have imagined that one day he would be watching his son blast off into outer space?

The ground rumbled and shook and the power was overwhelming as the *Challenger* slowly lifted skyward, seemingly hanging suspended, then blasting upward out over the Atlantic, a thick plume of smoke trailing majestically behind it. On board, Jim sat back, cool as ice, the g's pinning him to the seat. On the monitor in Mission Control, his pulse registered a laid-back 72. Pretty calm for a guy about to try to save the American taxpayers 80 million simoleons out there in the blackness of space. Vallarie was sure her heart was going about 150.

Fear wasn't part of Jim's astronaut equation. He had flown combat, dodged heat-seeking missiles, landed jets on a heaving carrier deck in the middle of the night . . . which, as every fighter jock knew, took ten

times the daring of riding a rocket into space. And besides, NASA officials had reported that the chances of anything going wrong with the
Challenger or any of the other space shuttles was in the neighborhood of
100,000 to 1. But even if the odds were only 10 to 1, Jim would have
been right there where he was, staring out the window at the earth
below. At six-three, 205 pounds, he was now the largest man ever in
space.

The Ox in Orbit.

He had gotten the flight he wanted—Mission 11. In addition to its
scientific experiments, the main goal of the mission was the rescue of
Solar Max, an $80 million taxpayer satellite that had been launched to
study the sun's atmosphere but instead was up there just cruising around
the earth every ninety minutes, doing nothing but wasting money. The
mission would require two men, Ox and his close friend Ed "Pinky"
Nelson, to perform an EVA to fix Solar Max. (EVA stood for extravehicu-
lar activity . . . also known on earth as a spacewalk.)

When the crew for Mission 11 had first been selected, Jim did not
think he would be one of the astronauts selected for the EVA because
there was only one size EVA suit and he was too big for it. An EVA suit
wasn't something off the rack at Sears—the cost was $1.5 million per
unit. But NASA dipped into the till and had one designed specifically for
him. Not bad for a guy whose parents couldn't afford to buy him desert
boots in high school. Now all he had to do was crawl out there into the
black void of space at 17,500 miles an hour and do what he'd been
training two years to do. And if he screwed up? It would only cost John
Q. Public $80 million. Or if he *really* screwed up? He would be the first
man lost in space. He slept like a log his first night in space.

The *Challenger* crew was blasted awake by ground control in Houston to
the sound of the Cal Fight Song. It was time for Ox to chug his Tang and
go to work and earn his salary, which was now up to $39,000 a year. As
he and Pinky slipped into their EVA suits, shuttle pilot Dick Scobee
maneuvered the spacecraft to within 100 feet of Solar Max, which was
like tailgating the bumper of a guy going 100 on the Ventura Freeway,
only 1,750 times faster. Ox and Pinky crawled through the cargo-bay
doors . . . and there they were . . . in outer space, the earth spinning
250 miles below.

Using a Buck Rogers jet-powered backpack, Pinky edged toward the
satellite. As he did, Ox attached himself to a long robot arm, which
would be his work station while he did his delicate repair job. He had
total confidence in his close friend Pinky, who had a Ph.D. in astron-

omy, a B.A. in English, wrote poetry in German, spoke four languages, and had played a scrappy second base in college. Their work was being televised back to hundreds of millions of viewers on earth.

Pinky attempted to dock with Solar Max, a procedure he had practiced a thousand times in training in simulator tanks, but the triggering device malfunctioned, sending it tumbling helplessly out of control. For several hours the crew and the people in Mission Control worked to correct the wild spinning, but all efforts proved futile. Ox and Pinky had to return to the shuttle, their mission on the brink of an embarrassing defeat. Eighty million dollars gone poof in space. The mood on board was somber, depressed. The network news and the wire services headlined their failure. Two years of training was about to be for naught. NASA officials termed the situation "not optimistic." For his part, Ox was cool and collected, reading his manuals, his indefatigable can-do spirit still in place.

That night, while the crew slept, engineers at the Goddard Space Flight Center in Maryland worked around the clock to stop Solar Max's wild tumbling. By morning they had done it. A victory for American technology. That day mission specialist T. J. Hart maneuvered the robot arm into position to grab it; then the next day Ox and Pinky zipped back into their spacesuits and went back out to try again. This time Pinky was able to maneuver the satellite into position, and then Ox, standing at the end of the fifty-foot robot arm, went to work, replacing a 400-pound attitude-control system. He opened a panel, and using a specially designed space wrench, delicately removed twenty-two small screws buried under a maze of wires. "Whoops," he said, dropping one of the screws, watching it float off into infinite orbit. His job, which would have been hard enough on the ground, was complicated by the blackness of space, zero gravity, and the thick gloves he was wearing. It was the equivalent of performing brain surgery at the bottom of a swimming pool while wearing boxing gloves. But he did it.

Mission Control was so pumped that they rewarded his efforts with an unscheduled one-hour ride with the Buck Rogers backpack, a ride that was televised by the networks. He was out there zooming around as if it was just another day at Rainie Falls. Pinky and he had discussed what he might say when his microphone was on—some profound words for the folks back on earth, perhaps "Oh, look, there's the face of God." No, better not, they decided.

"The view is incredible!" he gushed instead.

The next day USA Today bannered his success on page one. "Mr. Spacewrench," they called him. Pi KA's least likely hero.

. . . .

He was sitting at a desk in a small room with fellow astronaut Mike Lounge at the Air National Guard in Houston, on alert. It was a year after his heroics with Solar Max. He and Lounge had both been assigned to Mission 20, which was originally designed as a satellite deployment effort. They were monitoring the progress of a shuttle mission currently in space. Things on board were not going well. LEASAT 3, a communication satellite manufactured by Hughes Aircraft, had just gone lifeless thirty-three seconds after being launched out of the shuttle into orbit. It was now $85 million worth of lifeless, worthless space junk.

Jim and Lounge immediately began hatching a rescue plan. Jim took an envelope from his pocket and began scribbling down mathematical equations on the back side. He called NASA to get the data on the moment of inertia, then using Lounge's wristwatch computer for the calculations, they convinced themselves it wasn't a lost cause.

But first they had to sell their idea. They took it to NASA officials, who were intrigued. Over the next several weeks Jim, Lounge, and the rest of the crew for Mission 20 began putting together the specifics of a scenario for a rescue mission, with drawings and all the calculations. NASA had to be convinced it wasn't too dangerous. One reason was that the satellite was too unstable; another was that it was filled with thousands of gallons of potentially explosive fuel. Not a good combo. But Jim and the crew were able to persuade NASA.

The next step was to sell Hughes Aircraft, which had already collected $80 million in insurance from Lloyds of London. So Jim and the rest of the crew hopped into their T-38s and jetted out to L.A. to make their pitch. It was Jim, whose voice had been rendered squeaky by a bad case of laryngitis, who made the presentation to a hundred of the company's top officials. Following an all-night meeting with engineers, the plan was given the go-ahead. Flight readiness, including training and the manufacture of the necessary hardware, which normally took two years, would have to be accomplished in four months.

So in essence, what Jim and the crew had done was create a rescue mission and then sell it too. Now all that was left was to pull it off. Potentially, there was more danger in this rescue effort than on any of the other space shuttle missions. Lift-off was scheduled for August 1985.

At Mission Control at Cape Kennedy, Vallarie, who had a bad case of hives, anxiously watched the monitors. She knew something was desperately wrong. She looked at the EKG. Jim's heartbeat, which had never gone over 80 on the first mission, was at 120. His voice came over the speaker filled with urgency.

"This is screwed!" he said, voice quivering. He was outside the *Discovery*, 219 miles above the earth, and for the first time in the history of space exploration, an astronaut was in serious jeopardy of becoming a human satellite forever.

To Vallarie, this mission seemed doomed and cursed from the beginning. First there had been the off-again, on-again rescue effort, and then the launch had been postponed twice, the first time by bad weather, the second by a faulty backup computer. And by all rights, the lift-off itself should have been delayed. A severe storm system spawned by Hurricane Elena had brought ominous black clouds hovering over the Kennedy Space Center, but NASA had ignored their own rule for not blasting off in rain or through potential lightning, and ordered the launch. They got lucky . . . this time.

After reaching orbit, commander Joe Engle had closed the *Discovery* to within thirty-five feet of the spinning 15,000-pound satellite filled with hydrazine, a highly flammable fuel. Ox had crawled through the cargo door and attached his feet to the restraints at the end of the long robot arm as Lounge maneuvered him to within inches of the satellite. A malfunction in the arm's computer control added to the peril.

It had taken Ox thirty minutes, but he had finally attached a grappling bar to the satellite, and using his considerable strength, pushed it enough to stop its rotation, then held on tight while the robot arm brought him and the satellite back to the payload bay. It was his job to hold it in place—no small feat—while astronaut Bill Fisher opened up a panel and did what amounted to a hot-wire to get it jump-started. Ox realized the task was considerably more formidable than he had calculated on the back of the envelope back in Houston. One problem was that the grappling bar had been designed for a spinning satellite—but the motion had stopped, rendering the capturing device useless. Ox had to dream up a plan right on the spot. Without really explaining his idea to ground control, he just grabbed the satellite by hand. A very tricky maneuver. Another problem was that Fisher, an emergency room doctor, was having trouble with the wiring. The longer he took, the more dangerous it was for Ox, who was straining so hard wrestling with the huge 15,000-pound satellite and exerting so much pressure on his boots that he was afraid that the boots would split open. If they did, he was dead.

But the boots didn't split, and Fisher was finally able to finish the wiring. After seven hours outside, Ox reentered the *Discovery* to rest his exhausted body and replenish the oxygen in his suit. What he had just done was the equivalent of wrestling a house. The next day he went back outside for four more hours to complete the project. Once it was done, he heaved with all his muscle power and shoved the satellite away from the spacecraft and out into orbit . . . making him the first man in history to launch a satellite by hand.

Vallarie walked her elderly patient down the hall, taking him to the bathroom. He had tubes coming out of everywhere. She heard someone call her name, and turned to see another nurse moving toward her in a hurry, waving a magazine. It was the week after Jim's latest space heroics.

"Look!" the nurse exclaimed. "Your husband's picture is in *Time*. God, you must really feel honored to be married to an astronaut."

"What the hell am I, sewer water?" she replied, continuing toward the bathroom.

Ox was out of town on the NASA public relations trail again. Since his first flight, he had hopscotched the globe—Ottawa, Rome, Lisbon, South Chicago. He had received a congratulatory telegram from the ex-governor of California Jerry Brown; his birthplace, Fresno, which he moved from when he was three, named him an honorary citizen; he was invited to be the commencement speaker at the Cal School of Engineering and at Mills High, his alma maters. Pi KA, the fraternity he never felt comfortable in, awarded him its national Distinguished Service Award. He'd heard from goat brothers he hadn't talked to in twenty years. He had already been assigned his third flight.

In a space program that some aviation purists had accused of turning astronauts into nothing more than robots, Ox had not only physically pushed himself to the edge of the envelope on his second mission; his was also an engineering and marketing triumph, as he had played a crucial role in designing and selling the project. A triple-threat astronaut. Because of NASA's team-oriented concept for their shuttle program, and America's growing complacency with its launches, the shuttle astronauts were not being singled out for the glory and widespread individual acclaim of the original astronauts. People knew the name Sally Ride, and that was it. But within the TFNG fraternity, his accomplishment was well noted, recognized as perhaps the greatest all-around individual input into a flight in space history. But he and Vallarie still needed her salary as a nurse to make ends meet.

As she neared the bathroom with her patient, she felt a warm sensation on her leg. The man had lost it, peeing all over her right side. And at that same moment, Ox was in Peoria speaking to the Kiwanis, modestly telling them about the importance of space exploration.

Feeling the urine run down her stocking into her shoe, Vallarie yelled to her friend walking away with the magazine. "I'm not lucky to be married to an astronaut," she intoned. "He's lucky to be married to a nurse."

On the morning of January 28, 1986, Jim was at the Johnson Space Center in Houston, training for his third flight in May. At the Kennedy Space Center in Florida, the crew of seven were already on board the *Challenger,* waiting word on whether they would be allowed to fly. Freezing cold weather was threatening to postpone the mission—an engineer at Rockwell in California was watching by closed-circuit TV and had just called Mission Control urging a delay because of the ice. But Jim knew from experience that those astronauts up there already strapped to their seats were antsy to get going. His close friend Dick Scobee, who had piloted the Solar Max flight and was the commander of this flight, the twenty-fifth mission in the shuttle program, was ready to fly. Scobee had helped Jim build his backyard swimming pool; they had flown their homemade airplane cross-country together. The final countdown continued.

For several weeks Jim and Vallarie had been talking about quitting NASA. Vallarie, for all her Houston network of friends and social activities and nursing job at the hospital, was serious about moving back to California. She was tired of Jim being away from home so much. It was a hard decision: Jim still loved being an astronaut and working atop the pyramid; NASA was like family, a feeling of closeness through the whole organization; their best friends were the TFNGs and their families. But it was also time to start thinking about financial security. He was in his forties and after seventeen years in the Navy and NASA, he had no pension. With NASA he was now making $55,000, but that was as high as he could go. He had started sending out his résumé, figuring there should be somebody interested in hiring a guy with a Ph.D. in fluid mechanics and a couple of trips to outer space to his credit. One place that had already shown an interest was the engineering department at Cal.

He watched on the NASA television monitor as the *Challenger* blasted off. (The networks had stopped covering the lift-offs, considering them too uneventful.) He knew what the seven men and women on board were feeling, lying on their backs, the g's pressing them against their seats, looking up at a bright blue sky ahead, feeling the adrenaline rush and the sense of accomplishment. At seventy seconds into the flight he heard his friend Scobee say, "Roger, go with throttle up." Then came a violent, primal, imperceptible explosion. Suddenly a fireball and brilliant shades of orange and red and billowing white clouds formed a monster as the *Challenger* disintegrated and fell into the Atlantic. In Houston, he stared at the monitor screen in baffled horror. "Obviously, a major malfunction," said the flight announcer.

America wept. Jim wept. Those were his intimate friends and colleagues, his TFNG drinking buddies at Jason's. Christa McAuliffe excepted, he had shared seven intense years with them. At the memorial service in Houston, with the band playing funeral hymns and President Reagan delivering a eulogy that spoke of the bravery and noble sacrifice of America's newest heroes, four T-38 jets—the trainers in which he and Judy Resnik had flown to speaking engagements all over the country— roared overhead, a fifth plane symbolically missing. He tried to ease his grief with matter-of-factness machismo and the observation that they "died doing something they loved," but this was a man who got tears in his eyes every time he watched his daughter play the piano, and who, according to Vallarie, cried over Purina Dog Chow commercials.

NASA put future shuttle flights on hold after the tragedy, so Jim stepped up his job search. In mid-1986 he was offered a job as the manager of space technologies for the Defense and Space Division for Bechtel, the world's largest engineering company, headquartered in San Francisco. He accepted, but with a proviso—he didn't want to be the company's token astronaut. He was serious about making a contribution and being in a decision-making position. That was one thing he disliked about NASA . . . that the astronauts were just along for the ride with no real designed input, his second flight notwithstanding. His time at Bechtel would be spent more on the business side than on engineering— he'd have his own budget and lots of autonomy. He was sad to be leaving NASA, but also proud of what he had accomplished: he had logged 338 hours in orbit; he was the largest man ever in space; he was the first man to launch a satellite by hand; and he had set the record for the greatest number of hours (22) outside the spacecraft during flight.

"All that hero stuff was fine," observed Vallarie after they moved to California, "but he really wasn't getting the chance to use all his smarts with NASA."

67

Loren

A billion here and a billion there and pretty soon you're talking big money.
—Senator Everett Dirksen

On Halloween 1984, Loren's newly formed company, Whitney Financial Group, Inc., had purchased an insurance company. Hayseed was going big time, no more messing around with piddling little hundred-grand commissions for selling the dirt for new mini-malls. Whitney agreed to pay a cool 28 mil for Pine Top Insurance, a subsidiary of the Greyhound Corporation. Break out the Dom Pérignon.

At the age of forty-two, Loren finally had it made, climbing up there on the porch where the big dogs play. So he had thought. But it had taken only a few months for the foundation of his porch to start crumbling, and as he sat behind the wheel of his Mercedes on this day in 1985 heading to his fancy new office in the Greyhound Tower in downtown Phoenix, he had an anxious knot in his stomach.

He had spent the previous year working on the deal for Pine Top, which was in the reinsurance business (insuring a portion of assumed risks of other insurance companies). He had been shaking and baking with the sharpies from the New York investment world and the company vice presidents of Greyhound, a diversified billion-dollar company for which the bus business generated only a small portion of its profits. (Greyhound's consumer products included Dial soap, Fruit of the Loom,

Armour franks.) He was no insurance hayseed: he'd spent mucho hours studying the financial statements of Pine Top, learning the tricks of the insurance racket. He had already drawn $300,000 in up-front money to take care of business, a mere drop in the bucket for a company supposedly raking in millions.

In the back of his mind, he had this dream that when the premiums started rolling in, he might just mosey back to Trowbridge and kick back and live on the ranch. Return to his roots. He had been hustling deals for twenty-five years, and maybe now that he was going to be hauling in the megabucks, it was time to think about pulling over to the slow lane. But it was just an idea. He had to sock away a few million first.

And now that he was a father—Garrett was eighteen months old and Rita was expecting again—he couldn't be quite the free spirit he'd always been. Or could he? When Garrett was born in Phoenix in November 1983, Loren hadn't even bothered to show up to see his offspring for six weeks. He was too busy cutting deals and moving fast. He didn't want to give Rita, Garrett's mother, the impression he was committed to settling down. He breezed in and out, and the nights he didn't stay at Rita's apartment, which were frequent, she could only guess where he was. He came and went as he pleased, and if she didn't like it, then "tough shit." If she wanted their boy to have a real father, not a fake one like his dad, then she'd just have to take him the way he was because he wasn't changing "any more than I already have."

He parked his car and breezed through the lobby of the Greyhound Tower, headed for his twenty-third-floor office. Two building security guards stood in front of the elevator, arms folded, feet spread. He punched the "up" button.

"You can't go up there, Mr. Hawley," said one of the guards. Loren laughed, but the man wasn't kidding. The chief financial officer of Greyhound, a man Loren had argued with and tossed out of his office the day before, had signed an order having Loren barred from the Greyhound Tower. Seems that Loren, after a closer examination of Pine Top's financial statements, had accused the big dogs of Greyhound and their accountants of playing fast and loose in representing the financial condition of Pine Top at the time the agreement was reached. According to his calculations, they had sold him a company that was insolvent to a tune in excess of $100 million, and now they were trying to cover their tracks, attempting to take back the deal and bully him down the road.

Deciding not to bulldoze his way by the security guards, he turned and left the Greyhound Tower . . . and went off to find himself a good lawyer. In time, he would file a lawsuit in the United States District

Court in Arizona against the Greyhound Corporation and his former partners in Whitney, charging them with breach of contract, fraud, deceit, misrepresentation, and racketeering (RICO). Serious stuff. Country hardball. He was seeking $1.2 billion in damages. He vowed that Greyhound wouldn't have any buses left when he was through with them.

Despite all the hassles, he loved his work. It was still "the deal" that impassioned him and impelled him helplessly in search of the big score. He moved in a world where suspicion abounded, everybody was the enemy, control was necessary, all was fair, and there was no substitute for victory. And he loved it. The way he saw it, Greyhound had destroyed the best thing he had ever done—putting that insurance deal together. He'd been fouled. He wasn't after them for the money, he claimed. It was to exonerate himself and to prove they'd screwed with the wrong guy. By his count, he had been to court ten times since he'd entered the business world after college, and not counting his little glitch with the IRS, he had won every legal battle. He believed Greyhound would keep the string alive.

In 1987, Rita gave birth to their second son, Colin, and although Loren had begun to warm to the idea of being a father, he still wasn't ready to give up the "tomatoes" and settle down and be a family man. He and Rita continued to live apart, Loren sometimes not contacting her for days. She was hopeful a second child would reel him in, despite signs and words to the contrary. "I just want to be part of your life," she told him.

Loren's father had passed away, suffering a heart attack while making love to his second wife. For the last ten years of his life, Hal Hawley had been sober, deeply involved in Alcoholics Anonymous; but he and Loren had never reconciled the chasm between them. Loren had reacted to his death with little emotion.

There also now appeared to be an irreconcilable chasm between Loren and Craig. Their twenty-three-year friendship had disintegrated into a bitter feud. They were kaput, angry enemies, no longer speaking. Money was the root of the problem. According to Craig, Loren had cheated him out of "a ton" of money; but the way Loren saw it, Craig was a "hypocrite" and was trying to blame Loren for his own financial irresponsibility.

In early 1986 a fire had gutted the ranch house in Trowbridge, burning a hundred years of family tradition to the ground. Loren promised his mother that he would have it rebuilt, and persuaded Ron, his old pledge brother and teammate, to moonlight from his job with the state to make preliminary architectural plans for a new ranch house. Because Loren had lived in Phoenix for almost ten years, he and Ron had not seen much of each other since Ron moved to Sacramento in 1977; still, even though they were opposites in lifestyle and sensibilities and disagreed over the size of the fireplace, there remained a fondness between them that had been forged back in their days of enduring the wrath of Big Ben in the fraternity and Coach Walsh on the practice field.

As Ron set to work on the design plans, Loren started to talk more seriously about leaving Arizona and moving back to Trowbridge after the house was rebuilt. This left Rita wondering where she and their sons fit into the picture. The more he spoke of returning to California, the more she pressured him for a commitment. There were days he hinted that she and the boys could move with him; and there were days he told her he had no intention of making her a part of his life.

"If you keep hounding me and trying to tell me what I should do," he said, "I'll guarantee you'll never see me again. And you don't want those boys growing up without a father, do you?"

68

Larry

It is not true that life is one damned thing after another—it is one damned thing over and over.
—Edna St. Vincent Millay

The letter was postmarked Dothan, Alabama. It was from a nine-year-old boy requesting my autograph on my 1968 baseball card. He'd gotten my address, I presumed, from the *Baseball Address List*, a publication that lists the addresses of every player who ever played in the big leagues, even if it was only one game. It seemed ironic—I had no credit cards and two dollars to my name—yet here was a kid from down in Dixie who had more money in his piggy bank than I did in my checking account wanting my autograph on a piece of cardboard.

I was tempted to keep the card. I'd lost mine during one of my many moves. To the boy it was a 1968 card number 348 in a series of 490; to me it was a sentimental reminder of my brush with glory. But I signed it and mailed it back. Then I caught the bus to the baseball-card shop to buy my own baseball card.

It was 1984. In President Reagan's trickle-down economy, I was living below the trickle. But the editor at *Oregon* magazine had promised that "the check was in the mail" for my latest story. Sherry, my long-legged, big-dimpled, blue-eyed roommate from New Orleans, was asking ponderous questions about the future of our relationship and how I planned to support Wendy when she moved in with us in a month. I was having trouble committing to taking out the trash, let alone six months down the line. I only had two keys on my key chain—one to her apartment, the other to the Prince, her pickled '66 Plymouth Valiant.

The number 14 bus pulled to a stop in front of the baseball-card shop and I hustled off. "Do you have a 1968 rookie card number 348?" I asked, modestly preferring to ask for myself by number rather than name.

The clerk checked his stock, then shook his head. "Sorry," he said. "We sell quite a few of that card. He's a teacher around here and his students come in and buy them."

Shall I tell him? Nah. "How about a 1969 rookie card number 454?" I inquired. (I set a big-league record, of sorts, by being on a rookie card two years in a row.)

He pulled two cards from his file. "You're in luck," he said. "Do you want both of them?"

"How much?" I asked.

"Forty-five cents apiece," he said. "That's our lowest-priced card."

I decided to invest 80 percent of my remaining net worth and purchased both cards, which didn't leave me enough for bus fare home. I hoofed the five miles, turning on the six o'clock news as soon as I walked in the door. The TV set was in its last days, the picture a sickly pea green.

"You gotta be shittin' me!" I exclaimed.

Right there on the screen, big as life in living pea green, floating untethered and unencumbered through outer space, was my old fraternity brother "Piss 'n' Moan," a.k.a. Ox. I had no idea he was an astronaut —the last I remembered of him he and his buddy Toad were dancing in goat barf. And now President Reagan was talking to him on a satellite hookup, telling him that he had "made all America very proud of what you're doing up there and what the future holds for all of us with regard to this opening up of that great frontier of space." (Which was exactly what the script NASA had sent Reagan directed him to say.)

I noted the contrast. An ex-goat soaring up there in outer space on the technological frontier, doing the right stuff, the earth spinning below, while my life seemed so pedestrian and local in comparison. It wasn't that I thought of myself as having the wrong stuff; it was more a case of not having any stuff.

Watching Ox spacewalk raised more questions about the trajectory of my own life. Questions of success and failure. So many questions . . .

such as how in this world was I going to pull it together before Wendy came to live with me?

From my upstairs bedroom I could hear weird noises coming from Wendy's room downstairs. Shrill and irritating. I hesitated to investigate, but it was definitely intruding on my Saturday-morning sleep.

It was 1985. I had pulled it together. Sort of. Two weeks before Wendy had moved down from Seattle to live with me and Sherry, I abandoned the life of the free-lance artist to go to work for Nike, the Oregon-based shoe giant. It was a regular, responsible nine-to-five gig. My official job title was Marketing Projects Director, Nike International, which was corporate double-talk for "we don't know what to do with this guy now that we've hired him." I was spending my days churning out in-house copy about Air Jordan and all the latest scoops in footwear fashion. For my efforts I was bringing home a steady if unspectacular $2,000 monthly paycheck, decent health benefits, and lots of great sneakers to replace my worn-out K mart Specials. I was suddenly in the trickle. We moved into a comfortable four-bedroom rented house in a nice neighborhood and I bought a ten-year-old Datsun with four forward gears. There was, however, one slight problem with my new life as the organization man. I hated it, and my boss too. My father, as always, was quick with the solution. "Keep your nose to the grindstone," he advised. "And don't let the bastards get you down."

The noise from Wendy's room grew even shriller and more irritating. I figured it was probably her newest heavy metal album. She and her cohort in metalmania, Jennifer, a curly blonde with poured-on black jeans and a seductress smile, had been front row center the night before at the long-awaited Metallica concert on the group's "Kill 'Em All" tour. Metallica was taxing my fundamental belief in the First Amendment in a way I was sure Elvis never did to my mom.

Wendy's fascination with heavy metal puzzled me—I thought her sunny disposition more suited to a Bee Gee's concert. I was clinging to the hope that metalmania, like her weight, would soon be a thing of the past. For fourteen years I had been a Disneyland Dad to her, making sure her weekend visits were special times—but now that she was living under my roof, I was asking her to clean her room and do the dishes. Real Dad demands. I could see changes. She was enrolled at Portland Community College; she had a part-time job in a day-care center; she was taking an aerobics class; her eating habits were improving. I wasn't ready to declare myself Father of the Year, but I was pleased.

When the noise downstairs persisted, I went to explore. As I descended the stairs, I heard voices and laughter. Male voices. Wendy heard me coming and was waiting at the bottom of the stairs, her $3,000 orthodontia smile (that took me six years to pay) lighting the hallway.

"Guess who's here!" She was beaming.

Judging from her excitement, I was ready to guess Tom Cruise or Rob Lowe. Foolish me.

"It's the drummer and lead singer for Metallica!" she exuded. "They're here . . . in our house! Can you believe it!"

"They spent the night?"

"You don't understand, Dad," she continued. "They are the *greatest* band in the world!"

Foolish me again, here I'd been thinking it was Iron Maiden. So if they're so great, I wondered, then why don't they have a swanky room at the Marriott? I was afraid to ask for details. One voice inside advised me to get these scumbag pseudo-musicians out of my house, and how dare they take advantage of my vulnerable daughter. But on second thought, how were these guys any different than I had been as a clean-cut ballplayer breezing in and out of towns and leaving behind a trail of one-night stands? Was Wendy going to be emotionally scarred from this ten years down the line? I hoped not. I doubted it. I headed for the kitchen for a bowl of Grape-Nuts. As I sat at the nook crunching away, I looked up to see one of the Monsters of Rock wander in to check out the offerings in the fridge. Wendy introduced us. His name was Lars Ulrich. What was I supposed to say to a Rock Legend? Should I ask him what I might expect on his next album? Or show him my baseball card to prove I was somebody too? I just waved a friendly greeting. Being the Good Father. I was in the bathroom when Lars and his Metallica cohort left, missing my chance to wish them good luck on the rest of their "Kill 'Em All" Tour.

Sherry was threatening to move out, convinced that ours was a dead-end relationship. She was right. I wasn't giving her what she needed—commitment, passion, emotional support. In the search for true intimacy, I'd lost the horizon. I had a pocketful of excuses: I'd been burned twice already at the altar; I didn't want to be vulnerable again; I didn't trust myself to be faithful; I didn't want to start another family; I was afraid there was too much difference in our ages (fourteen years). I couldn't bring myself to say that I wanted to end it—we'd been together eighteen months—so I acted cool and distant, forcing her hand. The final straw was when I stayed out all night. She left the next day, but not before verbally unloading.

"I know this is what you want," she said, bags packed, standing at the door. "To be rid of me. But you don't have the balls to tell me, so you show me in your own little way. Last night made me realize one frightening fact. You have no respect for me. How could you be so cold and mean and inconsiderate? Consider yourself lucky that you don't feel the hurt I'm feeling. I wanted us to work more than anything I've ever wanted in my life. Not anymore. I just hope that as long as I live I never get involved with somebody like you again. What kind of man are you, Larry?"

I had been guilty of luring her in, then pushing her away. I was into a pattern. Charm them off their feet, move in together, then get cold feet. I was afraid to commit, yet unwilling to be alone. Before Sherry there had been Julie, the lawyer. She too was attractive, childless, younger, and involved in a failing relationship when I met her. And like both my ex-wives, Julie and Sherry had grown up with either no father or else a weak relationship with him.

Yes, a definite pattern. Over and over.

Sherry had raised the question of what kind of man I was. Her words echoed through my mind after she'd left. I certainly wasn't purposefully trying to be a butt hole. I guess it was part of the whole male thing—the need to think I was in control, strong, unconquerable, manly. Every time I started to feel vulnerable, I put up a wall. Torpedoed the love boat.

There was a desperate edge to Kathi's voice. There usually was when she called to tell me about her latest tête-à-tête with Sarah, only this time it was more frantic. They had been at each other's throats since she had split up from her second husband, and her new boyfriend, a carpenter who'd never had children of his own, had moved in and installed a get-tough program. Sarah wanted no part of him and made no bones about it.

"I can't handle it anymore," Kathi cried. "I want her to come and live with you."

Sign me up, I said, ready and willing. Sarah was twelve, very blond, very stubborn. A handful. Stormy. Sulky. Smart. Sometimes, she could be as sweet as she wanted to be. She and Wendy, seven years older, loved each other immensely but picked and sniped at each other relentlessly, competing for Father's attention. Thankfully, they would have their own rooms at opposite ends of the hall downstairs. I was upstairs.

I was finally getting my wish—to have both of my daughters live with me. Mr. Mom. Wendy, nineteen, was maturing, beginning to envision a world beyond Metallica. She had started seeing a therapist, admitting to me for the first time that she had been unhappy for years. She went on a new diet and lost weight. A glow that had been missing since junior high reappeared, and for the first time in her life, she had a steady boyfriend. He was studying to be an engineer, and his biggest flaw seemed only to be the fact he was twenty years old going on eleven. He looked remarkably similar to me at that age.

I too had found a new love interest. Her name was Marcie and she was the office manager of Nike International, the same job my father had at Douglas Aircraft. She had radiant brown hair, green eyes, a degree in sociology from Lewis and Clark College, and rowed competitively. She was five-eight, soft-spoken, a native Oregonian, pro-choice, and fit the familiar pattern—fifteen years younger, childless, coming out of a failed relationship, daughter of an alcoholic father. So, of course, I asked her to move in. And there I was again. Over and over. Marcie, who was adamant about not wanting children of her own, took a deep breath and braced herself for the experience. So did I.

Between us, Marcie and I were making $60,000 a year at Nike. But in September 1986 she quit, objecting to what she saw as the company's sexist and racist policies. She enrolled in a master's program for social workers, specializing in family therapy. (Perhaps she thought she would need it to survive with Larry and his girls.) The financial shock of her quitting had not quite settled in when I was given my pink slip in a big layoff following a major downturn in Nike's profits. So long Shoe Biz, hello free-lance again. From $60,000 to zero in an Oregon minute. I hated the corporate life anyway.

Now what? I was forty-five, unemployed, twice divorced, with my third live-in girlfriend in four years, supporting my two daughters, one a twenty-year-old semi-Metallica groupie, the other a willful thirteen-year-old going through puberty mad at her mom. I had a baseball card worth forty-five cents, an expired teaching certificate, a crummy car, and a piddling severance check from Nike. And an idea about writing a book about my fraternity brothers. But first I needed to make some money free-lancing.

One of my assignments over the next several months was to go to Florida during spring training and write a feature story on baseball star Dale Murphy. I used the occasion to visit Hedy, who had moved to Florida in the seventies. She was now seventy-four. It had been eighteen years since I had last seen her. Denise had told me that lately her mom had been through some tough times, physically and financially, and that it would be a nice gesture if I paid her a visit.

She was living in a prosaic apartment building in North Bay Village, Florida, just north of Miami. A weathered, pale green stucco, with a tiny swimming pool in a central courtyard. Many of the residents were Cuban. I scanned the names on the mailboxes, searching for hers. There it was, wedged between Javier and Martinez: Hedy Lamarr. Her name, once marqueed on movie theaters all across the land, was now printed ingloriously on a strip of plastic tape above her rusted mail slot.

I headed up the stairs. Hedy answered the door and ushered me inside her small one-bedroom apartment. It was jam-packed with antiques and small remnants of her million-dollar past. Prominently displayed on a shelf was an autographed photo of economist Louis Rukeyser, whom Hedy claimed was the ultimate guru on financial matters and was going to lead her to riches. All I knew of Hedy's finances was that she had received a modest settlement in the seventies when she took legal action against Mel Brooks for naming a horse after her in *Blazing Saddles.*

She looked surprisingly well—maybe a bit severe with the penciled eyebrows and red-tinted hair, but incredibly fit for a woman in her seventies, her figure trim, her mind still sharp. Her greeting was warm and friendly. When she noticed I wasn't wearing a watch, she retreated to her bedroom and returned with a handsome gold timepiece with a brown leather strap.

"This used to belong to Clark Gable," she said. "You can have it."

Wearing my new watch, I escorted her to a nearby restaurant. The maître d' explained it would be a thirty-minute wait. That was no problem, I said. But Hedy was still operating on 1945 superstar time and was convinced we should be seated immediately. I feared a scene as she moved toward the maître d'. I intercepted her, persuading her that the wait would give us a nice chance to chat in the bar instead. When we were finally seated for dinner, she barely touched her food. After finishing my meal, I resisted the urge to switch plates and polish off the rest of her seafood platter, remembering that she had once told Denise that my table manners were strictly plebeian. I was trying to convince her that her granddaughter, whom she hadn't seen in fifteen years, was being raised properly.

Following dinner we returned to her apartment to watch the Golden Globe Awards on television. I asked her why she had not appeared in a film or on TV in over two decades. She explained that the roles had been there but the right money hadn't.

I ended our visit with a promise to keep in touch and to take good care of her granddaughter. She hugged me and wished me well, presenting me with an autographed M-G-M studio portrait of herself from her glory years. It was inscribed: "To my favorite son-in-law, with love."

April 1987. Dripping wet, I hopped out of the shower to answer the phone. I was home alone and didn't want to risk missing the phone call I hoped would change my life. Richard Pine, my newly found New York literary agent, had promised to call as soon as he heard from the eight publishing companies to whom he had submitted my 39-page book proposal which promised to detail the lives of five fraternity brothers from Berkeley.

I had met Pine on a trip to New York to research an article that *Sports Illustrated* had assigned me to write on the Baseball Alumni Team (BAT), an organization dedicated to providing financial assistance to needy former major-league ballplayers and their families. Pine, a thirty-something Ivy Leaguer whose father had been a literary agent for twenty-five years, had been recommended to me by Mark Christensen, a Portland writer he represented. After meeting with Pine in New York and learning of his interest in my book idea, I returned to Portland, finished the story for *Sports Illustrated,* and then spent a month writing the proposal, an endeavor that depleted the few bucks I had left in my checking account. I assumed it would take several months to get a response from New York. It took five days.

"Six publishers bid on your proposal," said Pine as I dripped water all over the living-room floor. "Four of the bids are in the low six figures."

Did he say six figures? I tapped the phone to make sure it wasn't a bad connection. Yes, he said it . . . *six figures!*

"Are you positive?" I asked.

"Spend the money!" he replied.

By the end of the day, we had reached an agreement with Doubleday and I was looking at the new-car ads in the *Oregonian.* When Marcie and my daughters returned home late that afternoon, they found me floating near the ceiling.

"Spend the money!" I instructed.

Three months later I set out for California in my new Honda on the first of my fourteen trips to the Golden State in search of the stories of my long-lost fraternity brothers.

69

Steve

Death is nature's warning to slow down.
—John Maynard Keynes

Ayris's slow healing from Steve's death had been compounded by raising a daughter who would never know her father, as well as the onerous responsibility of dealing with the lawsuits and legal entanglements. He had died without a will, or insurance, or legal contracts on property he owned; and the family of Dennis Velucci, the man who was also killed in the crash, had sued the estate for a half million dollars.

There had been a problem determining the exact cause of the crash and who was at the controls when the plane went down. Velucci was also a pilot. The toxology report showed *no* trace of alcohol or drugs in Steve's system. The police report showed that *no* controlled substances had been found inside the cockpit. The rumors had been unfounded. The investigation by the Federal Aviation Administration concluded that when the homemade plane was climbing after a touch-and-go landing in the slough, the engine lost power and was unable to maintain proper airspeed and the plane went into a dive. The cause was "overweighting." Due to the lightweight nature of the aircraft, its maximum cockpit weight capacity when fully fueled on takeoff, as it was the day of the crash, was 285 pounds. Steve and Velucci had a combined weight of 350. According to the FAA's final report, "loss of life resulted from pilot's inaccurate preflight calculations," and the FAA investigators ruled that Steve had been the pilot. Eventually, Steve's estate paid $50,000 in 1984 to Velucci's family, half of which was paid by Ayris.

Ayris moved to San Anselmo in Marin County. She remarried in 1986; her new husband was a San Francisco psychiatrist and she continued her work as an art therapist. But the subject of Steve's attitude toward women was one which continued to bemuse her. In private, he had been a gentle, loving, affectionate man. At the same time, she felt he'd been unconsciously hostile, especially toward her as "his" woman and because she represented women. Her life with Steve had helped her realize how much she allowed for male domination and deprecation. Steve had taught her so much about herself, not because he really knew her, but because she had to look at who she was while she was with him long after he died.

She knew that deep in his heart Steve had loved her and Filaree. And other people. Even some women. He had an empathic way; he was able to talk to and listen to women. Early on he saw the value of women's rights, yet he flagrantly violated them.

He had been in a hurry to be his "own man," to not conform, to be known, to have money. He had been driven by some deep double messages in his life.

Steve had the complex combination of sensitivity toward others and total disregard for their welfare. For Ayris, it had taken her life with him for her to know she could not ever live like that again, to see how demeaning and how pitiful it was and how common it can be in our Western culture, and indeed in much of the world.

70

Loren

Do other men for they would do you. That's the true business precept.
—Charles Dickens

It had been two years since Loren's Pine Top Insurance deal had unraveled. The lawsuit against Greyhound, which had consumed most of his time and resources, was seriously bogged down in legal muck, not even close to a trial date. It was time, he had decided, to get on with his life and make some money, to work a few land deals . . . or in his words, "get back to the basics, the blocking and tackling." That was his business plan.

He was down to his last hundred grand, he claimed.

It was also time, he had concluded, to move back to California and settle down, replant his roots. Construction had started on the rebuilding of the family ranch house in Trowbridge, and he was dividing his time between there and Arizona. He planned to pour his sweat into rebuilding the ranch house, every nail, every brick, every cabinet. It was Ron's architectural design he would be following. His goal was to finish the house by the end of the year and then move in and raise his two "pride and joys," Garrett and Colin, who were in Phoenix with Rita.

After eight years in Phoenix, he was anxious to move back home. Part of it had to do with the fact that he thought it would be healthier for his sons to grow up in the country. Part of it was because he thought the

land boom in Arizona had peaked. And part of it was because the Greyhound deal had left a sour taste in his mouth. And part of it was safety.
An ex-felon who had been involved in a land deal Loren was negotiating
was found with a bullet through his head in Loren's business partner's
backyard. Loren wasn't a suspect in the unsolved case, but he took it as a
clue that the business climate might be a little healthier in California.
He was also still being hounded by the IRS about paying the taxes on the
income he didn't file back in the seventies that landed him in Lompoc.

But, he kept telling himself, he wouldn't change a thing. He'd lived by
two simple rules: don't walk away and don't cheat anyone. He was like
Rocky. He dreamed big. He'd made millions, he'd spent millions. Not
bad for a hayseed from Marysville.

Loren's voice echoed all the way down the hall of the office complex.
"You stupid cocksucker!" he bellowed. "I should fire your fuckin' ass!"

The object of his scorn was Ed, his porky all-purpose gofer with the
Texas drawl, his jailbird buddy from Lompoc. Upon Ed's parole, he had
tracked down Loren and convinced him to hire him as his chauffeur,
administrative assistant, and chief sycophant. Loren was Ed's mentor,
teaching him how to wheel and deal in the real estate business. But now
Ed had messed up big time, losing Loren's checkbook.

"Go find it!" Loren instructed. "And don't come back until you do."

The phone rang. It was Rita, calling to find out how soon he'd be back
to the apartment. She had left the boys with her mother in Phoenix and
flown to California to spend a few days with Loren in Sacramento to
check on the progress of the ranch house. Given the dubious future of
their relationship—they weren't married and he'd vowed they never
would be—she was apprehensive about moving to a place where the
nearest supermarket was fifteen miles away and the only person she
would know within fifty zip codes would be Loren's mom, a woman she
got along with about as well as broken glass.

"I'll be there when I fuckin' get there!" he snapped. "I've got a meeting
this afternoon. Or in case you forgot, I work for a living. Or did you think
I paid all the bills by magic?" He slammed down the receiver.

"Fuckin' cunt," he mumbled to himself. "She flies up here and thinks
she owns my time." They had gone out to dinner the night before, and
when they got into an argument, Loren walked out of the restaurant,
leaving her no choice but to take a cab back to the apartment.

He shuffled a few legal papers from the Greyhound suit, then went off
to a business meeting. He was dressed in dark slacks, starched white
shirt open at the collar, and ostrich-skin cowboy boots. The meeting was

with John Morgan, described by Loren as a "big California money man." It was a meeting to discuss a possible deal on a parcel of raw land in Carefree near Phoenix, owned by a man who, according to Loren, was in financial trouble and needed to unload it quick for cash. Loren's role was to put the buyer and seller together. At this stage of the deal, he still wasn't sure whose side of the transaction he was working for, although he considered it an honor to be meeting with Morgan, a man who owned thousands of acres of San Joaquin farmland, cattle, restaurants, buildings, and a casino in Las Vegas. Morgan had recently sold a hotel in Vegas to a Japanese investor who had allegedly outbid Merv Griffin, Donald Trump, and Melvin Davis. The BIG hitters.

On the drive to the meeting in his Mercedes, Loren thought briefly about his father. He couldn't remember what year Hal had died, or even if he had gone to the funeral. He also brooded about his split with Craig. He and Craig had not seen or talked to each other in two years. Their twenty-five-year friendship was in ruins. Craig, who was now the executive director of the American Pain and Stress Clinic in Denver and a deacon in his church, claimed that Loren had screwed him out of a lot of money. They'd had great times together. But now Craig was telling people he couldn't trust Loren anymore.

Loren's version of the demise of the friendship was very different than Craig's. As he saw it, Craig had always liked to use him as a scapegoat. And he had always let him, figuring Craig had a fragile ego that needed it. But as far as Loren was concerned, Craig had blown his own money with his lifestyle. It wasn't Loren's fault Craig was always going to Vegas and Tahoe and throwing money away. Loren thought Craig was a hypocrite, going to Bible study in Denver and pretending to be so pure. Loren had tried to help him, but Craig just wouldn't listen. He'd spent a lot of time over the years straightening out Craig's life; he'd saved Craig's football career, he claimed. Craig would get down and depressed, and then Loren would have to build his ego back up. Craig had said that Loren had used him in business. What a joke, Loren mused. Nobody could make money off Craig's name. When he had been traded by Dallas to New York, business people wanted nothing to do with him. The way Loren saw it, he'd lost a shitload of money because of Craig. Every time he was around him, his financial graph went down. They'd been great friends, like brothers, and he'd always love him, but Craig was confused. That's all there was to it.

Loren and Morgan met at Fat's, an oak-paneled restaurant and bar in Sacramento's Old Town. Morgan, who arrived twenty minutes late, was a huge man, a 300-pounder dressed in cowboy boots and shirt, Levi's jeans and jacket, and a ten-gallon hat. He was accompanied by a large Native American who looked like a cross between Jim Thorpe and Herman Munster, and was fingering a very large-caliber bullet. Morgan flopped down into a chair and flipped a huge wad of hundred-dollar bills on the table. He signaled for the waitress, ordering two rounds of drinks and four plates of hors d'oeuvres. He instructed Loren to put his wallet back in his pocket.

Two hours and six rounds of drinks later, they still had not discussed "the deal." Morgan preferred to talk about his idea of starting a Playmate of the Month at his casino. It would be a Las Vegas contest; one month all the contestants would be secretaries, the next month waitresses, and so on. It was pure gold, they agreed, a foolproof plan providing unlimited access to hundreds of beautiful women, all of them dying to be the casino's playmate.

Loren interrupted the playmate discussion just long enough to tell Morgan about his lawsuit against Greyhound. It was a ploy to whet Morgan's appetite in case somewhere down the line he needed a deep pocket to prevent Greyhound from dragging the case out for so long that he was no longer able to financially afford to fight them. It was not until they stood up to leave that the subject of the property in Arizona was mentioned.

"It's a great piece of dirt," Loren explained. "It's adjacent to the proposed site of a new basketball arena for the Phoenix Suns. You might want to hop on your plane and take a look at it."

"I'll let you know," replied Morgan.

That was it—out of a two-hour meeting a total of thirty seconds was devoted to "the deal." Afterward, Loren deemed the meeting a big success. He thought of it as setting the table. You don't want to flap like a duck, that's the way he looked at it. People were his business. This was a done deal.

Leaving the meeting, he drove his big blue Mercedes across town toward his apartment, a triumphant smile on his face, country music blaring on the radio. Suddenly, he started honking his horn and flapping like a duck. He had spotted his mother in her little blue Mercedes convertible, a car that once belonged to Craig. She too was on her way to the apartment. Rita had called her, crying hysterically, asking her if she could bring her some Valium.

The apartment was located in a huge complex, 500 units, four swimming pools, two rec rooms, carports, yuppiemobiles, speed bumps. Genevieve arrived first, disappearing quickly into the apartment. When

Loren pulled into his carport, Ed was standing there with a big stained-tooth grin. He had the checkbook. It had fallen under the front seat of the Bronco that Loren let him drive to run errands.

"Good thing for you, boy," said Loren, lingering in the parking lot to discuss possible dinner plans. Genevieve hustled back out of the apartment, urgently summoning him inside. He trudged off behind her, then reemerged a minute later wearing a pained expression.

"Rita's in there totally freaking out, gasping for air," he said to Ed. "She thinks she's having a damn heart attack. Now I have to take her to the damn hospital. Fucking tomatoes! I swear, they're always pulling shit like this."

71

Jim

We can't all be heroes because somebody has to sit on the curb and clap as they go by.
—Will Rogers

Jim was now a senior vice president with the Bechtel Corporation in San Francisco. He and Vallarie had purchased a rambling three-bedroom ranch-style atop a hill at the end of a cul-de-sac in the rustic suburb of Lafayette, a quiet, rural community nestled among the oak trees, pyracantha bushes, and riding trails of the East Bay hills. Before World War II, Lafayette had been a quiet farming village, but in the postwar building boom, bedrooms blossomed where corn had grown. According to its Chamber of Commerce, the 8,690 households in the town had a mean income of $45,800 in 1987 and the average three-bedroom house sold for $247,000.

Inside Jim's home, the pictures on the walls told a story of his adventurous spirit—photos of him going over Class VI Rainie Falls as a young river guide, him climbing into his F-4 on the deck of the *Ranger,* him floating untethered in outer space wearing his jet-powered backpack. On his desk was a snapshot of him shaking hands with George Bush; in the vestibule was a framed portrait painted by his father of him in his NASA space suit. And on the refrigerator door, next to all the magnetized letters and a notice for the next Burton Valley School PTA meeting, was a group photo of the seven friends who died on the *Challenger*, a magnetic heart placed right in the center.

In only four years with Bechtel, Jim had been promoted from program manager to vice president to senior vice president. And he had the goodies to prove it—new vacation lot at Tahoe, new van for Vallarie, new golf clubs. He was flying all over the world "chasing business." He took several trips to Saudi Arabia, where Bechtel was the head contractor in the building of an entire city. Business was booming. He also traveled around the globe as a member of ASE (Association of Space Explorers), and he usually took Vallarie on these trips. They were in Holland as guests at an international conference on space when Vallarie found herself at a gala dinner seated at a table with several of the wives of Russian cosmonauts. At first, she was intimidated, but it turned out great. "We really bonded because we came to the conclusion that no matter what country it is, men are all the same," she told friends later. "Those Russian guys are just like ours, trying to blame their wives every time a sock is missing."

In 1987 Vallarie had worked part-time as a nurse for a family practitioner in Walnut Creek, but quit after only two months on the job. "I wasn't cut out to be a suburban nurse," she'd told Jim. "I've got better things to do than wipe noses for a bunch of snotty brats." The last straw was when the doctor asked her to vacuum the office. "I didn't go four years to nursing school so I could do floors," she replied. "Sorry, but I don't even do my own floors."

Then she had taken on another part-time job, this one as a salesperson for Krups, demonstrating cookware in department stores. When she first told Jim she'd accepted the job, he just rolled his eyes. On one occasion when she'd been eager to show him a new five-minute training video she'd received, and flicked off the six o'clock news to insert her tape into the VCR, Jim instructed her to switch back to the news.

"I've watched your stupid space hero video a million times," she said. "It won't hurt you to take five lousy minutes to watch 'The Magic of Soufflé.' Or don't you care what I do?"

Next, she had quit the job as a Krups demonstrator after only nine months. "I've got more important things to do with my life than stand around and show a bunch of frustrated housewives how to fry sausage," she told Jim. Now she was a part-time receptionist for a marketing consultant firm in Oakland. "It's great," she liked to say. "I get to look cute in my little business suits and have yuppie businessmen hit on me at the water cooler. But please, I am not a receptionist. I am a support person . . . just as I am a helpmate for my strong and virile husband."

But in her more reflective moments, she admitted that Jim had a healthy respect for women, a trait she attributed to his mother and grandmother's strong influence when he was growing up, as well as having worked closely at NASA with powerful women such as Sally Ride and Judy Resnik.

Dressed in his NASA blue flight suit, Jim navigated the morning traffic of Lafayette on his way to Burton Valley Grade School, where he was the star attraction of the 9 A.M. assembly at his daughters' school, the second time in two years that he'd been asked and obliged. He worried that he was about to become officially overexposed as a celebrity in Lafayette, having recently served as the featured speaker at the Lafayette branch of the University Women's Club, where he received a standing ovation after being introduced as "a true American hero." Of all the guys in the fraternity back in 1962, he would have been everyone's last choice for the role, including his buddy Toad, who had not committed suicide as rumored, but had died of a massive pulmonary thromboembolism at the age of thirty-seven in 1981.

Jim parked his dented Chevy pickup in front of the school and headed for the cafeteria, where Vallarie was helping set up the metal folding chairs. Her primary role with the school, however, was to help raise money to pay for staff and supplies to keep alive the science and art programs that had been axed due to cuts in the school budget. She was in charge of licking envelopes, because, as she put it, the chairperson didn't want her on the phone committee, afraid of what she'd say to the people who refused to contribute. Her other volunteer position was meet director for the girls' Lafayette Moraga Youth Swim Club.

As Jim walked into the cafeteria, he was joined by a swarm of wide-eyed second-graders, including his youngest, Tori, who took her daddy's hand, beaming like the Player of the Year in Show and Tell. He was determined to be involved in Tori and Jamie's lives. He had mostly pleasant memories of his own childhood, but if there was one thing he would have changed, other than his father's frequent unemployment, it would have been that his parents had shown more of an interest in his scouting and his sports. He wasn't going to repeat that mistake, making every effort to attend his daughters' soccer matches, swim meets, and piano recitals. His big regret as a parent was that he'd missed all of that with Jenny, his daughter from his first marriage. Living hundreds of miles away had made it tough, relegating him to phone calls and visits during the summer. He had faithfully paid his child support for sixteen years. Jenny was a senior in high school in San Diego, soon to enroll at the

University of Oregon, but there wasn't the closeness that he had with Tori and Jamie. Even though he still resented the way his first wife, Patty, had dumped him as soon as he got home from Vietnam, his one consolation was that she had done an excellent job in raising Jenny.

"Boys and girls," announced the principal, "please welcome Burton Valley's most famous resident." Three hundred wiggling kids applauded.

Jim knew better than to give them the wonders-of-outer-space lecture. He went straight to the projector, opening with the scene of him in a Jell-O fight at zero gravity. And of course 300 kids howled and squealed. When the film was over, he went right to the questions and answers. One hundred arms strained for the ceiling.

"Are you really Tori's dad?"

"How do you go to the bathroom up there?"

"Were you scared?"

"What's it like in space?"

Realizing that he might be all day answering questions and miss his eleven o'clock meeting at Bechtel, he wrapped up the session, waved goodbye, and headed for his car, stopping to kiss Tori on the way out the door. He never did answer the question about how he went to the bathroom up there.

Jim took off for San Francisco and Vallarie returned to the house. She popped an English muffin in the toaster and poured a cup of coffee from her Krups coffeemaker. As she walked by Jim's rolltop desk in the living room, she opened a handwritten letter sitting on top. It was addressed to him, but she always opened his mail. Trust wasn't a problem in their marriage. After reading the letter, her eyes teared.

A month earlier she and Jim and the girls had left for Tahoe on a Saturday morning for a weekend of skiing. On the way up, he stopped at a hospital in Sacramento to talk to a ten-year-old boy who was dying of leukemia and had asked the Make-A-Wish Foundation if he could talk to an astronaut. While Vallarie and the girls waited in the lobby, Jim had gone upstairs to visit with the boy. He thought it would take fifteen minutes. He was gone two hours. There was no skiing that day. The letter was from the boy's parents, informing Jim that their child had died, but they wanted him to know that his visit was the happiest day of their son's life.

Vallarie put the letter back on the desk. That's so like him, she thought, brushing away a tear. He never would have said anything about that letter. Jim could discover a cure for cancer and he'd come home from work that day and she'd ask him how it went at the office and he'd just shrug and say, "Okay." She loved him, yes, she did . . . even if she had to share him.

72

Ron

I tell you the past is a bucket of ashes.
—Carl Sandburg

In 1988 Ron was an associate architect with the Parks and Recreation Department in Sacramento, working on restoration of historical buildings, currently assigned to assist in the redesign of the new visitors' center on the property of the Hearst Castle at San Simeon. After divorcing Bertena in 1985, he had married Connie, his third wife. Two things they had in common were that they both had degrees from Cal and they both very much wanted to have a child.

After marrying Connie, he had rented out his stucco tract home in Sacramento and moved into her house in Stockton, a fifty-mile commute south of Sacramento. Located in the upper San Joaquin Valley, it is an inland port on the Sacramento River, which carries California's rich agricultural harvest to San Francisco Bay. It was easier, they decided, for him to commute to work every day in a state van than it was for her to drive to her teaching job in Modesto. And besides, her house was much nicer; it was in an exclusive development built around a man-made lake, with community swimming pool, wide streets, circular driveways, and manicured lawns. Connie's house—and Ron was resolute always in pointing out that it was "her" house—was a custom-designed ranch-style, with a landscaped front lawn and a backyard easement to the lake.

Thus far in their marriage, their conjugal efforts to have a child had been unsuccessful. They weren't through trying.

Connie was a stickler for neatness. The house was immaculate, every throw pillow perfectly fluffed, every copy of *Town and Country* and *Architectural Digest* neatly stacked. In the kitchen the handles of the coffee cups all pointed west and the spice rack was arranged alphabetically. The pastel soap balls in the bathroom matched the towels. Whenever Ron entered the house, he diligently removed his wing tips and left them on the front porch. He was also quick to drop to his hands and knees to remove any crumbs he might drop on the sepia carpet. And this was a veteran of fraternity food fights where spaghetti was left to hang like stalactites from the dining-room ceiling.

October 1988. On a warm fall afternoon Ron was standing on the Pi KA porch, scanning the postgame football throng streaming down Piedmont Avenue. He had just watched his alma mater get thrashed by USC . . . just like when he was a player. He was dressed in brown slacks, brown wing tips, white shirt, no tie, with his Cal letterman's sweater draped around his shoulders. He had tried to put it on earlier in the day, but the new spare tire he was carrying made it too snug. He continued eyeing the crowd, not in hopes of spotting an old cheerleader or an ex-goat brother—he was looking for his son Royce. They were supposed to meet in front of the fraternity. Ron was anxious, partially because he was eager to spend the evening with his son, and partially because he was concerned about Connie, who was back home in Stockton. She was pregnant and not feeling well. The possibility of a miscarriage was at the front of both of their minds.

When Ron had first received the news that Connie was pregnant, he was thrilled. But there was much to think about. Such as concerns about her health. She would be forty when the baby was born, and she had already lost a baby in the past. But assuming that everything went well, what then? He was fast approaching fifty . . . and the more he thought about it, the more he worried that he was too old to be starting fatherhood all over again. And of course he wanted to be the Good Father. That would be how he could redeem his past failures, he hoped, a way to relieve his lingering guilt and to patch the hole in his psyche. He had a mission.

He also viewed a new child as something of a Catch-22. If he was the Good Father to this new child, he worried that it might hurt his tenuous relationship with Royce, now twenty. Ron was concerned that if he was all huggy and lovey and buying gifts for the newborn it would seem unfair to Royce, whose childhood had been empty of much emotional or financial support from his father. He also worried that his attention to a new baby would further anger Anna, who was still calling him to demand support money, despite the fact that he was no longer legally responsible for sending it. She contended that because he was now making close to $50,000 a year, it was his moral obligation to help her financially, just as she had supported him during his troubled times twenty years earlier.

What also scared Ron about Connie's pregnancy was that he still wasn't secure in the marriage. They had been together three years and he felt as if he was still on trial, auditioning for the part, one screw-up away from being sent packing. This would not be a screw-up of infidelity or physical abuse or alcohol; it had to do with issues of intimacy and tenderness. Or at least that's what he thought. There were also questions of compatibility. His friends thought her to be tense and unyielding; he had taken her to a Big Game party in Palo Alto, a function attended by his old teammates and fraternity brothers, and her apparent discomfort at the gathering made others in the room uneasy. In recent months she had told him he was negligent and unmindful. Not to mention messy. Ron feared that once the baby was born, she would say, "Thank you very much but I think I'll do it on my own from here." He would be out the door and gone. Zero for three as a father. And that scared him.

He continued to watch for Royce, who was living by himself in the tough Tenderloin district of San Francisco and working as a bicycle messenger boy, which helped pay for rent and the photography classes that he hoped would someday lead to a career. Royce had inherited his father's and grandfather's artistic interest, but there had been a time in the not too distant past when Ron worried that Royce's only involvement in photography would be a mug shot in a post office. Royce had been a disaffected teenager, dropping out, fighting with his mother, experimenting with drugs, brushing against the law. At one point, he lived out of the back seat of the old Chevy that Ron had helped him buy. Anna, who had found Jesus, was absolutely convinced her son had fallen into the devil's hands. But in the past year, he was slowly letting loose some of his miscreant ways. Ron sent him money from time to time to help him with living expenses.

Royce finally arrived; he was dressed all in black, his wavy black hair slicked back, his skin light like his father's. He was to the young fraternity brothers standing in front of the house what Elvis was to Pat Boone. Coeds turned to gawk. So did their mothers. He was six-three, 180, angular features, high cheekbones . . . an air of rebellion and brooding, but with an engaging smile. "He's gorgeous," a young woman whispered.

Ron introduced him to several ex-goat brothers. He had asked Royce to meet him at the fraternity, not because he wanted to show his friends what a hunk he had sired, but rather to expose another part of himself to Royce, to let him meet a few of his friends from his past and learn more about who his dad really was. For so many years Ron had tried to conceal that from him, ashamed of who he was.

After a brief stay at the frat, they turned to leave. The small gathering of goat brothers were plotting an evening of food and drink, and it was suggested to Ron that he catch up after he'd taken Royce out to dinner. He declined the offer, determined to spend the evening with his son as promised.

"Besides," he added, "I told Connie I'd be home before midnight. If I'm late, she just may have all my stuff waiting for me out on the porch." He chuckled.

Spring 1989. Dressed in dirty coveralls and work boots, Ron worked furiously in the backyard of his rental house in Sacramento, removing debris and loading concrete chunks from an old patio into a wheelbarrow. He was clearing a site to build a deck. He enjoyed the physical labor, a break from his forty-hour week behind a desk.

Ron had been promoted from his job as an associate architect with Parks and Recreation to a supervisory position with the Department of Corrections. The state was in the process of designing four new prisons. For eleven years he'd worked for the state, and for eleven years he'd been an exemplary and reliable employee, well liked by his co-workers. His plan was to stay with the state until retirement.

He had come to Sacramento today not only to work on his rental property but also because Michael, his one-year-old son, had a cold and Connie was afraid Ron would spread more germs or wake the baby from his nap if he stayed around the house.

Ron was trying his hardest to be the Good Father, but he still constantly wrestled with doubts about his performance. Much of the time he felt as if he was in the way. He also wondered if Connie was trying too hard to be the Perfect Mom; she rarely relaxed and treated every sneeze as if it was terminal diphtheria. And now, incredibly, she was pregnant again.

Issues of parenting were dividing them. He was trying to sort it out, take stock of his life. He had contacted many old friends and all his major women—Jackie, Joyce, Kristi, Anna, Bertena—in an effort to sort through old baggage and bury old ashes. Apologize for misdeeds. It had been a catharsis. Loose ends had been tied up. He was hopeful it would help him in his relationship with Connie.

The one relationship from the past that he wasn't having any success in smoothing over was Anna. She seemed to be unable, even after twenty years, to let go of her pain. After he'd become a father again, she wrote him and quoted long scriptures from the Bible and told him of the sadness in her heart for having lost out on the opportunity to experience a normal family life with him and of her concern for Royce.

Anna frustrated him. So did the fact that he was almost fifty and he still did not have financial security. There was no money socked away to pay for college educations, or retirement, or resort property, or to take care of his parents. (His mom was in a rest home in L.A., barely able to recognize him when he came to visit.) It also frustrated him that he wasn't doing anything with his art. He thought about painting pictures and taking drawing classes. But he didn't. And never a day went by that he didn't think of his first son, wondering if he was healthy and happy, wondering if he would ever get to meet him. Of all the loose ends in his life, that was the one he'd most like to tie up.

Winter of 1990. Ron was tired and discouraged . . . and sleeping in the garage. At night, as a frigid wave swept through the San Joaquin Valley, he shivered against the cold and wrapped himself in blankets on a cot, the freezing air swooping in under the garage door. He could hear the faint cries coming from the nursery. Ryan, his infant son, needed to be fed. Or maybe that was Michael crying. Sometimes it was hard for Ron to distinguish the difference through the garage wall. He was sleeping in the garage so that Connie could get a good night's sleep. She was working full-time and taking the kids to day care as well as doing the housework.

Ron was not supposed to come home until after 7:30, when the boys were already in bed. He hoped that Connie would soon allow him to move back inside. But he worried that she had decided she would be better off raising the children by herself. It was more than just the babies. She had talked of separation. The story was familiar—he wasn't satisfying her emotional needs. She talked about how they had so little in common. There were complaints that he watched too much football . . . and that he didn't read enough books . . . and that he wasn't nurturing enough.

It was now a nightly struggle for him to keep warm in the garage. He was fifty years old . . . and yet there he was, sleeping next to the rear tires of his wife's silver BMW, watching his icy breath dance across the blackness, and worrying about his sons.

73

Loren

But when a son is called on too early, the one thing that boy did wrong is that he didn't save his mother. He didn't make her happier, or take away her pain. He failed to replace his (inadequate) father, and so the father is in shame, but the son is in guilt, because he should have been able to do it . . . A man may marry "the wrong woman" in the midst of his guilt; another may become impotent. Still another may become a compulsive seducer, and so continue to feel guilt over never satisfying any woman's emotional needs.
—Robert Bly, *Iron John*

It was two days after Mother's Day 1989. Rita was on the edge, ready to crack, feeling as if she might hyperventilate again as she had that day she thought she was having a heart attack. Loren was in Phoenix on business and had promised to call her on Mother's Day . . . but there was no call, no card, no flowers. Nothing.

The previous night she had lain awake trembling, unable to sleep, staring at the phone, trying to find the courage to call him. To confront him. She didn't even know for certain where he was staying in Phoenix. She had also stared at the closet and the suitcases on the floor, trying to get up the courage to leave. To be strong. Her year at the ranch had been the worst of her life, a nightmare.

She was trapped in Trowbridge. She had moved to the ranch when construction on the house was finished in 1988, packing up Garrett, four, and Colin, two, and her blind hopes. She had lived in Phoenix her whole life, but the possibilities at the ranch seemed so idyllic: clean air and wide-open spaces for the boys; a spacious new two-story, four-bedroom house surrounded by hundred-year-old elm trees; a barn, carriage house, and workshop in back; a dog as gentle as Old Yeller; roosters crowing in the morning. Old-fashioned country living. Loren had been blunt—their only chance at a relationship, he'd said, was if she moved to California with the boys. His "pride and joys." She believed him. He wouldn't commit to marriage, but he'd promised that they would be a family, and go on picnics together, and dress up the boys and go out to dinner, and be the happiest family. It sounded exactly the way she always wanted it. She bought the spiel. He was a master salesman, so believable, so filled with qualities she wanted in a man—strong, smart, dynamic.

But there'd been no picnics. No happy family. From the day she moved in, it had been one big living hell for her, stuck out in the middle of nowhere, lonely, neglected, verbally steamrolled. He was gone half the time, back to Phoenix, doing his business, keeping her marooned. Or had she marooned herself? She admitted that sometimes she felt like nothing more than his breeding stock, the blue-eyed blonde who gave him the towheaded boys he claimed he wanted. Her only salvation was those boys and her job selling major appliances at Sears—she commuted into Sacramento three days a week, leaving the boys with a babysitter.

She had asked herself a thousand times why she stayed, allowed herself to be trapped, allowed herself to be chained to such a loveless relationship. Part of it was the children, of course. She didn't want her boys to grow up without a father. And part of it was money. She was trying to squirrel away money from her Sears paycheck, plotting her escape. But without financial help from Loren, which she knew he'd never agree to, she didn't think she could make it on her own. And part of it was hope. There was her blind desire to have it be the way she had always dreamed, the way Loren had promised.

But how much longer could she take it, the verbal abuse, the neglect? She had told him that things needed to change and he told her about the concessions he'd already made and how he wasn't going to change any more. She'd told him she needed more attention and he rambled on about the pressures of his business. Business came first, he said. His battle with Greyhound was still unresolved, buried deeper than ever under mountains of legal briefs after three years. He was shuttling between Trowbridge and Phoenix, always a dozen deals going at once. Always leaving her stranded with the kids. His "done deal" with the fat cat Morgan never got past the drinks and snacks at the bar. Rita couldn't understand why Loren didn't just take the $5 million he claimed Greyhound had offered to settle out of court. Was he lying? Or why didn't he just pay off the IRS and get them off his back, once and for all? When she pressed him on it, he'd replied, "What the hell do you know about business? You've never been to college. I suppose working at Sears makes you an expert." When she pressed him on why he treated her the way he did, he told her it was because she woke up in the morning and the first thing she did every day was start pecking on him. He had admitted he felt trapped, caught between a relationship he didn't want and the sons he wanted to raise. Parenting, he said, was a chance to teach Garrett and Colin how the world works, to show them the difference between right and wrong. He would be ten times the parent his father was—he would show affection and "spank the living wee-wee" out of them when they needed it. And he wasn't going to let their mother smother them the way it had happened to him. He would set the rules. But as far as Rita was concerned, Loren was a "Santa Claus Dad"—great at playing games, but when it came to the real parenting, he was nowhere to be found. He had threatened to fight her for custody if she tried to take off with the boys. That was in one breath. Then he told her he wouldn't bat an eye if she took off. "Go stick your head in the sand, or take the boys to Alaska, or fly off to wherever your little vigil in search of a hero takes you," he'd said. "Good luck and good riddance."

When she had finally summoned her courage to phone him in Phoenix on the day after Mother's Day, she was sobbing. "I don't know what you want me to do, Loren," she'd said. "I'm home. I'm a mom. I work. But I don't feel I exist. I'm having a hard time feeling that there's anybody out there who cares. It's just a nightmare. A nightmare. Loren, I have to be held, I have to be told I'm loved and that you miss me. Please talk to me. All I'm asking is to be part of your life. I'm asking for help, for talk."

He told her that her life was better than it's ever been.

"I have no life," she responded.

He told her not to call him again if all she was going to do was selfishly bitch. Then he hung up.

Her mind was made up. She would talk to him when he got home, and then she would gather up the boys, tell them that she was sorry that she had to do this, and then take off. She didn't know where she would go, or how she would get there, or what she would use for money. But no matter what, it had to be better than the hell she was living in.

·   ·   ·   ·   ·

Four months later. Heading for a business meeting, Loren was dressed for the kill—tan slacks, white shirt, beige sports coat, no tie, ostrich-skin cowboy boots. The prey was two venture capitalists. The bait was his scheme to market a revolutionary new "can't miss" asbestos sealant and fire retardant, a product that could cure America's asbestos woes. The venue was a conference room at the Oakland Airport. The payoff could be "zillions." All he had to do was get the venture capitalists to shell out two million up front to get the ball rolling. Today.

The big surprise was—or was it?—that Rita was still living at the ranch. The even bigger shock, according to both of them, was that the relationship was doing better than it had in the ten years they had known each other. They only disagreed on what caused the change.

At first, when Loren came back from Phoenix, Rita decided not to confront him. Instead, she retreated somewhere inside herself and concentrated on taking care of the boys and figuring out how she was going to get away. She kept her mouth shut and didn't confront him. And then for reasons not totally clear to her, Loren began to communicate. Maybe it was because the court had ruled in his favor in a preliminary hearing with Greyhound. Or maybe it was because she and the boys totally ignored him on Father's Day. Or maybe it was because he figured out that she'd given up and was serious about leaving with the boys. When they finally talked, she told him if he didn't change she was dust on the highway. He agreed to try. He didn't promise to roll over and play dead— he let her know that men think differently than women, and that he was the one with the college education, and that he was the one who had the important business. She'd heard all that a million times, but what made it different was that there was a pleasantness she'd never seen before. She was proud of herself for having stood up to him. On his next trip to Phoenix he called every night; he took her and the boys to Disneyland, and even hired a babysitter to come to their hotel room so that just the two of them could go out for dinner; he promised to fix up the carriage house so that she could use it to start a day-care center, which is what he'd wanted her to do ever since she'd moved to the ranch.

Rita was convinced the change in Loren was night and day. He disagreed. It was Rita who had changed, he believed, not him. Before, she had been ungiving, unseeing, always fighting him. Now she was showing faith in the way he was handling things. She was suddenly realizing that he had built the ranch house for their future, and that when he was off wheeling and dealing he was doing it for the family. She was accepting the fact that he needed to concentrate 110 percent on his deals and couldn't be bothered with the petty stuff. And she was understanding that he had hundreds and hundreds of girls in his past, but now he was ready to settle down and raise his boys, happy to be back home and creating something positive. Rita had finally learned, he believed, to just walk away instead of trying to challenge him, because when she did that, she was going to lose. On that they agreed.

Loren was the last to arrive at the meeting at the Oakland Airport. On one side of the table were the two venture capitalists—an impeccably stylish woman of Chinese ancestry in a white business suit and an eloquent gray-haired Jewish man who was a former philosophy professor at Cal. Joining Loren on his side of the table was his business adviser, Bob Grant, an M.B.A. from Harvard, and Ed, the ex-con from Texas. Ed, who was wearing jeans and a faded black golf shirt that didn't quite cover his belly, had made two trips to Arkansas to talk to the man who had invented, patented, and manufactured the asbestos sealant and fire retardant in a small garage in the woods. The man currently had a representative of a minority-owned marketing company in the South trying to distribute it, but Ed and Loren were convinced he would turn both manufacturing and marketing rights over to them . . . if they flashed $50,000 in front of him.

"The first thing we gotta do," said Ed to open the meeting, "is get rid of that dumb nigger they got doing the marketing down there in Arkansas."

The Chinese woman's and the former philosophy professor's mouths dropped. Loren, seeing the venture capital flying out the window just fifteen seconds into the meeting, jumped to the rescue. "I think what Ed meant to say," he said diplomatically, apologetically, "was that the potential for this product is unlimited."

Loren had done his homework, spending a month learning about asbestos and sealants and what the competition was. For thirty minutes he laid out a silky-smooth presentation with videos and graphs and technical talk of the product's properties and reliabilities. He presented business plans, marketing strategies, contract proposals. He talked of escrow, equity performance contracts, general partnerships, operating capital, letters of intent, receivables. In the words of his Harvard M.B.A. adviser, it was a "genius" of a presentation.

"The secret to life is financing," he concluded. The venture capitalists were duly impressed. They shook hands and promised to get back to him soon.

After the meeting, Loren turned to Ed. "It's a done deal," he said, beaming. "That chick was eating it up."

·   ·   ·   ·

As the spring of a new decade neared in Trowbridge, the world around it was changing with astonishing and unpredictable speed: the Berlin Wall was tumbling down, the Cold War was thawing out, and one Sunday after church, Loren and Rita had gone on a picnic. With their two blond towheads beside them, they strolled through a field of wildflowers. It was just as Loren had promised three years earlier, just as Rita had dreamed.

Loren had a smile on his face. The venture capital for the asbestos sealant wasn't yet a "done deal," but it was still a possibility, one of the many irons he had cooking: a ranch near Visalia . . . a housing development in the Mother Lode . . . a new mall in Yuba City. And his sixth lawyer on the Greyhound suit was telling him things were looking good. A settlement with the IRS was even a possibility.

Rita was smiling too. She was no longer working at Sears; her day-care center was up and running and already had ten kids enrolled. But what was even more exciting for her, a change she couldn't have imagined in her wildest dreams on Mother's Day, was that she was now Mrs. Loren Hawley.

74

Larry

No man knows his true character until he has run out of gas, purchased something on the installment plan and raised an adolescent.
—Mercelene Cox

It was 1988. Sarah was a sophomore in high school and was so mad at me she was ready to clobber me upside my head with her Esprit bag. I had just grounded her for the second weekend in a row, dealing a crushing blow to her vigorous social life. This time it was for multiple offenses —fifteen minutes late for curfew, not cleaning her room, talking on the phone after her 11 P.M. weekday bedtime.

"Grounding doesn't work!" she screamed, stomping toward her room. "And neither do your stupid rules."

Sarah had been living with me full-time for two hectic years. She visited her mother, who lived ten miles away, once a month. Their relationship was combative, neither of them willing to give ground. Most of the time, I had the feeling I was alone in raising Sarah through the turbulence of her adolescent years. I had neither asked for nor was I receiving child support. Wendy, twenty-two, had moved back to Seattle after living with me for three years and was working in a day-care center, living in an apartment, struggling with her weight. Marcie and I had been together two years; she had finished graduate school and was working as a family therapist with sexually and emotionally abused children.

We shared the $525 monthly rent on our modest three-bedroom bunga-low. I worked at home, sometimes going days without leaving the house, obsessed with writing about my goat brothers. Most of my advance from my publisher was spent on research trips to California. While I was gone, usually for a week at a time, Marcie watched over Sarah. They were not close, basically just coexisting, waging their disputes through me, interacting only when necessary or when I was out of town.

Infuriated at being grounded, Sarah slammed her door. "I hate you!" she yelled.

Part of me wanted to bust in her room and wash her mouth out with the Paul Mitchell shampoo I'd just bought her. Another part of me wanted to sit down on the floor and cry. I was doing everything I could to provide Sarah with as normal a home life as possible: I was there for her when she went to school in the morning, there for her when she got home in the afternoon; I attended parent-teacher conferences, drove her to the mall, cooked her meals; and to make sure she knew I was no longer a father driving backward through life, I typed out a set of rules so there'd be no misunderstandings. Dream on. We butted heads, fre-quently, and I never knew for sure if I was doing the right thing, or losing my cool, or in over my head as a parent. We got into yelling matches that rattled the neighbors' windows. Nothing I'd learned at Cal in the early sixties came remotely close to preparing me to raise an adolescent in the late eighties. Back then, I'd assumed that was women's work.

Sarah returned to the living room to resume the battle. "None of my friends can believe you make me be in bed by eleven on school nights," she claimed.

"I don't care what your friends say," I said.

"You treat me as if I'm some sort of horrible kid," she replied. "Maybe I'm not perfect, but what if I was into crack and stuff like that?"

My problems with her were indeed lightweight compared to "crack and stuff like that." Still, she could be punishing in her sulky funks. Our first year together had been a real struggle. She was angry—at her mom, at me, at the world; she cut school, got C's and D's, pouted around the house. But she had made huge strides in our second year together. I had impressed on her that we were in this for the duration; we had gone to counseling together several times. She had gone from near failing in her classes to all A's and B's; she was working two hours a day as a waitress in a retirement home, babysitting regularly, buying her own clothes, smiling more, decorating her room with posters of James Dean and River Phoenix. She always looked as if she just stepped off the pages of *Sassy;*

the boys circled the block trying to get her to take notice; the phone rang off the hook every night . . . and it was never for me.

"Sarah, I'm not saying you're a bad kid," I said. "It's just that you're old enough to be more responsible."

"I am, too, responsible."

I pointed out that in the last week she had broken her retainer, left her coat at school, lost her house key, and failed to return a library book on time. Not to mention the aggravation of the rap music blaring from her stereo, a form of music I ranked just above Metallica in listening pleasure.

"See what I mean," she said. "All you ever do is criticize. I never hear you say anything about the good things I do."

"That's not true," I countered.

And on and on we carped. All I could do was cross my fingers and wonder how we were going to make it all the way through her high school years together. I assumed that it would have to be love that carried us through.

My big literary advance was dwindling rapidly, consumed by my trips to interview the goats and by the rising cost of existence. In November, I was supposed to meet Loren at the Rusty Duck in Sacramento for dinner. He was late. Nothing surprising about that. I ordered a drink in the bar and waited. Nothing surprising about that either. Then I ordered another drink and waited some more. I called his house. No answer. I called his mom—she seemed to always know where he was.

"That Loren can be such a booger to get a hold of," she said, echoing an old refrain.

I ordered another drink, then told the hostess I was ready to be seated for dinner. Maybe Loren was on his way. I ordered a half carafe of wine to go with my grilled halibut. And that was the last thing I remembered until I looked in my rearview mirror and saw the flashing red and blue lights of the Sacramento County sheriff's car. I was fifteen miles from the Rusty Duck and had no clue as to how or why I got there. The officer said he stopped me because I was weaving in my lane. I couldn't walk a straight line, recite the alphabet, or touch my nose. I blew a 1.6, twice the legal limit.

So I was charged with driving under the influence, again. I spent the night sitting on a stainless-steel bench in the Sacramento County Jail, head down, avoiding the cold stare of the thug with the big tattoo sitting next to me. The bench was cold too, as was the ugly truth.

. . . .

On my way to interview Ayris the next day at her house in Marin County, I drove across the Golden Gate Bridge and parked in the vista turnout on the north side of the bridge. I removed a brown paper bag from the trunk and started walking back across the bridge, the bag under my arm. My wrists still hurt from where the sheriff's handcuffs had cut into my skin.

As I walked south across the bridge, I thought about what had happened the night before in Sacramento. The truth was inescapable. But still, I didn't think I fit the profile: I hardly ever had booze in the house . . . neither of my parents was an alcoholic . . . I could go months without a beer . . . I never drank in the morning . . . I didn't pass out in the gutter . . . I didn't get into drunken brawls . . . I didn't miss work because of hangovers. Sure, I liked to get loose at a party every now and then—I'd been doing it since the days of Pi KA. And yes, I enjoyed a bottle of wine with dinner. Or a few cocktails at a bar. I was just an ordinary social drinker, I believed. My only problem was that I had been unlucky to have been caught driving under the influence. Twice.

Actually, there were probably fifty times that I'd opened my eyes in the morning and couldn't remember anything from the night before. Once, I borrowed a friend's car and lost it. (It showed up two days later in a towing lot.) Another time I passed out in the middle of the entrance road to the Lair of the Bear and almost got mistaken for a speed bump. And the night I got the bejeebers beat out of me in 1968 in San Francisco, separating my shoulder, never to pitch in another big-league game . . . I was full of a dozen bourbon on the rocks. And another truth was that almost all of my worst arguments with women had been fueled by booze, such as the night I'd fired casserole around my living room.

Halfway across the Golden Gate Bridge, I stopped and stared off toward Berkeley to the east. It was a perfect fall day, crisp and clear, whitecaps sparkling on the Bay. I let a young couple walk past me, then reached in the brown paper bag and pulled out a half-empty bottle of gin. With a ceremonial kiss on the label, I poured the contents over the side.

Then I reached back in the bag and drew out a Baggie with a half ounce of homegrown Oregon killer weed. For twenty years I had been smoking marijuana, probably averaging a joint a night. That was approximately 7,300 joints. I was a hypocrite, warning Sarah about the dangers of drugs and alcohol, then *literally* sneaking off behind the garage to steal a couple quick tokes. Sometimes I'd take a clean shirt and my bottle of Listerine to get rid of any telltale odor before I came back inside.

I emptied the dope out of the bag and watched it drift out over the Bay. It was November 20, 1988. I was forty-six.

1989. I was off on another junket to California, this time to interview the fathers. I had talked to the mothers on my previous trip. Before leaving Oregon, I had been reading the new literature about all the defective men in our society who had grown up with "not enough father," and how these "father-hungry sons" were shelling out a thousand bucks to gather in the woods for a weekend of chest pounding and tribal chanting to get in touch with their absent fathers. The way I figured it, I was saving a thousand bucks by driving instead to Hemet, California, to meet face to face with my dad. That's where he and Mom have resided since 1982. They live in a deluxe mobile home park near the epicenter of the Southern California desert's golf boom. Dad plays golf five days a week, has two scotch and waters before dinner, and drives a ten-year-old Chevy Celebrity. His life is basic, uncomplicated, straight-ahead. There is almost a daring to the simplicity he has brought to his life. He lives on social security and his pension from forty years on the job with Douglas Aircraft.

Dad has never hugged me or told me he loved me. On the rare occasions when he writes me a letter, he simply signs it "Dad." When we are together, we talk of career, events, activities—we do not delve into feelings and emotions. I have never discussed my two divorces with him. (Nor did I tell him about my excesses with alcohol and pot . . . until now.) I asked him once what was the secret to the longevity of his marriage and he simply replied, "Your mother." That was the closest I ever saw him come to getting a tear in his eye.

Yet without any demonstrative affection from him, I have never once questioned his unfailing love. Our bond is pure and easy, and maybe the gurus of those men's groups would say it is incomplete, but it works for me. He is a man of unbridled optimism, and he always instructed me that all I had to do was keep my nose to the grindstone and the everlasting promise of sunshine and security was mine forevermore. That optimism was Nellie's patrimony.

Still, at times I feel like the colorized version of his life: I've divorced more Democrats than he's ever voted for; I've thrown more casseroles than he's ever cooked; I've driven backward more in one morning than he did his entire life; I've quit more jobs in a week than he ever held. We watched Ollie North's testimony before the Senate hearing on the Iran-Contra scandal together, and when Dad remarked that he thought North was a hero, I nearly gagged on my political correctness. We settled our disagreement by not talking about it. Rather than wage a family debate, he went into the other room and practiced his putting.

Although I never knew my paternal grandfather—he was killed by a hit-and-run driver just as he was starting to make money in real estate in the San Fernando Valley—when Dad told me in 1989 how Grandpa pursued his dreams, sometimes blindly and irresponsibly, I felt an instant affinity, sensed a secret inheritance that helped explain the trajectory of my own peculiar path. Yet my father, the generation linking us, was a product of the Depression, almost a martyr to responsibility and security. His life was a steady line marching across the page, while mine was a series of bolts shooting off the margins. My daughters, having lived with my dream-chasing, seem guided by an acquisitive pragmatism, as if they too feel the pull across a generation to their own sweet and steady Grandpa. Riding the Colton pendulum.

When I was a boy growing up, I knew of my father's love of baseball. It made sense that I would grow up and become a professional ballplayer, that I would in some way live out his dream. What surprised me, perhaps as much as anything I discovered in researching this book, was learning from him at the dining-room table in Hemet in 1989 that he had been the sports editor of the Santa Monica Junior College newspaper and that his goal in life had been to become a writer, a goal that was wiped away by the Depression. He had *never* told me that before. Not even when I became a writer. But surely, just as his influence steered me toward baseball, a silent paternal force also must have been guiding me toward writing. The few letters he has written me have always been flawless in grammar and syntax.

I called home, and Sarah proudly reported that she had received an A+ on her term paper in sophomore English and that she was now thinking about majoring in journalism when she went to college. I was even more certain that a paternal force was working there too. As they say, it's in the genes.

In March 1989, Wendy called from Seattle. During the last two years she had made big gains in personal growth. She was a woman, no longer a girl. She had a great sense of humor; she was astute, artistic, motivated, culturally hip. She was taking classes toward her degree in early childhood education. But as soon as I heard her voice that day, I knew something was wrong. Seriously wrong. She choked back tears.

"I need help, Dad," she pleaded.

My first thought was money. Or that her boyfriend had roughed her up. Or that she'd crashed her car.

"I have an eating disorder," she confessed.

I soon learned that during the three years she had lived with me she was bulimic, losing the weight she did by purging after meals. I never suspected. In the past several months, however, she had stopped purging. She was now compulsively overeating. It might be a whole pie, or she might make the circuit from Burger King to Taco Bell to McDonald's. She was huge. Her breathing and mobility were impaired. It was life-threatening.

It seemed easy enough to assign blame: that she had inherited her father's addictive, compulsive personality; that she had decided she didn't want to compete against her beautiful mother and movie star grandmother; that everyone had put too much pressure on her to be slim. But those were easy answers to a complex problem. This was life or death we were talking about, not who or what was to blame.

What she needed, we agreed, was to get professional clinical help as an inpatient. She had already inquired into the cost of the clinics available in Seattle; the cheapest was $12,000 for a month's stay. Insurance wouldn't cover it, and I had come to realize that after I had paid Uncle Sam, my agent, American Express, and the grocery bill, I didn't have enough money left in savings to cover it. I told her I'd call her back the next day. I felt helpless.

What happened next was divine providence. I went to the mailbox and it contained the usual bills and assorted junk. It also included my monthly newsletter from the Major League Baseball Players' Association, one of the perks of my two innings in the major leagues. This publication was usually something I glanced at and threw away, but today my eye caught a story about former baseball pitching great Sam McDowell, a recovering alcoholic who had helped establish a recovery program for former major-leaguers and their families. The program covered alcohol, drugs, and "other" addictions. I was able to reach him on the phone that evening and he told me the program had connections with a clinic in Florida that was allegedly the Betty Ford Clinic for eating disorders. There was a big problem, however. The cost for a minimum one-month stay was $22,500.

"Let me see what I can do," he said. "I'll get back to you."

I expected to hear from him in a couple of weeks. He called back in five minutes. The Major League Baseball Players' Association had agreed to pick up the tab, and not only that, they would pay Wendy's air fare from Seattle to Florida. She was to leave in three days. That sum of $22,500 was almost three times as much as I made in my best year as a player.

I drove to Seattle to break the news to her, and at the same time interview her mom for this book. It was during that interview that I first learned of Denise's affair with her Greenwich Village lover twenty-one years earlier, a revelation that neither surprised nor bothered me. (It would have collapsed me in 1968.)

After I told Wendy the good news about the clinic in Florida, we hugged and bowed to the Baseball Gods. It was delightfully odd. When I was growing up I had dreamed of the exhilaration of one day being the hero of the seventh game of the World Series and being introduced as a big celebrity by Ed Sullivan on his show. I assumed that would be the pinnacle of my career. I never came close to realizing that dream, of course. But eighteen years after my last pitch, as I looked into the hope in Wendy's beautiful green eyes, I now knew the true payoff for my two innings in the Show. And did I mention that I struck out Vada Pinson on a slider at the knees to leave Charlie Hustle stranded on third?

Epilogue

Where Are They Now?

I remember a quote from one of John Barth's novels—I think it was *Giles Goat-Boy:* "Self-knowledge is always bad news." Which sort of runs up against Plato's (was it Plato? Hey, I was no scholar, remember?) "The unexamined life is not worth living." But hell, both seem to apply here. And as long as I'm giving out Larry's Anthology of Epigrams, let's not forget Scott Fitzgerald's "Gatsby believed in the green light, the orgiastic future . . ."

In being honest about myself and my friends, I've joined the bad news with the good. We may have been representative of middle-class American males at a certain time and in a certain place. We were dreamers, we were romantics, we were floorboarding it through that green light, the orgiastic future was *now.* Even Jim the Ox was a dreamer, a romantic, and in his own way a Gatsby kind of guy who believed that if you worked hard, if you were disciplined, you could make it, and he did. And remember, he was romantic enough to believe in the fly-boy esprit de corps. Back in 1962, he struck me as a boring bowl of pudding, perhaps because he was, even then, mature and disciplined. Maturity and discipline —I guess the rest of us could have used more of each as we hippity-hopped along the dark crevices leading to middle age. Middle age. Did I say that? Yes. I'm zeroing in on fifty. Fifty. Did I say that?

Are we a mature and disciplined bunch now, the four who've survived? Have we grown? Dear reader, as those eighteenth-century dudes used to say, I leave it up to you.

But let me at least point you in the right direction. Let me give you, if not a Summing Up, at least an answer to Where Are They Now?

Steve. We know where he is. Or where the earthly part of him is. Stashed away in a vault in a marble slab in Sacto Town. But I can't believe that his spirit isn't hovering around somewhere, waiting for the good news from me. So here it is: I should let him know that the last time I saw his son Dennis, he had a ponytail and was playing in a Sacramento rock-and-roll band. And he should also know that his mom and dad, whom he battled all the way to the end, poured their hearts and souls into making Dennis feel a part of the Radich family after the plane crash, trying to atone for Steve's negligence; they had Dennis over for dinner, took him to football games down in Berkeley, where, by the way, they named the football weight room in Steve's honor. And if Steve doesn't think his dad was proud of him, then he didn't see the tears in Mr. Radich's eyes when he showed me Steve's scrapbooks. I should also let Steve know that his daughter Filaree was a straight-A student in high school, beautiful beyond words, dancing in the Marin Ballet Company, a joy to be around, soon to start Cal. God, would that make him happy. And I know Steve would be happy to read that Ayris is doing well too, living in San Anselmo, showing her artwork in Bay Area galleries, and, most surprisingly, a mother again, having given birth to a son at the age of forty-two.

Even though Steve was a New Age kind of guy and wasn't into material things, I have no doubt he'd enjoy knowing that he'd be stinky rich by now. Last I heard, his younger brother, who took over running South City Honda after he died, had just bought a million-dollar house. And the beautiful Safeway checker Miss Vicki, the last love of his life? Well, she went on to be a county sheriff for a while, then a hairdresser, and still carries his picture in her wallet. And his close friend Don Cobleigh? Well, he's now my close friend too, working hard to keep his construction company afloat during the recession of the early nineties.

And as long as I'm running it all down for Steve, I should let him know that there hasn't been a single day since he nose-dived into that pear orchard that I haven't thought about him and missed him. He's in my heart. Forever.

Whenever all the obsessive, compulsive, abusive behavior I was uncovering in these stories depressed me, I would think of Vallarie and Jim. Mr. and Mrs. Ox. She hates to be called that. She told me so very explicitly, making sure I realized she was not just an appendage of her successful husband . . . then she turned around two minutes later and introduced me to a friend as "Hedy Lamarr's former son-in-law."

Mr. and Mrs. Ox are living the American dream with their two adorable kids, nice house on a cul-de-sac, two cars in the garage, and the happy marriage. The only thing missing is the picket fence.

"How'd you get to be so lucky?" I asked.

"Luck?" railed Vallarie. "Luck has nothing to do with it. We work our ass off at it. It's not luck that we have two great kids. We pay attention to them. Let's face it, I'm a supermom and a great cook; I know Domino's number by heart. I'm great in bed. Tomorrow I'll crochet afghans for the girls' beds while I'm waiting in the car to pick them up from soccer practice. So don't talk to me about luck!"

In four short years with Bechtel, Jim has zoomed to the top, from program manager to VP to partner. I hesitate to say it, but he truly does have "the right stuff." I have no doubt that he is the man I'd want in my raft if I was headed over Rainie Falls without a paddle. And Hurricane Vallarie is taking to her new career as a "professional job applicant" and school volunteer. There were times I thought she could make it as a stand-up comic, but there was also a time or two when I wanted to slip a Sominex into her wineglass. Like the night Jim was sitting at the dining-room table telling me about courting his first wife and Vallarie decided it was time to vacuum full blast all around us for twenty minutes, nearly sucking my tape recorder right off the table. Or the night Jim and I were recounting the horrors of Hell Week and Hurricane Vallarie was in the living room pretending to watch television, only she was really listening to us, interrupting at every chance, demanding an answer to her question: "Why do men act like such jerks?" Jim ignored her, pouring himself another glass of wine. The Ox Man. If he has a tragic flaw, I'd have to say it is his short irons. But now that he's a member of one of the Bay Area's snazziest country clubs, he should have that squared away soon.

One of the rewards of this journey has been reuniting with Ron Vaughn. He's a warm, friendly, and compassionate man. I am not ashamed to say that I love him.

In the summer of 1991 Ron moved out of his wife's garage in Stockton into a one-bedroom apartment in Sacramento. His fear had been well founded—Connie decided she would be better off raising their two sons by herself. They are separated; Ron pays child support and day care, sees the boys once a week, and still hopes for reconciliation. "I sleep on a futon on the living-room floor of my apartment and keep a crib and a bed in the bedroom for the boys when they come to visit," he said.

The good news is that he was optimistic. Another bit of good news is that he is taking art classes. He's been threatening to do it since he dropped out of the class his mother enrolled him in in junior high, worried at the time that his buddies would think he was a sissy. Well, his buddies don't think that about him anymore. And just as he was in the fraternity, he is still the most loveable, big-hearted goat of all.

The last time I saw Loren was at his ranch house in Trowbridge. It was a perfect evening, the sun just starting to go down. We were sitting on the new patio he had just built behind the house. Loren was relaxing on a deck chair, pointing to where he planned to build a tennis court and a swimming pool. Things were going his way: his new lawyer for the Greyhound case—his sixth one in five years—said things were looking good; the IRS was offering him a revised settlement; the asbestos deal was on the back burner but he'd received some initial seed money to set up a project development office in Yuba City; he'd canned his ex-jailbird buddy Ed; he'd closed two real estate development deals for a couple hundred grand to "pay the bills"; and he was the volunteer junior varsity football coach at the local high school.

Rita, looking happy and tan and as healthy as a family picnic, was tending to the hot dogs on the barbecue. Garrett and Colin, blond and cuter than any two kids have a right to be, were playing nerf football and wiffle baseball all around their dad, who was teaching them the stuff that once made him the greatest athlete in all of Yuba County . . . and nearby Sutter County too. It was a scene so idyllic and family that Norman Rockwell would have had trouble finding enough bright colors to do it justice. They had all been to church earlier in the day. Hard to believe that less than a year earlier Rita had called Loren "the cruelest man on earth" and he had called her "the stupidest bitch." The scene gave hope to the claim that change is possible, even if it's glacial.

"So, Loren," I said, tossing a perfect spiral to Garrett in the corner of the patio, "if you could go back and do it all over again, what would you do differently?"

"Wouldn't change a damn thing," he asserted.

In September 1991, Loren was diagnosed to have cancer of the throat and underwent a nine-hour operation at the University of California at Davis Medical Center. The surgeon removed sixty percent of his tongue, as well as 120 lymph glands. Loren also had to undergo two months of intensive chemotherapy. His doctors were guardedly confident that they caught the cancer in time and that, with physical therapy, he will be able to regain his speech. They were unequivocal in stating that the cancer was caused by alcohol.

"I don't stray too far from home anymore," said Loren. "This has definitely changed my outlook on life. I couldn't have made it without Rita."

As for me, I'm still living in Portland in the same house I've been in for five years . . . which is the longest I've been in one place since I left home for Cal in 1960. And I've had the same girlfriend for six years . . . which is the longest I've been with any woman since I snipped the old apron strings. And it has been over three years since that day I stood on the Golden Gate Bridge and gave the heave-ho to the dope and booze . . . and I'm still clean and sober. I didn't go to AA meetings, and I've never been 12-stepped, and I think Nancy Reagan's "Just Say No" campaign is a bunch of Pollyanna crap, but I'm hanging tough and before long my car insurance rates will be back into triple digits.

It has been four long years since I started research on this book. Seems like forever. The same day I'm mailing the manuscript to my publisher, I am also driving Sarah down I-5 to Eugene, where she will be starting her freshman year at the University of Oregon. I'm thinking I'm in store for some major postpartum letdown. The last five years have been intense between Sarah and me. Big-time father-daughter stuff. There were times during her tempestuous senior year in high school when I had my doubts: such as the nightmare of teaching her to drive a stick-shift; the prom-from-hell when I wouldn't let her stay out all night; the period after my Big Literary Advance ran out and it was all I could do to scrape together lunch money for her, let alone worry about buying her a new back-to-school wardrobe at the Gap like "every other kid in school." But I am proud, proud, proud of her—she hung tough with me, we hung tough together. She and her mom are doing much better too. In fact, Kathi is going to ride down to Eugene with us for the big send-off. On the ride back to Portland I may try to pin her down on what she *really* thought was my one tragic flaw—you know, the final question she dodged in "The Newlywed Game." On second thought, we've been getting along pretty well lately, so I think I'll just keep it chatty. I'm good at that.

Wendy is now twenty-five, working as an assistant for an environmental lawyer in Seattle, chipping away at her education a class at a time. Her month in the eating-disorder clinic in Florida, sponsored by the Major League Baseball Players' Association, was a miracle. She lost weight and now she is fighting the battle of recovery one day at a time, as they say. It is a struggle, but she is, in every way, beautiful.

ACKNOWLEDGMENTS

Obviously, there are many people to thank. First, Richard Pine, my agent, my friend, my literary ace of staff. It was his enthusiasm and encouragement that launched this project and rode with it until the very end. Then there's my editor, Herman Gollob, who was not only invaluable in his editorial suggestions and advice, but patient beyond the call of duty, especially when the months I was overdue turned into years.

I must express my respect and gratitude to the Goats—Jim van Hoften, Loren Hawley, and Ron Vaughn. It wasn't always easy, my intrusions, my dredging up sometimes painful memories. Their candor and cooperation made this book possible. And Ayris Hatton has my undying affection.

When my advance was long gone, it was the generous support of friends that carried me through. So a special thanks to Katherine Dunn, Don Cobleigh, Dick Solomon, and Pete Donoghue. After I've paid them all back, I'll still be in their debt. And there's no way I can ever repay my best friend, John Strawn, for all his moral and financial support.

Above all, I want to thank my family. I can't imagine parents more supportive than mine. I am blessed. And when I was lost in composition, my two beautiful daughters, Wendy and Sarah, were indulgent and understanding of my obsession (except when I grounded Sarah). I love them immensely, and then some.

And finally, there's Marcie. She was always there, through all the ups and downs, and all the times I despaired about my efforts. She never stopped believing. And do you know what she did for me when I finally staggered to the finish? She treated me to ten days in Hawaii. I'll never be able to thank her enough. But I'll try.